Contents

108

100

Time Out

New York

timeout.com/newyork

Time Out Guides Ltd
Universal House
251 Tottenham Court Road
London W1T 7AB
United Kingdom
Tel: +44 (0)20 7813 3000
Fax: +44 (0)20 7813 6001
Email: guides@timeout.com
www.timeout.com

Published by Time Out Guides Ltd, a wholly owned subsidiary of Time Out Group Ltd. Time Out and the Time Out logo are trademarks of Time Out Group Ltd.

Previous editions 1990, 1992, 1994, 1997, 1998, 1999, 2000, 2001, 2002, 2003, 2004, 2005, 2006, 2007, 2008, 2009, 2011, 2012, 2013.

10 9 8 7 6 5 4 3 2 1

This edition first published in Great Britain in 2014 by Ebury Publishing.
A Random House Group Company
20 Vauxhall Bridge Road, London SW1V 2SA

Random House Australia Pty Ltd 20 Alfred Street, Milsons Point, Sydney, New South Wales 2061, Australia

Random House New Zealand Ltd 18 Poland Road, Glenfield, Auckland 10, New Zealand

Random House South Africa (Pty) Ltd Isle of Houghton, Corner Boundary Road & Carse O'Gowrie, Houghton 2198, South Africa

Random House UK Limited Reg. No. 954009

Distributed in the US and Latin America by Publishers Group West (1-510-809-3700)

For further distribution details, see www.timeout.com.

ISBN: 978-1-84670-325-6

A CIP catalogue record for this book is available from the British Library.

Printed and bound in China by Leo Paper Products Ltd.

The Random House Group Limited supports The Forest Stewardship Council® (FSC®), the leading international forest-certification organisation. Our books carrying the FSC label are printed on FSC®-certified paper. FSC is the only forest-certification scheme supported by the leading environmental organisations, including Greenpeace. Our paper procurement policy can be found at www.randomhouse.co.uk/environment.

MIX
Paper from responsible sources
FSC www.fsc.org FSC® C020056

364

267

157

Time Out New York

Editorial
Editor Lisa Ritchie
Deputy Editor Ros Sales
Listings Editors Julianna Flamio, Jennifer M Wood
Proofreader Marion Moisy
Indexer Marion Moisy

Editorial Director Sarah Guy
Management Accountant Margaret Wright

Design
Senior Designer Kei Ishimaru
Designer Thomas Havell
Group Commercial Senior Designer Jason Tansley

Picture Desk
Picture Editor Jael Marschner
Deputy Picture Editor Ben Rowe
Freelance Picture Researchers Lizzy Owen

Advertising
Managing Director of Advertising St John Betteridge
Advertising Sales Ari Ben, Dan Kenefick, Deborah Maclaren, Christy Stewart

Marketing
Senior Publishing Brand Manager Luthfa Begum
Head of Circulation Dan Collins

Production
Production Controller Katie Mulhern-Bhudia

Time Out Group
Chairman & Founder Tony Elliott
Chief Executive Officer Tim Arthur
Publisher Alex Batho
Group IT Director Simon Chappell
Group Marketing Director Carolyn Sims

Contributors
New York's Top 20 Lisa Ritchie and contributors to *Time Out New York* magazine. **New York Today** Howard Halle. **Diary** Lisa Ritchie and contributors to *Time Out New York* magazine. **Explore** Rebecca Fishbein, Julianna Flamio, Christina Izzo, Richard Koss, Howard Halle, Patty Lee, Marley Lynch, Lee Magill, Amy Plitt, Lisa Ritchie, Jennifer M Wood and contributors to *Time Out New York* magazine. **Hotels** Lisa Ritchie. **Children** Lee Magill. **Film & TV** Joshua Rothkopf (*Dinner at the Movies* Chris Schonberger). **Gay & Lesbian** Ethan LaCroix. **Performing Arts** Adam Feldman, Gia Kourlas, Matthew Love, Jenna Scherer, Steve Smith. **Nightlife** Adam Feldman, Sophie Harris, Matthew Love, Hank Shteamer, Steve Smith, Bruce Tantum. **Escapes & Excursions** Lisa Ritchie, Jennifer M Wood and contributors to *Time Out New York* magazine. **History** Richard Koss, Kathleen Squires. **Architecture** Eric P Nash. **Essential Information** Julianna Flamio, Lisa Ritchie.

Maps JS Graphics Ltd (john@jsgraphics.co.uk). Bronx map data supplied by Creative Force Maps

Cover and pull-out map photography Maurizio Rellini/SIME/4Corners Images

Back cover photography Clockwise from top left: Luboslav Tiles/Shutterstock.com; Pola Damonte/Shutterstock.com; Filip Wolak; pio3/Shutterstock.com; Refinery Hotel, New York

Photography pages 2/3, 394/395 dibrova/Shutterstock.com; 4 (top), 108, 118, 342 stockelements/Shutterstock.com; 5 (top), 344/345, 364, 365 Evan Joseph; 5 (bottom left), 267 Francine Daveta; 7, 24 (top right), 28 (middle), 47, 73, 93, 121, 122 (right), 181, 192, 312, 341 Sean Pavone/Shutterstock.com; 10 (left) Luciano Mortula/Shutterstock; 10 (right), 46, 208, 210, 264 (bottom), 285 Jonathan Perugia; 11, 15 (top), 20, 42 (top left), 122 (left), 130, 138, 233, 286 littleny/Shutterstock.com; 12 (top) pisaphotography/Shutterstock.com; (middle) Adriano Castelli/Shutterstock.com; (bottom) Chris Parypa Photography/Shutterstock.com; 13 (top and middle) Songquan Deng/Shutterstock.com; 14 (top), 145 Cristina Muraca/Shutterstock.com; 15 (bottom), 16 (top), 84, 85, 104, 120, 124, 160, 186, 243 Wendy Connett; 16 (bottom), 32 (bottom), 36 (bottom) A Katz/Shutterstock.com; 17 (top), 55 (bottom right), 110, 185, 191, 224, 227, 240/241, 263, 268, 270, 275 Filip Wolak; 18/19 Stan Honda/AFP/Getty Images; 23 Francis Dzikowski; 24 (left) James A. Harris/Shutterstock.com; 26 (top) Richard Bond/Alamy; (bottom) Jodie Love; 27, 139 Erika Cross/Shutterstock.com; 28 (top) Carlos Neto/Shutterstock.com; 30, 272 (top left) JStone/Shutterstock.com; 32 (top), 37, 282, 289 (bottom) Lev Radin/Shutterstock.com; 32 (middle) Gerard Lazaro/Shutterstock.com; 35 Debby Wong/Shutterstock.com; 38 (top) Thierry Guinet/Shutterstock; 38 (bottom), 172, 232, 242, 264 (top), 315 (middle) Alys Tomlinson; 41, 67, 88, 134 Caroline Voagen Nelson; 43 (bottom) Manish Gosalia; 44/45 Andrey Bayda/Shutterstock.com; 48 Donald Bowers/Shutterstock.com; 50 onairda/Shutterstock.com; 51 (top) Keith Sherwood/Shutterstock.com; 51 (bottom), 63, 81, 82 (right), 87, 116, 128, 136, 153, 203, 231, 265, 287, 289 (top), 313, 315 (top and bottom) Michael Kirby; 53, 56 Bokic Bojan/Shutterstock.com; 55 (top and bottom left) Daniel Krieger; 57, 78, 167, 204 Virginia Rollison; 58, 245 Lee Magill; 59 (top) vvoe/Shutterstock.com; (bottom) Kenneth Summers/Shutterstock.com; 61 David Persson/Shutterstock.com; 62 Jakob N. Layman; 64 Paul Matthew/Shutterstock.com; 80, 91 Stocksnapper/Shutterstock.com; 82 (left), 318 Daniel M. Silva/Shutterstock.com; 89 (top left) Amy Barkow; (middle) Andres Ramirez; (bottom) © Nigel Young/Foster + Partners; 92 Gabriele Stabile; 94 Patti McConville/Alamy; 98, 133 Loren Wohl; 101,102, 184, 189 (top and middle) Paul Wagtouicz; 106, 107 pio3/Shutterstock.com; 125 David Regen; 129, 228 Richard Cavalleri/Shutterstock.com; 132 (bottom) Francesco Tonelli; 135 Jessica Lin; 140, 216 Vladimir Korostyshevskiy/Shutterstock.com; 141 Olimpio Fantuz/SIME/4Corners Images; 148, 228 Manamana/Shutterstock.com; 151 Samuel Borges/Shutterstock.com; 154 (left) Tatiana Morozova/Shutterstock.com; (right) ldphotoro/Shutterstock.com; 161 ciapix/Shutterstock.com; 162 Dimitar Kunev/Shutterstock.com; 170 Ritu Manoj Jethani/Shutterstock.com; 173 David Heald © Solomon R. Guggenheim Foundation, New York; 176 Michael Bodycomb © The Frick Collection; 179 (clockwise from top left, apart from bottom right) Elizabeth Felicella, Matt Flynn/Cooper-Hewitt, National Design Museum, Ken Pelka/Cooper-Hewitt, National Design Museum, Bo Hovgaard, Ali Elai/Cooper-Hewitt, National Design Museum; 194, 271, 288 Leonard Zhukovsky/Shutterstock.com; 195, 272 (top right), 338 photo.ua/Shutterstock.com; 196 rSnapshotPhotos/Shutterstock.com; 200 Kristina Williamson; 212 Jennifer Arnow; 213, 249, 250 Jolie Ruben; 217 Elzbieta Sekowska/Shutterstock.com; 219 Gabriela Herman; 220 Beth Levendis; 237 Jannis Tobias Werner/Shutterstock.com; 246 cdrin/Shutterstock.com; 253 United Artists/Photofest; 255 Glynnis Jones/Shutterstock.com; 256 Bex Wade; 257 Zenith Richards; 259 (top) Magda Biernat; (bottom) Andrew Werner; 262 Jena Cumbo; 269 Mindy Tucker; 274 Ben Rosenzweig; 276 Luboslav Tiles/Shutterstock.com; 279 Anton Oparin/Shutterstock.com; 280 Nigel Spiers/Shutterstock.com; 284, 290, 297, 298 Matthew Murphy; 293 Jon Simon; 294 Brian Rogers; 295 Ian Douglas; 296 ValeStock/Shutterstock.com; 299 (top) Joan Marcus; (bottom) Northfoto/Shutterstock.com; 300 Francis Dzikowski; 301 Alick Crossley; 303 Francis Dzikowski/Esto; 307 Aislinn Weidele; 308 Julieta Cervantes; 309 EsDevlin; 310/311 Stephen St. John/Getty Images; 314 John A. Anderson/Shutterstock.com; 316 (right) Thomas Hart Shelby; 319 Jerry L. Thompson; 321 Aspen Photo/Shutterstock.com; 322/323 Pola Damonte/Shutterstock.com; 324 Science Museum/SSPL/NMM/Getty Images; 326 Buyenlarge/Getty Images; 331 Everett Collection Historical/Alamy; 332 New York Daily News/Getty Images; 337 Emin Kuliyev/Shutterstock.com; 351 Annie Schlechter; 354 Phillip Ennis

The following images were supplied by the featured establishments: pages 4 (bottom), 5 (bottom right), 14 (bottom), 17 (bottom), 22, 24 (bottom), 25, 28 (bottom), 33, 43 (top), 68, 71, 72, 76, 79, 86, 89 (top right), 90, 97, 100, 105, 111, 113, 115, 119, 126 (top right and bottom), 144, 150, 156, 157, 158, 164, 165, 168, 178, 179 (bottom right), 182, 189 (bottom left and right), 206, 214, 215, 218, 223, 230, 235, 236, 238, 254, 261, 266, 273, 283, 316 (top and bottom left), 317, 346, 347, 349, 355, 357, 359, 360, 362, 363, 366, 367, 368, 370

About the Guide

GETTING AROUND

Each sightseeing chapter contains a street map of the area marked with the locations of sights and museums (❶), restaurants (❶), cafés and bars (❶), and shops (❶). There are also street maps of New York at the back of the book, along with an overview map of the city and subway maps. In addition, there is now a detachable fold-out street map inside the back cover.

THE ESSENTIALS

For practical information, including visas, disabled access, emergency numbers, lost property, websites and local transport, see the Essential Information section. It begins on page 344.

THE LISTINGS

Addresses, phone numbers, websites, transport information, hours and prices are all included in our listings, as are selected other facilities. All were checked and correct at press time. However, business owners can alter their arrangements at any time, and fluctuating economic conditions can cause prices to change rapidly.

The very best venues in the city, the must-sees and must-dos in every category, have been marked with a red star (★). In the sightseeing chapters, we've also marked venues with free admission with a FREE symbol.

PHONE NUMBERS

New York has a number of area codes. Manhattan uses 212 and 646, while Brooklyn, Queens, the Bronx and Staten Island are served by 718 and 347. Even if you're dialling from within the area you're calling, you'll need to use the area code, always preceded by 1.

From outside the US, dial your country's international access code (00 from the UK) or a plus symbol, followed by the number as listed in the guide; here, the initial '1' serves as the US country code. So, to reach the Metropolitan Museum of Art, dial +1-212 535 7710. For more on phones, *see p382*.

FEEDBACK

We welcome feedback on this guide, both on the venues we've included and on any other locations that you'd like to see featured in future editions. Please email us at guides@timeout.com.

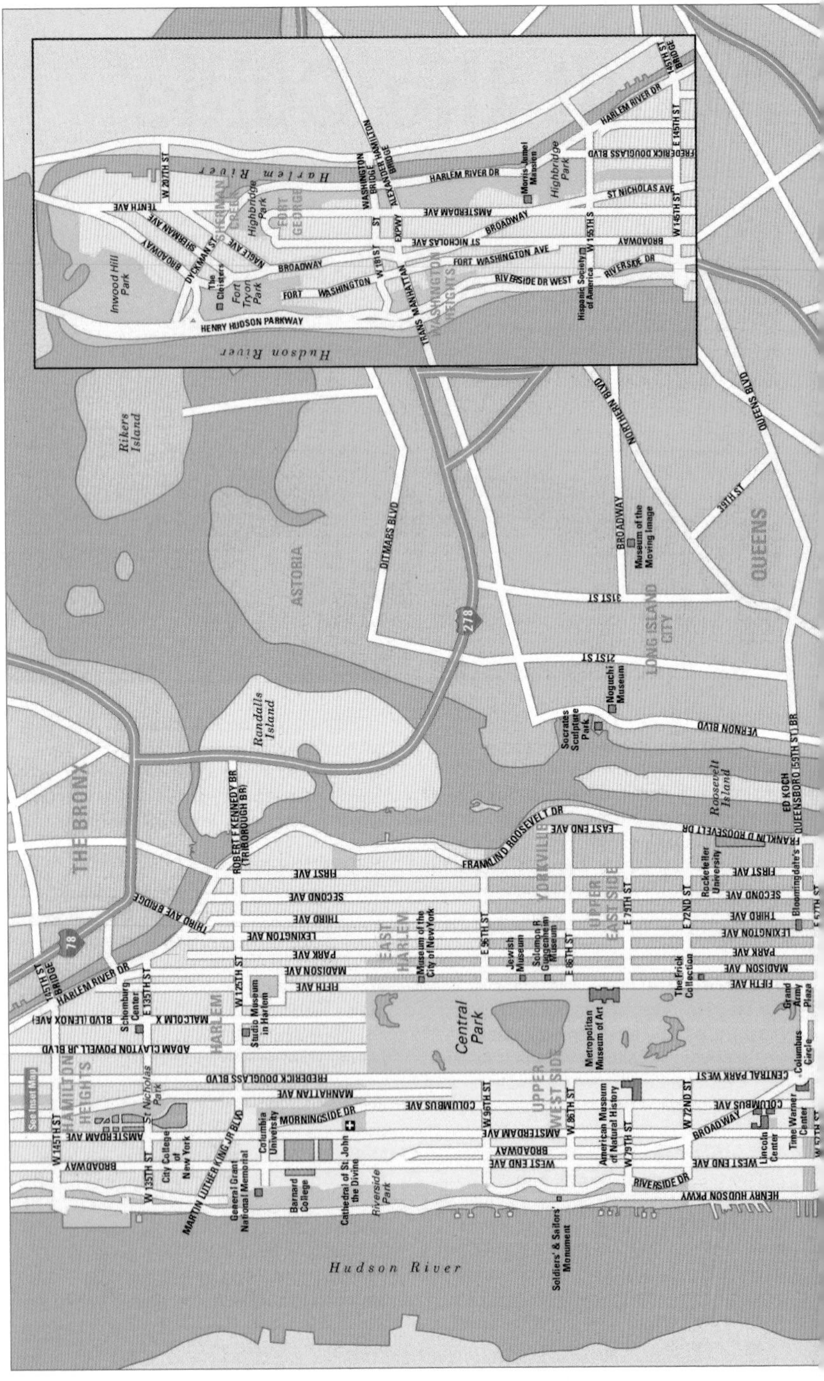

Harlem River
HARLEM RIVER DR
W 207TH ST
TENTH AVE
SHERMAN AVE
SHERMAN CREEK
Highbridge Park
FORT GEORGE
NAGLE AVE
DYCKMAN ST
BROADWAY
Inwood Hill Park
The Cloisters
Fort Tryon Park
FORT WASHINGTON
WASHINGTON BRIDGE
ALEXANDER HAMILTON BRIDGE
W 181ST
ST NICHOLAS AVE
AMSTERDAM AVE
TRANS MANHATTAN EXPWY
WASHINGTON HEIGHTS
FORT WASHINGTON AVE
RIVERSIDE DR WEST
RIVERSIDE DR
Morris-Jumel Mansion
Hispanic Society of America
W 155TH ST
FREDERICK DOUGLASS BLVD
145TH ST BRIDGE
E 145TH ST
W 145TH ST
HENRY HUDSON PARKWAY
Hudson River
Rikers Island
ASTORIA
DITMARS BLVD
NORTHERN BLVD
QUEENS BLVD
39TH ST
QUEENS
BROADWAY
Museum of the Moving Image
31ST ST
LONG ISLAND CITY
21ST ST
278
Noguchi Museum
Socrates Sculpture Park
VERNON BLVD
Randalls Island
Roosevelt Island
ED KOCH QUEENSBORO 59TH ST BR
THE BRONX
ROBERT F KENNEDY BR (TRIBOROUGH BR)
FRANKLIN D ROOSEVELT DR
EAST END AVE
YORKVILLE
FIRST AVE
SECOND AVE
THIRD AVE
THIRD AVE BRIDGE
LEXINGTON AVE
PARK AVE
MADISON AVE
FIFTH AVE
78
145TH ST BRIDGE
HARLEM RIVER DR
EAST HARLEM
Museum of the City of New York
E 96TH ST
Jewish Museum
Solomon R Guggenheim Museum
E 86TH ST
UPPER EAST SIDE
E 79TH ST
E 72ND ST
Rockefeller University
The Frick Collection
Bloomingdale's
Grand Army Plaza
E 57TH ST
Central Park
Metropolitan Museum of Art
W 125TH ST
Studio Museum in Harlem
MALCOLM X BLVD (LENOX AVE)
Schomburg Center
E 135TH ST
HARLEM
ADAM CLAYTON POWELL JR BLVD
See Inset Map
HAMILTON HEIGHTS
St Nicholas Park
FREDERICK DOUGLASS BLVD
CENTRAL PARK WEST
Columbus Circle
MANHATTAN AVE
COLUMBUS AVE
MORNINGSIDE DR
W 96TH ST
UPPER WEST SIDE
W 86TH ST
American Museum of Natural History
W 79TH ST
W 72ND ST
Time Warner Center
Lincoln Center
AMSTERDAM AVE
W 145TH ST
City College of New York
W 135TH ST
Columbia University
Cathedral of St. John the Divine
Barnard College
Riverside Park
General Grant National Memorial
MARTIN LUTHER KING JR BLVD
WEST END AVE
RIVERSIDE DR
Soldiers' & Sailors' Monument
HENRY HUDSON PKWY
Hudson River

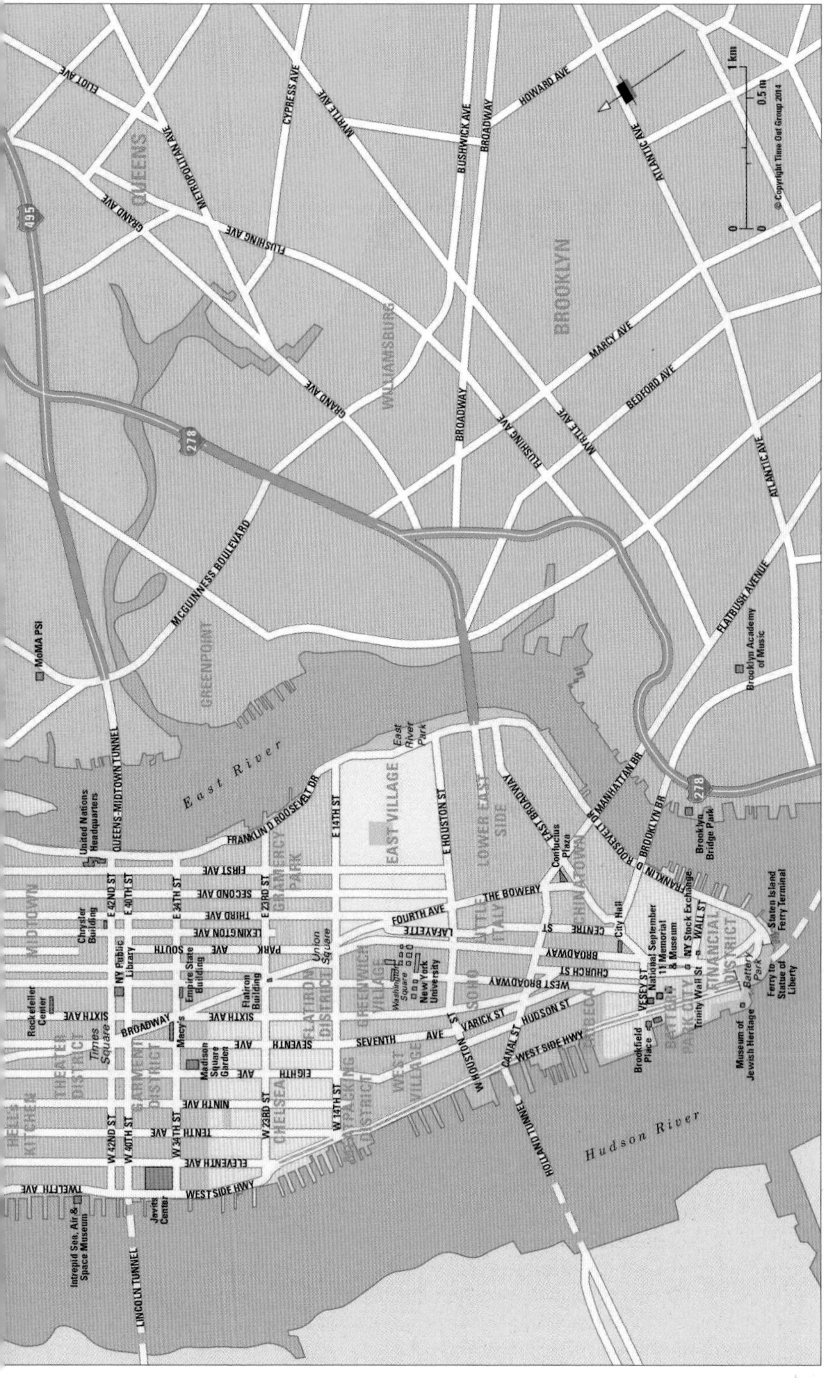
QUEENS
BROOKLYN
WILLIAMSBURG
GREENPOINT
MIDTOWN
THEATER DISTRICT
HELL'S KITCHEN
GARMENT DISTRICT
CHELSEA
GRAMERCY PARK
FLATIRON DISTRICT
MEATPACKING DISTRICT
WEST VILLAGE
GREENWICH VILLAGE
EAST VILLAGE
LOWER EAST SIDE
SOHO
LITTLE ITALY
CHINATOWN
TRIBECA
BATTERY PARK CITY
FINANCIAL DISTRICT
East River
Hudson River
East River Park
ELIOT AVE
GRAND AVE
METROPOLITAN AVE
FLUSHING AVE
CYPRESS AVE
MYRTLE AVE
BUSHWICK AVE
BROADWAY
HOWARD AVE
ATLANTIC AVE
MARCY AVE
BEDFORD AVE
FLATBUSH AVENUE
MCGUINNESS BOULEVARD
QUEENS-MIDTOWN TUNNEL
FRANKLIN D ROOSEVELT DR
MANHATTAN BR
BROOKLYN BR
EAST BROADWAY
THE BOWERY
FOURTH AVE
LAFAYETTE
CENTRE ST
CHURCH ST
WEST BROADWAY
VARICK ST
HUDSON ST
CANAL ST
W HOUSTON ST
E HOUSTON ST
E 14TH ST
W 14TH ST
E 23RD ST
W 23RD ST
E 34TH ST
W 34TH ST
E 40TH ST
W 40TH ST
E 42ND ST
W 42ND ST
FIRST AVE
SECOND AVE
THIRD AVE
LEXINGTON AVE
PARK AVE SOUTH
SIXTH AVE
SEVENTH AVE
EIGHTH AVE
NINTH AVE
TENTH AVE
ELEVENTH AVE
TWELFTH AVE
WEST SIDE HWY
VESEY ST
WALL ST
HOLLAND TUNNEL
LINCOLN TUNNEL
495
278
MoMA PS1
United Nations Headquarters
Chrysler Building
NY Public Library
Rockefeller Center
Times Square
Empire State Building
Macy's
Madison Square Garden
Flatiron Building
Union Square
Washington Square
New York University
Jevits Center
Intrepid Sea, Air & Space Museum
Confucius Plaza
City Hall
National September 11 Memorial & Museum
NY Stock Exchange
Trinity Wall St
Brookfield Place
Battery Park
Museum of Jewish Heritage
Ferry to Statue of Liberty
Staten Island Ferry Terminal
Brooklyn Bridge Park
Brooklyn Academy of Music
0
0.5 m
1 km
© Copyright Time Out Group 2014

New York's Top 20

From iconic skyscrapers to massive sandwiches, we count down the essentials.

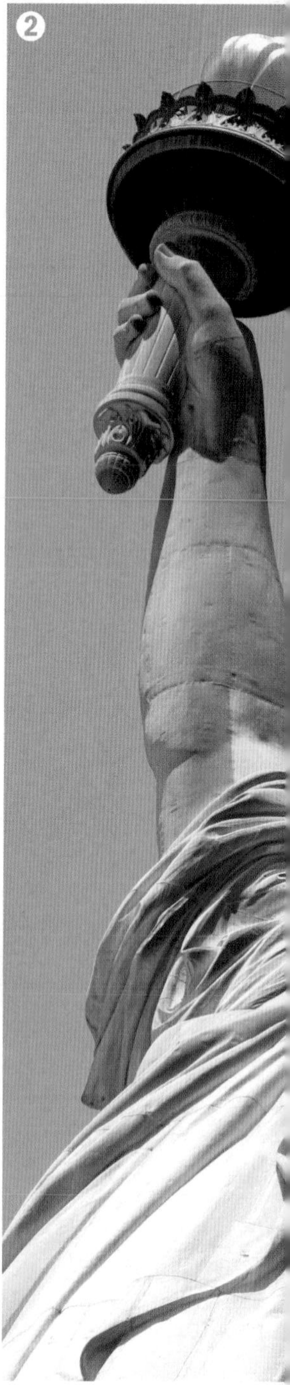

1 Empire State Building
(page 64)

King Kong recognised the Empire State's skyscraper supremacy when he commandeered the iconic tower. It may no longer be the city's tallest building, but until 1 World Trade Center's observation deck opens in 2015, it is the highest lookout point. Brave the crowds to escape the urban jungle and get a pigeon's eye panorama of the metropolis and beyond.

2 Statue of Liberty
(page 54)

Symbolic and surreal (a monumental statue-cum-lighthouse?), Lady Liberty was a beacon to millions of immigrants who subsequently shaped the city, and America. Impressive viewed from land, up close she is an immense marvel. A climb to the crown affords an exhilarating view of New York Harbor and the chance to see the literal nuts and bolts of Frédéric Auguste Bartholdi's creation.

3 Metropolitan Museum of Art
(page 180)

Not only does this massive institution – comprising 17 curatorial collections and more than two million objects – preserve such treasures as an Egyptian temple from c15 BC, but it is in a state of constant self-improvement. The American Wing, the European Paintings Galleries and the Costume Institute have all recently received impressive revamps and in autumn 2014, the museum unveils its new tree-shaded front plaza. Since the suggested admission now grants you entry to the Cloisters, its uptown medieval outpost, in the same week, the sum doesn't seem quite so steep.

4 Museum of Modern Art

(page 152)

You could spend a day getting lost in the permanent collection, which showcases some of the best-known works by Picasso, Van Gogh and other modern masters. But equally essential are the museum's other elements, including an attached cinema that combines arthouse fare and more accessible offerings, a sculpture garden with works by Rodin and Moore, and the Modern, one of the best restaurants in the city.

5 Solomon R Guggenheim Museum

(page 182)

When it was completed in 1959, Frank Lloyd Wright's curved concrete edifice ruffled a few art-world feathers, including those of Willem de Kooning and Robert Motherwell, who complained their art was not best appreciated from the museum's ramps. Today, the iconic spiral – Wright's only building in Manhattan – is considered as much a work of art as the paintings it houses (which include masterpieces by Picasso, Chagall and Kandinsky).

6 Central Park

(page 168)

Urban visionaries Frederick Law Olmsted and Calvert Vaux sought a harmonious balance of scenic elements: pastoral (the open lawn of the Sheep Meadow), formal (the linear, tree-lined Mall) and picturesque (the densely wooded paths of the Ramble). Today, the 843-acre plot draws millions of visitors to its skyscraper-bordered vistas in all

seasons: sunbathers and picnickers in summer, ice-skaters in winter, and bird-watchers in spring and autumn. It's also an idyllic venue for beloved cultural events like Shakespeare in the Park and the New York Philharmonic's annual open-air performances.

7 Brooklyn Bridge
(page 197)

No mere river crossing, this span is an elegant reminder of New York's history of architectural innovation. When it opened in 1883, the Brooklyn Bridge was the longest suspension bridge in the world. Stride along its wide wood-planked promenade from lower Manhattan and discover the pleasure of arriving at a completely different and very pleasant destination (Dumbo) on foot – with an expansive vista of New York Harbor, the Statue of Liberty and downtown's skyscrapers along the way.

8 9/11 Memorial & Museum
(page 57)

It was a decade in the making, but New York finally got a suitably awe-inspiring memorial of the terrible event that shook the city to its core. It's impossible not to feel moved as you gaze at the monumental waterfalls cascading down the sides of the vast chasms where the Twin Towers once stood. Above you, the soaring 1 World Trade Center serves as a reminder that this town never stays down for long. And the long-awaited 9/11 Memorial Museum should be open by the time you read this.

9 Times Square
(page 144)

Larger than life, brash, lurid and utterly hypnotic. For more than a century, the Crossroads of the World has provided an eye-popping arena for news, entertainment and advertising. Even the most jaded New Yorkers have to admit that the ever-shifting illuminated tableau is dazzling viewed from the top of the red steps behind TKTS – and you can pick up some cheap theatre tickets while you're there. The crowds in today's family-friendly Times Square can be infuriating (about 300,000 people pass through daily), but the recently pedestrianised zone is getting new paved plazas and granite seating, which should improve the experience.

9

10 Soho shopping
(page 66)

Yes, the former artists' enclave has become an outdoor shopping mall. But have you ever seen one so exquisite? Avoid the Saturday crowds and wander amid the pristine warehouses hung with fire escapes like so much costume jewellery, popping in and out of the ground-level retail ranging from cult designer boutiques (Alexander Wang, Phillip Lim) to luxury labels (Prada, Chanel) and cheaper chains (Madewell, Topshop). There are even outposts of Barneys and Bloomingdale's, and plenty of good brunch choices – we recommend Jack's Wife Freda (*see p66*) – in the area.

10

11 Lincoln Center
(page 286)

The largest campus of its kind in the world, this Upper West Side institution is home to a staggering array of theatre, music, dance and film. Construction began in 1959 with the help of John D Rockefeller III, largely in an effort to provide new stomping grounds for the Metropolitan Opera, the New York Philharmonic and the Juilliard School.

Today the complex encompasses 30 venues and 11 world-class resident organisations that mount thousands of events each year. After a campus-wide renovation, it's looking better than ever. Standing in Josie Robertson Plaza at twilight, with the fountain spouting white-lit jets of water and the lobby of the Met glowing golden behind it, is one of Manhattan's more transporting experiences.

12 The High Line
(page 118)

There's something uniquely New York about this eyrie. Built on an abandoned railway track, the space is ingenious in its use of reclaimed industrial detritus, a necessity in footage-starved Manhattan. The pathway takes you above the city while keeping you rooted in urban life – where else can you walk through a field of wildflowers or sprawl on a lush lawn as taxis zoom along the street beneath you? Keep an eye out for iconic sights (from the Statue of Liberty to the Empire State Building) and intriguing art installations.

13 Katz's Delicatesen
(page 85)

New York may be known for its delis, but these kosher canteens are a dying breed, and some celebrated pastrami purveyors don't live up to their overstuffed reputations. Plastered with shots of famous noshers, Katz's delivers on more than 125 years of history. Hand-carved and bookended with rye bread, the tender smoked meat is piled high and served with just a slick of mustard.

101 IDEAS
Looking for even more inspiration? Visit www.timeout.com/newyork for a full list of the best things to do in every season.

14 Washington Square Park
(page 108)

The beatniks, folkies and hippies who flocked to this park are still there, though sporting slightly different facial hair from their predecessors. During warmer months, the park is one of the city's best people-watching spots, as musicians and street artists perform in the shadow of the Stanford White-designed Washington Arch. The park is fresh from a controversial, multimillion-dollar renovation, which has spruced it up with more benches, lawns and flower beds.

15 Radio City Music Hall
(page 277)

New York City is full of legendary performance venues, but few match Radio City Music Hall in terms of sheer elegance. Designed by Donald Deskey, the art deco interior features opulent chandeliers, while the stage and proscenium are meant to resemble a setting sun. Although it's probably best known as the home of the Rockettes, a plethora of noteworthy performers have graced its boards, including Lady Gaga and Leonard Cohen.

16 Chelsea gallery district
(page 125)

We're not suggesting you skip the essential museums on our list, but in west Chelsea's contemporary-art mecca you can often catch museum-calibre shows without spending a dime. The former industrial buildings have been converted into more than 200 galleries, from sleek blue-chip salons to densely packed warrens of smaller art spaces.

18 The Panorama of the City of New York
(page 227)

Located on the grounds of two World's Fairs, the Queens Museum holds one of Gotham's most intriguing curiosities: The Panorama of the City of New York, a 9,335-square-foot scale model of the five boroughs, created for the 1964 exposition and featuring Lilliputian models of landmarks. And following the museum's recent renovation and expansion, the Little Apple will debut a new mini skyscraper – a replica of 1 World Trade Center.

19 Carbone
(page 110)

Like a *Godfather* hangout on steroids, this 2013 opening evokes old-school Little Italy, but it's more fantastical set piece than history-bound throwback. The waiters have the smooth steps and cool banter of celluloid pros, and the menu, which opens as wide as *The New York Times*, reads like an encyclopedia of red-checkered classics. But co-chefs Rich Torrisi and Mario Carbone have made such dramatic improvements, you'll barely recognise anything.

17 Brooklyn Flea
(page 203)

New Yorkers aren't content with merely shopping at the weekend, they want a complete cultural experience that involves local artisans, people-watching and cult eats. Since its debut more than five years ago, the Flea has elevated the vintage-and-craft market concept, spawning several offshoots as well as imitators. The food-only spin-off Smorgasburg – a glutton's paradise packed with up to 100 vendors – gives you the opportunity to taste your way across the city in one convenient spot.

20 Williamsburg clubbing
(page 209)

With its largely low-rise architecture (for now, before the condos take over), Williamsburg feels like a small town with an unusually high concentration of bars and gig spots. Hop from laid-back spaces showcasing local talent to Output (*see p264*), one of the city's best dance clubs.

New York Today

A new mayor, a new era?

TEXT: HOWARD HALLE

At the stroke of midnight on 1 January 2014, outside his home in the Park Slope section of Brooklyn, Bill de Blasio was sworn in as the 109th Mayor of New York City by New York State Attorney General Eric Schneiderman. Twelve hours later, the ceremony was repeated on the steps of City Hall in Lower Manhattan. This time the oath of office was administered by none other than former President Bill Clinton. Officially, Clinton's involvement was meant as thanks for de Blasio's service as campaign manager for Hillary Clinton's successful US Senate bid during the 2000 campaign. Unofficially, his presence underlined the importance attached to de Blasio's election as New York's first Democratic Mayor in a generation – an event seen as potentially momentous not only by members of his party, but also by national pundits, who wondered whether his victory signalled a wider shift in the American body politic.

East River State Park.

The more salient question, perhaps, is what does de Blasio's win as an unabashed progressive mean for New York? His ascension has been met in some quarters with fears of a return to the bad old days of high crime and vandalism, when squeegee men harassed motorists and graffiti writers despoiled the subways. This attitude is a reflection of a certain paradox about New York – its long-held reputation as a liberal bastion conflicts with the political reality over the past 20 years, as the city entrusted its political fortunes to Republicans, and its economic fate to Wall Street.

This combination has served New Yorkers well, at least in the broadest sense. Rampant crime is a distant memory, and huge swathes of the five boroughs have been developed or renovated. The amount of parkland – along the Hudson, East River and the Brooklyn waterfront, and cutting through the Meatpacking District and the heart of Chelsea in the form of the High Line – has been vastly increased. And while the rest of the country plunged into the Great Recession after the 2008 financial collapse, New York managed to sail through the hard times relatively unscathed – due in no small measure to federal government bailing out the same investment banks that had precipitated the crisis in the first place. In no time at all, it seemed, both the stock market and the city's real estate values resumed their relentless skyward march.

A TALE OF TWO CITIES

The main recipients of these benefits are the very top tier of the income bracket, the so-called One Percent – which, in terms of the real distribution of wealth, is more like the .01 per cent. For everyone else, including some households that were once thought to be affluent, but even more so for the poor and working class, living in New York has become a struggle. This disparity became impossible to ignore, especially as the reign of Gotham's billionaire mayor, Michael Bloomberg (who had exploited the financial crisis to amend the city charter and wrest himself a third term) grew increasingly imperious in tone. It was this perception of inequality that brought the candidacy of Bloomberg's anointed successor, City Council speaker Christine Quinn (who had helped to pave the way for the Mayor's additional term) crashing down in flames during the Democratic primary, pushing de Blasio to the fore. It was also the reason de Blasio's campaign decrying a 'tale of two cities' (one rich, the other poor) led to a crushing defeat of Republican nominee Joe Lhota, the former MTA chairman. To resounding success, de Blasio had run not only against his nominal opponent, but also against Mayor Bloomberg.

De Blasio's most concrete promise as a candidate was a proposed tax on the wealthy to pay for a universal preschool programme, a much-needed boon for working families. He also promised a fairer shake to workers in contract negotiations with the unions representing city employees. The contracts were actually up during Bloomberg's final term, but instead of tackling the thorny task of achieving long-term agreements, Bloomberg settled for short-term extensions, leaving the problem of reaching a final resolution to his successor. Undoubtedly, de Blasio is aware that another famously liberal New York Mayor, John Lindsay, endured crippling strikes in 1966 and 1968 by transport workers, teachers and sanitation employees over the same contract renewals; just as undoubtedly, de Blasio would prefer that history not repeat itself.

Among other measures, the new Mayor has indicated that he will sharply curtail the NYPD's controversial 'stop-and-frisk' policy, which basically targeted young of men of colour, allowing the police to detain and search them for contraband – especially guns – on thin legal pretexts. More often than not, the dragnet hauled in the innocent rather than the guilty, and statistically, it made no real impact on crime.

As for quality-of-life issues, de Blasio sides with animal rights activist who want to abolish Central Park's famed horse carriage rides, condemning the practice as cruel. A pet project of Bloomberg's – a standardised fleet of Nissan-built 'taxis of tomorrow' – isn't expected to survive, mainly because cab-fleet owners against the idea were major contributors to de Blasio's campaign. Yet so far, the new mayor has not indicated what he will do. In any case, the project is stuck in legal limbo by a lawsuit by fleet owners claiming that neither the mayor nor the Taxi and Limousine Commission have the right to dictate what make of vehicle can be used as cabs. As for other Bloomberg initiatives – the smoking ban, the prohibition on large sugared soft drinks – de Blasio has already stated that these will remain.

In other words, so far the new mayor has scarcely conducted himself like a Bolshevik. He's staffed his administration with experienced hands, including people who had worked for Bloomberg. His highest profile appointment, that of Police Commissioner, went to William Bratton, the top cop under Mayor Rudolph Giuliani during the early 1990s, when crime in New York was at its worst and the effort to stem it required heavy lifting. De Blasio appointed a renowned educator as Chancellor of New York's public school system (in sharp contrast to Bloomberg, who had selected a close friend – a magazine publisher – for the post, with disastrous consequences).

'In most respects... New York remains as it has been under Bloomberg: a gleaming metropolis moving inexorably forward as if on autopilot.'

THE HIGH LIFE

In most respects, however, New York remains as it has been under Bloomberg: a gleaming global metropolis moving inexorably forward as if on autopilot. All the major development projects initiated under Bloomberg remain underway. The extension of the 7 train to West 34th Street and Tenth Avenue opens in autumn 2014, and the first leg of the long-delayed Second Avenue subway (from E 63rd to E 96th Streets) is on track for its debut two years later. The first part of the massive Hudson Yards neighbourhood being built over the MTA rail yards on the far West Side – an 80-storey skyscraper at West 33rd Street and Tenth Avenue – is rising, and media giant Time Warner has just announced that it will be moving its headquarters there. Just a block over, another huge high-rise project, Manhattan West, is being erected over another part of the rail yards extending to Ninth Avenue.

Up on 57th Street, 'the billionaire boys' club' condo tower designed by French architect Christian de Portzamparc presides over the skyline as the tallest residential structure in New York. Better known as One57, it earned its nickname because its apartments, which can occupy anywhere from one to three entire floors, cost upwards of $90 to $100 million dollars. It's marketed towards international plutocrats looking for a pied-à-terre and a safe place to park some of their wealth. But these moneyed elites have no intention of becoming New Yorkers in any meaningful sense: most of them are expected to spend little time, if any, in their new castles in the clouds. Furthermore, buyers receive tax subsidies allowing them to purchase their homes more readily. When confronted with complaints that these absentee residents add little to the life of the city, and indeed, raise the cost of real estate for everyone, Bloomberg, during his final days in office, replied that he'd like to see even more billionaires move to town. The wave of global rich roosting here is unlikely to abate anytime soon. One57 represents the vanguard of similar buildings with similar architectural pedigrees being built nearby. Also in midtown, the Museum of Modern Art announced that it will proceed with its controversial plan to tear down the former American Folk Art Museum building as part of a 40,000 square foot expansion that will include space in yet another skyscraper, this time conceived by starchitect Jean Nouvel – a cystralline confection slated for West 53rd Street near Sixth Avenue.

BOOMING BOROUGHS

If there is one part of New York utterly transformed by the Bloomberg years, it is, of course, Brooklyn, where redevelopment continues apace. True, there were some snags there as well with the ongoing Atlantic Yards saga. Although the centrepiece Barclays Center arena has quickly become known for hosting superstar concerts by Jay-Z, Beyoncé, Rihanna and the like, the *Wall Street Journal* reported that the venue lagged 'tens of millions of dollars behind projections for operating income' in its first year. Meanwhile the complex's developer Bruce Ratner put a temporary halt in the construction of the first of 15 towers slated for the area, just as he negotiated the sale of a 70 per cent stake in the site to a Chinese concern. His promises to create affordable housing within the development – a key reason for the project's approval –

One57.

Theater for a New Audience.

have yet to materialise, much to the consternation of local politicians.

But the Barclays Center is just one facet of a considerable cultural shift to the second borough. The Downtown Brooklyn Cultural District continues to expand with the autumn 2013 opening of a gleaming modernist box housing the Theater for a New Audience, among other arts venues. The debut was hot on the heels of the Brooklyn Academy of Music's new Fisher Building, which contains a flexible theatre-cum-studio. Along with plans for a cultural space within another high-rise that is underway, the area will soon rival Lincoln Center as a performing-arts hub. Developments are also afoot for waterfront areas of Williamsburg and Greenpoint, which are still magnets for the young and hip, but will soon be clogged with condos beyond the reach of the heroines of *Girls*. Not to be outdone, Queens will see the city begin its $3 billion clean-up and redevelopment of the Willets Point area, while in the Bronx, there are hopes for a new major league soccer stadium to be built near Yankee Stadium. And in the not too distant future, Cornell University will be opening a world-class tech camp on Roosevelt Island.

So New York today is pretty much as it has been for a while, in spite of the various traumas inflicted upon it during the last decade or so – the World Trade Center attacks, the 2003 blackout, the 2008 financial meltdown, Hurricane Sandy in 2012. That is to say things are proceeding fairly smoothly, and it's unlikely de Blasio will change that or want to. Indeed, the de Blasio era seems off to a quiet start, so much so, that the media has had to focus on minor stories: would he, unlike Bloomberg, move his family from their Brooklyn brownstone to the mayoral residence, Gracie Mansion? (He did); how well will he cope with the city's first major snowstorm under his watch? (Quite well, actually, though the storm turned out to be not so major); did he really eat pizza with a fork and knife? (Yes. Get over it).

In truth, de Blasio has been fortunate with respect to the moment he presides over. For all of its inequality, the New York he's inherited is a city free of major crisis – unlike Giuliani (who had to deal with a Gotham that seemed out of control), or Bloomberg (who was sworn in in the aftermath of 9/11). De Blasio has major challenges to face – not only his own promise to right the city's economic wrongs, but also the impact of global warming and rising sea levels on New York that are sure to become more apparent as time goes on. In the long run, though, de Blasio's legacy will rest on the New York he bequeaths to his successor.

Itineraries

Make the most of every New York minute with our three-day tour of the metropolis.

Day 1

8AM Start your New York odyssey downtown, where Manhattan began and where millions of immigrants embarked on a new life. Get an organic caffeine jolt at Jack's Stir Brew Coffee (p60), then stroll over to the recently revamped Pier 15 for great views of the East River and the Brooklyn Bridge. Head further south if you want to hop on the free Staten Island Ferry for classic panoramas of New York Harbor and the Statue of Liberty.

11AM Now it's time to explore some of the traditional immigrant neighbourhoods, just a few subway stops away, that helped to create the character of the metropolis. Chinatown, Little Italy and the Lower East Side are within easy walking distance of one another and their borders are increasingly blurred. For a late morning snack, try Nom Wah Tea Parlor (p74), Chinatown's oldest dim sum venue, or grab a Super Heebster bagel from Russ & Daughters (p91), an LES purveyor of

Jewish delicacies for more than a century. To get a sense of how the ancestors of many New Yorkers lived, tour one of the reconstructed immigrants' apartments at the Lower East Side Tenement Museum (p83).

2PM The neighbourhood has changed considerably since its turn-of-the-19th-century squalor. Not only is it bursting at the seams with idiosyncratic shops – boutique-cum-bar the Dressing Room (p90) and rockin' clothier the Cast (p88), for example – it's also now a booming art district.

Gallery-hop the art spaces in the vicinity (see p89 for our picks). If you get peckish, stop by Katz's Delicatessen (p85) for an overstuffed pastrami on rye. Afterwards, there is more boundary-pushing creativity on display at the New Museum of Contemporary Art (p84). From here, cross the Bowery into Nolita for chic indie shops including jewellery designer Erica Weiner (p79) and LA-born boutique Creatures of Comfort (p78).

7PM Although the dining options in Little Italy are unremarkable, Nolita now has some great new-school Italian restaurants, including Torrisi Italian Specialties (p78) and Estela (p77).

9PM After dinner, amble back to the Lower East Side for a night of bar hopping and burlesque – we recommend Attaboy (p86), and the Slipper Room (p266) – or cross the river to Williamsburg, the city's new nightlife nerve centre, to catch a gig at offbeat indie venues like Pete's Candy Store (p276) or dance until dawn at Output (p264).

Clockwise from top left: **Staten Island Ferry; Chinatown; Creatures of Comfort; Attaboy.**

Day 2

9AM A short break in the Big Apple involves some tough choices: the Upper East Side's Museum Mile alone is lined with half a dozen world-class institutions. Fortify yourself with sumptuous pastries and exquisite coffee at Café Sabarsky (p182) as you mull over your itinerary. If you opt for the Metropolitan Museum of Art (p180), you can either take a brisk two-hour essentials tour or forget the rest of the itinerary entirely – the vast museum is home to more than two million objects. Don't miss the recently rehung European Paintings Galleries, the Temple of Dendur and the newly renovated Costume Institute among the many highlights. The Iris & B Gerald Cantor Roof Garden offers a view over Central Park, as well as a new installation each year, in the warmer months. Afterwards, even if you decide you can't manage another Museum Mile institution, walk a few blocks north to the Guggenheim (p182) to admire the curvaceous lines of its Frank Lloyd Wright-designed exterior. Now it's time to ease your art-saturated brain with a stroll in the park. Enter at 79th or 76th Street and walk south to admire the picturesque Conservatory Water, or cross East Drive and try to snag a table at the outdoor bar at the Loeb Boathouse to gaze at the somewhat incongruous sight of gondolas on the lake over drinks.

1PM Grab a taxi on Fifth Avenue (or walk through the park) to the Museum of Modern Art (p152). If you happen to be in town on a Friday, it's worth noting it stays open until 8pm. Before you take in the superb collection of art and design, lunch at the more affordable bar of MoMA's destination restaurant, the Modern.

5PM Once you've had your fill of Alsatian-inspired fare and modern masterpieces, it's time to get high. Rockefeller Center's Top of the Rock (p152) is a less-mobbed alternative to the Empire State Building – and affords a good view of the latter iconic structure.

8PM Evening, though, brings more dilemmas. Should you head back uptown for a global contemporary twist on soul food and live music at Red Rooster in Harlem (p190)? Or maybe it would be better to stick to midtown for a dozen Long Island oysters at the Grand Central Oyster Bar & Restaurant (p156), followed by a Broadway or Off-Broadway show. It's simply a matter of taste.

Top: **Loeb Boathouse**. Bottom: **Grand Central Oyster Bar & Restaurant**.

On and off the High Line

A disused freight-train track reborn as a public park-cum-promenade, the High Line has existed in its current incarnation for only half a decade, but it is already one of the most popular spots with visitors and locals alike. The lush, landscaped green strip provides a verdant pathway between the somewhat hedonistic Meatpacking District and the still-evolving neighbourhood of Hell's Kitchen, cutting through the city's main gallery district in Chelsea. You could easily spend an entire day traversing its length, disembarking to enjoy attractions, eateries and bars along the way.

The urban sanctuary has a less-than-serene history. Back in the early days of the 20th century, when freight-bearing trains competed with horses, carts and pedestrians on Tenth Avenue, the thoroughfare was so treacherous it earned the moniker 'Death Avenue'. In an attempt to counteract the carnage, mounted men known as 'West Side Cowboys' would ride in front of the train, waving red flags to warn of its imminent approach. These urban cowboys lost their jobs when the West Side Improvement Project finally raised the railway off street level and put it up on to an overhead trestle – the High Line – in 1934. Originally stretching from 34th Street to Spring Street, the line fell into disuse after World War II as trucks replaced trains. A southern chunk was torn down in the 1960s, and, after the last train ground to a halt in 1980, local property owners lobbied for its destruction. However, thanks to the efforts of railroad enthusiast Peter Obletz and, later, the Friends of the High Line, the industrial relic was saved. A decade after the group began advocating for its reuse as a public space, the first phase of New York's first elevated public park opened in summer 2009 (the second leg followed two years later).

Start your expedition in the Meatpacking District, where upscale shops include designer department store Jeffrey New York (p119) and independent boutiques including Owen (p119) and antique jewellers Doyle & Doyle (p119). You can combine retail therapy with a jolt of caffeine at the Rag & Bone General Store (p119), which has an on-site coffee bar.

From here, it's just a couple of blocks to the southernmost entrance to the High Line (p118), on Washington Street, at Gansevoort Street. As you mount the stairs, you'll notice a steel-and-glass structure to your left. The new home of the Whitney Museum of American Art (p113), opening in spring 2015, has 50,000 square feet of indoor exhibition space, plus alfresco terrace galleries.

As you stroll north alongside trees, flowers and landscaped greenery, keep an eye out for several interesting features. Commanding an expansive river view, the 'sun deck' between 14th and 15th Streets has wooden deck chairs that can be rolled along the original tracks, plus a water feature for cooling your feet. Just past 15th Street, the High Line cuts through the loading dock of the former Nabisco factory. This conglomeration of 18 structures, built between the 1890s and the 1930s, now houses Chelsea Market (75 Ninth Avenue, between 15th & 16th Streets, www.chelseamarket.com). Alight here if you want to shop in the ground-floor food arcade for artisanal bread, wine, baked goods and freshly made ice-cream, among other treats. From around late April until late October, however, food vendors set up on the High Line itself, and you can stop for a tipple at seasonal open-air café, the Porch, at 15th Street, which serves local wine and beer from cult vino spot Terroir (p103).

Top: **The High Line's 'sun deck'**. Middle: **Chelsea Market**. Bottom: **The Porch**.

HIGH LAWN

Between 22nd and 23rd Streets, a 4,900-square-foot lawn and reclaimed teak seating steps are a prime people-watching perch.

The elevated walkway provides a great vantage point for viewing the surrounding architecture; you will see not only iconic structures like the Statue of Liberty and the Empire State Building, but also newer buildings such as Frank Gehry's 2007 headquarters for Barry Diller's InterActiveCorp (555 W 18th Street, at West Side Highway), which comprises tilting glass volumes that resemble a fully rigged tall ship.

By now it's probably time for brunch. Descend the stairs at 20th Street for Cookshop (p124), which serves eggs with applewood bacon and seasonal variations on French toast. Nearby, the iconic Empire Diner (p124) recently reopened, now helmed by celebrity chef Amanda Freitag. At time of writing, it was open evenings only, but the chef has plans to extend the hours, so keep an eye on the website for updates.

Fortified, you're ready for some cultural sustenance. In the 1980s, many of New York's galleries left Soho for what was then an industrial wasteland on the western edge of Chelsea. Today, blue-chip spaces and numerous less exalted ones attract swarms of art aficionados to the area between Tenth and Eleventh Avenues from 19th to 29th

Streets (see p125 Gallery-Hopping Guide for our picks). If you have limited time, hit 24th Street, which has a concentration of high-profile spaces. At the street's western corner, check out the 19-storey apartment building at 200 Eleventh Avenue. Designed by Annabelle Selldorf, it has a car elevator, allowing residents to bring their prized motor up to their door. A couple of blocks north is a notable example of industrial architecture, the 1929 Starrett-Lehigh Building (601 W 26th Street, at Eleventh Avenue). If you want to pick up a souvenir, stop by arty bookshop Printed Matter (see p127).

Your art tour isn't over when you resume your High Line perambulation (there are stairs at 23rd and 26th Street). The park itself is a platform for creativity and has a dedicated curator of temporary site-specific installations, so keep an eye out for changing installations along its length.

In late 2014, the first phase of the final section of the High Line, skirting the under-construction mixed-use complex Hudson Yards, is slated to open; until then, you'll reach the end of the line at 30th Street.

From here, you can walk or take a taxi to Hell's Kitchen. At Gotham West Market (p149), a contemporary take on a food court, you can sample food from several cult eateries including new arrival from Tokyo, IvanRamen. Otherwise, Ninth Avenue in the 40s and 50s is packed with inexpensive restaurants serving just about any ethnic cuisine you can think of. Afterwards,the bright lights of Broadway (and Off Broadway), a few blocks away, beckon. Score cut-price Broadway tickets at TKTS (p144), or see high-level cabaret at 54 Below (p283), located in the bowels of legendary nightspot Studio 54.

NEW YORK FOR FREE

Some of the best things in the city are literally priceless.

SUMMER SAVINGS

When the temperature soars, the populace heads outside for superb events, from the star-studded plays of Shakespeare in the Park to big-name concerts downtown in the River to River Festival.

CASHLESS CULTURE

Time it right and you can visit many top institutions at no charge. On Friday nights, the Museum of Modern Art stays open late and admission – including films – is waived, while on the first Saturday of most months the Brooklyn Museum lays on live performances in addition to evening admission. New York also has many fine museums that are always free, including the National Museum of the American Indian, the Museum at FIT and the American Folk Art Museum.

CHEAPSKATES' CRUISE

It's no secret that the Staten Island Ferry provides thrilling panoramas of New York Harbor and the Statue of Liberty during its brief crossing. You can also cruise to Red Hook on New York Water Taxi's IKEA Express Shuttle (p373), which is free on weekends and has an outdoor deck to take in the skyline en route.

GARDEN VARIETY

Offering more than mere greenery, New York's parks are filled with diversions, from the art-studded High Line to Brooklyn Bridge Park's vintage carousel.

GET IN ON THE ACT

Free entertainment isn't only on the streets. At some of the Upright Citizens Brigade Theater's long-running comedy shows, the laughs are on them, and you can catch Thursday-night concerts at Lincoln Center's David Rubenstein Atrium.

Diary

Plan ahead with our year-round guide to the best celebrations and shows.

New Yorkers hardly struggle to find something to celebrate. The venerable city-wide traditions are well known, but don't miss the neighbourhood shindigs: you can soak up the local vibe at quirky annual events such as Brooklyn's Mermaid Parade or East Village beatnik bash Howl!, and take advantage of free summer concerts and outdoor films in the city's green spaces, such as Bryant, Central and Madison Square Parks. For more festivals and events, check out the other chapters in the Arts & Entertainment section. Before you set out or plan a trip around an event, it's wise to call or check online first as dates, times and locations are subject to change. For the latest listings, consult Time Out New York magazine or www.timeout.com/newyork.

Spring

Armory Show
Piers 92 & 94, Twelfth Avenue, at 55th Street, Hell's Kitchen (1-212 645 6440, www.thearmoryshow.com). Subway C, E to 50th Street. **Date** early Mar. **Map** p399 B22.
Although its name pays homage to the 1913 show that introduced avant-garde European art to an American audience, this contemporary international art mart debuted in 1999. Now held on the Hudson River, it has expanded to include 21st-century work.

St Patrick's Day Parade
Fifth Avenue, from 44th to 86th Streets, Midtown to Upper East Side (www.nycstpatricksparade.org). **Date** 17 Mar. **Map** p398 E24, p400 E18.
This massive march is even older than the United States – it was started by a group of homesick Irish conscripts from the British army in 1762. If you feel like braving huge crowds and potentially nasty weather, you'll see thousands of green-clad merrymakers strutting to the sounds of pipe bands.

Easter Parade
Fifth Avenue, from 49th to 57th Streets, Midtown (1-212 484 1222). Subway E, M to Fifth Avenue-53rd Street. **Date** late Mar/early Apr. **Map** p398 E23-E22.
Annual procession where participants show off elaborately constructed hats – we're talking noggin-toppers shaped like the NYC skyline or the Coney Island Cyclone. Starting at 10am on Easter Sunday, Fifth Avenue becomes a car-free promenade of gussied-up crowds milling around and showing off their extravagant bonnets.

Tribeca Film Festival
Date Apr.
See p252.

Sakura Matsuri (Cherry Blossom Festival)
For listings, *see p206* **Brooklyn Botanic Garden**. **Date** late Apr.
The climax to the cherry blossom season, when the BBG's 220 trees are in flower, the annual *sakura matsuri* celebrates both the blooms and Japanese culture with concerts, traditional dance, manga exhibitions and tea ceremonies.

TD Five Boro Bike Tour
Lower Manhattan to Staten Island (1-212 870 2080, www.bikenewyork.org). **Date** early May. **Map** p396 E34.
Thousands of cyclists take over the city for a 40-mile, car-free Tour de New York. Advance registration is required if you want to take part. The route begins near Battery Park, moves up through Manhattan and makes a circuit of the boroughs before winding up at Staten Island's Fort Wadsworth for a festival.

PUBLIC HOLIDAYS

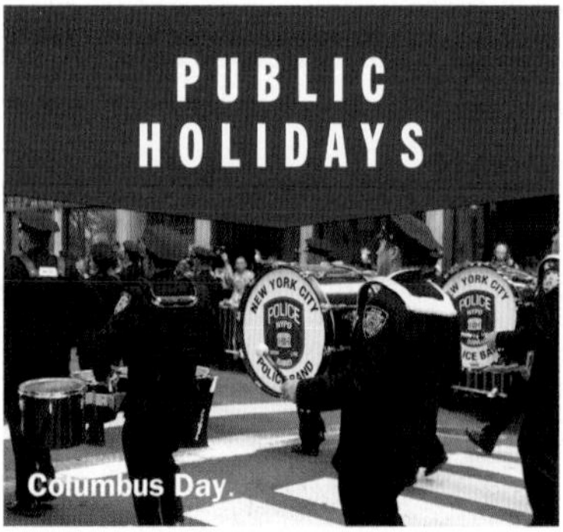
Columbus Day.

Memorial Day
26 May 2014, 25 May 2015

Independence Day
4 July

Labor Day
1 Sept 2014, 7 Sept 2015

Columbus Day
13 Oct 2014, 12 Oct 2015

Veteran's Day
11 Nov

Thanksgiving Day
27 Nov 2014, 26 Nov 2015

Christmas Day
25 Dec

New Year's Day
1 Jan

Martin Luther King, Jr Day
19 Jan 2015

Presidents Day
16 Feb 2015

Thanksgiving Day.

Frieze Art Fair New York

Randalls Island Park, (www.friezenewyork.com).
Date early/mid May.

The New York edition of the tent-tastic London art fair first arrived on Randalls Island in 2011. A global array of around 190 galleries set up shop under a temporary structure overlooking the East River, and several contemporary artists are commissioned to create site-specific works.

Lower East Side Festival of the Arts

Theater for the New City, 155 First Avenue, between 9th & 10th Streets, Lower East Side (1-212 254 1109, www.theaterforthenewcity.net). Subway L to First Avenue; 6 to Astor Place.
Date late May. **Map** p397 F28.

Theater for the New City runs this annual celebration of artistic diversity. Over the course of three days, the venue's four theatres feature more than 70 theatrical troupes, poetry readings, aerial dance, films and family-friendly programming. Food and craft vendors set up outside.

Washington Square Outdoor Art Exhibit

Various streets surrounding Washington Square Park, from University Place, at 13th Street, to Schwartz Plaza, at 3rd Street, Greenwich Village

Top: **TD Five Boro Bike Tour.** Bottom: **SummerStage.**

(1-212 982 6255, www.wsoae.org). Subway A, B, C, D, E, F, M to W 4th Street; N, R to 8th Street-NYU. **Date** late May/early June & late Aug/early Sept. **Map** p397 E28/29.

In 1931, Jackson Pollock and Willem de Kooning propped up a few of their paintings on the sidewalk near Washington Square Park and called it a show. A lot has changed since then: now, more than 125 artists and artisans exhibit at the Washington Square Outdoor Art Exhibit. If you miss it in May and June, you'll have another chance to browse in late summer.

Summer

Howl! Festival

Various East Village locations (1-212 466 6666, www.howlfestival.com). **Date** early June. **Map** p397.

A reading of Allen Ginsberg's seminal poem kicks off this three-day arts fest – a grab bag of art events, film screenings, poetry readings, performance art and much more.

SummerStage

Rumsey Playfield, Central Park, entrance on Fifth Avenue, at 72nd Street, Upper East Side (1-212 360 2777, www.summerstage.org). Subway 6 to 68th Street-Hunter College.
Date June-Aug. **Map** p399 E20.

Now held in parks across the city, these concerts embody summer for many New Yorkers, and break down the boundaries between artistic mediums. Rockers, world music stars, orchestras and other performers take over the main stage in Central Park at this very popular, mostly free annual series. Show up early or plan to listen from outside the enclosure gates (not a bad option if you bring a blanket and snacks).

Shakespeare in the Park

Date June-Aug.
See p308.

Celebrate Brooklyn!

Prospect Park Bandshell, Prospect Park West, at 9th Street, Park Slope, Brooklyn (1-718 855 7882, www.bricartsmedia.org). Subway F to Seventh Avenue. **Date** June-Aug. **Map** p404 T12.

Community arts organisation BRIC launched this series of outdoor performances to revitalise Prospect Park, and now the festival is Brooklyn's premier summer fête. It includes music, dance, film and spoken word acts. A $3 donation is requested and there's an admission charge for some shows.

National Puerto Rican Day Parade

Fifth Avenue, from 44th to 79th Streets, Midtown to Upper East Side (1-718 401 0404, www.nationalpuertoricandayparade.org).
Date early June. **Map** p398 E24-p399 E19.

A whopping 80,000 Nuyoricans take part in the march, including vejigantes (carnival dancers), colourful floats and live salsa and reggaetón bands at this freewheeling celebration of the city's largest Hispanic community and its culture.

Egg Rolls & Egg Creams Festival

For listings, *see p84* **Museum at Eldridge Street**. **Date** early June. **Map** p396 F31.

This block party celebrates the convergence of Jewish and Chinese traditions on the Lower East Side, with klezmer music, acrobats, Torah scribes, tea ceremonies and, of course, plenty of the titular treats.

Governors Ball Music Festival

Randalls Island Park (www.governorsballmusic festival.com). **Date** early June.

Catch big names in rock, pop and hip hop at this three-day outdoor festival. Recent headliners have included the Strokes, Jack White, TV on the Radio, local-boys-made-good Vampire Weekend, dubstep renegade Skrillex, UK house sensation Disclosure and soul fantasist Janelle Monáe.

Big Apple Barbecue Block Party

Madison Square Park, Flatiron District (www.bigapplebbq.org). **Date** early June. **Map** 404 E26.

Get your fill of the best 'cue around as the country's top pit masters band together for this two-day outdoor carnivore's paradise. Live music, chefs' demos and tips are also on the menu.

Museum Mile Festival

Fifth Avenue, from 82nd to 105th Streets, Upper East Side (1-212 606 2296, www.museummilefestival.org). **Date** early June.
Map p399 E19-p400 E16.

Nine of the city's most prestigious art institutions – including the Guggenheim, the Met and the Museum of the City of New York – open their doors to the public free of charge. Music, dance and children's activities turn this into a 23-block-long celebration, but you'll have to arrive early to stand a chance of getting into the museums themselves.

★ River to River Festival

Various venues along the West Side & southern waterfronts of Manhattan (1-212 219 9401, www.rivertorivernyc.com). **Date** Mid-late June.
Lower Manhattan organisations present hundreds of free events – from walks to all manner of arts performances – at various waterside venues. Past performers have included Patti Smith, Laurie Anderson and Angélique Kidjo.

★ Mermaid Parade

Coney Island, Brooklyn (1-718 372 5159, www.coneyisland.com). Subway D, F, N, Q to Coney Island-Stillwell Avenue. **Date** 3rd Sat in June.
Glitter-covered semi-nude revellers, aquatically adorned floats and classic cruisers fill Surf Avenue for this annual art parade.

★ Midsummer Night Swing

Damrosch Park at Lincoln Center Plaza, W 62nd Street, between Columbus and Amsterdam Avenues, Upper West Side (1-212 721 6500, www.midsummernightswing.org). Subway 1 to 66th Street-Lincoln Center. **Date** late June-mid July. **Map** p399 C21.
Lincoln Center's Damrosch Park is turned into a giant dancefloor as bands play salsa, Cajun, swing and other music. For three weeks (Tue-Sat), each night's party is devoted to a different dance style, and is preceded by lessons. Beginners are, of course, welcome.

★ NYC LGBT Pride March

From Fifth Avenue, at 36th Street, to Christopher Street, Midtown to West Village (1-212 807 7433, www.nycpride.org). **Date** late June.
Downtown Manhattan becomes a sea of rainbow flags as lesbian, gay, bisexual and transgendered people from the city and beyond parade down Fifth Avenue in commemoration of the 1969 Stonewall Riots. After the march, there's a massive street fair and a dance on the West Side piers.

Warm Up

Date late June-early Sept.
See p267.

Macy's Fourth of July Fireworks

1-212 494 4495, www.macys.com/fireworks.
Date 4 July.
The city's star Independence Day attraction is also the nation's largest Fourth of July fireworks display. Traditionally launched from barges on the East River, in 2009 the fireworks moved to the Hudson, and they have remained there for the last five years; call or check the website to be certain of the location. The pyrotechnics start at around 9pm, but you'll need to scope out your vantage point much earlier than that for a reasonable view. Keep in mind, however, that spectators are packed like sardines at prime public spots, so many choose to keep their distance.

New York Philharmonic Concerts in the Parks

Date July.
See p289 **Everything Under the Sun**.

Harlem Week

Various Harlem locations (1-212 862 8477, www.harlemweek.com). Subway B, C, 2, 3 to 135th Street. **Date** late July-late Aug. **Map** p401.
Get into the groove at this massive culture fest, which began in 1974 as a one-day event. Harlem Day is still the centrepiece of the event, but 'Week' is now a misnomer; besides the street fair serving up music, art and food along 135th Street, a wealth of concerts, films, dance performances, fashion and sports events are on tap for more than a month.

Summer Restaurant Week

www.nycgo.com/restaurantweek. **Date** late July/early Aug.
Twice a year, for two weeks or more at a stretch, some of the city's finest restaurants dish out three-course prix-fixe lunches for $25; some places also offer dinner for $38. For the full list of participating restaurants, visit the website. You'll need to make reservations well in advance.

Lincoln Center Out of Doors

For listings, *see p286* **Lincoln Center**.
Date late July-mid Aug.
Free dance, music, theatre, opera and more make up the programme over the course of three weeks at this family-friendly and ambitious festival.

New York International Fringe Festival

Various venues (1-212 279 4488, www.fringenyc.org). **Date** early-late Aug.
Wacky and sometimes wonderful, downtown's Fringe Festival – inspired by the Edinburgh original – shoehorns hundreds of arts performances into 16 theatre-crammed days.
► *See p308 for more information on Off-Off Broadway shows.*

US Open

USTA Billie Jean King National Tennis Center, Flushing Meadows Corona Park, Queens (1-718 760 6200, www.usopen.org). **Date** late Aug-early Sept.
For two weeks every summer, Flushing, Queens, becomes the centre of the tennis universe when it hosts the final Grand Slam event of the year.

Autumn

West Indian-American Day Carnival Parade

Eastern Parkway, from Schenectady Avenue to Flatbush Avenue, Crown Heights, Brooklyn (1-718 467 1797, www.wiadcacarnival.org).

Subway 2, 3 to Grand Army Plaza; 3, 4 to Crown Heights-Utica Avenue. **Date** early Sept. **Map** p404 W11-U11.
This Caribbean celebration is never short on costumed stilt dancers, floats blaring soca and calypso music, and plenty of flags from countries such as Barbados, Jamaica, and Trinidad and Tobago. Look for vendors stationed along Eastern Parkway selling island eats like jerk chicken, curry goat and oxtail.

Feast of San Gennaro

Mulberry Street, between Canal & Houston Streets; Grand Street, between Baxter & Mott Streets; Hester Street, between Baxter & Mott Streets, Little Italy (1-212 768 9320, www.sangennaro.org). Subway B, D, F, M to Broadway-Lafayette Street; J, N, Q, R, Z, 6 to Canal Street. **Date** mid-late Sept. **Map** p398 F30.
Celebrate the martyred third-century bishop and patron saint of Naples at this 11-day festival that fills the streets of Little Italy every year. Come after dark, when sparkling lights arch over Mulberry Street and the smells of frying *zeppole* (custard- or jam-filled fritters) and sausages hang in the sultry air. On the final Saturday in September, a statue of San Gennaro is carried in a Grand Procession outside the Most Precious Blood Church (109 Mulberry Street, between Canal & Hester Streets).

Next Wave Festival

For listings, *see p285* **Brooklyn Academy of Music. Date** Sept-Dec.
The festival is among the most highly anticipated of the city's autumn culture offerings, as it showcases only the very best in avant-garde music, dance, theatre and opera. Legends like John Cale, Meredith Monk and Steve Reich are among the many luminaries the festival has hosted.

Dumbo Arts Festival

Various locations in Dumbo, Brooklyn (1-718 488 8588, www.dumboartsfestival.com). Subway A, C to High Street; F to York Street. **Date** late Sept. **Map** p405 S9-T9.
Dumbo has been an artists' enclave for decades, and this weekend of art appreciation is hugely popular. Expect gallery shows, open studios, installations, concerts, dance and other arts events.

Atlantic Antic

Atlantic Avenue, from Fourth Avenue to Hicks Street, Brooklyn (1-718 243 1414, www.atlanticave.org). Subway B, Q, 2, 3, 4, 5 to Atlantic Avenue; D, N, R to Pacific Street. **Date** late Sept. **Map** p404 T10-S10.
More than 500 food and craft vendors and several stages close down a busy Brooklyn artery for the annual Atlantic Antic. Spanning ten blocks and cutting through four neighbourhoods, it's billed as NYC's largest street fair, and features local bands and cult Brooklyn food and drink.

BARKING MAD

Check out the wackiest events on the NYC calendar.

AIR SEX WORLD CHAMPIONSHIPS

Late June, www.airsexworld.com
Like an adult air-guitar tournament, this competition lets punters display their skills playing an imaginary...um...instrument. Hosted by comedian Chris Trew, the rules are simple: no nudity, all orgasms must be simulated and there must be an imaginary partner or object involved in your act. A panel of judges (comics, sex professionals) adjudicate the first round, with the audience choosing the eventual winner. New York is but one stop on the Air Sex World Championships' nationwide tour – regional winners throw down in Austin, Texas, at the end of the year.

TOMPKINS SQUARE PARK HALLOWEEN DOG PARADE

Late Oct, www.firstrunfriends.org
To see a plethora of puppies in adorable outfits, head to this canine costume parade, which has been an East Village institution for more than two decades. The getups are remarkably elaborate and conceptual; in 2013 they included Evita, ET and one of the sandworms from *Beetlejuice*. Enterprising owners stand to win prizes if their dog is selected Best in Show.

NO PANTS SUBWAY RIDE

January, www.improveverywhere.com
Improv Everywhere's annual barefaced, bare-legged mission began in January 2002 with a handful of operatives in one car on the downtown 6 train, but it's grown into a well-publicised mass event. Admittedly, it's not the mildly subversive, playful prank it was – it's now a chance for New Yorkers to perform a cheeky feat while supported by thousands of fellow residents. For unsuspecting visitors, it's a surreal spectacle. *Photo above.*

★ New York Film Festival
Date late Sept-mid Oct.
See p252.

★ Open House New York Weekend
1-212 991 6470, www.ohny.org. **Date** mid Oct.
More than 150 of the city's coolest and most exclusive architectural sites, private homes and landmarks open their doors during a weekend of urban exploration. Behind-the-scenes tours and educational programmes are also on offer.

CMJ Music Marathon & Film Festival
Various venues (1-212 235 7027, www.cmj.com).
Date mid Oct.
The annual *College Music Journal* schmooze-fest draws fans and music-industry types to one of the best showcases for new rock, indie, hip hop and electronica acts. The Film Festival, which runs in tandem, includes a wide range of feature and short films.

New York City Wine & Food Festival
Various locations (www.nycwff.org). **Date** mid Oct.
The Food Network's epicurean fete offers four belt-busting days of tasting events and celebrity-chef demos.

★ Village Halloween Parade
Sixth Avenue, from Spring to 16th Streets, Greenwich Village (www.halloween-nyc.com).
Date 31 Oct. **Map** p397 E30-D27.
The sidewalks at this iconic Village shindig are always packed beyond belief. For the best vantage point, don a costume and watch from inside the parade (the line-up starts at 6.30pm on Sixth Avenue, at Spring Street; the parade kicks off at 7pm).

Winter

New York Comedy Festival
Various venues (www.nycomedyfestival.com).
Date early Nov.
This five-day laugh fest features both big names (Jerry Seinfeld, Louis CK and Ricky Gervais in recent years) and up-and-comers.

ING New York City Marathon
Staten Island side of the Verrazano-Narrows Bridge to Tavern on the Green in Central Park (1-212 423 2249, www.ingnycmarathon.org).
Date early Nov.
Around 45,000 runners hotfoot it through all five boroughs over a 26.2-mile course. We recommend Fourth Avenue in Park Slope, Brooklyn; First Avenue between 60th and 96th Streets in Manhattan; or Central Park South – to get a good view.

Radio City Christmas Spectacular
For listings, *see p277* **Radio City Music Hall**.
Date early Nov-late Dec.

Top: **Mermaid Parade** (*see p34*). Bottom: **New Year's Eve in Times Square.**

IN THE KNOW
FORWARD THINKING

If you want to attend high-profile events like the Next Wave Festival (*see p34*) and New York Film Festival (*see above*), it's wise to book ahead. Hotly anticipated screenings and shows sell out quickly, so monitor the website as early as possible before your trip. BAM announces the Next Wave lineup in spring, for example, and the NYFF opens booking about three weeks in advance.

High-kicking precision dance troupe the Rockettes and an onstage nativity scene with live animals are the rather kitsch attractions at this annual homage to the Yuletide season.

Macy's Thanksgiving Day Parade & Balloon Inflation

Central Park West, at 77th Street, to Macy's, Broadway, at 34th Street, Upper West Side to Midtown (1-212 494 4495, www.macys.com/parade). **Date** late Nov. **Map** p399 D19-404 D25.

At 9am on Thanksgiving Day, the stars of this nationally televised parade are the gigantic balloons, the elaborate floats and good ol' Santa Claus. The evening before, New Yorkers brave the cold night air to watch the rubbery colossi take shape at the inflation area around the Museum of Natural History (beginning at 79th Street & Columbus Avenue).

Rockefeller Center Tree-Lighting Ceremony

Rockefeller Center, Fifth Avenue, between 49th & 50th Streets, Midtown West (1-212 332 6868, www.rockefellercenter.com). Subway B, D, F, M to 47th-50th Streets-Rockefeller Center. **Date** late Nov. **Map** p398 E23.

Proceedings start at 7pm, but this festive celebration is always mobbed, so get there early. The actual lighting takes place at the end of the programme; most of the two-hour event is devoted to celebrity performances (Mary J Blige and Jewel were among the recent human luminaries). Then the 30,000 LEDs covering the massive evergreen are switched on to mass oohs and aahs. If this doesn't sound like fun, there's plenty of time to view the tree over the holidays.

Unsilent Night

Washington Square Arch, Fifth Avenue, at Waverly Place, to Tompkins Square Park, Greenwich Village to East Village (www.unsilentnight.com). Subway A, B, C, D, E, F, M to W 4th Street. **Date** mid Dec. **Map** p397 E28-G28.

This trippy musical performance piece, dreamed up by composer Phil Kline, is downtown's arty, secular answer to Christmas carolling. Boom-box-toting participants gather under the Washington Square Arch, where they are given a cassette or CD of one of four different atmospheric tracks; you can also download the Unsilent Night app and sync up via smartphone. Everyone then presses play at the same time and marches through the streets of New York, blending their music and filling the air with a beautiful, echoing 45-minute piece.

New Year's Eve in Times Square

Times Square, Theater District (1-212 768 1560, www.timessquarenyc.org). Subway N, Q, R, S, 1, 2, 3, 7 to 42nd Street-Times Square. **Date** 31 Dec. **Map** p398 D24.

Get together with a million others and watch the giant illuminated Waterford Crystal ball descend amid a blizzard of confetti and cheering. Arrive by 3pm (earlier if the weather is nice) to stake out a spot in the Broadway-Seventh Avenue bowtie and be prepared to stay put. There are no public restrooms or food vendors, and leaving means giving up your spot. It may sound like no fun, but this is really the best kind of holiday masochism and your endurance will be rewarded with celebrity performances held across two stages, beginning at 6pm. Forget toasting the new year with champagne, though: public drinking is illegal in NYC.

New Year's Day Marathon Benefit Reading

Poetry Project at St Mark's Church, 131 E 10th Street, at Second Avenue (1-212 674 0910, www.poetryproject.org). **Date** 1 Jan.

Around 140 of the city's best poets, artists and performers gather at St Mark's Church in-the-Bowery and, one after another, recite their work to a hall full of listeners. Some big-name bohemians (past participants have included Philip Glass and Patti Smith) step up to the mic during this spoken-word spectacle, organised by the Poetry Project.

Winter Restaurant Week

For listings, *see p34* **Summer Restaurant Week**. **Date** late Jan/early Feb.

The Winter Restaurant Week provides yet another opportunity to sample delicious gourmet food at highly palatable prices.

Chinese New Year

Around Mott Street, Chinatown (www.betterchinatown.com). Subway J, N, Q, R, Z, 6 to Canal Street. **Date** late Jan/Feb. **Map** p396 E/F31.

Gung hay fat choy!, the greeting goes. Chinatown bustles with colour and is charged with energy during the two weeks of the Lunar New Year. The firecracker ceremony – which includes lion dances and food and craft vendors as well as the pyrotechnics – and parade are key events.

New York's Best

Check off the essentials with our list of hand-picked highlights.

View of Manhattan from Empire State Building.

The Cloisters.

Sightseeing

VIEWS

Empire State Building p151
The borough-spanning views are worth the inevitable wait.

Top of the Rock p152
The lines are shorter to this still-breathtaking perch.

Brooklyn Heights Promenade p196
Postcard-worthy views from this riverside strip.

Brooklyn Bridge p197
The city's most scenic pedestrian crossing.

Times Square p151
Climb the TKTS steps for a 360-degree light show.

ART

Metropolitan Museum of Art p180
A mammoth era- and globe-spanning collection.

Museum of Modern Art p152
Modern masterpieces and much more.

Solomon R Guggenheim Museum p182
Frank Lloyd Wright's building is the real treasure.

The Cloisters p193
A magical melange of medieval buildings set in a riverside park.

New Museum of Contemporary Art p84
Ground-breaking art in a striking structure.

Noguchi Museum p224
A serene sanctuary for sculpture in Queens.

HISTORY
Lower East Side Tenement Museum p83
See how immigrants lived in this erstwhile slum.
New-York Historical Society p165
A revamp shook the dust from this impressive collection.
Museum of the City of New York p181
Engaging city-centric exhibitions.
American Museum of Natural History p164
The famous dioramas have been restored.

OUTDOORS
Central Park p169
Manhattan's back yard.
Governors Island p51
An island retreat just minutes from lower Manhattan.
Brooklyn Bridge Park p197
Lush lawns, knockout views and NYC's coolest carousel.
The High Line p118
All aboard the elevated park-cum-walkway.

RELIGIOUS BUILDINGS
St Patrick's Cathedral p153
A white marble confection with a Tiffany altar.
Cathedral Church of St John the Divine p171
It may be unfinished but it's still awe-inspiring.
St Paul's Chapel p54
One of the finest Georgian buildings in America.
Eldridge Street Synagogue p84
A major restoration included a Kiki Smith-designed window.

ICONS
Statue of Liberty p54
This American icon is truly a marvel.
National September 11 Memorial & Museum p58
A monumental tribute as dramatic as it is moving.
Chrysler Building p155
A dazzling art deco homage to the automobile.
Flatiron Building p130
This early skyscraper still impresses.
Yankee Stadium p231
The new limestone arena is a worthy successor to the 'House that Ruth Built'.
Coney Island Cyclone p217
Take a teeth-rattling ride on this classic roller coaster – if you dare.

CURIOSITIES
Museum p71
A bizarre collection displayed in a disused elevator shaft.
City Reliquary p210
All manner of Gotham ephemera and memorabilia.

CHILDREN
Brooklyn Children's Museum p243
The world's oldest kids' museum is bang up to date.
Bronx Zoo p242
Explore a real urban jungle, with elephants, tigers and hissing cockroaches!
New Victory Theater p244
Exciting international youth-targeted productions.

Eating & drinking

INSTITUTIONS
Barney Greengrass p165
Massive egg and fish platters and delightfully gruff staff.

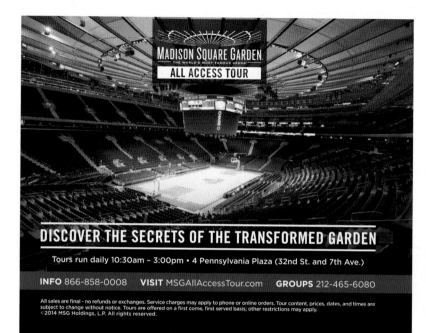

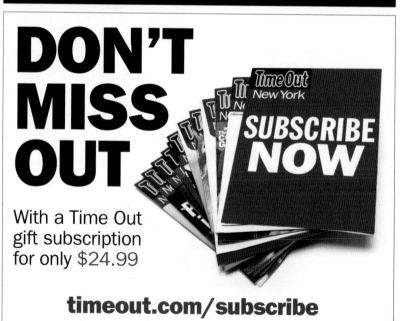

Katz's Delicatessen p85
Film-set looks and celebrated pastrami sandwiches.
Peter Luger p214
Steakhouses come and go, but Luger is the original.
Grand Central Oyster Bar p156
The classic spot for bivalves and cocktails.
McSorley's Old Ale House p102
Houdini was just one of the regulars at this historic pub.

BLOWOUTS
Per Se p166
The perfect meal – but it comes at a price.
Chef's Table at Brooklyn Fare p202
A memorable meal if you can secure a sought-after seat.
The NoMad p134
Elegant dining in plush, Paris-inspired surroundings.

AMERICAN
The Dutch p65
A raucous restaurant and oyster bar from hot chef Andrew Carmellini.
Shake Shack p167
Danny Meyer's burger stand is now a chain, but still delivers prime patties.
Mighty Quinn's p99
The barbecue craze is back and this is one of the best.

MODERN MELTING POT
Carbone p110
The food is as satisfying as the retro setting at this reimagined mob supper club.
Chez Sardine p115
A Québécois chef turns his hand to sushi.
Momofuku Ssäm Bar p99
Contemporary Korean from David Chang.
Pok Pok NY p202
A renowned Portland chef brings his touch to Thai.
RedFarm p116
Imaginative riffs on dim sum.
Red Rooster Harlem p190
Soul food from a Swedish-raised, Ethiopian toque.

BRUNCH
Allswell p213
Reliable diner-style dishes in Williamsburg.
Jack's Wife Freda p66
Creative riffs on late-morning grub at great prices.
Cookshop p124
Seasonal variations on classics like French toast.

BARS
Raine's Law Room p134
Exquisite cocktails are mixed in the 'kitchen' of this bar-less speakeasy.
PDT p102
The phonebooth entry is fun, but the drinks are the main event.
Terroir p103
Well-picked wines and gourmet nibbles at this down-to-earth wine bar.
The Commodore p214
Ultimate Brooklyn neo-dive.
Bohemian Hall & Beer Garden p225
A remnant of Queens quaffing history.

Shopping

CONCEPT
Dover Street Market p158
Rei Kawakubo's arty Comme mega-boutique has arrived.
Fivestory p177
Chic clothing and homewares in a townhouse setting.
Opening Ceremony p68
Gold-standard avant-garde looks, books and music.
Modern Anthology p201
Everything a fashionable male needs.

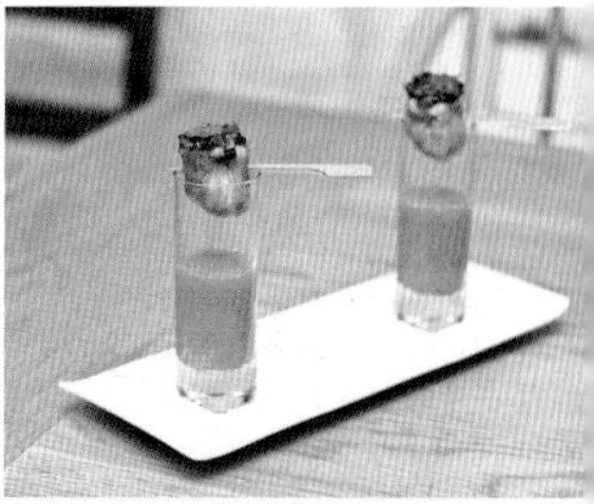

RedFarm.

Brooklyn Flea.

FOOD & DRINK

Eataly p136
An entire country's worth of flavours under one roof.

Bond Street Chocolate p103
Decadent sweets for grown-up tastes.

Dominique Ansel Bakery p67
Home of the cult Cronut.

Russ & Daughters p91
Superb smoked fish and other delicacies at this 100-year-old purveyor.

GIFTS & SOUVENIRS

Magpie p168
Eco-friendly handmade goods.

Bowne & Co Stationers p60
Hand-printed cards and stationery in a wonderfully old-fashioned store.

Aedes de Venustas p117
A boudoir-style stash of hard-to-find scents.

By Brooklyn p204
Gifts from bags to edibles, all made in the borough.

BOOKS & MUSIC

Other Music p104
Genre-crossing indie fare.

Strand Book Store p105
A browser's paradise on several floors.

Housing Works Bookstore Café p67
A great literary hangout that's all in a good cause.

Rough Trade p216
Vinyl lives at this UK import, which also hosts gigs.

LOCAL DESIGNERS

Erica Weiner p79
Great collection of unusual, affordable baubles.

(3x1) p166
Made-in-New York denim.

In God We Trust p67
Get the Brooklyn look – well-priced gear for guys and gals.

ANTIQUES & VINTAGE

Brooklyn Flea p203
Bric-a-brac, locally designed wares and artisanal food.

Mantiques Modern p127
A mad mix of bizarre and beautiful items.

What Goes Around Comes Around p69
The fashion insiders' choice for era-spanning clothing.

CHILDREN

Books of Wonder p154
An indie bookstore with a bakery attached.

Egg p154
Classic kids' clothing with contemporary flair.

FAO Schwarz p171
The ultimate New York City toy box.

DEPARTMENT STORES

Barneys New York p177
A contemporary twist on the department store.

Bergdorf Goodman p154
The ultimate Upper East Side designer institution.

Century 21 p57
Bargains galore at this rummagers' paradise.

Nightlife

CLUBS

Output p264
An underground vibe and a killer sound system.

Cielo p264
A surprisingly attitude-free dance hub.

Slipper Room p265
The city's burlesque bastion is back and better than ever.

MUSIC

Bowery Ballroom p273
Prime venue for indie bands.

Rockwood Music Hall p277
Sample a smorgasbord of up-and-coming acts.

Radio City Music Hall p277
The glitzy setting turns a concert into an event.

Radio City Music Hall.

Rockwood Music Hall.

Small's p282
The authentic hole-in-the-wall Village jazz joint you've been looking for.

Joe's Pub p276
Performers of all genres: alt-cabaret, comedy, rock and more.

GENRE-CROSSING VENUES

Le Poisson Rouge p277
A varied programme in a historic Village space.

The Bell House p272
Expect anything from quiz shows to DJs and burlesque.

Arts

FESTIVALS

River to River p34
Partake of free culture in waterside locations with hundreds of free events.

Shakespeare in the Park p33
It's worth queuing for hours (take a picnic!) for these gratis al fresco shows.

Next Wave Festival p35
Adventurous theatre, dance and music at BAM.

Mermaid Festival p34
Exotic sea creatures parade around Coney Island in this flamboyant fête.

THEATRE

Public Theater p305
The East Village landmark stages ambitious works.

Brooklyn Academy of Music p301
Big stars are often on the bill of BAM's reworked classics.

Sleep No More p301
An immersive, eerie riff on Macbeth.

Soho Rep p308
Diverse offerings at this innovative Off Broadway stage.

THREE SLEEPS

The Jane (p354)
Greenwich Hotel (p347)
The NoMad (p359)

FILM

Film Forum p249
A well-loved non-profit cinema with exciting programming.

Film Society of Lincoln Center p251
Host of the prestigious New York Film Festival.

Nitehawk Cinema p250
Get dinner and a movie.

CLASSICAL & DANCE

Lincoln Center p286
Home of the Metropolitan Opera, New York Phil and New York City Ballet.

Carnegie Hall p285
A grand setting for luminaries and emerging stars alike.

Bargemusic p287
An enchanting waterside music venue.

THE
LION KING
7 Av
ONE WAY
W 43 ST
FRIDAYS
www.LG.com
NOW
HUNGER GAMES
AUGUST 18
NEW YORK DOLLS
GENTLEMEN'S CLUB
7J40
NEW YORK
7J40c

Explore

The Financial District

Commerce has been the backbone of New York's prosperity since its earliest days as a Dutch Colony. The southern tip of Manhattan quickly evolved into the Financial District because, in the days before telecommunications, banks put their headquarters near the port. The oldest part of the city, lower Manhattan is the city's financial, legal and political powerhouse, but as the arrival point for the 19th-century influx of immigrants, it played another vital role in the city's evolution.

This part of town is still in flux, as more than a decade of construction moves towards completion. The new World Trade Center is finally taking shape and, in the wake of Hurricane Sandy's damage, the South Street Seaport is being transformed from a touristy eyesore into a waterfront destination where locals will want to stroll, shop and relax.

Statue of Liberty.

Don't Miss

1 Governors Island A tranquil retreat minutes from Manhattan (*p51*).

2 Statue of Liberty Ascend to the crown for a breathtaking vista (*p54*).

3 Dead Rabbit Grocery & Grog A lesson in booze history (*p54*).

4 National September 11 Memorial & Museum A suitably monumental tribute (*p58*).

5 Century 21 Paradise for bargain lovers (*p57*).

Bowling Green.

BATTERY PARK TO WALL STREET

Subway J, Z to Broad Street; R to Whitehall Street-South Ferry; 1 to South Ferry; R, 1 to Rector Street; 2, 3, 4, 5 to Wall Street; 4, 5 to Bowling Green.

It's easy to forget that Manhattan is an island – what with all those gargantuan skyscrapers obscuring your view of the water. Until, that is, you reach the southern point, where salty ocean breezes are reminders of the millions of immigrants who travelled on steamers in search of prosperity, liberty and a new home. This is where they landed, after passing through Ellis Island's immigration and quarantine centres.

On the edge of Battery Park, **Castle Clinton** was one of several forts built to defend New York Harbor against attacks by the British in the War of 1812 (others included Castle Williams on Governors Island, Fort Gibson on Ellis Island and Fort Wood, now the base of the Statue of Liberty). After serving as an aquarium, immigration centre and opera house, the sandstone fort is now a visitors' centre and ticket booth for **Statue of Liberty** and **Ellis Island** tours (*see p54*), as well as an intimate, open-air setting for concerts. The park is a key venue of the annual **River to River Festival** (*see p34*) – a summertime celebration of downtown culture and the city's largest free arts festival.

Joining the throngs making their way to Lady Liberty, you'll head south-east along the shore, where several ferry terminals jut into the harbour. Among them is the **Whitehall Ferry Terminal**, the boarding place for the famous **Staten Island Ferry**. Constructed in 1907, the terminal was severely damaged by fire in 1991, but was completely rebuilt in 2005. More than 75,000 passengers take the free, 25-minute journey to Staten Island each day; most are commuters but many are tourists, taking advantage of the views of the Manhattan skyline and the Statue of Liberty. Before the Brooklyn Bridge was completed in 1883, the **Battery Maritime Building** (11 South Street, between Broad & Whitehall Streets) served as a terminal for the ferry services between Manhattan and Brooklyn. Now, it's the launch point for a ferry to tranquil **Governors Island** (*see p51* **Island Getaway**). On the park's northern waterfront, the 1886 Pier A Harbor House, once the HQ for the harbour police, is reopening as a massive dining and drinking destination (www.piera.com).

Just north of Battery Park you'll find the triangular **Bowling Green**, the city's oldest park and a popular lunchtime spot for Financial District workers; it's also the front lawn of the

IN THE KNOW
THE BULL'S BALLS

On Bowling Green's northern side stands a three-and-a-half-ton bronze sculpture of a bull (symbolising the bull, or rising, share market). The statue was deposited without permission outside the Stock Exchange by guerrilla artist Arturo di Modica in 1989 and has since been moved by the city to its current location on the Green. The bull's enormous balls are often rubbed for good luck by tourists (and perhaps the occasional broker).

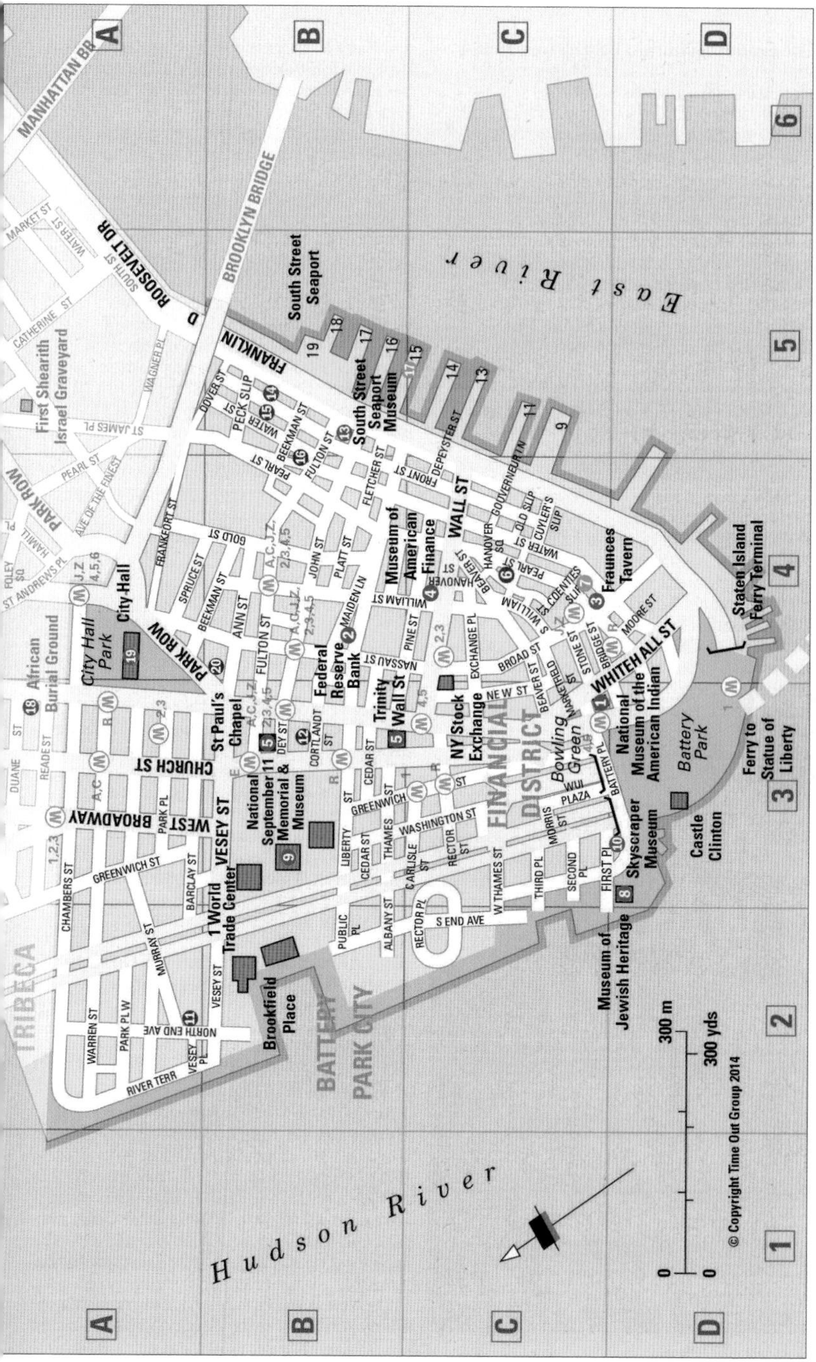
East River
Hudson River
South Street Seaport
South Street Seaport Museum
Museum of American Finance
Federal Reserve Bank
Trinity Wall St
NY Stock Exchange
FINANCIAL DISTRICT
Fraunces Tavern
Staten Island Ferry Terminal
National Museum of the American Indian
Bowling Green
Battery Park
Castle Clinton
Ferry to Statue of Liberty
Skyscraper Museum
Museum of Jewish Heritage
BATTERY PARK CITY
Brookfield Place
1 World Trade Center
National September 11 Memorial & Museum
St Paul's Chapel
City Hall Park
City Hall
African Burial Ground
First Shearith Israel Graveyard
TRIBECA
BROOKLYN BRIDGE
MANHATTAN BR
ROOSEVELT DR
FRANKLIN D
WALL ST
WHITEHALL ST
VESEY ST
WEST BROADWAY
CHURCH ST
PARK ROW
300 m
300 yds
© Copyright Time Out Group 2014

EXPLORE

Alexander Hamilton US Custom House, now home to the **National Museum of the American Indian** (*see p50*).

Dwarfed by the surrounding architecture, the **Stone Street Historic District** is a small pocket of restored 1830s buildings on the eponymous winding cobblestoned lane, also encompassing South William and Pearl Streets and Coenties Alley. Office workers and tourists frequent its restaurants and bars, including the boisterous **Ulysses' Folk House** (95 Pearl Street, between Broad Street & Hanover Square, 1-212 482 0400, www.ulyssesnyc.com) and **Stone Street Tavern** (52 Stone Street, between Broad Street & Hanover Square, 1-212 785 5658, www.stonestreettavernnyc.com).

Although the neighbourhood is bisected vertically by the ever-bustling Broadway, it's the east–west **Wall Street** (or 'The Street' in trader lingo) that's synonymous with the world's greatest den of capitalism. The name derives from a defensive wooden wall built in 1653 to mark the northern limit of New Amsterdam, and despite its huge significance, the thoroughfare is less than a mile long. At its western intersection with Broadway, you'll find the Gothic Revival spire of **Trinity Wall Street** (*see p54*). The original church burned down in 1776, and a second was demolished in 1839; the current version became the island's tallest structure when it was completed in 1846. **St Paul's Chapel** (*see p54*), the church's older satellite, is one of the finest Georgian structures in the US.

Wall Street.

A block to the east of Trinity is the **Federal Hall National Memorial** (26 Wall Street, at Nassau Street, 1-212 825 6990, www.nps.gov/feha, closed Sat, Sun), an august Greek Revival building and – in a previous incarnation – the site of George Washington's first inauguration. It was along this stretch that corporate America made its first audacious architectural statements; a walk eastwards offers much evidence of what money can buy. Structures include the **Bankers Trust Building** at 14 Wall Street (at Broad Street), completed in 1912 and crowned by a seven-storey pyramid modelled on the Mausoleum of Halicarnassus; **40 Wall Street** (between Nassau & William Streets), which battled the Chrysler Building in 1929 for the title of world's tallest building (the Empire State trounced them both in 1931); and the former **Merchants' Exchange** at 55 Wall Street (between Hanover & William Streets), with its stacked rows of Ionic and Corinthian columns, giant doors and a remarkable ballroom. Back around the corner is the **Equitable Building** (120 Broadway, between Cedar & Pine Streets), whose greedy use of vertical space helped to instigate the zoning laws that now govern skyscrapers; stand across the street from the building to get the best view. Nearby is the **Federal Reserve Bank** (*see p53*), with its huge gold vault.

The nerve centre of the US economy is the **New York Stock Exchange** (11 Wall Street, between Broad & New Streets, www.nyse.nyx.com). For security reasons, the Exchange is no longer open to the public, but the street outside offers an endless pageant of brokers, traders and their minions. For a lesson on Wall Street's influence over the years, visit the **Museum of American Finance** (*see p53*).

Sights & Museums

FREE Alexander Hamilton US Custom House/National Museum of the American Indian

1 Bowling Green, between State & Whitehall Streets (1-212 514 3700, www.nmai.si.edu). Subway R to Whitehall Street-South Ferry; 1 to South Ferry; 4, 5 to Bowling Green. **Open** 10am-5pm Mon-Wed, Fri-Sun; 10am-8pm Thur. **Admission** free. **Map** p49 C3 ❶

Cass Gilbert's magnificent Beaux Arts Custom House, completed in 1907, housed the Customs Service until 1973, when the federal government moved it to the newly built World Trade Center complex. Four monumental figures by Lincoln Memorial sculptor Daniel Chester French – representing America, Asia, Europe and Africa – flank the impressive entrance. The panels surrounding the elliptical rotunda dome were designed to feature

ISLAND GETAWAY

The former military HQ is now an arty seasonal sanctuary.

A 172-acre chunk of prime waterside real estate that can never be developed into luxury condos, **Governors Island** (*see p53*) is a secluded anomaly a scant 800 yards from lower Manhattan. The verdant commons and stately red-brick buildings evoke an Ivy League campus by way of a colonial New England village – oddly emptied of its inhabitants.

The peaceful backwater has had a tumultuous history. Initially a seasonal fishing and gathering ground for the Lenape Indians, it had plentiful nut trees, earning it the name 'Noten Eylant' when the Dutch arrived in the 1620s. In 1674, the British secured it for 'the benefit and accommodation of His Majesty's Governors'. Perhaps the most colourful of these was Edward Hyde, Viscount Cornbury, Governor of New York and New Jersey from 1702 to 1708. A cousin of Queen Anne, he was alleged to be a cross-dresser (a portrait, said to be of Lord Cornbury in drag, is in the collection of the New-York Historical Society, *see p165*).

The island's strategic position cemented its future as a military outpost (by the late 19th century it was the army's headquarters for the entire eastern US), and it still retains a significant chunk of its military-era construction, including Fort Jay, started in 1776, and Castle Williams, completed in 1812. When the army began to outgrow the space, excavated soil from the Lexington Avenue subway line was used to enlarge the island by 103 acres.

The modest patch has been the backdrop for some huge events. In 1909, it launched the first overwater flight, when Wilbur Wright circled the Statue of Liberty before flying back. Such legendary figures as Generals Ulysses S Grant and Douglas MacArthur had stints on the island.

Today, as well as providing a peaceful setting for cycling (bring a bike, or rent one on arrival), the island hosts a programme of events (see website for schedule). There are even plans for a day spa. In 2012, construction began on a new park, and 30 acres of green space are open to the public for the 2014 season. The Hammock Grove, with hammocks set among 1,500 trees, offers shady reclining, and 14 acres of lawn include two ball fields. Eventually, new hills constructed from the debris of demolished buildings will provide even more spectacular viewpoints for harbour panoramas.

EXPLORE

Alexander Hamilton US Custom House. See p50.

murals, but this wasn't realised until the 1930s, when local artist Reginald Marsh was commissioned to decorate them under the New Deal's Works Progress Administration; the paintings depict a ship entering New York Harbor.

In 1994, the National Museum of the American Indian's George Gustav Heye Center, a branch of the Smithsonian, moved into the first two floors of the building. On the second level, the life and culture of Native Americans are illuminated in three galleries radiating out from the rotunda. The permanent exhibition, 'Infinity of Nations', displays 700 of the museum's wide-ranging collection of Native American art and objects, from decorated baskets to elaborate ceremonial headdresses, organised by geographical region. Changing exhibitions showcase contemporary artwork. On the ground floor, the Diker Pavilion for Native Arts & Culture is the city's only dedicated showcase for Native American performing arts.

FREE Federal Reserve Bank

Visitors' entrance: 44 Maiden Lane, between Nassau & William Streets (1-212 720 6130, www.ny.frb.org/aboutthefed/visiting.html). Subway 2, 3, 4, 5 to Wall Street. **Tours** (reservations required) 11.15am, noon, 12.45pm, 1.30pm, 2.15pm, 3pm Mon-Fri. **Admission** free. **Map** p49 B4 ❷

For security reasons, tours of this important financial institution must be booked well in advance – the easiest way to do this is online, as a calendar feature shows availability – and a photo ID must be presented upon admission. Descend 50ft below street level and you'll find the world's largest known supply of monetary gold (over 12,000 tons, worth more than $300 billion), stored in a gigantic vault that rests on the solid bedrock of Manhattan Island. Visitors learn about the New York Fed's safeguarding of the precious metal, and the responsibilities and actions of the Federal Reserve.

Fraunces Tavern Museum

2nd & 3rd Floors, 54 Pearl Street, at Broad Street (1-212 425 1778, www.fraunces tavern museum.org). Subway J, Z to Broad Street; 4, 5 to Bowling Green. **Open** noon-5pm daily. **Admission** $7; $4 reductions; free under-6s & active military. **Map** p49 C4 ❸

True, George Washington slept here, but there's little left of the original 18th-century tavern he favoured during the Revolution. Fire-damaged and rebuilt in the 19th century, it was reconstructed in its current Colonial Revival style in 1907. The museum itself features period rooms, a collection of 800 reproduction regimental flags, paintings devoted to events of the Revolutionary War, and such Washington relics as a lock of his hair. It was here, after the British had finally been defeated, that Washington took tearful farewell of his troops and vowed to retire from public life. Luckily, he had a change of heart six years later and became the country's first president. You can still raise a pint in the bar, which is now run by Dublin's Porterhouse Brewing Company.

★ FREE Governors Island

1-212 440 2202, www.govisland.com. Subway R to Whitehall Street-South Ferry; 1 to South Ferry; 4, 5 to Bowling Green. Then take ferry from Battery Maritime Building at Slip no.7. **Open** Late May-late Sept 10am-6pm Mon-Fri; 10am-7pm Sat, Sun (see website for hours and ferry schedule). **Admission** *Ferry* $2 round trip; free under-12s; free 10am-noon Sat, Sun.
See p51 **Island Getaway**.

Museum of American Finance

48 Wall Street, at William Street (1-212 908 4110, www.moaf.org). Subway R, 1 to Rector Street; 2, 3, 4, 5 to Wall Street. **Open** 10am-4pm Tue-Sat. **Admission** $8; $5 reductions; free under-7s; free Sat through 2014. **Map** p49 C4 ❹

Situated in the old headquarters of the Bank of New York, the permanent collection traces the history of Wall Street and America's financial markets. Displays in the stately banking hall include a bearer bond made out to President George Washington and ticker tape from the morning of the stock market crash of 1929.

★ Statue of Liberty & Ellis Island Immigration Museum

Liberty Island (1-212 363 3200, www.nps.gov/stli). Subway R to Whitehall Street-South Ferry; 1 to South Ferry; 4, 5 to Bowling Green; then take Statue of Liberty ferry (1-201 604 2800, 1-877 523 9849, www.statuecruises.com), departing roughly every 30mins from gangway 4 or 5 in southernmost Battery Park. **Open** ferry runs 9.30am-3.30pm daily. Purchase tickets online, by phone or at Castle Clinton in Battery Park. **Admission** $17; free-$14 reductions.

The sole occupant of Liberty Island, Liberty Enlightening the World stands 305ft tall from the bottom of her base to the tip of her gold-leaf torch. Intended as a gift from France on America's 100th birthday, the statue was designed by Frédéric Auguste Bartholdi (1834-1904). Construction began in Paris in 1874, her skeletal iron framework crafted by Gustave Eiffel (the man behind the Tower), but only the arm with the torch was finished in time for the centennial in 1876. In 1884, the statue was finally completed – only to be taken apart to be shipped to New York, where it was unveiled in 1886. It served as a lighthouse until 1902, and as a welcoming beacon for millions of immigrants. These 'tired…poor…huddled masses' were evoked in Emma Lazarus's poem 'The New Colossus', written in 1883 to raise funds for the pedestal and engraved inside the statue in 1903.

With a free Monument Pass, available only with ferry tickets reserved in advance, you can enter the pedestal and view the interior through a glass ceiling. Access to the crown costs an extra $3 and must be reserved in advance.

A half-mile across the harbour from Liberty Island is the 32-acre Ellis Island, gateway for over 12 million people who entered the country between 1892 and 1954. In the Immigration Museum (a former check-in depot), three floors of photos, interactive displays and exhibits pay tribute to the hopeful souls who made the voyage. Tickets can be purchased online, by phone or at Castle Clinton in Battery Park. *Photo p46.*

FREE Trinity Wall Street & St Paul's Chapel

Trinity Wall Street *89 Broadway, at Wall Street (1-212 602 0800, www.trinitywallstreet.org). Subway R, 1 to Rector Street; 2, 3, 4, 5 to Wall Street.* **Open** 7am-6pm Mon-Fri; 8am-4pm Sat; 7am-4pm Sun. **Admission** free. **Map** p49 E33.
St Paul's Chapel *209 Broadway, between Fulton & Vesey Streets (1-212 602 0800, www.trinitywallstreet.org). Subway A, C, J, Z, 2, 3, 4, 5 to Fulton Street.* **Open** 10am-6pm Mon-Sat; 7am-6pm Sun. **Admission** free. **Map** p49 B3 ❺

Trinity Church was the island's tallest structure when it was completed in 1846 (the original burned down in 1776; a second was demolished in 1839). A set of gates north of the church on Broadway allows access to the adjacent cemetery, where cracked and faded tombstones mark the final resting places of dozens of past city dwellers, including such notable New Yorkers as founding father Alexander Hamilton, business tycoon John Jacob Astor and steamboat inventor Robert Fulton. The church museum displays historic diaries, photographs, sermons and burial records.

Six blocks to the north, Trinity's satellite, St Paul's Chapel, is more important architecturally. The oldest building in New York still in continuous use (it dates from 1766), it is one of the nation's most valued Georgian structures.

▶ *For Trinity's dirt-cheap Concerts at One series, see p291.*

Restaurants & Cafés

Adrienne's Pizzabar

54 Stone Street, between Coenties Alley & Mill Street (1-212 248 3838). Subway R to Whitehall Street-South Ferry; 2, 3 to Wall Street. **Open** 11.30am-midnight Mon-Sat; 11.30am-10pm Sun. **Pizzas** $14-$19. **Map** p49 C4 ❻ **Pizza**

Good, non-chain eateries are scarce in the Financial District, but this bright, modern pizzeria on quaint Stone Street provides a pleasant break from the crowded thoroughfares – there are outside tables from April through November. The kitchen prepares nicely charred pies with delectable toppings such as the rich *quattro formaggi*. If you're in a hurry, you can eat at the 12-seat bar, or opt for the sleek, wood-accented dining room to savour small plates and main courses such as baked sea scallops and ravioli *al formaggio*.

Bars

★ Dead Rabbit Grocery & Grog

30 Water Street, at Broad Street (1-646 422 7906, www.deadrabbitnyc.com). Subway R to Whitehall Street-South Ferry. **Open** 11am-4am daily. **Map** p49 C4 ❼

At this time-capsule nook, you can drink like a boss – Boss Tweed, that is. Belfast bar vets Sean Muldoon and Jack McGarry have conjured up a rough-and-tumble 19th-century tavern in a red-brick landmark. Resurrecting long-forgotten quaffs is nothing new in NYC, but the Dead Rabbit's sheer breadth of mid 19th-century libations eclipses the competition, spanning 100-odd bishops, fixes, nogs and smashes. The fruit-forward Byrrh Wine Daisy, era-appropriate in its china teacup with moustache guard, is particularly well wrought.

EXPLORE

Dead Rabbit Grocery & Grog.

WORLD TRADE CENTER & BATTERY PARK CITY

Subway A, C, J, Z, 2, 3, 4, 5 to Fulton Street; E to World Trade Center; R to Cortlandt Street; 4, 5 to Bowling Green.

The streets around the site of the former World Trade Center have been drawing the bereaved and the curious since that harrowing day in September 2001. The worst attack on US soil took nearly 3,000 lives and left a gaping hole where the Twin Towers had once helped to define the New York skyline. After the site was fenced off, there wasn't much to see for almost a decade. Construction on the new World Trade Center complex, which will eventually include five office buildings, a performing arts centre and a transit hub designed by Santiago Calatrava, has been plagued by infighting, missed deadlines and budget overruns, but the National September 11 Memorial opened as planned on the tenth anniversary of the attacks (*see p58* **A Fitting Memorial**). The **National September 11 Museum** opens its doors in late spring 2014, and the development's centrepiece skyscraper, **1 World Trade Center** (the renamed Freedom Tower) – now the tallest building in America – counts media giant Condé Nast among its tenants. Santiago Calatrava's dramatic PATH/subway transport hub, scaled back due to budget constraints, is due for completion in 2015, but a Calatrava-designed 600-foot-long, marble-clad pedestrian corridor – soon to be lined with high-end stores – now links the PATH station and the granite-and-glass corporate/retail/dining complex **Brookfield Place** (from Liberty to Vesey Streets, between the Hudson River & West Street, 1-212 417 7000, www.brookfieldplaceny.com). Overlooking a marina, the complex hosts numerous free arts events in its Winter Garden and is undergoing a major upgrade to its restaurant and retail offerings. A gallery above a food market due to open by publication of this guide includes outposts of popular NYC eateries such as East Village barbecue spot Mighty Quinn's (*see p99*) – good news given the scarcity of decent grub in the area.

Brookfield Place abuts **Battery Park City**, a 92-acre planned community devised in the 1950s to replace decaying shipping piers with new apartments, green spaces and schools. It's a man-made addition to the island, built on soil and rocks excavated from the original World Trade Center construction site and sediment dredged from New York Harbor. Home to

Robert F Wagner Jr Park.

roughly 10,000 people, the neighbourhood was devastated after 9/11, and nearly half of its residents moved away, although the area has been improved with new commercial development drawn by economic incentives. Visitors can enjoy its esplanade, a favoured route for bikers, skaters and joggers, and a string of parks that runs north along the Hudson River from Battery Park.

Providing expansive views of the Statue of Liberty and Ellis Island at its southernmost reaches, the stretch is dotted with monuments and sculptures. Close by the marina is the 1997 **Police Memorial** (Liberty Street, at South End Avenue), a granite pool and fountain that symbolically trace the lifespan of a police officer through the use of moving water, with names of the fallen etched into the wall. The **Irish Hunger Memorial** (Vesey Street, at North End Avenue) is here too, paying tribute to those who suffered during the famine from 1845 to 1852. Designed by artist Brian Tolle and landscape architect Gail Wittwer-Laird, the quarter-acre memorial incorporates vegetation, soil and stones from Ireland's 32 counties, and a reproduction of a 19th-century Irish cottage.

To the north, **Nelson A Rockefeller Park** (north end of Battery Park City, west of River Terrace) attracts sun worshippers, kite flyers and soccer players in the warm-weather months. Look out for Tom Otterness's whimsical sculpture installation, *The Real World*. Just east is **Teardrop Park** (between Warren & Murray Streets, east of River Terrace), a two-acre space designed to evoke the bucolic Hudson River Valley, and to the south are the inventively designed **South Cove** (on the Esplanade, between First & Third Place), with its quays and island, and **Robert F Wagner Jr Park** (north of Historic Battery Park, off Battery Place), where an observation deck offers fabulous views of both the harbour and the Verrazano-Narrows Bridge; below it, Louise Bourgeois's Eyes gaze over the Hudson from the lawn. The **Museum of Jewish Heritage** (*see below*), Gotham's memorial to the Holocaust, is on the edge of the green. Across the street at the **Skyscraper Museum** (*see p57*), you can learn about the buildings that have created the city's iconic skyline.

Sights & Museums

Museum of Jewish Heritage: A Living Memorial to the Holocaust

Edmond J Safra Plaza, 36 Battery Place, at First Place (1-646 437 4202, www.mjhnyc.org). Subway 4, 5 to Bowling Green. **Open** 10am-5.45pm Mon, Tue, Thur, Sun; 10am-8pm Wed; 10am-5pm Fri (until 3pm Nov-mid Mar); 10am-3pm eve of Jewish hols. **Admission** $12; $7-$10 reductions; free under-13s, members; free 4-8pm Wed. **Map** p49 D3 ❽

This museum explores Jewish life before, during and after the Nazi genocide. The permanent collection includes documentary films, thousands of photos and 30,000 artefacts, many donated by Holocaust survivors and their families, which are displayed on rotation. The Keeping History Center brings the collection to life with interactive displays, including 'Voices of Liberty', a soundscape of émigrés' and refugees' reactions to arrival in the United States – made all the more poignant juxtaposed with the museum's panoramic views of Ellis Island and the Statue of Liberty. Special exhibitions tackle historical events or themes. The Memorial Garden features English artist Andy Goldsworthy's *Garden of Stones*, 18 fire-hollowed boulders embedded with dwarf oak saplings.

★ National September 11 Memorial & Museum

Enter on Albany Street, at Greenwich Street (1-212 266 5211, www.911memorial.org). Subway A, C, J, Z, 2, 3, 4, 5 to Fulton Street; E to World Trade Center; N, R, 1 to Rector Street. **Open** See website for information. **Map** p49 B3 ❾

Until construction is completed on the World Trade Center site, visitors must reserve timed entry passes to the memorial online or at the 9/11 Memorial Preview Site (20 Vesey Street, at Church Street), where you can learn about the development of the memorial and museum through models, renderings, films and artefacts. *See p58* **A Fitting Memorial**.

Skyscraper Museum

39 Battery Place, between Little West Street & 1st Place (1-212 968 1961, www.skyscraper.org). Subway 4, 5 to Bowling Green. **Open** noon-6pm Wed-Sun. **Admission** $5; $2.50 reductions. **Map** p49 D3 ❿

The only institution of its kind in the world, this modest space explores high-rise buildings as objects of design, products of technology, real-estate investments and places of work and residence. A large part of the single gallery (a mirrored ceiling gives the illusion of height) is devoted to temporary exhibitions. A substantial chunk of the permanent collection relates to the Word Trade Center, including original models of the Twin Towers and the new 1 World Trade Center. Other highlights of the display are large-scale photographs of lower Manhattan's skyscrapers from 1956, 1976 and 2004, and a 1931 silent film documenting the Empire State Building's construction. *Photo p59.*

► *For more on the history of New York's skyscrapers, see p341* **Race to the Top**.

Restaurants & Cafés

North End Grill

104 North End Avenue, at Murray Street (1-646 747 1600, www.northendgrillnyc.com). Subway A, C to Chambers Street; E to World Trade Center; 2, 3 to Park Place. **Open** 11.30am-2pm, 5.30-10pm Mon-Thur; 11.30am-2pm, 5.30-10.30pm Fri; 11am-2pm, 5.30-10.30pm Sat; 11am-2.30pm, 5.30-9pm Sun. **Main courses** $26-$58. **Map** p49 A2 ⓫ **American**

Danny Meyer brings his Midas touch to Battery Park City for this instant classic. The place has all the hallmarks of a Meyer joint: effortless, affable service; a warm, buzzy space; and cooking that's easy and accessible. Chef Floyd Cardoz puts his stamp on the seasonal menu, devoting an entire section to eggs and adding doses of fire and spice. We were impressed by composed plates such as wood-fired lamb loin shingled on a bed of green lentils seasoned with mint.

Shops & Services

Century 21

22 Cortlandt Street, between Broadway & Church Street (1-212 227 9092, www.c21stores.com). Subway A, C, J, Z, 2, 3, 4, 5 to Fulton Street; E to World Trade Center; R to Cortlandt Street. **Open** 7.45am-9pm Mon-Wed; 7.45am-9.30pm Thur, Fri; 10am-9pm Sat; 11am-8pm Sun. **Map** p49 B3 ⓬ **Fashion**

A Marc Jacobs cashmere sweater for less than $200? Stella McCartney sunglasses for a mere $40? No, you're not dreaming – you're shopping at Century 21. You may have to rummage to unearth a treasure, but with savings of up to 65% off regular prices, it's worth it.

North End Grill.

A FITTING MEMORIAL

Pay your respects, and be awed, at the 9/11 Memorial and Museum.

In spring 2013, the final piece of the World Trade Center site's centrepiece tower was hoisted into place. At 1,776 feet, 1 World Trade Center (formerly known as the Freedom Tower) has surpassed the Empire State Building in height and is the tallest skyscraper in the Western Hemisphere. After years of stalled construction, the new WTC is almost complete.

For most of the decade following 9/11, those who made the pilgrimage to Ground Zero were confronted by an impenetrable fence, and although plans for the site's redevelopment were announced in 2003, there wasn't much evidence of progress. Yet, as the tenth anniversary of the attacks loomed, construction surged, and the 9/11 Memorial opened to visitors on 11 September 2011.

The **National September 11 Memorial & Museum** (*see p57*) occupies half of the WTC site's 16 acres. The memorial itself, Reflecting Absence, designed by architects Michael Arad and Peter Walker, comprises two one-acre 'footprints' of the destroyed towers, with 30-foot man-made waterfalls – the country's largest – cascading down their sides. Bronze parapets around the edges are inscribed with the names of those who died. As the title makes clear, the intention is to convey a powerful sense of loss. The museum pavilion, designed by Snøhetta – the Oslo-based firm behind its home city's New Norwegian National Opera & Ballet building (2008) – rises between the waterfalls. Its web-like glass atrium houses two steel trident-shaped columns salvaged from the base of the Twin Towers.

When the museum opens, around the time of publication of this guide, visitors will be able to descend to the vast spaces of the original foundations alongside a remnant of the Vesey Street staircase known as the 'Survivors' Stairs', used by hundreds escaping the carnage. The collection commemorates the victims of both the 1993 and 2001 attacks on the World Trade Center. Survivors and victims' families have donated items and helped to weave personal tales of people who died in the towers. One gallery is devoted to artists' responses to the events, and items like the East Village's Ladder Company 3 fire truck, which was dispatched to the towers with 11 firefighters who died during the rescue, are on display.

Other locations 1972 Broadway, between 66th & 67th Streets, Upper West Side (1-212 518 2121); 472 86th Street, between Fourth & Fifth Avenues, Bay Ridge, Brooklyn (1-718 748 3266).

SOUTH STREET SEAPORT

Subway A, C, J, Z, 2, 3, 4, 5 to Fulton Street.

New York's fortunes originally rolled in on the swells that crashed into its harbour. The city was perfectly situated for trade with Europe and, after 1825, goods from the Western Territories arrived via the Erie Canal and the Hudson River. By 1892, New York was also the point of entry for millions of immigrants. The **South Street Seaport** is the best place to appreciate this port heritage.

If you enter the Seaport area from Water Street, the first thing you're likely to spot is the whitewashed **Titanic Memorial Lighthouse**. It was originally erected on top of the Seaman's Church Institute (Coenties Slip & South Street) in 1913, the year after the great ship sank, but was moved to its current location at the intersection of Pearl and Fulton Streets in 1976. Check out the magnificent views of the Brooklyn Bridge from this bit of the district.

When New York's role as a vital shipping hub diminished during the 20th century, the South Street Seaport area fell into disuse, but a massive redevelopment project in the mid 1980s saw old buildings converted into restaurants, bars, chain stores and the **South Street Seaport Museum** (*see below*). **Pier 17** once supported the famous Fulton Fish Market, a bustling, early-morning trading centre dating back to the mid 1800s. However, in 2006 the market relocated to a larger facility in the Hunts Point area of the Bronx. Interest in Pier 17 dwindled after redevelopment in the 1980s, but a plan by SHoP Architects will replace the now-shuttered mall with a mixed-use complex, including a marina and a global food market. The city's East River Esplanade and Piers Project has landscaped the stretch of waterfront between the Battery Maritime Building and Fulton Street; **Pier 15** has been transformed into a bi-level lounging space, comprising a lawned viewing deck above a maritime education centre and the **Watermark** (*see p60*), a stylish glass-enclosed bar.

South Street Seaport Museum.

Sights & Museums

South Street Seaport Museum
12 Fulton Street, between South & Water Streets (1-212 748 8600, www.southstreetseaport museum.org). Subway A, C, J, Z, 2, 3, 4, 5 to Fulton Street. **Open** Call or see website for information. **Admission** Call or see website for information. **Map** p49 B5 ⓭

EXPLORE

Founded in 1967, the South Street Seaport Museum celebrates the maritime history of New York City's 19th-century waterfront. However, at time of writing it was still closed due to damage from 2012's Hurricane Sandy and a reopening date had yet to be determined. The museum shop, comprising Bowne Printers and Bowne & Co Stationers (*see right*), has remained open. The institution also has a fleet of historic vessels on Pier 16, including the 1607 lightship *Ambrose* and the 1885 schooner *Pioneer*, which offers excursions along the East River from May through October.

Restaurants & Cafés

Barbalu

225-227 Front Street, between Beekman Street & Peck Slip (1-646 918 6565, www.barbalu.com). Subway A, C, J, Z, 2, 3, 4, 5 to Fulton Street. **Open** 10am-10pm daily. **Main courses** $14-$22. **Map** p49 B5 ⓮ **Italian**

Former Barbarini owners Stefano Barbagallo and Adriana Luque bounced back from Hurricane Sandy with this 120-seat Italian eaterie at the same location. The husband-and-wife team scaled back the retail area, making space for a skylighted dining room packed with wooden two-tops. Slide into a brown banquette for classics like mozzarella-and-eggplant caponatina, fettuccine with shrimp and tomatoes, and *torta di pinoli* (pine-nut cake). At the expanded bar area, find charcuterie and cheese plates along with Italian wines.

Jack's Stir Brew Coffee

222 Front Street, between Beekman Street & Peck Slip (1-212 227 7631, www.jacksstirbrew.com). Subway A, C, J, Z, 2, 3, 4, 5 to Fulton Street. **Open** 6.30am-7pm Mon-Fri; 7am-7pm Sat, Sun. **Coffee** $2.50-$5.50. **Map** p49 B5 ⓯ **Café**

Java fiends convene at this award-winning caffeine spot that offers organic, shade-grown beans and a homey vibe. Coffee is served by espresso artisans with a knack for oddball concoctions, such as the super-silky Mountie latte, infused with maple syrup. **Other locations** 138 W 10th Street, between Greenwich Avenue & Waverly Place, West Village (1-212 929 0821).

IN THE KNOW
THE GHOST SUBWAY STATION

If you take the 6 train to its last downtown stop, Brooklyn Bridge-City Hall, ignore the recorded entreaty to get off. Stay aboard while the train makes its U-turn loop before heading uptown and you'll get a glimpse of the original 1904 City Hall Station (out of use since 1945) and its brass chandeliers, vaulted ceilings, tile mosaics and skylights.

Shops & Services

★ Bowne Printers and Bowne & Co Stationers

209-211 Water Street, between Fulton & Beekman Streets (1-646 628 2707). Subway A, C, J, Z, 2, 3, 4, 5 to Fulton Street. **Open** 11am-7pm daily. **Map** p49 B5 ⓰ **Gifts & stationery**

South Street Seaport Museum's re-creation of a 19th-century print shop doesn't just look the part: the platen presses – hand-set using antique letterpress and type from the museum's collection – also turn out custom and small-batch stationery and cards. Next door, Bowne & Co. Stationers, founded in 1775, sells hand-printed cards, prints, journals and other gifts.

Bars

Watermark

Pier 15, between Fletcher Street & Maiden Lane (1-212 742 8200, www.watermarkny.com). Subway A, C, J, Z, 2, 3, 4, 5 to Fulton Street; 2, 3 to Wall Street. **Open** *Apr-Dec* 11am-11pm daily. *Jan-Mar* 11am-6pm daily. **Map** p49 C5 ⓱

Sip local craft beers accompanied by sea-inspired bar bites like lobster rolls and crab cakes at this contemporary waterfront bar – the skyline views through the floor-to-ceiling windows are spectacular. In summer, the bar also doles out cones of Ben & Jerry's ice-cream, sorbets and frozen yoghurt, fit for indulging your inner kid as you soak up rays on the outdoor deck.

CIVIC CENTER & CITY HALL PARK

Subway J, Z to Chambers Street; R to City Hall; 2, 3 to Park Place; 4, 5, 6 to Brooklyn Bridge-City Hall.

The business of running New York takes place in the grand buildings in and around **City Hall Park**, an area that formed the budding city's northern boundary in the 1700s. The park itself was renovated just before the millennium, and pretty landscaping and abundant benches make it a popular lunching spot for office workers.

At the park's southern end, a granite 'time wheel' tracks its history. At the northern end of the park, **City Hall** (*see p61*) houses the mayor's office and the chambers of the City Council. When City Hall was completed in 1812, its architects were so confident that the city would grow no further north that they didn't bother to put any marble on its northern side. Nevertheless, the building is a beautiful blend of Federalist form and French Renaissance detail. Overlooking the park from the west is Cass Gilbert's famous **Woolworth Building** (233 Broadway, between Barclay Street & Park Place), the tallest building in the world when it opened in 1913. The neo-Gothic skyscraper's

EXPLORE

City Hall Park.

grand spires, gargoyles, vaulted ceilings and church-like interior earned it the moniker 'the Cathedral of Commerce'.

Behind City Hall, on Chambers Street, is the 1872 Old New York County Courthouse; it's popularly known as the **Tweed Courthouse**, after William 'Boss' Tweed (*see p329*), leader of the political machine Tammany Hall, who pocketed some $10 million of the building's $14 million construction budget. What he didn't steal bought a beautiful edifice, with exquisite Italianate detailing. These days, it houses the city's Department of Education and a New York City public school, but it's also open for tours (1-212 788 2656, www.nyc.gov/designcommission). To the east, other civic offices and services occupy the one million square feet of office space in the 1914 **Manhattan Municipal Building** at 1 Centre Street. This landmark limestone structure, built by McKim, Mead & White, also houses New York City's official gift shop (www.nyc.gov/citystore, closed Sat, Sun).

The houses of crime and punishment are located in the **Civic Center**, near Foley Square, once the site of the city's most notorious 19th-century slum, Five Points. These days, you'll find the State Supreme Court in the **New York County Courthouse** (60 Centre Street, at Pearl Street), a hexagonal Roman Revival building; the rotunda is decorated with a mural called *Law Through the Ages*. The **Thurgood Marshall United States Courthouse** (40 Centre Street, between Duane & Pearl Streets) is a Corinthian temple crowned with a golden pyramid.

The **Criminal Courts Building & Manhattan Detention Complex** (100 Centre Street, between Leonard & White Streets) is still known as 'the Tombs', a nod to the original 1838 Egyptian Revival building – or, depending on who you ask, its current grimness. There's no denying that the hall's great granite slabs and looming towers are downright lugubrious.

Nearby, the **African Burial Ground** (*see below*) was officially designated a National Monument in 2006.

Sights & Museums

FREE African Burial Ground National Monument

Duane Street, between Broadway & Centre Streets, behind 290 Broadway (1-212 637 2019, www.nps.gov/afbg). Subway J, Z to Chambers Street; R to City Hall; 4, 5, 6 to Brooklyn Bridge-City Hall. **Open** *Mar-Mid Nov* 9am-5pm daily. *Visitor centre* 10am-4pm Tue-Sat. **Admission** free. **Map** p49 A3 ⓲

The African Burial Ground is a small remnant of a 6.6-acre unmarked gravesite where between 10,000 and 20,000 enslaved Africans were buried. The burial ground, which closed in 1794, was unearthed during the construction of a federal office building in 1991 and later designated a National Monument. In 2007, a stone memorial, designed by architect Rodney Leon, was erected; the tall, curved structure draws heavily on African architecture and contains a spiral path leading to an ancestral chamber.

FREE City Hall

City Hall Park, from Vesey to Chambers Streets, between Broadway & Park Row (1-212 788 2656, www.nyc.gov/designcommission). Subway J, Z to Chambers Street; R to City Hall; 2, 3 to Park Place; 4, 5, 6 to Brooklyn Bridge-City Hall. **Open** *Tours* (individuals) noon Wed, 10am Thur; (groups) 10.30am Mon. Reservations required. **Admission** free. **Map** p49 A4 ⓳

Designed by French émigré Joseph François Mangin and John McComb Jr, the fine, Federal-style City Hall was completed in 1812. Tours take in the City Council Chamber and the Governor's Room, with its collection of American 19th-century political portraits and historic furnishings (including George Washington's desk). Individuals can book (at least two days in advance) for the Thursday morning tour; alternatively, sign up before 11.45am on Wednesday at the NYC tourism kiosk at the southern end of City Hall Park on the east side of Broadway, at Barclay Street for the first come, first-served tour at noon that day.

Shops & Services

J&R Music & Computer World

1 Park Row, at Beekman Street (1-212 238 9000, www.jr.com). Subway A, C to Broadway-Nassau Street. **Open** 10am-7pm Mon-Wed; 10am-7.30pm Thur, Fri; 11am-7pm Sat, Sun. **Map** p49 B4 ⓴
Electronics

This block-long electronics emporium stocks a plethora of electronic and electrical goods – from MP3 players and TVs to kitchen appliances.

EXPLORE

Soho & Tribeca

In the 1960s and '70s, artists colonised what had become a post-industrial wasteland south of Houston Street, squatting in abandoned warehouses. Eventually, they worked with the city to rezone and restore them. Others followed suit in the Triangle Below Canal, which was once the site of the city's main produce market. Today, many of the old factory buildings in Soho and Tribeca are occupied by designer stores and high-end restaurants, and those once-spartan loft spaces are among the most desirable real estate in the city. But you can still find pockets of experimental culture in this consumer paradise, in the form of scattered art galleries and Off and Off-Off Broadway theatres. Even if you're not shopping or dining, take a walk in the area to admire a well-preserved architectural legacy with a uniquely New York character.

Brushstroke.

Don't Miss

1 Drawing Center A bastion of culture in shop-saturated Soho (*p64*).

2 The Dutch A new American classic (*p65*).

3 Opening Ceremony Cutting-edge designers go for gold (*p68*).

4 Museum Mini masterpiece (*p71*).

5 Brushstroke This East-West collaboration serves a memorable feast (*p69*).

Bo
concept
PH
SALE
SALE

Greene Street.

SOHO

Subway A, C, E, 1 to Canal Street; C, E, 6 to Spring Street; N, R to Prince Street; 1 to Houston Street.

Now a retail mecca of the highest order, **Soho** was once a hardscrabble manufacturing zone with the derisive nickname Hell's Hundred Acres. In the 1960s, it was earmarked for destruction by over-zealous urban planner Robert Moses, but its signature cast-iron warehouses were saved by the artists who inhabited them as cheap live-work spaces. The **King & Queen of Greene Street** (respectively, 72-76 Greene Street, between Broome & Spring Streets, and 28-30 Greene Street, between Canal & Grand Streets) are both fine examples of the area's beloved architectural landmarks. The most celebrated of Soho's cast-iron edifices, however, is the five-storey **Haughwout Building**, at 488-492 Broadway, at Broome Street. Designed in 1857, it featured the world's first hydraulic lift (still in working condition).

After landlords sniffed the potential for profits in converting old loft buildings, Soho morphed into a playground for the young, beautiful and rich. It can still be a pleasure to stroll around the cobblestoned side streets on weekday mornings, and there are some standout shops in the area, but the large chain stores and sidewalk-encroaching street vendors along Broadway create a shopping-mall-at-Christmas crush on weekends. Although many of the galleries that made Soho an art capital in the 1970s and '80s decamped to Chelsea and, more recently, the Lower East Side, some excellent art spaces remain, including the recently expanded **Drawing Center**.

Sights & Museums

★ Drawing Center
35 Wooster Street, between Broome & Grand Streets (1-212 219 2166, www.drawingcenter.org). Subway A, C, E, 1 to Canal Street. **Open** noon-6pm Wed, Fri-Sun; noon-8pm Thur. **Admission** $5; $3 reductions; free under-12s; free 6-8pm Thur. **Map** p65 C2 ❶

This non-profit standout recently expanded its gallery space by 50%. Now comprising three galleries, the Drawing Center assembles shows of museum-calibre legends such as Philip Guston, James Ensor and Willem de Kooning, but also 'Selections' surveys of newcomers. Art stars such as Kara Walker and Chris Ofili received some of their earliest NYC exposure here.

New York City Fire Museum
278 Spring Street, between Hudson & Varick Streets (1-212 691 1303, www.nycfiremuseum.org). Subway C, E to Spring Street; 1 to Houston Street. **Open** 10am-5pm daily. **Admission** $8; $5 reductions. **Map** p65 B1 ❷

An active firehouse from 1905 to 1959, this museum is filled with all manner of life-saving gadgetry, from late 18th-century hand-pumped fire engines to present-day equipment.

Restaurants & Cafés

Balthazar
80 Spring Street, between Broadway & Crosby Street (1-212 965 1414, www.balthazarny.com). Subway N, R to Prince Street; 6 to Spring Street. **Open** 7.30-11.30am, noon-5pm, 6pm-midnight Mon-Thur; 7.30-11.30am, noon-5pm, 6pm-1am Fri; 8am-4pm, 6pm-1am Sat; 8am-4pm, 5.30pm-midnight Sun. **Main courses** $20-$45. **Map** p65 D1 ❸ **French**

At dinner, this iconic faux-vintage brasserie is perennially packed with rail-thin lookers dressed to the nines. But it's not only fashionable – the kitchen rarely makes a false step and the service is surprisingly friendly. The $165 three-tiered seafood platter casts an impressive shadow, and the roast chicken with garlic mashed potatoes for two is *délicieux*.

★ The Dutch

131 Sullivan Street, at Prince Street (1-212 677 6200, www.thedutchnyc.com). Subway C, E to Spring Street. **Open** 11.30am-3pm, 5.30pm-11pm Mon-Wed; 11.30am-3pm, 5.30pm-midnight Thur, Fri; 10am-3pm, 5.30pm-midnight Sat; 10am-3pm, 5.30pm-11pm Sun. **Main courses** $21-$38. **Map** p65 C1 ❹ **American**

Andrew Carmellini, Josh Pickard and Luke Ostrom – the white-hot team behind Italian hit Locanda Verde (*see p70*) – turned to American eats for their sophomore effort. The Dutch offers late-night hours and a freewheeling menu, completing Carmellini's progression from haute golden boy (Café Boulud, Lespinasse) to champion of lusty plates and raucous settings. Carmellini plays off the country's diverse influences with a broad spectrum of dishes. Mini fried-oyster sandwiches, dry-aged steaks and peel 'n' eat prawns all get their due. Drop by the airy oak bar, with its adjacent oyster room, to sip one of the extensive selection of American whiskies.

Ed's Lobster Bar

222 Lafayette Street, between Kenmare & Spring Streets (1-212 343 3236, www.lobsterbarnyc.com). Subway 6 to Spring Street. **Open** noon-3pm, 5-11pm Mon-Thur; noon-3pm, 5pm-midnight Fri; noon-midnight Sat; noon-9pm Sun. **Main courses** $18-$36. **Map** p65 D1 ❺ **Seafood**

If you secure a place at the 25-seat marble seafood bar or one of the few tables in the whitewashed eaterie, expect superlative raw-bar eats, delicately fried clams and lobster served every which way: steamed, grilled, broiled, chilled, stuffed into a pie and – the crowd favourite – the lobster roll. Here, it's a buttered bun stuffed with premium chunks of meat and a light coating of mayo. Note that the place serves lobster rolls only at the bar on weekday afternoons (3-5pm).

$ La Esquina

114 Kenmare Street, between Cleveland Place & Lafayette Street (1-646 613 7100, www.esquinanyc.com). Subway 6 to Spring Street. **Open** *Taqueria* 11am-2am daily. *Café* noon-midnight Mon-Thur; noon-1am Fri; 11am-1am Sat; 11am-midnight Sun. *Restaurant* 6pm-2am daily. **Tacos** $3.50. **Main courses** *Café* $9-$16; *restaurant* $18-$32. **Map** p65 D1 ❻ **Mexican**

La Esquina comprises three dining and drinking areas: first, a street-level *taqueria*, serving a short-order menu of tacos and Mexican *tortas*. Around the

EXPLORE

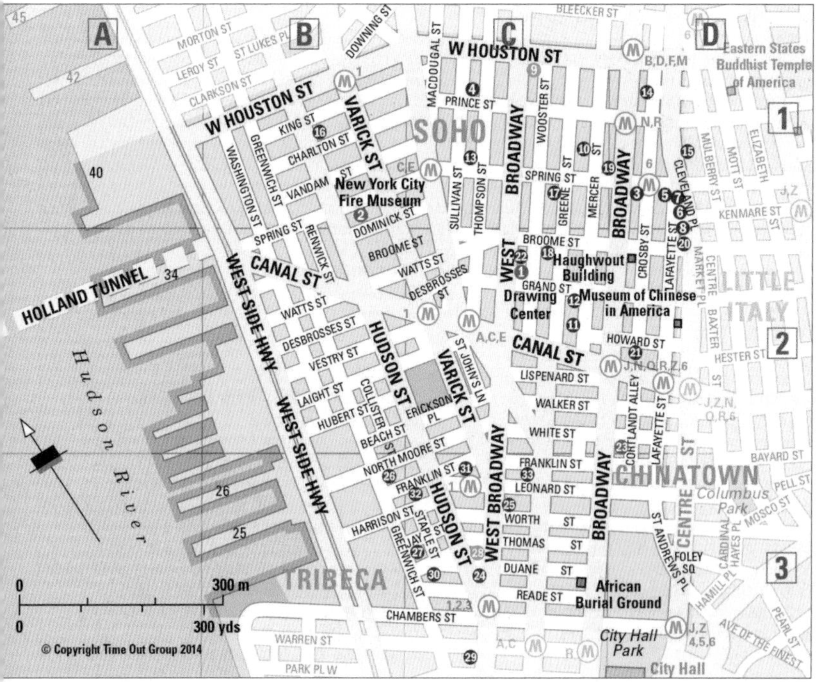

corner is a 30-seat café, its shelves stocked with books and old vinyl. Lastly, there's a dungeonesque restaurant and lounge accessible through a back door of the *taqueria* (to enter, you have to confirm that you have a reservation). It's worth the hassle: a world of Mexican murals, fine tequilas, *huitlacoche* (Mexican truffle) *quesadillas* and crab *tostadas* awaits.
Other locations Café de la Esquina at Wythe Diner, 225 Wythe Avenue, between Metropolitan Avenue & North 3rd Street, Williamsburg, Brooklyn (1-718 393 5500).

Jack's Wife Freda

224 Lafayette Street, between Kenmare & Spring Streets (1-212 510 8550, www.jackswifefreda.com). Subway 6 to Spring Street.
Open 9.45am-midnight Mon-Sat; 9.45am-10pm Sun. **Main courses** $15-$33. **Map** p65 D1 ❼
Café
Keith McNally protégé Dean Jankelowitz is behind this charming café. The 45-seat spot – sporting dark-green leather banquettes, brass railings and marble counters – serves homey fare, like Jankelowitz's grandmother's matzo ball soup made with duck fat or a skirt steak sandwich served alongside hand-cut fries.

★ Osteria Morini

218 Lafayette Street, between Broome & Spring Streets (1-212 965 8777, www.osteriamorini.com). Subway 6 to Spring Street. **Open** 11.30am-11pm daily. **Main courses** $28-$38. **Map** p65 D2 ❽
Italian
Michael White is one of New York's most prolific and successful Italian-American chefs, and this terrific downtown homage to a classic Bolognese tavern is his most accessible restaurant. The toque spent seven years cooking in Italy's Emilia-Romagna region, and his connection to the area surfaces in the resturant's rustic food. Handmade pastas are fantastic across the board, while superb meats might include porchetta with crisp, crackling skin and potatoes bathed in pan drippings.

Bars

★ Pegu Club

2nd Floor, 77 W Houston Street, at West Broadway (1-212 473 7348, www.pegucclub.com). Subway B, D, F, M to Broadway-Lafayette Street; N, R to Prince Street.
Open 5pm-2am Mon-Thur, Sun; 5pm-4am Fri, Sat. **Map** p65 C1 ❾
Audrey Saunders, the drinks maven who turned Bemelmans Bar (*see p177*) into one of the city's most respected cocktail lounges, is behind this sleek liquid destination. Tucked away on the second floor, the sophisticated spot was inspired by a British officers' club in Burma. The cocktail list features classics culled from decades-old booze bibles, and gin is the key ingredient – these are serious drinks for grown-up tastes.

Shops & Services

Soho's converted warehouses are packed with just about every major fashion brand you can think of, from budget and mid-priced international chains like H&M and Topshop to A-list designer labels like Chanel and Prada, plus stores selling home goods, cosmetics, food and more. These are our favourite independent shops.

3.1 Phillip Lim

115 Mercer Street, between Prince & Spring Streets (1-212 334 1160, www.31philliplim.com). Subway N, R to Prince Street; 6 to Spring Street.
Open 11am-7pm Mon-Sat; noon-6pm Sun.
Map p65 C1 ❿ **Fashion**
Since Phillip Lim debuted his collection in 2005, the New York-based designer has amassed a devoted international following for his simple yet strong silhouettes and beautifully constructed tailoring with a twist. His Soho boutique gathers together his award-winning collections for men and women, plus his cult accessories, under one roof.

(3x1)

15 Mercer Street, between Howard & Grand Streets (1-212 391 6969, www.3x1.us). Subway A, C, E, J, N, Q, R, Z, 1, 6 to Canal Street. **Open** 11am-7pm Mon-Sat; noon-6pm Sun. **Map** p65 C2
⓫ **Fashion**
Denim obsessives who are always looking for the next It jeans have another place to splurge: (3x1) creates entirely limited-edition styles sewn in the store. Designer Scott Morrison, who previously launched Paper Denim & Cloth and Earnest Sewn, fills the large, gallery-like space with a variety of jeans (prices start at $185 for women, $265 for men) and other denim pieces such as shorts and miniskirts. Watch the construction process take place in a glass-walled design studio in the middle of the boutique.

Alexander Wang

103 Grand Street, between Greene & Mercer Streets (1-212 977 9683, www.alexanderwang.com).

IN THE KNOW
WHERE THERE'S SMOKE

Despite the strict city-wide smoking ban, you can still indulge your habit in a few places that could prove a percentage of their income came from selling tobacco products when the ban was enforced. If you enjoy a cigarette, or even a cigar, with your cocktail, stop by Soho bar **Circa Tabac** (32 Watts Street, between Sixth Avenue & Thompson Street, 1-212 941 1781, www.circatabac.com).

EXPLORE

Subway J, N, Q, R, Z, 6 to Canal Street. **Open** 11am-7pm Mon-Sat; noon-6pm Sun. **Map** p65 C2 ⓬ **Fashion**
Anna Wintour-approved designer Alexander Wang has amassed a cultlike following of voguish downtown types. The Parsons dropout, who launched his eponymous line in 2007, was propelled to fashion royalty in 2008 after scoring a Council of Fashion Designers of America award. With chalky-white marble display pedestals and overstuffed leather couches, his luxurious and spacious flagship boutique offers the wunderkind's chic-but-casual men's and women's clothing, handbags and showstopping shoes, plus the lower-priced T by Alexander Wang line.

Dominique Ansel Bakery

189 Spring Street, between Sullivan & Thompson Streets (1-212 219 2773, www.dominiqueansel.com). Subway C, E to Spring Street. **Open** 8am-7pm Mon-Sat; 9am-7pm Sun. **Map** p65 C1 ⓭ **Food & drink**
Dominique Ansel honed his skills as executive pastry chef at Daniel for six years before opening this innovative patisserie. In 2013, his croissant-doughnut hybrid, the Cronut, created a frenzy in foodie circles and put his ingenious creations into the spotlight. If you can't get your hands on a Cronut, try the DKA – a caramelized, flaky take on the croissant-like Breton speciality *kouign amann.* And his cotton-soft mini cheesecake, an ethereally light gâteau with a brûléed top, leaves the dense old New York classic sputtering in its dust.

Osteria Morini. *See p65.*

IN THE KNOW
SOHO'S ITALIAN LEGACY

Just west of West Broadway, tenement- and townhouse-lined streets contain remnants of the Italian community that once dominated the area, including **St Anthony of Padua Roman Catholic Church** (155 Sullivan Street, at Houston Street), dedicated in 1888. You'll still find old-school neighbourhood flavour at **Pino's Prime Meat Market** (149 Sullivan Street, 1-212 475 8134, closed Sun). The iconic Vesuvio Bakery is now occupied by **Birdbath Neighborhood Green Bakery** (160 Prince Street, between Thompson Street & West Broadway, 1-646 556 7720, www.buildagreenbakery.com), which has kept the old-fashioned façade intact.

★ Housing Works Bookstore Café

126 Crosby Street, between Houston & Prince Streets (1-212 334 3324, www.housingworksbookstore.org). Subway B, D, F, M to Broadway-Lafayette Street; N, R to Prince Street; 6 to Bleecker Street. **Open** 10am-9pm Mon-Fri; 10am-5pm Sat, Sun. **Map** p65 D1 ⓮ **Books & music**
This endearing two-level space – which stocks literary fiction, non-fiction, rare books and collectibles – is also a peaceful spot to relax in over coffee or wine. All proceeds go to providing support services for people living with HIV/AIDS. Both emerging writers and the literati take the mic at the store's readings.

In God We Trust

265 Lafayette Street, between Prince & Spring Streets (1-212 966 9010, www.ingodwetrustnyc.com). Subway N, R to Prince Street; 6 to Spring Street. **Open** noon-8pm Mon-Sat; noon-7pm Sun. **Map** p65 D1 ⓯ **Accessories**
Designer Shana Tabor's cosy antique-furnished stores cater to that appealing vintage-intellectual aesthetic, offering locally crafted collections for men and women. The store's line of well-priced, cheeky accessories is a highlight – for example, gold heart-shaped pendants engraved with blunt sayings like 'Boring' or 'Blah Blah Blah', rifle-shaped tie bars, and a wide selection of retro sunglasses for only $20 a pair. *Photo p68.*
Other locations 129 Bedford Avenue, between North 9th & 10th Streets, Williamsburg, Brooklyn (1-718 384 0700); 70 Greenpoint Avenue, between Milton & Franklin Streets, Greenpoint, Brooklyn (1-718 389 3545).

Jacques Torres Chocolate

350 Hudson Street, between Charlton & King Streets, entrance on King Street (1-212 414 2462, www.mrchocolate.com). Subway 1 to Houston

Street. **Open** 8.30am-7pm Mon-Fri; 9am-7pm Sat; 10.30am-6.30pm Sun. **Map** p65 B1 ⑯ **Food & drink**

Walk into Jacques Torres's glass-walled shop and café, and you'll be surrounded by a Willy Wonka-esque factory that turns raw cocoa beans into luscious chocolate goodies before your eyes. As well as selling the usual assortments, truffles and bars (plus more unusual delicacies such as chocolate-covered cornflakes and Cheerios), the shop serves deliciously rich hot chocolate, steamed to order.

Other locations throughout the city.

★ Kiki de Montparnasse

79 Greene Street, between Broome & Spring Streets (1-212 965 8150, www.kikidm.com). Subway N, R to Prince Street; 6 to Spring Street. **Open** 11am-7pm Mon, Sun; 11am-8pm Tue-Sat. **Map** p65 C1 ⑰ **Lingerie**

This erotic luxury boutique channels the spirit of its namesake, a 1920s sexual icon and Man Ray muse, with a posh array of tastefully provocative contemporary lingerie in satin and French lace. Look out for novelties such as cotton tank tops with built-in garters and panties embroidered with saucy legends.

Kirna Zabete

477 Broome Street, between Greene & Wooster Streets (1-212 941 9656, www.kirnazabete.com). Subway N, R to Prince Street. **Open** 11am-7pm Mon-Sat; noon-6pm Sun. **Map** p65 C2 ⑱ **Fashion**

Since relocating a block from their original boutique, founders Beth Buccini and Sarah Easley have more space to display their edited collection of coveted designer clothing and accessories – more than 25 labels are new to the store, including Valentino, Nina Ricci and Roland Mouret. True to the duo's aesthetic, the 10,000sq ft space features black-and-white striped hardwood floors and neon signs displaying quirky mantras such as 'life is short, buy the shoes'.

★ Kiosk

41 Union Sq W (entrance: 22 E 17th) Th&F 12-7

2nd floor, 95 Spring Street, between Broadway & Mercer Street, Soho (1-212 226 8601, http://kioskkiosk.com). Subway 6 to Spring Street. **Open** noon-7pm Mon-Sat. **Map** p65 C1 ⑲ **Accessories/homewares**

Don't be deterred by the graffiti-covered stairway that leads up to this gem of a shop. Alisa Grifo has collected an array of inexpensive items – mostly simple and functional but with a strong design aesthetic – from around the world, such as cool Japanese can openers, colourful net bags from Germany and Shaker onion baskets handmade in New Hampshire. Kiosk may be relocating, so call or check the website before visiting.

Odin

199 Lafayette Street, between Broome & Kenmare Streets (1-212 966 0026, www.odinnewyork.com). Subway 6 to Spring Street. **Open** 11am-8pm Mon-Sat; noon-7pm Sun. **Map** p65 D2 ⑳ **Fashion**

The Norse god Odin is often portrayed sporting an eye patch and shabby robes. That may have been stylish in medieval Scandinavia, but to make it in NYC, he'd have to pick up some Engineered Garments, Rag & Bone or Our Legacy gear from this upscale men's boutique. Also look out for White Mountaineering, a Japanese brand that combines high-function fabrics with a fashionable aesthetic.

Other locations 328 E 11th Street, between First & Second Avenues, East Village (1-212-475 0666); 106 Greenwich Avenue, between Jane & W 13th Streets, West Village (1-212 243 4724).

★ Opening Ceremony

33-35 Howard Street, between Broadway & Lafayette Street (1-212 219 2688, www.openingceremony.us). Subway J, N, Q, R, Z, 6 to Canal Street. **Open** 11am-8pm Mon-Sat; noon-7pm Sun. **Map** p65 D2 ㉑ **Fashion**

The name references the Olympic Games; each year the store assembles hip US designers (Band of

In God We Trust. *See p67.*

IN THE KNOW
NEIGHBOURHOOD PORTMANTEAUS

Soho and Tribeca are early examples of an NYC phenom: catchy, contracted neighbourhood names largely driven by real estate agents trying to generate buzz. Recent inventions include NoMad (North of Madison Square Park), Dumbo (Down Under the Manhattan Bridge Overpass) and even Rambo (Right Around the Manhattan Bridge Overpass).

Outsiders, Alexander Wang, Patrik Ervell, Rodarte and its own house label) and pits them against the competition from abroad. The store is so popular it has expanded upwards, adding a book and music section upstairs and a men's shop next door.
▶ *There's an additional OC outpost at the Ace Hotel, see p359.*

What Goes Around Comes Around

351 West Broadway, between Broome & Grand Streets (1-212 343 1225, www.whatgoesaroundnyc.com). Subway A, C, E, 1 to Canal Street. **Open** 11am-8pm Mon-Sat; noon-7pm Sun. **Map** p65 C2 ㉒ **Fashion**

A favourite among the city's fashion cognoscenti, this downtown vintage destination sells highly curated stock alongside its own retro label. Style mavens particularly recommend it for 1960s, '70s and '80s rock T-shirts, pristine Alaïa clothing and vintage fur coats.

TRIBECA

Subway A, C, E, 1 to Canal Street; 1 to Franklin Street; 1, 2, 3 to Chambers Street.

In just two decades, the Triangle Below Canal Street has morphed from an isolated, run-down corner to a wealthy enclave with a family- and celebrity-heavy demographic. Robert De Niro has been a key figure in the area's transformation, founding the **Tribeca Film Center** (375 Greenwich Street, at Franklin Street) with partner Jane Rosenthal in 1988, which contains industry magnet and neighbourhood stalwart **Tribeca Grill** (1-212 941 3900). A few blocks away, De Niro's **Tribeca Cinemas** (54 Varick Street, at Laight Street, 1-212 941 2001, www.tribecacinemas.com) hosts premières and glitzy parties, when it isn't serving as a venue for the **Tribeca Film Festival** (*see p252*). In 2008, the actor unveiled the **Greenwich Hotel** (*see p347*).

The preponderance of large, hulking former industrial buildings gives Tribeca an imposing profile, but fine small-scale cast-iron architecture still stands along White Street and the parallel thoroughfares. Upscale eateries and, increasingly, retail cater to the well-heeled locals.

Sights & Museums

★ FREE Museum

Cortlandt Alley, between Franklin & White Streets (no phone, www.mmuseumm.com). Subway J, N, Q, R, Z, 6 to Canal Street. **Open** noon-6pm Sat, Sun. Admission free. **Map** p65 D2 ㉓
See p71 **Small Wonder**.

Restaurants & Cafés

★ Brushstroke

30 Hudson Street, at Duane Street (1-212 791 3771, www.davidbouley.com). Subway 1, 2, 3 to Chambers Street. **Open** 5.30-10pm Mon-Sat. **Tasting menus** $85-$135. **Map** p65 C3 ㉔ **Japanese**

Prominent local chef David Bouley's name may be behind this venture, but he's not in the kitchen, having handed the reins over to talented import Isao Yamada, who turns out some of the most accomplished Japanese food in the city. The ever-changing seasonal menu is best experienced as an intricate multicourse feast inspired by the Japanese *kaiseki*. A meal might start with crab *chawanmushi* (egg custard) with Oregon black truffles, before building slowly towards a subtle climax. In keeping with the basic tenets of this culinary art form, the savoury procession concludes with a rice dish – top-notch *chirashi* or seafood and rice cooked in a clay casserole – and delicate sweets such as creamy soy-milk panna cotta. The sushi bar is run by Tokyo-trained chef Eiji Ichimura, who serves a traditional Edomae-style omakase.

Landmarc Tribeca

179 West Broadway, between Leonard & Worth Streets (1-212 343 3883, www.landmarc-restaurant.com). Subway 1 to Franklin Street. **Open** 11am-midnight daily. **Main courses** $17-$40. **Map** p65 C3 ㉕ **Eclectic**

This downtown dining destination quickly distinguished itself among its Tribeca competitors by serving heady bistro dishes (bone marrow, crispy sweetbreads) until midnight, and stocking the wine list with reasonably priced half bottles. Chef-owner Marc Murphy focuses on the tried and trusted: *frisée aux lardons*, braised lamb shank and several types of mussels. Metal beams and exposed brick add an unfinished edge to the elegant bi-level space. Those who have little restraint when it comes to sweets will appreciate the dessert menu: miniature portions cost just $4 a pop and a tasting of six goes for $20.
Other locations 3rd Floor, Time Warner Center, 10 Columbus Circle, at Broadway, Upper West Side (1-212 823 6123).

Locanda Verde

377 Greenwich Street, at North Moore Street (1-212 925 3797, www.locandaverdenyc.com). Subway 1 to Franklin Street. **Open** 7-11am, 11.30am-3pm, 5.30-11pm Mon-Fri; 8am-3pm, 5.30-11pm Sat, Sun. **Main courses** $19-$35. **Map** p65 B3 ㉖ **Italian**

This buzzy eaterie in Robert De Niro's Greenwich Hotel features bold family-style fare that's best enjoyed as a bacchanalian banquet. Steak *tartara* piedmontese with hazelnuts, truffles and crispy *guanciale* (pork jowel bacon) won't last long in the middle of the table. Nor will the 'grandmother's' ravioli, stuffed with veal, pork and beef. This is one of those rare Italian restaurants with desserts worth saving room for – try the decadent La Fantasia di Tiramisu for two.

Telepan Local

329 Greenwich Street, between Duane & Jay Streets (1-212 966 9255, www.telepanlocal.com). Subway 1, 2, 3 to Chambers Street. **Open** 11.30am-11.30pm Mon-Thur; 11.30am-12.30am Fri, Sat; 11am-11.30pm Sun. **Main courses** $6-$20. **Map** p65 C3 ㉗ **American**

Bill Telepan had a busy 2013 – along with redesigning his Michelin-starred Upper West Side flagship, the locavore champion also opened this more casual small-plates spot, with shareable snacks like foie gras doughnuts and shrimp poppers with green-chili aioli. To sate more ample appetites, it also offers heftier fare such as grilled short ribs and quail à l'orange.

Other locations 72 West 69 Street, at Columbus Avenue, Upper West Side (1-212 580 4300).

EXPLORE

Bars

Weather Up Tribeca

159 Duane Street, between Hudson Street & West Broadway (1-212 766 3202, www.weatherupnyc.com). Subway 1, 2, 3 to Chambers Street. **Open** 5pm-2am daily. **Map** p65 C3 ㉘

At Kathryn Weatherup's tony Manhattan drinkery, a spin-off of her popular Prospect Heights bar, the well-balanced cocktail list features a regularly rotating mix of classics and original quaffs. Pair the booze with smart snacks such as grilled cheese sandwiches and steak tartare.

Other locations 589 Vanderbilt Avenue, between Bergen & Dean Streets, Prospect Heights, Brooklyn (no phone).

Shops & Services

Babesta Threads

66 West Broadway, between Murray & Warren Streets (1-212 608 4522, www.babesta.com). Subway 1, 2, 3 to Chambers Street. **Open** 11am-7pm Mon-Fri; noon-6pm Sat, Sun. **Map** p65 C3 ㉙ **Children**

Husband-and-wife team Aslan and Jenn Cattaui fill their cosy store with the stuff kids love – Rowdy Sprout concert tees, Uglydolls and eco-friendly clothing that'll make parents envious. The shop focuses on the under-six set, but there are also pieces for children aged up to 12 from popular lines such as Mini Rodini.

Nili Lotan

188 Duane Street, between Greenwich & Hudson Streets (1-212 219 9784, www.nililotan.com). Subway 1, 2, 3 to Chambers Street. **Open** noon-7pm Mon-Sat; noon-6pm Sun. **Map** p65 C3 ㉚ **Fashion**

The sparsely hung women's garments in Israeli designer Nili Lotan's airy, all-white store and studio look like art pieces on display in a gallery. Perfectly cut, largely monochrome wardrobe staples such as silk camisoles and dresses, oversized cashmere sweaters and crisply tailored menswear-inspired shirts appeal to minimalists with a penchent for luxury.

Patron of the New

151 Franklin Street, between Hudson & Varick Streets (1-212 966 7144, www.patronofthenew.com). Subway A, C, E to Canal Street; 1 to Franklin Street. **Open** 11am-7pm Mon-Sat; noon-6pm Sun. **Map** p65 C3 ㉛ **Fashion**

This avant-garde fashion emporium showcases an international collection of unique guys' and gals' clothing, accessories, beauty products and housewares from both illustrious and under-the-radar designers, including Balmain, Nicolas Andreas Taralis and Denis Colomb. Most goods carry hefty price tags, but there are some affordable jewellery, accessories and gifts such as soaps and candles.

Shinola

177 Franklin Street, between Greenwich & Hudson Streets (1-917 728 3000, www.shinola.com). Subway A, C, E to Canal Street; 1 to Franklin Street. **Open** 11am-7pm Mon-Sat; noon-6pm Sun. **Map** p65 C3 ㉜ **Fashion**

Motor City may be in dire financial straits but there is no denying the cool factor of the struggling metropolis. The first NYC location of the Detroit-based brand Shinola showcases a range of American-manufactured watches, bicycles, leather goods and other items. A 1930s bronze map that used to hang in Rockefeller Center adorns the industrial-edged store, which includes an outpost of cult East Village café the Smile.

Steven Alan

103 Franklin Street, between West Broadway & Church Street (1-212 343 0692, www.stevenalan.com). Subway 1 to Franklin Street. **Open** 11.30am-7pm Mon-Wed, Fri, Sat; 11.30am-8pm Thur; noon-6pm Sun. **Map** p65 C3 ㉝ **Fashion**

Known for well-crafted cotton shirts in an array of stripes, checks and solid colours, Steven Alan also assembles cultish boutique brands for men and women in its flagship store. In addition to the house label, browse clothing by Acne, Band of Outsiders and Engineered Garments, plus handbags and shoes.

SMALL WONDER

NYC's tiniest museum occupies a Tribeca elevator shaft.

Institutions like the Metropolitan Museum of Art are home to thousands of treasures. At the other end of the spectrum, there's **Museum** (*see p69*), a 60-square-foot repository in an abandoned Tribeca freight elevator. Finding it feels like an adventure in itself – it's on Cortlandt Alley, a narrow throughway located between Broadway and Lafayette Streets.

The walk-in-closet-size space showcases a mishmash of found objects and artefacts donated by hobbyists; its holdings include an index card detailing a pot dealer's pricing scale, and – allegedly – the shoe that was thrown at President George W Bush in Iraq in 2008. The museum's founders, indie filmmakers Alex Kalman, Josh Safdie and Benny Safdie say they're not legally allowed to reveal the donor of this particular piece of history. Museum was a logical extension of the filmmaking process, explains Alex Kalman. 'We've made a lot of work that is very much rooted in exploring the humanity of the world around us, so in a way we've been collecting moments by capturing them on video. Then at a certain point we started collecting actual objects – objects that we would consider proof of things, or that blew our minds – so we started amassing them over a couple of years. Then we said, let's open an institution for this language.'

The exhibits for each season, lasting roughly six months, are acquired in various ways, including via a submissions email address. Season 3, on view for much of 2014, includes a selection of *Screw* magazine founder Al Goldstein's transcribed personal Dictaphone notes, memorabilia from one of Saddam Hussein's palaces, and part of a collection of 200 mosquitoes killed mid-bite amassed by a traveller in New Delhi. 'That works for us on a bunch of different levels,' says Kalman of the latter, 'but on the simplest aesthetic level the almost-abstract forms they take are beautiful.'

Though Kalman acknowledges the humour inherent in the displays, he stresses that Museum is not merely an esoteric joke. 'We know that it's small, but its basically saying, these are not the things we're creating in society because we think they're important or valuable, these are the things we're creating because they are the things we want and need, and that tells us a lot about our psychology and who we are. It's trying to paint a very big portrait of humanity through the collection of our smallest things.'

Although Museum is only open at weekends, viewers can also get a peek at the space when it's closed – look for the small peepholes in a metal door between Franklin and White Streets. 'We love that part of it, that it's lit and alive 24/7,' says Kalman. If we're in the studio late and look down the alley, we often see people huddled outside looking in the windows.'

Chinatown, Little Italy & Nolita

Take a walk in the area south of Broome Street and east of Broadway, and you'll feel as though you've entered not just a different country but a different continent. You won't hear much English spoken on the streets of Manhattan's Chinatown, which are packed with exotic-produce stands, herb emporiums, cheap jewellers, snack vendors and restaurants. As New York City's largest Asian community continues to grow, it merges with neighbouring Little Italy. Between Chinatown and Nolita (North of Little Italy), with its hotspots, the historically Italian district has long been shrinking, but you can still get a taste of the old neighbourhood in its cafés and red-sauce eateries.

Nom Wah Tea Parlor.

Don't Miss

1 Museum of Chinese in America A stylish evocation of the Chinese-American story (*p74*).

2 Nom Wah Tea Parlor For a taste of Chinatown's history (*p74*).

3 Xi'an Famous Foods Celeb chef-approved cheap eats (*p76*).

4 Torrisi Italian Specialties Old-world Little Italy reinvented (*p78*).

5 Erica Weiner Unique (and affordable) local trinkets (*p79*).

廣州駕駛學校
EASTERN DRIVING SCHOOL
60號怡豐商場
MANHATTAN
BR.
ONE WAY

CHINATOWN

Subway F to East Broadway; J, N, Q, R, Z, 6 to Canal Street.

A steady flow of new arrivals keeps this neighbourhood – one of the largest Chinese communities outside Asia – full to bursting, with thousands of residents packed into the area surrounding East Canal Street. Some eventually decamp to one of NYC's three other Chinatowns in Sunset Park, Brooklyn, and Flushing and Elmhurst in Queens.

Mott and Grand Streets are lined with fish-, fruit- and vegetable-stocked stands selling some of the best and most affordable seafood and produce in the city – you'll see buckets of live eels and crabs, square watermelons and piles of hairy rambutans. Street vendors sell satisfying snacks such as pork buns and sweet egg pancakes by the bagful. Canal Street glitters with cheap jewellery and gift shops, but beware furtive vendors of (undoubtedly fake) designer goods. Between Kenmare and Worth Streets, Mott Street is lined with restaurants representing the cuisine of virtually every province of mainland China and Hong Kong; the Bowery, East Broadway and Division Street are just as diverse. Adding to the mix are myriad Indonesian, Malaysian, Thai and Vietnamese eateries and shops. The busy streets get even wilder during the **Chinese New Year** festivities (*see p37*).

Explore the Chinese experience on these shores at the stylish **Museum of Chinese in America**, which reopened in 2009 in much larger premises. The **Eastern States Buddhist Temple of America** (64 Mott Street, between Bayard & Canal Streets, 1-212 925 8787), founded in 1962, is one of the country's oldest Chinese Buddhist temples.

IN THE KNOW
MANHATTAN BRIDGE

It may lack the lore of the Brooklyn and Queensboro bridges, but this sweeping steel suspension bridge, completed in 1909, is among the city's most beautiful. The stone archway, near the junction of Broadway and Canal Street, was designed by New York Public Library architects Carrère and Hastings and modelled on the 17th-century Porte St Denis in Paris.

Sights & Museums

Museum of Chinese in America

215 Centre Street, between Grand & Howard Streets (1-212 619 4785, www.mocanyc.org). Subway J, N, Q, R, Z, 6 to Canal Street. **Open** 11am-6pm Tue, Wed, Fri-Sun; 11am-9pm Thur. **Admission** $10; $5 reductions; free under-12s; free Thur. **Map** p75 A3 ❶

Designed by prominent Chinese-American architect Maya Lin, MoCA reopened in an airy former machine shop in 2009. Its interior is loosely inspired by a traditional Chinese house, with rooms radiating off a central courtyard and areas defined by screens. The core exhibition traces the development of Chinese communities in the US from the 1850s to the present through objects, images and video. Innovative displays (drawers open to reveal artwork and documents, portraits are presented in a ceiling mobile) cover the development of industries such as laundries and restaurants in New York, Chinese stereotypes in pop culture, and the suspicion and humiliation Chinese-Americans endured during World War II and the McCarthy era. A mocked-up Chinese general store evokes the feel of these multi-purpose spaces, which served as vital community lifelines for men severed from their families under the 1882 Exclusion Act that restricted immigration. There's also a gallery for special exhibitions.

Restaurants & Cafés

$ Big Wing Wong

102 Mott Street, between Canal & Hester Streets (1-212 274 0696). Subway J, N, Q, R, Z, 6 to Canal Street. **Open** 7am-9.30pm daily. **Main courses** $5-$20. **No credit cards. Map** p75 B3 ❷ **Chinese**

See p76 **Chinatown 101**.

★ $ Nom Wah Tea Parlor

13 Doyers Street, between Bowery & Pell Street (1-212 962 6047, www.nomwah.com). Subway J, N, Q, R, Z, 6 to Canal Street; J, Z to Chambers Street. **Open** 10.30am-9pm Mon-Thur, Sun; 10.30am-10pm Fri, Sat. **Main courses** $2-$10. **Map** p75 B4 ❸ **Chinese**

New York's first dim sum house, Nom Wah opened in 1920 and was owned by the same family for more than three decades. The current owner, Wilson Tang, has revamped it in a vintage style true to the restaurant's archival photographs. He also updated the kitchen and did away with cooking dim sum en masse. Now, each plate (ultra-fluffy oversized roasted-pork buns, flaky fried crêpe egg rolls) is cooked to order. *Photo p72.*

Ping's

22 Mott Street, between Mosco & Pell Streets (1-212 602 9988, www.pingsnyc.com). Subway J, N, Q, R, Z, 6 to Canal Street. **Open** 10.30am-11pm Mon-Fri; 9am-11pm Sat, Sun. **Main courses** $7-$80. **Map** p75 B4 ❹ **Chinese**

The bank of fish tanks near the entrance suggests the speciality. Go for something you haven't tried: bite-sized pieces of boneless smelt deep-fried to a golden yellow and served with a mix of Szechuan peppercorns

EXPLORE

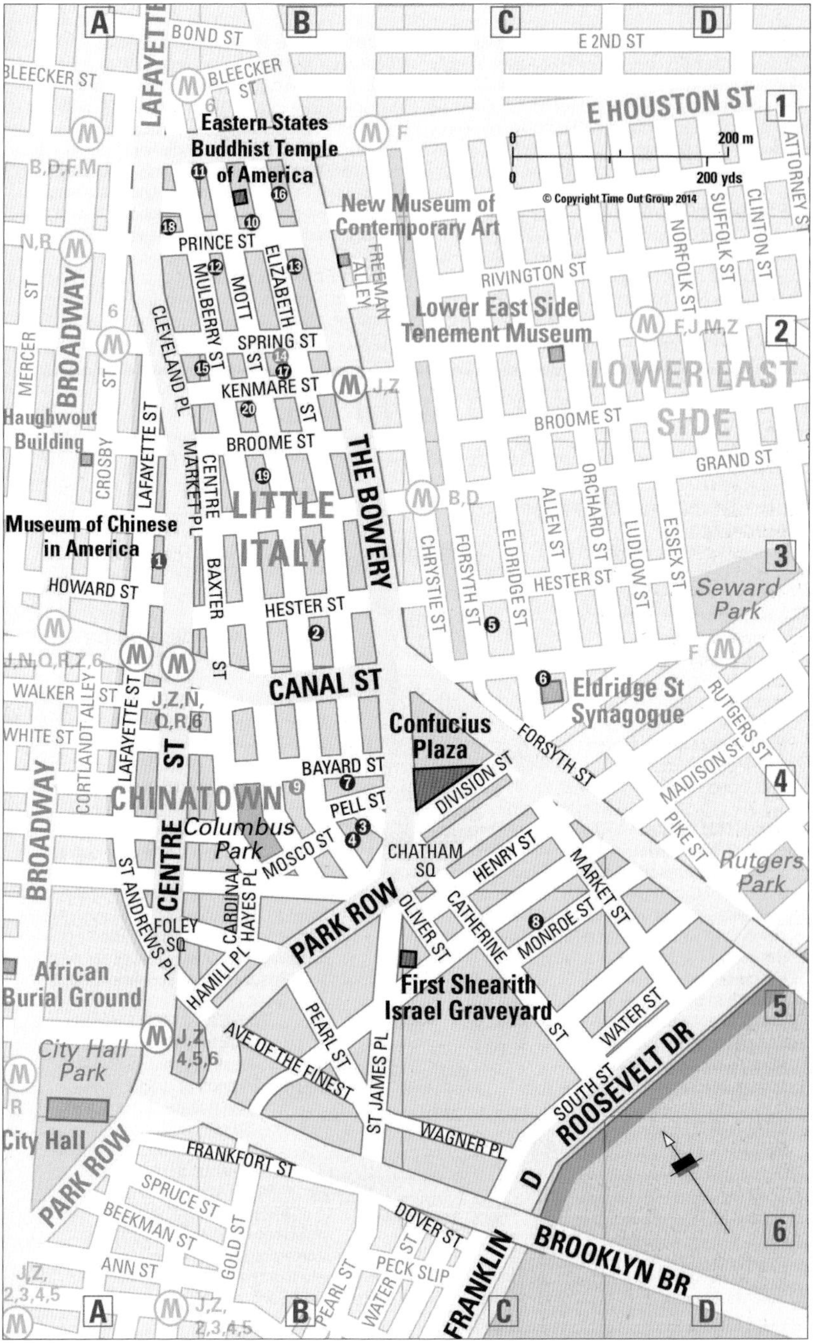
A
B
C
D
1
2
3
4
5
6
BOND ST
E 2ND ST
BLEECKER ST
LAFAYETTE
E HOUSTON ST
Eastern States
Buddhist Temple
of America
B,D,F,M
F
0
200 m
200 yds
© Copyright Time Out Group 2014
New Museum of
Contemporary Art
N,R
PRINCE ST
MULBERRY ST
MOTT
ELIZABETH
FREEMAN ALLEY
RIVINGTON ST
NORFOLK ST
SUFFOLK ST
CLINTON ST
ATTORNEY ST
BROADWAY
MERCER
CLEVELAND PL
SPRING ST
Lower East Side
Tenement Museum
F,J,M,Z
LOWER EAST
SIDE
KENMARE ST
J,Z
Haughwout
Building
CROSBY
LAFAYETTE ST
MARKET PL
CENTRE
BROOME ST
THE BOWERY
GRAND ST
LITTLE
ITALY
B,D
CHRYSTIE ST
FORSYTH ST
ELDRIDGE ST
ALLEN ST
ORCHARD ST
LUDLOW ST
ESSEX ST
Museum of Chinese
in America
BAXTER
HOWARD ST
HESTER ST
Seward
Park
J,N,Q,R,Z,6
J,Z,N,
Q,R,6
WALKER ST
WHITE ST
CORTLANDT ALLEY
CANAL ST
Confucius
Plaza
Eldridge St
Synagogue
RUTGERS ST
FORSYTH ST
MADISON ST
BAYARD ST
DIVISION ST
PELL ST
CHINATOWN
Columbus
Park
MOSCO ST
CHATHAM
SQ
HENRY ST
MARKET ST
PIKE ST
Rutgers
Park
ST ANDREWS PL
CENTRE ST
FOLEY
SQ
CARDINAL HAYES PL
PARK ROW
OLIVER ST
CATHERINE
MONROE ST
African
Burial Ground
HAMILL PL
First Shearith
Israel Graveyard
WATER ST
PEARL ST
City Hall
Park
J,Z
4,5,6
AVE OF THE FINEST
ST JAMES PL
SOUTH ST
ROOSEVELT DR
City Hall
FRANKFORT ST
WAGNER PL
PARK ROW
SPRUCE ST
BEEKMAN ST
GOLD ST
DOVER ST
ANN ST
FRANKLIN
BROOKLYN BR
PECK SLIP
PEARL ST
WATER ST
J,Z,
2,3,4,5

EXPLORE

and salt. Big steamed oysters benefit from a splash of Ping's celebrated house-made XO sauce – a spicy condiment made of dried shrimp, scallops and garlic. The sliced sautéed conch is set off by snappy snow peas and a tangy fermented shrimp sauce. Those exotic flavours, plus touches like tablecloths, justify prices that are a notch above the Chinatown norm.

$ Prosperity Dumpling

46 Eldridge Street, between Canal & Hester Streets (1-212 343 0683). Subway J, N, Q, R, Z, 6 to Canal Street. **Open** 7am-9.30pm daily. **Dumplings** $1/4. **No credit cards. Map** p75 C3 ❺ **Chinese**
See below **Chinatown 101**.

$ Super Taste Restaurant

26 Eldridge Street, at Canal Street (1-646 283 0999). Subway F to East Broadway. **Open** 10.30am-10.30pm daily. **Main courses** $4.50-$6. **No credit cards. Map** p75 C4 ❻ **Chinese**
In a sea of cheap Chinatown noodle bars, Super Taste stands out. Watch the cook hand pull your Lanzhou-style la mian, the Chinese relative of Japanese ramen, which is served in a soup with toppings that vary from beef tendon to eel – for little more than $5.

$ Xi'an Famous Foods

67 Bayard Street, between Elizabeth & Mott Streets (no phone, www.xianfoods.com). Subway J, N, Q, R, Z, 6 to Canal Street. **Open** 11.30am-9pm

CHINATOWN 101

Too much choice in Chinatown? Here are the essentials.

DOLLAR DUMPLINGS: PROSPERITY DUMPLING
This pint-size dumpling den serves one of the best budget meals in Chinatown: four pan-fried pot stickers for a buck. A plump, hand-made wrapper – chewy with crisp, griddle-pressed edges – is folded around a juicy pork-and-chive filling, its rich flavour at odds with the cheap price. *See above.*

Prosperity Dumpling.

ROASTED DUCK: BIG WING WONG
You'll be confused when you show up to this old-school Cantonese joint – the outside inexplicably says 102 Noodles Town. But clarity hits when you taste a slice of the roasted duck, with its fatty, succulent meat and crackly, burnished mahogany skin. You can get the bird over rice or congee, but purists stick to a mere drizzle of hoisin. *See p74.*

Big Wing Wong.

EGG TART: BREAD TALK
The litmus test of a good Chinatown bakery is its *dan ta* (egg custard tart), and there's no tastier tartlet than the one at this Two Bridges bakery (47 Catherine Street, between Madison & Monroe Streets, 1-917 832 4784). What sets the three-bite sweet apart is its melt-in-the-mouth custard filling, eggy-sweet but not cloying, wrapped in a buttery, crisp-around-the-edges crust. A dollar buys you two.

MASSAGE: FISHION HERB CENTER
At the end of an AstroTurfed alley off Mott Street is an unexpected gem (107 Mott Street, between Canal & Hester Streets, 1-212 966 8771, www.fishionherbcenter.com). In 15 linoleum-floored, semi-private rooms, therapists dole out a combination of Chinese acupressure and shi-atsu massage (30 minutes for $20), while foot massages (40 minutes for $25) are dispensed at armchairs in the downstairs communal area. Reservations recommended.

STREET CART: LING'S SWEET MINI CAKES
Nestled amid sidewalk stands of dragon fruit and rice rolls, this Canal Street cart (between Baxter & Mulberry Streets) doles out $1 paper bags filled with 15 quarter-size balls of batter. Pillow-soft with a crisp exterior, the puffs are made to order in a special waffle iron and taste like the sweet cross between a fortune cookie and a French madeleine.

Mon-Thur, Sun; 11.30am-9.30pm Fri, Sat. **Main courses** $3-$10. **No credit cards**. **Map** p75 B4 ❼ **Chinese**
This cheap Chinese chainlet, which got the seal of approval from celebrity chef Anthony Bourdain, highlights the mouth-tingling cuisine of Xi'an, an ancient capital along China's Silk Road. Claim one of the 35 stools and nosh on spicy noodles or a cumin-spiced burger for less than $5.

Shops & Services

Downtown Music Gallery

13 Monroe Street, between Catherine & Market Streets (1-212 473 0043, www.downtownmusic gallery.com). Subway J, Z to Chambers Street; 4, 5, 6 to Brooklyn Bridge-City Hall. **Open** noon-6pm Mon-Wed; noon-7pm Thur-Sun. **Map** p75 C5 ❽ **Books & music**
Many landmarks of the so-called downtown music scene have shuttered, but as long as DMG persists, the community will have a sturdy anchor. The shop stocks the city's finest selection of avant-garde jazz, contemporary classical, progressive rock and related styles.

★ Sun's Organic Garden

79 Bayard Street, between Mott and Mulberry Streets (1-212 566 3260). Subway J, N, Q, R, Z, 6 to Canal Street. **Open** 10.30am-7.30pm daily. **Map** p75 B4 ❾ **Food & drink**
Owner Lorna Lai knows her teas the way a sommelier knows terroir. Curious sippers peruse the well-stocked shelves of the Hong Kong native's nook, which boasts more than a thousand jarred loose-leaf varieties from around the world, available by the ounce. Lai's house-made herbal blends are standouts, in exotic flavours like holy basil and bilberry.

LITTLE ITALY & NOLITA

Subway B, D, F, M to Broadway-Lafayette Street; J, N, Q, R, Z, 6 to Canal Street; J, Z to Bowery; N, R to Prince Street; 6 to Spring Street.

Abandoning the dismal tenements of the Five Points district (in what is now the Civic Center and part of Chinatown), immigrants from Naples and Sicily began moving to **Little Italy** in the 1880s. The area once stretched from Canal Street to Houston Street, between Lafayette Street and the Bowery, but these days only the blocks immediately surrounding Mulberry Street exude a strong Italian presence. As families prospered in the 1950s, they moved to the outer boroughs and suburbs.

Another telling change in the district: **St Patrick's Old Cathedral** (260-264 Mulberry Street, between Houston & Prince Streets) no longer holds services in Italian, but in English and Spanish. Completed in 1809 and restored after a fire in 1868, this was the city's premier Catholic church until it was demoted upon consecration of the Fifth Avenue cathedral of the same name. But ethnic pride remains: Italian-Americans flood in from across the city during the 11-day **Feast of San Gennaro** (*see p35*).

Touristy cafés and restaurants line Mulberry Street between Broome and Canal Streets, but pockets of the past linger nearby. Long-time residents still buy fresh mozzarella from **DiPalo's Fine Foods** (200 Grand Street, at Mott Street, 1-212 226 1033). Legend has it that the first pizzeria in New York was opened by Gennaro Lombardi on Spring Street in 1905. **Lombardi's** moved down the block in 1994 (32 Spring Street, at Mott Street, 1-212 941 7994), but still serves its signature clam pies. Today the area's restaurants are largely undistinguished grills and pasta houses, but two reliable choices are **Il Cortile** (125 Mulberry Street, between Canal & Hester Streets, 1-212 226 6060) and **La Mela** (167 Mulberry Street, between Broome & Grand Streets, 1-212 431 9493). Drop in for dessert at **Caffè Roma** (385 Broome Street, at Mulberry Street, 1-212 226 8413), which opened in 1891.

Nolita became a magnet for pricey boutiques and trendy eateries in the 1990s. Elizabeth, Mott and Mulberry Streets, between Houston and Spring Streets, in particular, are home to hip shops.

Restaurants & Cafés

$ Café Habana

17 Prince Street, at Elizabeth Street (1-212 625 2001, www.ecoeatery.com). Subway N, R to Prince Street; 6 to Spring Street. **Open** 9am-midnight daily. **Main courses** $10-$17.50. **Map** p75 B2 ❿ **Cuban**
Trendy Nolita types storm this chrome corner fixture for a taste of the addictive grilled corn: golden ears doused in fresh mayo, chargrilled, and generously sprinkled with chilli powder and grated cotija cheese. Staples include a Cuban sandwich of roasted pork, ham, melted swiss and sliced pickles, and crisp beer-battered catfish with spicy mayo. At the takeaway next door, you can get that corn-on-a-stick to go.
Other locations Habana Outpost, 757 Fulton Street, at South Portland Avenue, Fort Greene, Brooklyn (open Apr-Oct, 1-718 858 9500).

Estela

47 E Houston Street, between Mott & Mulberry Streets (1-212 219 7693, www.estelanyc.com). Subway B, D, F, M to Broadway-Lafayette Street; 6 to Bleecker Street. **Open** 5.30-11pm Mon-Sat; 5.30-10.30pm Sun. **Main courses** $16-$33. **Map** p75 A1 ⓫ **American creative**
The fashionable cookie-cutter decor – exposed brick, globe lights, hulking marble bar – may suggest you've stumbled into yet another bustling rustic restaurant-cum-bar that's not worth the wait. But there is more to this Mediterranean-tinged spot

Estela. *See p77.*

than meets the eye: primarily, the talent of Ignacio Mattos, the imaginative Uruguayan-born chef, who strained to sell his brand of 'primitive modern' cooking to a Williamsburg crowd at Isa. Here, he has reined in his modernist tendencies with an ever-changing, mostly small-plates menu that pivots from avant-garde towards intimate. Highlights might include beef tartare with tart pickled elderberries, a musty baseline note from fish sauce and crunchy sunchoke (Jerusalem artichoke) chips, egg with gigante beans and cured tuna, and a creamy panna cotta with honey.

★ Parm & Torrisi Italian Specialties

Parm *248 Mulberry Street, between Prince & Spring Streets (1-212 993 7189, www.parmnyc.com).* **Open** 11am-11pm Mon-Wed, Sun; 11am-midnight Thur-Sat. **Sandwiches** $9-$14.
Torrisi Italian Specialties *250 Mulberry Street, between Prince & Spring Streets (1-212 965 0955, www.torrisinyc.com).* **Open** 5.30-11pm Mon-Thur; noon-2pm, 5.30-11pm Fri-Sun. **Prix fixe** $100. *Subway N, R to Prince Street; 6 to Spring Street.* **Map** p75 B2 ⓬ **Italian**

Young guns Mario Carbone and Rich Torrisi, two fine-dining vets, brought a cool-kid sheen to red-sauce plates in 2010, when they debuted Torrisi Italian Specialties, a deli by day and haute eaterie by night. People lined up for their buzzworthy sandwiches (outstanding herb-rubbed roast turkey, classic cold cuts or chicken parmesan) and hard-to score dinner seats, packing the joint until it outgrew the space. The pair smartly split the operations, devoting their original flagship to tasting menus and transplanting the sandwich offerings to fetching diner digs next door.

Public

210 Elizabeth Street, between Prince & Spring Streets (1-212 343 7011, www.public-nyc.com). Subway N, R to Prince Street; 6 to Spring Street. **Open** 6pm-1am Mon-Thur; 6pm-2am Fri; 10.30am-3.30pm, 6pm-2am Sat; 10.30am-3.30pm, 6pm-midnight Sun. **Main courses** $21-$35. **Map** p75 B2 ⓭ **Eclectic**

This sceney restaurant is moodily lit and industrially chic. Reflecting pan-Pacific, Middle Eastern and South-east Asian influences, the menu offers creative dishes such as grilled kangaroo on coriander falafel, or ricotta cavatelli with carrot bolognese, Thai basil and cashew pesto, all paired with interesting wines.

Bars

Mother's Ruin

18 Spring Street, between Elizabeth & Mott Streets (no phone, www.mothersruinnyc.com). Subway J, Z to Bowery; 6 to Spring Street. **Open** 11am-4am Mon-Fri; noon-4am Sat, Sun. **Map** p75 B2 ⓮

At this airy Nolita drinkery, co-owners Timothy Lynch and Richard Knapp bring in a rotating cast of star bartenders to sling classic and contemporary drinks. The laid-back space – done up with a cream tin ceiling, exposed brick and weathered-wood bar – also offers a full menu of globally inflected bites.

Shops & Services

Creatures of Comfort

205 Mulberry Street, between Kenmare & Spring Streets (1-212 925 1005, www.creaturesofcomfort.us). Subway 6 to Spring Street; N, R to Prince Street. **Open** 11am-7pm Mon-Sat; noon-7pm Sun. **Map** p75 B2 ⓯ **Fashion**

Jade Lai opened Creatures of Comfort in Los Angeles in 2005 and brought her cool-girl aesthetic east five years later. Occupying the former home of the 12th police precinct, the New York offshoot offers a similar mix of pricey but oh-so-cool pieces from various avant-garde lines, such as MM6 Maison Martin Margiela, Acne and Isabel Marant's Etoile, plus the store's own-label bohemian basics, and shoes and accessories.

Christian Siriano

252 Elizabeth Street, between E Houston & Prince Streets (1-212 775 8494, www.christianvsiriano.com). Subway B, D, F, M

to Broadway-Lafayette Street. **Open** 11.30am-7pm Mon-Sat; noon-6pm Sun. **Map** p75 B1 ⓰ **Fashion**
This 1,000sq ft flagship boutique was personally designed by the hotshot *Project Runway* season-four winner. You'll find the glam evening wear that propelled Siriano to success – such as beaded gowns and cocktail dresses – displayed on mannequins throughout the shop, but if you don't have a red-carpet event on your calendar, there are plenty of reasonably priced separates and accessories to paw through, along with his current Payless footwear collection (starting at just $30).

★ Erica Weiner

173 Elizabeth Street, between Kenmare & Spring Streets (1-212 334 6383, www.ericaweiner.com). Subway C, E to Spring Street. **Open** noon-8pm daily **Map** p75 B2 ⓱ **Accessories**
Erica Weiner sells her own bronze, brass, silver and gold creations – many under $100 – alongside vintage and reworked baubles. Old wooden cabinets and stacked crates showcase rings and charm-laden necklaces, the latter laden with the likes of tiny dangling harmonicas and steel penknives. Other favourites include brass ginkgo-leaf earrings, and moveable-type-letter necklaces for your favourite wordsmith.

McNally Jackson

52 Prince Street, between Lafayette & Mulberry Streets (1-212 274 1160, www.mcnallyjackson.com). Subway N, R to Prince Street; 6 to Spring Street. **Open** 10am-10pm Mon-Sat; 10am-9pm Sun. **Map** p75 A2 ⓲ **Books & music**
Owned by Sarah McNally, daughter of the folks behind Canada's fine independent McNally Robinson, this appealing bookstore stocks a distinctly international selection of novels and non-fiction titles. A wide range of readings and events – which have included such well-known figures as Garrison Keillor, Hari Kunzru and Siri Hustvedt – take place in its comfortable downstairs space.

New & Almost New

171 Mott Street, between Broome & Grand Streets, Nolita (1-212 226 6677, www.newandalmostnew.com). Subway B, D to Grand Street; J, Z to Bowery; 6 to Spring Street. **Open** 1-5pm Mon, Sun; noon-6.30pm Tue-Sat. **Map** p75 B3 ⓳ **Fashion**
Germophobe label-lovers, rejoice: 40% of the merchandise on sale at this resale shop is actually brand new. Owner Maggie Chan hand-selects every piece, ensuring its quality and authenticity. Among the items hanging on the racks you'll find pieces from lofty labels such as Prada, Chanel and Hermès. Prices range from as low as $15 up to around $600.

Warm

181 Mott Street, between Broome & Kenmare Streets (1-212 925 200, www.warmny.com). Subway J, Z to Bowery; 6 to Spring Street. **Open** noon-7pm Mon-Sat; noon-6pm Sun. **Map** p75 B2 ⓴ **Fashion/accessories**
The husband-and-wife owners of this appealing boutique, Rob Magnotta and Winnie Beattie, curate an eclectic selection of women's threads and accessories, alongside fragrances and body products, vintage books and items for the home, all influenced by the couple's globe-trotting surfer lifestyle. The laid-back looks include urban boho-chic clothing from Vanessa Bruno, Giada Forte and Maison Olga, and handcrafted jewellery by artist Suzannah Wainhouse.

IN THE KNOW
THE MOB WAS HERE

Little Italy is the site of several notorious Mafia landmarks. The brick-fronted store now occupied by a shoe boutique (247 Mulberry Street, between Prince & Spring Streets) was once the Ravenite Social Club, where Mafia kingpin John Gotti made his deals until his arrest in 1990. Mobster Joey Gallo was shot and killed in 1972 while celebrating his birthday at Umberto's Clam House, which has since moved around the corner to 132 Mulberry Street, between Grand & Hester Streets (1-212 431 7545).

Creatures of Comfort.

EXPLORE

Lower East Side

Once better known for bagels and bargains, the Lower East Side is now brimming with vintage and indie-designer boutiques, fashionable bars and contemporary art galleries. In fact, the former slum has been so radically altered by the forces of gentrification, it was placed on the National Trust for Historic Preservation's annual list of the 11 most endangered historic places in 2008. But new development hasn't yet destroyed the character of the erstwhile centre of immigrant life. You can still explore remnants of the old Jewish neighbourhood that the Marx Brothers and George Gershwin called home, including 100-year-old food purveyors, a magnificently restored synagogue and recreated tenement apartments.

Katz's Delicatessen.

Don't Miss

1 Lower East Side Tenement Museum See how the other half really lived (*see p83*).

2 Museum at Eldridge Street This restored synagogue is an inspirational sight (*see p84*).

3 New Museum of Contemporary Art Cutting-edge exhibitions in a cool building (*see p84*).

4 Katz's Delicatessen Your chance to have what she had (*see p85*).

5 Russ & Daughters Get a new-school bagel at this old-school shop (*see p91*).

NEW YORK USA

Lower East Side Tenement Museum.

LOWER EAST SIDE

Subway B, D to Grand Street; F to East Broadway; F to Delancey Street or Lower East Side-Second Avenue; J, Z to Bowery; J, M, Z to Delancey-Essex Streets.

In the 19th century, tenement buildings were constructed on the Lower East Side, a roughly defined area south of Houston Street and west of the East River, to house the growing number of German, Irish, Jewish and Italian immigrants – by 1900 it was the most populous neighbourhood in the US. The appalling conditions of these overcrowded, unsanitary slums were captured by photographer and writer Jacob Riis in *How the Other Half Lives* in 1890; its publication spurred activists and prompted the introduction of more humane building codes. The dwellings have since been converted or demolished, but you can see how newcomers once lived by visiting the recreated apartments of the **Lower East Side Tenement Museum** (*see p83*).

IN THE KNOW GRAVE SECRETS

Although the gate is usually locked, catch a glimpse of the **First Shearith Israel Graveyard** (55-57 St James Place, between James & Oliver Streets), the final resting place of the country's first Jewish community; some gravestones date from 1683, including those of Spanish and Portuguese Jews who fled the Inquisition.

The neighbourhood was also the focal point of Jewish culture in New York. Between 1870 and 1920, hundreds of synagogues and religious schools thrived alongside Yiddish newspapers, social-reform societies and kosher bakeries. Vaudeville and classic Yiddish theatre also prospered here. Today, most of these places are long gone, but vestiges of Jewish life can be found amid the Chinese businesses spilling over from sprawling Chinatown and the ever-multiplying fashionable boutiques, restaurants and bars. The **Eldridge Street Synagogue** (*see p84*), which has undergone extensive renovation, still has a small but vital congregation. Heading east down Canal Street rewards with a view of the façade of the **Sender Jarmulowsky Bank** (on the corner of Canal & Orchard Streets), which catered to Jewish immigrants until its collapse in 1914; note the seated classical figures flanking the clock above the doorway. Further down Canal, at the corner of Ludlow, you'll find the former home of the **Kletzker Brotherly Aid Association**, a lodge for immigrants from Belarus still marked by the Star of David and the year of its opening, 1892. The **Forward Building** (175 E Broadway, at Canal Street) was once the headquarters of the *Jewish Daily Forward*, a Yiddish-language paper that had a peak circulation of 275,000 in the 1920s; it's now home to multimillion-dollar condominiums.

Those looking for a taste of the old Jewish Lower East Side should grab a table at **Katz's Delicatessen** (*see p85*). Opened in 1888, this kosher deli continues to serve some of the best pastrami in New York (and was the site of Meg

Ryan's famous 'fauxgasm' scene in *When Harry Met Sally*…). **Essex Street Market** (www.essexstreetmarket.com), which opened in 1940 as part of La Guardia's plan to get pushcarts off the streets, contains a mix of high-quality vendors selling cheese, coffee, sweets, produce, fish and meat.

By the 1980s, when young artists and musicians began moving into the area, it was a patchwork of Asian, Latino and Jewish enclaves. Hipster bars and music venues sprang up on and around Ludlow Street, creating an annex to the East Village. That scene still survives, at spots like the **Bowery Ballroom** and **Cake Shop** (for both, *see p273*), but rents have risen dramatically and some stalwarts have closed.

These days, visual art is the Lower East Side's main cultural draw. Dozens of storefront galleries have opened in the vicinity over the past decade (for our picks, *see p89* **Gallery-Hopping Guide**). In 2007, the **New Museum of Contemporary Art** (*see p84*) decamped here from Chelsea, opening a $50-million building on the Bowery. A narrow glass tower designed by Norman Foster, a block north at 257 Bowery, opened in 2010 as the HQ for established art dealers **Sperone Westwater** (*see p89*), whose high-profile stable includes Bruce Nauman, Susan Rothenberg and William Wegman.

Although the **Orchard Street** bargain district – a row of shops selling utilitarian goods such as socks, sportswear and luggage, and beloved of hagglers – persists, the strip is at the centre of a proliferation of small indie shops. More mainstream commercial gloss is encroaching on the area in the form of high-rise hotels and apartment buildings, but as the area continues to change, groups such as the Lower East Side Conservancy are working to preserve its unique character.

Sights & Museums

★ Lower East Side Tenement Museum

Visitors' centre, 103 Orchard Street, at Delancey Street (1-212 982 8420, www.tenement.org). Subway F to Delancey Street; J, M, Z to Delancey-Essex Streets. **Open** *Museum shop & ticketing* 10am-6.30pm Mon-Wed, Fri-Sun; 10am-8.30pm Thur. **Tours** 10.30am-5pm Mon-Wed, Fri-Sun; 10am-8pm Thur (see website for schedule). **Admission** $22-$25; $17-$20 reductions. **Map** p83 B2 ❶

This fascinating museum – actually a series of restored tenement apartments at 97 Orchard Street – is accessible only by guided tour, which start at the visitors' centre at 103 Orchard Street. Tours often sell out, so it's wise to book ahead.

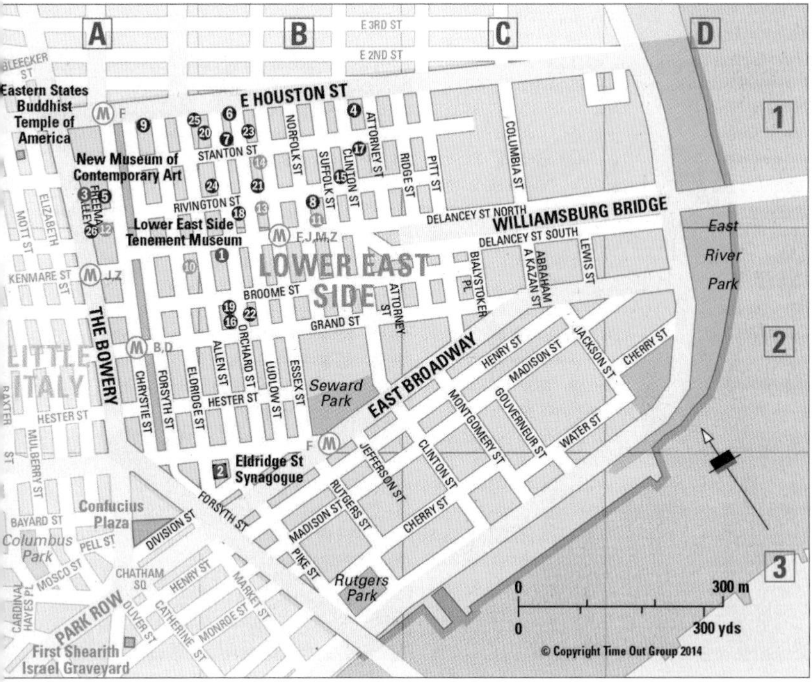

'Hard Times' visits the homes of an Italian and a German-Jewish clan; 'Sweatshop Workers' explores the apartments of two Eastern European Jewish families as well as a garment shop where many of the locals would have found employment; and 'Irish Outsiders' unfurls the life of the Moore family, who are coping with the loss of their child. Families may want to stop by quarters once occupied by a Sephardic Jewish Greek family and speak to an interpreter in period costume channelling the 14-year-old daughter of the house, Victoria Confino. A new tour, 'Shop Life' explores the diverse retailers that occupied the building's storefronts, including a 19th-century German saloon. From mid March through December, the museum also conducts themed daily walking tours of the Lower East Side ($22-$45; $17-$40 reductions).

★ Museum at Eldridge Street (Eldridge Street Synagogue)

12 Eldridge Street, between Canal & Division Streets (1-212 219 0302, www.eldridgestreet.org). Subway F to East Broadway. **Open** 10am-5pm Mon-Thur, Sun; 10am-3pm Fri. **Admission** $10; $6-$8 reductions; free under-5s; free Mon. **Map** p83 B3 ❷

With an impressive façade that combines Moorish, Gothic and Romanesque elements, the first grand synagogue on the Lower East Side is now surrounded by dumpling shops and Chinese herb stores, but rewind about a century and you would have found delicatessens and *mikvot* (ritual bathhouses). For its first 50 years, the 1887 synagogue had a congregation of thousands and doubled as a mutual-aid society for new arrivals in need of financial assistance, healthcare and employment. But as Jews left the area and the congregation dwindled, the building fell into disrepair.

A 20-year, $19.5-million facelift has restored its splendour; the soaring main sanctuary features hand-stencilled walls and a resplendent stained-glass rose window with Star of David motifs. The renovations were completed in autumn 2010, with the installation of a new stained-glass window designed by artist Kiki Smith and architect Deborah Gans. The admission price includes a guided tour (see website for schedule). In the new orientation centre, touch-screen displays highlight the synagogue's architecture, aspects of worship and local history, including other (extant or long-vanished) Jewish landmarks.

★ New Museum of Contemporary Art

235 Bowery, between Prince & Stanton Streets (1-212 219 1222, www.newmuseum.org). Subway N, R to Prince Street; 6 to Spring Street. **Open** 11am-6pm Wed, Fri-Sun; 11am-9pm Thur. **Admission** $16; $10-$14 reductions; free under-18s (accompanied by an adult). Pay what you wish 7-9pm Thur. **Map** p83 A1 ❸

Having occupied various sites for 30 years, New York City's only contemporary art museum finally got its own purpose-built space in late 2007.

EXPLORE

Museum at Eldridge Street (Eldridge Street Synagogue).

Katz's Delicatessen.

Dedicated to emerging media and under-recognised artists, the seven-floor space is worth a look for the architecture alone – a striking, off-centre stack of aluminium-mesh-clad boxes designed by the cutting-edge Tokyo architectural firm Sejima + Nishizawa/SANAA. Two ongoing exterior installations by Chris Burden add to the drama: the artist's 36ft-high *Twin Quasi Legal Skyscrapers* (2013) perch on the roof and his 30ft-long *Ghost Ship* (2005) hangs on the façade. The museum's café is run by the folks behind Hester Street Market, offering artisanal eats by a selection of local vendors. At weekends, don't miss the fabulous views from the minimalist seventh-floor Sky Room.

Restaurants & Cafés

Clinton Street Baking Company & Restaurant

4 Clinton Street, between E Houston & Stanton Streets (1-646 602 6263, www.clintonstreetbaking.com). Subway F to Lower East Side-Second Avenue; J, M, Z to Delancey-Essex Streets. **Open** 8am-4pm, 6-11pm Mon-Fri; 9am-4pm, 6-11pm Sat; 8am-6pm Sun. **Main courses** $9-$23. **No credit cards before 6pm**. **Map** p83 B1 ❹ **Café**

The warm buttermilk biscuits and fluffy plate-size pancakes at this pioneering little eaterie are reason enough to face the brunch-time crowds. If you want to avoid the onslaught, the homey place is just as reliable for both lunch and dinner. Try the $15 beer and burger special (6-8pm Mon-Thur): 8oz of Black Angus topped with swiss cheese and caramelised onions, served with a beer.

Freemans

2 Freeman Alley, off Rivington Street, between Bowery & Chrystie Street (1-212 420 0012, www.freemansrestaurant.com). Subway F to Lower East Side-Second Avenue; J, Z to Bowery. **Open** 11am-4pm, 6-11.30pm Mon-Fri; 10am-4pm, 6-11.30pm Sat, Sun. **Main courses** $15-$32. **Map** p83 A1 ❺ **American creative**

Located at the end of a graffiti-marked alley, Freemans, with its colonial tavern meets hunting lodge style, is an enduring hit with retro-loving New Yorkers. Garage-sale oil paintings and moose antlers serve as backdrops to a curved zinc bar, while the menu recalls a simpler time – devils on horseback (prunes stuffed with stilton cheese and wrapped in bacon); rum-soaked ribs, the meat falling off the bone with a gentle nudge of the fork; and stiff cocktails that'll get you good and sauced.

★ Katz's Delicatessen

205 E Houston Street, at Ludlow Street (1-212 254 2246, www.katzsdelicatessen.com). Subway F to Lower East Side-Second Avenue. **Open** 8am-10.45pm Mon-Wed; 8am-2.45am Thur; 24hrs Fri (from 8am), Sat; closes 10.45pm Sun. **Sandwiches** $12-$18. **Map** p83 B1 ❻ **American**

A visit to Gotham isn't complete without a stop at a quintessential New York deli, and this Lower East Side survivor is the real deal. You might get a kick out of the famous faces (from Bill Clinton to Ben Stiller) plastered to the panelled walls, or the spot where Meg Ryan faked it in *When Harry Met Sally…*, but the real stars of this cavernous cafeteria are the thick-cut pastrami sandwiches and crisp-skinned all-beef hot dogs – the latter a mere $3.45.

IN THE KNOW
BETTER THAN SEX?

Want to order what Meg Ryan had in that famous 'faking it' scene in **Katz's Delicatessen** (*see above*) in the film *When Harry Met Sally…*? Ask for turkey on rye (with coleslaw and a pickle).

Mission Cantina.

Mission Cantina
172 Orchard Street, at Stanton Street (1-212 254 2233, www.missioncantinanyc.com). Subway F to Lower East Side-Second Avenue. **Open** noon-3pm, 5.30pm-midnight Tue-Sun. **Tacos** $5-$6. **Shared plates** $35. **Map** p83 B1 ❼ **Mexican**
Rock-star chef Danny Bowien changes up the tune for his highly anticipated sophomore act, turning from his brand of innovative Szechuan eats to thoughtful Mexican fare. At a 40-seat hangout located down the block from Mission Chinese Food, which was closed for renovation at time of writing, he reworks classic dishes, like rotisserie chicken stuffed with rice. Tacos also get the Bowien touch: fresh tortillas made with Anson Mills corn are topped with such rotating fillings as rotisserie pork and house-made Oaxacan-style cheese. Mexican beer accompanies the South of the Border food, and – as at his other spots – a portion of sales will be donated to a local charity.

Schiller's Liquor Bar
131 Rivington Street, at Norfolk Street (1-212 260 4555, www.schillersny.com). Subway F to Delancey Street; J, M, Z to Delancey-Essex Streets. **Open** 11am-1am Mon-Thur; 11am-3am Fri; 10am-3am Sat; 10am-1am Sun. **Main courses** $15-$27. **Map** p83 B1 ❽ **Eclectic**
At this artfully reconstructed faux-vintage hangout, the menu is a mix of French bistro (steak frites), British pub (fish and chips) and good ol' American (cheeseburger), while the wine menu famously hawks a down-to-earth hierarchy: Good, Decent, Cheap. As at Keith McNally's other establishments, folks pack in for the scene, triple-parking at the curved central bar for elaborate cocktails and star sightings.

$ Yonah Schimmel Knish Bakery
137 E Houston Street, between Eldridge & Forsyth Streets (1-212 477 2858, www.knishery.com). Subway F to Lower East Side-Second Avenue.
Open 9am-7pm Mon-Thur, Sun; 9am-9pm Fri, Sat (extended hours in summer). **Knishes** $3.50-$5. **Map** p83 A1 ❾ **Bakery-Café**
This neighbourhood stalwart has been doling out its carb-laden goodies since 1910. About 20 rotating varieties are available, including blueberry, chocolate-cheese and pizza flavour, but traditional potato, kasha and spinach knishes are the most popular.

Bars

Attaboy
134 Eldridge Street, between Broome & Delancey Streets (no phone). Subway F to Delancey Street; J, M, Z to Delancey-Essex Streets. **Open** 6.45pm-3.30am daily. **Map** p83 A2 ❿
Occupying the original Milk and Honey (*see p134*) digs and run by alums Sam Ross and Michael McIlroy, Attaboy has a livelier, lighter air than Sasha Petraske's big-league cocktail den. The tucked-away haunt has kept the same bespoke protocol as its forebear: at the brushed-steel bar, suspender-clad drinks slingers stir off-the-cuff riffs to suit each customer's preference. Wistful boozers can seek solace in Petraske-era standard-bearers, like Ross's signature Penicillin, a still-inspiring blend of Laphroaig ten-year, honey-ginger syrup and lemon.

Back Room

102 Norfolk Street, between Delancey & Rivington Streets (1-212 228 5098). Subway F to Delancey Street; J, M, Z to Delancey-Essex Streets. **Open** 7.30pm-3am Mon-Thur, Sun; 7.30pm-4am Fri, Sat. **Map** p83 B1 (11)

For access to this ersatz speakeasy, look for a sign that reads 'The Lower East Side Toy Company'. Pass through the gate, walk down an alleyway, up a metal staircase and open an unmarked door to find a convincing replica of a 1920s watering hole. Cocktails are poured into teacups, and bottled beer is brown-bagged before being served. Patrons must be 25 or older on Fridays and Saturdays. The dress code is casual, but note that in a departure from the Jazz Age sensibility, real fur is banned in the bar.

Schiller's Liquor Bar.

Loreley

7 Rivington Street, between Bowery & Chrystie Street (1-212 253 7077, www.loreleynyc.com). Subway J, Z to Bowery. **Open** noon-1am Mon, Tue, Sun; noon-2am Wed; noon-3am Thur; noon-4am Fri, Sat. **Map** p83 A1 (12)

Perhaps bar owner Michael Momm, aka DJ Foosh, wanted a place where he could spin to his heart's content. Maybe he missed the *biergartens* of his youth in Cologne. Whatever. Just rejoice that he opened Loreley. Twelve draughts and eight bottled varieties of Germany's finest brews are available, along with wines from the country's Loreley region and a full roster of spirits. Or try one of the speciality cocktails, such as the Zimtschnitte with Captain Morgan, Cointreau, cinnamon and fresh orange.

Spitzer's Corner

101 Rivington Street, at Ludlow Street (1-212 228 0027, www.spitzerscorner.com). Subway F to Delancey Street; J, M, Z to Delancey-Essex Streets. **Open** noon-4am Mon-Fri; 10am-4am Sat, Sun. **Map** p83 B1 (13)

Referencing the Lower East Side's pickle-making heritage, the walls at this rustic gastropub are made from salvaged wooden barrels. The formidable beer list – 40 rotating draughts – includes New York's Southern Tier IPA. Mull over your selection, with the help of appetising tasting notes, at one of the wide communal tables. The gastro end of things is manifest in the menu of quality pub grub, such as truffle mac and cheese or grilled fish sliders.

Two-Bit's Retro Arcade

153 Essex Street, between Rivington & Stanton Streets (1-212 477 8161, www.twobitsretro arcade.com). Subway F to Lower East Side-Second Avenue; J, M, Z to Delancey-Essex Streets. **Open** 5pm-2am Mon-Thur; 5pm-4am Fri; 1pm-4am Sat; 1pm-2am Sun. **Map** p83 B1 (14)

Joystick addicts, take note: this gamer haven offers titles dating back to the 1980s (Pac-Man, Popeye, Final Fight, Donkey Kong), as well as pinball (Fun

Two-Bit's Retro Arcade. See p87.

House, Twilight Zone). After you've grabbed a beer, pause for a moment to admire the video-game-character illustrations inlaid in the bar. One tip: try to make it here by early evening, before the lines to play become three dudes deep.

Shops & Services

★ Alife Rivington Club

158 Rivington Street, between Clinton & Suffolk Streets (1-212 432 7200, www.alifenewyork.com). Subway F to Delancey Street; J, M, Z to Delancey-Essex Streets. **Open** noon-7pm Mon-Sat; noon-6pm Sun. **Map** p83 B1. ⓯ **Accessories**

Whether you're looking for a simple white trainer or a trendy graphic style, you'll want to gain entry to this 'club', which stocks a wide range of major brands such as Nike (including sought-after re-issues like Air Jordan), Adidas and New Balance. You'll also find lesser-known names including the shop's own label.

The Cast

71 Orchard Street, between Broome & Grand Streets (1-212 228 2020, www.thecast.com). Subway F to Delancey Street; J, M, Z to Delancey-Essex Streets; B, D to Grand Street. **Open** noon-8pm Mon-Sat; noon-6pm Sun. **Map** p83 B2 ⓰ **Fashion**

At the core of Chuck Guarino's rock 'n' roll-inspired collection is the trinity of well-cut denim, superior leather jackets based on classic motorcycle styles, and the artful T-shirts that launched the label in 2004. The ladies have their own line, covering similar ground.

Curvaceous K

179 Stanton Street, between Attorney & Clinton Streets (1-646 684 3175, www.curvaceousk.com). Subway F to Delancey Street; J, M, Z to Delancey-Essex Streets. **Open** 2-7pm Mon, Tue, Sun; 2-8pm Thur, Fri, Sat. **Map** p83 B1 ⓱ **Fashion**

Lifelong New Yorker Kathy Sanchez ditched her desk job in marketing to bring NYC something it was missing – a full-figure fashion boutique, catering to a considerably underserved market of plus-size women (US sizes 14-24). She searched high and low for the best, most affordable curvy-girl threads, by labels such as Melissa Masse, Igigi, Mynt 1792 and Jessica Simpson.

Dear: Rivington

95 Rivington Street, between Ludlow & Orchard Streets (1-212 673 3494, www.dearrivington.com). Subway F to Delancey Street; J, M, Z to Delancey-Essex Streets. **Open** noon-7pm daily. **Map** p83 B1 ⓲ **Fashion/homewares**

The glass storefront is a stage for Moon Rhee and Hey Ja Do's art installation-like displays; inside the white bi-level space, head downstairs for their own

GALLERY-HOPPING GUIDE

Plan a culture crawl of this hot art 'hood with our curated list.

Canada.

Miguel Abreu Gallery.

Over the past ten years, the Lower East Side has seen a steady migration of young dealers, aided by the relocation of the New Museum of Contemporary Art to the Bowery. These are a few of our favourites.

Canada *333 Broome Street, between Bowery & Chrystie Street (1-212 925 4631, www.canadanewyork.com).* **Open** 11am-6pm Wed-Sun.
One of the first of the Lower East Side galleries, Canada continues to keep it real with a programme that reflects a funky DIY aesthetic.

Rachel Uffner Gallery.

Eleven Rivington *11 Rivington Street, between Bowery & Chrystie Street (1-212 982 1930, www.eleven rivington.com).* **Open** noon-6pm Wed-Sun.
The offshoot of the Van Doren Waxter Gallery offers an impeccable uptown vibe in small-storefront form.

Lisa Cooley *107 Norfolk Street, between Delancey & Rivington Streets (1-212 680 0564, www.lisa-cooley.com).* **Open** 10am-6pm Wed-Sun.
Lisa Cooley's roster of artists seems to share a penchant for Conceptualist sleight-of-hand, mixed with unexpected materials.

Miguel Abreu Gallery *36 Orchard Street, between Canal & Hester Streets (1-212 995 1774, www.miguelabreugallery.com).* **Open** 11am-6.30pm Wed-Sun.
A filmmaker as well as founding member of the legendary Threadwaxing alternative space in Soho (now closed), Miguel Abreu represents conceptually inspired artists.

Rachel Uffner Gallery *70 Suffolk Street, between E Houston & Stanton Streets (1-212 274 0064, www.racheluffner gallery.com).* **Open** 10am-6pm Wed-Sun.
Uffner, who cut her teeth at Christies, showcases a small but eclectic stable.

Sperone Westwater *257 Bowery, between E Houston & Stanton Streets (1-212 999 7337, www.speronewestwater. com).* **Open** 10am-6pm Tue-Sat.
Started in 1975, this gallery now occupies a purpose-built showcase designed by starchitect Norman Foster.

Sperone Westwater.

Obsessive Compulsive Cosmetics.

Victorian-inspired line and select pieces by avant-garde Japanese labels such as Comme des Garçons and Yohji Yamamoto. Upstairs is a fascinating archive of vintage homewares, art and objects, including framed antique silhouettes, old globes and tins, plus contemporary handmade pottery.

The Dressing Room

75A Orchard Street, between Broome & Grand Streets (1-212 966 7330, www.thedressingroomnyc.com). Subway B, D to Grand Street; F to Delancey Street; J, M, Z to Delancey-Essex Streets. **Open** 1pm-midnight Tue, Wed; 1pm-2am Thur-Sat; 1-8pm Sun. **Map** p83 B2 ⓳ **Fashion**

At first glance, the Dressing Room may look like any Lower East side lounge, thanks to a handsome wood bar, but this co-op cum watering hole rewards the curious. The adjoining room displays designs by indie labels alongside select vintage pieces, and there's a second-hand clothing exchange downstairs.

The Hoodie Shop

181 Orchard Street, between E Houston & Stanton Streets (1-646 559 2716, www.thehoodieshop.com). Subway F to Lower East Side-Second Avenue. **Open** noon-9pm Mon-Sat; noon-7pm Sun. **Map** p83 B1 ⓴ **Fashion**

Up to 50 different brands of hooded apparel for both men and women are showcased in this 1970s-inspired boutique, from retro zip-ups to army-print utility jackets. The shop has a DJ booth and movie screen for late-night shopping parties and other in-store events.

Edith Machinist

104 Rivington Street, between Essex & Ludlow Streets (1-212 979 9992, www.edithmachinist.com). Subway F to Delancey Street; J, M, Z to Delancey-Essex Streets. **Open** noon-7pm Tue, Thur, Sat; noon-6pm Fri, Sun. **Map** p83 B1 ㉑ **Fashion/accessories**

An impeccable assemblage of leather bags, shoes and boots is the main draw here, but you'll also find a whittled-down collection of clothes, including a small men's section. The store is closed some Mondays, so call before visiting.

Moo Shoes

78 Orchard Street, between Broome & Grand Streets (1-212 254 6512, www.mooshoes.com). Subway F to Delancey Street; J, M, Z to Delancey-Essex Streets. **Open** 11.30am-7.30pm Mon-Sat; noon-6pm Sun. **Map** p83 B2 ㉒ **Accessories**

Cruelty-free footwear is far more fashionable than it once was. Moo stocks a variety of brands for men and women, such as Vegetarian Shoes and Novacas, plus styles from independent designers such as Elizabeth Olsen, whose arty line of high heels and handbags is anything but hippyish.

★ Obsessive Compulsive Cosmetics

174 Ludlow Street, between E Houston & Stanton Streets (1-212 675 2404, www.occmakeup.com). Subway F to Lower East Side-Second Avenue. **Open** 11am-7pm Mon-Sat; noon-6pm Sun. **Map** p83 B1 ㉓ **Health & beauty**

Creator David Klasfeld founded OCC in the kitchen of his Lower East Side apartment in 2004. The make-up artist has since expanded his 100% vegan and cruelty-free cosmetics line from just two shades of lip balm to an extensive assortment of bang-for-your-buck beauty products. In the downtown flagship, you can browse more than 40 shades of nail polish and nearly 40 loose eye-shadow powders, among other products, but we especially like the Lip Tars, which glide on like a gloss but have the matte finish and saturated pigmentation of a lipstick.

Reed Space

151 Orchard Street, between Rivington & Stanton Streets (1-212 253 0588, www.thereedspace.com). Subway F to Delancey Street; J, M, Z to Delancey-Essex Streets. **Open** 1-7pm Mon-Fri; noon-7pm Sat, Sun. **Map** p83 B1 ㉔ **Fashion/accessories**

Reed Space is the brainchild of Jeff Ng (AKA Jeff Staple), who has worked on product design and branding with the likes of Nike and Timberland. The store stocks local and international urban clothing brands – such as 10.Deep and Undefeated – and footwear, including exclusive Staple collaborations. Art books and culture mags are shelved on an eye-popping installation of four stacked rows of white chairs fixed to one wall.

★ Russ & Daughters

179 E Houston Street, between Allen & Orchard Streets (1-212 475 4880, www.russanddaughters.com). Subway F to Lower East Side-Second Avenue. **Open** 8am-8pm Mon-Fri; 9am-7pm Sat; 8am-5.30pm Sun. **Map** p83 A1 ㉕ **Food & drink**

The daughters in the name have given way to great-grandchildren, but this Lower East Side institution (est 1914) is still run by the same family. Specialising in smoked and cured fish and caviar, it sells about ten varieties of smoked salmon, eight types of herring (pickled, salt-cured, smoked and so on) and many other Jewish-inflected Eastern European delectables. Bagels are available to take away – try the Super Heebster, filled with baked salmon, fluffy whitefish salad, horseradish-dill cream cheese and wasabi-infused flying-fish roe.

Spiritual America

5 Rivington Street, between Bowery & Chrystie Street (1-212 960 8564, www.spiritualameri.ca). Subway F to Lower East Side-Second Avenue; J, Z to Bowery; 6 to Spring Street. **Open** noon-8pm Mon-Fri; 11am-7pm Sat, Sun. **Map** p83 A1 ㉖ **Fashion/accessories**

Housed in the same storefront (and operating under the same name) as artist Richard Prince's original pop-up exhibition in 1983, this minimalist shop stocks a mix of European and American labels (Vanessa Bruno, Damir Doma, Derek Lam) and wares by up-and-coming designers. Using the airy feel of a gallery as inspiration, Parisian-born owner Claire Lemétais has outfitted the space with custom light-sculpture installations and rammed-earth-crafted countertops. We're especially taken with the boutique's selection of cool shoes and accessories.

EXPLORE

Russ & Daughters.

East Village

Originally part of the Lower East Side, the East Village developed its distinct identity as a countercultural hotbed in the 1960s. By the dawning of the Age of Aquarius, rock clubs thrived on almost every corner. But in the '70s, the neighbourhood took a dive as drugs and crime prevailed – although that didn't stop the influx of artists and punk rockers. In the early '80s, East Village galleries were among the first to display the work of groundbreaking artists like Jean-Michel Basquiat and Keith Haring.

The blocks east of Broadway between Houston and 14th Streets may have lost some of their edge, and the former tenements are increasingly occupied by young professionals and trust-fund kids, but humanity in all its guises converges in the parks, bargain restaurants, indie record stores and grungy watering holes on First and Second Avenues and St Mark's Place.

Momofuku Ssäm Bar.

Don't Miss

1 Merchant's House Museum Explore this frozen-in-time (and purportedly haunted) house (*p95*).

2 Big Gay Ice Cream Shop It's out, it's proud and it's delicious (*p96*).

3 Momofuku Ssäm Bar Star chef David Chang reinterprets Korean classics (*p99*).

4 PDT The secret entrance only thrills once, but the drinks warrant return visits (*p102*).

5 Strand Book Store This well-stocked indie is an NYC institution (*p105*).

EAST VILLAGE

Subway B, D, F, M to Broadway-Lafayette Street; F to Lower East Side-Second Avenue; N, R to 8th Street-NYU; L to First Avenue or Third Avenue; 6 to Astor Place or Bleecker Street.

From the 1950s to the '70s, **St Marks Place** (E 8th Street, between Lafayette Street & Avenue A) was a hotbed of artists, writers, radicals and musicians, including WH Auden, Abbie Hoffman, Lenny Bruce, Joni Mitchell and GG Allin. The grungy strip still fizzes with energy well into the wee hours, but these days, it's packed with cheap eateries, shops selling T-shirts, tourist junk and pot paraphernalia, and tattoo parlours.

A short walk north brings you to **St Mark's Church in-the-Bowery** (131 E 10th Street, at Second Avenue, 1-212 674 6377, www.stmarksbowery.com). Built in 1799, the Federal-style church sits on the site of Peter Stuyvesant's farm; the old guy himself, one of New York's first governors, is buried in the adjacent cemetery. Regular services are still held, and the church is home to several cultural organisations, including the Poetry Project and the Incubator Arts Project.

Cutting between Broadway and Fourth Avenue south of East 8th Street, **Astor Place** is the site of the **Cooper Union**. Comprising schools of art, architecture and engineering, it was the only free private college in the United States but the institution announced that it would have to start charging partial tuition fees in 2014. It was here, in February 1860, that Abraham Lincoln gave his celebrated Cooper Union Address, which argued for the regulation (though not abolition) of slavery and helped to propel him into the White House.

During the 19th century, Astor Place marked the boundary between the slums to the east and some of the city's most fashionable homes. **Colonnade Row** (428-434 Lafayette Street, between Astor Place & E 4th Street) faces the distinguished Astor Public Library building, which theatre legend Joseph Papp rescued from demolition in the 1960s. Today, the old library houses the **Public Theater** (*see p305*), a platform for first-run American plays, and cabaret venue **Joe's Pub** (*see p276*). Nearby,

Merchant's House Museum

the **Merchant's House Museum** (*see p95*) is a perfectly preserved specimen of upper-class domestic life in the 1800s.

Below Astor Place, Third Avenue (one block east of Lafayette Street) becomes the **Bowery**. For decades, the street languished as a seedy strip and the home of missionary organisations catering to the down and out. Although the sharp-eyed can find traces of the old flophouses, and the more obvious Gothic Revival headquarters of **Bowery Mission** at no.227 (between Rivington & Stanton Streets), the thoroughfare has been cleaned up and repopulated with high-rise condo buildings, restaurants, nightspots and hotels.

Elsewhere in the neighbourhood, East 7th Street is a stronghold of New York's Ukrainian community, of which the focal point is the Eastern Catholic **St George's Ukrainian Catholic Church** at no.30. The **Ukrainian Museum** (222 E 6th Street, between Second & Third Avenues, 1-212 228 0110, www.ukrainianmuseum.org, closed Mon, Tue) houses folk and fine art and archival materials from that country. One block over, there's often a long line of loud fraternity types waiting at weekends to enter **McSorley's Old Ale House** (*see p102*). Festooned with aged photos, yellowed newspaper articles and dusty memorabilia, the 1854 Irish tavern is purportedly the oldest continually operating pub in New York and the spot where Lincoln repaired after giving his Cooper Union Address. Representing a different corner of the globe, **Curry Row** (East 6th Street, between First & Second Avenues) is lined with Indian restaurants that are popular with budget-minded diners.

IN THE KNOW SPINNING '60S

Astor Place is marked by a steel cube that has sat on a traffic island by the entrance to the 6 train since 1968. With a little elbow grease, the cube, whose proper title is Alamo, will spin on its axis.

Alphabet City (which gets its name from its key avenues: A, B, C and D) stretches towards the East River. It was once an edgy Puerto Rican neighbourhood with links to the drugs trade, but its demographic has dramatically shifted over the past 20 years. Avenue C is also known as Loisaida Avenue, a rough approximation of 'Lower East Side' when pronounced with a Hispanic accent. Two churches on 4th Street are built in the Spanish colonial style: **San Isidro y San Leandro** (345 E 4th Street, between Avenues C & D) and **Iglesia Pentecostal Camino Damasco** (289 E 4th Street, between Avenues B & C). The **Nuyorican Poets Café** (236 E 3rd Street, between Avenues B & C, East Village, 1-212 505 8183, www.nuyorican.org), a clubhouse for espresso-drinking wordsmiths since 1974, is known for its Friday-night poetry slams, in which performers wage lyric battles before a score-keeping audience.

Dating from 1834, **Tompkins Square Park** (from 7th to 10th Streets, between Avenues A & B), honours Daniel D Tompkins, governor of New York from 1807 to 1817, and vice-president during the Monroe administration. Over the years, this 10.5-acre park has been a site for demonstrations and rioting. The last major uprising occurred in 1991, when the city evicted squatters from the park and renovated it to suit the influx of affluent residents. Along with dozens of 150-year-old elm trees (some of the oldest in the city), the landscaped green space has basketball courts, playgrounds and dog runs, and remains a place where bongo beaters, guitarists, multi-pierced teenagers, hipsters, local families and vagrants mingle.

North of Tompkins Square, around First Avenue and 11th Street, are remnants of earlier communities: discount fabric dealers, Italian cheese shops, Polish butchers and two great Italian coffee and cannoli houses: **De Robertis** (176 First Avenue, between 10th & 11th Streets, 1-212 674 7137, www.derobertiscaffe.com) and **Veniero's Pasticceria & Caffè** (342 E 11th Street, between First & Second Avenues, 1-212 674 7070, www.venierospastry.com).

Merchant's House Museum

29 E 4th Street, between Lafayette Street & Bowery (1-212 777 1089, www.merchantshouse.org). Subway B, D, F, M to Broadway-Lafayette Street; 6 to Bleecker Street. **Open** noon-5pm Mon, Thur-Sun. *Guided tour* 2pm. **Admission** $10; $5 reductions; free under-12s. **Map** p95 A2 ❶

Merchant's House Museum, the city's only fully preserved 19th-century family home, is an elegant, late

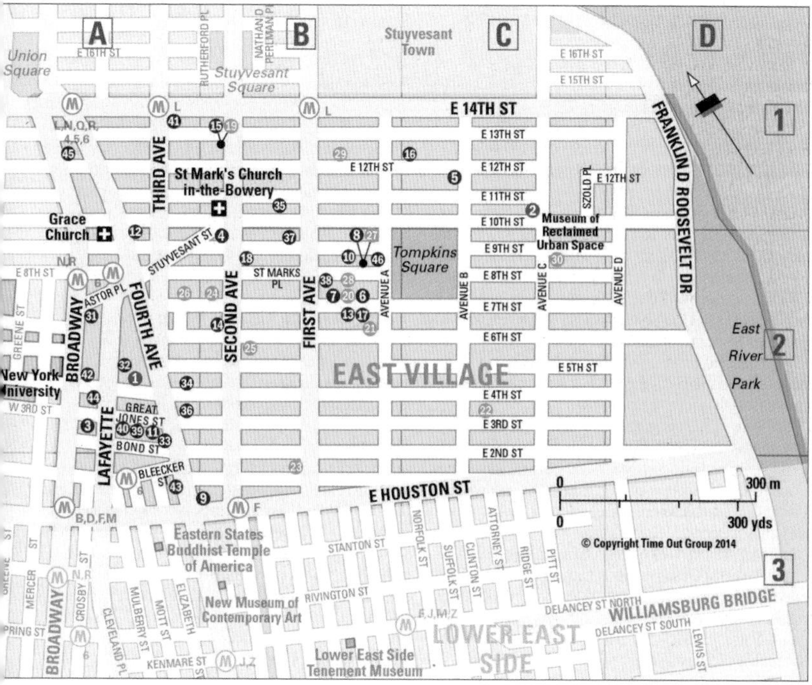

IN THE KNOW
METAL LANDMARK

The cover of Led Zeppelin's 1975 album *Physical Graffiti* depicts the apartment buildings at 96 and 98 St Marks Place.

Federal-Greek Revival property kitted out with the same furnishings and decorations it contained when it was inhabited from 1835 by hardware tycoon Seabury Tredwell and his family. Three years after Tredwell's eighth daughter died in 1933, it opened as a museum. You can peruse the house at your own pace, following along with the museum's printed guide, or opt for the 2pm guided tour. Be sure to ascend to the servants' quarters on the renovated fourth floor, and note the original bell that summoned the four Irish immigrant maids at the top of the stairs.

Museum of Reclaimed Urban Space

155 Avenue C, between 9th & 10th Streets (1-646 833 7764, www.morusnyc.org). Subway L to First Avenue. **Open** 11am-7pm Tue, Thur-Sun. **Admission** *Suggested donation* $5. **Map** p95 C1 ❷

See p97 **The People's Museum**.

Restaurants & Cafés

Acme

9 Great Jones Street, between Broadway & Lafayette Street (1-212 203 2121, www.acmenyc.com). Subway B, D, F, M to Broadway-Lafayette Street; 6 to Bleecker Street. **Open** 6-11pm Mon-Wed; 6pm-midnight Thur, Fri; 11am-3pm, 6pm-midnight Sat; 11am-3pm, 6-11pm Sun. **Main courses** $10-$38. **Map** p95 A2 ❸ **Scandinavian**

The Scandinavian food scene – known for the extreme locavore cooking showcased at restaurants like Copenhagen's Noma – is suddenly the hottest on earth. And Nordic cuisine has finally arrived in NYC, thanks to Danish chef Mads Refslund, who co-founded Noma with superstar Ren Redzepi (but left after a year to do his own thing). Formerly a Cajun dive, the once-grungy spot has been transformed into a raffish and chic downtown bistro, featuring a retro mix of contemporary art and antiques. Refslund's menu delivers an easy introduction to the avant-garde cuisine of Northern Europe, unpretentious and moderately priced. Refslund's new-wave bistro fare features some unusual pairings, but even the most oddball combinations work. His spin on steak tartare marries hand-cut raw bison with delicious sweet shrimp – an elemental surf-and-turf spooned like retro canapés into bitter endive and radicchio leaves. The big family-style portions of meat, fish and fowl that round out the collection of shareable plates are even more down-to-earth.

Alder

157 Second Avenue, between 9th & 10th Streets (1-212 539 1900, www.aldernyc.com). Subway L to Third Avenue; 6 to Astor Place. **Open** 6-11pm daily. **Main courses** $11-$25. **Map** p95 B2 ❹ **Gastropub**

James Beard Award-winning chef Wylie Dufresne cultivated his modernist, tongue-in-cheek approach at wd~50. At the original nucleus of North American avant-garde cuisine, which opened in 2003, he created curiosities like deep-fried mayonnaise and scrambled-egg ravioli. At his gastropub, Alder, Dufresne is still challenging the orthodoxy of serious cooking, presenting familiar flavours in surprising new frameworks: the wrappers in a pigs-in-a-blanket riff, for example, are Pepperidge Farm hot-dog buns, flattened in a pasta machine and fried into crisp jackets as gratifying as any puff pastry. But you can also eat quite simply here if you want to, with a pub cheese platter or bowl of New England clam chowder. Intriguing tapped cocktails like the Dr Dave's 'Scrip Pad, made with rye, amaro, smoked maple and yuzu, are sold in full-size or short portions, so you can taste your way through the lot. *Photo p98.*

Back Forty

190 Avenue B, at 12th Street (1-212 388 1990, www.backfortynyc.com). Subway L to First Avenue. **Open** 6-11pm Mon-Thur; 6pm-midnight Fri; 11am-3pm, 6pm-midnight Sat; 11am-3.30pm, 6-10pm Sun. **Main courses** $12-$38. **Map** p95 C1 ❺ **American**

Peter Hoffman (the pioneering chef who launched the market-driven restaurant Savoy, now occupied by his second Back Forty location) is behind this East Village seasonal-eats tavern. Pared-down farmhouse chic prevails in the decor and on the menu. House specialities include juicy grass-fed burgers, served with a spicy home-made ketchup and pickle. The spacious back garden, open in warmer months, is a bonus. **Other locations** 70 Prince Street, at Crosby Street, Soho (1-212 219 8570).

★ Big Gay Ice Cream Shop

125 E 7th Street, between First Avenue & Avenue A (1-212 533 9333, www.biggayicecream.com). Subway L to First Avenue. **Open** 1pm-midnight daily (see website for reduced winter hours). **Ice-cream** $4-$8. **Map** p95 B2 ❻ **Ice-cream**

Ice-cream truckers Doug Quint and Bryan Petroff now have two brick-and-mortar shops dispensing their quirky soft-serve creations. Toppings run the gamut from cayenne pepper to bourbon-butterscotch sauce, or opt for one of the signature combos like the Salty Pimp (vanilla ice-cream, dulce de leche, sea salt and chocolate dip) or the Bea Arthur (vanilla ice-cream, dulce de leche and crushed Nilla wafers). **Other locations** 61 Grove Street, at Seventh Avenue South, West Village (1-212 533 9333).

THE PEOPLE'S MUSEUM

A monument to local activism takes root in the East Village.

While the word 'museum' tends to evoke a sense of permanence, the **Museum of Reclaimed Urban Space** (*see p96*) resides in more ephemeral digs. 'The museum is actually in the most famous squat in New York City right now,' explains co-founder Bill Di Paola. As the founding director of advocacy group Time's Up!, Di Paola has fought for bikers' rights and environmental causes for 25 years; his new project with co-founder and Time's Up volunteer Laurie Mittelmann builds on his experience on picket lines and in rallies to show how activism can spark community change.

Known as C-Squat, the five-floor walk-up has housed activists, down-on-their-luck artists and members of several punk bands (including Leftover Crack, Old Skull and Nausea) from the 1970s to the present. 'People can knock on the door and sleep there, and work there,' says Di Paola. 'They play shows in the basement.'

The fight to establish and maintain spots like C-Squat has been waged in community gardens and abandoned buildings around New York City. Di Paola and Mittelmann spent two years gathering documents from local residents related to events such as the 1988 Tompkins Square Park Riot, which erupted when Community Board 3 tried to impose a 1am closing time on the outdoor space. 'It was an incredible battle about curfew and public spaces, the struggle between corporations and community,' explains Di Paola. Zines from art and activist centre ABC No Rio, an Occupy Wall Street banner and a Time's Up! energy bike that helped power Zuccotti Park during its occupation in 2011 illustrate how city residents created, protected and took back community spaces. Other pieces commemorate lost causes, such as a map painted on the museum's floor that marks battlegrounds like the 5th Street Squat, which the city knocked down in 1997. Volunteers also lead daily tours to places including La Plaza Cultural (www.laplaza cultural.com), a once-illegal plot that is now an official community garden, and the Christodora House, a former social services building that became a symbol of gentrification following its conversion in the '80s into a pricey East Village co-op.

Di Paola hopes that highlighting the history of local protests and subsequent victories might inspire a new generation of activists. 'A lot of people like to do the quick fix...especially with the Occupy Wall Street kids,' says Di Paola. 'People can get involved in their community and make proper choices about what they buy. The solution is all around us. We don't really need a revolution. We just need to support things that already work.'

$ Caracas Arepa Bar

93½ E 7th Street, between First Avenue & Avenue A (1-212 228 5062, www.caracasarepabar.com). Subway F to Lower East Side-Second Avenue; 6 to Astor Place. **Open** noon-11pm daily. **Arepas** $7-$8.50. **Map** p95 B2 ❼ **Venezuelan**

This endearing spot, with bare-brick walls and tables covered with flower-patterned vinyl, zaps you straight to Caracas. Each *arepa* is made from scratch daily; the pita-like pockets are stuffed with a choice of a dozen fillings, such as the classic beef with black beans, cheese and plantain, or chicken with chorizo and avocado. Top off your snack with a *cocada*, a thick and creamy coconut milkshake made with freshly grated cinnamon.

Other locations 291 Grand Street, between Havemeyer & Roebling Streets, Williamsburg, Brooklyn (1-718 218 6050).

$ Crif Dogs

113 St Marks Place, between First Avenue & Avenue A (1-212 614 2728, www.crifdogs.com). Subway L to First Avenue; 6 to Astor Place. **Open** noon-2am Mon-Thur, Sun; noon-4am Fri, Sat. **Hot dogs** $2.50-$5. **Map** p95 B2 ❽ **American**

You'll recognise this place by the giant hot dog outside, bearing the come-on 'Eat me'. Crif offers the best Jersey-style dogs this side of the Hudson: handmade smoked pork tube-steaks that are deep-fried until they're bursting out of their skins. While they're served in various guises, including the Spicy Redneck (bacon-wrapped and covered in chilli, coleslaw and jalapeños) and the Chihuahua (bacon-wrapped with sour cream and avocado), the classic with mustard and kraut is the most popular. If you're wondering why there are so many people hanging around near the public phone booth at night, it's because there's a trendy cocktail bar, PDT (*see p102*), concealed behind it.

Other locations 555 Driggs Avenue, at North 7th Street, Williamsburg, Brooklyn (1-718 302 3200).

DBGB Kitchen & Bar

299 Bowery, at E Houston Street (1-212 933 5300, www.dbgb.com/nyc). Subway B, D, F, M to Broadway-Lafayette Street; 6 to Bleecker Street. **Open** noon-11pm Mon; noon-midnight Tue-Thur; noon-1am Fri; 11am-1am Sat; 11am-11pm Sun. **Main courses** $14-$42. **Map** p95 B3 ❾ **French**

This big, buzzy brasserie – chef Daniel Boulud's most populist venture – stands out for its kitchen-sink scope. Around ten rotating types of sausage,

Alder. *See p96.*

EXPLORE

from Thai-accented to Tunisian, are served alongside burgers, various pieces of offal and haute bistro fare. The best way to get your head around it all is to bring a large group and sample as much of the range as possible, including ice-cream sundaes or sumptuous cakes.

► *For more of Daniel Boulud's output, see p176 and p98.*

Dirt Candy

430 E 9th Street, between First Avenue & Avenue A (1-212 228 7732, www.dirtcandynyc.com). Subway L to First Avenue; 6 to Astor Place.
Open 5.30-10pm Tue, Wed; 5.30-10.30pm Thur-Sat. **Main courses** $18-$21. **Map** p95 B2 ⑩
Vegetarian

The shiny, futuristic environment here makes the place look more like a chic nail salon than a restaurant. Chef-owner Amanda Cohen has created an unlikely space to execute her less-likely ambition: to make people crave vegetables. And she mostly succeeds. Elaborate dishes might include a pungent portobello mousse accompanied by truffled pear and fennel compote, or stone-ground grits served with corn cream, pickled shiitake mushrooms, *huitlacoche* (Mexican truffle) and a tempura poached egg. With vegan-friendly options for desserts, Cohen has created a menu that's suitable for omnivores. Note that the restaurant may be relocating.

► *Another excellent veggie option is Pure Food & Wine, see p139.*

Il Buco Alimentari & Vineria

53 Great Jones Street, between Bowery & Lafayette Streets (1-212 837 2622, www.ilbucovineria.com). Subway B, D, F, M to Broadway-Lafayette Street; 6 to Bleecker Street. **Open** 7am-midnight Mon-Thur; 7am-1am Fri; 9am-1am Sat; 9am-11pm Sun. **Main courses** $19-$45. **Map** p95 A2 ⑪ **Italian**

Il Buco has been a mainstay of the downtown dining scene since the 1990s and a pioneer in the sort of rustic Italian food now ubiquitous in the city. Owner Donna Leonard took her sweet time (18 years, to be exact) to unveil her first offshoot, Il Buco Alimentari & Vineria. It was worth the wait: the new hybrid bakery, food shop, café and trattoria is as confident as its decades-old sibling with sure-footed service, the familial bustle of a neighbourhood pillar, and heady aromas of wood-fired short ribs and salt-crusted fish drifting from an open kitchen.
Other locations Il Buco, 47 Bond Street, between Bowery & Lafayette Street, East Village (1-212 533 1932).

Ippudo NY

65 Fourth Avenue, between 9th & 10th Streets (1-212 388 0088, www.ippudony.com). Subway 6 to Astor Place. **Open** 11am-3.30pm, 5-11.30pm Mon-Thur; 11am-3.30pm, 5pm-12.30am Fri, Sat; 11am-10.30pm Sun. **Ramen** $15-$16. **Map** p95 A2 ⑫
Japanese

This sleek outpost of a Japanese ramen chain is packed mostly with Nippon natives who queue up for a taste of 'Ramen King' Shigemi Kawahara's *tonkotsu* – a pork-based broth. About half a dozen varieties include the Akamaru Modern, a smooth, buttery soup topped with scallions, cabbage, a slice of roasted pork and pleasantly elastic noodles. Avoid non-soup dishes such as the oily fried-chicken wings. Long live the Ramen King – just don't ask him to move beyond his speciality.
Other locations 321 W 51st Street, between Eighth & Ninth Avenues, Midtown West (1-212 974 2500).

★ Kyo Ya

94 E 7th Street, between First Avenue & Avenue A (1-212 982 4140). Subway 6 to Astor Place.
Open 5.30-11.30pm Mon-Sat; 5.30-10.30pm Sun.
Main courses $28-$42. **Map** p95 B2 ⑬
Japanese

The city's most ambitious Japanese speakeasy is marked only by an 'Open' sign, but in-the-know diners still find their way inside. The food, presented on beautiful handmade plates, is gorgeous: maitake mushrooms are fried in the lightest tempura batter and delivered on a polished stone bed. Sushi is pressed with a hot iron on to sticky vinegar rice. The few desserts are just as ethereal as the savoury food.

Mighty Quinn's

103 Second Avenue, at E 6th Street (1-212 677 3733, www.mightyquinnsbbq.com). Subway 6 to Astor Place. **Open** 11.30am-11pm Mon-Thur, Sun; 11.30am-midnight Fri, Sat. **Barbecue.**
Map p95 B2 ⑭ **American**

Drummer-turned-chef Hugh Mangum first hawked his Texalina (Texas spice meets Carolina vinegar) specialities at his immensely popular stand at Smorgasburg (*see p203*). When the operation went bricks-and-mortar, the hungry throngs followed. Lines of customers snake through the steel-tinged East Village joint, watching as black-gloved carvers give glistening meat porn a dash of Maldon salt before slinging it down the assembly line. Dry-rubbed brisket is slow-smoked for 22 hours, and the Jurassic-sized beef rib is so impossibly tender that one bite will quiet the pickiest barbecue connoisseur. *Photo p100.*

★ Momofuku Ssäm Bar

207 Second Avenue, at 13th Street (1-212 254 3500, www.momofuku.com). Subway L to First or Third Avenue; L, N, Q, R, 4, 5, 6 to 14th Street-Union Square. **Open** 11.30am-3.30pm, 5pm-midnight Mon-Thur, Sun; 11.30am-3.30pm, 5pm-1am Fri, Sat. **Main courses** $20-$25.
Map p95 B1 ⑮ **Korean**

At chef David Chang's second modern Korean restaurant, waiters hustle to noisy rock music in the 50-seat space, which feels expansive compared with its Noodle Bar predecessor's crowded counter dining. Try the wonderfully fatty pork-belly

Mighty Quinn's. *See p99.*

steamed bun with hoisin sauce and cucumbers, or one of the ham platters. But you'll need to come with a crowd to sample the house speciality, *bo ssäm* (a slow-roasted hog butt that is consumed wrapped in lettuce leaves, with a dozen oysters and other accompaniments); it serves six to eight people and must be ordered in advance. David Chang has further expanded his E Vill empire with a bar, Booker and Dax (*see p101*) at this location, and a sweet annexe, Milk Bar (one of several in the city), across the street.

Other locations Má Pêche, 15 West 56th Street, between Fifth & Sixth Avenues, Midtown West (1-212 757 5878); Momofuku Ko, 163 First Avenue, at 10th Street, East Village (1-212 500 0831); Momofuku Noodle Bar, 171 First Avenue, between 10th & 11th Streets, East Village (1-212 777 7773); Milk Bar, throughout the city.

Northern Spy Food Co

511 E 12th Street, between Avenues A & B (1-212 228 5100, www.northernspyfoodco.com). Subway L to First Avenue. **Open** 10am-4pm, 5.30-11pm Mon-Fri; 10am-3.30pm, 5.30-11pm Sat, Sun. **Main courses** $22-$27. **Map** p95 C1 16 **American**

Named after an apple indigenous to the North-east, Northern Spy serves locally sourced meals at reasonable prices. The frequently changing menu is based almost entirely on what's in season. The food isn't fancy, but it satisfies: a recent dish paired toothsome pastured pork loin in a rich pork jus with sautéed leeks, green cabbage and brussels-sprout leaves.

★ $ Porchetta

110 E 7th Street, between First Avenue & Avenue A (1-212 777 2151, www.porchettanyc.com). Subway F to Lower East Side-Second Avenue; L to First Avenue; 6 to Astor Place. **Open** 11.30am-10pm Mon-Thur, Sun; 11.30am-11pm Fri, Sat. **Sandwiches** $10-$12. **Map** p95 B2 17 **Café**

This small, subway-tiled space has a narrow focus: central Italy's classic boneless roasted pork. The meat – available as a sandwich or a platter – is amazingly moist and tender, having been slowly roasted with rendered pork fat, seasoned with fennel pollen, herbs and spices and flecked with brittle shards of skin. The other menu items (a mozzarella sandwich, humdrum sides) seem incidental; the pig is the point.

Veselka

144 Second Avenue, at 9th Street (1-212 228 9682, www.veselka.com). Subway L to Third Avenue; 6 to Astor Place. **Open** 24hrs daily. **Main courses** $14-$18. **Map** p95 B2 18 **Eastern European**

When you need food to soak up the mess of drinks you've consumed in the East Village in the early hours, it's worth remembering Veselka: a relatively inexpensive Eastern European restaurant with plenty of seats, which is open 24 hours a day. Hearty appetites can get a platter of classic Ukrainian grub: pierogies, goulash, kielbasa, beef stroganoff or bigos stew. For dessert, try the *kutya* (traditional Ukrainian pudding made with berries, walnuts, poppy seeds and honey).

Bars

Booker and Dax

207 Second Avenue, at 13th Street (entrance on 13th Street) (1-212 254 3500, www.momofuku.com). Subway L to Third Ave; L, N, Q, R, 4, 5, 6 to 14th Street-Union Square. **Open** 6pm-2am Mon-Thur, Sun; 6pm-3am Fri, Sat. **Map** p95 B1 ⑲

This tech-forward cocktail joint, housed next to Momofuku Ssäm Bar (*see p92*), showcases the boozy tinkerings of wizardly Dave Arnold, the International Culinary Center director of culinary technology. Glasses are chilled with a pour of liquid nitrogen, and winter warmers, like the Friend of the Devil (Campari, sweet vermouth, rye, Pernod, bitters, absinthe), are scorched with a Red Hot Poker, a rod with a built-in 1,500-degree heater created by Arnold. He also showcases new techniques for creating fizzy drinks, like the Gin and Juice, made with Tanqueray gin and grapefruit juice that is clarified in a centrifuge, then carbonated in a CO^2-pressurised cocktail shaker.

Bourgeois Pig

111 E 7th Street, between First Avenue & Avenue A (1-212 475 2246, www.bourgeoispigny.com). Subway F to Lower East Side-Second Avenue; 6 to Astor Place. **Open** 6pm-2am daily. **Map** p95 B2 ⑳

Ornate mirrors and antique chairs give this small, red-lit wine and fondue joint a decidedly decadent feel. The wine list is well chosen, and although the hard stuff is verboten here, mixed concoctions based on wine, champagne or beer – such as the Provence Punch, featuring champagne, elderflower, white peach, lemon and orange bitters – cater to cocktail aficionados.

Death & Company

433 E 6th Street, between First Avenue & Avenue A (1-212 388 0882, www.deathandcompany.com). Subway F to Lower East Side-Second Avenue; 6 to Astor Place. **Open** 6pm-2am Mon-Thur, Sun; 6pm-3am Fri, Sat. **Map** p95 B2 ㉑

The nattily attired mixologists are deadly serious about drinks at this pseudo speakeasy with gothic flair (don't be intimidated by the imposing wooden door). Black walls and cushy booths combine with chandeliers to set a luxuriously sombre mood. The inventive cocktails are matched by top-notch food, including crispy oysters with pickled jalapeno relish and lime cream.

Elsa

217 E 3rd Street, between Avenues B & C (1-917 882 7395, www.elsabar.com). Subway F to Lower East Side-Second Avenue. **Open** 6pm-4am daily. **Map** p95 C2 ㉒

At this stylish boîte, named for the iconoclastic 1930s clothing designer Elsa Schiaparelli, nods to couture include framed fashion sketches and three tap lines that flow through a vintage sewing machine. Perch on a white wooden banquette to enjoy speciality cocktails such as the Black Book (bourbon, jalapeño and spices, including cinnamon and cardamom).

Golden Cadillac

13 First Avenue, at 1st Street (1-212 995 5151, www.goldencadillacnyc.com). Subway F to Lower East Side-Second Avenue. **Open** 5pm-2am Mon-Wed; 5pm-4am Thur-Fri; 11am-4am Sat; 11am-2am Sun. **Map** p95 B3 ㉓

Nostalgic for the 1970s, drinks historian Greg Boehm (owner of barware emporium Cocktail Kingdom) and James True (former manager of the Pegu Club) have joined forces for this ode to the seedy decade. At the 55-seat spot – outfitted with a wooden canopy bar and patterned wallpaper – the powerhouse duo revives maligned classics like the Harvey Wallbanger, whiskey sour and Disco Daiquiri (a frosty mix of overproof rum, lime and sugar). To match the throwback quaffs, executive chef Miguel Trinidad crafts a menu of retro comfort eats from vintage food magazines –

Golden Cadillac.

devilled eggs, a shrimp Louie salad with Treasure Island dressing, and deep-fried Monte Cristo sliders with maple syrup.

Jimmy's No. 43

43 E 7th Street, between Second & Third Avenues (1-212 982 3006, www.jimmysno43.com). Subway F to Lower East Side-Second Avenue; 6 to Astor Place. **Open** noon-2am Mon-Thur; noon-4am Fri, Sat; 11.30am-2am Sun. **Map** p95 B2 ㉔

You could easily miss this worthy subterranean spot if it weren't for the sign painted on a doorway over an inconspicuous set of stairs. Descend them and you'll encounter burnt-yellow walls displaying taxidermy, mismatched wood tables and medieval-style arched passageways that lead to different rooms. Beer is a big attraction here, with about a dozen quality selections on tap (and more in the bottle), many of which also make it into the slow-food dishes filled with organic ingredients.

Mayahuel

304 E 6th Street, between First & Second Avenues (1-212 253 5888, www.mayahuelny.com). Subway F to Lower East Side-Second Avenue; 6 to Astor Place. **Open** 6pm-2am daily. **Map** p95 B2 ㉕

Tequila and its cousin, mezcal, are the focus at this haute cantina. The inventive cocktail menu features the Red Baron, a smoky, spicy mix of mezcal, red pepper, basil, lemon, absinthe and cayenne salt. The East 6th cocktail is a liquid campfire of tequila, Jamaican rum, apple brandy, sweet vermouth, cynar and smoked salt. The craftsmanship in the drinks is equalled in the bar menu, which features juicy pork bellies with papaya and mango salsa.

★ McSorley's Old Ale House

15 E 7th Street, between Second & Third Avenues (1-212 473 9148, www.mcsorleysnewyork.com). Subway F to Lower East Side-Second Avenue. **Open** 11am-1am Mon-Sat; 1pm-1am Sun. **No credit cards. Map** p95 A2 ㉖

Ladies should probably leave the Blahniks at home. In traditional Irish-pub fashion, McSorley's floor has been thoroughly scattered with sawdust to take care of the spills and other messes that often accompany the consumption of large quantities of cheap beer. Established in 1854, McSorley's became an institution by remaining steadfastly authentic and providing only two choices to its customers: McSorley's Dark Ale and McSorley's Light Ale.

★ PDT

113 St Marks Place, between First Avenue & Avenue A (1-212 614 0386, www.pdtnyc.com). Subway L to First Avenue; 6 to Astor Place. **Open** 6pm-2am Mon-Thur, Sun; 6pm-4am Fri, Sat. **Map** p95 B2 ㉗

Word has gotten out about 'Please Don't Tell', the faux speakeasy inside gourmet hot dog joint Crif Dogs (*see p98*), so it's a good idea to reserve a booth in advance. Once you arrive, you'll notice people lingering outside an old wooden phonebooth near the front. Slip inside, pick up the receiver and the host opens a secret panel to the dark, narrow space. The serious cocktails surpass the gimmicky entry: try the house old-fashioned, made with bacon-infused bourbon, which leaves a smoky aftertaste.

Proletariat

102 St Marks Place, between First Avenue & Avenue A (1-212 777 6707, www.proletariatny.com). Subway 6 to Astor Place. **Open** 5pm-2am daily. **Map** p95 B2 ㉘

Proletariat is a much-deserved look into no-holds-barred beer geekdom, blissfully free of TVs and generic pub grub. With just 12 stools and a space so tight that clunky menus have been replaced with a QR code (scan it with your smartphone), brewhounds get the type of intimacy usually afforded only to the cocktail and wine crowds. The

Proletariat.

expert servers have a story for every keg they tap, from the newest local brews to obscure New Zealand ales and deep cuts from the Belgian canon. Sure, the name out front may feel ironic when you're sipping a $10 pour of a Norwegian saison you can't pronounce, but Gotham's beer scene is ready for a place that doesn't compromise.

★ Terroir

413 E 12th Street, between First Avenue & Avenue A (1-646 602 1300, www.wineis terroir.com). Subway L to First Avenue; L, N, Q, R, 4, 5, 6 to 14th Street-Union Square. **Open** 5pm-2am Mon-Sat; 5pm-midnight Sun. **Map** p95 B1 ㉙

The surroundings are stripped-back basic at this wine-bar offspring of nearby restaurant Hearth – the focus is squarely on the drinks. Co-owner and oeno-evangelist Paul Grieco preaches the powers of terroir – grapes that express a sense of place – and the knowledgeable waitstaff deftly help patrons to navigate nearly 50 by-the-glass options. Pair the stellar sips with the restaurant-calibre small plates.

Other locations 24 Harrison Street, between Greenwich & Hudson Streets, Tribeca (1-212 625 9463); 439 Third Avenue, between 30th & 31st Streets, Murray Hill (1-212 481 1920); 284 Fifth Avenue, at 1st Street, Park Slope, Brooklyn (1-718 832 9463).

The Wayland

700 E 9th Street, at Avenue C (1-212 777 7022, www.thewaylandnyc.com). Subway L to First Avenue. **Open** 5pm-4am daily. **Map** p95 C2 ㉚

East Village boozers have been stumbling further down the alphabet for years now, but it's taken evolving Avenue C time to develop the critical mass necessary to attract a late-night buzz. At this fun-loving bar, solicitous staff, a young and attractive crowd and the likelihood of a spontaneous singalong around the piano all contribute to a convivial vibe that makes you want to call for another round. An old-fashioned riff called I Hear Banjos ($12) – made with apple pie moonshine, rye whiskey and apple-spice bitters – comes with a ceremonious puff of applewood smoke, captured in an overturned glass that's placed over the drink.

Shops & Services

Astor Place Hairstylists

2 Astor Place, at Broadway (1-212 475 9854, www.astorplacehairnyc.com). Subway N, R to 8th Street-NYU; 6 to Astor Place. **Open** 8am-8pm Mon, Sat; 8am-9pm Tue-Fri; 9am-6pm Sun. **No credit cards. Map** p95 A2 ㉛ **Health & beauty**

The army of barbers at Astor Place does everything from neat trims to more complicated and creative shaved designs. You can't make an appointment, but you can call ahead; otherwise, just take a number and wait outside with the crowd. Sunday mornings are usually quieter. Cuts start at $16.

Astor Wines & Spirits

399 Lafayette Street, at 4th Street (1-212 674 7500, www.astorwines.com). Subway N, R to 8th Street-NYU; 6 to Astor Place. **Open** 9am-9pm Mon-Sat; noon-6pm Sun. **Map** p95 A2 ㉜ **Food & drink**

High-ceilinged, wide-aisled Astor Wines is a terrific place to browse for wines of every price range, vineyard and year – which makes it a favourite hunting ground for the city's top sommeliers. Sakés and spirits are also well represented.

Bond No. 9

9 Bond Street, between Broadway & Lafayette Street (1-212 228 1732, www.bondno9.com). Subway B, D, F, M to Broadway-Lafayette Street; 6 to Bleecker Street. **Open** 11am-8pm Mon-Fri; 10am-7pm Sat; noon-6pm Sun. **Map** p95 A2 ㉝ **Health & beauty**

The collection of scents here pays olfactory homage to New York City. Choose from more than 60 'neighbourhoods' and 'sensibilities', including Wall Street, Park Avenue, Eau de Noho, High Line – even Chinatown (but don't worry, it smells of peach blossoms, gardenia and patchouli, not fish stands). The arty bottles and neat, colourful packaging are particularly gift friendly.

Other locations throughout the city.

★ Bond Street Chocolate

63 E 4th Street, between Bowery & Second Avenue (1-212 677 5103, www.bondst chocolate.com). Subway 6 to Bleecker Street. **Open** noon-8pm Tue-Sat; 1-6pm Sun. **Map** p95 A2 ㉞ **Food & drink**

Former pastry chef Lynda Stern's East Village spot is a grown-up's candy store, with quirky chocolate confections in shapes ranging from gilded Buddhas (and other religious figures) to skulls, and flavours from elderflower to bourbon and absinthe.

Buffalo Exchange

332 E 11th Street, between First & Second Avenues (1-212 260 9340, www.buffalo exchange.com). Subway L to First Avenue. **Open** 11am-8pm Mon-Sat; noon-7pm Sun. **Map** p95 B1 ㉟ **Fashion**

This popular buy-sell-trade clothing shop spans all sartorial tastes, from Forever 21 to Marc Jacobs. You could score a pair of 7 for All Mankind jeans for $25, current-season Manolo Blahniks for $250 or a Burberry men's wool coat for $135.

Other locations 114 W 26th Street, at Sixth Avenue, Chelsea (1-212 675 3535); 504 Driggs Avenue, at North 9th Street, Williamsburg, Brooklyn (1-718 384 6901); 109 Boerum Place, between Pacific & Dean Streets, Boerum Hill, Brooklyn (1-718 403-0490).

DQM
7 E 3rd Street, between Bowery & Second Avenue (1-212 505 7551, www.dqmnewyork.com). Subway F to Lower East Side-Second Avenue. **Open** 11.30am-7.30pm Mon-Sat; noon-6pm Sun. **Map** p95 A2 ㊱ **Fashion**
DQM founder – and professional skateboarder – Chris Keeffe stocks a range of top-shelf streetwear in this wittily designed shop. As well as a line-up of the latest sneaks by Adidas and Vans, DQM sells its own-label T-shirts, chinos and button-downs.
Other locations Vans DQM General, 93 Grand Street, at Greene Street, Soho (1-212 226 7776).

★ Fabulous Fanny's
335 E 9th Street, between First & Second Avenues (1-212 533 0637, www.fabulousfannys.com). Subway L to First Avenue; 6 to Astor Place. **Open** noon-8pm daily. **Map** p95 B2 ㊲ **Accessories**
Formerly a Chelsea flea market booth, this two-room shop is the city's best source of period glasses, stocking more than 30,000 pairs of spectacles, from Jules Verne-esque wire rims to 1970s rhinestone-encrusted Versace shades.

Fun City Tattoo
94 St Marks Place, between First Avenue & Avenue A (1-212 353 8282, www.funcitytattoo.com). Subway N, R to 8th Street-NYU; 6 to Astor Place. **Open** noon-10pm daily. **No credit cards. Map** p95 B2 ㊳ **Tattoo parlour**

Future Perfect.

Jonathan Shaw started inking locals from his apartment nearly 40 years ago (back when tattooing was illegal) and then opened the storefront Fun City in the early 1990s. The legendary figure has retired to South America, but his New York City institution – which has served the likes of Johnny Depp, Jim Jarmusch, Dee Dee Ramone and Sepultura's Max Cavalera – continues its operations in the East Village. Fun City's five current artists – 'Big' Steve Pedone, Mina Aoki, Claire Vuillemot, Benjamin Haft and John Raftery – can do most anything, from lettering and Japanese to American traditional.

★ Future Perfect
55 Great Jones Street, between Bowery & Lafayette Street (1-212 473 2500, www.thefutureperfect.com). Subway 6 to Bleecker Street. **Open** 10am-7pm Mon-Fri; noon-7pm Sat; noon-5pm Sun; also by appointment. **Map** p95 A2 ㊴ **Homewares**
Championing avant-garde interior design, this innovative store showcases international and local talent – it's the exclusive US stockist of Dutch designer Piet Hein Eek's furniture and pottery. Look out for Kiel Mead's quirky gold and silver jewellery.

★ Great Jones Spa
29 Great Jones Street, at Lafayette Street (1-212 505 3185, www.greatjonesspa.com). Subway 6 to Astor Place. **Open** 9am-10pm daily. **Map** p95 A2 ㊵ **Health & beauty**
Based on the theory that water brings health, Great Jones is outfitted with a popular water lounge complete with subterranean pools, saunas, steam rooms and a three-and-a-half-storey waterfall. Access to the 15,000sq ft paradise is complimentary with services over $100 – treat yourself to a divinely scented body scrub, a massage or one of the many indulgent packages. Alternatively, a three-hour pass costs $50.

Kiehl's
109 Third Avenue, between 13th & 14th Streets (1-212 677 3171, www.kiehls.com). Subway L to Third Avenue; N, Q, R, 4, 5, 6 to 14th Street-Union Square. **Open** 10am-8pm Mon-Sat; 11am-6pm Sun. **Map** p95 A1 ㊶ **Health & beauty**
The apothecary founded on this East Village site in 1851 has morphed into a major skincare brand, but the products, in their minimal packaging, are still good value and effective. Lip balms and the thick-as-custard Creme de Corps have become cult classics. The Upper East Side location (157 E 64th Street, between Lexington & Third Avenues, 1-917 432 2503) houses the first Kiehl's spa; the Hell's Kitchen store (678 Ninth Avenue, at 47th Street, 1-212 956 2891) has a barber shop.
Other locations throughout the city.

★ Other Music
15 E 4th Street, between Broadway & Lafayette Street (1-212 477 8150, www.othermusic.com). Subway B, D, F, M to Broadway-Lafayette Street;

6 to Bleecker Street. **Open** 11am-9pm Mon-Fri; noon-8pm Sat; noon-7pm Sun. **Map** p95 A2 ㊷ **Books & music**
Other Music opened in the shadow of Tower Records in the mid 1990s, a pocket of resistance to chain-store tedium. Now the Goliath across the street is gone, but tiny Other Music carries on. Whereas the shop's mish-mash of indie rock, experimental music and stray slabs of rock's past once seemed adventurous, the curatorial foundation has proved prescient amid the emergence of mixed-genre venues in the city.

Patricia Field
306 Bowery, between Bleecker & E Houston Streets (1-212 966 4066, www.patriciafield.com). Subway 6 to Bleecker Street. **Open** 11am-8pm Mon-Thur, Sun; 11am-9pm Fri, Sat. **Map** p95 A3 ㊸ **Fashion/health & beauty**
The iconic redheaded designer and stylist has moved her flamboyant boutique two doors down, into a space that's nearly double the size, combining Field's former apartment with a vacated store behind it – her old bedroom is now a full-service hair salon. Funky ladies' threads include daringly short crop tops and thigh-high faux snake boots, while flamboyant fellas will find Keith Haring for House of Field T-shirts and Joy Rich sweat pants. Stock up on whimsical accessories such as polka-dot shades, taxi cab-shaped wristlets by Betsey Johnson and cube-shaped rings.

Screaming Mimi's
382 Lafayette Street, at 4th Street (1-212 677 6464, www.screamingmimis.com). Subway B, D, F, M to Broadway-Lafayette Street; N, R to Prince Street; 6 to Bleecker Street. **Open** noon-8pm Mon-Sat; 1-7pm Sun. **Map** p95 A2 ㊹ **Fashion**
This vintage mecca has been peddling men's and women's clothing and accessories since 1978. Owner Laura Wills travels the world, scouting eclectic finds that span the 1950s to the 1990s, and organises clothing racks by decade. Do you need sunglasses from the 1970s? How about a Duran Duran T-shirt from the '80s? Head upstairs to check out higher-end garments by designers such as Hattie Carnegie, Jean Paul Gaultier and Vivienne Westwood.

★ Strand Book Store
828 Broadway, at 12th Street (1-212 473 1452, www.strandbooks.com). Subway L, N, Q, R, 4, 5, 6 to 14th Street-Union Square. **Open** 9.30am-10.30pm Mon-Sat; 11am-10.30pm Sun. **Map** p95 A1 ㊺ **Books & music**
Established in 1927, the Strand has a mammoth collection of more than two million discount volumes (both new and used), and the store is made all the more daunting by its chaotic, towering shelves and sometimes crotchety staff. You can find just about anything here, from that out-of-print Victorian book on manners to the kitschiest of sci-fi pulp. The rare book room upstairs closes at 6.15pm.
► *There's a seasonal Strand kiosk on the edge of Central Park at Fifth Avenue and 60th Street (Apr-Dec 10am-dusk, weather permitting).*

Sustainable NYC
139 Avenue A, between 9th Street & St Marks Place (1-212 254 5400, www.sustainable-nyc.com). Subway L to First Avenue; 6 to Astor Place. **Open** 8am-10pm Mon-Fri; 9am-10pm Sat, Sun. **Map** p95 B2 ㊻ **Gifts & souvenirs**
This gift-centric shop houses a wealth of eco-minded goods within its green walls: organic shampoos and beauty products; Fairtrade chocolate; frames, jewellery, clutch bags and other gifts made from recycled metals and materials such as computer keys; and sun-powered BlackBerry chargers. The on-site café serves fair trade coffee and locally made treats.

IN THE KNOW ROCK RELICS

Pay your respects to the neighbourhood's late, legendary music venues, including the Dom (23 St Mark's Place, between Second & Third Avenues), where the Velvet Underground often headlined – the building is now a condo. The hallowed CBGB, once the unofficial home of US punk, which fostered legends such as the Ramones, Talking Heads and Patti Smith, is now occupied by swanky menswear shop John Varvatos (315 Bowery, at Bleecker Street, 1-212 358 0315, www.johnvarvatos.com). The store has preserved a section of the club's flyer-plastered wall behind glass.

Greenwich Village & West Village

Anchored by New York University, Greenwich Village, along with its western adjunct the West Village, is one of the most picturesque parts of the city. The stomping ground of the Beat Generation is no longer a cheap-rent bohemian paradise, but it's still a pleasant place for idle wandering, dining in excellent restaurants and hopping between bars and cabaret venues. The Meatpacking District, which over the past two decades has evolved from gritty industrial zone to gay cruising spot to hedonistic consumer playground, has a flashier feel. But the arrival of the new Whitney Museum in 2015 will bring an injection of culture to the neighbourhood.

High Line.

Don't Miss

1 Washington Square Park The heart of Village life (*p108*).

2 Caffe Reggio Forgo artisanal beans to soak up a vintage vibe (*p110*).

3 Carbone A cinematic replica of an old-school red-sauce joint (*p110*).

4 RedFarm Reinvented Chinese fare (*p116*).

5 High Line The elevated park is one of the city's most popular attractions (*p118*).

Jefferson Market Library.

GREENWICH VILLAGE

Subway A, B, C, D, E, F, M to W 4th Street; L, N, Q, R, 4, 5, 6 to 14th Street-Union Square; N, R to 8th Street-NYU; 1 to Christopher Street-Sheridan Square.

Stretching from Houston Street to 14th Street, between Broadway and Sixth Avenue, **Greenwich Village** has been inspiring bohemians for almost a century. Now that it has become one of the most expensive neighbourhoods in the city, you need a lot more than a struggling artist's or writer's income to inhabit its leafy streets.

Great for people-watching, **Washington Square Park** attracts a disparate cast of characters that takes in hippies, students and street musicians. Skateboarders clatter near the base of the Washington Arch, a modestly sized replica of Paris's Arc de Triomphe, built in 1895 to honour George Washington. The 9.75-acre Village landmark recently received a $16-million redesign.

In the 1830s, the wealthy began building handsome townhouses around the square. A few of those properties are still privately owned and occupied, but many others have become part of the ever-expanding NYU campus. The university also owns the Washington Mews, a row of charming 19th-century former stables that line a tiny cobblestoned alley just to the north of the park between Fifth Avenue and University Place. Several famed literary figures, including Henry James (author of the celebrated novel which took its title from the square), Herman Melville, Edith Wharton, Edgar Allan Poe and Eugene O'Neill, lived on or near the square. In 1871, the local creative community founded the **Salmagundi Club** (47 Fifth Avenue, between 11th & 12th Streets, 1-212 255 7740, www.salmagundi.org), America's oldest artists' club. Now situated north of Washington Square on Fifth Avenue, it has galleries that are open to the public.

Greenwich Village continues to change with the times, for the better and for the worse. In the 1960s, **8th Street** was the closest New York got to San Francisco's hippie Haight Street; Jimi Hendrix's **Electric Lady Studios** is still at 52 West 8th Street, between Fifth & Sixth Avenues. Although the strip was until recently a procession of piercing parlours, punky boutiques and shoe stores, it has been smartened up with the arrival of popular purveyors like **Stumptown Coffee Roasters** (*see p111*) and a boutique hotel, the **Marlton** (*see p353*). Once the dingy but colourful domain of Beat poets and folk and jazz musicians, the well-trafficked section of **Bleecker Street** between La Guardia Place and Sixth Avenue is now an overcrowded stretch of poster shops, cheap restaurants and music venues for the college crowd. Renowned hangouts such as Le Figaro Café (184 Bleecker Street, at MacDougal Street), Kerouac's

IN THE KNOW
DYLAN'S VILLAGE

Bob Dylan resided at 94 MacDougal Street (on a row of historic brownstones near Bleecker Street) through much of the 1960s, performing in Washington Square Park and at clubs such as **Café Wha?** and the **Bitter End** (for both, *see p109*).

favourite, are no more, but a worthy alternative is **Caffe Reggio** (*see p110*), the oldest coffeehouse in the village. Nearby, a former literati favourite of the likes of Hemingway and Fitzgerald, **Minetta Tavern** (*see p111*), has been rehabilitated by golden-touch restaurateur Keith McNally.

Although 1960s hotspot **Cafe Wha?** (115 MacDougal Street, between Bleecker & W 3rd Streets, 1-212 254 3706, www.cafewha.com) is now running on the fumes of its illustrious past, it has a decent house band. Nearby, the **Bitter End** (147 Bleecker Street, between La Guardia Place & Thompson Street, 1-212 673 7030, www.bitterend.com) has proudly championed the singer-songwriter – including a young Bob Dylan – since 1961.

The famed Village Gate jazz club at the corner of Bleecker and Thompson Streets – which staged performances by Miles Davis, Nina Simone and John Cage – closed in 1993. However, in 2008, **(Le) Poisson Rouge** (*see p277*) opened on the site with a similar mission to present diverse genres under one roof.

Not far from here, in the triangle formed by Sixth Avenue, Greenwich Avenue and 10th Street, you'll see the Gothic-style **Jefferson Market Library** (a branch of the New York Public Library). The lovely flower-filled garden facing Greenwich Avenue was once the site of the Women's House of Detention, which was torn down in 1974. Mae West did a little time there in 1926, on obscenity charges stemming from her Broadway show *Sex*.

Just behind the library, off 10th Street, lies **Patchin Place**, which was home to some of the leading luminaries of New York's literary pantheon. This cul-de-sac lined with brick houses built during the mid 19th century is off limits to the public, but through the gate you can make out no.4, where the poet and staunch foe of capitalisation ee cummings resided from 1923 to 1962; and no.5, where Djuna Barnes, author of *Nightwood*, lived from 1940 to 1982. Indeed, cummings would reportedly check on the reclusive Barnes by calling 'Are you still alive, Djuna?' though his neighbour's window.

Sights & Museums

FREE AIA Center for Architecture

536 La Guardia Place, between Bleecker & W 3rd Streets (1-212 683 0023, www.cfa.aiany.org). Subway A, B, C, D, E, F, M to W 4th Street.
Open 9am-8pm Mon-Fri; 11am-5pm Sat.
Admission free. **Map** p109 D2 ❶
Designed by architect Andrew Berman, this three-storey building is a fitting home for architectural

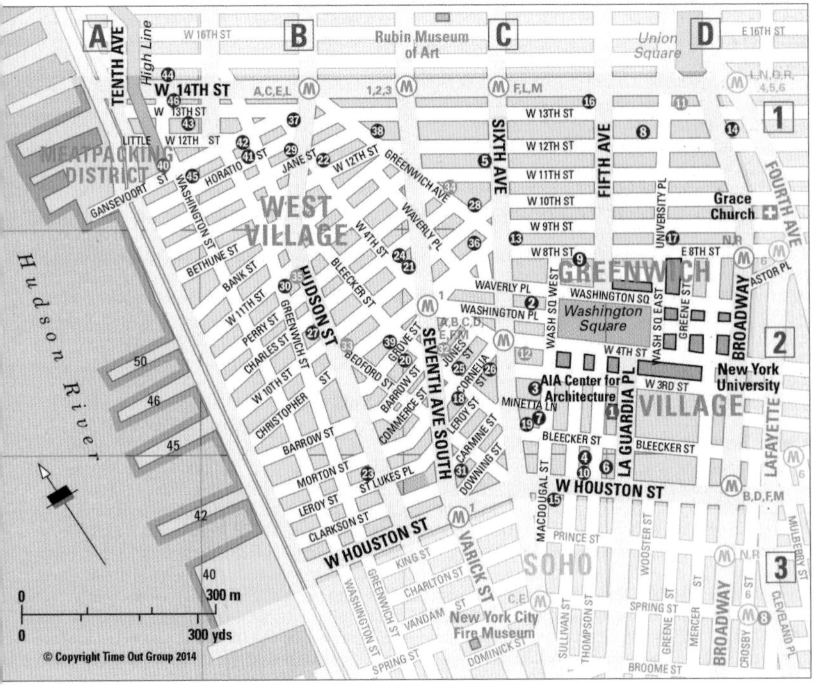

Carbone.

debate: the sweeping, light-filled design is a physical manifestation of AIA's goal of promoting transparency in terms of both access and programming. Berman cut away large slabs of flooring at the street and basement levels, converting underground spaces into bright, museum-quality galleries.

Restaurants & Cafés

Blue Hill

75 Washington Place, between Washington Square West & Sixth Avenue (1-212 539 1776, www.bluehillfarm.com). Subway A, B, C, D, E, F, M to W 4th Street. **Open** 5-11pm Mon-Sat; 5-10pm Sun. **Main courses** $32-$38. **Map** p109 C2 ❷ **American**

More than a mere crusader for sustainability, Dan Barber is also one of the most talented cooks in town, building his menu around whatever's at its peak on the family farm in Great Barrington, Massachusetts, and the not-for-profit Stone Barns Center for Food and Agriculture in Westchester, New York (home to a sibling restaurant), among other suppliers. The evening may begin with a sophisticated seasonal spin on a pig-liver terrine and move on to a sweet slow-roasted parsnip 'steak' with creamed spinach and beet ketchup.

Caffe Reggio

119 MacDougal Street, at W 3rd Street (1-212 475 9557, www.caffereggio.com). Subway A, B, C, D, E, F, M to W 4th Street. **Open** 8am-3am Mon-Thur; 8am-4am Fri, Sat; 9am-3am Sun. **Main courses** $10-$11. **No credit cards. Map** p109 C2 ❸ **Café**

Legend has it that the original owner of this classic café introduced Americans to the cappuccino in 1927 and, apart from its acquired patina, we bet the interior hasn't changed much since then. It's since traded in the coal-fuelled espresso machine for a sleeker Caffe Sacco model, but you can still admire the old custom chrome-and-bronze contraption on the bar. Tuck into a house-made tiramisu and espresso under the Italian Renaissance paintings.

★ Carbone

181 Thompson Street, between Bleecker & Houston Streets (1-212 254 3000, www.carbonenewyork.com). Subway C, E to Spring Street. **Open** noon-2pm, 5.30pm-midnight Mon-Fri; 5.30pm-midnight Sat, Sun. **Main courses** $21-$52. **Map** p109 C3 ❹ **Italian**

Nostalgia specialists Rich Torrisi and Mario Carbone honour Gotham's legendary red-sauce relics (Rao's, Bamonte's) with their high-profile revamp of historic Rocco's Ristorante. Suave, tuxedo-clad waiters – Bronx accents intact, but their burgundy threads designed by Zac Posen – tote an avalanche of complimentary extras: chunks of chianti-infused parmesan, olive-oil-soaked 'Grandma Bread' and slivers of smoky prosciutto. Follow updated renditions of classic pasta like a spicy, über-rich rigatoni vodka with mains such as sticky cherry-pepper ribs and lavish takes on tiramisu for dessert.

Kin Shop

469 Sixth Avenue, between 11th & 12th Streets (1-212 675 4295, www.kinshopnyc.com). Subway F, M to 14th Street; L to Sixth Avenue. **Open** 11.30am-3pm, 5.30-10pm Mon-Wed; 11.30am-3pm, 5.30-11pm Thur-Sat; 11.30am-3pm, 5-10pm Sun. **Main courses** $19-$32. **Map** p109 C1 ❺ **Thai**

Top Chef champ Harold Dieterle channels his Southeast Asian travels into the menu at this eaterie, which serves classic Thai street food alongside more upmarket Thai-inspired dishes. The traditional fare seems extraneous, but Dieterle's auteur creations are often inspired. A salad of crispy oysters, slivered celery and fried pork belly is bright and refreshing, while a cheffy riff on massaman curry features long-braised goat with a silky sauce infused with toasted coconut, fried shallots and purple yams.

Lupa

170 Thompson Street, between Bleecker & W Houston Streets (1-212 982 5089, www.luparestaurant.com). Subway A, B, C, D, E, F, M to W 4th Street. **Open** 11.30am-midnight daily. **Main courses** $18-$25. **Map** p109 C3 ❻ **Italian**

No mere 'poor man's Babbo' (Mario Batali's other and pricier restaurant around the corner), this convivial trattoria offers communal dining, reasonably priced wines and hit-the-spot comfort food. Come for classic Roman fare such as punchy rigatoni with skate and broccoli rabe, or gumdrop-shaped ricotta gnocchi.

► *For Mario Batali's sprawling Italian food emporium Eataly, see p136; for Casa Mono, the celeb chef's take on a tapas bar, see p139.*

Corkbuzz Wine Studio. *See p112.*

Minetta Tavern

113 MacDougal Street, between Bleecker & W 3rd Streets (1-212 475 3850, www.minettatavernny.com). Subway A, B, C, D, E, F, M to W 4th Street. **Open** 5.30pm-1am Mon, Tue; noon-2.30pm, 5.30pm-1am Wed-Fri; 11am-3pm, 5.30pm-1am Sat, Sun. **Main courses** $19-$35. **Map** p109 C2 ❼ **Eclectic**

Thanks to restaurateur extraordinaire Keith McNally's spot-on restoration, the Minetta is as buzzy now as it must have been when it was frequented by Hemingway and Fitzgerald in its heyday. The big-flavoured bistro fare includes classics such as roasted bone marrow, trout meunière topped with crabmeat, and an airy Grand Marnier soufflé. But the most illustrious thing on the menu is the Black Label burger. You might find the $28 price tag a little hard to swallow, but the superbly tender sandwich – essentially chopped steak in a bun smothered in caramelised onions – is worth every penny.

► *For less expensive but equally acclaimed burgers, see Corner Bistro (p115) and Shake Shack (p166).*

$ Num Pang Sandwich Shop

21 E 12th Street, between Fifth Avenue & University Place (1-212 255 3271, www.numpangnyc.com). Subway L, N, Q, R, 4, 5, 6 to 14th Street-Union Square. **Open** 11am-10pm Mon-Sat; noon-9pm Sun. **Sandwiches** $7.50-$12. **No credit cards. Map** p109 D1 ❽ **Cambodian**

At this small shop, the rotating varieties of *num pang* (Cambodia's answer to the Vietnamese *banh mi*) include pulled *duroc* pork with spiced honey, peppercorn catfish, and hoisin veal meatballs, each stuffed into crusty baguettes. There's counter seating upstairs, or get it to go and eat in nearby Washington Square Park.

Other locations 140 E 41st Street, between Lexington & Third Avenues, Midtown East (1-212 867 8889); 1129 Broadway, between 25th & 26th Streets, Gramercy & Flatiron (1-212 647 8889); Chelsea Market, 75 Ninth Avenue, between 15th & 16th Streets, Chelsea (1-212 390 8851).

Stumptown Coffee Roasters

30 W 8th Street, at MacDougal Street (1-347 414 7802, www.stumptowncoffee.com). Subway A, B, C, D, E, F, M to W 4th Street. **Open** 7am-8pm daily. **Coffee** $2.50-$5.50. **Map** p109 C2 ❾ **Café**

The lauded Portland, Oregon, outfit has expanded its New York holdings – which include a branch inside the Ace Hotel – with this stand-alone café. Coffee purists can find single-origin espresso from a La Marzocco GS3 machine and slow brews prepared via java-geek speciality drips like Chemex pour-overs, ceramic filter-cone Bee House drippers or a siphon vacuum brewer. It also offers the chain's full line of 20 seasonal coffees, plus pastries from Momofuku Milk Bar, Ovenly and Doughnut Plant.

EXPLORE

ZZ's Clam Bar

169 Thompson Street, between Bleecker & W Houston Streets (1-212 254 3000, www.zzsclambar.com). Subway B, D, F, M to Broadway-Lafayette Street; 6 to Bleecker Street. **Open** 6pm-1am Tue-Sat. **Main courses** $18-$56. **Map** p109 C3 ⑩ **Seafood**

A powerhouse trio – Rich Torrisi, Mario Carbone and Jeff 'ZZ' Zalaznick – continues its neo-Italian-American hot streak (including Carbone and Parm) with a 12-seat raw bar highlighting first-rate cocktails and crudo. At the marble bar, acclaimed barman Thomas Waugh (Death & Company) concocts the likes of rum, house-made coconut cream, acacia honey and lime juice served in a frozen coconut. In bar-friendly small plates, the chefs explore raw fish in all forms, with East Coast oysters on the half-shell and the titular clams. Composed crudos might feature *shimaaji* (striped horse mackerel) tartare topped with whipped ricotta and Petrossian caviar.

Bars

Corkbuzz Wine Studio

13 E 13th Street, between Fifth Avenue & University Place (1-646 873 6071, www.corkbuzz.com). Subway L, N, Q, R, 4, 5, 6 to 14th Street-Union Square. **Open** 4.30pm-midnight, Mon-Wed; 4.30pm-1am Thur-Sat; 11am-3pm, 4.30pm-midnight Sun. (Call or see website for summer hours.) **Map** p109 D1 ⑪

This intriguing and elegant hybrid, owned by the world's youngest female master sommelier, Laura Maniec, comprises a restaurant, wine bar and educational centre. Staff preach the Maniec gospel to patrons as they navigate 35 by-the-glass options and around 250 bottles. *Photo p111.*

Vol de Nuit Bar (aka Belgian Beer Lounge)

148 W 4th Street, between Sixth Avenue & MacDougal Street (1-212 982 3388, www.voldenuitbar.com). Subway A, B, C, D, E, F, M to W 4th Street. **Open** 4pm-midnight Mon-Wed, Sun; 4pm-1am Thur; 4pm-2am Fri, Sat. **Map** p109 C2 ⑫

Duck through an unmarked doorway and find yourself in a red-walled Belgian bar that serves brews exclusively from the motherland. Clusters of European grad students knock back glasses of Corsendork and Triple Kermeliet – just two of 13 beers on tap and 22 by the bottle. Moules and frites – served with one of a dozen sauces – are the only eats available (not Monday).

Shops & Services

CO Bigelow Chemists

414 Sixth Avenue, between 8th & 9th Streets (1-212 533 2700, www.bigelowchemists.com). Subway A, B, C, D, F, M to W 4th Street; 1 to Christopher Street. **Open** 7.30am-9pm Mon-Fri; 8.30am-7pm Sat; 8.30am-5pm Sun. **Map** p109 C2 ⑬ **Health & beauty**

Established in 1838, Bigelow is the oldest apothecary in America. Its appealingly old-school line of toiletries includes such tried-and-trusted favourites as Mentha Lip Shine, Barber Cologne Elixirs and Lemon Body Cream. The spacious, chandelier-lit store is packed with natural and homeopathic remedies, organic skincare products and drugstore essentials – and the place still fills prescriptions.

Forbidden Planet

832 Broadway, between 12th & 13th Streets (1-212 473 1576, www.fpnyc.com). Subway L, N, Q, R, 4, 5, 6 to 14th Street-Union Square. **Open** 9am-10pm Mon, Tue, Sun; 9am-midnight Wed-Sat. **Map** p109 D1 ⑭ **Books & music**

Embracing both pop culture and the cult underground, the Planet takes comics seriously. You'll also find graphic novels, manga, action figures, DVDs and more.

Harry's Corner Shop

64 MacDougal Street, at Houston Street (1-646 964 5193, www.harrys.com/cornershop). Subway 1 to Houston Street. **Open** 11am-8pm Mon-Fri; 10am-7pm Sat. **Map** p109 C3 ⑮ **Barber**

Warby Parker co-founder Jeff Raider and business partner Andy Katz-Mayfield launched grooming brand Harry's in 2013 and opened the e-commerce platform's first 1920s-esque barbershop. Aside from affordable cuts ($35) and shaves ($30), the shop offers clients a completely individualised appointment: barbers use iPads to snap headshots and update digital profiles of each customer. The merchandise stocked on ash-wood shelves includes Harry's razors and shave cream, plus gents' essentials like Hanes white cotton tees, Sleepy Jones striped socks, and Best Made Belgian dart sets.

Reminiscence

74 Fifth Avenue, between 13th & 14th Streets (1-212 243 2292, www.reminiscence.com). Subway L, N, Q, R, 4, 5, 6 to 14th Street-Union Square. **Open** 10am-8pm Mon-Sat; noon-7pm Sun. **Map** p109 C1 ⑯ **Fashion/accessories**

When Stewart Richer began crafting newsboy hats out of salvaged denim in the 1970s, he had no intention of starting a lifelong business. But his designs proved so popular with buyers, he decided to open his own storefront, selling his handmade clothing and accessories alongside vintage items. Having held four locations around the city, the shop recently relocated to its original Greenwich Village spot. Specialising in quirky threads from the 1960s to the '80s, Reminiscence is known for its inexpensive collection of street-ready and costume duds for both men and women. Snatch up unisex deep-dyed cotton tie-string overalls, Hawaiian-print skirts and authentic Swiss Army surplus bags.

MUSEUM ON THE MOVE

Four reasons to get excited about the Whitney's new downtown digs.

Once the gritty domain of wholesale butchers and gay nightspots with evocative names such as the Mineshaft and the Ramrod, the Meatpacking District became a fashionable hub in the 1990s and early noughties before giving way to more mainstream popularity. What the neighbourhood has lacked, however, is culture – though since 2009, the High Line has provided a direct pedestrian link to Chelsea's galleries (and plenty of temporary public art installations along its length). That is set to change in spring 2015, when the **Whitney Museum of American Art** (*see p176*) opens its striking new digs at the southern foot of the park.

After earlier plans to expand its Upper East Side building were scrapped in the face of local opposition, the museum broke ground on its downtown home in 2011. Designed by Renzo Piano, the nine-storey, steel-and-glass building is on track to be the first LEED Gold-rated green art museum in NYC. The dramatic, asymmetrical structure features a series of outdoor terraces that rise like steps above the High Line. At 200,000 square feet, it is roughly three times the size of the old premises. For the first time, there will be space for a comprehensive display of the collection. Here are four features to look forward to:

Free exhibits A 8,500-square-foot public plaza beneath the High Line leads to the cantilevered glass entrance. Inside, you'll find a ground-floor restaurant helmed by dining guru Danny Meyer, a gift shop and a free-admission lobby gallery.

Transporting art Four elevators, commissioned by Richard Artschwager before his death in 2013, have a dual function as passenger lifts and an art installation, entitled *Six in Four.* Using six themes that have featured in the artist's work since the 1970s – door, window, table, basket, mirror and rug – they will transport visitors not only to the upper floors, but also to an alternative reality.

Viewings with a view Terraces on the fifth, sixth and seventh floors let you take in sculptures and installations while admiring views of the Hudson River and city landmarks including the Empire State Building and One World Trade Center. The eighth-floor café also has outside seating.

After-hours events The new building includes a 170-seat theatre with retractable seating that can adapt to a variety of programming, from dance and concerts to contemporary films, after the galleries are closed.

Meurice Garment Care

31 University Place, between 8th & 9th Streets (1-212 475 2778, www.garmentcare.com). Subway N, R to 8th Street-NYU. **Open** 7.30am-6pm Mon-Fri; 9am-6pm Sat; 10am-3pm Sun. **Map** p109 D2 ⑰ **Drycleaner**

This longstanding family-run dry cleaners prides itself on attention to detail. Knitwear is cleaned using a hydrocarbon process, which substitutes a gentler petroleum-based solvent for the traditional perchloroethylene, and very delicate fabrics, including vintage items and shearlings, are hand-cleaned. Be prepared to pay for this superior service; dry cleaning starts at about $15 for a skirt.

Other locations 245 E 57th Street, between Second & Third Avenues, Midtown (1-212 759 9057).

Murray's Cheese

254 Bleecker Street, between Sixth & Seventh Avenues (1-212 243 3289, www.murrayscheese.com). Subway A, B, C, D, E, F, M to W 4th Street. **Open** 8am-8pm Mon-Sat; 9am-7pm Sun. **Map** p109 C2 ⑱ **Food & drink**

For the last word in curd, New Yorkers have been flocking to Murray's since 1940 to sniff out the best international and domestic cheeses. The helpful staff will guide you through hundreds of stinky, runny, washed-rind and aged comestibles.

► *Murray's also has an outpost in Grand Central Terminal, plus a Cheese Bar at 264 Bleecker Street.*

EXPLORE

Porto Rico Importing Co

201 Bleecker Street, between Sixth Avenue & MacDougal Street (1-212 477 5421, www.portorico.com). Subway A, B, C, D, E, F, M to W 4th Street. **Open** 8am-9pm Mon-Sat; noon-7pm Sun. **Map** p109 C2 ⑲ **Food & drink**

This small, family-run store, established in 1907, has earned a large following for its terrific range of coffee beans, including its own prepared blends. Prices are reasonable, and the selection of teas also warrants exploration.

Other locations 40½ St Marks Place, between First & Second Avenues, East Village (1-212 533 1982); Essex Market, 120 Essex Street, between Delancey & Rivington Streets, Lower East Side (1-212 677 1210); 636 Grand Street, between Manhattan Avenue & Leonard Street, Williamsburg, Brooklyn (1-718 782 1200).

WEST VILLAGE

Subway A, C, E, 1, 2, 3 to 14th Street; L to Eighth Avenue; 1 to Christopher Street-Sheridan Square.

In the early 20th century, the **West Village** was largely a working-class Italian neighbourhood. These days, the highly desirable enclave is home to numerous celebrities (including Claire Danes, Hugh Jackman, and Sarah Jessica Parker and Matthew Broderick), but a low-key, everyone-knows-everyone feel remains. The area west of Sixth Avenue to the Hudson River, from 14th Street to Houston Street, possesses the quirky geographical features that moulded the Village's character. Only here could West 10th Street cross West 4th Street, and Waverly Place cross… Waverly Place. One of the oldest parts of the Village, it retains a street layout based the original settlers' horse paths.

Locals and visitors crowd bistros along Seventh Avenue and Hudson Street, and patronise the high-rent shops on this stretch of Bleecker Street, including no fewer than three Marc Jacobs boutiques. Venture on to the side streets for interesting discoveries, such as sumptuous perfume parlour **Aedes de Venustas** (*see p117*) on Christopher Street. The area's bohemian population may have dwindled years ago, but a few old landmarks remain. Solemnly raise a glass in the **White Horse Tavern** (*see p117*), a favourite of such literary luminaries as Ezra Pound, James Baldwin, Norman Mailer and Dylan Thomas, who included it on his last drinking binge before his death in 1953. On and just off Seventh Avenue South are jazz and cabaret clubs, including the **Village Vanguard** (*see p282*).

The West Village is also a historic gay neighbourhood, although the current scene has mostly migrated north to Hell's Kitchen. The **Stonewall Inn** (*see p260*), on Christopher Street, was the site of the 1969 riots that marked the birth of the modern gay-liberation movement. In **Christopher Park**, which faces the bar, is George Segal's *Gay Liberation*, a piece composed of plaster sculptures of two same-sex couples that commemorates the street's pivotal role in gay history.

Restaurants & Cafés

Buvette

42 Grove Street, between Bedford & Bleecker Streets (1-212 255 3590, www.ilovebuvette.com). Subway 1 to Christopher Street-Sheridan Square. **Open** 8am-2am Mon-Fri; 10am-2am Sat, Sun. **Main courses** $12-$15. **Map** p109 C2 ⑳ **French**

Chef Jody Williams has filled every nook of tiny, Gallic-themed Buvette with old picnic baskets, teapots and silver trays, among other vintage ephemera. The food is just as thoughtfully curated – Williams's immaculate renditions of coq au vin, duck rillettes or intense, lacquered wedges of tarte Tatin arrive on tiny plates, in petite jars or in miniature casseroles, her time-warp flavours recalling an era when there were still classic bistros on every corner.

Rosemary's. *See p116.*

★ Chez Sardine

183 W 10th Street, at W 4th Street (1-646 360 3705, www.chezsardine.com). Subway A, B, C, D, E, F, M to W 4th Street; 1 to Christopher Street-Sheridan Square. **Open** 5.30-11pm Mon-Wed; 5.30pm-1am Thur, Fri; 11am-2.45pm, 5.30pm-1am Sat; 11am-2.45pm, 5.30-11pm Sun. **Main courses** $19-$24. **Map** p109 C2 ㉑ **Eclectic/Japanese**

Prolific restaurateur Gabriel Stulman's fifth Village venture is a cross-cultural izakaya. The slim restaurant's sardine-can-size kitchen, run by Fedora's (*see right*) Mehdi Brunet-Benkritly, sends out wild riffs on sushi, like Scottish salmon with pretzels and lime cream or chopped beef with sea urchin. The inspiration and compact dimensions are steeped in Japan. The execution, though, is pure Quebecois gluttony, with a smoked cheddar grilled cheese sandwich oozing melted foie gras; and pancakes stacked with briny roe, fish tartare and tangy yoghurt.

$ Corner Bistro

331 W 4th Street, at Jane Street (1-212 242 9502). Subway A, C, E to 14th Street; L to Eighth Avenue. **Open** 11.30am-4am Mon-Sat; noon-4am Sun. **Burgers** $6.75-$8.75. **No credit cards. Map** p109 B1 ㉒ **American**

There's only one reason to come to this legendary pub: it serves what some New Yorkers say are the city's best burgers – plus the beer is just $3 for a mug of McSorley's. The patties are no-frills and served on a flimsy paper plate. To get one, you may have to queue for a good hour, especially on weekend nights; if the wait is too long for a table, try to slip into a space at the bar.

Other locations 47-18 Vernon Boulevard, at 47th Road, Long Island City, Queens (1-718 606 6500).

► *For other top-ranking burgers, see Minetta Tavern (see p111) and Shake Shake (p166).*

EN Japanese Brasserie

435 Hudson Street, at Leroy Street (1-212 647 9196, www.enjb.com). Subway 1 to Houston Street. **Open** noon-2.30pm, 5.30-10.30pm Mon-Thur; noon-2.30pm, 5.30-11.30pm Fri; 11am-2.30pm, 5.30-11.30pm Sat; 11am-2.30pm, 5.30-10.30pm Sun. **Main courses** $14-$34. **Map** p109 B3 ㉓ **Japanese**

The owners of this popular spot aim to evoke a sense of Japanese living in the multi-level space. On the ground floor are tatami-style rooms; on the mezzanine are recreations of a living room, dining room and library of a Japanese home from the Meiji era. But the spacious main dining room is where the action is. Highlights of chef Abe Hiroki's menu include freshly made scooped tofu served with a soy-dashi mix; miso-marinated, broiled Alaskan black cod; and Berkshire pork belly braised in sansho miso. Try the saké and shochu flights.

Fedora

239 W 4th Street, between Charles & W 10th Streets (1-646 449 9336, www.fedoranyc.com). Subway A, B, C, D, E, F, M to W 4th Street; 1 to Christopher Street-Sheridan Square. **Open** 5.30pm-midnight Mon, Sun; 5.30pm-2am Tue-Sat. **Main courses** $24-$30. **Map** p109 B2 ㉔ **Eclectic**

This French-Canadian knockout is part of restaurateur Gabriel Stulman's West Village mini-empire (his other local eateries are Joseph Leonard, Jeffrey's Grocery, Italian spot Perla and eclectic Japanese joint Chez Sardine; *see left*). Mehdi Brunet-Benkritly produces some of the most exciting toe-to-tongue cooking in town, plying epicurean hipsters with Quebecois party food that's eccentric, excessive and fun – crisp pig's head with *enoki*, for example, or maple-smoked salmon with almonds and curry cream.

★ Kesté Pizza & Vino

271 Bleecker Street, between Cornelia & Jones Streets (1-212 243 1500, www.kestepizzeria.com). Subway 1 to Christopher Street-Sheridan Square. **Open** noon-3.30pm, 5-11pm Mon-Thur; noon-11.30pm Fri, Sat; noon-10.30pm Sun. **Pizzas** $13-$23. **Map** p109 C2 ㉕ **Pizza**

If anyone can claim to be an expert on Neapolitan pizza, it's Kesté's Roberto Caporuscio: as president of the US branch of the Associazione Pizzaiuoli Napoletani, he's the top dog for the training and certification of *pizzaioli*. At his intimate, 46-seat space, it's all about the crust – blistered, salty and elastic, it could easily be eaten plain. Add ace toppings such as sweet-tart San Marzano tomato sauce, milky mozzarella and fresh basil, and you have one of New York's finest pies.

► *Roberto Caporuscio also had a hand in superior Theater District pizza place, Don Antonio by Starita (see p148).*

Pearl Oyster Bar

18 Cornelia Street, between Bleecker & W 4th Streets (1-212 691 8211, www.pearloyster bar.com). Subway A, B, C, D, E, F, M to W 4th Street. **Open** noon-2.30pm, 6-11pm Mon-Fri; 6-11pm Sat. **Main courses** $23-$36. **Map** p109 C2 **26 Seafood**

There's a good reason this convivial, no-reservations, New England-style fish joint always has a queue – the food is outstanding. Signature dishes include the lobster roll (sweet, lemon-scented meat laced with mayonnaise on a butter-enriched bun) and a contemporary take on bouillabaisse: a briny lobster broth packed with mussels, cod, scallops and clams, topped with an aïoli-smothered croûton.

★ RedFarm

529 Hudson Street, between Charles & W 10th Streets (1-212 792 9700, www.redfarmnyc.com). Subway 1 to Christopher Street-Sheridan Square. **Open** 5-11.45pm Mon-Fri; 11am-2.30pm, 5-11.45pm Sat; 11am-2.30pm, 5-11pm Sun. **Main courses** $19-$49. **Map** p109 B2 **27 Chinese**

The high-end ingredients and whimsical plating at Ed Schoenfeld's interpretive Chinese restaurant have helped to pack the dining room since opening night. Chef Joe Ng is known for his dim sum artistry: scallop and squid *shu mai* come skewered over shot glasses of warm carrot ginger bisque – designed to be eaten and gulped in rapid succession; other nouveau creations include Katz's pastrami-stuffed egg rolls and shrimp dumplings decorated with 'eyes' and pursued on the plate by a sweet-potato Pac-Man. **Other locations** 2170 Broadway, between 76th & 77th Streets, Upper West Side (1-212 724 9700).

Rosemary's

18 Greenwich Avenue, at 10th Street (1-212 647 1818, www.rosemarysnyc.com). Subway A, B, C, D, E, F, M to W 4th Street. **Open** 11.30am-4.30pm, 5pm-midnight Mon-Fri; 10am-4pm, 5pm-midnight Sat, Sun. **Main courses** $12-$24. **Map** p109 C1 **28 Italian**

While gastronomy isn't the primary focus in most of the pheromone factories clustered on this stretch of Seventh Avenue, this rustic, farmhouse-vibe celebrity magnet ought to be packed with food fanatics. Chef Wade Moises, who worked for Mario Batali at Babbo and Lupa, is a talent to watch. Pair pasta with one of the showstopping large-format feasts – big platters for two that in fact serve three or four. House-made cavatelli with braised beef, heirloom tomato sauce and fresh cherry tomatoes is a mellow foil for the chef's *carne misti*, a mountain of espresso-glazed pork ribs, smoky lamb shoulder and super-succulent whey-brined chicken. *Photo p115.*

$ 'sNice

45 Eighth Avenue, at 4th Street (1-212 645 0310, www.snicecafe.com). Subway A, C, E to 14th Street; L to Eighth Avenue. **Open** 7.30am-10pm daily. **Sandwiches/salads** $9.25. **Map** p109 B1 **29 Café/Vegetarian**

If you're looking for a laid-back place in which to read the papers, do a little laptopping, and enjoy cheap, simple and satisfying veggie fare, then 'sNice is nice indeed. Far roomier than it appears from its windows, the bare-brick café has what may well be the largest menu in the city, scrawled on the wall, giving thorough descriptions of each sandwich and salad. **Other locations** 150 Sullivan Street, between Houston & Prince Streets, Soho (1-212 253 5405); 315 Fifth Avenue, at 3rd Street, Park Slope, Brooklyn (1-718 788 2121).

The Spotted Pig

314 W 11th Street, at Greenwich Street (1-212 620 0393, www.thespottedpig.com). Subway A, C, E to 14th Street; L to Eighth Avenue. **Open** noon-2am Mon-Fri; 11am-2am Sat, Sun. **Main courses** $20-$32. **Map** p109 B2 **30 Eclectic**

White Horse Tavern.

With a creaky interior that recalls an ancient pub, this Anglo-Italian hybrid from Ken Friedman and chef April Bloomfield is still hopping more than a decade after opening. The gastropub doesn't take reservations and a wait can always be expected. The burger is a must-order: a secret blend of ground beef grilled rare (unless otherwise specified) and covered with gobs of pungent roquefort. It arrives with a tower of crispy shoestring fries tossed with rosemary. Indulgent desserts, like the flourless chocolate cake, are worth loosening your belt for.

$ Sweet Revenge

62 Carmine Street, between Bedford Street & Seventh Avenue (1-212 242 2240, www.sweetrevengenyc.com). Subway A, B, C, D, E, F, M to W 4th Street; 1 to Christopher Street-Sheridan Square. **Open** 7am-11pm Mon-Thur; 7am-12.30am Fri; 10.30am-12.30am Sat; 10.30am-10pm Sun. **Cupcakes** $3.50. **Map** p109 C3 ㉛ **Café**

Baker Marlo Scott steamrollered over the cupcake's innocent charms: at her café/bar, she pairs her confections with wine or beer; where there were pastel swirls of frosting, there are now anarchic spikes of peanut butter, cream cheese and milk-chocolate icing. In the process, she saved the ubiquitous treat from becoming a cloying cliché. Gourmet sandwiches and other plates cater to non-sweet-tooths.

Bars

Blind Tiger Ale House

281 Bleecker Street, at Jones Street (1-212 462 4682, www.blindtigeralehouse.com). Subway A, B, C, D, E, F, M to W 4th Street; 1 to Christopher Street-Sheridan Square. **Open** 11.30am-4am daily. **Map** p109 C2 ㉜

Brew geeks descend upon this hops heaven for boutique ales and more than two dozen daily rotating, hard-to-find drafts (like Southern Tier Krampus and Singlecut Half-Stack). The clubby room features windows that open on to the street. Late afternoons and early evenings are ideal for serious sippers enjoying plates of Murray's Cheese, while the after-dark set veers dangerously close to Phi Kappa territory.

★ Employees Only

510 Hudson Street, between Christopher & W 10th Streets (1-212 242 3021, www.employeesonlynyc.com). Subway 1 to Christopher Street-Sheridan Square. **Open** 6pm-3.30am daily. **Map** p109 B2 ㉝

This Prohibition-themed bar cultivates an exclusive vibe, but there's no cover and no hassle at the door. Pass by the palm reader in the window (it's a front) and you'll find an amber-lit art deco interior where formality continues to flourish: servers wear custom-designed frocks and bartenders are in waitstaff whites. But the real stars are cocktails such as the West Side, a lethal mix of lemon vodka, lemon juice, fresh mint and club soda.

Gottino

52 Greenwich Avenue, between Charles & Perry Streets (1-212 633 2590, www.gottinony.com). Subway 1 to Christopher Street-Sheridan Square. **Open** 8am-2am Mon-Fri; 10am-2am Sat, Sun. **Map** p109 C1 ㉞

Jockey for a seat at this narrow enoteca – there are just five tables in addition to the long marble bar. It's worth the crush. The all-Italian wine list is complemented by a menu of choice nibbles, divided into salumi and cheese on one side, and delectable prepared bites on the other.

White Horse Tavern

567 Hudson Street, at 11th Street (1-212 989 3956). Subway 1 to Christopher Street-Sheridan Square. **Open** 11am-2am Mon-Thur, Sun; 11am-4am Fri, Sat. **No credit cards. Map** p109 B2 ㉟

Popular lore tells us that in 1953, Dylan Thomas pounded 18 straight whiskeys here before expiring in his Chelsea Hotel residence – a portrait of him now hangs in the middle room, above his favourite table in the corner. Now the old-school bar and its adjacent outdoor patio play host to a yuppie crowd and clutches of tourists, drawn by the outdoor seating, a fine selection of beers – and the legend.

Shops & Services

Aedes de Venustas

9 Christopher Street, between Greenwich Avenue & Waverly Place (1-212 206 8674, www.aedes.com). Subway A, B, C, D, F, M to W 4th Street; 1 to Christopher Street-Sheridan Square. **Open** noon-8pm Mon-Sat; 1-7pm Sun. **Map** p109 C2 ㊱ **Health & beauty**

Decked out like a 19th-century boudoir, this perfume collector's palace devotes itself to ultra-sophisticated fragrances and high-end skincare lines, such as Diptyque, Santa Maria Novella and its own glamorously packaged range of fragrances, candles and room sprays. Hard-to-find scents, such as Serge Lutens perfumes, line the walls.

Darling

1 Horatio Street, at Eighth Avenue (1-646 336 6966, www.darlingnyc.com). Subway A, C, E to 14th Street; L to Eighth Avenue. **Open** noon-7pm Mon-Sat; noon-6pm Sun. **Map** p109 B1 ㊲ **Fashion**

Ann Emonts Sherman's two-floor boutique is a great place to pick up a special-occasion number. Not only is the lower level stocked with dramatic pieces from the 1950s to the recent past, the former Broadway and Off-Broadway costume designer has a discerning eye for cherry-picking reasonably priced dresses from popular labels like BB Dakota, Karina and Bailey 44 that meet her girly aesthetic. For a finishing touch, check out the jewellery by Lotus, Alosh and Sally Kay displayed near the register.

Meatpacking District.

Flight 001
96 Greenwich Avenue, between Jane & W 12th Streets (1-212 989 0001, www.flight001.com). Subway A, C, E to 14th Street; L to Eighth Avenue. **Open** 11am-8pm Mon-Sat; noon-6pm Sun. **Map** p109 B1 ㊳ **Travel**

As well as a tasteful selection of luggage by the likes of Lipault, Rimowa and Hideo, this one-stop shop carries everything for the chic jet-setter, including fun travel products such as novelty patterned eye masks and emergency totes that squash down to tennis ball size, plus 'essentials' such as expanding hand-towel tablets and single-use packets of Woolite.

Other locations 132 Smith Street, between Bergen & Dean Streets, Boerum Hill, Brooklyn (1-718 243 0001).

Whittemore House
45 Grove Street, at Bleecker Street (1-212 242 8880, www.whittemorehousesalon.com). Subway 1 to Christopher Street-Sheridan Square. **Open** 11am-8pm Tue; noon-8pm Wed; noon-9pm Thur, Fri; 10am-6pm Sat. **Map** p109 B2 ㊴ **Health & beauty**

Victoria Hunter and Larry Raspanti, who each spent more than 15 years at Bumble & Bumble, opened this hair salon in an 1830s mansion (one of the three oldest buildings in NY). The decor features faux-decayed stencilled walls and boudoir chairs. Cuts (from $105) and natural-looking colour, achieved through the house hair-painting technique (from $225), come courtesy of some of New York's best stylists.

MEATPACKING DISTRICT

Subway A, C, E to 14th Street.

The north-west corner of the West Village has been known as the **Meatpacking District** since the area was dominated by the wholesale meat industry in the early 20th century. As business waned, gay fetish clubs took root in derelict buildings and, until the 1990s, the area was a haunt for transsexual prostitutes. In more recent years, however, hip eateries and designer boutiques have moved in. Frequent mentions on *Sex and the City,* along with the arrival of swanky hotel **Gansevoort Meatpacking NYC** (*see p353*) in the noughties cemented the area's reputation as a mainstream consumer playground. Nightclubs, including **Cielo** (*see p264*) and **Le Bain** (*see p263*), continue to draw after-dark pleasure seekers.

The 2009 opening of freight-track-turned-park the **High Line** (*see below*) has brought even bigger crowds to the area. Slick style hotel the **Standard** (*see p354*) straddles the elevated park at West 13th Street, and its seasonal Biergarten, nestled beneath it, is a great spot for a pint. Ironically, the arrival of the luxury hotel unintentionally restored some of the area's old raunchy reputation when the *New York Post* reported that naked hotel guests were putting on explicit shows in their glass-fronted rooms for the passersby below.

Sights & Museums

High Line
1-212 500 6035, www.thehighline.org. **Open** usually 7am-10pm daily (hours vary seasonally; see website for updates). **Map** p109 A1 ㊵

Running from Gansevoort Street in the Meatpacking District through Chelsea's gallery district to 30th Street, this slender, sinuous green strip – formerly an elevated freight train track – has been designed by landscape architects James Corner Field Operations and architects Diller Scofidio + Renfro. In autumn 2012, construction began on the final section, which will open in three phases, starting in late 2014. Stretching from 30th to 34th Streets, it skirts the West Side Rail Yards, which are being developed into a long-planned residential and commercial complex, Hudson Yards. *See also p122..*

EXPLORE

Restaurants & Cafés

Fatty Crab

643 Hudson Street, between Gansevoort & Horatio Streets (1-212 352 3592, www.fattycrab.com). Subway A, C, E to 14th St; L to Eighth Avenue. **Open** noon-11pm Mon-Wed; noon-midnight Thur, Fri; 11am-midnight Sat; 11am-11pm Sun. **Main courses** $16-$35. **Map** p109 B1 ㊶ **Malaysian**

This Malaysian-inspired eaterie reflects chef Zak Pelaccio's cunning take on South-east Asian cuisine: who knew you could squeeze slow-cooked lamb, shallot raisin sambal, chillies and Vietnamese mint between slices of Pepperidge Farm bread for a killer tea sandwich? The classic Malaysian chilli crab makes an appearance, but it doesn't come cheap. Far better bang for your buck is the short rib *rendang*, a tender chunk of meat braised in lemongrass-chilli and coconut. This packed spot takes no reservations, but turnover is quick – hard wooden chairs squeezed behind tiny tables in the single red-walled room don't encourage tarrying.

Shops & Services

Blow

Second Floor, 34 Gansevoort Street, at Hudson Street (1-212 989 6282, www.blowny.com). Subway A, C, E to 14th Street. **Open** 7.30am-8pm Mon-Fri; 10am-8pm Sat; noon-6pm Sun. **Map** p109 B1 ㊷ **Health & beauty**

Launched as a scissor-free blow-dry bar in 2005, this award-winning salon was at the vanguard of the trend. It later diversifed into other services, but has recently returned to its roots, so to speak, to concentrate on expertly executed 'blowouts' ($50), to use the local parlance. You can also opt for an updo, such as a chic ponytail, twist or chignon.

► *There's now a Blow outpost in Macy's (see p144).*

Owen.

Doyle & Doyle

412 W 13th Street, between Ninth Avenue & Washington Street (1-212 677 9991, www.doyledoyle.com). Subway A, C, E to 14th Street; L to Eighth Avenue. **Open** noon-7pm Mon-Wed, Fri-Sun; noon-8pm Thur. **Map** p109 A1 ㊸ **Accessories**

Whether your taste is art deco or nouveau, Victorian or Edwardian, gemologist sisters Elizabeth and Pamela Doyle, who specialise in vintage and antique jewellery, will have that one-of-a-kind item you're looking for, including engagement and eternity rings. In 2013, they packed up their curated archive and moved from the Lower East Side to larger premises in the Meatpacking District. The sisters have also launched their own collection of new heirlooms.

Jeffrey New York

449 W 14th Street, between Ninth & Tenth Avenues (1-212 206 1272, www.jeffreynewyork.com). Subway A, C, E to 14th Street; L to Eighth Avenue. **Open** 10am-8pm Mon-Wed, Fri; 10am-9pm Thur; 10am-7pm Sat; 12.30-6pm Sun. **Map** p109 A1 ㊹ **Fashion**

Jeffrey Kalinsky, a former Barneys shoe buyer, was a Meatpacking District pioneer when he opened his namesake store in 1999. Designer clothing abounds here – by Yves Saint Laurent, L'Wren Scott, Céline and Christopher Kane, among others. But the centrepiece is without doubt the shoe salon, which features the work of Manolo Blahnik, Prada and Christian Louboutin, as well as newer names to watch.

Owen

809 Washington Street, between Gansevoort & Horatio Streets (1-212 524 9770, www.owennyc.com). Subway A, C, E to 14th Street; L to Eighth Avenue. **Open** 11am-7pm Mon-Sat; noon-6pm Sun. **Map** p109 B1 ㊺ **Fashion**

FIT grad Phillip Salem founded this upscale boutique featuring more than 30 emerging and already-established brands. Anchoring the stock is Phillip Lim's cool, urban menswear and edgy dresses by Alexander Wang. The modern threads for both genders are displayed atop quartz slab tables and hung on blackened steel bars.

★ Rag & Bone General Store

425 W 13th Street, at Washington Street (1-212 249 3331, www.rag-bone.com). Subway A, C, E to 14th Street. **Open** 11am-8pm Mon-Sat; noon-7pm Sun. **Map** p109 A1 ㊻ **Fashion**

The downtown outpost of this enduringly hip brand, which began as a denim line in 2002, was once a meat factory, and it retains much of that industrial vibe with unfinished concrete floors, brick walls and an original Dave's Quality Veal sign. Sip a latte from the in-store Jack's Stir Brew Coffee before or after browsing the impeccably cut jeans, luxurious knitwear and well-tailored jackets for men and women.
Other locations throughout the city.

EXPLORE

Chelsea

Formerly a working-class Irish and Hispanic neighbourhood, the corridor between 14th and 29th Streets west of Sixth Avenue emerged as the nexus of New York's queer life in the 1990s. Due to rising housing costs and the protean nature of the city's cultural landscape, it's since been eclipsed by Hell's Kitchen to the north (just as Chelsea once overtook the West Village), but you'll still find bars, restaurants and shops catering to the once-ubiquitous 'Chelsea boys'. The cityscape shifts from leafy side streets lined with pristine 19th-century brownstones to an array of striking industrial and contemporary architecture on the far west side. In recent years, the local buzz has shifted to the previously neglected Hudson-hugging strip that has evolved into the city's main gallery district. But it's the transformation of a disused elevated freight train track snaking through the area into the High Line – already one of the city's most popular parks – that's really drawing crowds to this patch.

Mantiques Modern.

Don't Miss

1 Chelsea gallery district Around 200 art spaces in just ten blocks (*p125*).

2 Museum at FIT A must for fashion-conscious folk – and it's free (*p123*).

3 Cookshop This art-world favourite is great for brunch (*p124*).

4 Printed Matter For arty souvenirs (*p127*).

5 Mantiques Modern An atmospheric trove of unique objects (*p127*).

KOBRA

Chelsea Market.

CHELSEA

Subway A, C, E, 1, 2, 3 to 14th Street; C, E, 1 to 23rd Street; L to Eighth Avenue; 1 to 18th Street or 28th Street.

In the 1980s and '90s, many of New York's contemporary galleries left Soho for the once-desolate western edge of Chelsea (*see p125* **Gallery-Hopping Guide**). Today, internationally recognised spaces such as **Mary Boone Gallery**, **Gagosian Gallery** and **Gladstone Gallery**, as well as numerous less exalted names, attract swarms of art aficionados. The High Line has brought even more gallery-hoppers to the area as it provides a verdant pathway from the boutique- and restaurant-rich Meatpacking District to the art enclave. Traversing the elevated promenade, you'll pass through the old loading dock of the former Nabisco factory, where the first Oreo cookie was made in 1912. This conglomeration of 18 structures, built between the 1890s and the 1930s, now houses **Chelsea Market** (75 Ninth Avenue, between 15th & 16th Streets, www.chelseamarket.com). The ground-floor food arcade offers artisanal bread, wine, baked goods and freshly made ice-cream, among other treats.

Also among the area's notable industrial architecture is the **Starrett-Lehigh Building** (601 W 26th Street, at Eleventh Avenue). The stunning 1929 structure was left in disrepair until the dot-com boom of the late 1990s, when media companies, photographers and designers snatched up its loft-like spaces.

While some of the Hudson River piers, which were once terminals for the world's grand ocean liners, remain in a state of ruin, the four that lie between 17th and 23rd Streets have been transformed into mega sports centre **Chelsea Piers** (*see p127*).

To get a glimpse of how Chelsea looked back when it was first developed in the 1880s, stroll along **Cushman Row** (406-418 W 20th Street, between Ninth & Tenth Avenues) in the Chelsea Historic District. Just to the north is the block-long **General Theological Seminary of the Episcopal Church** (440 W 21st Street, between Ninth & Tenth Avenues). The seminary's land was part of the estate known as Chelsea, owned by poet Clement Clarke Moore, author of *A Visit from St Nicholas* (more commonly known as *'Twas the Night Before Christmas*), and the guest wing has been converted into the **High Line Hotel** (*see p357*).

A hostelry with a more notorious history is nearby. The **Chelsea Hotel** on West 23rd Street has been a magnet for creative types since it first opened in 1884; Mark Twain was an early guest. The list of those who have stayed here reads like an international *Who's Who* of the artistic elite: Sarah Bernhardt (who slept in a coffin), William Burroughs (who wrote *Naked Lunch* here), Dylan Thomas, Janis Joplin and Jimi Hendrix, to name a few. In the 1960s, it was the stomping ground of Andy Warhol's coterie of superstars, and the location of his 1966 film *The Chelsea Girls*. It's still home to about 95 permanent residents, working artists among them, but the Chelsea, recently acquired by fashionable boutique-hotel developer

IN THE KNOW STREET ART

While in Chelsea's gallery district, don't overlook the outdoor art installation *7000 Oaks* by German artist Joseph Beuys: 18 pairings of basalt stones and trees on W 22nd Street, between Tenth and Eleventh Avenues. Maintained by Dia Art Foundation (diaart.org), the piece is a spin-off of a five-year international effort, begun in 1982 at Germany's Documenta 7 exhibition, to enact social and environmental change by planting 7,000 trees.

King & Grove (www.kingandgrove.com), was undergoing renovations at the time of writing and not taking reservations for short-term guests.

The weekend flea markets tucked between buildings along 25th Street, between Seventh Avenue and Broadway, have shrunk in recent years (casualties of development), but you'll still find a heady assortment of clothes, furnishings, cameras and knick-knacks at the rummage-worthy **Antiques Garage** (*see p127*).

Not far from here, the Fashion Institute of Technology, on 27th Street, between Seventh and Eighth Avenues, counts Calvin Klein, Nanette Lepore and Michael Kors among its alumni. The school's **Museum at FIT** mounts free exhibitions.

Sights & Museums

FREE Museum at FIT

Building E, Seventh Avenue, at 27th Street (1-212 217 4558, www.fitnyc.edu/museum). Subway 1 to 28th Street. **Open** noon-8pm Tue-Fri; 10am-5pm Sat. **Admission** free. **Map** p123 D1 ❶

The Fashion Institute of Technology owns one of the largest and most impressive clothing collections in the world, including some 50,000 garments and accessories dating from the 18th century to the present. Under the directorship of fashion historian Dr Valerie Steele, the museum showcases a rotating selection from the permanent collection, as well as temporary exhibitions focusing on individual designers or the role that fashion plays in society.

Rubin Museum of Art

150 W 17th Street, at Seventh Avenue (1-212 620 5000, www.rmanyc.org). Subway A, C, E to 14th Street; L to Eighth Avenue; 1 to 18th Street. **Open** 11am-5pm Mon, Thur; 11am-9pm Wed; 11am-10pm Fri; 11am-6pm Sat, Sun. **Admission** $15; $10 reductions; free under-13s; free 6-10pm Fri. **Map** p123 D3 ❷

Dedicated to Himalayan art, the Rubin is a very stylish museum – a fact that falls into place when you learn that the six-storey space was once occupied by famed fashion store Barneys. The ground-floor café, where you can sample inexpensive Himalayan dishes, used to be the accessories department, and retail lives on in the colourful gift shop. A dramatic central spiral staircase ascends to the galleries, where rich-toned walls are classy foils for the serene statuary and intricate, multicoloured textiles. The second level is dedicated to 'Gateway to Himalayan Art', a yearly rotating display of selections from the permanent collection of more than 2,000 pieces from the second century to the present day. The upper floors are devoted to changing exhibitions. *Photo p124.*

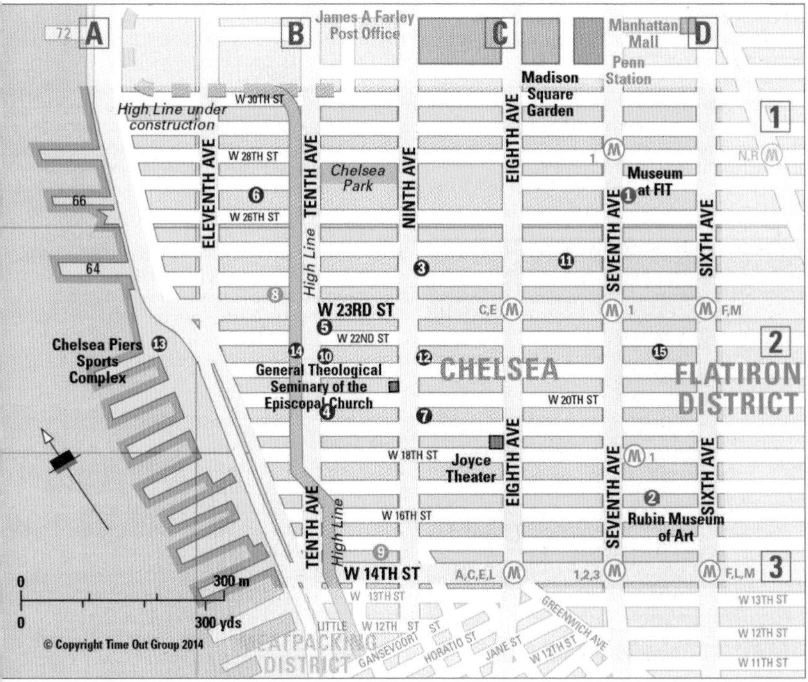

IN THE KNOW VINO AL FRESCO

From around late April until late October, food vendors set up on the High Line, and you can stop for a tipple at seasonal open-air café, the Porch, at 15th Street, which serves local wine and beer from cult vino spot Terroir (*see p103*).

Restaurants & Cafés

Co

230 Ninth Avenue, at 24th Street (1-212 243 1105, www.co-pane.com). Subway C, E to 23rd Street. **Open** 5-11pm Mon; 11.30am-11pm Tue-Sat; 11am-10pm Sun. **Pizzas** $9-$20. **Map** p123 C2 ❸ **Pizza**

This unassuming pizzeria was the restaurant debut of Jim Lahey, whose Sullivan Street Bakery supplies bread to many top restaurants. Lahey's crust is so good, in fact, it doesn't need any toppings (try the Pizza Bianca, sprinkled with sea salt and olive oil). The most compelling individual-sized pies come from non-traditional sources, such as the ham and cheese, essentially a croque-monsieur in pizza form.

★ Cookshop

156 Tenth Avenue, at 20th Street (1-212 924 4440, www.cookshopny.com). Subway C, E to 23rd Street. **Open** 8-11am, 11.30am-4pm, 5.30-11.30pm Mon-Fri; 10.30am-4pm, 5.30-11.30pm Sat; 10.30am-4pm, 5.30-10pm Sun. **Main courses** $22-$42. **Map** p123 B2 ❹ **American creative**

Chef Marc Meyer and his wife/co-owner Vicki Freeman want Cookshop to be a platform for sustainable ingredients from independent farmers. True to this mission, the ingredients are consistently top-notch, and the menu changes daily. While organic ingredients alone don't guarantee a great meal, Meyer knows how to let the flavours speak for themselves, and Cookshop scores points for getting the house-made ice-cream to taste as good as Ben & Jerry's.

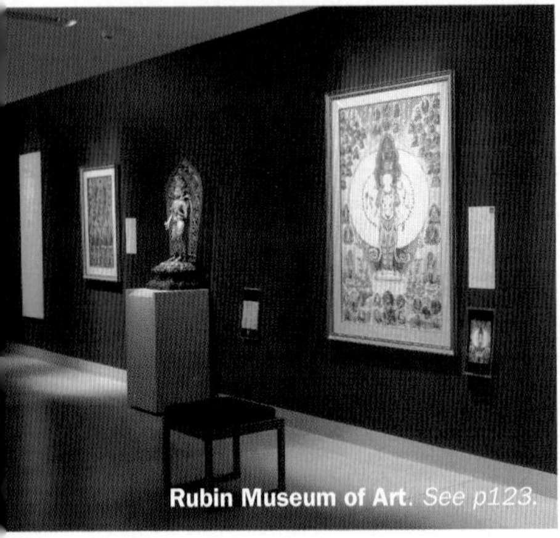

Rubin Museum of Art. *See p123.*

Empire Diner

210 Tenth Avenue, at 22nd Street (1-212 596 7523, www.empire-diner.com). Subway C, E to 23rd Street. **Open** 5.30-10pm Mon-Thur, Sun; 5.30-11pm Fri, Sat (hrs may be extended). **Main courses** $17-$28. **Map** p123 B2 ❺ **American**

See p126 **The Non-Greasy Spoon**.

The Heath

McKittrick Hotel, 530 W 27th Street, between Tenth & Eleventh Avenues (1-212 564 1662, www.theheathnyc.com). Subway 1 to 28th Street. **Open** 5-11pm daily. **Main courses** $18-$35. **Map** p123 B1 ❻ **American/British**

Punchdrunk – the London troupe behind the hit *Macbeth*-inspired production *Sleep No More* (*see p301*) – has premiered a 150-seat restaurant underneath its seasonal rooftop bar, Gallow Green. Chef RL King crafts a menu of modern American and British fare, such as chicken with charred broccoli, apples and hazelnuts, and a short-rib-and-chanterelle-mushroom pie. Cocktails with names like the gin-based Hull Executive and the Aberdonian Sour (Scotch, orgeat syrup, red wine float) bow to the company's UK roots.

Tipsy Parson

156 Ninth Avenue, between 19th & 20th Streets (1-212 620 4545, www.tipsyparson.com). Subway C, E to 23rd Street. **Open** 11.30am-midnight Mon-Fri; 10am-1am Sat; 10am-11pm Sun. **Main courses** $24-$34. **Map** p123 C ❼ **American regional**

Julie Wallach's Chelsea restaurant channels the experience of dining at home – if home happens to be a charming country cottage stocked with knick-knacks, that is. The nostalgic food is grounded firmly in the Deep South. A tasty down-home twist on a burger comes topped with pimento cheese (grits and bacon optional), accompanied by batter-fried pickles. Macaroni and cheese features a complex medley of cheddar, gruyère and grana padano, with crumbled corn bread and fresh *cavatelli*. For dessert, try the namesake Tipsy Parson – a boozy trifle.

Bars

Half King

505 W 23rd Street, between Tenth & Eleventh Avenues (1-212 462 4300, www.thehalfking.com). Subway C, E to 23rd Street. **Open** 11am-4am Mon-Fri; 9am-4am Sat, Sun. **Map** p123 B2 ❽

Don't let their blasé appearance fool you – the creative types gathered at the Half King's yellow pine bar are probably as excited as you are to catch a glimpse of the part-owner, author Sebastian Junger. While you're waiting, order one of the 16 draught beers – including several local brews – or a seasonal cocktail.

EXPLORE

GALLERY-HOPPING GUIDE

Hit these essential stops in the city's premier contemporary-art hub.

From West 19th Street to West 29th Street, between Tenth and Eleventh Avenues, converted industrial spaces are crammed with around 200 art spaces. Here, you'll find group shows by up-and-comers, blockbuster exhibitions from big names and a slew of provocative work. Note that galleries are generally closed or operate on an appointment-only basis on Mondays, and are open 10am-6pm Tuesday to Saturday. In summer, however, many keep different hours and close at weekends. Some may shut up shop for two weeks or a month at a stretch in July or August, so call before visiting. Below are our highlights.

Cheim & Read *547 W 25th Street, between Tenth & Eleventh Avenues (1-212 242 7727, www.cheimread.com).*
The international artists here include such superstars as Diane Arbus and Jenny Holzer.

David Zwirner *519, 525 & 533 W 19th Street, between Tenth & Eleventh Avenues (1-212 727 2070, www.davidzwirner.com).*
Zwirner mixes museum-quality shows of historical figures with a head-turning array of contemporary artists.

Gagosian Gallery *555 W 24th Street, between Tenth & Eleventh Avenues (1-212 741 1111, www.gagosian.com).*
Larry Gagosian's mammoth (20,000sq ft) contribution to 24th Street's galleries opened in 1999.

Gladstone Gallery *515 W 24th Street, between Tenth & Eleventh Avenues (1-212 206 9300, www.gladstonegallery.com).*
Gladstone is strictly blue-chip, with an emphasis on daring conceptual art.

Luhring Augustine *531 W 24th Street, between Tenth & Eleventh Avenues (1-212 206 9100, www.luhringaugustine.com).*
An impressive index of artists includes Rachel Whiteread, Christopher Wool and Pipilotti Rist.

Mary Boone Gallery *541 W 24th Street, between Tenth & Eleventh Avenues (1-212 752 2929, www.maryboonegallery.com).*
Boone made her name in the 1980s, representing Julian Schnabel and Jean-Michel Basquiat, among others, and continues to produce hit shows featuring young artists.

Matthew Marks Gallery *523 W 24th Street, between Tenth & Eleventh Avenues (1-212 243 0200, www.matthewmarks.com).*
Opened in 1991, the Matthew Marks gallery was a driving force behind Chelsea's transformation into an art destination.

Tanya Bonakdar Gallery *521 W 21st Street, between Tenth & Eleventh Avenues (1-212 414 4144, www.tanyabonakdargallery.com).*
This elegant space reps such powerhouse names as New York City *Waterfalls* maestro Olafur Eliasson.

Yossi Milo *245 Tenth Avenue, between West 24th & West 25th Streets (1-212 414 0370, www.yossimilo.com).*
Yossi Milo's impressive roster of camera talent encompasses emerging artists as well as more established photographers.

THE NON-GREASY SPOON

An iconic Chelsea diner is back, with a celebrity chef behind the counter.

The Empire Diner (*see p124*) has always had nostalgia permeating its stainless-steel walls. A Chelsea fixture since 1976, when Jack Doenias, Carl Laanes and Richard Ruskay took over a run-down former greasy spoon, the 1940s Fodero dining car spoke of an earlier era. The chrome-edged interior was an Edward Hopper time-warp of rotating stools, leather booths and subway tiles, with a dash of piano-parlour elegance – a 1930 Steck upright regularly provided mood music.

Despite the space's retro leanings, the round-the-clock eaterie kept a finger on the pulse of ever-changing Chelsea, establishing itself as a major force in helping to transform the neighbourhood. During the disco-ball decadence of the '70s, counter stools were dominated by club-hopping drag queens and leather daddies hungry for after-hours chilli sundaes. The nightclub debauchery slowed in the 1980s, with the boxcar comfortably mellowing into a coffee-pouring haven until the '90s art-world boom, which ushered in gallery glitterati and celebrities including Madonna, Steven Spielberg and Woody Allen (who lovingly immortalised the iconic spot in his 1979 film, *Manhattan*).

The haute hash house remained a tourist destination until lease issues forced it to close in 2010. After an unsuccessful reboot by the team behind Union Square canteen the Coffee Shop, the diner remained shuttered, its future uncertain.

Now the Chelsea landmark is getting an injection of star power. Amanda Freitag had been one of New York's most high-profile free agents since parting ways with the Harrison, where she was executive chef, in 2010. Despite reaching celebrity-chef status through appearances on *Chopped* and *Iron Chef*, there was still one space left to fill on Freitag's résumé – running her own restaurant.

In 2013, the Chelsea resident announced she was taking over the Empire, preserving its vintage looks – with era-appropriate additions like black-and-white portraits, grey vinyl booths and a soda fountain – but giving the menu a contemporary, locavore revamp. Elevated fare includes smoked whitefish wrapped up with radishes in crêpes, matzo-ball soup luxuriously laced with bone marrow, and Greek salad studded with charred octopus. The ice-cream for the pecan-sprinkled banana splits is churned in house, a move in line with the en-vogue artisanal bent of New York's food scene. But diner purists take heart: there are also patty melts and buttermilk pancakes.

The Tippler

Chelsea Market, 425 W 15th Street, between Ninth & Tenth Avenues (1-212 206 0000, www.thetippler.com). Subway A, C, E to 14th Street; L to Eighth Avenue. **Open** 4pm-2am Mon-Thur, Sun; 4pm-4am Fri, Sat. **Map** p123 B3 ⑨

Even at its most packed, there's still a fair amount of room to manoeuvre in this expansive lounge, which means you won't have too much trouble finding a space at the long marble bar. The menu includes a number of draft and bottled beers, plus wines from around the world, but you'd be remiss not to try at least one of the speciality cocktails, such as the Gin & Chronic (Plymouth gin, hops, spiced lime, tonic).

Shops & Services

192 Books

192 Tenth Avenue, between 21st & 22nd Streets (1-212 255 4022, www.192books.com). Subway C, E to 23rd Street. **Open** 11am-7pm daily. **Map** p123 B2 ⑩ **Books & music**

In an era when many an indie bookshop has closed, 192, open since 2003, is proving that quirky boutique booksellers can make it after all. Owned and 'curated' by art dealer Paula Cooper and her husband, editor Jack Macrae, the store offers a strong selection of art books and literature, as well as tomes on history, current affairs, music, science and nature. The phenomenal reading series brings in top authors of the calibre of Joan Didion, Zadie Smith and Mark Strand.

Antiques Garage

112 W 25th Street, between Sixth & Seventh Avenues (1-212 243 5343, www.annexmarkets.com). Subway F, M to 23rd Street. **Open** 9am-5pm Sat, Sun. **No credit cards**. **Map** p123 C2 ⑪ **Homewares**

Designers (and the occasional celebrity) hunt regularly at this flea market in a vacant parking garage. Strengths include old prints, vintage clothing and household paraphernalia. The weekend outdoor Hell's Kitchen Flea Market, run by the same people, features a mix of vintage clothing and textiles, furniture and bric-a-brac.

Other locations 39th Street, between Ninth & Tenth Avenues, Hell's Kitchen.

Billy's Bakery

184 Ninth Avenue, between 21st & 22nd Streets (1-212 647 9956, www.billysbakerynyc.com). Subway C, E to 23rd Street. **Open** 9.30am-11pm Mon-Thur; 9.30am-midnight Fri, Sat; 9am-9pm Sun. **Map** p123 C2 ⑫ **Food & drink**

If you crave a large serving of nostalgia, come here for such super-sweet delights as classic cupcakes, coconut cream pie, Hello Dollies (indulgent graham cracker treats) and Famous Chocolate Icebox Cake, all dispensed in a retro setting.

Other locations 75 Franklin Street, between Broadway & Church Street, Tribeca (1-212 647 9958).

IN THE KNOW
A VICIOUS MURDER

The Hotel Chelsea gained punk-rock notoriety on 12 October 1978, when Sex Pistol Sid Vicious stabbed girlfriend Nancy Spungen to death in Room 100.

Chelsea Piers

Piers 59-62, W 18th to 23rd Streets, at Twelfth Avenue (1-212 336 6666, www.chelseapiers.com). Subway C, E to 23rd Street. **Open** times vary; phone or check website for details. **Map** p123 A2 ⑬ **Sport**

Chelsea Piers is still the most impressive all-in-one athletic facility in New York. Between the ice rink (Pier 61, 1-212 336 6100), the bowling alley (between Piers 59 & 60, 1-212 835 2695), the driving range (Pier 59, 1-212 336 6400) and scads of other choices, there's definitely something for everyone. The Field House (between Piers 61 & 62, 1-212 336 6500) has a climbing wall, a gymnastics centre, batting cages, basketball courts and indoor turf fields. At the Sports Center Health Club (Pier 60, 1-212 336 6000), you'll find a gym complete with comprehensive weight deck and cardiovascular machines, plus classes covering everything from boxing to triathlon training in the pool.

★ Printed Matter

195 Tenth Avenue, between 21st & 22nd Streets (1-212 925 0325, www.printedmatter.org). Subway C, E to 23rd Street. **Open** 11am-7pm Mon-Wed, Sat; 11am-8pm Thur, Fri. **Map** p123 B2 ⑭ **Books & music**

This non-profit organisation is devoted to artists' books – from David Shrigley's deceptively naïve illustrations to provocative photographic self-portraits by Matthias Herrmann – and operates a public reading room as well as a shop. Works by unknown and emerging artists share shelf space with those by veterans such as Yoko Ono and Edward Ruscha.

★ Mantiques Modern

146 W 22nd Street, between Sixth & Seventh Avenues (1-212 206 1494, www.mantiquesmodern.com). Subway 1 to 23rd Street. **Open** 10.30am-6.30pm Mon-Fri; 11am-7pm Sat, Sun. **Map** p123 D2 ⑮ **Homewares**

Walking into this two-level shop is a little like stumbling upon the private collection of a mad professor. Specialising in industrial and modernist furnishings, art and accessories from the 1880s to the 1980s, Mantiques Modern is a fantastic repository of beautiful and bizarre items, from kinetic sculptures and early 20th-century wooden artists' mannequins to a Soviet World War II telescope. Pieces by famous designers such as Hermès sit side by side with natural curiosities, and skulls (in metal or Lucite), crabs, animal horns and robots are all recurring themes. *Photo p120.*

Gramercy & Flatiron

Lying east of Chelsea, the Gramercy and Flatiron neighbourhoods contain some of the city's most distinctive architecture – including the famous wedge-shaped building that gave the Flatiron District its name – and several inviting green spaces. Unfortunately, you'll probably only get tantalising over-the-gate glimpses of pretty Gramercy Park, which remains the exclusive preserve of residents of the surrounding buildings. But in recent years, the attractions for visitors have multiplied in this part of town, with the arrival of new museums, restaurants and shops, including the country's first Museum of Mathematics and Italian-food mecca Eataly.

Madison Square Park

Don't Miss

1 Flatiron Building The lovely structure that gave the nabe its name (*p130*).

2 Madison Square Park A picturesque patch with an adventurous public-art programme (*p130*).

3 ABC Carpet & Home The city's finest furniture store is home to a first-rate restaurant (*p136*).

4 The NoMad Arguably the best roast chicken in town (*p134*).

5 Raines Law Room This sophisticated pseudo-speakeasy mixes perfect cocktails (*p134*).

Madison Square Park.

FLATIRON DISTRICT & UNION SQUARE

Subway F, M to 14th Street; L, N, Q, R, 4, 5, 6 to 14th Street-Union Square; L to Sixth Avenue; N, R, 6 to 23rd Street or 28th Street.

Taking its name from the distinctive wedge-shaped **Flatiron Building**, this district extends from 14th to 29th Streets, between Sixth and Lexington Avenues. (However, as with many NYC neighbourhoods, the borders are disputed and evolving – NoMad is slowly catching on as the new name for the blocks north of Madison Square Park.) The area was once predominantly commercial, home to numerous toy manufacturers and photography studios – it's still not uncommon to see models and actors strolling to and from their shoots. However, in the 1980s, the neighbourhood became more residential, as buyers were drawn to its 19th-century brownstones and early 20th-century industrial architecture. Clusters of restaurants and shops soon followed. By the turn of the millennium, many internet start-ups had moved to the area, earning it the nickname 'Silicon Alley'.

There are two major public spaces in the locale: Madison Square Park and Union Square. Opened in 1847, **Madison Square Park** (from 23rd to 26th Streets, between Fifth & Madison Avenues) is the more stately of the two. In the 19th century, the square was a highly desirable address. Winston Churchill's grandfather resided in a magnificent but since-demolished mansion at Madison Avenue and 26th Street; Edith Wharton also made her home in the neighbourhood and set many of her high-society novels here. By the 1990s, the park had become a decaying no-go zone given over to drug dealers and the homeless, but it got a much-needed makeover in 2001 thanks to the efforts of the Madison Square Park Conservancy (www.madisonsquarepark.org), which has created a programme of cultural events, including Mad Sq Art, a year-round 'gallery without walls', featuring sculptural, video and installation exhibitions from big-name artists. A further lure is restaurateur Danny Meyer's original **Shake Shack** (for a review of a bricks-and-mortar branch, *see p167*), which attracts queues in all weathers for its burgers – considered by many New Yorkers to be top of the heap.

The square is surrounded by illustrious buildings. Completed in 1909, the **Metropolitan Life Tower** (1 Madison Avenue, at 24th Street) was modelled on the Campanile in Venice's Piazza San Marco (an allusion as commercial as it was architectural, for Met Life Insurance wished to remind people that it had raised funds for the Campanile after its fall two years earlier). The **Appellate Division Courthouse** (35 E 25th Street, at Madison Avenue) features one of the most beautiful pediments in the city, while Cass Gilbert's **New York Life Insurance Company Building** (51 Madison Avenue, at 26th Street) is capped by a golden pyramid that's one of the skyline's jewels.

The most famous of all Madison Square's edifices, however, lies at the southern end. The **Flatiron Building** (175 Fifth Avenue, between 22nd & 23rd Streets) was the world's first steel-frame skyscraper, a 22-storey Beaux Arts edifice clad conspicuously in white limestone and glazed terracotta. But it's the unique triangular shape (like an arrow pointing northward to indicate the city's progression uptown) that has drawn sightseers since it opened in 1902. Legend has it that a popular

1920s catchphrase originated at this corner of 23rd Street – police would give the '23 skidoo' to ne'er-do-wells trying to peek at ladies' petticoats as the unique wind currents that swirled around the building blew their dresses upward. Speaking of rampant libidos: the nearby **Museum of Sex** (*see right*) houses an impressive collection of salacious ephemera.

In the 19th century, the neighbourhood went by the moniker of Ladies' Mile, thanks to the ritzy department stores that lined Broadway and Sixth Avenue. These retail palaces attracted the 'carriage trade', wealthy women who bought the latest imported fashions and household goods. By 1914, most of the department stores had moved north, leaving their proud cast-iron buildings behind. Today, the area is peppered with chain clothing stores, bookshops and tasteful home-furnishing shops such as **ABC Carpet & Home** (*see p136*).

The Flatiron District's other major public space, **Union Square** (from 14th to 17th Streets, between Union Square East & Union Square West) is named after neither the Union of the Civil War nor the labour rallies that once took place here, but simply for the union of Broadway and Bowery Lane (now Fourth Avenue). Even so, it does have its radical roots: from the 1920s until the early '60s, it was a favourite spot for tub-thumping political oratory. Following 9/11, the park was home to candlelit vigils and became a focal point for the city's grief. Formerly grungy, the park is fresh from a rolling renovation project started in the 1980s. It's best known as the home of the **Union Square Greenmarket** (*see p137*). The square is flanked by a variety of large businesses, including a **Barnes & Noble** bookstore (www.barnesandnoble.com) that hosts an excellent programme of author events.

Sights & Museums

Museum of Mathematics (MoMath)

11 E 26th Street, between Fifth & Madison Avenues (1-212 542 0566, www.momath.org). Subway N, R, 6 to 23rd Street. **Open** 10am-5pm daily (10am-2.30pm 1st Wed of each mth). **Admission** $16; free-$10 reductions. **Map** p131 A2 ❶
See p135 **Go Figure**.

Museum of Sex

233 Fifth Avenue, at 27th Street (1-212 689 6337, www.museumofsex.com). Subway N, R, 6 to 28th Street. **Open** 10am-8pm Mon-Thur, Sun; 10am-9pm Fri, Sat. **Admission** $17.50; $15.25 reductions. Under-18s not admitted.
Map p131 A1 ❷

EXPLORE

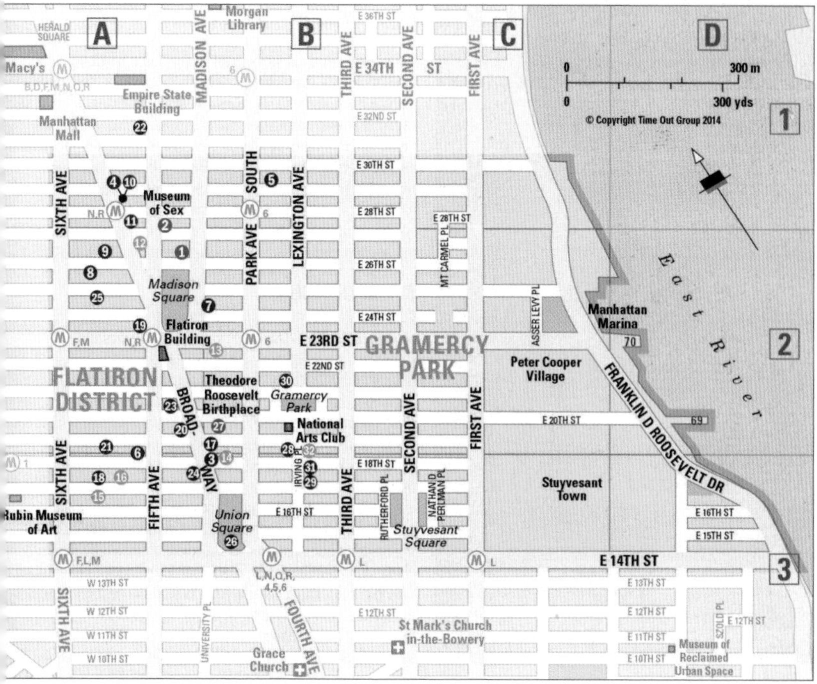

Situated in the former Tenderloin district, which bumped and ground with dance halls and brothels in the 1800s, MoSex explores its subject within a cultural context. Highlights of the permanent collection of more than 15,000 objects range from the tastefully erotic to the outlandish: an 1890s anti-onanism device looks as uncomfortable as the BDSM gear donated by a local dominatrix, and there is kinky art courtesy of Picasso and Keith Haring. Rotating exhibitions in the three-level space include the likes of 'The Sex Lives of Animals'. The gift shop stocks books and arty sex toys, while the museum's bar dispenses aphrodisiac cocktails, stimulating soft drinks and light bites.

ABC Kitchen.

Restaurants & Cafés

★ ABC Kitchen

35 E 18th Street, between Broadway & Park Avenue South (1-212 475 5829, www.abckitchennyc.com). Subway L, N, Q, R, 4, 5, 6 to 14th Street-Union Square. **Open** noon-3pm, 5.30-10.30pm Mon-Wed; noon-3pm, 5.30-11pm Thur; noon-3pm, 5.30-11.30pm Fri; 11am-3.30pm, 5.30-11.30pm Sat; 11am-3.30pm, 5.30-10pm Sun. **Main courses** $15-$39. **Map** p131 B2 ❸ **Eclectic**

The haute green cooking at Jean-Georges Vongerichten's artfully decorated restaurant inside landmark Flatiron furniture store ABC Carpet & Home is based on the most gorgeous ingredients from up and down the East Coast. Local, seasonal bounty finds its way into fresh salads, home-made pastas, whole-wheat pizzas and locally sourced fish. A signature sundae of salted caramel ice-cream, candied peanuts and popcorn with chocolate sauce reworks the kids' treat to thrill a grown-up palate. ABC delivers one message overall: food that's good for the planet needn't be any less opulent, flavourful or stunning to look at.

★ The Breslin Bar & Dining Room

Ace Hotel New York, 16 W 29th Street, at Broadway (1-212 679 1939, www.thebreslin.com). Subway N, R to 28th Street. **Open** 7am-4pm, 5.30pm-midnight daily. **Main courses** $21-$48. **Map** p131 A1 ❹ **Eclectic**

The third project from restaurant savant Ken Friedman and Anglo chef April Bloomfield, the Breslin broke gluttonous new ground. Expect a wait at this no-reservations hotspot – quell your appetite at the bar with an order of scrumpets (fried strips of lamb belly). The overall ethos might well be described as late-period Henry VIII: groaning boards of house-made terrines feature thick slices of guinea hen, rabbit and pork. The pig's foot for two – half a leg, really – could feed the full Tudor court. Desserts include amped-up childhood treats like ice-cream sundaes.

$ The Cannibal

113 E 29th Street, between Park & Lexington Avenues (1-212 686 5480, www.thecannibalnyc.com). Subway 6 to 28th Street. **Open** 11am-11.30pm daily. **Small plates** $11-$18. **Map** p131 B1 ❺ **American creative**

Run by restaurateur Christian Pappanicholas and connected to his Belgian-American eaterie, Resto, the Cannibal is an unusual retail-restaurant hybrid – a beer store and a butcher but also a laid-back place to eat and drink. The meat counter supplies whole beasts for Resto's large-format feasts, but the carnivore's paradise is otherwise autonomous, with its own chef, Preston Clark (formerly of Jean Georges), and beer director, Julian Kurland. The food is best ordered in rounds, pairing beer and bites – wispy shavings of Kentucky ham, pâtés, sausages and tartares – as you sample some of the 450 selections on the drinks list.

Hanjan.

$ The City Bakery

3 W 18th Street, between Fifth & Sixth Avenues (1-212 366 1414, www.thecitybakery.com). Subway L, N, Q, R, 4, 5, 6 to 14th Street-Union Square. **Open** 7.30am-7pm Mon-Fri; 8am-7pm Sat; 9am-6pm Sun. **Salad bar** $14/lb. **Map** p131 A3 ❻ **Café**

Pastry genius Maury Rubin's loft-size City Bakery is jammed with shoppers loading up on creative baked goods such as maple bacon biscuits and unusual salad bar choices (grilled pineapple with ancho chilli, or beansprouts with smoked tofu, for example). There's also a small selection of soups, pizzas and hot dishes. But never mind all that: the thick, incredibly rich hot chocolate with fat house-made marshmallows is justly famed, and the moist 'melted' chocolate-chip cookies are divinely decadent.

Eleven Madison Park

11 Madison Avenue, at E 24th Street (1-212 889 0905, www.elevenmadisonpark.com). Subway N, R, 6 to 23rd Street. **Open** 5.30-10pm Mon-Wed, Sun; noon-1pm, 5.30-10pm Thur-Sat. **Tasting menu** $225. **Map** p131 B2 ❼ **American creative**

Chef Daniel Humm and impresario partner Will Guidara – who bought Eleven Madison Park from their old boss, legendary restaurateur Danny Meyer – are masters of reinvention. And once again, they've hit on a winning formula, this time for a 16-course Gotham-themed meal – marked by stagecraft and tricks – that departs from the city's upper echelons of Old World-dominated fine dining. On a recent meal, a glass cloche rose over a puff of smoke, unveiling smoked sturgeon above smouldering embers. Rib eye, aged an astonishing 140 days, was served with a side of oxtail jam with melted foie gras and whipped potato icing that's as rich as it sounds, and a waiter performed a card trick with a chocolate pay off – a nod to the city's old street-corner shysters.

Hanjan

36 W 26th Street, between Broadway & Sixth Avenue (1-212 206 7226, www.hanjan26.com). Subway N, R to 28th Street. **Open** noon-2.15pm, 5.30pm-1am Mon-Fri; 5.30pm-1am Sat. **Main courses** $10-$24. **Map** p131 A2 ❽ **Korean**

Hanjan is a shining example of a *joomak*, the Korean equivalent of the English gastropub. Expect a barrage of deeply satisfying dishes: glutinous rice cakes licked with spicy pork fat; crispy scallion pancakes studded with local squid; and skewers of fresh chicken thighs that you can swab with funky *ssam-jang*. Each plate packs its own surprises, but the whole feast is tied together by a soulful bass note melding sweetness, spice and just the right amount of fishy funk.

Hill Country

30 W 26th Street, between Broadway & Sixth Avenue (1-212 255 4544, www.hillcountryny.com). Subway N, R to 28th Street. **Open** noon-10pm Mon-Wed, Sun; noon-11pm Thur; noon-midnight Fri, Sat. **Main courses** $12-$30. **Map** p131 A2 ❾ **American barbecue**

The guys behind Hill Country are about as Texan as Donald Trump in a stetson, but the cooking is an authentic, world-class take on the restaurant's namesake region. Dishes feature sausages imported from barbecue stalwart Kreuz Market of Lockhart, Texas, and two options for brisket: go for the 'moist' (read: fatty) version for full flavour. Beef shoulder emerges from the smoker in 20lb slabs, and tips-on pork ribs are hefty, with just enough fat to imbue proper flavour. Desserts, such as jelly-filled cupcakes with peanut butter frosting, live out some kind of *Leave It to Beaver* fantasy, though June Cleaver wouldn't approve of the two dozen tequilas and bourbons on offer.

The John Dory Oyster Bar

Ace Hotel New York, 1196 Broadway, at 29th Street (1-212 792 9000, www.thejohndory.com). Subway N, R to 28th Street. **Open** noon-midnight daily. **Small plates** $11-$29. **Map** p131 A1 ❿ **Seafood**

EXPLORE

April Bloomfield and Ken Friedman's original John Dory in the Meatpacking District was an ambitious, pricey endeavour, but its reincarnation in the Ace Hotel is an understated success. Tall stools face a raw bar stocked with a rotating mix of East and West Coast oysters, all expertly handled and impeccably sourced. True to form, the rest of Bloomfield's tapas-style seafood dishes are intensely flavoured – cold poached lobster with tomalley vinaigrette, for example, or chorizo-stuffed squid with smoked tomato.

★ The NoMad

1170 Broadway, at 28th Street (1-212 796 1500, www.thenomadhotel.com). Subway N, R to 28th Street. **Open** 5.30-10.30pm Mon-Thur; 5.30-11pm Fri, Sat; 5.30-10pm Sun. **Main courses** $20-$37. **Map** p131 A1 11 **American**

Another restaurant from chef Daniel Humm and front-of-house partner Will Guidara, who are also behind Eleven Madison Park *(see p133)*, the NoMad features plush armchairs around well-spaced tables and a stylish return to three-course dining. The food, like the space, exudes unbuttoned decadence: a slow-cooked egg stars in one over-the-top starter, with mushrooms, black garlic and kale for crunch. And while there are plenty of rich-man roast chickens for two in New York, the amber-hued bird here – with a foie gras, brioche and black truffle stuffing under the skin – is surely the new gold standard, well worth its $79 price tag.

Bars

230 Fifth

230 Fifth Avenue, at 27th Street (1-212 725 4300, www.230-fifth.com). Subway N, R to 28th Street. **Open** 4pm-4am Mon-Fri; 10am-4am Sat, Sun. **Map** p131 A2 12

The 14,000sq ft roof garden atop an anonymous office building dazzles with truly spectacular views, including a close-up of the Empire State Building, but the glitzy indoor lounge – with floor-to-ceiling windows, wraparound sofas and bold lighting – shouldn't be overlooked. While the sprawling outdoor space gets mobbed on sultry nights, it's less crowded during the cooler months when heaters, fleece robes and hot ciders turn it into a winter hotspot.

Milk & Honey.

Milk & Honey

30 E 23rd Street, between Madison Avenue & Park Avenue South (no phone, www.mlkhny.com). Subway N, R, 6 to 23rd Street. **Open** 6.15pm-3am daily. **Map** p131 B2 13

In 2000, Sasha Petraske recast the mould for the Gotham cocktail bar with Milk & Honey, the reservations-only temple of mixology guarded by a secret phone number. More than a decade and countless imitations later, he shocked the booze cognoscenti by his moving his legendary bar to the Flatiron neighbourhood. Ditching the reservations-only policy, the relocated, expanded and now democratic drinkery now operates on a first come, first served basis, but cocktail menus are still absent. Ask for one of the bar's contemporary classics like the ginger-and-Scotch Penicillin.

Old Town Bar & Grill

45 E 18th Street, between Broadway & Park Avenue South (1-212 529 6732, www.oldtownbar.com). Subway L, N, Q, R, W, 4, 5, 6 to 14th Street-Union Square. **Open** 11.30am-11.30pm Mon-Fri; 10am-11.30pm Sat; 11am-10pm Sun. **Map** p131 B3 14

Amid the swank food and drink sanctums sprouting around Park Avenue South, this classic tavern remains a shrine to unchanging values. Belly up to the bar and drain a few pints alongside the regulars who gather on stools 'south of the pumps' (their lingo for taps). If you work up an appetite, skip the much-praised burger in favour of the chilli dog: a grilled and scored all-beef Sabrett with spicy homemade beef-and-red-kidney-bean chilli.

★ Raines Law Room

48 W 17th Street, between Fifth & Sixth Avenues (no phone, www.raineslawroom.com). Subway F, M to 14th Street; L to Sixth Avenue. **Open** 5pm-2am Mon-Thur; 5pm-3am Fri, Sat; 8pm-1am Sun. **Map** p131 A3 15

There's no bar to belly up to at this louche lounge. In deference to its name (which refers to an 1896 law that was designed to curb liquor consumption), drinks are prepared in a half-hidden back room known as 'the kitchen'. While this reduces the noise level in the plush, upholstered space, it also robs you of the opportunity to watch the bar staff at work. The cocktail list includes classics, and variations thereof.

GO FIGURE

Mathematics + high-tech interactive exhibits = fun.

NYC has museums dedicated to everything from tenement housing to copulation. So it's no surprise that the least-favourite subject of sixth-graders everywhere finally landed its very own tribute – the country's first Museum of Mathematics (*see p131*). MoMath replaces lectures and textbooks with more than 30 eclectic exhibits covering topics such as algebra and geometry.

Designed for visitors of all ages, the museum aims to eliminate the intimidation factor and 'show how everyone can experience and enjoy mathematical exploration at their own level', according to hedge-funder-turned-co-executive director Glen Whitney.

There's plenty to intrigue and amaze. Think a ride on a square-wheeled trike could never be smooth? Find out just how bump-free it can be when you take said tricycle over a sunflower-shaped track, where the petals create strategically placed catenaries – curves used in geometry and physics – that make a level ride possible. Elsewhere, you can pass 3-D objects (or even your own body) through the laser-light 'Wall of Fire', and the lasers will display the objects as two-dimensional cross-sections (a cone becomes a triangle and circle, for instance). Or collaborate with a pair of fellow visitors to pan, zoom and rotate your own video cameras to create a single composite image, which can be manipulated into a bevy of interesting 'Feedback Fractals' (or fragmented shapes). If you like what you see on the live projection screen, click the snapshot button to save the image to your profile so that you can print a copy before you leave.

MoMath uses state-of-the-art technology to personalise visits: patrons' ticket stubs are wirelessly tracked, and exhibits adapt based on user preferences from the first few electronic displays. For example, if you opt for more in-depth explanations, in Spanish, later displays will default to those settings.

JJ Hat Center.

EXPLORE

Rye House
11 W 17th Street, between Fifth & Sixth Avenues (1-212 255 7260, www.ryehousenyc.com). Subway F, M to 14th Street; L to Sixth Avenue. **Open** noon-11pm Mon-Thur; noon-midnight Fri; 11am-midnight Sat; 11am-11pm Sun. **Map** p131 A3 ⑯
As the name suggests, American spirits are the emphasis at this dark, sultry bar. As well as bourbons and ryes, there are gins, vodkas and rums, most distilled in the States. Check out the jalapeño-infused Wake-up Call, one of the venue's most popular bourbon cocktails. While the focus is clearly on drinking, there's excellent upscale pub grub, such as truffle grilled cheese or potato pierogies.

Shops & Services

★ ABC Carpet & Home
888 Broadway, at 19th Street (1-212 473 3000, www.abchome.com). Subway L, N, Q, R, 4, 5, 6 to 14th Street-Union Square. **Open** 10am-7pm Mon-Wed, Fri, Sat; 10am-8pm Thur; 11am-6.30pm Sun. **Map** p131 B2 ⑰ **Homewares**
Most of ABC's 35,000-strong carpet range is housed in the store across the street at no.881 – except the rarest rugs, which reside on the sixth floor of the main store. Browse everything from organic soap to hand-beaded lampshades on the bazaar-style ground floor. On the upper floors, furniture spans every style, from slick European minimalism to antique oriental and mid-century modern. The Bronx warehouse outlet has discounted furnishings, but prices are still steep.
Other locations ABC Carpet & Home Outlet, 1055 Bronx River Avenue, between Bruckner Boulevard & Westchester Avenue, Bronx (1-718 842 8772).

Books of Wonder
18 W 18th Street, between Fifth & Sixth Avenues, Flatiron District (1-212 989 3270, www.booksofwonder.com). Subway F, M to 14th Street; L to Sixth Avenue; 1 to 18th Street. **Open** 10am-7pm Mon-Sat; 11am-6pm Sun. **Map** p131 A3 ⑱ **Books & music**
The only independent children's bookstore in the city features titles new and old (rare and out-of-print editions), plus a special collection of Oz books. The store also always has a good stock of signed books and children's book art, and the on-site bakery makes a visit even more of a treat.

Eataly
200 Fifth Avenue, between 23rd & 24th Streets (1-212 229 2560, www.eataly.com). Subway F, M, N, R to 23rd Street. **Open** 10am-11pm daily. **Map** p131 A2 ⑲ **Food & drink**
This massive foodie destination from Mario Batali and Joe and Lidia Bastianich sprawls across 50,000sq ft. A spin-off of an operation by the same name just outside of Turin, the complex encompasses six restaurants and a rooftop beer garden. Adjacent retail areas offer gourmet provisions, including artisanal breads baked on the premises, fresh mozzarella, salumi and a vast array of olive oils.

Fishs Eddy
889 Broadway, at 19th Street (1-212 420 9020, www.fishseddy.com). Subway N, R to 23rd Street. **Open** 10am-9pm Mon; 9am-9pm Tue-Sat; 10am-8pm Sun. **Map** p131 A2 ⑳ **Homewares**
Penny-pinchers frequent this barn-like space for sturdy dishware and glasses – surplus stock or recycled from restaurants, ocean liners and hotels (plain

white side plates are a mere 99¢). But there are plenty of affordable, freshly minted kitchen goods too. Add spice to mealtime with glasses adorned with male or female pole-dancers, plates printed with the Brooklyn or Manhattan skyline and Floor Plan dinnerware – from $10 for a 'studio' side plate, NYC real estate has never been so cheap!

Idlewild Books

12 W 19th Street, between Fifth & Sixth Avenues (1-212 414 8888, www.idlewildbooks.com). Subway F, M to 14th Street; L to Sixth Avenue. **Open** noon-7.30pm Mon-Thur; noon-6pm Fri, Sat; noon-5pm Sun. **Map** p131 A2 ㉑ **Books & music**

Idlewild stocks travel guides to more than 100 countries and all 50 US states, which are grouped with related works of fiction and non-fiction. The shop also has a large selection of works in French, Spanish and Italian and offers an ongoing series of foreign language classes.

Other locations 249 Warren Street, between Court & Smith Streets, Cobble Hill, Brooklyn (1-718 403 9600).

★ JJ Hat Center

310 Fifth Avenue, between 31st & 32nd Streets (1-212 239 4368, www.porkpiehatters.com). Subway B, D, F, M, N, Q, R to 34th Street-Herald Square. **Open** *Jan-Sept* 9am-6pm Mon-Fri; 9.30am-5.30pm Sat. *Oct-Dec* 9am-6pm Mon-Fri; 9.30am-5.30pm Sat; noon-5pm Sun. **Map** p131 A1 ㉒ **Accessories**

Trad hats may be back in fashion, but this venerable shop, in business since 1911, is oblivious to passing trends. Dapper gents sporting the shop's wares will help you choose from more than 4,000 fedoras, pork pies, caps and other styles on display in the splendid, chandelier-illuminated, wood-panelled showroom. Prices start at $35 for a wool-blend cap. In 2011, the store opened the first of its two satellite stores, which operate under the name Pork Pie Hatters.

IN THE KNOW
MYSTERIES OF THE METRONOME

It's not uncommon to see passers-by perplexed by the **Metronome**, a massive sculptural installation attached to 1 Union Square South that bellows steam and generates a barrage of numbers on a digital read-out. Although they appear strange, they're not random numbers – the 15-digit display is actually a clock indicating the time relative to midnight. There's a detailed explanation at the website of Kristin Jones and Andrew Ginzel, the artists responsible; see www.jonesginzel.com.

Other locations 440 East 9th Street, between 1st Avenue & Avenue A, East Village (1-212 260 0408); 441 Metropolitan Avenue, between Marcy & Meeker Avenues, Williamsburg, Brooklyn (1-347 457 6519).

LA Burdick

5 E 20th Street, between Fifth Avenue & Broadway (1-212 796 0143, www.burdickchocolate.com). Subway N, R to 23rd Street. **Open** 8.30am-9pm Mon-Sat; 10am-7pm Sun. **Map** p131 A2 ㉓ **Food & drink**

Best known for its petite chocolate penguins and mice, the family-owned, New Hampshire-based chocolatier now has a shop and café in NYC. Pastries share space in the display cases with marzipan, dipped caramels and a selection of truffles. Ponder the choices over a cup of dark, white or milk hot chocolate, or plump for dealer's choice with the assorted boxes.

Paragon Sporting Goods

867 Broadway, at 18th Street (1-212 255 8889, www.paragonsports.com). Subway L, N, Q, R, 4, 5, 6 to 14th Street-Union Square. **Open** 10am-8.30pm Mon-Fri; 10am-8pm Sat; 11am-7pm Sun. **Map** p131 A3 ㉔ **Sports equipment**

Three floors of equipment and clothing for almost every activity, from the everyday (a slew of gym gear and trainers) to the more niche (badminton, kayaking) make this a prime one-stop sports-gear spot.

Showplace Antique & Design Center

40 W 25th Street, between Fifth & Sixth Avenues (1-212 633 6063, www.nyshowplace.com). Subway F, M to 23rd Street. **Open** 10am-6pm Mon-Fri; 8.30am-5.30pm Sat, Sun. **Map** p131 A2 ㉕ **Fashion/homewares**

Set over four expansive floors, this indoor market houses more than 200 high-quality dealers selling everything from Greek and Roman antiquities to vintage radios. Among the highlights are Joe Sundlie's spot-on-trend vintage pieces from Lanvin and Alaïa, and Mood Indigo – arguably the best source in the city for collectable bar accessories and dinnerware. The array of Bakelite jewellery and table accessories, Fiestaware and novelty cocktail glasses is dazzling, and it's a wonderful repository of art deco cigarette cases, lighters and New York memorabilia.

Union Square Greenmarket

From 16th to 17th Streets, between Union Square East & Union Square West (1-212 788 7476, www.grownyc.org/greenmarket). Subway L, N, Q, R, 4, 5, 6 to 14th Street-Union Square. **Open** 8am-6pm Mon, Wed, Fri, Sat. **Map** p131 B3 ㉖ **Market**

Shop elbow-to-elbow with top chefs for locally grown produce, handmade breads and baked goods, preserves and cheeses at the city's flagship farmers' market around the periphery of Union Square Park. Between Thanksgiving and Christmas, a holiday market sets up shop. *Photo p138.*

GRAMERCY PARK

Subway L to Third Avenue; L, N, Q, R, 4, 5, 6 to 14th Street-Union Square; N, R, 6 to 23rd Street.

A key to **Gramercy Park**, the tranquil, gated square at the bottom of Lexington Avenue, between 20th and 21st Streets, is one of the most sought-after treasures in all the five boroughs. For the most part, only residents of the beautiful surrounding townhouses and apartment buildings have access to the park, which was developed in the 1830s to resemble a London square. The park is flanked by two private clubs; members of both also have access to the square. One is the **Players Club** (16 Gramercy Park South, between Park Avenue South & Irving Place, 1-212 475 6116, www.theplayersnyc.org), inspired by London's Garrick Club. It's housed in an 1847 brownstone formerly owned by Edwin Booth, the celebrated 19th-century actor and brother of John Wilkes Booth, Abraham Lincoln's assassin. Next door at no.15 is the Victorian Gothic Revival Samuel J. Tilden House, which houses the **National Arts Club** (1-212 475 3424, www.nationalartsclub.org, closed Sat, Sun & July, Aug). The busts of famous writers (Shakespeare, Dante) along the façade were chosen to reflect Tilden's library, which, along with his fortune, helped to create the New York Public Library. The NAC's galleries are open to non-members, but call before visiting as they may close for private events or between shows.

Leading south from the park to 14th Street, Irving Place is named after author Washington Irving (although he never actually lived here). Near the corner of 15th Street sits **Irving Plaza** (*see p274*), a music venue. At the corner of Park Avenue South and 17th Street is the final base of the once-omnipotent Tammany Hall political machine. Built in 1929, it now houses the New York Film Academy. Popular local hangout **71 Irving Place Coffee & Tea Bar** (*see p141* is a good place to revive oneself with a cup of New York State-roasted java. A few blocks away from here is the **Theodore Roosevelt Birthplace** (*see below*), a national historic site.

The largely residential area bordered by 23rd and 30th Streets, Park Avenue and the East River is known as **Kips Bay** after Jacobus Kip, whose farm covered the area in the 17th century. Third Avenue is the district's main thoroughfare, and a locus of restaurants representing a variety of eastern cuisines, including Afghan, Tibetan and Turkish.

Sights & Museums

FREE Theodore Roosevelt Birthplace National Historic Site

28 E 20th Street, between Broadway & Park Avenue South (1-212 260 1616, www.nps.gov/thrb). Subway 6 to 23rd Street. **Tours** hourly 10am-4pm Tue-Sat, except noon. **Admission** free. **Map** p131 B2 ㉗

The brownstone where the 26th President of the United States was born, and where he lived until he was 14 years old, was demolished in 1916. But it was re-created after his death in 1919, complete with authentic period furniture (some from the original house), personal effects and a trophy room. The house can only be explored by guided tour.

Union Square Greenmarket. *See p137.*

EXPLORE

Gramercy Park.

Restaurants & cafés

$ 71 Irving Place Coffee & Tea Bar

71 Irving Place, between 18th & 19th Streets (1-212 995 5252, www.irvingfarm.com). Subway L, N, Q, R, 4, 5, 6 to 14th Street-Union Square. **Open** 7am-10pm Mon-Fri; 8am-10pm Sat. **Sandwiches** $10-$11. **Map** p131 B2 ㉘ **Café**

Irving Farm's beans are roasted in a 100-year-old carriage house in the Hudson Valley; fittingly, its Gramercy Park café, which occupies the ground floor of a stately brownstone, also has a rustic edge. Breakfast (granola, oatmeal, croissants, bagels), sandwiches and salads accompany the excellent java.

Other locations 88 Orchard Street, at Broome Street, Lower East Side (1-212 228 8880); 89 E 42nd Street, Grand Central Terminal, Midtown (1-212 983 4242); 224 W 79th Street, between Amsterdam Avenue & Broadway, Upper West Side (1-212 874 7979).

Casa Mono

52 Irving Place, at 17th Street (1-212 253 2773, www.casamononyc.com). Subway L to Third Avenue; N, Q, R, 4, 5, 6 to 14th Street-Union Square. **Open** noon-midnight daily. **Small plates** $9-$25. **Map** p131 B3 ㉙ **Spanish**

Offal-loving chef-partners Mario Batali and Andy Nusser broke new ground in NYC with their adventurous Spanish fare: crispy pigs' ears, fried sweetbreads with fennel, foie gras with *cinco cebollas* (five types of onion), or fried duck egg with black truffles. For a cheaper option, the attached Bar Jamón (125 E 17th Street; open 5pm-2am Mon-Fri; noon-2am Sat, Sun) offers tapas, Ibérico hams and Spanish cheeses.

Maialino

Gramercy Park Hotel, 2 Lexington Avenue, between E 21st & E 22nd Streets (1-212 777 2410, www.maialinonyc.com). Subway 6 to 23rd Street. **Open** 7.30-10am, noon-2pm, 5.30-10.30pm Mon-Thur; 7.30-10am, noon-2pm, 5.30-11pm Fri; 10am-2.30pm, 5.30-11pm Sat; 10am-2.30pm, 5.30-10.30pm Sun. **Main courses** $23-$72. **Map** p131 B2 ㉚ **Italian**

Danny Meyer's first full-fledged foray into Italian cuisine is a dedicated homage to the neighbourhood trattorias that kept him well fed as a 20-year-old tour guide in Rome. Salumi and bakery stations between the front bar and the wood-beamed dining room – hog jowls and sausages dangling near shelves stacked with crusty loaves of bread – mimic a market off the Appian Way. Executive chef Nick Anderer's menu offers exceptional facsimiles of dishes specific to Rome, such as carbonara, braised tripe and suckling pig.

Pure Food & Wine

54 Irving Place, between 17th & 18th Streets (1-212 477 1010, www.purefoodandwine.com). Subway L, N, Q, R, 4, 5, 6 to 14th Street-Union Square. **Open** noon-4pm, 5.30-11pm daily. **Main courses** $22-$26. **Map** p131 B3 ㉛ **Vegetarian**

The dishes delivered to your table – whether out on the leafy patio or inside the ambient dining room – are minor miracles, not only because they look gorgeous and taste terrific, but also because they come from a kitchen that lacks a stove. Everything at Pure is raw and vegan, including the lasagna (with creamy macadamia nut and pumpkin seed 'ricotta'). Wines, most of which are organic, are top-notch, as are the desserts, including a classic vegan ice-cream sundae.

Bars

Pete's Tavern

129 E 18th Street, at Irving Place (1-212 473 7676, www.petestavern.com). Subway L, N, Q, R, W, 4, 5, 6 to 14th Street-Union Square. **Open** 11am-2.30am daily. **Map** p131 B3 ㉜

According to history buffs, in 1904, O Henry wrote his sentimental short story 'The Gift of the Magi' in what was then a quiet Gramercy pub. Today it's three deep at the bar, and O Henry would have a hard time parking it anywhere. Though Pete's – a Civil War-era survivor – draws its share of tourists, you'll also rub shoulders with neighbourhood types who slide into the wooden booths to snack on affordable Italian eats with standard suds (16 beers on tap include a hoppy house ale) bubbling in frosty mugs.

Midtown

Soaring office towers, crowded pavements and taxi-choked streets – that's the image most people have of the busy midsection of Manhattan. This part of town draws visitors to some of the city's best-known landmarks, including iconic skyscrapers like the Empire State Building and the Chrysler Building, the dazzling electronic spectacle that is Times Square and the Rockefeller Center, with its picturesque seasonal ice-skating rink. Fifth Avenue, the dividing line between Midtown West and Midtown East, is continuously clogged with shoppers from all over the world. But there's more to midtown than iconic architecture and commerce. On the far west side, the northern extension of the High Line is attracting galleries and shops, and rapidly gentrifying Hell's Kitchen has emerged as the city's hottest gaybourhood.

Rockefeller Center.

Don't Miss

1 Times Square The bright lights still razzle-dazzle (*p144*).

2 Empire State Building The world's most iconic skyscraper (*p151*).

3 Museum of Modern Art (MoMA) Art primer from the 19th century to the present (*p152*).

4 Don Antonio by Starita Pedigree pizza a throw from Broadway (*p148*).

5 Dover Street Market The classy, kooky Comme concept store is an essential browse (*p158*).

2013
TDK
YOUR BREAKFAST BFF
DUNKIN' DONUTS
LIME-A-RITA
SONY
The Art of the Brick
Discovery
ENTRANCE AROUND THE CORNER ON 44T
Hankook
driving emotion
FOX UFC SATURDAY
JOHNSON
MORAGA
McDONALD
ELLENBERGER
LAWLER
BAHADURZADA
CARMOUCHE
ANDRADE
SAT. JULY 27
LIVE ON FOX
WE'RE THE MILLERS
AUGUST 7TH
Kodak
Bank of Am
MARQUIS

HERALD SQUARE & THE GARMENT DISTRICT

Subway A, C, E, 1, 2, 3 to 34th Street-Penn Station; B, D, F, M, N, Q, R to 34th Street-Herald Square.

Seventh Avenue, aka Fashion Avenue, is the main drag of the **Garment District** (roughly from 34th to 40th Streets, between Broadway & Eighth Avenue) and where designers – and their seamstresses, fitters and assistants – feed America's multi-billion-dollar clothing industry. Delivery trucks and workers pushing racks of clothes clog streets lined with wholesale trimming, button and fabric shops. Many showrooms hold sample sales (*see p159* **In the Know**).

Taking up an entire city block, from 34th Street to 35th Street, between Broadway and Seventh Avenue, is the legendary **Macy's** (*see p144*). With one million square feet of selling space spread across nine floors, it's the biggest and busiest department store in the world. Facing Macy's, at the intersection of Broadway, 34th Street and Sixth Avenue, is **Herald Square**, named after a long-gone newspaper, the *New York Herald*. The lower section is known as **Greeley Square** after editor and reformer Horace Greeley, owner of the *Herald*'s rival, the *New York Tribune* (the two papers merged in 1924). Once seedy, the square now offers bistro chairs and tables that get crowded with shoppers and office lunchers in the warmer months. To the east, the many spas, restaurants and karaoke bars of small enclave **Koreatown** line 32nd Street, between Broadway and Fifth Avenue.

Located not in Madison Square but on Seventh Avenue, between 31st and 33rd Streets, **Madison Square Garden** (*see p271*) is home for the Knicks and Rangers, and has welcomed rock icons from Elvis to Lady Gaga as well as the Barnum & Bailey Circus and other big events. The massive arena is actually the fourth building to bear that name (the first two were appropriately located in the square after which they were named) and opened in 1968, replacing the grand old Pennsylvania Station razed four years earlier. This brutal act of architectural vandalism spurred the creation of the city's Landmarks Preservation Commission, which has saved many other edifices from a similar fate.

Beneath Madison Square Garden stands **Penn Station**, a claustrophobic catacomb serving 600,000 Amtrak, Long Island Rail Road and New Jersey Transit passengers daily and the busiest train station in America. A proposal to relocate the station across the street to the stately **James A Farley Post Office** (421 Eighth Avenue, between 31st & 33rd Streets) was championed by the late Senator Patrick Moynihan in the early 1990s. The project, which has stalled over the years, finally got the necessary funding and government approval, and Moynihan Station is expected to be completed in 2016.

EXPLORE

Restaurants & Cafés

Keens Steakhouse

72 W 36th Street, at Sixth Avenue (1-212 947 3636, www.keens.com). Subway B, D, F, M, N, Q, R to 34th Street-Herald Square. **Open** 11.45am-10.30pm Mon-Fri; 5-10.30pm Sat; 5-9.30pm Sun. **Main courses** $26-$58. **Map** p143 D4 ❶ **Steakhouse**

The ceiling and walls are hung with pipes, some from such long-ago Keens regulars as Babe Ruth, JP Morgan and Teddy Roosevelt. Even in these non-smoking days, you can catch a whiff of the restaurant's 125-plus years of history. Bevelled-glass doors, two working fireplaces and a forest's worth of dark wood suggest a time when 'Diamond Jim' Brady piled his table with bushels of oysters, slabs of seared beef and troughs of ale. The menu still lists a three-inch-thick mutton chop and the porterhouse (for two or three) holds its own against any steak in the city.

$ Mandoo Bar

2 W 32nd Street, between Fifth Avenue & Broadway (1-212 279 3075, www.mandoobarnyc.com). Subway B, D, F, M, N, Q, R to 34th Street-Herald Square. **Open** 11.30am-10pm daily. **Main courses** $12-$20. **Map** p143 D4 ❷ **Korean**

If the staff members filling and crimping dough squares in the front window don't give it away, we will – this wood-wrapped industrial-style spot elevates *mandoo* (Korean dumplings) above mere appetiser status. Six varieties of the tasty morsels are filled with such delights as subtly piquant kimchi, juicy pork, succulent shrimp and vegetables. Try them miniaturised, as in the Baby Mandoo, swimming in a soothing beef broth or atop soupy ramen noodles.

Shops & Services

B&H

420 Ninth Avenue, at 34th Street (1-212 444 6615, www.bhphotovideo.com). Subway A, C, E to 34th Street-Penn Station. **Open** 9am-7pm Mon-Thur; 9am-1pm Fri; 10am-6pm Sun. **Map** p143 D2 ❸ **Electronics & photography**

The ultimate one-stop shop for all your photographic, video and audio needs. In this huge store, goods are transported from the stock room via an overhead conveyor belt. Due to the largely Hasidic Jewish staff, the store is closed on Saturdays and Jewish holidays.

Juvenex

5th Floor, 25 W 32nd Street, between Fifth Avenue & Broadway (1-646 733 1330, www.juvenexspa.com). Subway B, D, F, M, N, Q, R to 34th Street-Herald Square. **Open** 24hrs daily. **Map** p143 D3 ❹ **Health & beauty**

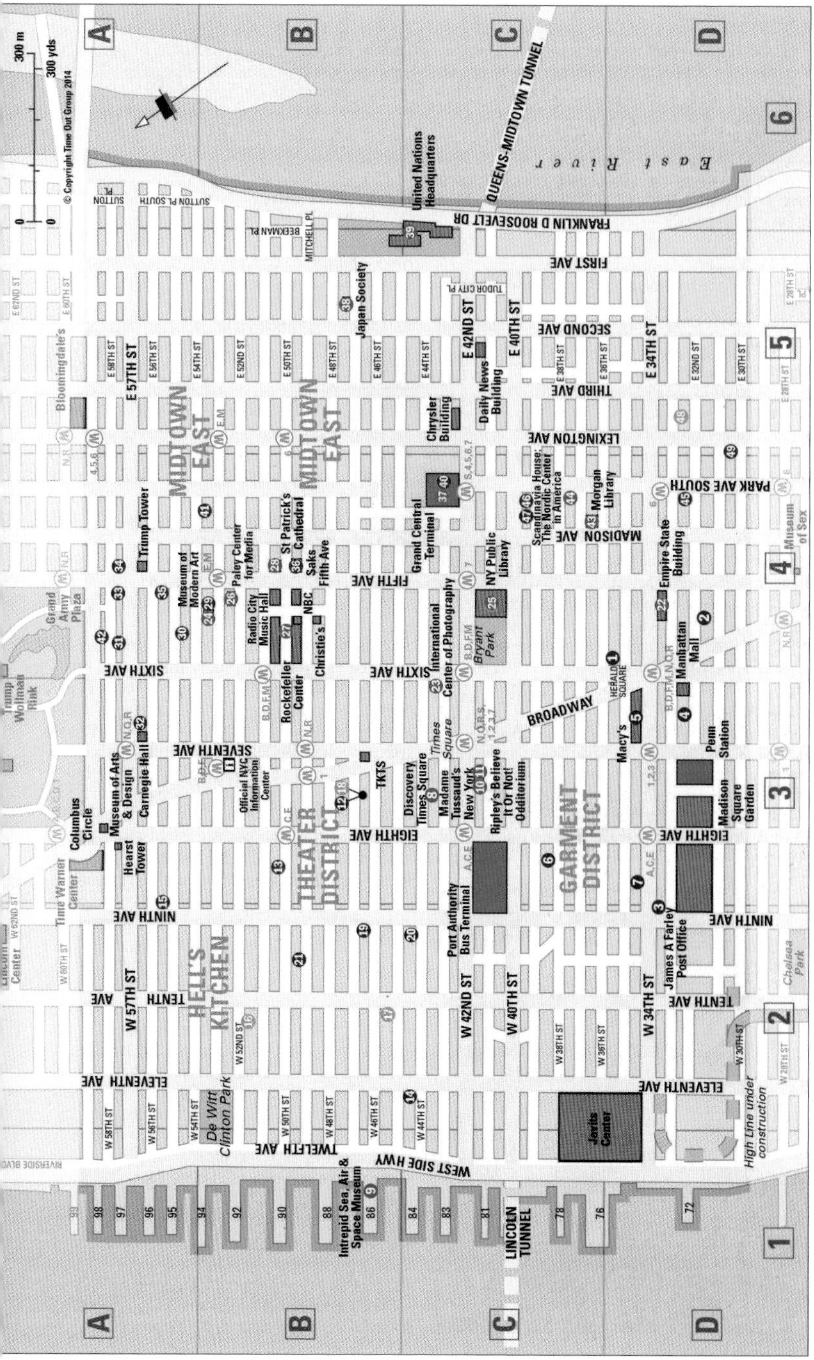

A
B
C
D
1
2
3
4
5
6
300 m
300 yds
© Copyright Time Out Group 2014
East River
QUEENS-MIDTOWN TUNNEL
LINCOLN TUNNEL
FRANKLIN D ROOSEVELT DR
WEST SIDE HWY
United Nations Headquarters
Japan Society
Chrysler Building
Daily News Building
Grand Central Terminal
Trump Tower
Museum of Modern Art
Paley Center for Media
St Patrick's Cathedral
Saks Fifth Ave
Radio City Music Hall
NBC
Christie's
Rockefeller Center
International Center of Photography
NY Public Library
Bryant Park
Scandinavia House: The Nordic Center in America
Morgan Library
Empire State Building
Manhattan Mall
Museum of Sex
Herald Square
Macy's
Penn Station
Madison Square Garden
James A Farley Post Office
Javits Center
Port Authority Bus Terminal
Ripley's Believe It Or Not! Odditorium
Madame Tussaud's New York
Discovery Times Square
Times Square
TKTS
Official NYC Information Center
Carnegie Hall
Museum of Arts & Design
Columbus Circle
Hearst Tower
Time Warner Center
Lincoln Center
Trump Wollman Rink
Grand Army Plaza
Bloomingdale's
Intrepid Sea, Air & Space Museum
De Witt Clinton Park
Chelsea Park
High Line under construction
MIDTOWN EAST
THEATER DISTRICT
GARMENT DISTRICT
HELL'S KITCHEN
FIRST AVE
SECOND AVE
THIRD AVE
LEXINGTON AVE
PARK AVE SOUTH
MADISON AVE
FIFTH AVE
SIXTH AVE
SEVENTH AVE
BROADWAY
EIGHTH AVE
NINTH AVE
TENTH AVE
ELEVENTH AVE
TWELFTH AVE
E 57TH ST
E 42ND ST
E 40TH ST
E 34TH ST
W 57TH ST
W 42ND ST
W 40TH ST
W 34TH ST
SUTTON PL
SUTTON PL SOUTH
BEEKMAN PL
MITCHELL PL
TUDOR CITY PL
RIVERSIDE BLVD

This bustling Koreatown relaxation hub may be slightly rough around the edges (frayed towels, dingy sandals), but we embrace it for its bathhouse-meets-Epcot feel (igloo saunas, tiled 'soaking ponds' and a slatted bridge), and 24-hour availability (it's women only between 7am and 5pm). A basic Purification Program – including soak and sauna, face, body and hair cleansing and a salt scrub – is great value at $115.

Macy's

151 W 34th Street, between Broadway & Seventh Avenue (1-212 695 4400, www.macys.com). Subway B, D, F, M, N, Q, R to 34th Street-Herald Square; 1, 2, 3 to 34th Street-Penn Station. **Open** 9am-9.30pm Mon-Sat; 11am-8.30pm Sun. **Map** p143 D3 ❺ **Department store**

It may not be as glamorous as New York's other famous stores but for sheer breadth of stock, the 34th Street behemoth is hard to beat. Mid-price fashion for all ages, big beauty names and housewares have traditionally been the store's bread and butter, but a $400 million redesign, wrapping up in late 2015, has introduced new luxury boutiques including Gucci and Burberry. The cosmetics department has been luxed-up with high-end brands such as Jo Malone London and Laura Mercier, plus a Blow hair-styling bar. Among the eateries is a contemporary trattoria.

▶ *If you need tourist guidance, stop by the store's Official NYC Information Center.*

Nepenthes New York

307 W 38th Street, between Eighth & Ninth Avenues (1-212 643 9540, www.nepenthesny.com). Subway A, C, E, 1, 2, 3 to 34th Street-Penn Station. **Open** noon-7pm Mon-Sat; noon-5pm Sun. **Map** p143 C3 ❻ **Fashion**

Well-dressed dudes with an eye on the Japanese style scene will already be familiar with this Tokyo fashion retailer. The narrow Garment District shop – its first US location – showcases expertly crafted urban-rustic menswear from house label Engineered Garments, such as plaid flannel shirts and work-wear-inspired jackets. There is also a small selection of its women's line, FWK.

Macy's.

Sam Ash Music

333 W 34th Street, between Eighth & Ninth Avenues (1-212 719 2299, www.samashmusic.com). Subway A, C, E to 34th Street-Penn Station. **Open** 10am-8pm Mon-Sat; 11am-7pm Sun. **Map** p143 D3 ❼ **Books & music**

Established in Brooklyn in 1924, this musical instrument emporium moved from Times Square's now-silent 'music row' in 2013. The 30,000sq ft store offers new, vintage and custom guitars of all varieties, along with amps, DJ equipment, drums, keyboards, recording equipment, turntables and an array of sheet music. **Other location** 113-25 Queens Boulevard, at 76th Road, Forest Hills, Queens (1-718 793 7983).

THE THEATER DISTRICT & HELL'S KITCHEN

Subway A, C, E to 42nd Street-Port Authority; N, Q, R, S, 1, 2, 3, 7 to 42nd Street-Times Square.

Times Square's evolution from a traffic-choked fleshpot to a tourist-friendly theme park has accelerated in the past few years. Not only has 'the Crossroads of the World' gained an elevated viewing platform atop the TKTS discount booth, from which visitors can admire the surrounding light show (*see p145* **Insider's Guide**), but also stretches of Broadway, from 47th to 42nd Streets and from 35th to 33rd Streets, have been designated pedestrian zones, complete with seating, in an effort to streamline midtown traffic and create a more pleasant environment for both residents and visitors. Permanent plazas, designed by National September 11 Museum architects Snøhetta, are being developed in the 'Bowtie' from 42nd to 47th Streets, featuring continuous paved areas and granite benches. The first section should be completed by publication of this guide and the remainder by 2015.

Originally Longacre Square, the junction of Broadway and Seventh Avenue, stretching from 42nd to 47th Streets, was renamed after the *New York Times* moved here in the early 1900s. The first electrified billboard graced the district in 1904, on the side of a bank at 46th and Broadway. The same year, the inaugural New Year's Eve party in Times Square doubled as the *Times*'s housewarming party in its new HQ. Today, about a million people gather here to watch a glittery mirrorball descend every 31 December.

The paper left the building only a decade after it had arrived (it now occupies an

INSIDER'S GUIDE TO TIMES SQUARE

Five local-approved things to do pre- or post-show.

TKTS booth staircase, Duffy Square.

1. RISE ABOVE IT ALL AND ADMIRE THE VIEW

Times Square may have lost most of its grit, but the spectacle is still exhilarating. While scoring cheap tickets to a show, ascend the TKTS ticket booth's red glass structural steps in Duffy Square (Broadway, at 47th Street; *see p144*) for an eye-popping panorama of the Great White Way. The glowing staircase was the brainchild of Australians John Choi and Tai Ropiha, who won a globe-spanning competition for a new design in 1999; it debuted in 2008.

2. STOP AND LISTEN

Steal a moment of relative quiet amid the clamour of this bustling intersection and experience sound in the name of art. Rising from a metal subway grate on Broadway, between 45th and 46th Streets, a 1977 sound installation by Max Neuhaus titled *Times Square* often competes with – but also depends upon – its environment. The surrounding architecture and a series of underground spaces amplify the piece, which evokes ringing church bells.

3. GET A TASTE OF OLD TIMES SQUARE

'Up until a few years ago, it was a very rough bar: the folks there were five to ten dollars away from being homeless, and the women looked like Tom Waits.' That's how Rich Brooks sums up **Smith's Bar & Restaurant** (701 Eighth Avenue, at 44th Street, 1-212 246 3268, www.smithsbar.com). Yet the comedian counts it among his favourite local spots. From the vintage neon sign to the 50-foot mahogany bar, the dive invokes pre-Disney Times Square, and prices for the standard pub grub (burgers, nachos, fish and chips) are mostly under $15.

4. CAMP IT UP WITH CABARET QUEENS

What good is singing alone in your room when you can sing along with showtunes at **Don't Tell Mama** (343 W 46th Street, between Eighth & Ninth Avenues, 1-212 757 0788, www.donttellmamanyc.com)? The line-up may include pop, jazz and musical-theatre singers, as well as comedians and drag artists. Performers often congregate in the no-cover (two-drink minimum) piano bar before and after their numbers.

5. SATISFY LATE-NIGHT CRAVINGS

The Bromberg brothers, the team behind the Blue Ribbon eateries (www.blueribbon restaurants.com), which built a reputation as after-hours hubs for restaurant workers, supply the snacks at the surprisingly unhyped **R Lounge** in the Renaissance Hotel (714 Seventh Avenue, at 48th Street, 1-212 261 5200, www.rloungetimessquare.com). Try the signature 'Northern fried' chicken wings ($12) – with a Manhattan, of course – while enjoying a ringside view of Times Square.

$84-million tower on Eighth Avenue, between 40th and 41st Streets). However, it retained ownership of its old headquarters until the 1960s, and erected the world's first scrolling electric news 'zipper' in 1928. The readout, now sponsored by Dow Jones, still trumpets the latest breaking stories.

Times Square is also the gateway to the **Theater District**, the zone between 41st Street and 53rd Street, from Sixth Avenue to Ninth Avenue, where extravagant shows are put on six days a week (Monday is the traditional night off). While numerous showhouses stage first-rate productions in the area, only 39 are officially Broadway theatres. The distinction is based on size rather than location or quality – Broadway theatres must have more than 500 seats.

The Theater District's transformation from the cradle of New York's sex industry began in 1984, when the city condemned properties along 42nd Street ('Forty Deuce', or 'the Deuce' for short), between Seventh and Eighth Avenues. A change in zoning laws meant adult-oriented venues must now subsist on X-rated videos rather than live 'dance' shows; the square's sex trade is now relegated to short stretches of Seventh and Eighth Avenues, just north and south of 42nd Street.

The streets to the west of Eighth Avenue are filled with eateries catering to theatregoers, especially the predominantly pricey, tourist-oriented places along **Restaurant Row** (46th Street, between Eighth and Ninth Avenues). Locals tend to walk west to Ninth Avenue – in the 40s and 50s, the Hell's Kitchen strip is tightly packed with inexpensive restaurants serving a variety of ethnic cuisines.

Recording studios, record labels, theatrical agencies and other entertainment and media companies reside in the area's office buildings. The **Brill Building** (1619 Broadway, at 49th Street) was once a hive of music publishers and producers; such luminaries as Jerry Lieber, Mike Stoller and Carole King wrote and auditioned their hits here.

Flashy attractions and huge retail stores strive to outdo one another in hopes of snaring the tourist throngs. The vast **Toys 'R' Us** (1514 Broadway, at 44th Street, 1-646 366 8800) boasts a 60-foot indoor Ferris wheel and a two-floor Barbie emporium.

West of the Theater District lies **Hell's Kitchen**. The precise origins of the name are unclear, but are no doubt connected to its emergence as an Irish-mob-dominated neighbourhood in the 19th-century – *The New York Times* claims that the first known documented reference was in that very paper in 1881, to describe an unsavoury tenement in the locale. In the 1950s, clashes between Irish and recently arrived Puerto Rican factions were dramatised in the musical *West Side Story*. It was a particularly violent incident in 1959, in which two teenagers died, that led to an attempt by local businesses to erase the stigma associated with the area by renaming it Clinton (taken from a park named after one-time mayor DeWitt Clinton). The new name never really took, and gang culture survived until the 1980s.

Today, the area has emerged as New York's hottest queer neighbourhood, with numerous bars and the city's first gay-oriented luxury hotel, **The Out NYC** (*see p257*). As gentrification takes hold, new apartment blocks are also springing up in the former wasteland near the Hudson River. This area is dominated by the massive, black-glass **Jacob K Javits Convention Center** (Eleventh Avenue, between 34th & 39th Streets), which hosts a never-ending schedule of large-scale trade shows. A couple of major draws are also here: the **Circle Line Terminal**, at Pier 83, the departure point for the cruise company's three-hour circumnavigation of Manhattan Island (*see p374*), and the **Intrepid Sea, Air & Space Museum** (*see below*), a retired aircraft carrier-cum-naval museum.

Sights & Museums

Discovery Times Square

226 W 44th Street, between Seventh & Eighth Avenues (1-866 987 9692, www.discoverytsx.com). Subway A, C, E to 42nd Street-Port Authority; N, Q, R, S, 1, 2, 3, 7 to 42nd Street-Times Square. **Open** 10am-7pm Mon, Tue, Sun; 10am-8pm Wed, Thur; 10am-9pm Fri, Sat. **Admission** $27; $19.50-$23.50 reductions; free under-4s. **Map** p143 C3 ❽

This Discovery Channel-sponsored exhibition centre stages big shows on such crowd-pleasing subjects as King Tut, Pompeii, the *Titanic* and the Harry Potter franchise.

Intrepid Sea, Air & Space Museum

USS Intrepid, Pier 86, Twelfth Avenue & 46th Street (1-212 245 0072, www.intrepidmuseum.org). Subway A, C, E to 42nd Street-Port Authority, then M42 bus to Twelfth Avenue or 15min walk. **Open** *Apr-Oct* 10am-5pm Mon-Fri; 10am-6pm Sat, Sun. *Nov-Mar* 10am-5pm daily. **Admission** $24; $12-$20 reductions; free under-3s, active & retired US military. **Map** p143 B1 ❾

Commissioned in 1943, this 27,000-ton, 898ft aircraft carrier survived torpedoes and kamikaze attacks in World War II, served during the Vietnam War and the Cuban Missile Crisis, and recovered two space capsules for NASA. It was decommissioned in 1974, then resurrected as an educational institution. On its flight deck and portside aircraft elevator are top-notch examples of American military might, including the US

Intrepid Sea, Air & Space Museum. See p147.

Navy F-14 Tomcat (as featured in *Top Gun*), an A-12 Blackbird spy plane and a fully restored Army AH-1G Cobra gunship helicopter. In summer 2011, the museum became home to the Enterprise (OV-101), the prototype NASA Orbiter, which was recently retired (entry to the Space Shuttle Pavilion costs extra).

Madame Tussauds New York

234 W 42nd Street, between Seventh & Eighth Avenues (1-866 841 3505, www.madametussauds.com/newyork). Subway A, C, E to 42nd Street-Port Authority; N, Q, R, S, 1, 2, 3, 7 to 42nd Street-Times Square. **Open** 10am-8pm Mon-Thur, Sun; 10am-10pm Fri, Sat. **Admission** $36; $29 reductions; free under-4s. **Map** p143 C3 ⑩

With roots in 18th-century Paris and founded in London in 1802, the world's most famous wax museum now draws celebrity-hungry crowds to more than a dozen locations worldwide. At the New York outpost, you can get a stalker's-eye view of paraffin doppelgangers of an array of political, sports, film and pop stars, from Barack Obama and Carmelo Anthony to Leonardo DiCaprio and Lady Gaga. A new crop of freshly waxed victims debuts every few months.

Ripley's Believe It or Not!

234 W 42nd Street, between Seventh & Eighth Avenues (1-212 398 3133, www.ripleysnewyork.com). Subway A, C, E to 42nd Street-Port Authority; N, Q, R, S, 1, 2, 3, 7 to 42nd Street-Times Square. **Open** 9am-1am daily (last entry midnight). **Admission** $33; $25 reductions; free under-4s. **Map** p143 C3 ⑪

Times Square might be a little whitewashed these days, but you can get a feel for the old freak show at this repository of the eerie and uncanny. Marvel at such bizarre artefacts as a six-legged cow, the world's largest collection of shrunken heads and a cache of weird art that includes a portrait of President Obama composed of 12,600 gumballs. Carrying a torch for gritty bygone attractions, Ripley's provides a platform for a new generation of sideshow acts with free weekend performances by the likes of Albert Cadabra, the human blockhead, at the entrance (see website for schedule).

Restaurants & Cafés

$ Café Edison

Hotel Edison, 228 W 47th Street, between Broadway & Eighth Avenue (1-212 354 0368). Subway N, Q, R to 49th Street; 1 to 50th Street. **Open** 6am-9.30pm Mon-Sat; 6am-7.30pm Sun. **Main courses** $7-$13. **No credit cards. Map** p143 B3 ⑫ **American**

This old-school no-frills eaterie draws tourists, theatregoers, actors and just about everyone else in search of deli staples such as cheese blintzes and giant Reuben sandwiches. The matzo ball soup is so restorative, you can almost feel it bolstering your immune system.

★ Don Antonio by Starita

309 W 50th Street, between Eighth & Ninth Avenues (1-646 719 1043, www.donantoniopizza.com). Subway C, E to 50th Street. **Open** 11.30am-11pm Mon-Thur; 11.30am-midnight Fri, Sat; 11.30am-10.30pm Sun. **Pizzas** $9-$23. **Map** p143 B3 ⑬ **Italian/Pizza**

Pizza aficionados have been busy colonising this pedigreed recent arrival, a collaboration between Kesté's (*see p115*) talented Roberto Caporuscio and his decorated Naples mentor, Antonio Starita. Start with tasty bites like the *fritattine* (a deep-fried spaghetti cake oozing *prosciutto cotto* and mozzarella sauce). The main event should be the habit-forming Montanara Starita, which gets a quick dip in the deep fryer before hitting the oven to develop its puffy, golden crust. Topped with tomato sauce, basil and intensely smoky buffalo mozzarella, it's a worthy new addition to the pantheon of classic New York pies.

Gotham West Market

600 Eleventh Avenue, between 44th & 45th Streets (1-212 582 7940, www.gothamwest market.com). A, C, E to 42nd Street-Port Authority. **Open** 7am-11pm Mon-Fri; 8am-11pm Sat, Sun. **Map** p143 C2 ⑭ **Eclectic**

In 2013, Hell's Kitchen welcomed this hip take on a food court, perfect for lunch or a quick pre-theatre bite. The 15,000sq ft retail-dining mecca is divided into eight culinary stalls – such as Blue Bottle Coffee and an outpost of gourmet grocer/cooking-supply store Brooklyn Kitchen – as well as a full-service NYC Velo bike shop. Dine-in or take-out options include Ivan Ramen Slurp Shop, where Tokyo noodle guru Ivan Orkin offers his famed *shio*, shoyu and chilli-sesame varieties; Little Chef, the salad-and-soup-focused offshoot of Caroline Fidanza's Saltie sandwich shop; El Colmado tapas bar from Seamus Mullen of Tertulia; and a cocktail-and-charcuterie outpost of the Cannibal (*see p132*). Seating is at chefs' counters or communal tables.

Kashkaval Garden

852 Ninth Avenue, between 55th & 56th Streets (1-212 245 1758, www.kashkavalgarden.com). Subway C, E to 50th Street. **Open** 4pm-2am daily. **Main courses** $12-$17. **Map** p143 A2 ⑮ **Mediterranean**

This charming tapas and wine bar evokes fondue's peasant origins, with deep cast-iron pots and generous baskets of crusty bread. Steer clear of the bland and rubbery kashkaval (a Balkan sheep's-milk cheese) and order the gooey gruyère and truffle. Or choose from the selection of tangy Mediterranean spreads – roasted artichoke dip with breadcrumbs or beet hummus – and the impressive roster of skewers. End the meal with the crowd-pleasing chocolate torte.

Bars

For gay bars in Hell's Kitchen, *see pp261-262*.

★ Ardesia

510 W 52nd Street, between Tenth & Eleventh Avenues (1-212 247 9191, www.ardesia-ny.com). Subway C, E to 50th Street. **Open** 5pm-midnight Mon-Wed; 5pm-2am Thur, Fri; 2pm-2am Sat; 2-11pm Sun. **Map** p143 B2 ⑯

Le Bernardin vet Mandy Oser's iron-and-marble gem offers superior wines in a relaxed setting. The 75-strong collection of international bottles is a smart balance of Old and New World options that pair beautifully with the varied selection of small plates. A grüner veltliner – a dry, oaky white from Austria – had enough backbone to stand up to a duck *banh mi* layered with spicy duck pâté and Sriracha aioli. One for the serious oenophile.

Pony Bar

637 Tenth Avenue, at 45th Street (1-212 586 2707, www.theponybar.com). Subway C, E to 50th Street. **Open** 3pm-4am Mon-Fri; noon-4am Sat, Sun. **Map** p143 B2 ⑰

The Theater District isn't known for civilised, non-chain bars, but you need only walk a couple of blocks west to this convivial paean to American microbrews. Choose from a constantly changing selection of two cask ales and 20 beers on tap; daily selections are artfully listed on signboards according to provenance and potency. Despite the expert curation, the prices are kept low (all beers cost $6).

Other locations 1444 First Avenue, at 75th Street, Upper East Side (1-212 288 0090).

Rum House

228 W 47th Street, between Seventh & Eighth Avenues (1-646 490 6924, www.edisonrum house.com). Subway N, Q, R to 49th Street. **Open** noon-4am daily. **Map** p143 B3 ⑱

In 2009, this rakish, 1970s-vintage piano bar in the Edison Hotel seemed destined to go the way of the Times Square peep show. But the team behind Tribeca mixology den Ward III has ushered in a second act, introducing some key upgrades (including serious cocktails) while maintaining the charmingly offbeat flavour of the place. Sip dark spirit-heavy tipples, such as a funky old-fashioned riff that showcases the rich, tropical complexity of Banks 5 Island Rum, while listening to a pianist or jazz trio most nights of the week.

Shops & Services

Amy's Bread

672 Ninth Avenue, between 46th & 47th Streets (1-212 977 2670, www.amysbread.com). Subway C, E to 50th Street; N, Q, R to 49th Street. **Open** 7.30am-10pm Mon, Tue; 7.30am-11pm Wed-Fri; 8am-11pm Sat; 8am-10pm Sun. **Map** p143 B2 ⑲ **Food & drink**

Whether you want sweet (double-chocolate pecan Chubbie cookies) or savoury (hefty French sourdough *boules*), Amy's never disappoints. Breakfast and snacks such as the grilled cheese sandwich (made with New York State cheddar) are served.

Other locations Chelsea Market, 75 Ninth Avenue, between 15th & 16th Streets, Chelsea (1-212 462 4338); 250 Bleecker Street, at Leroy Street, West Village (1-212 675 7802).

Domus

413 W 44th Street, at Ninth Avenue, Hell's Kitchen (1-212 581 8099, www.domusnew york.com). Subway A, C, E to 42nd Street-Port Authority. **Open** noon-8pm Tue-Sat; noon-6pm Sun. **Map** p143 C2 ⑳ **Homewares**

Scouring the globe for unusual design products is nothing new, but owners Luisa Cerutti and Nicki Lindheimer take the concept a step further; each year they visit a far-flung part of the world to forge links with and support co-operatives and individual craftspeople. The beautiful results, such as vivid baskets woven from telephone wire by South African Zulu tribespeople, reflect a fine attention to detail and a sense of place. It's a great spot for reasonably priced home goods and gifts, from Tunisian bath towels to Italian throws.

Fine and Dandy

445 W 49th Street, between Ninth & Tenth Avenues (1-212 247 4847, www.fineanddandyshop.com). Subway C, E to 50th Street. **Open** noon-8pm Mon, Wed-Sat; 1-8pm Sun. **Map** p143 B2 ㉑ **Accessories**

Following the success of several pop-ups around the city, owner Matt Fox opened his first permanent location in Hell's Kitchen. The accessories-only shop – decked out in flourishes such as collegiate trophies and ironing boards repurposed as tables – is a prime location for the modern gent to score of-the-moment retro accoutrements like bow ties, suspenders (braces) and spats. House-label printed ties are hung in propped-open vintage trunks, while patterned socks are displayed in old briefcases.

FIFTH AVENUE & AROUND

Subway B, D, F, M, N, Q, R to 34th Street-Herald Square; Subway B, D, F, M to 42nd Street-Bryant Park; B, D, F, M to 47-50th Streets-Rockefeller Center; E, M to Fifth Avenue-53rd Street; 7 to Fifth Avenue.

The stretch of Fifth Avenue between Rockefeller Center and Central Park South showcases retail palaces bearing names that were famous long before the concept of branding was developed. Bracketed by **Saks Fifth Avenue** (49th to 50th Streets; *see p155*) and **Bergdorf Goodman** (57th to 58th Streets; *see p154*), tenants include Gucci, Prada and Tiffany & Co (and the parade of big names continues east along 57th Street). Along with Madison Avenue uptown, this is the centre of high-end shopping in New York, and the window displays – particularly during the frenetic Christmas shopping season – are worth a look even if you're not buying.

Fifth Avenue is crowned by Grand Army Plaza at 59th Street, presided over by a gilded statue of General William Tecumseh Sherman. To the west stands the **Plaza** (*see p362*), the famous hotel that was home to fictional moppet Eloise. Stretching north above 59th Street (the parkside stretch is called Central Park South), is **Central Park** (*see pp169-170*).

Fifth Avenue is the main route for the city's many public processions: the **St Patrick's Day Parade** (*see p31*), the **LGBT Pride March** (*see p34*) and many others. Even without floats or marching bands, the sidewalks are generally teeming with shoppers and tourists. The most famous skyscraper in the world also has its entrance on Fifth Avenue: the **Empire State Building** (*see p151*), located smack-bang in the centre of midtown.

A pair of impassive stone lions, which were dubbed Patience and Fortitude by Mayor Fiorello La Guardia during the Great Depression, guard the steps of the beautiful Beaux Arts humanities and social sciences branch of the **New York Public Library** at 42nd Street, now officially named the Stephen A Schwarzman Building. Just behind the library is **Bryant Park**, a manicured lawn that hosts a popular outdoor film series in summer and an ice-skating rink in winter.

The luxury **Bryant Park Hotel** (*see p363*) occupies the former American Radiator Building on 40th Street. Designed by architect Raymond Hood in the mid 1920s, the structure is faced with near-black brick and trimmed in gold leaf. Alexander Woollcott, Dorothy Parker and her 'vicious circle' held court and traded barbs at the nearby **Algonquin** (*see p263*); the lobby is still a great place to meet for a drink. Just north of the park, on Sixth Avenue, is the always thought-provoking **International Center of Photography** (*see p151*).

Step off Fifth Avenue into **Rockefeller Center** (*see p152*) and you'll find yourself in a 'city within a city', an interlacing complex of 19 buildings housing corporate offices, retail space and the popular Rockefeller Plaza. After plans for an expansion of the Metropolitan Opera on the site fell through in 1929, John D Rockefeller

Fine and Dandy.

IN THE KNOW
EMPIRE STATE EXPRESS

If you're visiting the **Empire State Building** *(see below)*, allow at least two hours for queueing and viewing. To save time, bypass one of three lines by buying tickets online (the others, for security and entry, are unavoidable), and visit late at night, when most sightseers have turned in. Alternatively, springing for an express pass ($50) allows you to cut to the front.

Jr set about creating the complex to house radio and television corporations. Designed by Raymond Hood and many other prominent architects, Rock Center grew over the decades, with each new building conforming to the original master plan and art deco design.

On weekday mornings, a crowd gathers at the NBC network's glass-walled, ground-level studio (where the *Today* show is shot), at the south-west corner of Rockefeller Plaza and 49th Street. The complex is also home to art auction house **Christie's** (20 Rockefeller Plaza, 49th Street, between Fifth & Sixth Avenues, 1-212 636 2000, www.christies.com, 9am-5.30pm Mon-Fri, usually closed Sat, Sun); pop into the lobby to admire a mural by conceptualist Sol LeWitt.

When it opened on Sixth Avenue (at 50th Street) in 1932, **Radio City Music Hall** (*see p277*) was designed as a showcase for high-end variety acts, but the death of vaudeville led to a quick transition into what was then the world's largest movie house. Today, the art deco jewel hosts concerts and a traditional Christmas Spectacular featuring renowned precision dance troupe the Rockettes. Visitors can get a peek backstage, and meet one of the high-kicking dancers, on the Stage Door tour (every 30mins, 11am-3pm daily; $20, $15 reductions; see www.radiocity.com/tours.html for details).

Facing Rockefeller Center is the beautiful **St Patrick's Cathedral** (*see p153*). Famous couples from F Scott and Zelda Fitzgerald to Liza Minnelli and David Gest have tied the knot here; funeral services for such notables as Andy Warhol and baseball legend Joe DiMaggio were held in its confines. A few blocks north is the **Museum of Modern Art** (MoMA) and the **Paley Center for Media** (for both, *see p152*).

Sights & Museums

★ Empire State Building

350 Fifth Avenue, between 33rd & 34th Streets (1-212 736 3100, www.esbnyc.com). Subway B, D, F, M, N, Q, R to 34th Street-Herald Square.

Empire State Building.

Open 8am-2am daily (last elevator 1.15am). **Admission** *86th floor* $27; $21-$24 reductions; free under-6s. *102nd floor* $17 extra. **Map** p143 D4 ㉒

Financed by General Motors executive John J Raskob at the height of New York's skyscraper race, the Empire State sprang up in a mere 14 months, weeks ahead of schedule and $5 million under budget. Since its opening in 1931, it's been immortalised in countless photos and films, from the original *King Kong* to *Sleepless in Seattle*. Following the destruction of the World Trade Center in 2001, the 1,250ft tower resumed its title as New York's tallest building but has since been overtaken by the new 1 World Trade Center. The nocturnal colour scheme of the tower lights – recently upgraded to flashy LEDs – often honours holidays, charities or special events.

The enclosed observatory on the 102nd floor is the city's highest lookout point, but the panoramic deck on the 86th floor, 1,050ft above the street, is roomier. From here, you can enjoy views of all five boroughs and five neighbouring states too (when the skies are clear).

International Center of Photography

1133 Sixth Avenue, at 43rd Street (1-212 857 0000, www.icp.org). Subway B, D, F, M to 42nd Street-Bryant Park; N, Q, R, S, 1, 2, 3, 7 to 42nd Street-Times Square; 7 to Fifth Avenue. **Open** 10am-6pm Tue-Thur, Sat, Sun; 10am-8pm Fri. **Admission** $14; $10 reductions; free under-12s; pay what you wish 5-8pm Fri. **Map** p143 C3 ㉓

Since 1974, the ICP has served as a pre-eminent library, school and museum devoted to the photographic image. Photojournalism remains a vital facet of the centre's programming, which also includes contemporary photos and video. Recent shows in the two-floor exhibition space have focused on the work of Elliott Erwitt, Richard Avedon and Lewis Hine.

★ Museum of Modern Art (MoMA)

11 W 53rd Street, between Fifth & Sixth Avenues (1-212 708 9400, www.moma.org). Subway E, M to Fifth Avenue-53rd Street. **Open** 10.30am-5.30pm Mon-Thur, Sat, Sun; 10.30am-8pm Fri; 10.30am-8.30pm 1st Thur of the mth & every Thur in July, Aug. **Admission** (incl admission to film programmes) $25; $14-$18 reductions; free under-17s; free 4-8pm Fri. **Map** p143 B4 ㉔
After a two-year renovation based on a design by Japanese architect Yoshio Taniguchi, MoMA reopened in 2004 with almost double the space to display some of the most impressive artworks from the 19th, 20th and 21st centuries. The museum's permanent collection now encompasses seven curatorial departments: Architecture and Design, Drawings, Film, Media, Painting and Sculpture, Photography, and Prints and Illustrated Books. Highlights include Picasso's *Les Demoiselles d'Avignon*, Van Gogh's *The Starry Night* and Dali's *The Persistence of Memory* as well as masterpieces by Giacometti, Hopper, Matisse, Monet, O'Keeffe, Pollock, Rothko, Warhol and many others. Outside, the Philip Johnson-designed Abby Aldrich Rockefeller Sculpture Garden contains works by Calder, Rodin and Moore. The destination museum also contains a destination restaurant, the Modern, which overlooks the garden. If you find the prices too steep, dine in the bar, which shares the kitchen.

► *For MoMA PS1 in Queens, see p220.*

IN THE KNOW PUBLIC ART

While you're walking around midtown, keep an eye out for famous pieces of public art such as Robert Indiana's 12-foot-high, red-and-blue *LOVE* (Sixth Avenue at 55th Street) and Alexander Calder's red, mobile-like yet static *Saurien* (Madison Avenue at 57th Street). Next to Grand Central Terminal, the Grand Hyatt (109 E 42nd Street, 1-212 883 1234, www.grandhyatt newyork.com) shelters two ethereal marble heads by Barcelona-based artist Jaume Plensa. Other intriguing works, hidden within office buildings, need to be sleuthed out, such as the life-size nude sculpture between the revolving doors of 747 Third Avenue (between 46th & 47th Streets) – you get a surreal double-take glimpse as you pass through.

★ FREE New York Public Library

Fifth Avenue, at 42nd Street (1-917 275 6975, www.nypl.org). Subway B, D, F, M to 42nd Street-Bryant Park; 7 to Fifth Avenue. **Open** *Sept-June* 10am-6pm Mon, Thur-Sat; 10am-8pm Tue, Wed; 1-5pm Sun. *July, Aug* 10am-6pm Mon, Thur-Sat; 10am-8pm Tue, Wed (see website for gallery hours). **Admission** free. **Map** p143 C4 ㉕
Guarded by the marble lions Patience and Fortitude, this austere Beaux Arts edifice, designed by Carrère and Hastings, was completed in 1911. The building was renamed in honour of philanthropist Stephen A Schwarzman in 2008, but Gothamites still know it as the New York Public Library, although the city-wide library system consists of 91 locations. Free hour-long tours (11am, 2pm Mon-Sat; 2pm Sun, except July & Aug) take in the Rose Main Reading Room on the third floor, which at 297 feet long and 78 feet wide is almost the size of a football field. Specialist departments include the Map Division, containing some 431,000 maps and 16,000 atlases, and the Rare Books Division boasting Walt Whitman's personal copies of the first (1855) and third (1860) editions of *Leaves of Grass*.

The library also stages major exhibitions and events, including the excellent 'Live from the NYPL' series of talks and lectures from big-name authors and thinkers (see website for schedule).

Paley Center for Media

25 W 52nd Street, between Fifth & Sixth Avenues (1-212 621 6800, www.paleycenter.org). Subway B, D, F, M to 47-50th Streets-Rockefeller Center; E, M to Fifth Avenue-53rd Street. **Open** noon-6pm Wed, Fri-Sun; noon-8pm Thur. **Admission** $10; $5-$8 reductions. **No credit cards. Map** p143 B4 ㉖
Nirvana for telly addicts and pop-culture junkies, the Paley Center (formerly the Museum of Television & Radio) houses an immense archive of almost 150,000 radio and TV shows. Head to the fourth-floor library to search the system for your favourite episode of *Star Trek*, *Seinfeld*, or rarer fare, and watch it on your assigned console; radio shows are also available. A theatre on the concourse level is the site of frequent screenings, premières and high-profile panel discussions. There's also a small ground-floor gallery for themed exhibitions.

★ Rockefeller Center

From 48th to 51st Streets, between Fifth & Sixth Avenues (Tours & Top of the Rock 1-212 698 2000, NBC Studio Tours 1-212 664 3700, www.rockefellercenter.com). Subway B, D, F, M to 47-50th Streets-Rockefeller Center. **Open** *Tours* vary. *Observation deck* 8am-midnight daily (last elevator 11pm). **Admission** *Rockefeller Center tours* $17 (under-6s not admitted). *Observation deck* $27; $17-$25 reductions; free under-6s. *NBC Studio tours* $24; $21 reductions (under-6s not admitted). **Map** p143 B4 ㉗

EXPLORE

Museum of Modern Art (MoMA).

Constructed under the aegis of industrialist John D Rockefeller in the 1930s, this art deco city-within-a-city is inhabited by NBC, Simon & Schuster, McGraw-Hill and other media giants, as well as Radio City Music Hall, Christie's auction house, and an underground shopping arcade. Guided tours of the entire complex are available daily, and there's a separate NBC Studio tour (call the number above or see website for details).

The buildings and grounds are embellished with works by several well-known artists; look out for Isamu Noguchi's stainless-steel relief, *News*, above the entrance to 50 Rockefeller Plaza, and José Maria Sert's mural *American Progress* in the lobby of 30 Rockefeller Plaza (also known as the GE Building). But the most breathtaking sights are those seen from the 70th-floor Top of the Rock observation deck (combined tour/observation deck tickets are available). In the cold-weather months, the Plaza's sunken courtyard – eternally guarded by Paul Manship's bronze statue of Prometheus – transforms into a picturesque, if crowded, ice-skating rink..

FREE St Patrick's Cathedral

Fifth Avenue, between 50th & 51st Streets (1-212 753 2261, www.saintpatrickscathedral.org). Subway B, D, F, M to 47-50th Streets-Rockefeller Center; E, M to Fifth Avenue-53rd Street. **Open** 6.30am-8.45pm daily. **Admission** free. **Map** p143 B4 ㉘

The largest Catholic church in America, St Patrick's counts presidents, business leaders and movie stars among its past and present parishioners. The Gothic-style façade features intricate white-marble spires, but equally impressive is the interior, including the Louis Tiffany-designed altar, solid bronze baldachin, and the rose window by stained-glass master Charles Connick. Note that due to crucial restoration work, part of the exterior may still be under scaffolding in 2014.

► *Further uptown is another awe-inspiring house of worship, the Cathedral Church of St John the Divine; see p171.*

Restaurants & Cafés

Bar Room at the Modern

9 W 53rd Street, between Fifth & Sixth Avenues (1-212 333 1220, www.themodernnyc.com). Subway E, M to Fifth Avenue-53rd Street. **Open** 11.30am-3pm, 5-10.30pm Mon-Sat; 11.30am-3pm, 5-9.30pm Sun. **Main courses** $16-$35. **Map** p143 B4 ㉙ **American creative**

Those who can't afford to drop a pay cheque at award-winning chef Gabriel Kreuther's formal MoMA dining room, the Modern, can still dine in the equally stunning and less pricey bar at the front. The Alsatian-inspired menu is constructed of around 30 small and medium-sized plates (for example, liverwurst with pickled vegetables; slow-poached egg with lobster; spicy steak tartare with quail egg; and house-made country sausage with sauerkraut), which can be mixed and shared. Desserts come courtesy of pastry chef Marc Aumont, and the wine list is extensive, to say the least.

► *For the Museum of Modern Art, see p152.*

Benoit

60 W 55th Street, between Fifth & Sixth Avenues (1-646 943 7373, www.benoitny.com). Subway E, M to Fifth Avenue-53rd Street; F to 57th Street. **Open** 11.45am-3pm, 5.30-11pm Mon-Sat; 11.30am-3.30pm, 5.30-11pm Sun. **Main courses** $26-$48. **Map** p143 A4 ㉚ **French**

Alain Ducasse's classic brasserie attempts to reclaim 55th Street's former Francophile row. Come for successful, seasonality-snubbing relics like a cassoulet packed with hearty meat (pork loin, garlic sausage, duck confit) under a canopy of white beans. At the Sunday-only brunch, the dessert bar (per item $6, all-you-can-eat $18) offers a dozen seasonal pastries and tarts.

Betony

41 W 57th Street, between Fifth & Sixth Avenues (1-212 465 2400, www.betony-nyc.com). Subway F, N, Q, R to 57th Street. **Open** noon-2pm,

Grand Central Terminal.

5.30-10pm Mon-Thur; noon-2pm, 5.30-10.30pm Fri; 5.30-10.30pm Sat. **Main courses** $28-$37. **Map** p143 A4 ㉛ **American creative**
Eleven Madison Park alums Bryce Shuman and Eamon Rockey have created a rare treat: a serious New American restaurant that doesn't take itself too seriously. Hyper-professional service is softened with a heaping dose of humanity, and the fun-loving à la carte menu includes stellar riffs on crunchy fried pickles and toasty tuna melts. Dishes such as seared foie gras plugged with smoked ham hock and draped with crisp, vinegar-twanged kale combine upmarket cachet with down-home comforts.

Russian Tea Room

150 W 57th Street, between Sixth & Seventh Avenues (1-212 581 7100, www.russiantearoom nyc.com). Subway F, N, Q, R to 57th Street. **Open** 7am-11.30pm Mon-Fri; 11am-11.30pm Sat, Sun. **Main courses** $24-$48. **Map** p143 A3 ㉜ **Russian**
This refurbished 1920s icon has never looked better. Nostalgia buffs will be happy to hear that nothing's happened to the gilded-bird friezes or the famously tacky crystal-bear aquarium, although the food has not been frozen in time. Chef Marc Taxiera has at once modernised the menu – adding signature novelties such as sliders (mini burgers) – and brought back waylaid classics such as beef stroganoff and chicken kiev. In truth, however, the main reason to make for this tourist magnet is to luxuriate in the opulent setting.

Shops & Services

Bergdorf Goodman

754 Fifth Avenue, between 57th & 58th Streets (1-212 753 7300, www.bergdorfgoodman.com). Subway E, M to Fifth Avenue-53rd Street; N, Q, R to Fifth Avenue-59th Street. **Open** 10am-8pm Mon-Fri; 10am-7pm Sat; noon-6pm Sun. **Map** p143 A4 ㉝ **Department store**
Synonymous with understated luxury, Bergdorf's is known for designer clothes (the fifth floor is dedicated to younger, trend-driven labels) and accessories. For something more unusual, seek out Kentshire's wonderful cache of vintage jewellery on the ground floor. Descend to the basement for the wide-ranging beauty department. The men's store is across the street at 745 Fifth Avenue.

★ FAO Schwarz

767 Fifth Avenue, at 58th Street (1-212 644 9400, www.fao.com). Subway N, Q, R to Lexington Avenue-59th Street; 4, 5, 6 to 59th Street. **Open** 10am-8pm Mon-Thur, Sun; 10am-9pm Fri, Sat. **Map** p143 A4 ㉞ **Children**
Although it's now owned by the ubiquitous Toys 'R' Us company, this three-storey emporium is still the ultimate NYC toy box. Most people head straight to the 22ft-long floor piano that Tom Hanks famously tinkled in *Big*. Children will marvel at the giant stuffed animals, the detailed and imaginative Lego figures and the revolving Barbie fashion catwalk.

Henri Bendel

712 Fifth Avenue, at 56th Street (1-212 247 1100, www.henribendel.com). Subway E, M to Fifth Avenue-53rd Street; N, Q, R to Fifth Avenue-59th Street. **Open** 10am-8pm Mon-Sat; noon-7pm Sun. **Map** p143 A4 ㉟ **Department store**
While Bendel's merchandise (a mix of jewellery, fashion accessories, cosmetics and fragrances) is comparable to that of other upscale stores, it somehow seems more desirable when viewed in its opulent premises, a conglomeration of three 19th-century townhouses – and those darling brown-and-white

striped shopping bags don't hurt, either. If you find you haven't a thing to wear while you're in NYC but don't want to add to your luggage, you can select designer duds and accessories in the on-site showroom of popular e-tailer Rent the Runway. Bendel's is also the home of celebrity hairdresser Frédéric Fekkai's flagship salon.

Saks Fifth Avenue

611 Fifth Avenue, between 49th & 50th Streets, (1-212 753 4000, www.saksfifthavenue.com). Subway E, M to Fifth Avenue-53rd Street. **Open** 10am-8pm Mon-Sat; 11am-7pm Sun. **Map** p143 B4 ㊱ **Department store**

Although Saks maintains a presence in more than 30 American states, the Fifth Avenue location is the original, established in 1924 by New York retailers Horace Saks and Bernard Gimbel. The store features all the big names in fashion, from Armani to Yves Saint Laurent, including an expansive shoe salon that shares the eighth floor with a shop-cum-café from deluxe chocolatier Charbonnel et Walker. The opulent beauty hall is fun to peruse, and customer service is excellent, though retiring types might find it too aggressive.

MIDTOWN EAST

Subway E, M to Lexington Avenue-53rd Street; S, 4, 5, 6, 7 to 42nd Street-Grand Central; 6 to 51st Street.

Shopping, dining and entertainment options wane east of Fifth Avenue in the 40s and 50s. However, the area is home to many iconic landmarks and world-class architecture.

The 1913 **Grand Central Terminal** (*see right*) is the city's most spectacular point of arrival, although these days it welcomes only commuter trains from Connecticut and upstate New York. Looming behind the terminal, the **MetLife Building** (formerly the Pan Am Building) was the world's largest office tower when it opened in the 1960s. Other must-see buildings in the vicinity include **Lever House** (390 Park Avenue, between 53rd & 54th Streets), the **Seagram Building** (375 Park Avenue, between 52nd & 53rd Streets), the slanted-roofed **Citigroup Center** (from 53rd Street to 54th Street, between Lexington & Third Avenues) and the stunning art deco skyscraper that anchors the corner of Lexington Avenue and 51st Street, formerly the **General Electric Building** (and before that, the RCA Victor Building). A Chippendale crown tops the **Sony Building** (550 Madison Avenue, between 55th & 56th Streets), Philip Johnson's postmodern icon.

East 42nd Street has a wealth of architectural distinction, including the Romanesque Revival hall of the former **Bowery Savings Bank** (no.110) and the art deco details of the **Chanin Building** (no.122). Completed in 1930 by architect William Van Alen, the gleaming **Chrysler Building** (at Lexington Avenue) is a pinnacle of art deco architecture, paying homage to the automobile with vast radiator-cap eagles in lieu of traditional gargoyles and a brickwork relief sculpture of racing cars complete with chrome hubcaps. The **Daily News Building** (no.220), another art deco gem designed by Raymond Hood, was immortalised in the *Superman* films. Although the namesake tabloid no longer has its offices here, the lobby still houses its giant globe and weather instruments.

To the east lies the literally elevated **Tudor City** (between First & Second Avenues, from E 41st to E 43rd Streets), a pioneering 1925 residential development that resembles high-rise versions of England's Hampton Court Palace. At the end of 43rd Street is a terrace overlooking, and stairs leading down to, the **United Nations Headquarters** (*see p156*). Not far from here is the **Japan Society** (*see p156*).

IN THE KNOW LOFTY RETREAT

If you need respite from the traffic in Midtown East, slip into Tudor City, which perches on a hill between First and Second Avenues. The peaceful residential enclave features a charming park where you can rest your feet. Head for the development's east-facing terrace for an impressive view of the United Nations complex.

EXPLORE

Sights & Museums

FREE Grand Central Terminal

From 42nd to 44th Streets, between Vanderbilt & Lexington Avenues (audio tours 1-917 566 0008, www.grandcentralterminal.com). Subway S, 4, 5, 6, 7 to 42nd Street-Grand Central. **Map** p143 C4 ㊲

Each day, the world's largest rail terminal sees more than 750,000 people shuffle through its Beaux Arts threshold. Designed by Warren & Wetmore and Reed & Stern, the gorgeous transportation hub opened in 1913 with lashings of Botticino marble and staircases modelled after those of the Paris opera house. After midcentury decline, the terminal underwent extensive restoration between 1996 and 1998 and is now a destination in itself, with shopping and dining options, including the Campbell Apartment (1-212 953 0409), the Grand Central Oyster Bar & Restaurant (*see p156*), and a sprawling Apple Store (1-212 284 1800) on the East Balcony. Check the website for information about self-guided audio tours ($8; $6-$7 reductions).

▶ *For trains from Grand Central, see p372.*

Japan Society

333 E 47th Street, between First & Second Avenues (1-212 832 1155, www.japansociety.org). Subway E, M to Lexington Avenue-53rd Street; 6 to 51st Street. **Open** hrs vary. *Gallery* 11am-6pm Tue-Thur; 11am-9pm Fri; 11am-5pm Sat, Sun. **Admission** $12; $10 reductions; free under-16s; free 6-9pm Fri. **Map** p143 B5 ㊳

Founded in 1907, the Japan Society moved into its current home, complete with waterfall and bamboo garden, in 1971. Designed by Junzo Yoshimura, it was the first contemporary Japanese building in New York and is now the city's youngest official landmark. The gallery mounts temporary exhibitions on such diverse subjects as the art of anime, manga, video games and textile design.

United Nations Headquarters

Temporary visitors' entrance: First Avenue, at 47th Street (tours 1-212 963 8687, http://visit.un.org). Subway S, 4, 5, 6, 7 to 42nd Street-Grand Central. **Tours** 10.15am-4.15pm Mon-Fri. **Admission** $18; $9-$11 reductions (under-5s not admitted). **Map** p143 C5 ㊴

The UN is undergoing extensive renovations that have left the Secretariat building, designed by Le Corbusier, gleaming – though that structure is off-limits to the public. The hour-long public tours discuss the history and role of the UN, and visit the Security Council Chamber (when not in session) in the newly renovated Conference Building. The General Assembly Hall is currently closed for building work until autumn 2014 or later. Although some artworks and objects given by member nations are not on public display during this period, you can now see other pieces for the first time in years, such as Norman Rockwell's mosaic *The Golden Rule*, on the third floor of the Conference Building. Note that until the renovations are complete, tours must be booked in advance online.

IN THE KNOW
MAD MEN IN MIDTOWN

Fans of the retro TV series may want to stop by some of the *Mad Men* locations. The fictional firm's original premises is at 405 Madison Avenue (between 47th & 48th Streets), but in season four, the newly formed Sterling Cooper Draper Pryce moved into Rock Center's Time & Life Building (1271 Sixth Avenue, between 50th & 51st Streets). The building's lobby has landmark status, so it hasn't changed much since the '60s. Grand Central Oyster Bar (*see right*) was the setting for an iconic scene – Don dupes boss Roger into a clam-eating/vodka-drinking contest before the latter famously vomits in front of clients. The nearby Roosevelt Hotel (45 E 45th Street, at Madison Avenue, 1-212 661 9600, www.theroosevelthotel.com) was Don's crash pad after Betty kicked him out before their final split.

Restaurants & Cafés

Grand Central Oyster Bar & Restaurant

Grand Central Terminal, Lower Level, 42nd Street, at Park Avenue (1-212 490 6650, www.oysterbarny.com). Subway S, 4, 5, 6, 7 to 42nd Street-Grand Central. **Open** 11.30am-9.30pm Mon-Sat. **Main courses** $18-$32. **Map** p143 C4 ㊵ **Seafood**

The legendary Grand Central Oyster Bar has been a fixture of the gorgeous hub that shares its name since 1913. The surly countermen at the mile-long bar (the best seats in the house) are part of the charm. Avoid the more complicated fish concoctions and play it safe with a reliably awe-inspiring platter of iced, just-shucked oysters (there can be a whopping 30 varieties to choose from, including many from nearby Long Island).

► *For more on the iconic transport hub, see p155.*

The Monkey Bar

Hotel Elysée, 60 E 54th Street, between Madison & Park Avenues (1-212 288 1010, www.monkeybarnewyork.com). Subway E, M to Lexington Avenue-53rd Street; 6 to 51st Street. **Open** 11.30am-10pm Mon-Fri; 5.30-10pm Sat. **Main courses** $25-$55. **Map** p143 B4 ㊶ **American**

After the repeal of Prohibition in 1933, this one-time piano bar in the swank Hotel Elysée (*see p364*) became a boozy clubhouse for the glitzy artistic figures of the age, among them Tallulah Bankhead, Dorothy Parker and Tennessee Williams. The Monkey Bar is now owned by publishing titan Graydon Carter, who has brought new buzz to the historic space. Perched at the bar with a pitch-perfect glass of Gonet-Medeville champagne or ensconced in a red leather booth with a plate of fettuccine carbonara with bacon lardons,

EXPLORE

Salvation Taco. See p159.

you'll find yourself seduced by that rare alchemy of old New York luxury and new-school flair.

Quality Meats

57 W 58th Street, between Fifth & Sixth Avenues (1-212 371 7777, www.qualitymeatsnyc.com). Subway F, N, Q, R to 57th Street; N, Q, R to Fifth Avenue-59th Street. **Open** 11.30am-3pm, 5-10.30pm Mon-Wed; 11.30am-3pm, 5-11.30pm Thur, Fri; 5-11.30pm Sat; 5-10pm Sun. **Main courses** $21-$47. **Map** p143 A4 42 **Steakhouse**

Michael Stillman – son of the founder of landmark steakhouse Smith & Wollensky – is behind this highly stylised industrial theme park complete with meat-hook light fixtures, wooden butcher blocks, white tiles and exposed brick. Lespinasse-trained chef Craig Koketsu nails the steaks (including a $110 double-rib steak) and breathes new life into traditional side dishes. Pudding-like corn crème brûlée and the airy 'gnocchi & cheese', a clever take on mac and cheese, are terrific. High-concept desserts are best exemplified by the outstanding coffee-and-doughnuts ice-cream crammed with chunks of the fritters and crowned with a miniature doughnut.

Shops & Services

For our pick of the stores on Fifth Avenue, *see p150.*

MURRAY HILL

Murray Hill spans 30th to 40th Streets, between Third and Fifth Avenues. Townhouses of the rich and powerful were once clustered around Madison and Park Avenues, including the home of Pierpont Morgan; his private library is now the **Morgan Library & Museum** (*see right*), which houses some 500,000 rare books, prints, manuscripts, and objects. These days, the neighbourhood is populated mostly by upwardly mobiles fresh out of university, and only a few streets retain their former elegance. One is **Sniffen Court** (150-158 E 36th Street, between Lexington & Third Avenues), an unspoiled row of 1864 carriage houses located within earshot of the Queens Midtown Tunnel's ceaseless traffic.

Sights & Museums

★ Morgan Library & Museum

225 Madison Avenue, at 36th Street (1-212 685 0008, www.themorgan.org). Subway 6 to 33rd Street. **Open** 10.30am-5pm Tue-Thur; 10.30am-9pm Fri; 10am-6pm Sat; 11am-6pm Sun. **Admission** $18; $12 reductions; free under-13s; free 7-9pm Fri. **Map** p143 C4 43

This Madison Avenue institution began as the private library of financier Pierpont Morgan, and is his cultural gift to the city. Building on the collection Morgan amassed in his lifetime, the museum houses first-rate works on paper, including drawings by Michelangelo, Rembrandt and Picasso; three Gutenberg Bibles; a copy of *Frankenstein* annotated by Mary Shelley; manuscripts by Dickens, Poe, Twain, Steinbeck and Wilde; sheet music handwritten by Beethoven and Mozart; and an original edition of Dickens's *A Christmas Carol* that's displayed every Yuletide. A massive renovation and expansion orchestrated by Renzo Piano brought more natural light into the building and doubled the available exhibition space. The final phase restored the original 1906 building, designed by McKim, Mead & White. Visitors can now see Morgan's spectacular library (the East Room), with its 30ft-high book-lined walls and murals designed by Henry Siddons Mowbray (who also painted the ceiling of the restored Rotunda).

Scandinavia House – The Nordic Center in America

58 Park Avenue, at 38th Street (1-212 779 3587, www.scandinaviahouse.org). Subway S, 4, 5, 6, 7 to 42nd Street-Grand Central. **Open** varies. *Gallery* noon-6pm Tue, Thur-Sat; noon-7pm Wed; noon-5pm Sun (Dec only). **Admission** varies. **Map** p143 C4 44

DOVER STREET MARKET NEW YORK

Rei Kawakubo brings her Comme concept store Stateside.

Murray Hill isn't exactly a fashionable district. For years dominated by the hard-partying post-frat set, the neighbourhood has recently been gaining more sophistication, but it still lacked destination retail – until the biggest fashion happening of 2013 hit the corner of Lexington Avenue and 30th Street. Just before Christmas, the third **Dover Street Market** (*see p159*) opened in the former home of the New York School of Applied Design, bringing Comme des Garçons designer Rei Kawakubo's quirky, upscale interpretation of a London fashion market to NYC.

Like the original Dover Street Market – named for its London location – DSMNY is a multilevel store containing an eclectic mix of more than 75 labels with displays that blur the line between art and commerce. It also has an outpost of the Rose Bakery, though here,the cult Paris eaterie isn't perched on the top floor but given a prominent spot just inside the entrance.

A transparent elevator whisks visitors through the seven-floor consumer playground. Three pillars running through six of the levels have been transformed into art installations: a stripey patchwork knitted sheath by Magda Sayeg, London Fieldworks' wooden metropolis, and 3D collages by 'junk sculptor' Leo Sewell. On the third floor, a cave-like covered staircase titled 'Biotopological Scale-Juggling Escalator' by Arakawa and Gins leads up to a showroom spotlighting emerging talent, such as Central Saint Martins graduate Phoebe English and Russian artist/designer Gosha Rubchinskiy. If you hear music while browsing on the ground or fourth levels, it's likely to be emanating from one of two sound sculptures composed of old audio equipment by Brooklyn-based Calx Vive (more are in the pipeline).

All of the Comme lines – more than 15 of them – are here, alongside mini boutiques for luxury labels like Louis Vuitton and Prada, streetwear brands such as Nike, Supreme and Undercover and a raft of cool names – Christopher Kane, Casely Hayford, Raf Simons and Simone Rocha, among them The individual style of each vendor creates an intriguingly varied experience – on the third level, for example, a tribal-themed display of Michael Costiff's World Archive, a collection of global adornments such as enormous nose plugs from Papua New Guinea, shares floor space with Azzedine Alaïa's sleek monochrome salon.

One of the city's top cultural centres, Scandinavia House serves as a link between the US and the Scandinavian nations, and offers a full schedule of film screenings, lectures and art exhibitions. An outpost of Smörgås Chef (open 11am-10pm Mon-Sat, 11am-5pm Sun), serves tasty Swedish meatballs, and the shop is a showcase for chic Scandinavian design.

Restaurants & Cafés

Artisanal

2 Park Avenue, at 32nd Street (1-212 725 8585, www.artisanalbistro.com). Subway 6 to 33rd Street. **Open** 11.45am-2.45pm, 5-9.45pm Mon-Wed; 11.45am-2.45pm, 5-10.45pm Thur, Fri; 11am-3.45pm, 5-10.45pm Sat; 10.30am-3.45pm, 5-8.45pm Sun. **Main courses** $24-$50. **Map** p143 D4 ⑮ **French**

As New York's bistros veer towards uniformity, Terrance Brennan's high-ceilinged deco gem makes its mark with an all-out homage to fromage. Skip the appetisers and open with fondue, which comes in three varieties. Familiar bistro fare awaits, with such dishes as steak frites, mussels, and chicken baked 'under a brick', but the curd gets the last word with the cheese and wine pairings. These selections of three cheeses – chosen by region, style or theme (for example, each one produced in a monastery) – are matched with three wines (or beers or even sakés) for a sumptuous and intriguing finale.

Kajitsu

125 E 39th Street, between Park & Lexington Avenues (1-212 228 4873, www.kajitsunyc.com). Subway S, 4, 5, 6, 7 to 42nd Street-Grand Central. **Open** 11.45am-1.45pm, 5.30-10pm Tue-Sat; 5.30-10pm Sun (closed 1st day of each month). **Tasting menus** $55-$85. **Map** p143 C4 ⑯ **Japanese/vegetarian**

There's no shortage of cheap ramen joints in post-grad mecca Murray Hill, but house-made soba crowned with shaved black truffles? That's only at Kajitsu. The minimalist, Michelin-starred den displays a devotion to produce, influenced by the monk-approved *shojin-ryori* (vegetarian) tradition. The sublime fare has made it a cult favourite among top-notch toques like Momofuku's David Chang. In the small, bare dining room or at the eight-seat chef's counter, choose from three ever-changing menus – four courses, eight or a counter-only omakase – each paired with sake if you like (they'll split a single pairing between two people if you ask nicely).

Salvation Taco

145 E 39th Street, between Lexington & Third Avenues (1-212 865 5800, www.salvationtaco.com). Subway S, 4, 5, 6, 7 to 42nd Street-Grand Central. **Open** 7am-5pm, 5.30pm-midnight daily. **Main courses** $13-$38. **Map** p143 C4 ⑰ **Mexican**

The decor – coloured Christmas lights, fake fruit – may evoke that Cancun vacation, but the fiesta fare doled out at this Murray Hill cantina off the lobby of the Pod 39 hotel (*see p365*) has an upscale bent, thanks to April Bloomfield and Ken Friedman (of the Spotted Pig and the Ace Hotel's Breslin). Exotic fillings include Moroccan-spiced lamb and Korean-barbecue-style beef. Even a margarita gets a chefly update with a zippy guajillo chili salt rim. *Photos pp156-157.*

Bars

Middle Branch

154 E 33rd Street, between Lexington & Third Avenues (1-212 213 1350). Subway 6 to 33rd Street. **Open** 5pm-2am daily. **Map** p143 D5 ⑱

In 2000, visionary barman Sasha Petraske paved the way for the modern cocktail bar with members-only Milk & Honey (*see p134*); since then, he and his acolytes have spread the liquid gospel with a rapidly expanding web of standout watering holes. His latest bar, Middle Branch – run by longtime Little Branch lieutenants Lucinda Sterling and Benjamin Schwartz – plants a flag for artisanal cocktails in post-frat epicentre Murray Hill. Unlike Little Branch, this is no sly speakeasy, hidden from the masses with a windowless façade and an unmarked ingress: the bi-level drinkery, sporting French doors that offer a glimpse inside, practically beckons passersby. As at Petraske's other highfalutin' joints, the razor-sharp focus is on classic cocktails and riffs (all $12), built with hand-cut ice and superior spirits.

Other locations Little Branch, 20 Seventh Avenue South, at Leroy Street, West Village (1-212 929 4360).

Shops & Services

★ Dover Street Market New York

160 Lexington Avenue, at 30th Street (1-646 837 7750, www.newyork.doverstreetmarket.com). Subway 6 to 28th or 33rd Street. **Open** 11am-7pm Mon-Sat; noon-6pm Sun. **Map** p143 D5 ⑲ **Fashion/accessories**

See p158 **Dover Street Market New York.**

IN THE KNOW SAMPLE SALES

Home to numerous designer studios and showrooms, New York's Garment District (*see p142*) hosts a weekly spate of sample sales. The best are listed in the Shopping & Style section of *Time Out New York* magazine and www.timeout.com/newyork. Other good resources are Racked (www.ny.racked.com), Top Button (www.topbutton.com) and Clothing Line (1-212 947 8748, www.clothingline.com), which holds sales for a variety of labels – from J Crew and Theory to Helmut Lang and Rag & Bone, at its showroom (Second Floor, 261 W 36th Street, between Seventh & Eighth Avenues).

EXPLORE

Upper West Side & Central Park

The four-mile-long stretch west of Central Park is culturally rich and cosmopolitan. In the late 19th century, lavish apartment buildings sprang up alongside newly completed Central Park. Then, in the 20th century, immigrants brought diverse shops and eateries to the avenues in between; some survive, but the arrival of new real estate and chain stores has had a homogenising effect.

The neighbourhood is home to museums, including the American Museum of Natural History and the New-York Historical Society, but its seat of culture is largely concentrated on venerated performing-arts complex Lincoln Center.

EXPLORE

American Museum of Natural History.

Don't Miss

1 American Museum of Natural History Nature comes to life at this revitalised classic (*p164*).

2 Museum of Arts and Design Curators get creative with inventive themed shows (*p164*).

3 Barney Greengrass The 'Sturgeon King' has reigned since 1908 (*p165*).

4 Central Park Spans everything from formal gardens and follies to rustic woodland (*p168*).

5 Cathedral Church of St John the Divine Prepare to be awed (*p171*).

UPPER WEST SIDE

Subway A, B, C, D, 1 to 59th Street-Columbus Circle; B, C to 72nd Street, 81st Street-Museum of Natural History, 86th Street, 96th Street or 103rd Street; 1, 2, 3 to 72nd Street or 96th Street; 1 to 66th Street-Lincoln Center, 79th Street, 86th Street or 103rd Street.

The gateway to the Upper West Side is **Columbus Circle**, where Broadway meets 59th Street, Eighth Avenue, Central Park South and Central Park West – a rare rotary in a city of right angles. The architecture around it could make anyone's head spin. At the entrance to Central Park, a 700-ton statue of Christopher Columbus is dwarfed by the **Time Warner Center** across the street, which houses offices, apartments, hotel lodgings and Jazz at Lincoln Center's stunning **Frederick P Rose Hall**. The first seven levels of the enormous glass complex are filled with high-end retailers and gourmet restaurants, such as **Per Se** (*see p166*). In 2008, the **Museum of Arts & Design** (*see p164)* opened in a landmark building on the south side of the circle, itself the subject of a controversial redesign.

A few blocks north, **Lincoln Center** (*see p286*), a complex of concert halls and auditoriums built in the early 1960s, is the home of the New York Philharmonic, the New York City Ballet, the Metropolitan Opera and a host of other notable arts organisations. The big circular fountain in the central plaza is a popular gathering spot – especially in summer, when amateur dancers converge on it to dance alfresco at **Midsummer Night Swing** (*see p34*).

The centre has completed a major overhaul that included a redesign of public spaces, refurbishment of the various halls and a new visitor centre, the **David Rubenstein Atrium** (Broadway, between W 62nd & W 63rd Streets). Conceived as a contemporary interior garden with lush planted walls, the Atrium stages free genre-spanning concerts on Thursday nights and sells week-of show discounted tickets to performances at Lincoln Center, plus other Manhattan venues (see www.lincolncenter.org for details). It's also the starting point for guided tours of the complex (1-212 875 5350, $18, $15 reductions), which, in addition to the hallowed concert halls, contains several notable artworks, including Henry Moore's *Reclining Figure* in the plaza near Lincoln Center Theater, and two massive music-themed paintings by Marc Chagall in the lobby of the Metropolitan Opera House. Nearby is the **New York Public Library for the Performing Arts** (40 Lincoln Center Plaza, at 65th Street, 1-212 870 1630, www.nypl.org, closed Sun); alongside its extraordinary collection of films, letters, manuscripts, videos and sound recordings, it stages concerts and lectures.

Around Sherman and Verdi Squares (from 70th to 73rd Streets, where Broadway and Amsterdam Avenue intersect), classic early 20th-century buildings stand cheek-by-jowl with newer high-rises. The jewel is the 1904 **Ansonia Hotel** (2109 Broadway, between 73rd & 74th Streets). Over the years, Enrico Caruso, Babe Ruth and Igor Stravinsky have lived in this Beaux Arts masterpiece; it was also the site of the Continental Baths, the gay bathhouse and cabaret where Bette Midler got her start, and Plato's Retreat, a swinging 1970s sex club.

After Central Park was completed, magnificently tall residential buildings rose up along **Central Park West** to take advantage of the views. The first of these great apartment blocks was the **Dakota** (at 72nd Street), so named because its location was considered remote when it was built in 1884. The fortress-like building is known as the setting for *Rosemary's Baby* and the site of John Lennon's murder in 1980 (Yoko Ono still lives there); other residents have included Judy Garland, Rudolph Nureyev, Lauren Bacall and Boris

San Remo Apartments. *See p164.*

IN THE KNOW
NEW-YORK, NEW-YORK

The New-York Historical Society's name is itself a historical preservation – placing a hyphen between 'New' and 'York' was common in the early 19th century. In fact, according to the Society, the *New York Times*, the paper of record, maintained the convention until 1896.

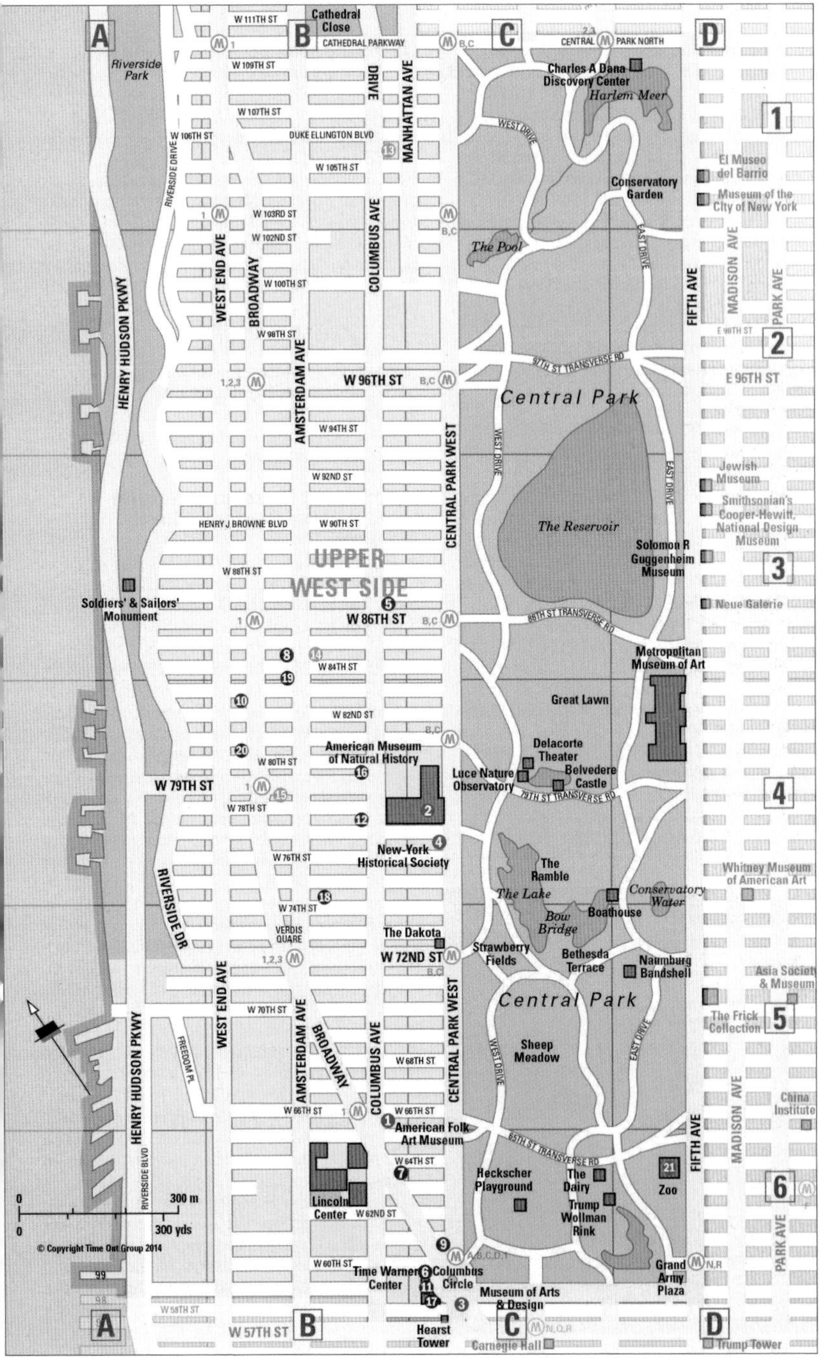
A
B
C
D
1
2
3
4
5
6
Cathedral Close
W 111TH ST
CATHEDRAL PARKWAY
CENTRAL PARK NORTH
Riverside Park
W 109TH ST
DRIVE
MANHATTAN AVE
Charles A Dana Discovery Center
Harlem Meer
W 107TH ST
W 106TH ST
DUKE ELLINGTON BLVD
WEST DRIVE
RIVERSIDE DRIVE
W 105TH ST
El Museo del Barrio
Conservatory Garden
Museum of the City of New York
W 103RD ST
W 102ND ST
COLUMBUS AVE
EAST DRIVE
The Pool
MADISON AVE
WEST END AVE
BROADWAY
W 100TH ST
FIFTH AVE
PARK AVE
HENRY HUDSON PKWY
W 98TH ST
E 98TH ST
AMSTERDAM AVE
97TH ST TRANSVERSE RD
W 96TH ST
E 96TH ST
Central Park
W 94TH ST
WEST DRIVE
CENTRAL PARK WEST
W 92ND ST
EAST DRIVE
Jewish Museum
Smithsonian's Cooper-Hewitt, National Design Museum
HENRY J BROWNE BLVD
W 90TH ST
The Reservoir
UPPER WEST SIDE
W 88TH ST
Solomon R Guggenheim Museum
Soldiers' & Sailors' Monument
Neue Galerie
W 86TH ST
86TH ST TRANSVERSE RD
Metropolitan Museum of Art
W 84TH ST
Great Lawn
W 82ND ST
American Museum of Natural History
Delacorte Theater
W 80TH ST
Luce Nature Observatory
Belvedere Castle
W 79TH ST
79TH ST TRANSVERSE RD
W 78TH ST
New-York Historical Society
W 76TH ST
The Ramble
RIVERSIDE DR
Whitney Museum of American Art
The Lake
Conservatory Water
W 74TH ST
Bow Bridge
Boathouse
VERDIS QUARE
The Dakota
W 72ND ST
Strawberry Fields
Bethesda Terrace
Naumburg Bandshell
Asia Society & Museum
W 70TH ST
Central Park
The Frick Collection
FREEDOM PL
W 68TH ST
Sheep Meadow
W 66TH ST
China Institute
American Folk Art Museum
65TH ST TRANSVERSE RD
RIVERSIDE BLVD
W 64TH ST
Heckscher Playground
The Dairy
Zoo
Lincoln Center
W 62ND ST
Trump Wollman Rink
0
300 m
300 yds
© Copyright Time Out Group 2014
W 60TH ST
Time Warner Center
Columbus Circle
Grand Army Plaza
Museum of Arts & Design
W 58TH ST
W 57TH ST
Hearst Tower
Carnegie Hall
Trump Tower

away by the co-op board when he tried to buy an apartment. You might recognise **55 Central Park West** (at 66th Street) from the movie *Ghostbusters*. Built in 1930, it was the first art deco building on the block. Heading north on Central Park West, you'll spy the massive twin-towered **San Remo Apartments** (at 74th Street), which also date from 1930. Rita Hayworth, Steven Spielberg, Tiger Woods and U2's Bono have been among the building's many celebrity residents over the years.

A few blocks to the north, the **New-York Historical Society** (*see p164*) is the city's oldest museum, founded in 1804. Across the street, at the glorious **American Museum of Natural History** (*see p164*), dinosaur skeletons, a planetarium and an IMAX theatre lure visitors of all ages.

To see West Siders in their natural habitat, queue at the perpetually jammed smoked fish counter at gourmet market **Zabar's** (*see p168*). The legendary (if scruffy) restaurant and delicatessen **Barney Greengrass**, the self-styled 'Sturgeon King' (*see p165*), has specialised in smoked fish, knishes and what may be the city's best chopped liver since 1908.

Riverside Park, a sinuous stretch of riverbank along the Hudson from 59th Street to 155th Street, was originally designed by Central Park's Frederick Law Olmsted, and subsequently extended. You'll probably see yachts, along with several houseboats, berthed at the **79th Street Boat Basin**. Several sites provide havens for quiet reflection. The **Soldiers' and Sailors' Monument** (89th Street, at Riverside Drive), built in 1902 by French sculptor Paul EM Duboy, honours Union soldiers who died in the Civil War; and a 1913 memorial (100th Street, at Riverside Drive) pays tribute to fallen firemen.

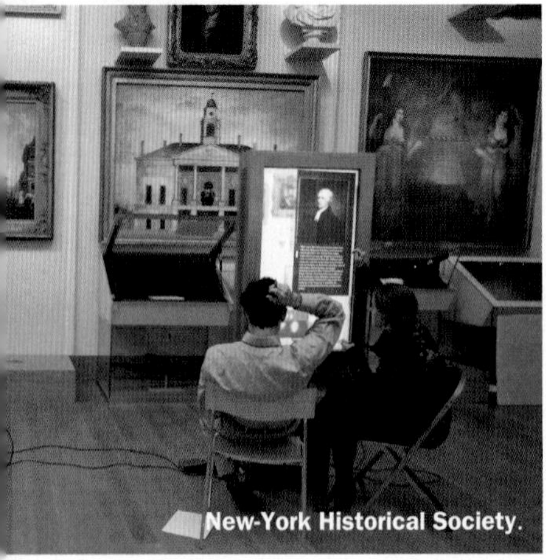
New-York Historical Society.

EXPLORE

FREE American Folk Art Museum

2 Lincoln Square, Columbus Avenue, at 66th Street (1-212 595 9533, www.folkartmuseum.org). Subway 1 to 66th Street-Lincoln Center. **Open** noon-7.30pm Tue-Sat; noon-6pm Sun. **Admission** free. **Map** p163 B5 ❶

Following a budget crisis that forced the American Folk Art Museum to give up its midtown premises, the institution is still going strong in the small original space it had retained as a second location. Its unparalleled holdings of folk art include more than 5,000 works from the late 18th century to the present. Exhibitions explore the work of self-taught and outsider artists, as well as showing traditional folk art such as quilts and needlework, and other decorative objects. You can purchase original handmade pieces in the large gift shop, and the museum regularly hosts free musical performances, inexpensive craft workshops and other events.

★ American Museum of Natural History/Rose Center for Earth & Space

Central Park West, at 79th Street (1-212 769 5100, www.amnh.org). Subway B, C to 81st Street-Museum of Natural History. **Open** 10am-5.45pm daily. **Admission** *Suggested donation* $22; $12.50-$17 reductions. **Map** p163 C4 ❷

The American Museum of Natural History's fourth-floor dino halls are home to the largest and arguably most fabulous collection of dinosaur fossils in the world. Nearly 85% of the bones on display were dug out of the ground by Indiana Jones types, but during the museum's mid 1990s renovation, several specimens were remodelled to incorporate more recent discoveries. The tyrannosaurus rex, for instance, was once believed to have walked upright, Godzilla-style; it now stalks prey with its head lowered and tail raised parallel to the ground. A new exhibition devoted to the winged reptiles known as pterosaurs is on view until January 2015.

The Hall of North American Mammals, part of a two-storey memorial to Theodore Roosevelt, reopened in autumn 2012 after extensive restoration to its formerly faded 1940s dioramas. The Hall of Human Origins houses a fine display of our old cousins, the Neanderthals, and the Hall of Biodiversity examines world ecosystems and environmental preservation. A life-size model of a blue whale hangs from the cavernous ceiling of the Hall of Ocean Life, while in the Hall of Meteorites, the focal point is Ahnighito, the largest iron meteor on display in the world, weighing in at 34 tons.

The spectacular Rose Center for Earth & Space offers insight into recent cosmic discoveries via shows in the Hayden Planetarium and a simulation of the origins of the Universe in the Big Bang Theater. The museum also screens digital nature films in 3D, and the roster of temporary exhibitions is thought-provoking for all ages.

Boulud Sud.

★ Museum of Arts & Design
2 Columbus Circle, at Broadway (1-212 299 7777, www.madmuseum.org). Subway A, B, C, D, 1 to 59th Street-Columbus Circle. **Open** 10am-6pm Tue, Wed, Sat, Sun; 10am-9pm Thur, Fri. **Admission** $16; $12-$14 reductions; free under-19s; pay what you wish 6-9pm Thur, Fri. **Map** p163 C6 ❸
This institution explores the importance of the creative practice with a permanent collection of art, craft and design items dating back to 1950 through the present. MAD brings together contemporary objects created in a wide range of media – including clay, glass, wood, metal and cloth – with a strong focus on materials and process. And in 2008 the museum crafted itself a new home. Originally designed in 1964 by Radio City Music Hall architect Edward Durell Stone to house Huntington Hartford's Gallery of Modern Art, 2 Columbus Circle was a windowless monolith that had sat empty since 1998. The redesigned ten-storey building now has four floors of exhibition galleries, including the Tiffany & Co Foundation Jewelry Gallery, as well as an education centre with workshop and studio spaces. Curators are able to display more of the 3,000-piece permanent collection, which includes porcelain ware by Cindy Sherman, stained glass by Judith Schaechter and ceramics by James Turrell. In addition to checking out temporary shows, you can also watch resident artists create works in studios on the sixth floor, while the ninth-floor bistro has views over the park.

★ New-York Historical Society
170 Central Park West, between 76th & 77th Streets (1-212 873 3400, www.nyhistory.org). Subway B, C to 81st Street-Museum of Natural History. **Open** 10am-6pm Tue-Thur, Sat; 10am-8pm Fri; 11am-5pm Sun. **Admission** $18; $6-$14 reductions; free under-4s. Pay what you wish 6-8pm Fri. **Map** p163 C4 ❹
Founded in 1804 by a group of prominent New Yorkers that included Mayor DeWitt Clinton, the New-York Historical Society is the city's oldest museum, originally based at City Hall. In autumn 2011, the society's 1904 building reopened after a three-year, $70-million renovation that opened up the interior spaces to make the collection more accessible to a 21st-century audience. The Robert H and Clarice Smith New York Gallery of American History provides an overview of the collection and a broad sweep of New York's place in American history – Revolutionary-era maps are juxtaposed with a piece of the ceiling mural from Keith Haring's Pop Shop (the artist's Soho store, which closed after his death in 1990). Touch-screen monitors offer insight into artwork and documents, and large HD screens display a continuous slide show of highlights of the museum's holdings, such as original watercolours from Audubon's *Birds of America* and some of its 132 Tiffany lamps. The auditorium screens an 18-minute film tracing the city's development, while downstairs the DiMenna Children's History Museum engages the next generation. The upper floors house changing exhibitions and the Henry Luce III Center for the Study of American Culture, a visible-storage display that spans everything from spectacles and toys to Washington's Valley Forge camp bed.

Restaurants & Cafés

★ Barney Greengrass
541 Amsterdam Avenue, between 86th & 87th Streets (1-212 724 4707, www.barneygreengrass.com). Subway B, C, 1 to 86th Street. **Open** 8.30am-6pm Tue-Sun. **Sandwiches** $9-$21. **No credit cards. Map** p163 B3 ❺ **American**
Despite decor that Jewish mothers might call 'schmutzy', this legendary deli is a madhouse at breakfast and brunch. Enormous egg platters come with the usual choice of smoked fish (such as sturgeon or Nova Scotia salmon). Prices are on the high side, but portions are large, and that goes for the sandwiches too. Or try the less costly items: matzo-ball soup, creamy egg salad or cold pink borscht served in a glass.

$ Bouchon Bakery
3rd Floor, Time Warner Center, 10 Columbus Circle, at Broadway (1-212 823 9366, www.bouchonbakery.com). Subway A, B, C, D, 1 to 59th Street-Columbus Circle. **Open** 8am-9pm Mon-Sat; 8am-7pm Sun. **Pastries** $1-$7. **Map** p163 C6 ❻ **Café**

IN THE KNOW
CAFE IN THE PARK

Near the Sheep Meadow, mid-park at 69th Street, you'll find an outpost of popular café Le Pain Quotidien in the former mineral springs (which once served health-giving water to park-goers). Indoor and outdoor seating is available for coffee, pastries, salads or the chain's signature tartines.

Chef Thomas Keller's café, in the same mall as his lauded fine-dining room Per Se (*see right*), lacks ambience, and the menu (soups, tartines, salads, sandwiches) is basic. But prices are much more palatable – a dry-cured ham and emmenthal baguette is around a tenner. Baked goods, including Keller's takes on American classics like Oreo cookies, are the highlights. **Other locations** 1 Rockefeller Plaza, at 49th Street, Midtown (1-212 782 3890).

Boulud Sud

20 W 64th Street, between Broadway & Central Park West (1-212 595 1313, www.danielnyc.com). Subway 1 to 66th Street-Lincoln Center. **Open** noon-11pm Mon-Fri; 11.30am-11pm Sat; 11.30am-10pm Sun. **Main courses** $22-$41. **Map** p163 B6 ❼ **Mediterranean**

At his most international restaurant yet, superchef Daniel Boulud highlights the new French cuisine of melting-pot cities like Marseille and Nice. With his executive chef, Travis Swikard, he casts a wide net – looking to Egypt, Turkey and Greece. Diners can build a full tapas meal from shareable snacks like octopus *à la plancha*, with marcona almonds and arugula. Heartier dishes combine Gallic finesse with polyglot flavours: sweet-spicy chicken tagine with harira soup borrows from Morocco. Desserts – such as grapefruit *givré* stuffed with sorbet, sesame mousse and rose-scented nuggets of Turkish delight – take the exotic mix to even loftier heights. *Photo p165.*

Celeste

502 Amsterdam Avenue, between 84th & 85th Streets (1-212 874 4559, www.celestenewyork.com). Subway 1 to 86th Street. **Open** 5-11pm Mon-Thur; 5-11.30pm Fri; noon-3pm, 5-11.30pm Sat; noon-3pm, 5-10.30pm Sun. **Main courses** $9-$16. **No credit cards. Map** p163 B3 ❽ **Italian**

This popular spot, offering authentic fare in a rustic setting, doesn't take reservations so a wait is to be expected. Once you're in, start with *carciofi fritti*: fried artichokes that are so light, they're evanescent. Three house-made pastas are prepared daily – the tagliatelle with shrimp, cabbage and pecorino stands out. Those who can manage a few more bites are advised to try the *pastiera*, a grain-and-ricotta cake flavoured with candied fruit and orange-blossom water.

Jean-Georges

Trump International Hotel & Tower, 1 Central Park West, at Columbus Circle (1-212 299 3900, www.jean-georgesrestaurant.com). Subway A, B, C, D, 1 to 59th Street-Columbus Circle. **Open** noon-2.30pm, 5.30-11pm Mon-Thur; noon-2.30pm, 5-11pm Fri-Sun. **Three-course prix fixe** $118. **Seven-course prix fixe** $198. **Map** p163 C6 ❾ **French**

Unlike many of its vaunted peers, the flagship of celebrated chef Jean-Georges Vongerichten has not become a shadow of itself: the top-rated food is still breathtaking. Velvety foie gras terrine is coated in a thin brûlée shell; other signature dishes include ginger-marinated yellowfin tuna ribbons with avocado and spicy radish. Pastry chef Joseph Murphy's inventive seasonal quartets, comprising four mini desserts, are always a delight. The more casual on-site Nougatine café is less expensive, but still provides a taste of its big brother.

Ouest

2315 Broadway, between 83rd & 84th Streets (1-212 580 8700, www.ouestny.com). Subway 1 to 86th Street. **Open** 5.30-9.30pm Mon, Tue; 5.30-10pm Wed, Thur; 5.30-11pm Fri; 5-11pm Sat; 11am-2pm, 5-9pm Sun. **Main courses** $27-$36. **Map** p163 B4 ❿ **American creative**

A prototypical local clientele calls chef-owner Tom Valenti's uptown stalwart – one of the neighbourhood's most celebrated restaurants – its local canteen. And why not? The friendly servers ferry pitch-perfect cocktails and rich, Italian-inflected cuisine from the open kitchen to immensely comfortable round red booths. Valenti adds some unexpected flourishes to the soothing formula: salmon gravadlax is served with a chickpea pancake topped with caviar and potent mustard oil, while the house-smoked sturgeon presides over frisée, lardons and a poached egg.

★ Per Se

4th Floor, Time Warner Center, 10 Columbus Circle, at Broadway (1-212 823 9335, www.perseny.com). Subway A, B, C, D, 1 to 59th Street-Columbus Circle. **Open** 5.30-10pm Mon-Thur; 11.30am-1.30pm, 5.30-10pm Fri-Sun. **Main courses** (in lounge) $30-$125. **Five-course prix fixe** $205 (Fri-Sun lunch only). **Nine-course tasting menu** $310. **Map** 163 C6 ⓫ **French**

Expectations are high at Per Se – and that goes both ways. You're expected to wear the right clothes (jackets are required for men), pay a non-negotiable service charge, and pretend you aren't eating in a shopping mall. The restaurant, in turn, is expected to deliver one hell of a tasting menu for $310. And it does. Dish after dish is flawless, beginning with Thomas Keller's signature Oysters and Pearls (a sabayon of pearl tapioca with oysters and caviar); an all-vegetable version is also available. If you can afford it, it's worth every penny, but avoid the à la carte option in the lounge, which offers miserly portions at high prices, making it less of a deal than the celebrated tasting menu in the formal dining room.

★ $ Shake Shack

366 Columbus Avenue, at 77th Street (1-646 747 8770, www.shakeshack.com). Subway B, C to 81st Street-Museum of Natural History; 1 to 79th Street. **Open** 10.45am-11pm daily. **Burgers** $5-$9. **Map** p163 B4 ⑫ **American**

The spacious offspring of Danny Meyer's wildly popular Madison Square Park concession stand is now one of several locations across the city. Shake Shack gets several local critics' votes for New York's best burger. Patties are made from fresh-ground, all-natural Angus beef, and the franks are served Chicago-style on potato buns and topped with Rick's Picks Shack relish. Frozen-custard shakes hit the spot, and there's beer and wine if you want something stronger. **Other locations** throughout the city.

Bars

Ding Dong Lounge

929 Columbus Avenue, between 105th & 106th Streets (1-212 663 2600, ww.dingdong lounge.com). Subway B, C to 103rd Street. **Open** 4pm-4am daily. **Map** p163 B1 ⑬

Goth chandeliers and kick-ass music mark this dark dive as punk – with broadened horizons. The tap pulls, dispensing half a dozen beers including Guinness, are sawn-off guitar necks, and the walls are covered with vintage concert posters (from Dylan to the Damned). The affable local clientele and mood-lit conversation nooks make it surprisingly accessible (even without a working knowledge of Dee Dee Ramone).

Jacob's Pickles

509 Amsterdam Avenue, between 84th and 85th Streets (212 470 5566, www.jacobspickles.com). Subway 1 to 86th Street. **Open** 11am-2am Mon-Thur; 11am-4am Fri; 9am-4am Sat; 9am-2am Sun. **Map** p163 B3 ⑭

This craft-beer-and-biscuit-slinging gastropub shoehorns a grab bag of tippling memes – Dixieland grub, house-made bitters, local wines on tap – into one rustic barroom. But while it may be trying a little too hard, there's plenty for brew geeks to get excited about, with more than two dozen taps offering an all-domestic lineup. The list is broken down by state, with a stable of Empire State breweries (Barrier, Radiant Pig, Singlecut) complemented by a constantly rotating roster of cross-country favourites from the likes of Maine Beer Co and Virginia's Blue Mountain Brewery. If you're feeling peckish, go for the namesake pickles or the biscuits in sausage gravy.

Manhattan Cricket Club

226 W 79th Street, between Amsterdam Avenue & Broadway (1-646 823 9252, www.burkeandwills ny.com). Subway 1 to 79th Street. **Open** 7pm-2am daily. **Map** p163 B4 ⑮

Upstairs from Australian bistro Burke & Wills, this gold-brocaded, cricket-inspired cocktail parlour is a polished upgrade from the shrimp-on-the-barbie kitsch that often plagues Aussie efforts. Summit Bar founder Greg Seider offers pricey but potent quaffs inspired by cricket hubs like India and South Africa. The I'll Have Another jolts a dark-and-stormy base of sweet rum and shaved ginger with the spice-heavy bite of garam masala-infused agave, while the kafir lime's sweetness tempers a smoky spritz of campfire essence in the vodka-based Bonfire of the Calamities.

EXPLORE

Jacob's Pickles.

Shops & Services

Alexis Bittar

410 Columbus Avenue, at 80th Street (1-646 590 4142, www.alexisbittar.com). Subway B, C to 81st Street-Museum of Natural History. **Open** 11am-7pm Mon-Sat; noon-6pm Sun. **Map** p163 B4 ⑯ **Accessories**

Alexis Bittar started out selling his jewellery from a humble Soho street stall, but now the designer has four shops in which to show off his flamboyant pieces, such as sculptural Lucite cuffs and oversized crystal-encrusted earrings. This uptown boutique is twice the size of the West Village, Upper East Side and Soho locations, and is meant to resemble a 1940s powder room, with silk wallpaper and art deco-style lights.

Other locations 465 Broome Street, between Greene & Mercer Streets, Soho (1-212 625 8340); 353 Bleecker Street, between Charles & 10th Streets, West Village (1-212 727 1093); 1100 Madison Avenue, between 82nd & 83rd Streets, Upper East Side (1-212 249 3581).

Shops at Columbus Circle

Time Warner Center, 10 Columbus Circle, at 59th Street (1-212 823 6300, www.theshopsatcolumbuscircle.com). Subway A, B, C, D, 1 to 59th Street-Columbus Circle. **Open** 10am-9pm Mon-Sat; 11am-7pm Sun (hours vary for some shops, bars and restaurants). **Map** p163 C6 ⑰ **Mall**

Nothing like your average Mall, the retail contingent of the 2.8 million-sq-ft Time Warner Center features upscale stores such as Coach, Cole Haan and LK Bennett for accessories and shoes, London shirt-maker Thomas Pink, Bose home entertainment, the fancy kitchenware purveyor Williams-Sonoma, as well as shopping centre staples J Crew, Aveda, and organic grocer Whole Foods. Some of the city's top restaurants (including Thomas Keller's gourmet destination Per Se, *p166*, and his café Bouchon Bakery, *p165*) have made it a dining destination that transcends the stigma of eating at the mall.

► *The Museum of Arts & Design next door has a gift shop selling handcrafted jewellery and design items; see p164.*

Levain Bakery

167 W 74th Street, between Columbus & Amsterdam Avenues (1-212 874 6080, www.levainbakery.com). Subway 1 to 79th Street. **Open** 8am-7pm Mon-Sat; 9am-7pm Sun. **Map** p163 B4 ⑱ **Food & drink**

Levain's cookies are a full 6oz, and the massive mounds stay gooey in the middle. The lush, brownie-like double-chocolate variety, made with extra-dark French cocoa and semi-sweet chocolate chips, is a truly decadent treat.

Other locations 2167 Frederick Douglass Boulevard (Eighth Avenue), between 116th & 117th Streets, Harlem (1-646 455 0952).

Magpie

488 Amsterdam Avenue, between 83rd & 84th Streets (1-646 998 3002, www.magpienewyork.com). Subway 1 to 86th Street. **Open** 11am-7pm Mon-Sat; 11am-6pm Sun. **Map** p163 B3 ⑲ **Homewares**

Sylvia Parker worked as a buyer at the American Folk Art Museum gift shop before opening this eco-friendly boutique. The funky space, which is decorated with bamboo shelving and recycled Hudson River driftwood, is packed with locally made, hand-crafted, sustainable and fair-trade items. Finds include vintage quilts, recycled-resin cuff bracelets, and Meow Meow Tweet soaps and candles, hand-made in Brooklyn.

Zabar's

2245 Broadway, at 80th Street (1-212 787 2000, www.zabars.com). Subway 1 to 79th Street. **Open** 8am-7.30pm Mon-Fri; 8am-8pm Sat; 9am-6pm Sun. **Map** p163 B4 ⑳ **Food & drink**

Zabar's is more than just a market – it's a genuine New York City landmark. It began life in 1934 as a tiny storefront specialising in Jewish 'appetising' delicacies and has gradually expanded to take over half a block of prime Upper West Side real estate. What never ceases to surprise, however, is its reasonable prices – even for high-end foods. Besides the famous smoked fish and rafts of delicacies, Zabar's has fabulous bread, cheese, olives and coffee, and an entire floor dedicated to gadgets and homewares.

Magpie.

IN THE KNOW BOATS & BEER

From late March through October (weather permitting), you can take in the view of the **79th Street Boat Basin** (*see p164*) with a beer and a burger at the no-reservations **Boat Basin Café** (www.boatbasincafe.com). The patio of this extremely popular spot overlooks the marina, but there's also an adjacent covered rotunda.

CENTRAL PARK

Numerous subway stations on multiple lines.

In 1858, the newly formed Central Park Commission chose landscape designer Frederick Law Olmsted and architect Calvert Vaux to turn a vast tract of rocky swampland into a rambling oasis of lush greenery. Inspired by the great parks of London and Paris, the Commission imagined a place that would provide city dwellers with respite from the crowded streets. It was a noble thought, but one that required the eviction of 1,600 mostly poor or immigrant inhabitants, including residents of Seneca Village, the city's oldest African-American settlement. Still, clear the area they did: when it was completed in 1873, it became the first man-made public park in the US.

Although it suffered from neglect at various points in the 20th century (most recently in the 1970s and '80s, when it gained a reputation as a dangerous spot), the park has been returned to its green glory thanks largely to the Central Park Conservancy. Since this not-for-profit civic group was formed in 1980, it has been instrumental in the park's restoration and maintenance.

The 1870 Victorian Gothic **Dairy** (midpark at 65th Street, 1-212 794 6564, www.centralparknyc.org, open 10am-5pm daily) houses one of Central Park Conservancy's five visitor centres and a gift shop; there are additional staffed information booths dotted around the park.

The southern section abounds with family-friendly diversions, including the **Central Park Zoo** (*see p170*), between 63rd & 66th Streets, the **Friedsam Memorial Carousel** (midpark, at 64th Street; *see p245* **Horsing Around**) and the **Trump Wollman Rink** (between 62nd & 63rd Streets; *see p247*), which doubles as a small children's amusement park in the warmer months. Come summer, kites, Frisbees and soccer balls seem to fly every which way across **Sheep Meadow**, the designated quiet zone that begins at 66th Street. Sheep did indeed graze here until 1934, but they've since been replaced by sunbathers improving their tans and scoping out the throngs. **Tavern on the Green** (Central Park West, at 67th Street), the landmark restaurant housed in the former shepherd's residence, closed in 2009, but a new seasonal eaterie should be open by publication of this guide. East of Sheep Meadow, between 66th and 72nd Streets, is the **Mall**, an elm-lined promenade that attracts street performers and in-line skaters. And just east of the Mall's Naumburg Bandshell is Rumsey Playfield – the main venue of the annual **SummerStage** series (*see p33*), an eclectic roster of free and benefit concerts in the city's parks.

One of the most popular meeting places (and loveliest spots) in the park is north of here, overlooking the lake: the grand **Bethesda Fountain & Terrace**, near the midpoint of the 72nd Street Transverse Road. *Angel of the Waters*, the sculpture in the centre of the fountain, was created by Emma Stebbins, the first woman to be granted a major public art commission in New York City. Be sure to admire the Minton-tiled ceiling of the ornate passageway that connects the plaza around the fountain to the Mall – after years of neglect in storage, the tiles, designed by Jacob Wrey Mould, were restored and reinstated in 2007. Mould also designed the intricate carved ornamentation of the stairways leading down to the fountain.

To the west of the fountain, near the West 72nd Street entrance, sits **Strawberry Fields**, which memorialise John Lennon, who lived in, and was shot in front of, the nearby Dakota Building (*see p162*). Also called the International Garden of Peace, it features a mosaic of the word 'imagine' that was donated by the city of Naples. More than 160 species of flowers and plants from all over the world flourish here, strawberries among them. Just north of the fountain is the **Loeb Boathouse** (midpark, between 74th & 75th Streets, 1-212 517 2233, www.thecentralparkboathouse.com). From here, you can take a rowing boat or a gondola out on the lake, which is crossed by the elegant Bow Bridge. The Loeb houses a restaurant and bar (closed dinner Nov-mid Apr), and lake views make it a lovely place for brunch or drinks.

Further north, the popular **Belvedere Castle** (*see p247*), a restored Victorian folly, sits atop the park's second-highest peak. Besides offering excellent views and a terrific setting for a picnic, it also houses the Henry Luce Nature Observatory. The nearby Delacorte Theater hosts **Shakespeare in the Park** (*see p308*), a summer run of free open-air performances of plays by the Bard and others. Further north still sits the **Great Lawn** (midpark, between 79th & 85th Streets), a sprawling stretch of grass that doubles as a rallying point for political protests and a concert spot for just about any act that can attract six-figure audiences. At other times, it's put to use by seriously competitive soccer, baseball and softball teams. East of the Great Lawn, behind the **Metropolitan Museum of Art** (*see p180*), is the **Obelisk**, a 69-foot hieroglyphics-covered granite monument dating from around 1500 BC, which was given to the US by the Khedive of Egypt in 1881.

In the mid 1990s, the **Reservoir** (midpark, between 85th & 96th Streets) was renamed in honour of the late Jacqueline Kennedy Onassis, who used to jog around it. A turn here gives great views of the skyscrapers rising above the park on the East and West Sides as well as midtown; in spring, the cherry trees that ring the reservoir path and the bridle path below it make it particularly beautiful.

In the northern section, the exquisite **Conservatory Garden** (entrance on Fifth Avenue, at 105th Street) comprises formal gardens inspired by English, French and Italian styles. At the top of the park, next to the Harlem Meer, the **Charles A Dana Discovery Center** (entrance at Malcolm X Boulevard/ Lenox Avenue, at 110th Street, 1-212 860 1374, www.centralparknyc.org, open 10am-5pm daily) operates a roster of activities, events and exhibitions. It also lends out fishing rods and bait (for 'catch and release' fishing, Apr-Oct); prospective fishermen need to take photo ID.

EXPLORE

Central Park Zoo

830 Fifth Avenue, between 63rd & 66th Streets (1-212 439 6500, www.centralparkzoo.org). Subway N, Q, R to Fifth Avenue-59th Street. **Open** *April-Nov* 10am-5pm Mon-Fri; 10am-5.30pm Sat, Sun; *Nov-Apr* 10am-4.30 daily. **Admission** (under-16s must be accompanied by an adult) $12; $7-$9 reductions; free under-3s. **Map** p163 D6 ㉑

A collection of animals has been kept in Central Park since the 1860s. But in its current form, Central Park Zoo dates only from 1988; it was renovated when operation of the zoo was assumed by the Wildlife Conservation Society. More than 180 species inhabit its 6.5-acre corner of the park, snow leopards and penguins among them. The Tisch Children's Zoo (*see p247*) is home to kid-friendly species, and the roving characters on the George Delacorte Musical Clock – perched atop a brick arcade between both zoos – delight little ones every half-hour.

MORNINGSIDE HEIGHTS

Subway B, C, 1 to 110th Street-Cathedral Parkway; 1 to 116th Street.

Morningside Heights runs from 110th Street (also known west of Central Park as Cathedral Parkway) to 125th Street, between Morningside Park and the Hudson River. The campus of **Columbia University** exerts a considerable influence over the surrounding neighbourhood, while the Cathedral Church of St John the Divine draws visitors from all over the city.

General Grant National Memorial.

One of the oldest universities in the US, Columbia was initially chartered in 1754 as King's College (the name changed after the Revolutionary War). It moved to its present location in 1897. If you wander into Columbia's campus entrance at 116th Street, you won't fail to miss the impressive **Low Memorial Building**, modelled on Rome's Pantheon. The former library, completed in 1897, is now an administrative building. The list of illustrious graduates includes Alexander Hamilton, Allen Ginsberg and Barack Obama.

Thanks to the large student population of Columbia and its sister school, Barnard College, the area has an academic feel, with bookshops, inexpensive restaurants and coffeehouses lining Broadway between 110th and 116th Streets. The façade of **Tom's Restaurant** (2880 Broadway, at 112th Street, 1-212 864 6137) will be familiar to *Seinfeld* aficionados, but the interior doesn't resemble Monk's Café, which was created on a studio set for the long-running sitcom.

The **Cathedral Church of St John the Divine** (*see p171*) is the seat of the Episcopal Diocese of New York. Subject to a series of construction delays and misfortunes, the enormous cathedral (larger than Paris's Notre Dame) is on a medieval schedule for completion: work is set to continue for a couple more centuries, although it has wrapped up for the time being. Just behind is the green expanse of **Morningside Park** (from 110th to 123rd Streets, between Morningside Avenue & Morningside Drive), while across the street is the **Hungarian Pastry Shop** (*see p171*), a great place for coffee and dessert and engaging graduate students in esoteric discussions.

North of Columbia, **General Grant National Memorial** (aka Grant's Tomb), the mausoleum of former president Ulysses S Grant, is located in Riverside Park. Across the street stands the towering Gothic-style **Riverside Church** (490 Riverside Drive, at 120th Street, 1-212 870 6700, www.theriversidechurchny.org), built in 1930. The tower contains the world's largest carillon: 74 bronze bells, played every Sunday at 10.30am, 12.30pm and 3pm.

★ Cathedral Church of St John the Divine

1047 Amsterdam Avenue, at 112th Street (1-212 316 7540, www.stjohndivine.org). Subway B, C, 1 to 110th Street-Cathedral Parkway. **Open** 7.30am-6pm daily. **Admission** *Suggested donation* $10. *Tours* $6-$15; $5-$12 reductions. **Map** p171 B2 ㉒

Construction of this massive house of worship, affectionately nicknamed 'St John the Unfinished', began in 1892 following a Romanesque-Byzantine design by George Heins and Christopher Grant LaFarge. In 1911, Ralph Adams Cram took over with a Gothic Revival redesign. Work came to a halt in 1941, when the US entered World War II. It resumed in earnest in 1979, but a fire in 2001 that destroyed the church's gift shop and damaged two 17th-century Italian tapestries further delayed completion. It's still missing a tower and a north transept, among other things, but the nave has been restored and the entire interior reopened and rededicated. No further work is planned… for now. In addition to Sunday services, the cathedral hosts concerts and tours (the Vertical Tour, which takes you the top of the building, is a revelation). It bills itself as a place for all people – and it certainly means it. Annual events include both winter and summer solstice celebrations, the Blessing of the Animals during the Feast of St Francis, which draws pets and their people from all over the city, and even a Blessing of the Bicycles every spring.

FREE General Grant National Memorial

Riverside Drive, at 122nd Street (1-212 666 1640, www.nps.gov/gegr). Subway 1 to 125th Street. **Open** *Visitor centre* 9am-5pm Mon, Thur-Sun. **Admission** free. **Map** p171 A1 ㉓

Although he was born in Ohio, Civil War hero and 18th president Ulysses S Grant lived in New York for the last five years of his life. More commonly referred to as Grant's Tomb, the neoclassical granite and marble mausoleum was completed in 1897; his wife, Julia, is also laid to rest here. The tomb is open for self-guided tours on the hour from 10am to 4pm; if you arrive between slots, the visitor centre offers exhibits and free talks by National Park Service rangers at 11.15am, 1.15pm and 3.15pm.

Restaurants & Cafés

Community Food & Juice

2893 Broadway, between 112th & 113th Streets (1-212 665 2800, www.communityrestaurant.com). Subway 1 to 110th Street-Cathedral Parkway. Open 8am-3.30pm, 5-9.30pm Mon-Thur, Sun; 8am-3.30pm, 5-10pm Fri; 9am-3.30pm, 5-10pm Sat; 9am-3.30pm, 5-9.30pm Sun. **Main courses** $14-$29. **Map** p171 A2 ㉔ **American**

Clinton Street Baking Company's UWS sibling is a neighbourhood brunch destination, but there's more to eating here than eggs and pancakes. Chef-co-owner Neil Kleinberg's dinner menu of global comfort food includes a formidable matzo-ball soup and a top-notch grass-fed burger with caramelised onions and Vermont cheddar. Vegetarians will be pleased by a range of creative salads and meatless sandwiches and main dishes.

Hungarian Pastry Shop

1030 Amsterdam Avenue, between 110th & 111th Streets (1-212 866 4230). Subway 1 to 110th Street-Cathedral Parkway. **Open** 7.30am-11.30pm Mon-Fri; 8.30am-11.30pm Sat; 8.30am-10.30pm Sun. **Pastries** $1-$4. **Map** p171 B2 ㉕ **Café**

So many theses have been dreamed up, procrastinated over or tossed aside in the Hungarian Pastry Shop since it opened more than five decades ago that the Columbia University neighbourhood institution merits its own dissertation. The java is strong enough to make up for the erratic array of pastries, and the Euro feel is enhanced by the view of St John the Divine cathedral from outdoor tables.

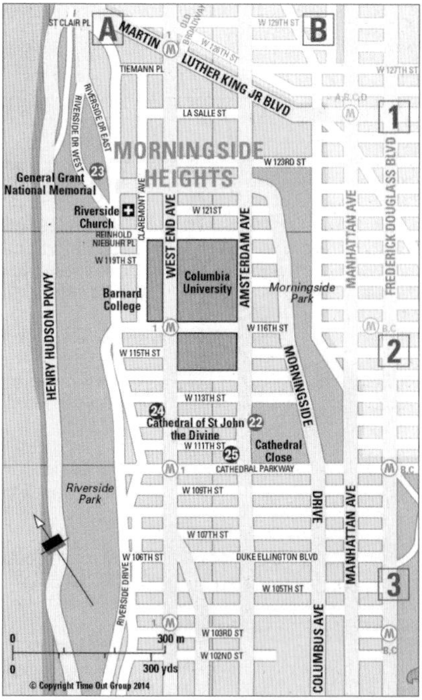

Upper East Side

Luxurious pre-war apartments owned by blue-blooded socialites, soigné restaurants filled with Botoxed ladies-who-lunch, exclusive designer boutiques... this is the clichéd image of the Upper East Side, and you'll see a lot of supporting evidence on Fifth, Madison and Park Avenues. Although Manhattan's super-rich now live all over town, the air of old money is most palpable east of Central Park. Drawn to the freshly landscaped green space in the late 19th century, the city's more affluent residents began building mansions and townhouses along Fifth Avenue. Many of these now house foreign consulates and some of the world-class institutions that draw hordes of visitors and New Yorkers to Museum Mile.

Metropolitan Museum of Art.

Don't Miss

1 Metropolitan Museum of Art The globe- and era-spanning behemoth is a must (*p180*).

2 Solomon R Guggenheim Museum Admire the stunning Frank Lloyd Wright building (*p182*).

3 Lexington Candy Shop A portal to classic NYC (*p176*).

4 Bar Pleiades Sophisticated sipping (*p177*).

5 Barneys New York The city's most fashionable department store (*see p177*).

LENOX HILL

Subway F to Lexington Avenue-63rd Street; 6 to 68th Street-Hunter College or 77th Street.

The swathe between Fifth and Lexington Avenues in the 60s and 70s, Lenox Hill encapsulates the classic Upper East Side. Along Fifth, Madison and Park, stately mansions and townhouses rub shoulders with deluxe apartment buildings guarded by uniformed doormen. The 1916 limestone structure at 820 Fifth Avenue (at 63rd Street) was one of the earliest luxury apartment buildings on the avenue, and still has just one residence per floor. And further north, Stanford White designed 998 Fifth Avenue (at 81st Street) in the image of an Italian Renaissance palazzo. Once home to the Seventh Regiment of the National Guard, the impressive 1881 **Park Avenue Armory** (643 Park Avenue, between 66th & 67th Streets, 1-212 616 3930, www.armoryonpark.org) contains a series of period rooms from the late 19th century, designed by such luminaries as Louis Comfort Tiffany and the Herter Brothers. The vast Wade Thompson Drill Hall has become one of the city's premier alternative spaces for art, concerts and theatre.

If you head east on 59th Street, you'll eventually reach the **Ed Koch Queensboro Bridge**, which was renamed in 2011 to honour the former mayor, and links to Queens. At Second Avenue you can catch the overhead tram to **Roosevelt Island**. The two-mile-long isle between Manhattan and Queens is largely residential. However, from 1686 to 1921, it went by the name of Blackwell's Island, during which time it was the site of an insane asylum, a smallpox hospital and a prison – notable inmates included Mae West, who served eight days here after being moved from the Women's House of Detention in the Village, and Emma Goldman, the anarchist, feminist and political agitator. In autumn 2012, **Franklin D Roosevelt Four Freedoms Park** (www.fdrfourfreedomspark.org) finally opened on the island's southern tip, 40 years after Mayor John Lindsay and Governor Nelson A Rockefeller announced the memorial. The plans languished until 2005, when an exhibition at Cooper Union revived interest in the project. Commemorating the 32nd President's famous 'four freedoms' speech, the park offers postcard-worthy skyline views.

IN THE KNOW ROOSEVELT ISLAND TRAM

Suspended on a cable, the tram to Roosevelt Island reaches a height of 250 feet on its brief journey. The fare is the same as a subway ride – MetroCards are accepted – and the views are spectacular.

Sights & Museums

Asia Society & Museum

725 Park Avenue, at 70th Street (1-212 288 6400, www.asiasociety.org). Subway 6 to 68th Street-Hunter College. **Open** *July, Aug* 11am-6pm Tue-Sun. *Sept-June* 11am-6pm Tue-Thur, Sat, Sun; 11am-9pm Fri. **Admission** $12; $7-$10 reductions; free under-16s (must be accompanied by an adult). Free 6-9pm Fri. **Map** p175 B5 ❶

The Asia Society sponsors study missions and conferences while promoting public programmes in the US and abroad. The headquarters' striking galleries host exhibitions of art from dozens of countries and time periods (from ancient India and medieval Persia to contemporary Japan); some are assembled from public and private collections, including the permanent Mr and Mrs John D Rockefeller III collection of Asian art. An attractive gift shop and a spacious, atrium-like café with a pan-Asian-inspired menu help to make the society a one-stop destination for anyone with even a passing interest in Asian culture.

China Institute

125 E 65th Street, between Park & Lexington Avenues (1-212 744 8181, www.chinainstitute.org). Subway F to Lexington Avenue-63rd Street; 6 to 68th Street-Hunter College. **Open** *Galleries* 10am-5pm Mon, Wed, Fri-Sun; 10am-8pm Tue, Thur. **Admission** $7; $4 reductions; free under-12s. Free to all 6-8pm Tue, Thur. **Map** p175 B5 ❷

With two small galleries, the China Institute is somewhat overshadowed by the nearby Asia Society, but the organisation mounts two substantial exhibitions a year, which include high-profile collections on loan from Chinese institutions. The institute also offers courses and arts events such as concerts and films.

Frick Collection

1 E 70th Street, between Fifth & Madison Avenues (1-212 288 0700, www.frick.org). Subway 6 to 68th Street-Hunter College. **Open** 10am-6pm Tue-Sat; 11am-5pm Sun. **Admission** (under-10s not admitted) $20; $10-$15 reductions. Pay what you wish 11am-1pm Sun. **Map** p175 B5 ❸

Industrialist, robber baron and collector Henry Clay Frick commissioned this opulent mansion with a view to leaving his legacy to the public. Designed by Thomas Hastings of Carrère & Hastings (the firm behind the New York Public Library) and built in 1914, the building was inspired by 18th-century British and French architecture.

In an effort to preserve the feel of a private residence, labelling is minimal, but you can opt for a free audio guide or pay $2 for a booklet. Works spanning the 14th to the 19th centuries include masterpieces

EXPLORE

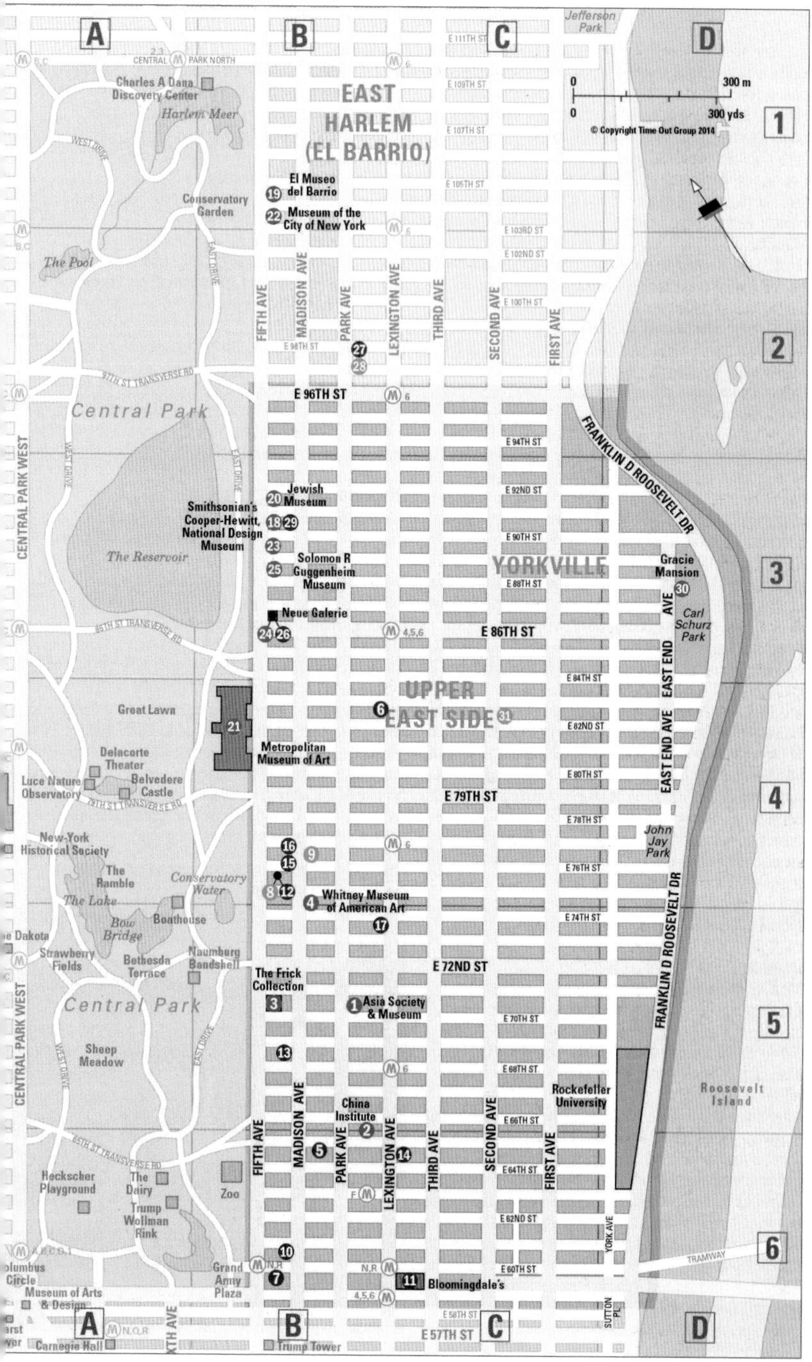
EAST HARLEM (EL BARRIO)
UPPER EAST SIDE
YORKVILLE
Central Park
El Museo del Barrio
Museum of the City of New York
Jewish Museum
Smithsonian's Cooper-Hewitt, National Design Museum
Solomon R Guggenheim Museum
Neue Galerie
Metropolitan Museum of Art
Whitney Museum of American Art
The Frick Collection
Asia Society & Museum
China Institute
Bloomingdale's
Gracie Mansion
Carl Schurz Park
John Jay Park
Rockefeller University
Roosevelt Island
Charles A Dana Discovery Center
Harlem Meer
Conservatory Garden
The Pool
The Reservoir
Great Lawn
Delacorte Theater
Luce Nature Observatory
Belvedere Castle
New-York Historical Society
The Ramble
The Lake
Conservatory Water
Bow Bridge
Boathouse
Strawberry Fields
Bethesda Terrace
Naumburg Bandshell
Sheep Meadow
Heckscher Playground
The Dairy
Trump Wollman Rink
Zoo
Grand Army Plaza
Museum of Arts & Design
Carnegie Hall
Trump Tower
FIFTH AVE
MADISON AVE
PARK AVE
LEXINGTON AVE
THIRD AVE
SECOND AVE
FIRST AVE
YORK AVE
EAST END AVE
SUTTON PL
FRANKLIN D ROOSEVELT DR
CENTRAL PARK WEST
CENTRAL PARK NORTH
E 96TH ST
E 86TH ST
E 79TH ST
E 72ND ST
E 57TH ST
TRAMWAY
© Copyright Time Out Group 2014

EXPLORE

by Rembrandt, Vermeer, Whistler, Gainsborough, Holbein and Titian, exquisite period furniture, porcelain and other decorative objects. Aficionados of 18th-century French art will find two rooms especially enchanting: the panels of the Boucher Room (1750-52) depict children engaged in adult occupations; the Fragonard Room contains the artist's series *Progress of Love* – four of the paintings were commissioned (and rejected) by Louis XV's mistress Madame du Barry. A gallery in the enclosed garden portico is devoted to decorative arts and sculpture.
▶ *For the Frick's excellent concert series, see p287.*

Whitney Museum of American Art

945 Madison Avenue, at 75th Street (1-212 570 3600, www.whitney.org). Subway 6 to 77th Street. **Open** 11am-6pm Wed, Thur, Sat, Sun; 1-9pm Fri. **Admission** $20; $16 reductions; free under-19s. Pay what you wish 6-9pm Fri. **Map** p175 B4 ❹

The Whitney is leaving the Upper East Side, but it isn't going quietly. A nearly museum-wide Jeff Koons retrospective (27 June-19 Oct 2014) is the instituion's blockbuster goodbye to the Marcel-Breuer-designed premises it has occupied since 1966. In spring 2015, the new Whitney – a nine-storey building designed by Renzo Piano at the foot of the High Line in the Meatpacking District – will open to the public. For the first time, there will be space for a comprehensive display of the collection (*see p113*).

When sculptor and art patron Gertrude Vanderbilt Whitney opened the museum in 1931, she dedicated it to living American artists. Today, the Whitney holds more than 19,000 pieces by around 2,900 artists, including Willem de Kooning, Edward Hopper, Jasper Johns, Georgia O'Keeffe and Claes Oldenburg. Yet its reputation rests primarily on its temporary shows – particularly the Whitney Biennial. Launched in 1932 and held in even-numbered years, it's the most prestigious and controversial assessment of contemporary art in the US.

Restaurants & Cafés

Daniel

60 E 65th Street, between Madison & Park Avenues (1-212 288 0033, www.danielnyc.com). Subway F to Lexington Avenue-63rd Street; 6 to 68th Street-Hunter College. **Open** 5.30-11pm Mon-Sat. **Three-course prix fixe** $125. **Map** p175 B6 ❺ **French**

The cuisine at Daniel Boulud's elegant fine-dining flagship, designed by Adam Tihany, is rooted in French technique with contemporary flourishes like fusion elements and an emphasis on local produce. Although the menu changes seasonally, it always includes a few signature dishes, such as the chef's oven-baked black sea bass with Syrah sauce, or the duo of beef – a sumptuous pairing of Black Angus short ribs and seared Wagyu tenderloin.

Other locations Café Boulud, 20 E 76th Street, between Fifth & Madison Avenues, Upper East Side (1-212 772 2600); Bar Boulud, 1900 Broadway, at 64th Street, Upper West Side (1-212 595 0303); DB Bistro Moderne, 55 West 44th Street, between Fifth & Sixth Avenues, Midtown West (1-212 391 2400).
▶ *For Boulud's Bowery brasserie DBGB, see p98; for Boulud Sud, see p166.*

★ Lexington Candy Shop

1226 Lexington Avenue, at 83rd Street (1-212 288 0057, www.lexingtoncandyshop.net). Subway 4, 5, 6 to 86th Street. **Open** 7am-7pm Mon-Sat; 8am-6pm Sun. **Main courses** $6-$14. **Map** p175 B4 ❻ **American**

You won't see much candy for sale here. Instead, you'll find a wonderfully preserved retro diner (it was founded in 1925), its long counter lined with chatty locals on their lunch hours, tucking into burgers and chocolate malts. If you come for breakfast, order the doorstop slabs of french toast.

Rôtisserie Georgette

14 E 60th Street, between Fifth & Madison Avenues (1-212 390 8060, www.rotisserieg.com). Subway N, Q, R to Fifth Avenue-59th Street. **Open** noon-2.30pm, 5.45-10pm Mon; noon-2.30pm, 5.45-11pm Tue-Fri; noon-3pm, 5.45-11pm Sat; 5.45-10pm Sun. **Main courses** $25-$45. **Map** p175 B6 ❼ **French/American**

Two Daniel Boulud vets strike out on their own with this 90-seat rotisserie, decorated with steel columns and caramel-coloured banquettes. Led by Georgette Farkas – the toque's publicist for nearly two decades – the restaurant showcases spit-fired roasts, including organic Zimmerman Farm chicken and rib-eye steak with béarnaise sauce. Former Boulud banquet chef David Malbequi helms the kitchen, turning out seasonal sides like pancetta-studded

Frick Collection. *See p174.*

EXPLORE

brussels sprouts and four takes on potatoes (roasted, fried, puréed and stuffed with black truffles). Legendary Daniel sommelier Jean-Luc Le Dû, now a wine shop owner, curates a vino list showcasing lesser-known French producers.

Bars

★ Bar Pleiades

The Surrey, 20 E 76th Street, between Fifth & Madison Avenues (1-212 772 2600, www.danielnyc.com). Subway 6 to 77th Street. **Open** noon-midnight daily. **Map** p175 B4 ❽

Designed as a nod to Coco Chanel, Daniel Boulud's bar is framed in black lacquered panels that recall an elegant make-up compact. The luxe setting and moneyed crowd might seem a little stiff, but the seasonally rotating cocktails are so exquisitely executed you won't mind sharing your banquette with a suit. Light eats are provided by Café Boulud next door.

Bemelmans Bar

The Carlyle, 35 E 76th Street, at Madison Avenue (1-212 744 1600, www.thecarlyle.com). Subway 6 to 77th Street. **Open** 11am-midnight Mon, Sun; 11am-12.30am Tue-Thur; 11am-1am Fri, Sat. **Map** p175 B4 ❾

The Plaza may have Eloise, but the Carlyle has its own children's book connection – the wonderful 1947 murals of Central Park by *Madeline* creator Ludwig Bemelmans in this, the quintessential classy New York bar. A jazz trio adds to the atmosphere every night at 9.30pm (a cover charge of $15-$30 applies when it takes up residence).

Shops & Services

Madison Avenue, between 57th and 86th Streets, is packed with international designer names: Alexander McQueen, Chloé, Derek Lam, Gucci, Prada, Lanvin, Ralph Lauren, Valentino and more.

★ Barneys New York

660 Madison Avenue, at 61st Street, Upper East Side (1-212 826 8900, www.barneys.com). Subway N, Q, R to Fifth Avenue-59th Street; 4, 5, 6 to 59th Street. **Open** 10am-8pm Mon-Fri; 10am-7pm Sat; 11am-6pm Sun. **Map** p175 B6 ❿ **Department store**

Barneys has a reputation for spotlighting more independent designer labels than other upmarket department stores, and has its own quirky-classic collection. The ground floor showcases luxe accessories, and cult beauty brands are in the basement. Head to the seventh and eighth floors for contemporary designer and denim lines.

Other locations 2151 Broadway, at 76th Street, Upper West Side (1-646 335 0978); 116 Wooster Street, between Prince & Spring Streets, Soho (1-212 965 9964); 194 Atlantic Avenue, at Court Street, Cobble Hill, Brooklyn (1-718 637 2234).

IN THE KNOW
POP ARTIST'S PAD

A sedate Upper East Side address might seem at odds with his avant-garde image, but Andy Warhol lived at 57 East 66th Street from 1974 to 1987.

Bloomingdale's

1000 Third Avenue, at 59th Street (1-212 705 2000, www.bloomingdales.com). Subway N, Q, R to Lexington Avenue-59th Street; 4, 5, 6 to 59th Street. **Open** 10am-8.30pm Mon-Sat; 10am-7pm Sun. **Map** p175 C6 ⓫ **Department store**

Ranking among the city's top tourist attractions, Bloomie's is a gigantic, glitzy department store stocked with everything from handbags to home furnishings. The glam beauty section includes an outpost of globe-spanning apothecary Space NK, and you can get a mid-shopping sugar fix at the on-site Magnolia Bakery. The hipper, compact Soho outpost concentrates on contemporary fashion and accessories, denim and cosmetics.

Other locations 504 Broadway, between Broome & Spring Streets, Soho (1-212 729 5900).

Cornelia Spa at the Surrey

2nd Floor, 20 E 76th Street, between Fifth & Madison Avenues (1-646 358 3600, www.corneliaspaatthesurrey.com). Subway 6 to 77th Street. **Open** 10am-8pm Mon-Fri; 9am-7pm Sat, Sun. **Map** p175 B4 ⓬ **Health & beauty**

Husband and wife Rick Aidekman and Ellen Sackoff have reopened this popular boutique spa, which closed in 2009, in a smaller hotel setting. The intimate yet luxurious oasis is designed to make you feel like you're lounging in your own living space, while a 'botanical tasting bar' serves savoury and sweet treats. Splurge on the Reparative Caviar and Oxygen Quench facial ($325), or a signature massage ($175), which combines deep-tissue, Swedish and shiatsu techniques.

Fivestory

18 E 69th Street, between Fifth & Madison Avenues (1-212 288 1338, www.fivestoryny.com). Subway 6 to 68th Street-Hunter College. **Open** 10am-6pm Mon-Wed, Fri; 10am-7pm Thur; noon-6pm Sat, Sun. **Map** p175 B5 ⓭ **Fashion**

At just 26 (with a little help from her fashion-industry insider dad), Claire Distenfeld opened this glamorous, grown-up boutique, which sprawls over two and a half floors of – yes – a five-storey townhouse. The space is stocked with clothing, shoes and accessories for men, women and children, plus select home items. The emphasis is on less-ubiquitous American and European labels, including Alexander Wang, Giambattista Valli and Acne, and Gianvito Rossi's seductively sleek footwear. *Photo p178.*

Fivestory. *See p177.*

Fix Beauty Bar

2nd Floor, 847 Lexington Avenue between 64th and 65th Streets (1-212 744 0800, www.fixbeautybar.com). Subway F to Lexington Avenue-63rd Street. **Open** 9am-7pm Mon, Tue; 9am-8pm Wed, Thur; 9am-9pm Fri, Sat; 9am-6pm Sun. **Map** p175 C6 ⓮ **Health & beauty**

Writer Karol Markowicz and Michelle Breskin, whose background is in real estate and finance, are taking the blow-dry bar phenomenon one step further, offering busy New Yorkers manicures ($15) and pedicures ($35) to accompany the affordable flat-rate blow-dries ($40) at their chic lavender-and-grey salon. Hairstyles are named after celebrities with instantly recognisable tresses, such as the Jen (sleek and pin-straight), the Taylor (soft, styled curls) and the Kim (full, dramatic waves).

Gagosian Shop

976 Madison Avenue, between 76th & 77th Streets (1-212 796 1224, www.gagosian.com). Subway 6 to 77th Street. **Open** 10am-7pm Mon-Sat. **Map** p175 B4 ⓯ **Gifts & souvenirs**

The art-gallery giant recently opened a 600sq ft gift shop, designed by Selldorf Architects, on the ground floor of its Upper East Side location. Posters, prints and publications are the main focus, but artist-designed home decor and objects pepper the offerings.

Lisa Perry

988 Madison Avenue, at 77th Street (1-212 431 7467, www.lisaperrystyle.com). Subway 6 to 77th Street. **Open** 10am-6pm Mon-Sat; noon-5pm Sun. **Map** p175 B4 ⓰ **Fashion**

Upon graduation from FIT in 1981, designer Lisa Perry launched her line of retro women's threads inspired by her massive personal collection of 1960s and '70s fashion. Ultrabright pieces, such as her signature colour-blocked minidresses, pop against the stark white walls of her Madison Avenue flagship. You'll also find the designer's cheerful accessories, such as candy-coloured duffel bags, and her mod home collection, which includes place mats and pillows.

Paul Molé Barber Shop

1034 Lexington Avenue, at 74th Street (1-212 535 8461, www.paulmole.com). Subway 6 to 77th Street. **Open** 7.30am-8pm Mon-Fri; 7.30am-6pm Sat; 9am-4pm Sun (except July, Aug). **No credit cards. Map** p175 B5 ⓱ **Health & beauty**

Best known for its precise shaves, this nostalgic barbers' has been grooming men since 1913 (John Steinbeck used to come here to be debearded). As well as its signature Deluxe Open Razor Shave ($40), you can get a haircut (from $39) and other services such as a scalp massage ($10).

MUSEUM MILE & CARNEGIE HILL

Subway 4, 5, 6 to 86th Street; 6 to 96th Street or 103rd Street.

Philanthropic gestures made by the moneyed classes over the past 130-odd years have helped to create an impressive cluster of art collections, museums and cultural institutions on the Upper East Side. Indeed, Fifth Avenue from 82nd to 105th Streets is known as **Museum Mile**, and for good reason: it's lined with more than half a dozen celebrated institutions. **El Museo del Barrio** (*see p180*) used to define the Mile's northern border, but the strip is lengthening: the future home of the **New Africa Center**, which will contain a museum (www.africanart.org), is at the corner of 110th Street, though the opening has been delayed by lack of funding.

Carnegie Hill, the northern blocks of the Upper East Side between Fifth and Lexington Avenues, takes its name from early resident Andrew Carnegie. The Scottish philanthropist bought a large chunk of then-rural land in 1898 to build a 64-room mansion, which is now home to the Smithsonian's Cooper-Hewitt, National Design Museum.

Sights & Museums

Smithsonian's Cooper-Hewitt, National Design Museum

2 E 91st Street, at Fifth Avenue (1-212 849 8400, www.cooperhewitt.org). Subway 4, 5, 6 to 86th Street. Closed until autumn 2014 (see website for updates). **Map** p175 B3 ⓲

The Cooper-Hewitt Museum began as a collection created for students of the Cooper Union for the Advancement of Science and Art by the Hewitt sisters – grand-daughters of the institution's founder, Peter Cooper – and opened to the public in 1897. Part of the Smithsonian since the 1960s, it is the only museum in the US solely dedicated to historic and

GRAND DESIGNS

Five highlights of the Cooper-Hewitt, National Design Museum

Home to 217,000 objects, the Cooper-Hewitt's Carnegie mansion is itself an example of ground-breaking design – the landmarked 64-room Georgian-style pile was among the first private homes to have an elevator, central heating and even a precursor of air-conditioning. Historic spaces such as the Teak Room, with its intricate wall panels and cabinets conceived by prominent interior designer Lockwood de Forest and hand-carved in India, have been painstakingly restored, and the addition of a 6,000-square-foot gallery on the third floor – formerly occupied by the National Design Library (now housed an adjacent building) – provides more room for rotating exhibitions.

Diller Scofidio + Renfro – the architects behind Lincoln Center's recent spruce-up – have created contemporary, interactive displays that respect the period surroundings. On the museum's reopening, the second floor will showcase a selection of 358 objects from the permanent collection – comprising wall coverings, textiles, product design, decorative arts, drawings, prints and graphic design – integrated in thematic displays. Here are five highlights:

STAIRCASE MODEL, EARLY 19TH CENTURY

The unique collection of 26 staircase models were mainly made in France by craftsmen to demonstrate their skills. Although it measures little more than two feet high, this piece is made of contrasting cut and inlaid mahogany, ebony, pear or sycamore and oak, and embellished with miniature Sèvres porcelain busts of Voltaire and Rousseau.

CONCEPT DESIGN FOR AIR JORDAN XIII SNEAKER, 1996

The Air Jordan sneaker was among the top cult design items of the 1990s. This rendering by the shoe's original designer, Tinker Hatfield, reflects the museum's commitment to collecting not only finished objects, but also drawings and prototypes that illuminate the design process.

OIL SKETCH, 'ATHENS, FROM THE NORTHWEST', 1869

Part of the museum's original collection, this sketch by Hudson River School painter Frederic Church reflects the museum's origins as a 'visual library' for Cooper Union students, which included preparatory sketches as well as the completed works. 'The real strength of our collection is 19th century,' says curatorial director, Cara McCarty, 'although in recent years we've been making a concerted effort to add to the contemporary collection.'

'RUSH HOUR 2/SHANGHAI', 2012

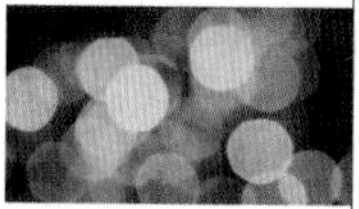

Danish textile designer Grethe Sørensen trained in traditional techniques but became increasingly interested in digital technology, both photography and the automated jacquard weaving process, explains McCarty. To create this wall hanging, the designer worked on graph paper to convert an image of oncoming traffic to the punch cards used in the operation of the loom.

LED WALLPAPER, 2013

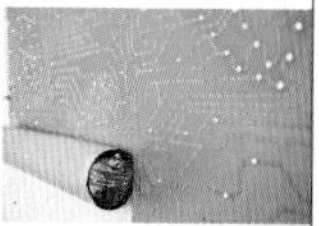

A prototype for this circuit-inspired wallpaper was first shown in 2007 as part of a retrospective of the German artist/lighting designer Ingo Maurer. 'Finally, they were able to put it into production,' says McCarty. The LED lights have been hand-placed on machine-printed paper and can be programmed to illuminate specific sections.

IN THE KNOW
NIGHT AT THE MUSEUM

Most of the city's major museums are free or pay what you wish one evening (usually Thursday or Friday) or afternoon of the week. Some enhance the experience with musical and other performances.

contemporary design. In 1976, it took up residence in the former home of steel magnate Andrew Carnegie. Autumn 2014 sees the completion of a three-year renovation and expansion project, which has increased the exhibition space by 60%. *See p179* **Grand Designs**.

El Museo del Barrio

1230 Fifth Avenue, at 104th Street (1-212 831 7272, www.elmuseo.org). Subway 6 to 103rd Street. **Open** 11am-6pm Wed-Sat. **Admission** *Suggested donation* $9; $5 reductions; free under-12s; free over-65s Wed. *Sept-Dec, Feb-May* Free 3rd Sat each mth. **Map** p175 B1 ⑲

Founded in 1969 by the artist and former MoMA curator Rafael Montañez Ortiz, El Museo del Barrio takes its name from its East Harlem locale (though this stretch of Fifth Avenue is considered to be part of the Upper East Side). Dedicated to the art and culture of Puerto Ricans and Latin Americans all over the US, El Museo reopened in autumn 2009 following a $35-million renovation. The redesigned spaces within the museum's 1921 Beaux Arts building provide a polished, contemporary showcase for the diversity and vibrancy of Hispanic art. The new galleries allow more space for rotating exhibitions from the museum's 6,500-piece holdings – from pre-Columbian artefacts to contemporary installations – as well as temporary shows.

Jewish Museum

1109 Fifth Avenue, at 92nd Street (1-212 423 3200, www.thejewishmuseum.org). Subway 4, 5, 6 to 86th Street; 6 to 96th Street. **Open** 11am-5.45pm Mon, Tue, Sat, Sun; 11am-8pm Thur; 11am-5.45pm Fri (11am-4pm Nov-Mar). Closed on Jewish holidays. **Admission** $15; $7.50-$12 reductions; free under-19s. Free Sat. Pay what you wish 5-8pm Thur. **Map** p175 B3 ⑳

The Jewish Museum is housed in a magnificent 1908 French Gothic-style mansion – the former home of the financier, collector and Jewish leader Felix Warburg. Inside, 'Culture and Continuity: The Jewish Journey' traces the evolution of Judaism from antiquity to the present day. The two-floor permanent exhibition comprises thematic displays of 800 of the museum's cache of 25,000 works of art, artefacts and media installations. The excellent temporary shows, which spotlight Jewish artists or related themes, appeal to a broad audience, and the museum recently launched a series of global film and video works, selected by 25 international curators, to be screened monthly over the next two years.

► *The Museum of Jewish Heritage: A Living Memorial to the Holocaust (see p56) and the Museum at Eldridge Street (see p84), both Downtown, further explore Jewish culture.*

★ Metropolitan Museum of Art

1000 Fifth Avenue, at 82nd Street (1-212 535 7710, www.metmuseum.org). Subway 4, 5, 6 to 86th Street. **Open** 10am-5.30pm Mon-Thur, Sun; 10am-9pm Fri, Sat. **Admission** *Suggested donation* (incl same-week admission to the Cloisters) $25; $12-$17 reductions; free under-12s. **Map** p175 B4 ㉑

Now occupying 13 acres of Central Park, the Metropolitan Museum of Art opened in 1880. The original Gothic Revival building was designed by Calvert Vaux and Jacob Wrey Mould, but is now almost completely hidden by subsequent additions. A redesign of the museum's four-block-long plaza is expected to be completed in autumn 2014, bringing new fountains and tree-shaded seating.

The first floor's north wing contains the collection of ancient Egyptian art and the glass-walled atrium housing the Temple of Dendur, moved en masse from its original Nile-side setting and now overlooking a reflective pool. The north-west corner is occupied by the American Wing, which underwent a multi-phase renovation that culminated in 2012 with the reopening of its Galleries for Paintings, Sculpture and Decorative Arts; the centrepiece is Emanuel Gottlieb Leutze's iconic 1851 painting *Washington Crossing the Delaware*. The wing's grand Engelhard Court is now more a sculpture court than an interior garden; the light-filled space is flanked by the façade of Wall Street's Branch Bank of the United States (saved when the building was torn down in 1915) and a stunning loggia designed by Louis Comfort Tiffany for his Long Island estate.

In the southern wing are the halls housing Greek and Roman art. Turning west brings you to the Arts of Africa, Oceania and the Americas collection; it was donated by Nelson Rockefeller as a memorial to his son Michael, who disappeared while visiting New Guinea in 1961. A wider-ranging bequest, the two-storey Robert Lehman Wing, is at the western end of the floor. This eclectic collection is housed in a recreation of the Lehman family townhouse and features works by Botticelli, Bellini, Ingres and Rembrandt, among others.

Upstairs, the central western section is dominated by the recently expanded and rehung European Paintings galleries, which hold an amazing reserve of old masters – the museum's five Vermeers are now shown together for the first time. To the south, the 19th-century European galleries contain some of the Met's most popular works – in particular the two-room Monet holdings and a colony of Van Goghs that includes his oft-reproduced *Irises*.

Walk eastward and you'll reach the galleries of the Art of the Arab Lands, Turkey, Iran, Central Asia and Later South Asia. In the north-east wing of the floor, you'll find the sprawling collection of Asian art; be sure to check out the ceiling of the Jain Meeting Hall in the South-east Asian gallery. If you're still on your feet, give them a deserved rest in the Astor Court, a tranquil recreation of a Ming Dynasty garden, or head up to the Iris & B Gerald Cantor Roof Garden (usually open May-Oct).

▶ *For the Cloisters, which houses the Met's medieval art collection, see p193.*

Museum of the City of New York

1220 Fifth Avenue, between 103rd & 104th Streets (1-212 534 1672, www.mcny.org). Subway 6 to 103rd Street. **Open** 10am-6pm daily. **Admission** *Suggested donation* $10; $6 reductions; $20 family; free under-13s. **Map** p175 B1 ㉒

A great introduction to New York, this institution contains a wealth of city history. *Timescapes*, a 22-minute multimedia presentation that illuminates the history of NYC, is shown free with admission every half hour. The museum's holdings include prints, drawings and photos of the city, decorative arts and furnishings, and a large collection of toys. The undoubted jewel is the amazing Stettheimer Dollhouse: it was created in the 1920s by Carrie Stettheimer, whose artist friends reinterpreted their masterpieces in miniature to hang on the walls. Look closely and you'll even spy a tiny version of Marcel Duchamp's famous *Nude Descending a Staircase*.

A rolling renovation has brought new galleries for temporary exhibitions, which spotlight the city from different angles. Renovations to the museum's North Wing, due to be completed in 2015, will provide space for a core exhibition about the city.

National Academy Museum

1083 Fifth Avenue, at 89th Street (1-212 369 4880, www.nationalacademy.org). Subway 4, 5, 6 to 86th Street. **Open** 11am-6pm Wed-Sun. **Admission** $15; $10 reductions; free under-12s. **Map** p175 B3 ㉓

Founded in 1825, the National Academy combines an art school, a museum and a professional association – academicians include Bill Viola, Chuck Close, Cindy Sherman and Frank Gehry, to name but a few. Housed in an elegant Fifth Avenue townhouse, the museum holds more than 7,000 works of American art, from the 19th century to the present, including paintings, sculptures, engravings and architectural drawings by the likes of Louise Bourgeois, Jasper Johns, Robert Rauschenberg and John Singer Sargent. The institution also regularly hosts temporary shows.

Neue Galerie

1048 Fifth Avenue, at 86th Street (1-212 628 6200, www.neuegalerie.org). Subway 4, 5, 6 to 86th Street. **Open** 11am-6pm Mon, Thur-Sun; 11am-8pm 1st Fri of the mth. **Admission** (under-16s must be accompanied by an adult; under-12s not admitted) $20; $10 reductions. Free 6-8pm 1st Fri of the mth. **Map** p175 B3 ㉔

IN THE KNOW
EYEING THE NEEDLE

The Central Park **Obelisk** (*see p169*), the only one in the entire western hemisphere, is best viewed from the Petrie European Sculpture Court in the Metropolitan Museum (*see p182*).

The elegant Neue Galerie is devoted entirely to late 19th- and early 20th-century German and Austrian fine and decorative arts. The creation of the late art dealer Serge Sabarsky and cosmetics mogul Ronald S Lauder, it has the largest concentration of works by Gustav Klimt and Egon Schiele outside of Vienna. There's also a bookstore, a small design shop and the ultra-refined Café Sabarsky (*see right*), serving modern Austrian cuisine and ravishing Viennese pastries.

★ Solomon R Guggenheim Museum

1071 Fifth Avenue, between 88th & 89th Streets (1-212 423 3500, www.guggenheim.org). Subway 4, 5, 6 to 86th Street. **Open** 10am-5.45pm Mon-Wed, Fri, Sun; 10am-7.45pm Sat. **Admission** $22; $18 reductions; free under-13s. Pay what you wish 5.45-7.45pm Sat. **Map** p175 B3 ㉕

The Guggenheim is as famous for its landmark building as it is for its impressive collection and daring temporary shows. The dramatic structure, with its winding, cantilevered curves, was designed by Frank Lloyd Wright. His only NYC building, apart from a private house on Staten Island, it caused quite a stir when it debuted 1959. In 1992, the addition of a ten-storey tower provided space for a sculpture terrace (with park views), a café and an auditorium; the museum also has a more upscale restaurant. Solomon R Guggenheim's original founding collection, amassed in the 1930s, includes 150 works by Kandinsky, in addition to pieces by Chagall, Picasso and Franz Marc and others; the Solomon R Guggenheim Foundation's holdings have since been enriched by subsequent bequests, including the Thannhauser Collection – which includes paintings by Impressionist and post-Impressionist masters such as Manet, Cézanne and Gaugin – and the Panza di Biumo Collection of American minimalist and conceptual art from the 1960s and '70s.

Restaurants & Cafés

★ Café Sabarsky

Neue Galerie, 1048 Fifth Avenue, at 86th Street (1-212 288 0665, www.cafesabarsky.com). Subway 4, 5, 6 to 86th Street. **Open** 9am-6pm Mon, Wed; 9am-9pm Thur-Sun. **Main courses** $16-$30. **Map** p175 B3 ㉖ **Austrian/Café**

Purveyor of indulgent pastries and whipped cream-topped *einspänner* coffee for Neue Galerie patrons by day, this sophisticated, high-ceilinged restaurant, inspired by a classic Viennese *kaffeehaus*, is helmed by chef Kurt Gutenbrunner of modern Austrian restaurant Wallsé. Appetisers are most adventurous – the creaminess of the spätzle is a perfect base for sweetcorn, tarragon and wild mushrooms – while main course specials, such as the wiener schnitzel tartly garnished with lingonberries, are capable yet ultimately feel like the calm before the *Sturm und Drang* of dessert. Try the *klimttorte*, which masterfully alternates layers of hazelnut cake with chocolate. Note that Café Sabarsky is closed on Tuesdays.

Dough Loco

1261 Park Avenue, between 97th & 98th Streets (1-212 876 1980, www.doughloco.com). Subway 6 to 96th Street. **Open** 7am-7pm daily. **Doughnuts** $3. **Map** p175 B2 ㉗ **Café**

Chef Corey Cova (Earl's Beer & Cheese, ABV) – known for funky dishes like a Spam-and-octopus salad and a foie gras Fluffernutter – rolls out eccentric haute doughnuts at this seven-seat bakery. Behind a counter crafted from old bowling alley lanes, find a rotating selection of oddball flavours like miso-maple and raspberrry-Sriracha alongside more traditional ones like cinnamon-sugar and chocolate. To drink: pour-overs and espressos made from Blue Bottle beans.

Penrose.

EXPLORE

Bars

Earl's Beer & Cheese

1259 Park Avenue, between 97th & 98th Street (1-212 289 1581, www.earlsny.com). Subway 6 to 96th Street. **Open** 4pm-midnight Mon, Tue; 11am-midnight Wed, Thur, Sun; 11am-2am Fri, Sat. **Map** p175 B2 ㉘

Tucked into the no-man's land between the Upper East Side and Spanish Harlem, this craft-beer cubby hole has the sort of community-hub vibe that makes you want to settle in. The well-priced rotating selection of American craft brews and slapdash set-up appeal to a neighbourhood crowd, but it's Momofuku Ssäm Bar alum Corey Cova's madcap bar menu that makes it destination-worthy. Try the NY State Cheddar – a grilled cheese with braised pork belly, fried egg and house-made kimchi. (Note that the kitchen closes at 11pm.) The crew has since opened a cocktail bar, the Guthrie Inn, next door (at the same address, 1-212 423 9900) and a wine bar, ABV (1504 Lexington Avenue, at 97th Street, 1-212 722 8959, www.abvny.com), a block east.

Shops & Services

Malin + Goetz

1266B Madison Avenue, between 90th & 91st Streets (1-212 226 1310, www.malinandgoetz.com). Subway 4, 5, 6 to 86th Street. **Open** 11am-7pm Mon-Fri; noon-7pm Sat; noon-6pm Sun. **Map** p175 B3 ㉙ **Health & beauty**

Matthew Malin and Andrew Goetz recently opened the third Manhattan location of their modern apothecary, showcasing their natural, locally manufactured line of unisex skin and hair products. Aluminium towers hold the full collection, including glycolic-acid peel pads, aluminium-free eucalyptus deodorant and sage styling cream. An alcove in the back wall displays candles and fragrances in unusual scents.

YORKVILLE

The atmosphere becomes noticeably less rarefied as you walk east from Central Park, with grand edifices giving way to bland modern apartment blocks and walk-up tenements. Not much remains of the old German and Hungarian immigrant communities that once filled **Yorkville**, the neighbourhood above 79th Street between Third Avenue and the East River, with delicatessens, beer halls and restaurants. However, one such flashback, open since 1936, is **Heidelberg** (1648 Second Avenue, between 85th & 86th Streets, 1-212 628 2332, www.heidelbergrestaurant.com), where dirndl-wearing waitresses serve up steins of Spaten and platters of sausages from the wurst-meisters at butcher shop Schaller & Weber a few doors up (1654 Second Avenue, 1-212 879 3047, closed Sun). Second Avenue in the 70s and 80s throbs with rowdy pick-up bars frequented by preppy, twentysomething crowds. But new craft-beer spot the **Penrose** (*see below*) has brought a bit of the indie-chic East Village uptown.

The only Federal-style mansion in Manhattan, **Gracie Mansion** stands at the eastern end of 88th Street. The stately pile has served as New York's official mayoral residence since 1942 – except during billionaire Michael Bloomberg's time in office. Since Bill de Blasio was elected in 2013, it is once again occupied. The mansion is fenced off, but much of the exterior can be seen from surrounding **Carl Schurz Park**.

One block from Gracie Mansion, the **Henderson Place Historic District** (at East End Avenue, between 86th & 87th Streets) contains 24 handsome Queen Anne row houses – commissioned by furrier and noted real-estate developer John C Henderson as servants' quarters – with their original turrets, double stoops and slate roofs.

Sights & Museums

Gracie Mansion

Carl Schurz Park, 88th Street, at East End Avenue (1-212 570 4778). Subway 4, 5, 6 to 86th Street. **Tours** Wed, call for information; reservations required. **Admission** $7; $4 reductions; free students. **No credit cards. Map** p175 D3 ㉚

This green-shuttered yellow edifice was built in 1799 by Scottish merchant Archibald Gracie as a country home. Today, the stately house is the focal point of tranquil Carl Schurz Park, named in honour of the German immigrant who became a newspaper editor and US senator. When mayor Michael Bloomberg declined to move in after taking up office in 2002, Gracie Mansion's living quarters were opened up to public tours for the first time in 60 years; tours of part of the house will continue now that Mayor de Blasio is in residence.

Bars

Penrose

1590 Second Avenue, between 82nd & 83rd Streets (1-212 203 2751, www.penrosebar.com). Subway 4, 5, 6 to 86th Street. **Open** 3pm-4am Mon-Thur; noon-4am Fri; 10.30am-4am Sat, Sun. **Map** p175 C4 ㉛

Named for a neighbourhood in Cork, Ireland, where two of the owners grew up, the Penrose stands apart from the Upper East Side's sports bars and fancier joints – its exposed-brick walls, retro decorative touches and curved wooden bar are casually sophisticated. The craft-brew list includes the malty NewBurgh Brown Ale from upstate New York; there's also Murphy's Stout and an extensive whiskey selection (Irish, American and Scotch). The comfort-food-heavy menu includes a thick, juicy Pat LaFrieda blend house burger.

Harlem & Upper Manhattan

Harlem is the cultural capital of black America – a legacy of the Harlem Renaissance, the cultural movement that spanned the 1920s. During the Jazz Age, white New Yorkers accepted Ellington's famous invitation to 'Take the A Train' uptown to the neighbourhood's celebrated nightclubs, but in the 1960s and '70s, crime and urban decay kept them away. Now Harlem's second renaissance, stalled by the recession, is back on track. The area isn't packed with sights, but it offers eclectic architecture, theatrical street life, historic churches with exuberant gospel choirs and a rejuvenated restaurant and bar scene.

Red Rooster.

Don't Miss

1 Studio Museum in Harlem Work by prominent and emerging black artists (*p188*).

2 Red Rooster Savour gourmet soul food at this cross-cultural canteen (*p190*).

3 Morris-Jumel Mansion George Washington slept here (*p193*).

4 The Cloisters A fairytale castle houses the Met's medieval collection (*p193*).

5 New Leaf Restaurant & Bar Good food for a good cause (*p193*).

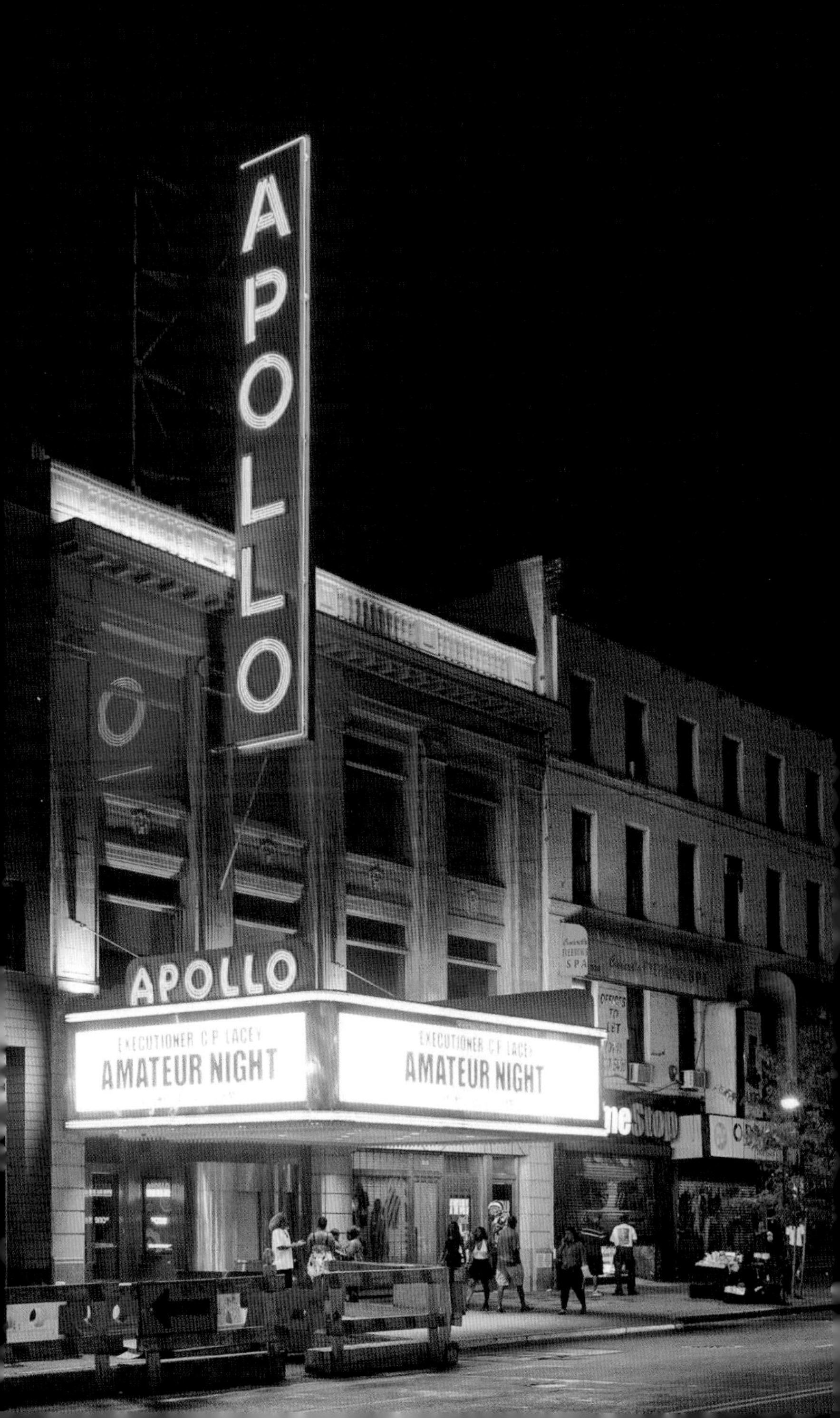
APOLLO
APOLLO
EXECUTIONER C.P. LACEY
AMATEUR NIGHT
EXECUTIONER C.P. LACEY
AMATEUR NIGHT
OFFICES TO LET

Harlem

WEST & CENTRAL HARLEM

Subway A, B, C, D to 125th Street; B, C to 116th Street or 135th Street; 1, 2, 3 to 125th Street.

The village of Harlem, named by Dutch colonists after their native Haarlem, was annexed by the City of New York in 1873. The extension of the elevated subway two decades later brought eager developers who overbuilt in the suddenly accessible suburb. The consequent housing glut led to cheap rents, and Jewish, Italian and Irish immigrants escaping the tenements of the Lower East Side snapped them up.

Around the turn of the 20th century, black Americans joined the procession into Harlem, their ranks swelled by the great migration from the Deep South. By 1914, the black population of Harlem had risen well above 50,000; by the 1920s, Harlem was predominately black and the country's most populous African-American community. This prominence soon attracted some of black America's greatest artists: writers such as Langston Hughes and Zora Neale Hurston and musicians including Duke Ellington, Louis Armstrong and Cab Calloway, an unprecedented cultural gathering known as the Harlem Renaissance. White New York took notice, venturing uptown – where the enforcement of Prohibition was lax – to enjoy the Cotton Club, Connie's Inn, Smalls Paradise and the Savoy Ballroom, which supplied the beat for the city that never sleeps.

The Depression killed the Harlem Renaissance, and deeply wounded Harlem. By the 1960s, the community had been ravaged by middle-class flight and municipal neglect. Businesses closed, racial tensions ran high, and the looting during the 1977 blackout was among the worst the city had seen. However, as New York's economic standing improved in the mid '90s, investment began slowly spilling into the area, spawning new businesses and the phalanxes of renovated brownstones that beckon the middle class (white and black). This moneyed influx's coexistence with Harlem's long-standing residents can be tense, but it is seldom volatile.

On 125th Street, Harlem's main artery, street preachers and mix-tape hawkers vie for the attentions of the human parade and the celebrated **Apollo Theater** (*see p272*) hosts concerts, a syndicated TV show and the classic Amateur Night every Wednesday – James Brown, Ella Fitzgerald, Michael Jackson and Lauryn Hill are among its starry alumni. A block east is the highly regarded **Studio Museum in Harlem** (*see p188*).

Although new apartment buildings, boutiques, restaurants and cafés are scattered around the neighbourhood, especially on Frederick Douglass Boulevard (Eighth Avenue) between 110th and 125th Streets, Harlem has managed to retain many of the buildings that went up around the turn of the century because redevelopers shunned it for so long. Of particular interest, the **Mount Morris Historic District** (from 119th to 124th Streets, between Malcolm X Boulevard/ Lenox Avenue & Mount Morris Park West) contains charming brownstones and a

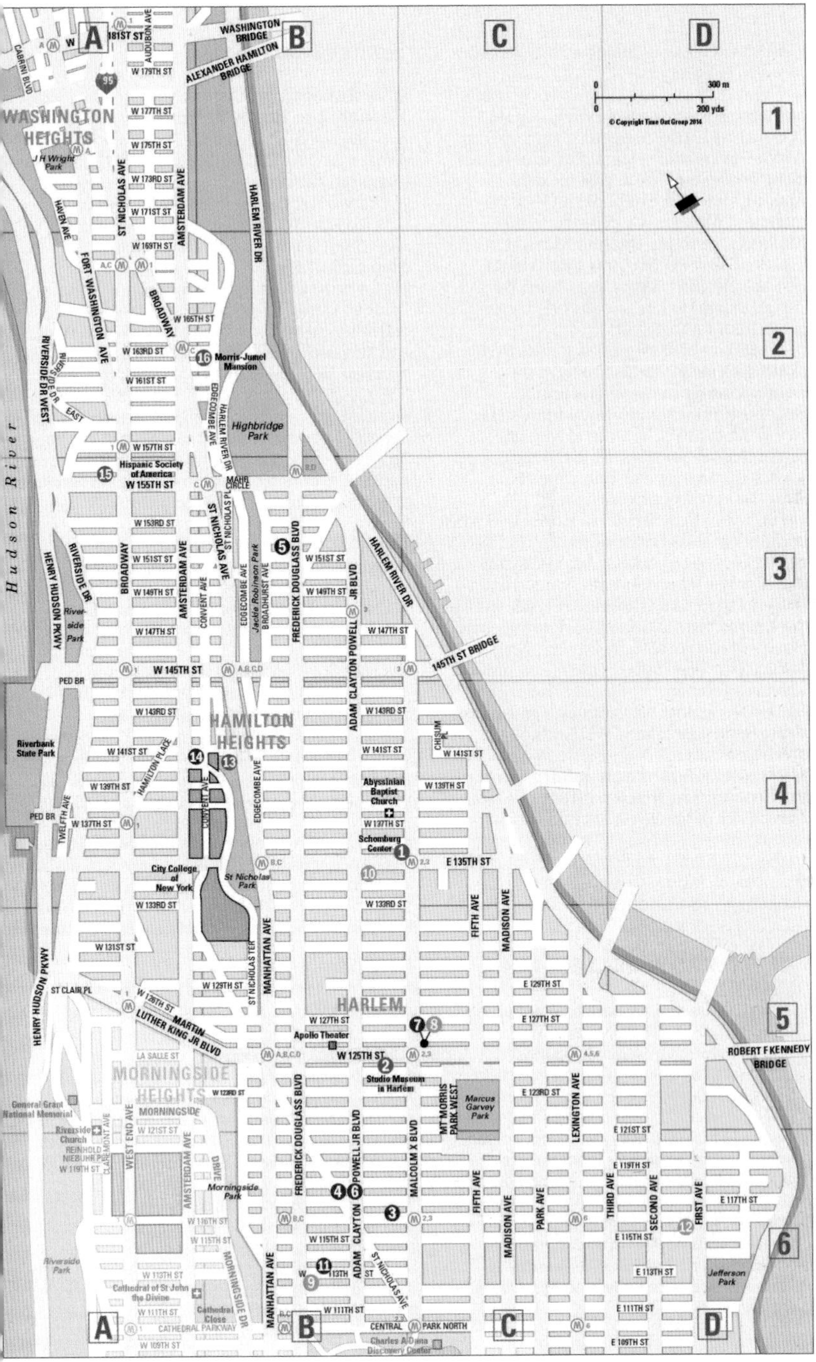

A
B
C
D
1
2
3
4
5
6
0
300 m
300 yds
© Copyright Time Out Group 2014
WASHINGTON HEIGHTS
HAMILTON HEIGHTS
HARLEM
MORNINGSIDE HEIGHTS
Hudson River
WASHINGTON BRIDGE
ALEXANDER HAMILTON BRIDGE
HARLEM RIVER DR
145TH ST BRIDGE
ROBERT F KENNEDY BRIDGE
W 181ST ST
W 179TH ST
W 177TH ST
W 175TH ST
W 173RD ST
W 171ST ST
W 169TH ST
W 165TH ST
W 163RD ST
W 161ST ST
W 157TH ST
W 155TH ST
W 153RD ST
W 151ST ST
W 149TH ST
W 147TH ST
W 145TH ST
W 143RD ST
W 141ST ST
W 139TH ST
W 137TH ST
E 135TH ST
W 133RD ST
W 131ST ST
W 129TH ST
E 129TH ST
W 127TH ST
E 127TH ST
W 125TH ST
W 123RD ST
E 123RD ST
W 121ST ST
E 121ST ST
W 119TH ST
E 119TH ST
E 117TH ST
W 116TH ST
W 115TH ST
E 115TH ST
W 113TH ST
E 113TH ST
W 111TH ST
E 111TH ST
W 109TH ST
E 109TH ST
CABRINI BLVD
AUDUBON AVE
ST NICHOLAS AVE
AMSTERDAM AVE
HAVEN AVE
FORT WASHINGTON AVE
BROADWAY
RIVERSIDE DR WEST
RIVERSIDE DR EAST
EDGECOMBE AVE
ST NICHOLAS PL
MAHR CIRCLE
RIVERSIDE DR
HENRY HUDSON PKWY
CONVENT AVE
Jackie Robinson Park
BROADHURST AVE
FREDERICK DOUGLASS BLVD
ADAM CLAYTON POWELL JR BLVD
CHISUM PL
PED BR
HAMILTON PLACE
TWELFTH AVE
ST NICHOLAS TER
MANHATTAN AVE
ST CLAIR PL
W 126TH ST
MARTIN LUTHER KING JR BLVD
LA SALLE ST
MORNINGSIDE
CLAREMONT AVE
WEST END AVE
MORNINGSIDE DRIVE
REINHOLD NIEBUHR PL
MALCOLM X BLVD
MT MORRIS PARK WEST
FIFTH AVE
MADISON AVE
PARK AVE
LEXINGTON AVE
THIRD AVE
SECOND AVE
FIRST AVE
CATHEDRAL PARKWAY
CENTRAL PARK NORTH
J H Wright Park
Highbridge Park
River-side Park
Riverbank State Park
St Nicholas Park
Morningside Park
Marcus Garvey Park
Riverside Park
Jefferson Park
Morris-Jumel Mansion
Hispanic Society of America
Abyssinian Baptist Church
Schomburg Center
City College of New York
Apollo Theater
Studio Museum in Harlem
General Grant National Memorial
Riverside Church
Cathedral of St John the Divine
Cathedral Close
Charles A Dana Discovery Center

collection of religious buildings in a variety of architectural styles.

The section of West 116th Street between St Nicholas Avenue and Morningside Park is known as **Little Senegal**, a strip of West African shops and restaurants. Continue east along 116th Street West, past the domed **Masjid Malcolm Shabazz** (no.102), the mosque of Malcolm X's ministry, to the **Malcolm Shabazz Harlem Market** (no.52, 1-212 987 8131), an outdoor bazaar that buzzes with vendors, most from West Africa, selling clothes, jewellery and other goods from covered stalls.

While most of the storied jazz clubs have closed, look out for the reopening of the **Lenox Lounge** (*see right* **Harlem's Second Renaissance**). **Showman's Bar** (375 W 125th Street, between St Nicholas & Morningside Avenues, 1-212 864 8941, www.showmansjazzclub.com, closed Sun), is another neighbourhood old-timer.

Further north is **Strivers' Row**, also known as the St Nicholas Historic District. On 138th and 139th Streets, between Adam Clayton Powell Jr Boulevard (Seventh Avenue) and Frederick Douglass Boulevard (Eighth Avenue), these harmonious blocks of brick townhouses were developed in 1891 by David H King Jr and designed by three different architects, one of whom was Stanford White. The enclave is so well preserved that the alleyway sign advising you to 'walk your horses' is still visible.

Harlem's rich history is stored in the archives of the nearby **Schomburg Center for Research in Black Culture** (*see right*). This branch of the New York Public Library contains more than five million documents, artefacts, films and prints relating to the cultures of peoples of African descent, with a strong emphasis on the African-American experience.

IN THE KNOW HALLELUJAH!

In the 1930s, the **Abyssinian Baptist Church** (132 Odell Clark Place/W 138th Street, between Malcolm X Boulevard/Lenox Avenue & Adam Clayton Powell Jr Boulevard/Seventh Avenue, 1-212 862 7474, www.abyssinian.org) was under the leadership of legendary civil rights crusader Adam Clayton Powell Jr. From the staid gingerbread Gothic exterior, you'd never suspect the energy that charges the church when the gospel choir gets into swing. Visitors are welcome to attend services on Sunday at 11am and Wednesday at 7pm, but get there early, and don't wear shorts or flip-flops.

Sights & Museums

FREE Schomburg Center for Research in Black Culture

515 Malcolm X Boulevard (Lenox Avenue), between 135th & 136th Streets (1-212 491 2200, www.nypl.org/locations/schomburg). Subway 2, 3 to 135th Street. **Open** *General & gallery* 10am-6pm Mon, Fri, Sat; 10am-8pm Tue-Thur. *Other departments* times vary. **Admission** free. **Map** p187 C4 ❶

Part of the New York Public Library, this institution holds an extraordinary trove of vintage literature and historical memorabilia relating to black culture and the African diaspora, much of which was amassed by notable bibliophile Arturo Alfonso Schomburg, who was curator from 1932 until his death in 1938. (It was posthumously renamed in his honour.) Note that parts of the collection can only be viewed on certain days by appointment; call or refer to the website. The centre also hosts regular exhibitions, concerts, films, lectures and tours.

Studio Museum in Harlem

144 W 125th Street, between Adam Clayton Powell Jr Boulevard (Seventh Avenue) & Malcolm X Boulevard (Lenox Avenue) (1-212 864 4500, www.studiomuseum.org). Subway 2, 3 to 125th Street. **Open** noon-9pm Thur, Fri; 10am-6pm Sat; noon-6pm Sun. **Admission** *Suggested donation* $7; $3 reductions; free under-12s. Free Sun. **No credit cards. Map** p187 B5 ❷

The first black fine arts museum in the United States when it opened in 1968, the Studio Museum is an important player in the art scene of the African diaspora. Under the leadership of director and chief curator Thelma Golden (formerly of the Whitney), this vibrant institution, housed in a stripped-down, three-level space, presents shows in a variety of media by black artists from around the world. The museum supports emerging visual artists of African descent through its coveted artist-in-residence programme.

Restaurants & Cafés

Amy Ruth's

113 W 116th Street, between Malcolm X Boulevard (Lenox Avenue) & Adam Clayton Powell Jr Boulevard (Seventh Avenue) (1-212 280 8779, www.amyruthsharlem.com). Subway 2, 3 to 116th Street. **Open** 11am-11pm Mon; 8.30am-11pm Tue-Thur; 8.30am-5.30am Fri; 7.30am-5.30am Sat; 7.30am-11pm Sun. **Main courses** $12.25-$23. **Map** p187 B6 ❸ **American regional**

This popular no-reservations spot is the place for soul food. Delicately fried okra is delivered without a hint of slime, and the mac and cheese is gooey inside and crunchy-brown on top. Dishes take their names from notable African-Americans – vote for the President Barack Obama (fried, smothered, baked or barbecued chicken).

HARLEM'S SECOND RENAISSANCE

The neighbourhood is hopping with hot restaurants and supper clubs.

Red Rooster.

Nearly a century after its famed cultural surge, Harlem is experiencing another exciting revival, this time of the culinary variety. Frederick Douglass Boulevard has become a de facto Restaurant Row, with buzzy eateries popping up along Eighth Avenue and throughout the area.

Marcus Samuelsson helped to pioneer the movement in 2011 when he opened his comfort-food sensation, **Red Rooster** (*see p190*), named after a legendary Harlem speakeasy once located at 138th Street and Seventh Avenue. The Ethiopian-born, Swedish-raised chef – himself a Harlem resident – created a destination as cool as any downtown spot, but with a distinctly uptown flavour, raking in critical acclaim for his refined soul food that honours both the nabe's history (fried chicken and waffles) and its multicultural residents (Dominican oxtail stew, Jamaican jerk chicken). A year later, Samuelsson expanded his Harlem holdings with **Ginny's Supper Club** (*see p190*), a jazzy ode to the swinging speakeasies and live-music lounges of the 1920s.

In autumn 2013, Richard Parsons and Alexander Smalls paid tribute to Harlem cuisine and music with two notable openings. Inside the historic Cecil Hotel space, the twosome revived Minton's Playhouse, the 1930s jazz lounge where Thelonious Monk served as house pianist and Dizzy Gillespie invented bebop. The new throwback supper club, **Minton's** (*see p190*), tips a hat to this musical past – a 1948 mural of Hot Lips Page anchors the stage and a house band plays nightly. Next door, the **Cecil** (*see p190*) braids together the far-reaching flavours of the African diaspora (citrus jerk bass, roasted poussin yassa) in a polished, gold-accented dining room.

Those aren't the only newbies in the neighbourhood. In December 2013, Harlem welcomed the wine-focused **Park 112** (*see p190*). And the progress will continue with a duo of projects from Richie Notar, owner of the Nobu chain. In spring 2014, he relaunches the fabled Lenox Lounge, a 1939 art deco bar where Billie Holiday and John Coltrane once performed; Mr Henry's Bakery, a New Orleans-style café from baker-turned-actor Dwight Henry. (*Beasts of the Southern Wild*) will follow.

Ginny's Supper Club.

The Cecil

210 W 118th Street, between Adam Clayton Powell Jr Boulevard (Seventh Avenue) and St Nicholas Avenue (1-212 866 1262, www.thececilharlem.com). Subway B, C to 116th Street. **Open** 5pm-midnight Mon-Thur; 5pm-1am Fri; 10am-1am Sat; 11am-11pm Sun. **Main courses** $19-$36. **Map** p187 B6 ❹ **Eclectic**
See p189 **Harlem's Second Renaissance**.

$ Charles' Country Panfried Chicken

2841 Frederick Douglass Boulevard (Eighth Avenue), between 151st & 152nd Streets (1-212 281 1800). Subway B, D to 155th Street. **Open** 11am-1am Mon-Thur; 11am-2am Fri, Sat; 11am-9pm Sun. **Main courses** $10.50-11.50. **Map** p187 B3 ❺ **American regional**
Fried chicken has made quite the comeback, and the guru of moist flesh and crackly skin, Charles Gabriel, has also made a triumphant return to Harlem with his resurrected restaurant. In addition to the poultry, you can feast on barbecued ribs, mac and cheese, collard greens, yams and other Southern favourites.

Minton's

206 W 118th Street, between Adam Clayton Powell Jr Boulevard (Seventh Avenue) and St Nicholas Avenue (1-212 243 2222, www.mintonsharlem.com). Subway B, C to 116th Street. **Open** 6pm-midnight Wed, Thur; 6pm-1am Fri, Sat; 5-11pm Sun. **Main courses** $25-$46. **Map** p187 B6 ❻ **American**
See p189 **Harlem's Second Renaissance**.

★ Red Rooster Harlem

310 Malcolm X Boulevard (Lenox Avenue), between 125th & 126th Streets (1-212 792 9001, www.redroosterharlem.com). Subway 2, 3 to 125th Street. **Open** 11.30am-3pm, 5.30-10.30pm Mon-Thur; 11.30am-3pm, 5.30-11.30pm Fri; 10am-3pm, 5-11.30pm Sat; 10am-3pm, 5-10pm Sun. **Main courses** $18-$36. **Map** p187 C5 ❼ **American**
With its hobnobbing bar scrum, potent cocktails and lively jazz, this buzzy eaterie serves as a worthy clubhouse for the new Harlem. Superstar chef Marcus Samuelsson (*see p189*) is at his most populist here, drawing on a mix of Southern-fried, East African, Scandinavian and French flavours. Harlem politicos mix at the teardrop bar with downtown fashionistas, swilling cocktails and gorging on rib-sticking food.

Bars

Ginny's Supper Club

310 Malcolm X Boulevard (Lenox Avenue), between 125th & 126th Streets (1-212 421 3821, www.redroosterharlem.com). Subway 2, 3 to 125th Street. **Open** 6-10pm Mon-Wed 7pm-2am Thur; 6pm-3am Fri, Sat; 10am & 12.30pm brunch seatings, 6-10pm Sun. **Map** p187 C5 ❽
This sprawling basement lounge is modelled after the Harlem speakeasies of the '20s. The menu, eclectic cocktails and a steady line-up of live music all revive the sophisticated supper club experience.

Park 112

2080 Fredrick Douglass Boulevard (Eighth Avenue), at 112th Street (1-646 524 6610, www.thepark112.com). Subway B, C to 110th Street-Cathedral Parkway. **Open** 5.30pm-midnight Mon-Wed; 5.30pm-2am Thur, Fri; 11am-2am Sat; 11am-11pm Sun. **Map** p187 B6 ❾
Styled with illuminated communal tables and brown-leather banquettes, this 90-seat restaurant and bar is equipped with a self-serve Enomatic wine machine. In addition to the 60-bottle wine list, you'll find global fare from Aquavit alum Kingsley John. Note that the kitchen closes at 11pm Mon-Wed, midnight Thur-Sat and 10pm Sun.

Shrine

2271 Adam Clayton Powell Jr Boulevard (Seventh Avenue), between 133rd & 134th Streets (1-212 690 7807, www.shrinenyc.com). Subway B, C, 2, 3 to 135th Street. **Open** 4pm-4am daily. **No credit cards**. **Map** p187 B4 ❿
Playfully adapting a sign left over from the previous tenants (the Black United Foundation), the Shrine advertises itself as a 'Black United Fun Plaza'. The interior is tricked out with African art and vintage album covers, and actual vinyl adorns the ceiling. Nightly concerts might feature indie rock, jazz, reggae or DJ sets. The cocktail menu aspires to similar diversity.

Shops & Services

Trunk Show Designer Consignment

275-277 W 113th Street, between Adam Clayton Powell Jr Boulevard (Seventh Avenue) & Frederick Douglass Boulevard (Eighth Avenue) (1-212 662 0009, www.trunkshowconsignment.com). Subway B, C to 110th Street-Cathedral Parkway. **Open** 1-8.30pm Tue-Fri; 1-7.30pm Sat; noon-6.30pm Sun. **Map** p187 B6 ⓫ **Fashion**
Modelling agent Heather Jones graduated from hosting oversubscribed pop-up trunk shows to co-opening this small Harlem storefront. Men's and women's threads and accessories range from edgier brands (Margiela, Rick Owens) to Madison Avenue labels (Gucci, Chanel, Céline), with in-season items marked down between 20% and 70%. The shop sometimes keeps erratic hours, so call first.

EAST HARLEM

Subway 6 to 110th Street or 116th Street.

East of Fifth Avenue is **East Harlem**, commonly called Spanish Harlem but also known to its primarily Puerto Rican residents as El Barrio.

EXPLORE

The Grange Bar & Eatery. See p192.

The traditional southern boundary with the Upper East Side is 96th Street, but is becoming increasingly blurred with gentrification. Its main east–west cross street, East 116th Street, shows signs of a recent influx of Mexican immigrants. The modest **Graffiti Hall of Fame** (106th Street, between Madison & Park Avenues) celebrates old- and new-school taggers in a schoolyard. Be sure to check out the nearby **El Museo del Barrio** (*see p180*), too.

Bars

For bars on the border of the Upper East Side and East Harlem, *see p183*.

Camaradas el Barrio Bar Restaurant

2241 First Avenue, at 115th Street (1-212 348 2703, www.camaradaselbarrio.com). Subway 6 to 116th Street. **Open** 3pm-3am Mon-Thur; 3pm-3.30am Fri, Sat; 3pm-midnight Sun. **Map** p187 D6 ⑫

Owner Orlando Plaza pays tribute to his Puerto Rican heritage at this lively bar, eaterie and nightspot. The look is downtown chic: exposed brick, rough-hewn wooden benches and a modest gallery. Grab a seat and sample 'Puerto Rican pub fare' from the tapas-style menu, or kick back over a pitcher of sangria and take in some live salsa or jazz.

HAMILTON HEIGHTS

Subway A, B, C, D, 1 to 145th Street; 1 to 137th Street.

Named after Alexander Hamilton, who owned an estate and a farm here, **Hamilton Heights** extends from 125th Street to the Trinity Cemetery at 155th Street, between Riverside Drive and St Nicholas Avenue. Hamilton's 1802 Federal-style house, the **Grange**, now a national memorial, recently reopened to visitors after being moved from 287 Convent Avenue around the corner to St Nicholas Park.

The neighbourhood developed after the West Side elevated train was built in the early 20th century; it's notable for the elegant turn-of-the-20th-century row houses in the **Hamilton Heights Historic District**, centred on the side streets off scenic **Convent Avenue** between 140th and 145th Streets – just beyond the Gothic Revival-style campus of the **City College of New York** (Convent Avenue, from 135th to 140th Streets).

Sights & Museums

FREE Hamilton Grange National Memorial

St Nicholas Park, 414 W 141st Street, near Convent Avenue (1-646 548 2310, www.nps.gov/hagr). Subway A, B, C, D to 145th Street.

Open *Visitor centre* 9am-5pm Wed-Sun. *Tours* 11am, noon, 1pm, 2pm, 4pm. **Admission** free. **Map** p187 B4 ⑬
The Federal-style estate of America's first Secretary of the Treasury was completed two years before he was shot in a duel with Vice President Aaron Burr. Rooms, accessed via park ranger-led tours, include Hamilton's study and the parlour, with his daughter's pianoforte. A short film about the founding father's life is shown in the visitor centre.

Restaurants & Cafés

The Grange Bar & Eatery

1635 Amsterdam Ave at 141st St (212-491 1635, www.thegrangebarnyc.com). Subway A, B, C, D to 145th Street; 1 to 137th Street-City College. **Open** 11.30am-4am Mon-Fri; 10.30am-4am Sat, Sun. **Main courses** $11-$25. **Map** p187 A4 ⑭
American
Harlem goes back to its rural roots at this locavore bistro and bar, outfitted with mason jars, weathered white-oak floors and antique chandeliers. Aric Sassi oversees a comfort-food menu rooted in seasonal produce; having scoured nearby farms, the chef dispatches dishes such as seared crab cakes with celery-parsnip slaw and a roast-beet salad with lime yogurt, almonds and goat-cheese croutons. At the 40ft-long butcher-block bar, cocktails designed by Dead Rabbit head bartender Jack McGarry include Grange Collins (Farmer's Gin, pomegranate liqueur, basil, lemon juice and soda) and Convent Stroll (Heaven Hill whiskey, ginger, honey, lemon juice and soda). *Photo p191.*

The Cloisters.

EXPLORE

Washington Heights & Inwood

Subway A, C, 1 to 168th Street-Washington Heights; A to 190th Street; C to 163rd Street-Amsterdam Avenue; 1 to 157th Street or 191st Street.

The area from West 155th Street to Dyckman (200th) Street is called **Washington Heights**; venture north of that and you're in Inwood, Manhattan's northernmost neighbourhood, where the Harlem and Hudson Rivers converge. An ever-growing number of artists and young families are relocating to these parts, attracted by the spacious pre-war buildings, big parks, hilly streets and (comparatively) low rents.

Washington Heights' main attraction is the **Morris-Jumel Mansion** (*see p193*), a stunning Palladian-style house that served as a swanky headquarters for George Washington during the autumn of 1776. But the small **Hispanic Society of America** (*see p193*), featuring a surprising collection of masterworks, is an overlooked gem.

Since the 1920s, waves of immigrants have settled in Washington Heights. In the post-World War II era, many German-Jewish refugees (among them Henry Kissinger and Dr Ruth Westheimer) moved to the western edge of the district. Broadway was once home to a small Greek population – opera singer Maria Callas lived here in her youth. But in the last few decades, the southern and eastern parts of the area have become predominantly Spanish-speaking due to a large population of Dominican settlers.

A trek along Fort Washington Avenue, from about 173rd Street to **Fort Tryon Park**, puts you in the heart of what is now called **Hudson Heights** – the posh area of Washington Heights. Start at the **George Washington Bridge**, the city's only bridge across the Hudson River. A pedestrian walkway (also a popular route for cyclists) allows for dazzling Manhattan views. Under the bridge on the New York side is a diminutive lighthouse. To see it up close, look for the footpath on the west side of Henry Hudson Parkway below 181st Street, which leads down to the riverside Fort Washington Park and the Hudson River Greenway, a popular route for walkers, joggers and cyclists.

North of the bridge is the beautiful Fort Tryon Park, and at the park's northern edge is the **Cloisters** (*see p193*), a museum built in 1938 using segments of five medieval cloisters shipped from Europe by the Rockefeller clan. It houses the Metropolitan Museum of Art's permanent medieval art collection.

Inwood stretches from Dyckman Street up to 218th Street, the last residential block in Manhattan. Dyckman buzzes with street life from river to river, but, north of that, the island narrows considerably and the parks along the western shoreline culminate in the seclusion of **Inwood Hill Park**, another Frederick Law Olmsted legacy. Some believe that this is the location of the legendary 1626 transaction between Peter Minuit and the Native American Lenapes for the purchase of a strip of land called Manahatta – a plaque at the south-west corner of the ballpark near 214th Street marks the purported spot. The 196-acre refuge contains the island's last swathes of virgin forest and salt marsh. Today, you can hike over the hilly terrain, liberally scattered with massive glacier-deposited boulders (called erratics) and picture Manhattan as it was before development.

Sights & Museums

★ The Cloisters

Fort Tryon Park, Fort Washington Avenue, at Margaret Corbin Plaza (1-212 923 3700, www.metmuseum.org). Subway A to 190th Street, then M4 bus or follow Margaret Corbin Drive north, for about the length of 5 city blocks, to the museum. **Open** *Mar-Oct* 10am-5.15pm daily. *Nov-Feb* 10am-4.45pm daily. **Admission** *Suggested donation* (incl same-day admission to Metropolitan Museum of Art) $25; $12-$17 reductions; free under-12s. **Map** p403 B3

Set in a lovely park overlooking the Hudson River, the Cloisters houses the Metropolitan Museum's medieval art and architecture collections. A path winds through the peaceful grounds to a castle that looks as if it's been there since the Middle Ages. In fact, it was built a mere 75 years ago, using pieces of five medieval French cloisters. The collection itself is an inspired trove of Romanesque, Gothic and Baroque treasures brought from Europe and assembled in a manner that somehow manages not to clash. Highlights are the famous Unicorn Tapestries (c1500), the 12th-century Fuentidueña Chapel and the Annunciation triptych by Robert Campin.

FREE Hispanic Society of America

Audubon Terrace, Broadway, between 155th & 156th Streets (1-212 926 2234, www.hispanicsociety.org). Subway 1 to 157th Street. **Open** 10am-4.30pm Tue-Sat; 1-4pm Sun. **Admission** free. **Map** p187 B9 ⑮

Though few people who pass this way seem aware of it, the Hispanic Society boasts the largest assemblage of Spanish art and manuscripts outside Spain. Goya's masterful *Duchess of Alba* greets you as you enter, while several haunting El Greco portraits can be found on the second floor. The collection is dominated by religious artefacts, including 16th-century tombs from the monastery of San Francisco in Cuéllar, Spain. Also among its holdings are decorative art objects and thousands of black and white photographs that document life in Spain and Latin America from the mid 19th century to the present. One of the highlights is Valencian painter Joaquín Sorolla y Bastida's *Vision of Spain*, comprising 14 monumental oils commissioned by the Society in 1911.

Morris-Jumel Mansion

65 Jumel Terrace, between 160th & 162nd Streets (1-212 923 8008, www.morrisjumel.org). Subway C to 163rd Street-Amsterdam Avenue. **Open** 10am-4pm Tue-Sun. **Admission** $5; $4 reductions; free under-12s. **Map** p187 C8 ⑯

Constructed in 1765, Manhattan's only surviving pre-Revolutionary pile was originally built for British governor Roger Morris but later served as General Washington's headquarters in the early months of the Revolutionary War. Later, an elderly Aaron Burr lived here after marrying widow Eliza Brown Jumel in 1833. (They divorced a year later.) The restored interior features many of the 19th-century French decorations of which Eliza was so fond. The handsome Palladian-style villa offers fantastic views. Its former driveway is now Sylvan Terrace, which has the longest continuous stretch (one block in total) of old wooden houses in all of Manhattan.

Restaurants & Cafés

New Leaf Restaurant & Bar

Fort Tryon Park, 1 Margaret Corbin Drive (212 568 5323, www.newleafrestaurant.com). Subway A to 190th Street; 1 to 191st Street. **Open** noon-3.30pm Mon; noon-9pm Tue-Thur; noon-10pm Fri; 11am-3.30pm, 6-10pm Sat; 11am-3.30pm, 6-9pm Sun. **Main courses** $18-$30. **Map** p403 B4 **American**

A seasonal American restaurant in lush Fort Tryon Park. In the warmer months have brunch on the patio; dinner in the 1930s former concessions building sees dishes such as own-made pappardelle with jumbo shrimp. Profits go to the New York Restoration Project, dedicated to the greening of the city.

Rusty Mackerel

209 Pinehurst Avenue, between 186th & 187th Streets (1-212 928 0584, www.rustymackerelny.com). Subway A to 190th Street. **Open** 5pm-11pm Mon-Wed; 5pm-midnight Thur, Fri; 11am-3pm, 5pm-midnight Sat; 11am-3pm, 5-11pm Sun. **Small plates** $5-$30. **Map** p403 B5 **Eclectic**

Uptown native James 'Mac' Moran (Olives, Chanterelle) plies Mediterranean small plates at this 35-seat Washington Heights restaurant. From an open kitchen, the chef sends out dishes that honour the neighbourhood's diversity: organic chicken with green harissa, octopus with romesco sauce, and cauliflower in a golden-raisin chimichurri. The drinks list includes a rhubarb-strawberry sangria on tap and six draft wines.

EXPLORE

Brooklyn

Not long ago, many Manhattanites baulked at the idea of crossing the East River for a day or night out. Times sure have changed. Not only is the second borough a destination in its own right, with a thriving cultural and food scene, but 'Brooklyn' has also become shorthand for a particular brand of indie cool, recognised the world over. Settled by the Dutch in the early 17th century, it was America's third largest municipality until its amalgamation with the four other boroughs that created New York City in 1898. Its many brownstones are a testament to a large and wealthy merchant class that made its money from the shipping trade. By the end of the 19th century, Brooklyn had become so prosperous, and its view of itself so grandiloquent, it built copies of the Arc de Triomphe (in Grand Army Plaza) and the Champs-Elysées (Eastern Parkway), and a greensward (Prospect Park) to rival Central Park.

Green-Wood Cemetery. *See p207.*

Don't Miss

1 Brooklyn Bridge Approach the borough on foot for spectactular panoramas (*p197*).

2 Pok Pok NY Thai food that's worth the trek (*p202*).

3 Vinegar Hill House A tucked-away gem in a time-warp street (*p201*).

4 Brooklyn Museum The second borough's answer to the Met is more manageble and less crowded (*p207*).

5 Green-Wood Cemetery Where the great, the good and the bad are buried (*p207*).

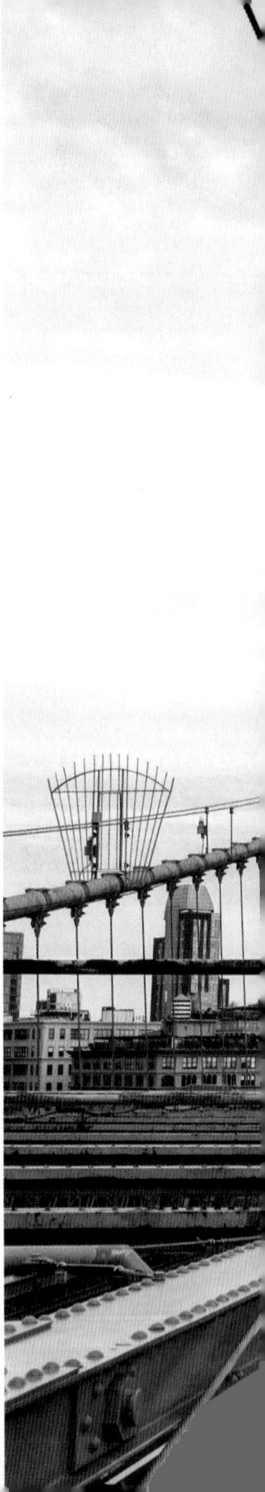

Brooklyn Heights Promenade.

BROOKLYN HEIGHTS & DUMBO

Brooklyn Heights – Subway A, C, F to Jay Street-Borough Hall; A, C, G to Hoyt-Schermerhorn; M, R to Court Street; 2, 3, 4, 5 to Borough Hall. Dumbo – Subway to A, C to High Street; F to York Street.

Home to well-to-do families and professionals lured by its proximity to Wall Street, **Brooklyn Heights** is where you'll find the idyllic leafy, brownstone-lined streets of Brooklyn legend. Thanks to the area's historic district status, it has many Greek Revival and Italianate row houses dating from the 1820s. Take a stroll down the gorgeous tree-lined streets – try Cranberry, Hicks, Pierrepont and Willow – to see the area at its best.

Given its serenity and easy access to Manhattan, it's not surprising that Brooklyn Heights has been home to numerous illustrious (and struggling) writers. Walt Whitman printed the first edition of *Leaves of Grass* at 98 Cranberry Street (in a building since demolished); Truman Capote wrote *Breakfast at Tiffany's* at 70 Willow Street; and Thomas Wolfe penned *Of Times and the River* at 5 Montague Terrace.

Henry and Montague Streets are the prime strips for shops, restaurants and bars. At the end of Montague, the **Brooklyn Heights Promenade** offers spectacular waterfront views of lower Manhattan, New York Harbor and the nearby **Brooklyn Bridge** (*see p197*), a marvel of 19th-century engineering. The grand **Borough Hall** (209 Joralemon Street, at Court Street), the seat of local government, stands as a monument to Brooklyn's past as an independent municipality. Completed in 1851 but only later crowned with a Victorian cupola, the Greek Revival edifice was renovated in the late 1980s. The building is linked to the **New York State Supreme Court** (360 Adams Street, between Joralemon Street & Tech Place) by **Cadman Plaza** (from Prospect Street to Tech Place, between Cadman Plaza East & Cadman Plaza West).

At the turn of the 19th century, **Dumbo** (Down Under the Manhattan Bridge Overpass) was a thriving industrial district; all kinds of manufacturers, including Brillo and Benjamin Moore, were based here, leaving behind a fine collection of factory buildings and warehouses; the most famous of these, the **Eskimo Pie Building** (100 Bridge Street, at York Street), with its embellished facade, was actually built for the Thomson Meter Company in 1908-09.

In the 1970s and '80s, these warehouses were colonised by artists seeking cheap live/work spaces, but playing out a familiar New York migration pattern, the area is now bursting with million-dollar apartments and high-end design shops. The spectacular views – taking in the Statue of Liberty, the lower Manhattan skyline and the Brooklyn and Manhattan Bridges – remain the same. The best vantage point is below the Brooklyn Bridge at the **Fulton Ferry Landing**, which juts out over the

East River at Old Fulton and Water Streets. It was here that General George Washington and his troops beat a hasty retreat by boat from the Battle of Brooklyn in 1776. It's now a stop on the East River Ferry service (*see p373*), which links to Manhattan and Queens. Along the same pier is the **Brooklyn Ice Cream Factory** (Fulton Ferry Landing, 1 Water Street, 1-718 246 3963, closed Mon Dec-Mar), located in a 1920s fireboat house. Next door, docked at the pier, is one of the borough's great cultural jewels: **Bargemusic** (*see p287*), a 100-foot steel barge that was built in 1899 but has staged chamber music concerts since the 1970s.

On both sides of the landing, **Brooklyn Bridge Park** (riverside, from the Manhattan Bridge to Atlantic Avenue) has been undergoing a rolling redesign that includes lawns, freshwater gardens, a water fowl-attracting salt marsh and the Granite Prospect, a set of stairs fashioned out of salvaged granite facing the Manhattan skyline. But the undoubted centrepiece is the vintage merry-go-round known as **Jane's Carousel** (between Main Street and the Brooklyn Bridge; *see p245* **Horsing Around**), which made its park debut in 2011 in a Jean Nouvel-designed pavilion in the section of park alongside the post-Civil War coffee warehouses, Empire Stores.

The artists who flocked to the area en masse in the 1970s and '80s maintain a presence in the local galleries, most of which support the work of emerging talent (*see p201* **In the Know**). Dumbo is also becoming a performing arts hotspot. You can catch anything from puppet theatre to a rock concert at **St Ann's Warehouse** (*see p307*). Another artsy venue, which has even more diverse programming – think burlesque, camp variety and contemporary classical – is the **Galapagos Art Space** (*see p273*), based in a quirky, LEED-certified green space.

Head east on Water or Front Street to discover one of Brooklyn's forgotten neighbourhoods. Once a rough and bawdy patch dotted with bars and brothels frequented by sailors and dockworkers, **Vinegar Hill**, between Bridge Street and the Navy Yard, earned the moniker 'Hell's Half Acre' in the 19th century. Only fragments of the enclave remain (parts of it were designated a historic district in the late 1990s), and it's considerably quieter today. Although inhabited, the isolated strips of early-19th-century row houses and defunct storefronts on Bridge, Hudson and Plymouth Streets, and a stretch of Front Street, have a ghost-town quality, heightened by their juxtaposition with a Con Edison generating station. For refreshment, seek out the enclave's tavern-like **Vinegar Hill House** (*see p201*).

IN THE KNOW LOVE LOCKS

Wondering why there are padlocks scattered on the fence on the Brooklyn Bridge? Couples attach them and throw the keys in the river as a symbol of everlasting love – until Department of Transportation workers cut them off, that is.

Sights & Museums

★ FREE Brooklyn Bridge

Subway A, C to High Street; J to Chambers Street; 4, 5, 6 to Brooklyn Bridge-City Hall. **Map** p198 D1 ❶

Designed by John Roebling, the Brooklyn Bridge was built in response to the harsh winter of 1867 when the East River froze over, severing connection between Manhattan and what was then the nation's third most populous city. When it opened in 1883, the 5,989ft-long structure was the world's longest bridge, and the first in the world to use steel suspension cables. Every day, 6,600 people walk or bike across the bridge's wide, wood-planked promenade, taking in views of New York Harbor, the Statue of Liberty and the skyscrapers of lower Manhattan.

► *You can also walk or bike into Brooklyn across the Manhattan or Williamsburg Bridges.*

Brooklyn Historical Society

128 Pierrepont Street, at Clinton Street, Brooklyn Heights (1-718 222 4111, www.brooklynhistory.org). Subway 2, 3, 4, 5 to Borough Hall. **Open** *Museum* noon-5pm Wed-Sat. *Gift shop* noon-5pm daily. *Library* 1-5pm Wed-Sat. **Admission** $10; $6 reductions; free under-13s. **Map** p198 D2 ❷

Founded in 1863, the BHS resides in a just-renovated landmark Queen Anne-style building. In addition to a major photo and research library – featuring historic maps and newspapers, notable family histories and archives from the area's abolitionist movement – it presents ongoing and temporary exhibitions. 'Brooklyn Abolitionists/In Pursuit of Freedom', scheduled to run until 2018, examines Kings County's antislavery movement in the 19th century and includes one of the most prized items in the BHS's collection: an original copy of the Emancipation Proclamation, signed by President Lincoln.

New York Transit Museum

Corner of Boerum Place & Schermerhorn Street, Brooklyn Heights (1-718 694 1600, www.mta.info/mta/museum). Subway A, C, G to Hoyt-Schermerhorn; 2, 3, 4, 5 to Borough Hall.
Open 10am-4pm Tue-Fri; 11am-5pm Sat, Sun. **Admission** $7; $5 reductions; free under-3s; free seniors Wed. **Map** p198 D3 ❸

Located in a historic 1936 IND subway station, this is the largest museum in the United States devoted to urban public transport history. Exhibits explore the social and practical impact of public transport on the development of greater New York; among the

EXPLORE

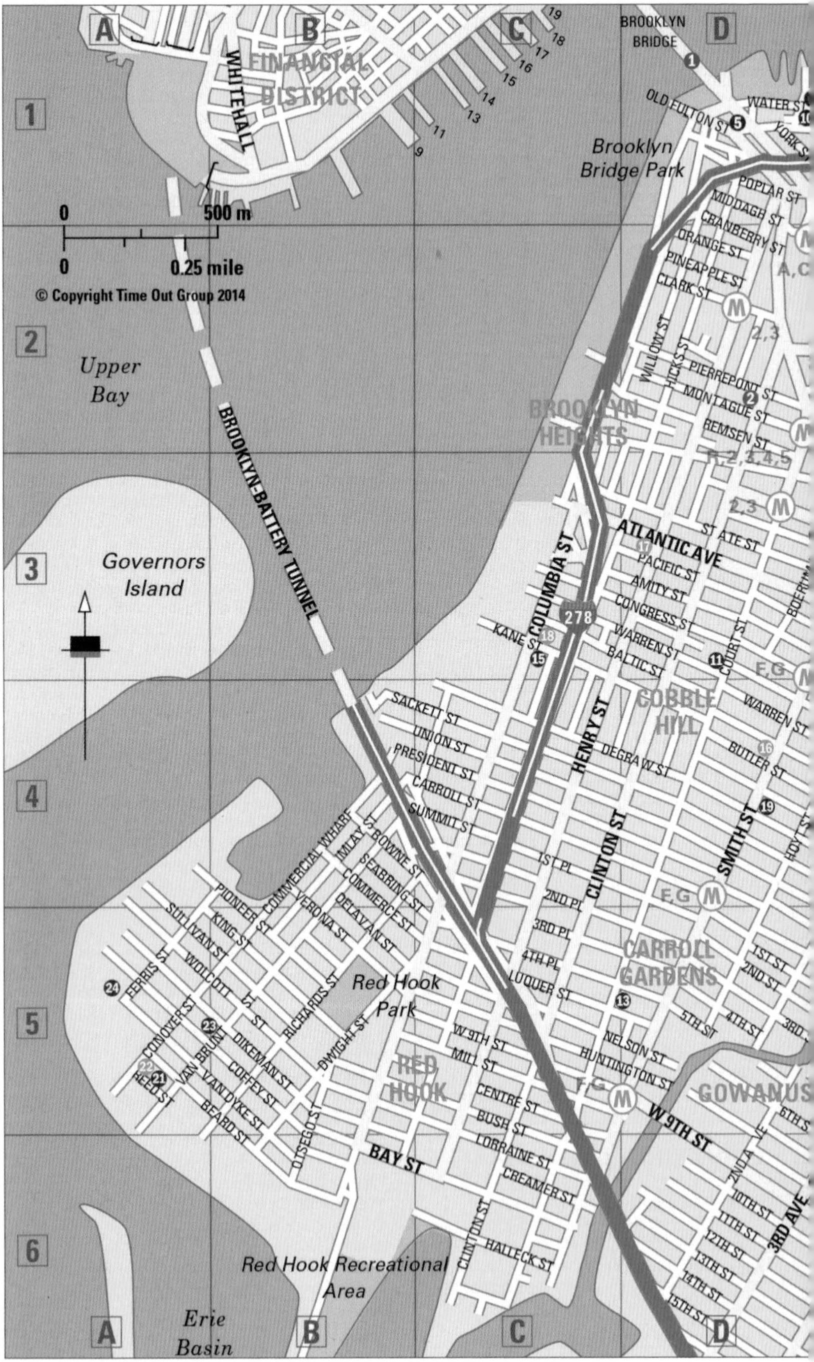
FINANCIAL DISTRICT
WHITEHALL
BROOKLYN BRIDGE
Brooklyn Bridge Park
OLD FULTON ST
WATER ST
YORK ST
POPLAR ST
MIDDAGH ST
CRANBERRY ST
ORANGE ST
PINEAPPLE ST
CLARK ST
WILLOW ST
HICKS ST
PIERREPONT ST
MONTAGUE ST
REMSEN ST
BROOKLYN HEIGHTS
STATE ST
ATLANTIC AVE
PACIFIC ST
AMITY ST
CONGRESS ST
WARREN ST
BALTIC ST
COURT ST
KANE ST
COLUMBIA ST
278
COBBLE HILL
HENRY ST
DEGRAW ST
BUTLER ST
SMITH ST
HOYT ST
BOERUM
CLINTON ST
1ST PL
2ND PL
3RD PL
4TH PL
LUQUER ST
CARROLL GARDENS
1ST ST
2ND ST
3RD
4TH ST
5TH ST
NELSON ST
HUNTINGTON ST
W 9TH ST
GOWANUS
6TH S
2ND AVE
3RD AVE
10TH ST
11TH ST
12TH ST
13TH ST
14TH ST
15TH ST
0
500 m
0
0.25 mile
© Copyright Time Out Group 2014
Upper Bay
Governors Island
BROOKLYN-BATTERY TUNNEL
SACKETT ST
UNION ST
PRESIDENT ST
CARROLL ST
SUMMIT ST
COMMERCIAL WHARF
IMLAY ST
BOWNE ST
SEABRING ST
COMMERCE ST
DELAVAN ST
VERONA ST
PIONEER ST
KING ST
SULLIVAN ST
WOLCOTT ST
FERRIS ST
CONOVER ST
VAN BRUNT
DIKEMAN ST
COFFEY ST
VAN DYKE ST
BEARD ST
REED ST
RICHARDS ST
DWIGHT ST
Red Hook Park
RED HOOK
W 9TH ST
MILL ST
CENTRE ST
BUSH ST
LORRAINE ST
CREAMER ST
BAY ST
OTSEGO ST
CLINTON ST
HALLECK ST
Red Hook Recreational Area
Erie Basin
A
B
C
D
1
2
3
4
5
6

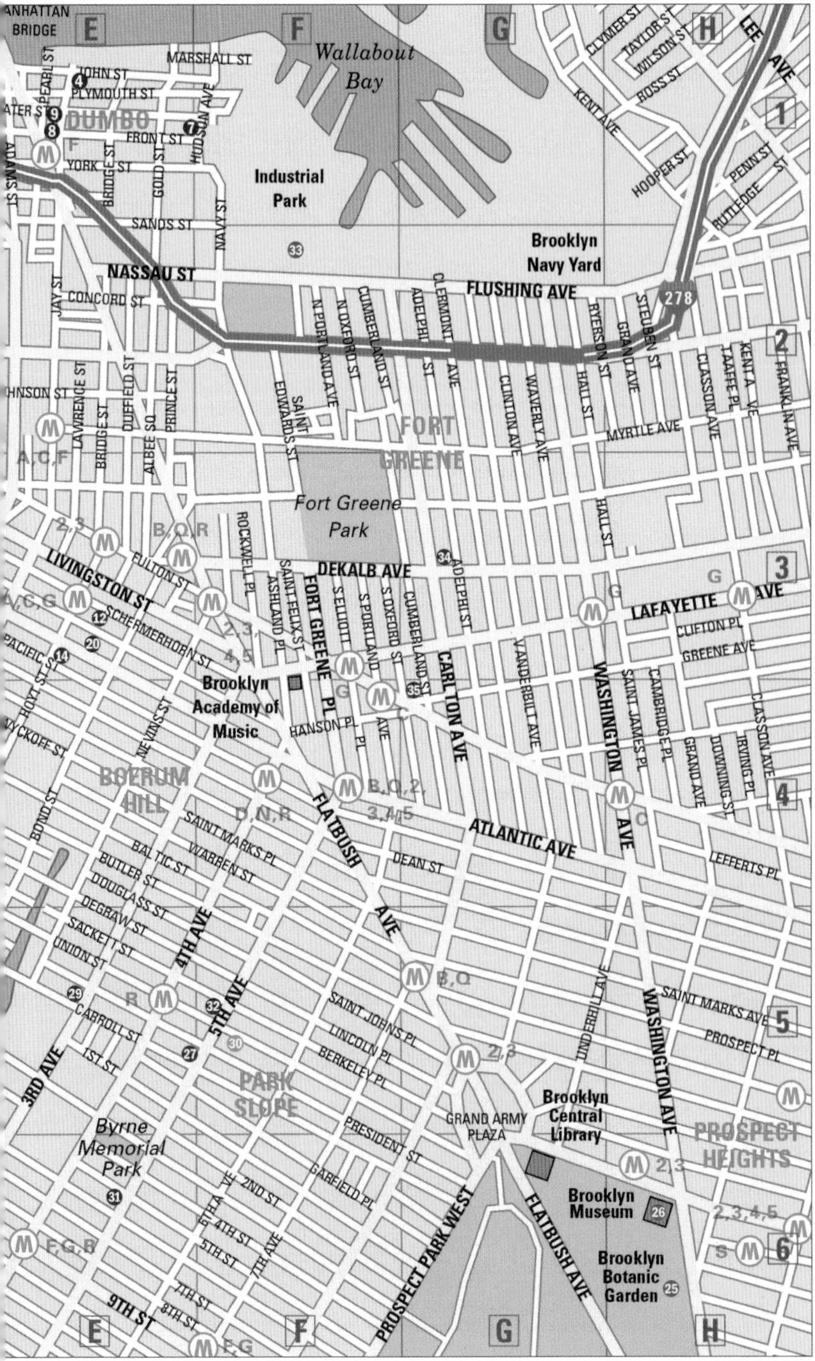

Wallabout Bay
Industrial Park
Brooklyn Navy Yard
DUMBO
FORT GREENE
Fort Greene Park
Brooklyn Academy of Music
BOERUM HILL
PARK SLOPE
Byrne Memorial Park
GRAND ARMY PLAZA
Brooklyn Central Library
Brooklyn Museum
Brooklyn Botanic Garden
PROSPECT HEIGHTS
MANHATTAN BRIDGE
FLUSHING AVE
NASSAU ST
MYRTLE AVE
DEKALB AVE
LAFAYETTE AVE
FULTON ST
LIVINGSTON ST
SCHERMERHORN ST
ATLANTIC AVE
FLATBUSH AVE
WASHINGTON AVE
CARLTON AVE
FORT GREENE PL
VANDERBILT AVE
4TH AVE
5TH AVE
3RD AVE
7TH AVE
PROSPECT PARK WEST
9TH ST
UNDERHILL AVE
LEE AVE

highlights is an engrossing walk-through display charting the construction of the city's century-old subway system, when fearless 'sandhogs' were engaged in dangerous tunnelling. A line-up of turnstiles shows their evolution from the 1894 'ticket chopper' to the current Automatic Fare Card model. But the best part is down another level to a real platform where you can board an exceptional collection of vintage subway and El ('Elevated') cars, some complete with vintage ads.
Other locations New York Transit Museum Gallery Annex & Store, Grand Central Terminal, adjacent to stationmaster's office, main concourse (1-212 878 0106; *see p372*).

Restaurants & Cafés

Brooklyn Roasting Company

25 Jay Street, between John & Plymouth Streets, Dumbo (1-718 522 2664, www.brooklynroasting.com). Subway A, C to High Street; F to York Street. **Open** 7am-7pm daily. **Coffee** $1.50-$5.25. **Map** p199 E1 ❹ **Café**
If you need a caffeine fix in Dumbo, stop by Brooklyn Roasting Company, supplier of Fairtrade, organic beans to many of the borough's best cafés. Savour the aromas wafting from the fuel-efficient roasting machine in the on-site 'espresso lab' and accompany your brew with baked goods or a sandwich from Brooklyn's Dough or Margo Patisserie.
Other locations 200 Flushing Avenue, at Washington Avenue, Fort Greene (1-718 858 5500).

Juliana's

19 Old Fulton Street, between Front & Water Streets, Dumbo (718 596 6700, www.julianaspizza.com). Subway A, C to High Street; F to York Street. **Open** 11.30am-11pm daily. **Pizzas** $16-$30. **Map** p198 D1 ❺ **Pizza**
For years, Manhattanites and tourists have crossed the Brooklyn Bridge and lined up for pizza at venerated Dumbo fixture Grimaldi's – but they may not be aware that founder Patsy Grimaldi sold the place more than a decade ago. In 2012, he burst out of retirement to reclaim his shop's first location, along with its original coal oven. This time, Grimaldi – who learned to spin dough at age 13 in his Uncle Patsy Lancieri's Harlem institution – named the spot after his mother. At Juliana's, the menu spotlights iconic red-sauce fare, including classic pizzas, such as sausage and broccoli rabe. But he's also mixed in a few nods to modern times: creative pizzas (such as a bagel-like riff with lox and goat cheese) and a proprietary chocolate-and-raspberry flavour from nearby Brooklyn Ice Cream Factory. Another throwback touch: an antique jukebox plays Patsy's favourite Sinatra tunes.

One Girl Cookies

33 Main Street, at Water Street, Dumbo (1-347 338 1268, www.onegirlcookies.com). Subway A, C to High Street; F to York Street. **Open** 8am-7pm Mon-Thur; 8am-8pm Fri; 9am-8pm Sat; 9am-7pm Sun. **Cookies** $2.75-$4. **Map** p198 D1 ❻ **Café**
Dawn Casale started baking cookies out of her Greenwich Village apartment in 2000 (hence the name), before hiring chef David Crofton to help – now married, they run two bakery-cafés. Pair your tea cookies or a whoopie pie with Red Hook-roasted Stumptown coffee. The spot also serves a rotating selection of craft beer, wine and snacks, such as a cheese plate in collaboration with Stinky Bklyn.
Other locations 68 Dean Street, between Smith Street & Boerum Place, Cobble Hill (1-212 675 4996).

Modern Anthology.

EXPLORE

IN THE KNOW
DUMBO ART PARTY

Each month, around 25 Dumbo galleries remain open late – some hosting special events – for the **1st Thursday Gallery Walk** (www.dumbo.is/culture). On the night, you can pick up a map at 111 Front Street (between Adams & Washington Streets), which houses many of the galleries.

★ Vinegar Hill House

72 Hudson Avenue, between Front & Water Streets, Dumbo (1-718 522 1018, www.vinegarhillhouse.com). Subway A, C to High Street; F to York Street. **Open** 6-11pm Mon-Thur; 6-11.30pm Fri; 10.30am-3.30pm, 6-11.30pm Sat; 10.30am-3.30pm, 5.30-11pm Sun. **Main courses** $16-$30. **Map** p199 E1 ❼ **American**

As it's hidden in a residential street in the forgotten namesake neighbourhood (now essentially part of Dumbo), tracking down Vinegar Hill House engenders a treasure-hunt thrill. In the cosy, tavern-like space, the daily-changing menu focuses on seasonal comfort foods. In the warmer months, linger over brunch in the secluded back garden.

Shops & Services

Egg

72 Jay Street, between Front & Water Streets, Dumbo (1-347 356 4097, www.egg-baby.com). Subway A, C to High Street; F to York Street. **Open** 10am-6pm Mon-Wed, Sun; 10am-7pm Thur-Sat. **Map** p199 E1 ❽ **Children**

Set in the old HQ of the Grand Union Tea Company, designer Susan Lazar's NYC store has a retro garment-factory vibe. Among her seasonally changing creations for babies and kids up to age eight, you might find striped infant bodysuits, print jersey dresses for girls, and peacoats for both genders.

★ Modern Anthology

68 Jay Street, between Front & Water Streets, Dumbo (1-718 522 3020, www.modernanthology.com). Subway A, C to High Street; F to York Street. **Open** 11am-7pm Mon-Sat; noon-6pm Sun. **Map** p199 E1 ❾ **Fashion/homewares**

Owners Becka Citron and John Marsala – the creative force behind the *Man Caves* TV series – have created a one-stop lifestyle shop that brings together vintage and contemporary homewares, alongside clothing, accessories and grooming products. Understatedly stylish dudes can update their wardrobes with classic shirts and sweaters by New York designers Ernest Alexander and Todd Snyder and USA-crafted footwear by Oak Street Bootmakers, among other labels. And what hip bachelor pad is complete without a stack of vintage issues of *Playboy* and barware?

Powerhouse Arena

37 Main Street, between Front & Water Streets, Dumbo (1-718 666 3049, www.powerhousearena.com). Subway A, C to High Street; F to York Street. **Open** 10am-7pm Mon-Fri; 11am-7pm Sat, Sun (extended hours in summer). **Map** p198 D1 ❿ **Books & music**

Also serving as a gallery and performance space, the Powerhouse Arena is the cavernous retail arm of Powerhouse Books, which produces coffee-table tomes on such diverse subjects as New York laundromats, celebrity dogs and the Brooklyn Navy Yard. **Other locations** Powerhouse on 8th, 1111 Eighth Avenue, between 11th & 12th Streets, South Slope (1-718 801 8375).

BOERUM HILL, CARROLL GARDENS & COBBLE HILL

Subway A, C, F to Jay Street-MetroTech; F, G to Bergen Street, Carroll Street; 2, 3, 4, 5 to Borough Hall.

A convenient if annoying real estate agents' contraction for these blurred-boundaried 'hoods, BoCoCa is a prime example of gentrification at work. Gone are the bodegas and cheap shoe shops along the stretch of Smith Street that runs from Atlantic Avenue to the Carroll Street subway stop; it's now lined with restaurants and upscale shops. The mile-long stretch of Atlantic Avenue between Henry and Nevins Streets, most of which falls under **Boerum Hill**, was once crowded with Middle Eastern restaurants and markets; one remaining stalwart is the **Sahadi Importing Company** (no.187, between Clinton & Court Streets, Cobble Hill, 1-718 624 4550, closed Sun), a neighbourhood institution that sells olives, spices, cheeses, nuts and other gourmet treats. These days, you'll find a slew of antique and modern furniture stores on the strip, including **City Foundry** (no.365, between Bond & Hoyt Streets, Boerum Hill; 1-718 923 1786, www.cityfoundry.com), which specialises in midcentury design and industrial-style pieces. Recently, clothing stores have moved in, such as **Hollander & Lexer** (no.369; *see p204*); there's even an nearby outpost of **Barneys New York** (no.194; *see p177*).

West of Smith Street, **Cobble Hill** has a palpable small-town feel. Here, **Court Street** is dotted with cafés and shops. Walk over the Brooklyn-Queens Expressway to the industrial waterfront and the excellent Thai spot **Pok Pok NY** (*see p202*).

Further south, you'll cross into the still predominantly Italian-American **Carroll Gardens**. Pick up a prosciutto loaf from **Caputo Bakery** (329 Court Street, between Sackett & Union Streets, 1-718 875 6871) or an aged *soppressata* salami from **G Esposito & Sons** (357 Court Street, between President

& Union Streets, 1-718 875 6863); then relax in **Carroll Park** (from President to Carroll Streets, between Court & Smith Streets) and watch the old-timers play *bocce* (lawn bowls).

Restaurants & Cafés

★ Blue Marble Ice Cream

196 Court Street, between Bergen & Warren Streets, Cobble Hill (1-718 858 0408, www.bluemarbleicecream.com). Subway F, G to Bergen Street. **Open** varies by season; usually 8am-10pm daily. **Ice-cream** $4-$8. **Map** p198 D3 ⓫ **Ice-cream**

With 30 rotating seasonal flavours, including sweet-tart strawberry, maple-toffee popcorn and sea salt caramel, Blue Marble is beloved by locals of all ages. Produced in NYC's only certified-organic ice-cream plant, it's a cut above standard scoops, and the shop also sells superior La Colombe coffee.

★ Chef's Table at Brooklyn Fare

200 Schermerhorn Street, at Hoyt Street, Boerum Hill (1-718 243 0050, www.brooklynfare.com/chefs-table). Subway A, C, G to Hoyt-Schermerhorn; B, N, Q, R to DeKalb Avenue; 2, 3 to Hoyt Street; 2, 3, 4, 5 to Nevins Street. **Open** *Seatings* 7pm & 7.45pm Tue, Wed; 6pm, 6.45pm, 9.30pm & 9.55pm Thur-Sat. **Prix fixe** $255. **Map** p199 E3 ⓬ **Eclectic**

Scoring a place at chef César Ramirez's 18-seat restaurant within the Brooklyn Fare supermarket takes determination: reservations are only taken on Mondays at 10.30am, six weeks before your desired booking. But the luxurious set dinner of approximately 20 courses is among the best small-plate cuisine in New York, and the dinner-party vibe is convivial: diners perch on stools around a prep table. The menu changes weekly, but might include such delicacies as a Kumamoto oyster reclining on crème fraîche and yuzu gelée or halibut served in a miraculous broth of dashi and summer truffles.

Frankies 457 Spuntino

457 Court Street, between Lucquer Street & 4th Place, Carroll Gardens (1-718 403 0033, www.frankiesspuntino.com). Subway F, G to Carroll Street. **Open** 11am-11pm Mon-Thur, Sun; 11am-midnight Fri, Sat. **Main courses** $15-$20. **Map** p198 C5 ⓭ **Italian**

This casual spuntino was an instant classic when it debuted in Carroll Gardens in 2004. The mavericks behind the place – collectively referred to as 'the Franks' Castronovo and Falcinelli – went on to become neighbourhood pillars, opening German-leaning steakhouse Prime Meats down the block and a coffee shop, Café Pedlar, in Cobble Hill. But their flagship remains as alluring as ever, turning out an impressive selection of cheeses, antipasti and cured meats, distinctive salads and exceptional pastas to a mostly local crowd. Cavatelli with hot sausage and browned sage butter is a staple, as are the flawless meatballs – feather-light orbs stuffed into a sandwich or served solo.
Other locations Frankies 570 Spuntino, 570 Hudson Street, at 11th Street, West Village (1-212 924 0818).

Mile End Deli

97A Hoyt Street, between Atlantic Avenue and Pacific Street, Boerum Hill (1-718 852 7510, www.mileenddeli.com). Subway A, C, G to Hoyt-Schermerhorn; 2, 3 to Hoyt Street. **Open** 11am-4pm, 5pm-midnight Tue-Fri; 10am-4pm, 5pm-midnight Sat; 10am-4pm, 5-10pm Sun. **Sandwiches** $9-$14. **Map** p199 E3 ⓮ **Deli**

New Yorkers have pastrami, Montrealers have smoked meat – luscious brisket that's been dry-rubbed, cured, smoked, steamed and hand cut, resulting in flavourful, delicious slices bound for mustard-slathered rye. This Montreal-style deli from Québécois Noah Bernamoff and his wife, Rae Cohen, serves the sandwiches in old-school fashion, along with other regional specialities – like the excellent poutine (including a smoked-meat riff), and, at brunch, a killer hash.
Other locations 53 Bond Street, between Bowery & Lafayette Street, East Village (1-212 529 2990).

★ Pok Pok NY

117 Columbia Street, at Kane Street, Cobble Hill (1-718 923 9322, www.pokpokny.com). Subway F, G to Bergen Street. **Open** 5.30-10.30pm daily. **Main courses** $10-$21. **Map** p198 C3 ⓯ **Thai**

James Beard Award-winning chef Andy Ricker's Brooklyn restaurant replicates the indigenous dives of Chiang Mai – a seasonal outdoor dining area is festooned with dangling plants, colourful oilcloths on the tables and second-hand seats. But what separates Pok Pok from other cultish Thai restaurants is the curatorial role of its minutiae-mad chef. Ricker highlights a host of surprisingly mild northern-Thai dishes, including a delicious sweet-and-sour Burmese-inflected pork curry, *kaeng hung leh*. His *khao soi*, the beloved meal-in-a-bowl from Chiang Mai – chicken noodle soup delicately spiced with yellow curry and topped with fried noodles for crunch – is accompanied here with raw shallots and pickled mustard greens.

Bars

Clover Club

210 Smith Street, between Baltic & Butler Streets, Cobble Hill (1-718 855 7939, www.cloverclubny.com). Subway F, G to Bergen Street. **Open** 4pm-2am Mon-Thur; noon-4am Fri; 10.30am-4am Sat; 10.30am-1am Sun. **Map** p198 D4 ⓰

Classic cocktails are the signature tipples at Julie Reiner's Victorian-styled cocktail parlour. Sours, fizzes, mules, punches and cobblers all get their due at the 19th-century mahogany bar. Highbrow snacks (fried oysters, steak tartare) accompany drinks like the eponymous Clover Club (with gin, raspberry syrup, egg whites, dry vermouth and lemon juice).

SUPERFLEA

Flea markets have morphed into food-and-culture destinations.

Rummaging in the city's outdoor flea markets has long been a favourite New York weekend pastime, but the past several years have seen the emergence of a more sophisticated breed of bazaar, offering high-quality crafts, gourmet snacks and even arts and entertainment, alongside vintage clothing, furniture and bric-a-brac. The popular **Brooklyn Flea** (www.brooklynflea.com) was launched in 2008 by Jonathan Butler, founder of Brooklyn real-estate blog Brownstoner.com, and Eric Demby, former PR man for the Brooklyn borough president, who identified Brooklyn as being ripe for a destination market. The original location (176 Lafayette Avenue, between Clermont & Vanderbilt Avenues, Fort Greene) is open from April until the third week of November on Saturdays, and includes around 150 vendors, selling a mix of vintage clothing, records, furnishings, locally designed fashion and crafts; there's also a small, family-friendly offshoot at a school in Park Slope (PS 321, 180 Seventh Avenue, between 1st & 2nd Street).

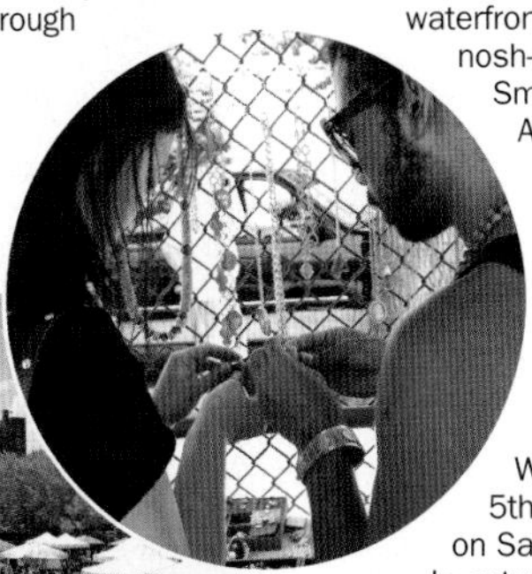

Brooklyn Flea.

Another location runs on Sundays (its 2014 location was still to be confirmed at the time of writing), while Williamsburg waterfront is the site of the nosh-only Saturday spin-off, Smorgasburg (90 Kent Avenue at N 7th Street), where you can sample NYC grub such as Red Hook Lobster Pound lobster rolls and Mighty Quinn's barbecue. In winter, the flea market moves indoors, to a sprawling space in Willamsburg (80 North 5th Street, at Wythe Avenue) on Saturday and Sunday.

In autumn 2013, the crowd-pleasing pop-up **Brooklyn Night Bazaar** (www.bkbazaar.com) found a permanent home in a 24,000-square-foot Greenpoint warehouse at 165 Banker Street, at Norman Avenue. On Friday nights from 7pm to 1am and Saturdays from 6pm to midnight, the market features a locally focused lineup of artists, craftspeople and food, including BrisketTown's top-flight barbecue and Ample Hills Creamery ice-cream. It also adds music to the mix – four to five bands, curated by a record label or publication, play each night – and Kelso and 21st Amendment are on tap in the beer garden. The sprawling emporium is also equipped with a minigolf course, ping-pong tables and arcade games.

And the phenomenon isn't limited to Brooklyn – on Saturdays from May through October, you can sample everything from locally made ice-cream to tacos as you browse vintage fashion, handmade jewellery and skincare at **Hester Street Fair** (Hester Street, at Essex Street, www.hesterstreetfair.com). Located on the site of a former Lower East Side pushcart market, it has around 60 vendors.

Whiskey Soda Lounge NY.

Long Island Bar

110 Atlantic Avenue, at Henry Street, Cobble Hill (1-718 625 8908). Subway F, G to Bergen Street; 2, 3, 4, 5 to Borough Hall. **Open** 5.30pm-midnight Mon-Thur, Sun; 5.30pm-2am Fri, Sat. **Map** p198 D3 17

A revivalist spirit is at the core of this retro-fitted bar from Toby Cecchini, which took over midcentury greasy spoon the Long Island Restaurant. But the cocktail vet does more than simply dig up old bones. The menu swaps the tortas that once powered neighbourhood blue-collars for Cecchini's fine-tuned list of six bedrock quaffs. Cecchini is a bit of a legend in cocktail-swilling circles – he created the modern Cosmo at the Odeon in 1987. Here you'll find a biting but balanced rye-and-Campari Boulevardier and a tart gimlet, given a fiery kick from ginger grated into the lime cordial. The iconic signage and old-line interior – terrazzo floors, Formica walls – have been preserved with an almost religious reverence, down to the faded cigarette burns that still cheetah-spot the gleaming art deco bar.

Whiskey Soda Lounge NY

115 Columbia Street, at Kane Street, Cobble Hill (1-718 797 4120, www.whiskeysodalounge-ny.com). Subway F, G to Bergen Street. **Open** 5.30pm-midnight daily. **Map** p198 C3 18

Andy Ricker's Thai canteen was conceived as a spillover spot for Pok Pok NY hopefuls, but the boozier kid bro is a destination in its own right, offering a highlight reel of *ahaan kap klaem* (Thai drinking food) and smartly tweaked cocktails. Not surprisingly, whiskey – commonly drunk with fizzy water in Thailand – is front and centre. There's a 30-plus roster of American slugs, as well as selections from Japan, Ireland and Canada. The low-ceilinged rec room is sparse – wood-panelled walls, drooping Christmas lights – but dashed with poppy touches of Bangkok-in-Brooklyn kitsch.

Shops & Services

By Brooklyn

261 Smith Street, between DeGraw & Douglass Streets, Carroll Gardens (1-718 643 0606, www.bybrooklyn.com). Subway F, G to Carroll Street. **Open** 11am-7pm Mon-Wed, Sun; 11am-8pm Thur-Sat. **Map** p198 D4 19 **Gifts & souvenirs**

Gaia DiLoreto's modern-day general store offers an array of New York-made goods, including pickles, soaps, T-shirts, jewellery, housewares, accessories and cookbooks by Brooklyn authors. Look out for Maptote borough-specific bags and Brooklyn Slate Co's burlap-wrapped reclaimed slate cheese boards.

Hollander & Lexer

369 Atlantic Avenue, between Bond & Hoyt Streets, Boerum Hill (1-718 797 9739, www.hollanderandlexer.com). **Open** 11am-7pm Mon-Sat; noon-6pm Sun. **Map** p199 E3 20 **Fashion**

Most of the men's and women's clothing displayed on vintage iron racks in this black-walled store is designed in Manhattan's Garment District. Owner Brian Cousins stocks lines, such as Kai D, Seyrig and his New York-made house label, which exude an old-fashioned focus on craftsmanship and high-quality fabrics that is also utterly contemporary.

RED HOOK

Subway F, G to Smith-9th Streets, then B61 bus.

To the south-west of Carroll Gardens, beyond the Brooklyn-Queens Expressway, the formerly rough-and-tumble industrial locale of **Red Hook** has long avoided urban renewal. In recent years, however, the arrival of gourmet mega-grocer Fairway and Swedish furniture superstore IKEA have served notice that gentrification is slowly moving in.

Luckily for its protective residents, the Hook still feels secluded, tucked away on a peninsula. While the area continues to evolve, its time-warp charm is still evident, and its decaying piers make a moody backdrop for empty warehouses and trucks clattering over cobblestone streets. The lack of public transport has thus far prevented it from becoming the next Williamsburg. From the Smith-9th Streets subway stop, it's either a half-hour walk south or a transfer to the B61 bus, although the **New York Water Taxi** (*see p373*) has improved the situation with its IKEA express shuttle from downtown Manhattan.

The area offers singular views of the Statue of Liberty and New York Harbor from **Valentino Pier**, and has an eclectic selection of bars, eateries and artists' studios. Look for the word 'Gallery' hand-scrawled on the doors of the **Kentler International Drawing Space** (353 Van Brunt Street, between Wolcott & Dikeman Streets, 1-718 875 2098, www.kentlergallery.org, closed Mon-Wed & Jan, Aug), or check the website of the **Brooklyn Waterfront Artists Coalition** (499 Van Brunt Street, at Beard Street Pier, 1-718 596 2506, www.bwac.org) for details of its large group shows at weekends in spring, summer and autumn; they're held in the BWAC's 25,000-square-foot exhibition space in a Civil War-era warehouse on the pier just south of Fairway.

Restaurants & Cafés

Brooklyn Crab

24 Reed Street, between Conover & Van Brunt Streets (1-718 643 2722, www.brooklyncrab.com). Subway F, G to Smith-9th Streets, then B61 bus. **Open** *Mid Mar-mid Oct* 11.30am-10pm Mon-Thur, Sun; 11.30am-11pm Fri, Sat. *Mid Oct-mid Mar* 11.30am-10pm Wed, Thur, Sun; 11.30am-11pm Fri, Sat. **Main courses** $11-$47. **Map** p198 A5 ㉑ **Seafood**

Channelling Maine's minigolf clam shacks, this hulking 250-seat spot brings games and seaside flavours to Red Hook's waterfront. Elevated on stilts, the three-storey stand-alone restaurant is done up with wharf-themed flourishes: lobster traps, fishing rods and a mounted shark's head. Gather friends for a round of minigolf, shuffleboard or cornhole (beanbag toss) outdoors, then grab a picnic table and dig into simple coastal fare, such as peel-and-eat shrimp, and steam pots brimming with crabs and lobster. Drinkers can sip margaritas and piña coladas or split a mixed bucket of five beers on the open-air roof deck, with views of New York's Upper Bay.

IN THE KNOW
THE TRUCK STOPS HERE

At weekends from May through October, Latin American food trucks descend on the corner of Bay and Clinton Streets, adjacent to the Red Hook Ballfields, to serve up some of the best street food in the city, including Ecuadoran *ceviche*, Salvadoran *papusas*, and Mexican tacos and *huaraches*. Originally catering to soccer players, the vendors now attract foodies from all over.

Bars

★ Sunny's Bar

253 Conover Street, between Beard & Reed Streets (1-718 625 8211, www.sunnysredhook.com). Subway F, G to Smith-9th Streets, then B61 bus. **Open** 8pm-4am Wed-Fri; 4pm-4am Sat; 4pm-11pm Sun (extended hrs in summer). **No credit cards. Map** p198 A5 ㉒

Restored after 2012's Hurricane Sandy dealt it a devastating blow, this unassuming wharfside tavern, which has been passed down in the Balzano family since 1890, is back in business. The bar buzzes with middle-aged and new-generation bohemians. Despite the nautical feel, you're more likely to hear bossa nova or bluegrass than sea shanties from the speakers.

Shops & Services

Erie Basin

388 Van Brunt Street, at Dikeman Street (1-718 554 6147, www.eriebasin.com). Subway F, G to Smith-9th Streets, then B61 bus. **Open** varies seasonally; usually noon-6pm Wed-Sat. **Map** p198 B5 ㉓ **Accessories**

For a unique keepsake, check out Russell Whitmore's finely honed collection of jewellery dating from the 18th century to the 1940s, from *fin de siècle* tortoiseshell studs to art deco cocktail rings (vintage engagement and wedding rings are a speciality). There's also a selection of furiture and decorative objects.

Steve's Authentic Key Lime Pie

185 Van Dyke Street, at Ferris Street (1-718 858 5333, www.stevesauthentic.com). Subway F, G to Smith-9th Streets, then B61 bus. **Open** varies; usually 11am-5pm Fri-Sun. **Map** p198 A5 ㉔ **Food & drink**

Flooding ravaged the original factory on Pier 41 during Hurricane Sandy, putting owner Steve Tarpin and his pastry lieutenants out of commission. They made their comeback on the next pier over. Inside the orange-hued bakery, you'll find his signature graham-cracker-crusted pies, filled with a condensed-milk custard laced with zesty lime juice, plus the Swingle, a tartlet dipped in dark Belgian chocolate.

PARK SLOPE, GOWANUS & PROSPECT HEIGHTS

Park Slope & Gowanus – Subway F to 7th Avenue or 15th Street-Prospect Park; F, G to Fourth Ave-9th Street; R to Union Street. Prospect Heights – Subway B, Q, Franklin Avenue S to Prospect Park; 2, 3 to Eastern Parkway-Brooklyn Museum or Grand Army Plaza; R to 25th Street.

Bustling with parents pushing baby strollers and herding lively children, **Park Slope** houses hip young families in Victorian brownstones and feeds them organically from the nation's oldest working food co-operative (only open to members). The neighbourhood's intellectual, progressive and lefty political heritage is palpable; local residents include Hollywood actors (Maggie Gyllenhaal and Peter Sarsgaard, John Turturro and Steve Buscemi, among others) and famous authors (Paul Auster and Jonathan Safran Foer).

Fifth Avenue is Park Slope's strip for restaurants, bars and shops, but recently interest has shifted west to **Gowanus**, the neighbourhood hugging the canal of the same name. It might seem baffling that anyone would want to build glitzy condos or big retail shops near a polluted waterway, but that's precisely what is happening. The canal was named a Superfund site in 2010, and the city and the Environmental Protection Agency are expected to work on clean-up for at least the next decade. That hasn't stopped businesses from moving in: all-purpose performance hub the **Bell House** (*see p272*), which opened in 2007, was among the first hotspots in the area, and the long-planned Whole Foods at the corner of Third Avenue and 3rd Street opened in 2013.

The western edge of Prospect Park is a section of the **Park Slope Historic District**. Brownstones and several fine examples of Romanesque Revival and Queen Anne residences grace these streets. Particularly charming are the brick edifices that line Carroll Street, Montgomery Place and Berkeley Place. Fans of writer-director Noah Baumbach, who grew up in these parts, may recognise the locale from 2005 hit *The Squid and the Whale*, much of which was set here.

Central Park may be bigger and far more famous, but **Prospect Park** (main entrance at Grand Army Plaza, Prospect Heights, 1-718 965 8999, www.prospectpark.org) has a more rustic quality. This masterpiece, which designers Frederick Law Olmsted and Calvert Vaux said was more in line with their vision than Central Park, is a great spot for birdwatching, especially with a little guidance from the **Prospect Park Audubon Center** at the Boathouse (*see p242*). You can pretend you've left the city altogether by hiking along the paths of the **Ravine District** (park entrances on Prospect Park West, at 3rd, 9th & 15th Streets), a landscape of dense woods, waterfalls and stone bridges in the park's centre.

Children enjoy riding the hand-carved horses at the antique carousel (Flatbush Avenue, at Empire Boulevard) and seeing real animals in the **Prospect Park Zoo** (park entrance on Flatbush Avenue, near Ocean Avenue, Prospect Heights, 1-718 399 7339, www.prospectpark zoo.com). A 15-minute walk from Prospect Park is the verdant necropolis of **Green-Wood Cemetery** (*see p207*).

Near the main entrance to Prospect Park sits the massive Civil War memorial arch at **Grand Army Plaza** (intersection of Flatbush Avenue, Eastern Parkway & Prospect Park West) and the imposing art deco central branch of the **Brooklyn Public Library** (10 Grand Army Plaza, Prospect Heights, 1-718 230 2100, www.bklynpubliclibrary.org). Around the corner are the tranquil **Brooklyn Botanic Garden** (*see below*) and the **Brooklyn Museum** (*see p207*).

To the north is the borough's biggest and most prominent new development, the 22-acre Atlantic Yards complex, on the edge of downtown Brooklyn, which encompasses more than 6,000 (yet-to-be-built) apartments and the **Barclays Center** (*see p271*), a major concert venue and the new home of the New Jersey Nets. Despite nine years of local opposition, contentious legal battles and the recession, the venue was christened by Jay-Z in autumn 2012.

Sights & Museums

Brooklyn Botanic Garden

990 Washington Avenue, at Eastern Parkway, Prospect Heights (1-718 623 7200, www.bbg.org). Subway B, Q, Franklin Avenue S to Prospect Park; 2, 3 to Eastern Parkway-Brooklyn Museum. **Open** *Mar-Oct* 8am-6pm Tue-Fri; 10am-6pm Sat, Sun. *Nov-Feb* 8am-4.30pm Tue-Fri; 10am-4.30pm Sat, Sun. **Admission** $10; $5 reductions; free under-12s. Free Tue; 10am-noon Sat. **Map** p199 H6 ㉕

Gowanus Canal.

This 52-acre haven of luscious greenery was founded in 1910. In spring, when Sakura Matsuri, the annual Cherry Blossom Festival, takes place, prize buds and Japanese culture are in full bloom. Linger in serene spots like the Japanese Hill-and-Pond Garden, the first Japanese-inspired garden built in the US, and the Shakespeare Garden, brimming with plants mentioned in the Bard's works. Start your stroll at the eco-friendly visitor centre – it has a green roof filled with 45,000 plants.

★ Brooklyn Museum

200 Eastern Parkway, at Washington Avenue, Prospect Heights (1-718 638 5000, www.brooklynmuseum.org). Subway 2, 3 to Eastern Parkway-Brooklyn Museum. **Open** 11am-6pm Wed, Fri-Sun; 11am-10pm Thur. Open 11am-11pm 1st Sat of mth (except Sept). **Admission** Suggested donation $12; $8 reductions; free under-12s. Free 5-11pm 1st Sat of mth (except Sept). **Map** p199 H6 26

Among the many assets of Brooklyn's premier institution are the third-floor Egyptian galleries. Highlights include the Mummy Chamber, an installation of 170 objects, including human and animal mummies. Also on this level, works by Cézanne, Monet and Degas, part of an impressive European art collection, are displayed in the museum's skylighted Beaux-Arts Court. The Elizabeth A Sackler Center for Feminist Art on the fourth floor is dominated by Judy Chicago's monumental mixed-media installation, *The Dinner Party*. The fifth floor is mainly devoted to American works, including Albert Bierstadt's immense *A Storm in the Rocky Mountains, Mt Rosalie*, and the Visible Storage-Study Center, where paintings, furniture and other objects are intriguingly juxtaposed. It's always worth checking the varied schedule of temporary shows and, reflecting the trend for destination museum eateries, the institution is the new home of Michelin-starred Brooklyn restaurant Saul. *Photo p208.*

★ FREE Green-Wood Cemetery

Fifth Avenue, at 25th Street, Sunset Park (1-718 210 3080, www.green-wood.com). Subway R to 25th Street. **Open** varies by season; usually 8am-5pm daily. **Admission** free. **Map** p404 S13

Filled with Victorian mausoleums, cherubs and gargoyles, hills and ponds, this lush 478-acre landscape is the resting place of some half-million New Yorkers, among them Jean-Michel Basquiat, Leonard Bernstein, Boss Tweed and Horace Greeley *Photo p194.*

Restaurants & Cafés

Al di là

248 Fifth Avenue, at Carroll Street, Park Slope (1-718 783 4565, www.aldilatrattoria.com). Subway R to Union Street. **Open** noon-3pm, 6-10.30pm Mon-Thur; noon-3pm, 6-11pm Fri; 11am-3.30pm, 5.30-11pm Sat; 11am-3.30pm, 5-10pm Sun. **Main courses** $10-$27. **Map** p199 E5 27 **Italian**

A fixture on the Slope's Fifth Avenue for more than a decade, this convivial, no-reservations restaurant is still wildly popular. Affable owner Emiliano Coppa orchestrates the inevitable wait with panache. Coppa's wife, co-owner and chef, Anna Klinger, produces northern Italian dishes with a Venetian slant. It would be hard to better her braised rabbit with black olives atop polenta, and even simple pastas, such as own-made tagliatelle *al ragù*, are superb. The full menu is also served in the restaurant's bar, which has a separate entrance around the corner on Carroll Street.

★ Four & Twenty Blackbirds

439 Third Avenue, at 8th Street, Gowanus (1-718 499 2917, www.birdsblack.com). Subway F, G, R to Fourth Ave-9th Street. **Open** 8am-7pm Mon-Fri; 9am-7pm Sat; 10am-6pm Sun. **Pie** $5.25/slice. **Map** p198 D6 28 **Café**

Emily and Melissa Elsen, the South Dakota-reared sisters who opened this cult bakery, learned pie-baking from their grandma, and her expert instruction is evident in varieties like lemon chess, salted caramel apple and the rich chocolate-and-custard Black Bottom Oatmeal. Settle in at one of this homey space's communal tables and savour a slice.

The Pines

284 Third Avenue, between Carroll & President Streets, Gowanus (1-718 596 6560, www.thepinesbrooklyn.com). Subway R to Union Street. **Open** 6-11pm Mon-Sat; 6-10pm Sun. **Main courses** $20-$36. **Map** p199 E5 29 **American**

With folding chairs and peeling tin walls, the Pines may seem an unlikely setting for ambitious fare from John Poiarkoff (previously at MoMA's fine-dining spot, the Modern). A recent meal started with torn hunks of craggy semolina bread, plated among rosettes of locally cured beef bresaola and a purée of fermented tangerine. Rich, gamey lamb neck was paired with butter-drenched kasha, fava beans and a sauce made with mentholy hyssop – a crafty surrogate for traditional mint jelly. The seasonal trellised backyard (open May-Oct) has it own dedicated menu of fire-licked dishes prepared on an open wood grill.

Bars

Union Hall

702 Union Street, between Fifth & Sixth Avenues, Park Slope (1-718 638 4400, www.unionhallny.com). Subway R to Union Street. **Open** 4pm-4am Mon-Fri; 1pm-4am Sat, Sun. **Map** p199 F5 30

Upstairs at Union Hall, couples chomp on mini burgers and sip microbrews in the gentlemen's club anteroom (decorated with Soviet-era globes, paintings of fez-capped men, fireplaces) – before battling it out on the clay bocce courts. Downstairs, in the taxidermy-filled basement, the stage hosts bands, comedians and off-beat events.

EXPLORE

Brooklyn Museum. *See p207.*

Shops & Services

Brooklyn Superhero Supply Company

372 Fifth Avenue, between 5th & 6th Streets, (1-718 499 9884, www.superherosupplies.com). Subway F, G, R to Fourth Ave-9th Street. **Open** varies; call before visiting. **Map** p198 E6 ㉛ **Gifts & souvenirs**

To unleash your inner superhero, stop by this purveyor of capes, X-ray goggles, truth serum and gallon tins of Immortality. Just be sure you adhere to the Vow of Heroism you must recite before your purchases are handed over. Proceeds benefit the 826NYC kids' writing centre behind a concealed door in the back of the store, so you can feel super about that, too.

Cog & Pearl

190 Fifth Avenue, at Sackett Street (1-718 623 8200, www.cogandpearl.com). Subway R to Union Street. **Open** noon-8pm Tue-Sat; noon-6pm Sun (reduced hrs in winter). **Map** p199 F5 ㉜ **Gifts & souvenirs**

This gift shop sells a melange of artist-made items including jewellery, fine art, home accessories and greeting cards. Look out for embroidered linen pillows by Brooklyn-based Coral & Tusk, gemstone rings by local jeweller Emily Amey and cool terrariums, complete with miniature figures, by Twig Terrariums.

FORT GREENE

Subway B, Q, R to DeKalb Avenue; B, D, N, Q, R, 2, 3, 4, 5 to Atlantic Avenue-Barclays Center; C to Lafayette Avenue; G to Fulton Street or Clinton-Washington Avenues.

With its stately Victorian brownstones and other grand buildings, Fort Greene has undergone a major revival over the past two decades. It has long been a centre of African-American life and business – Spike Lee, Branford Marsalis and Chris Rock have all lived here. **Fort Greene Park** (from Myrtle to DeKalb Avenues, between St Edwards Street & Washington Park) was conceived in 1846 at the behest of poet Walt Whitman (then editor of the *Brooklyn Daily Eagle*); its masterplan was fully realised by Olmsted and Vaux in 1867.

At the centre of the park stands the Prison Ship Martyrs Monument, erected in 1909 (from a design by Stanford White) in memory of 11,000 American prisoners who died on squalid British ships that were anchored nearby during the Revolutionary War.

Despite its name, the 34-floor **Williamsburgh Savings Bank**, at the corner of Atlantic and Flatbush Avenues, is in Fort Greene, not Williamsburg. The 512-foot-high structure was long the tallest in Brooklyn and, with its four-sided clocktower, one of the most recognisable features of its skyline. The 1927 building has been renamed One Hanson Place, and converted into (what else?) luxury condominiums.

Every Saturday, New Yorkers from across the five boroughs hit the **Brooklyn Flea** (*see p203* **Superflea**) in the yard of a public high school on Lafayette Avenue between Clermont & Vanderbilt Avenues. The combination of antiques, vintage clothes, indie crafts and food has proved so popular it's sparked several spin-offs and other markets in the borough.

Though originally founded in Brooklyn Heights, the **Brooklyn Academy of Music** (*see p285*) moved to its current site on Fort Greene's southern border in 1901. America's oldest operating performing arts centre, BAM was the home of the Metropolitan Opera until 1921; today, it's at the centre of a growing cultural district (*see p300* **Art of Brooklyn**). Almost as famous is the cheesecake at nearby **Junior's Restaurant** (386 Flatbush Avenue, at DeKalb Avenue,1-718 852 5257).

In addition to some funky shops, a slew of restaurants can be found on or near **DeKalb Avenue**, including South African institution **Madiba Restaurant** (*see below*).

Sights & Museums

FREE BLDG 92

63 Flushing Avenue, at Carlton Avenue (1-718 907 5992, www.bldg92.org). Subway A, C to High Street; F to York Street; G to Clinton-Washington Avenues. **Open** noon-6pm Wed-Sun. **Admission** free. **Map** p199 F2 ㉝

Located in the grounds of the Brooklyn Navy Yard, this small museum chronicles the mighty history of the former shipbuilding centre – which, at its peak during World War II, employed close to 70,000 people. Exhibits examine the yard's origins and significance throughout history, but the institution also looks to the manufacturing future of the space and the increasing number of businesses moving in each year (including Brooklyn Grange, which operates an apiary on site). The premises also has a café and rotating exhibitions, and offers weekend bus tours.

Restaurants & Cafés

Madiba Restaurant

195 DeKalb Avenue, between Carlton Avenue & Adelphi Street (1-718 855 9190, www.madibarestaurant.com). C to Lafayette Avenue; C, G to Clinton-Washington Avenues. **Open** 11am-11pm Mon-Thur, Sun; 11am-midnight Fri, Sat. **Main courses** $13-$25. **Map** p199 G3 ㉞
South African

Brooklyn's first South African eaterie honours the spirit of the late Nelson Mandela – Madiba is the legendary leader's clan name. Wooden chairs and folk art grace the convivial, high-ceilinged space, and live music ranges from Afrobeat to Afropop. The menu features fragrant curries and stews, as well as offbeat eats like thin, pleasantly gamey ostrich carpaccio and spicy prawns piri piri. The safari platter, loaded with cured, salted and dried beef tenderloin, is a presidential feast.

No. 7

7 Greene Avenue, between Cumberland & Fulton Streets (1-718 522 6370, www.no7restaurant.com). C to Lafayette Avenue; C, G to Clinton-Washington Avenues. **Open** 5.30-11pm Tue-Fri; noon-3pm, 5.30-11pm Sat; noon-3pm, 4-9pm Sun. **Main courses** $16-$25. **Map** p199 G4 ㉟
Eclectic

Given the constraints of this restaurant's tiny kitchen, chef Tyler Kord's eclectic cuisine – influenced by Asian and Eastern European flavours among others – is impressively bold. The menu changes frequently; on a recent visit, an unforgettable starter of crisp broccoli tempura was served with black-bean purée and a vinegary, citrus-spiked salad, and a hanger steak entrée featured pink slices of beef and toothsome kimchi-stuffed pierogi.

IN THE KNOW
BROOKLYN BADDIE

Alphonse (Al) Capone was born in 1899 in a house that stood just east of the Manhattan Bridge and south of the Brooklyn Navy Yard at 95 Navy Street; before moving to Chicago, he was a member of several local gangs, including the Brooklyn Rippers.

WILLIAMSBURG, GREENPOINT & BUSHWICK

Williamsburg – Subway G to Metropolitan Avenue; J, M, Z to Marcy Avenue; L to Bedford Avenue or Lorimer Street. Greenpoint – Subway G to Greenpoint Avenue or Nassau Avenue. Bushwick – Subway L to Jefferson Street or Morgan Avenue.

With a thriving music scene and an abundance of laid-back bars, small galleries and independent shops, **Williamsburg** – or 'Billyburg' as it's affectionately known – channels the East Village (just one stop away on the L train) in its heyday. But the area teeters on the brink of (or, some argue, has already fallen into) hipster cliché. Long before the trendsetters invaded, Williamsburg's waterfront location had made it ideal for industry. When the Erie Canal linked the Atlantic Ocean to the Great Lakes in 1825, the area became a bustling port. Companies such as Pfizer and Domino Sugar started here, but businesses had begun to abandon the area's huge industrial spaces by the late 20th century. The Domino refinery closed in 2004, and is currently being developed into apartments.

Bedford Avenue is the neighbourhood's main thoroughfare. By day, the epicentre of the strip is the **Bedford MiniMall** (no.218, between North 4th & North 5th Streets) – you won't find a Gap or Starbucks here, but you can browse an exceptionally edited selection of titles at **Spoonbill & Sugartown,**

EXPLORE

Booksellers (1-718 387-7322, www.spoonbillbooks.com) and sip some excellent coffee at the **Verb Café** (1-718 599 0977). The area has a constantly shifting array of cafés and eateries; south of the Williamsburg Bridge on Broadway, **Marlow & Sons** (*see p214*) was a pioneer in the kind of rustic aesthetic and farm-to-table `fare that's become the knee-jerk norm in Kings County. Nearby, New York institution **Peter Luger** (*see p214*) grills what most carnivores consider to be the best steak in the city.

You'll find chic shops dotted around the area, and the 'hood has more than 25 art galleries, which stay open late on the second Friday of every month. Pick up the free gallery guide *Wagmag* at local shops and cafés or visit www.wagmag.org for listings. However, Billyburg is better known for its music scene. Local rock bands and touring indie darlings play at **Music Hall of Williamsburg**, **Pete's Candy Store** and **Knitting Factory Brooklyn** (for all, *see p276)*.

Those with a nostalgic bent will enjoy quirky repository of NYC ephemera, **City Reliquary** (*see right*). Another local gem is the **Brooklyn Brewery** (79 North 11th Street, between Berry Street & Wythe Avenue, 1-718 486 7422, www.brooklynbrewery.com), housed in a former ironworks. The tasting room is open from Friday to Sunday, but visit during the happy 'hour' (Fridays 6-11pm) for $5 drafts. You can take a tour at weekends (every 30mins 1-5pm Sat; 1-4pm Sun).

With Williamsburg approaching hipster saturation point and rents rising accordingly, many of its young, creative residents seek cheaper digs nearby – which usually starts the gentrification cycle over again. **Greenpoint**, Williamsburg's northern neighbour, has been quietly undergoing a transformation of its own in the past decade. The former Polish stronghold's cachet recently rose even further this year, as the setting of HBO's *Girls*. The recently opened WNYC Transmitter Park, a 1.6-acre waterfront green space between Greenpoint Avenue and Kent Street that was once the site of the local public radio station's AM transmitter towers, offers a stellar view of the Manhattan skyline. Young, wealthy residents are moving into the neighbourhood in droves, leading to inevitable tensions between old and new denizens.

Bushwick has also attracted a creative demographic to its industrial spaces. In late spring, the annual **Bushwick Open Studios** (www.artsinbushwick.org) gives you a glimpse inside around 600 artists' work spaces, but you'll also see plenty of street art in the vicinity of the Morgan Avenue subway stop. Bounded by Bushwick Avenue to the north-west and Broadway to the south-west, this traditionally Latino neighbourhood has begun to sprout coffee shops, bars and vintage stores over the last few years, not to mention restaurants, such as acclaimed locavore eaterie **Roberta's** (*see p214*).

Sights & Museums

City Reliquary

370 Metropolitan Avenue, at Havemeyer Street, Williamsburg (1-718 782 4842, www.cityreliquary.org). Subway G to Metropolitan Avenue; L to Lorimer Street. **Open** noon-6pm Thur-Sun. **Admission** *Suggested donation* $5. **Map** p211 B3 36

This not-for-profit mini-museum of New York history reopened in 2012 after a renovation that coincided with its ten-year anniversary. Peruse Gotham ephemera such as memorabilia from both NYC World's Fairs,

Bedford Avenue. *See p209.*

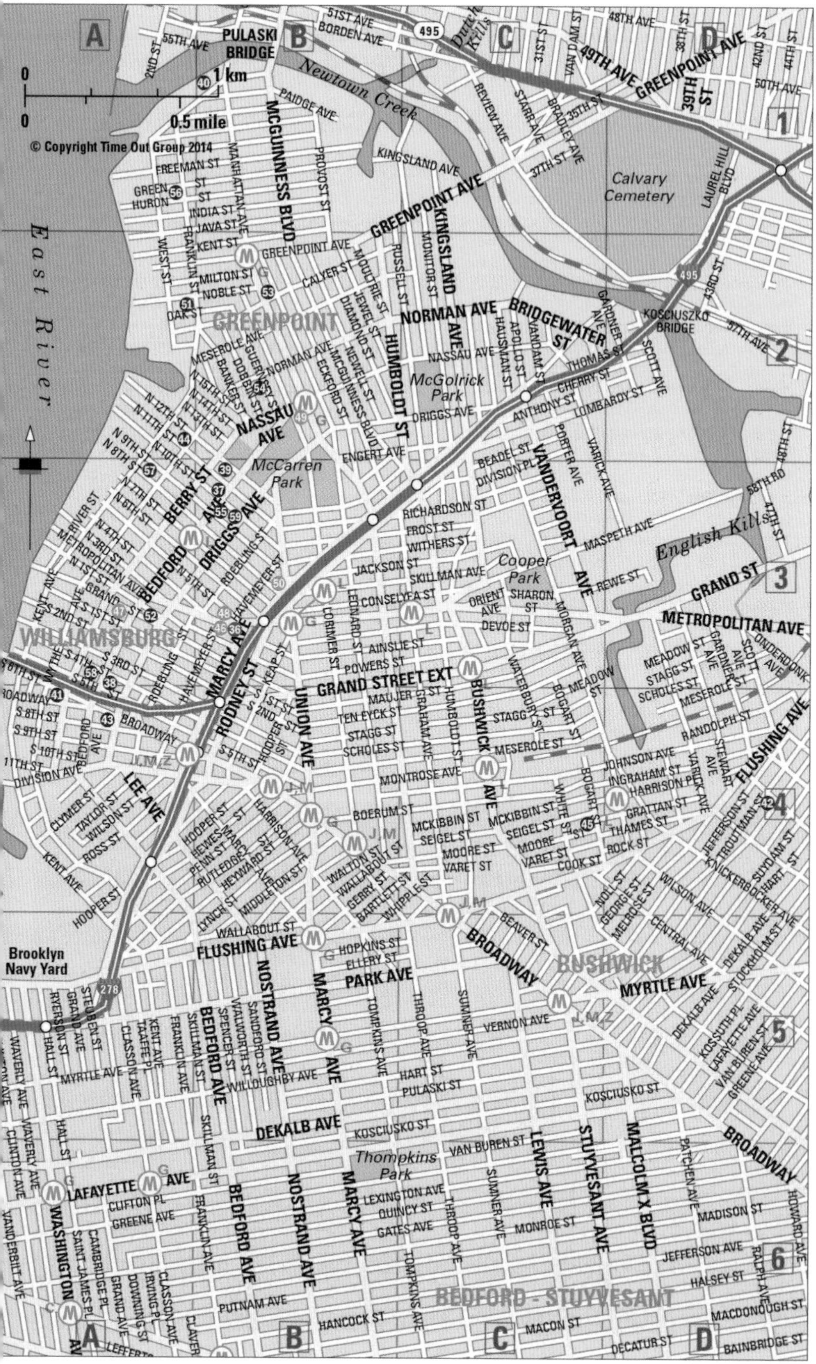
A
B
C
D
1
2
3
4
5
6
0
1 km
0
0.5 mile
© Copyright Time Out Group 2014
PULASKI BRIDGE
Newtown Creek
Dutch Kills
495
278
East River
Calvary Cemetery
GREENPOINT
WILLIAMSBURG
BUSHWICK
BEDFORD - STUYVESANT
McGolrick Park
McCarren Park
Cooper Park
Thompkins Park
English Kills
Brooklyn Navy Yard
KOSCIUSZKO BRIDGE
GREENPOINT AVE
MCGUINNESS BLVD
KINGSLAND AVE
NORMAN AVE
HUMBOLDT ST
BRIDGEWATER ST
NASSAU AVE
BERRY ST
BEDFORD AVE
DRIGGS AVE
MARCY AVE
RODNEY ST
LEE AVE
UNION AVE
GRAND STREET EXT
BUSHWICK AVE
VANDERVOORT AVE
GRAND ST
METROPOLITAN AVE
FLUSHING AVE
BROADWAY
MYRTLE AVE
PARK AVE
NOSTRAND AVE
DEKALB AVE
LAFAYETTE AVE
WASHINGTON AVE
LEWIS AVE
STUYVESANT AVE
MALCOLM X BLVD
LAUREL HILL BLVD
49TH AVE
39TH ST
MASPETH AVE
KENT AVE
WYTHE AVE
KOSCIUSKO ST

ON THE RECORD

Embark on a crate-digging crawl of Williamsburg and Greenpoint.

New record stores have recently sprung up in already crate-digger-friendly North Brooklyn making it a prime place for casual music lovers and serious vinyl collectors to spend an afternoon. In late 2013, revered UK indie retailer **Rough Trade** (*see p216*) opened its first Stateside outpost in a 15,000-square-foot Williamsburg warehouse, complete with in-house café. In addition to tens of thousands of all-new titles – roughly half of them vinyl and half CDs – the megastore sells music books, magazines and equipment, curates rotating art installations, and hosts gigs both ticketed and free from the likes of Television, Sky Ferreira and Sondre Lerche.

Rough Trade joins old timers like **Earwax** (*see p216*), which opened in 1991 (though the store recently relocated within the 'hood). The selection spans genres and decades, from buzzy indie pop to used funk, psychedelic and world music, and the insanely knowledgeable staff can always be counted on to provide some tuneful inspiration.

Just a few blocks north, Greenpoint is drawing record stores with cheaper rents than its gentrified neighbour. A recent addition to the growing LP nexus is the **Academy Record Annex** (*see p215*), which moved from its long-time home in Williamsburg to its current sunny digs by the Greenpoint waterfront. Expect serious buyers, reasonable prices and a massive collection of punk, rock & roll, jazz, soul and experimental records. Another local standby is the welcoming **Permanent Records** (*see p216*), with amiable folks behind the counter, a listening station and thousands of hand-picked, mostly used records and CDs, some of which go for as little as a dollar.

Nearby is **Co-Op 87 Records** (*see p216*), launched by the folks behind the valuable Kemado and Mexican Summer labels, whose offices are housed upstairs. The diminutive shop packs a punch with meticulously curated collector pieces, bootlegs and other rarities, from avant-garde electronica to classic rock. Trendsetting label **Captured Tracks** (*see p216*) also has its eponymous flagship in Greenpoint; in addition to stocking an ever-changing trove of vinyl, there are lots of cassettes, art books, vintage recording equipment and curation booths from local musicians. Don't be surprised to find yourself browsing alongside artists from the top-shelf Captured Tracks roster, such as DIIV's Zachary Cole Smith and Canadian troubadour Mac DeMarco.

Rough Trade.

EXPLORE

BrisketTown.

and hundreds of Lady Liberty figurines. Other idiosyncratic displays include a vintage barber-shop diorama furnished with a chair from Barber Hall of Famer Antonio Nobile's Bay Ridge, Brooklyn, shop, and a transplanted Chinatown newsstand.

Restaurants & Cafés

Allswell

124 Bedford Avenue, at North 10th Street, Williamsburg (1-347 799 2743, http://allswellnyc.com). Subway L to Bedford Avenue. **Open** 10am-2am Mon-Thur; 10am-4am Fri; 9am-4am Sat; 9am-2am Sun. **Main courses** $14-$36. **Map** p211 B3 37 **American**

Chef-owner Nate Smith, who earned his gastropub stripes at the Spotted Pig, broke out on his own with this laid-back Williamsburg tavern. The 47-seat space is done up with a reclaimed pine bar, vintage wallpaper in different patterns and brass-hunting-horn chandeliers with matching sconces. Choose from chefly bar grub (like smoked-trout spread or spicy pork-stuffed pastry rounds); heartier dishes (such as roasted lamb or shellfish stew); and greens (including a chicory salad with figs and pomegranate). The drinks list takes a locavore slant with small-production wines and craft beers on tap, plus a selection of market-driven cocktails.

BrisketTown

359 Bedford Avenue, between South 4th & 5th Streets, Williamsburg (1-718 701 8909, http://delaneybbq.com). Subway L to Bedford Avenue. **Open** 11am-11pm Mon-Thur, Sun; 11am-midnight Fri, Sat. **Main courses** $12-$25. **Map** p211 A3 38 **American barbecue**

New Jersey-born Daniel Delaney – a former journalist – might not seem like an obvious poster child for purist Texan 'cue. But the Yankee is turning out some seriously crave-worthy meat. Delaney takes the traditionalist route, coating chunks of heritage beef in salt and pepper before smoking them over oak-fuelled fire for 16 hours. That deep-pink brisket, along with remarkably tender pork ribs, draws Williamsburg's jeans-and-plaid set, who tuck in while indie tunes jangle over the speakers.

The Elm

160 North 12th Street, between Bedford Avenue & Berry Street, Williamsburg (1-718 218 1088, www.theelmnyc.com). Subway L to Bedford Avenue. **Open** 7am-11am, 6-10pm Mon-Wed; 7am-11am, 6-11pm Thur-Sat; 7am-10.45am, 11.30am-3pm, 6-10pm Sun. **Main courses** $18-$26. **Map** p211 B3 39 **French**

The ingenious and notoriously bullish Paul Liebrandt recently departed Tribeca's Corton – and the two Michelin stars he earned there – to bring a softened rendition of his art-cum-cuisine to the gleaming King & Grove hotel. Bare-wood tables and a wall of living vines make for pleasant gazing, but the tidy room feels as sterile and listless as an architectural rendering. A deeply soothing shellfish stew was anchored by brackish seaweed butter and crowned with a meaty hunk of halibut-like amadai, whose feathery scales boast a 'how did he do that?' crunch. On occasion, function succumbs to form on Liebrandt's painterly plates. Yet despite its fussiness, Liebrandt's food is too inspired to be stifled by the bland space.

Glasserie

95 Commercial Street, between Box Street & Manhattan Avenue, Greenpoint (1-718 389 0640, www.glasserienyc.com). Subway G to Greenpoint Avenue. **Open** 5.30-11pm Mon-Thur; 5.30pm-midnight Fri; 10am-4pm, 5.30pm-midnight Sat; 10am-4pm, 5.30-11pm Sun. **Shared plates** $19-$22. **Map** p211 B1 40 **Eclectic**

In an old industrial glass factory, Sara Kramer (Reynard, Blue Hill) and Sara Conklin (Cipriani) bring a touch of the breezy Mediterranean coast to the gritty Greenpoint waterfront. Kramer oversees a small-plates spread with a heavy emphasis on produce sourced from Pennsylvania's Lancaster Farm and upstate's Blooming Hill Farm. The menu spans Spain, Greece and the Middle East, in dishes such as lamb tartare alongside bulgur crackers, and a whole rabbit for two, served with flaky flatbread. At the horseshoe-shaped bar, the wine list focuses on exotic locales, including Croatia, Portugal and Morocco, and cocktails follow suit, spiced with ingredients like Aleppo peppers and muddled mint. Sea-foam-green walls conjure the ocean, and potted plants enliven the rustic 72-seat interior, outfitted in whitewashed brick and framed catalogue prints from the erstwhile factory. A terrace, transformed from the loading dock, provides coastal breezes. *Photo p214.*

Marlow & Sons

81 Broadway, between Berry Street & Wythe Avenue, Williamsburg (1-718 384 1441, www.marlowandsons.com). Subway J, M, Z to Marcy Avenue. **Open** 8am-midnight daily. **Main courses** $20-$30. **Map** p211 A4 41 **American creative**

In this charming oyster bar, restaurant and café, diners wolf down market-fresh salads, succulent brick chicken and the creative crostini of the moment (such as goat's cheese with flash-fried strawberries). In the back, an oyster shucker cracks open the catch of the day, while the bartender mixes the kind of potent drinks that helped to make the owners' earlier ventures (including the next-door Diner, a tricked-out 1920s dining car) successes.

Northeast Kingdom

18 Wyckoff Avenue, at Troutman Street, Bushwick (1-718 386 3864, www.north-east kingdom.com). Subway L to Jefferson Street. **Open** 11.30am-2.30pm, 6-11pm Mon-Wed; 11.30am-2.30pm, 6-11.30pm Thur, Fri; 11am-3pm, 6-11.30pm Sat; 11am-3pm, 6-11pm Sun. **Main courses** $15-$30. **Map** p211 D4 42 **American**

The mood inside this 28-seat eaterie is half cabin in the woods (wide-plank wood floors, clunky butcher-block tables) and half Grandma's living room (quaint sconces). In keeping with the country vibe, chef Kevin Adey uses meat and produce from local farms, including Brooklyn Grange, and foraged ingredients. The seasonal menu features such elevated fare as Hudson Valley foie gras and Rhode Island scallops alongside classics like an excellent burger.

★ Peter Luger

178 Broadway, at Driggs Avenue, Williamsburg (1-718 387 7400, www.peterluger.com). Subway J, M, Z to Marcy Avenue. **Open** 11.45am-10pm Mon-Thur; 11.45am-10.45pm Fri, Sat; 12.45-9.45pm Sun. **Steaks** $49-$199. **No credit cards. Map** p211 A4 43 **Steakhouse**

At Luger's old-school steakhouse, the choice is limited, but the porterhouse is justly famed. Choose from various sizes, from a small single steak to 'steak for four'. Although a slew of Luger copycats have prospered in the last several years, none has captured the elusive charm of this stucco-walled, beer hall-style eaterie, with worn wooden floors and tables, and waiters in waistcoats and bow ties.

Reynard

Wythe Hotel, 80 Wythe Avenue, at North 11th Street, Williamsburg (1-718 460 8004, www.wythehotel.com). Subway L to Bedford Avenue. **Open** 7am-midnight daily. **Main courses** $20-$30. **Map** p211 A2 44 **American creative**

The Wythe's sprawling restaurant is a Balthazar for Brooklyn, urbane and ambitious, mature and low-key. Its chef, Sean Rembold, serves casual breakfast and lunch to a drop-in crowd, including a terrifically earthy grass-fed burger. His menu, which changes often – sometimes daily – becomes much more serious at night. There's no fanfare at any time to his spare list of dishes, no trendy buzzwords, barely any descriptions at all. Rembold's thoughtful food, portioned to satisfy and priced to move, mostly speaks for itself.

★ Roberta's

261 Moore Street, between Bogart & White Streets, Bushwick (1-718 417 1118, www.robertaspizza.com). Subway L to Morgan Avenue. **Open** 11am-midnight Mon-Fri; 10am-midnight Sat, Sun. **Pizzas** $9-$16. **Map** p211 C4 45 **Italian**

This sprawling hangout has become the unofficial meeting place for Brooklyn's sustainable-food movement. Opened in 2008 by a trio of friends, Roberta's has its own on-site garden that provides some of the ingredients for its locally sourced dishes. The pizzas – like the Cheeses Christ, topped with mozzarella, taleggio, parmesan, black pepper and cream – are among Brooklyn's finest. The team recently opened Blanca, a sleek spot in the back, to showcase chef Carlo Mirarchi's acclaimed evening-only tasting menu (6-9pm Wed-Fri; 5-8pm Sat; $195).

Bars

The Commodore

366 Metropolitan Avenue, at Havemeyer Street, Williamsburg (1-718 218 7632). Subway J, M, Z to Marcy Avenue; L to Bedford Avenue. **Open** 4pm-4am Mon-Fri; 3pm-4am Sat, Sun. **Map** p211 B3 46

With its old arcade games, cheap Schaefer in a can and stereo pumping out the *Knight Rider* theme song, this Williamsburg gastrodive offers some of

Glasserie. *See p213.*

EXPLORE

Roberta's.

the city's best cheap-ass bar eats. The 'hot fish' sandwich, for one, is a fresh, flaky, cayenne-rubbed catfish fillet poking out of both sides of a butter-griddled sesame-seed roll. You'll be thankful it's available after a few rounds of the Commodore's house drink – a slushy, frozen piña colada.

Maison Premiere

298 Bedford Avenue, between Grand & South 1st Streets, Williamsburg (1-347 335 0446, www.maisonpremiere.com). Subway L to Bedford Avenue. **Open** 4pm-2am Mon-Wed; 4pm-4am Thur, Fri; 11am-4am Sat; 11am-2am Sun. **Map** p211 A3 47

Most of NYC's New Orleans-inspired watering holes choose debauched Bourbon Street as their muse, but this gorgeous salon embraces the romance found in the Crescent City's historic haunts. Belly up to the oval, marble-topped bar and get familiar with the twin pleasures of oysters and absinthe: two French Quarter staples with plenty of appeal in Brooklyn. The mythical anise-flavoured liqueur appears in 22 international varieties, in addition to a trim list of cerebral cocktails.

★ Spuyten Duyvil

359 Metropolitan Avenue, at Havermeyer Street, Williamsburg (1-718 963 4140, www.spuytenduyvilnyc.com). Subway L to Bedford Avenue; G to Metropolitan Avenue. **Open** 5pm-2am Mon-Thur; 5pm-4am Fri; 1pm-4am Sat; 1pm-2am Sun. **Map** p211 B3 48

Don't arrive thirsty. It takes at least ten minutes to choose from roughly 150 quaffs, a list that impresses even microbrew mavens. Most selections are middle-European regionals, and bartenders are eager to explain the differences among them. The cosy interior is chock-full of flea market finds, most of which are for sale. There's also a tasty bar menu of smoked meats, pâtés, cheeses and terrines.

Tørst

615 Manhattan Avenue, between Driggs & Nassau Avenues, Greenpoint (1-718 389 6034). Subway G to Nassau Avenue. **Open** noon-midnight Mon-Wed, Sun; noon-2am Thur-Sat. **Map** p211 B2 49

Danish for 'thirst', Tørst is helmed by legendary 'gypsy brewer' Jeppe Jarnit-Bjergsø and chef Daniel Burns, formerly of Noma in Copenhagen. These warriors are laying waste to tired ideas of what a great taproom should be, with a minimalist space that looks like a modernist log cabin, and rare brews from throughout Europe and North America. The ever-changing, 21-tap draft menu can move faster than a Swedish vallhund, but usually includes selections from Jarnit-Bjergsø's own Evil Twin Brewing. More than 100 bottled beers are also available. Tørst has more in common with a high-end wine bar than with your average local watering hole – well-heeled locals and pilgrimaging brew buffs quietly sip from designer wineglasses at the sleek white marble counter. Luksus, the restaurant hidden away in the back room, offers a tasting menu for $95 from 6.30pm to midnight Tuesday through Saturday.

Union Pool

484 Union Avenue, at Meeker Avenue, Williamsburg (1-718 609 0484, www.unionpool.com). Subway L to Lorimer Street; G to Metropolitan Avenue. **Open** 5pm-4am Mon-Fri; 1pm-4am Sat, Sun. **Map** p211 B3 50

This former pool-supply outlet now supplies booze to scruffy Williamsburgers, who pack the tin-walled main room's half-moon booths and snap saucy photo-kiosk pics. Bands strum away on the adjacent stage, while the spacious courtyard and outdoor bar is popular during the warmer months. Arrive early to kick back $5 draft beers and $6 house cocktails – happy hour is 5-9pm weeknights.

► *For more on the entertainment at Union Pool, see p279.*

Shops & Services

Academy Record Annex

85 Oak Street, between Franklin & West Streets, Greenpoint (1-718-218 8200, www.academyannex.com). Subway G to Greenpoint Avenue. **Open** noon-8pm daily. **Map** p211 A2 51 **Books & music**

See p212 **On the Record**.

Bird

203 Grand Street, between Bedford & Driggs Avenues, Williamsburg (1-718 388 1655, www.shopbird.com). Subway L to Bedford Avenue. **Open** noon-8pm Mon-Fri; 11am-7pm Sat; noon-7pm Sun. **Map** p211 A3 52 **Fashion**

A former assistant buyer at Barneys, Jen Mankins opened her first Bird boutique in Park Slope in 1999. Now fashion-forward Brooklyn (and Manhattan)

EXPLORE

Coney Island.

residents flock to three locations for up-and-coming local and international designers. The spacious LEED-certified green Williamsburg store stocks clothing and accessories for men and women. Rubbing shoulders on the racks are eclectic pieces by well-known and not-so-familiar names such as Acne, Isabel Marant, A Détacher, Tsumori Chisato and Black Crane.
Other locations 220 Smith Street, at Butler Street, Cobble Hill (1-718 797 3774); 316 Fifth Avenue, between 2nd & 3rd Streets, Park Slope (1-718 768 4940).

Captured Tracks
195 Calyer Street, between Manhattan Avenue & Leonard Street, Greenpoint (1-718 609 0871, www.capturedtracks.com). Subway G to Greenpoint Avenue or Nassau Avenue. **Open** noon-8pm daily. **Map** p211 B2 53 **Books & music**
See p212 **On the Record**.

Co-Op 87 Records
87 Guernsey Street, between Nassau & Norman Avenues, Greenpoint (1-347 294 4629, www.coop87records.tumblr.com). Subway G to Nassau Avenue. **Open** 11am-9pm daily. **Map** p211 B2 54 **Books & music**
See p212 **On the Record**.

Earwax
167 North 9th Street, between Bedford & Driggs Avenues, Williamsburg (1-718 486 3771, www.earwaxrecords.net). Subway L to Bedford Avenue. **Open** 11am-9pm daily. **Map** p211 B3 55 **Books & music**
See p212 **On the Record**.

Permanent Records
181 Franklin Street, between Green & Huron Streets, Greenpoint (1-718 383 4083, www.permanentrecords.info). Subway G to Greenpoint Avenue. **Open** noon-8pm daily. **Map** p211 A1 56 **Books & music**
See p212 **On the Record**.

Rough Trade
64 North 9th Street, between Kent & Wythe Avenues, Williamsburg (1-718 388 4111, www.roughtrade.com). Subway L to Bedford Avenue. **Open** 9am-11pm Mon-Sat; 10am-9pm Sun. **Map** p211 A3 57 **Books & music**
See p212 **On the Record**.

Swords-Smith
98 South 4th Street, between Bedford Avenue & Berry Street, Williamsburg (1-347 599 2969, www.swords-smith.com). Subway L to Bedford Avenue; J, M, Z to Marcy Avenue. **Open** noon-8pm Mon-Fri, Sun; 11am-8pm Sat. **Map** p211 A3 58 **Fashion**
Fashion vets Briana Swords (a former womenswear designer for Levi Strauss) and R Smith (a graphic designer whose credits include *Vogue*) are behind this boutique for men and women. The duo offers a carefully curated collection of clothing and accessories from between 70 and 80 up-and-coming designers – many of them locally based, such as Lucio Castro and Samantha Pleet – in the skylighted, minimalist space.

Woodley & Bunny
196 North 10th Street, at Driggs Avenue, Williamsburg (1-718 218 6588, www.woodleyandbunny.com). Subway L to Bedford Avenue; G to Nassau Avenue. **Open** 10am-9pm Mon-Fri; 9am-8pm Sat; 11am-7pm Sun. **Map** p211 B3 59 **Health & beauty**
With a prime Williamsburg location, Woodley & Bunny is the place to get the most cutting-edge crop (from $86 for women, from $66 for men) or colour, but there's a welcome emphasis on individuality at this laid-back beauty spot. Part salon, part apothecary, it also offers beauty treatments such as mini facials and eyebrow tweezing.

CONEY ISLAND & BRIGHTON BEACH

Subway B, Q to Brighton Beach; D, F, N, Q to Coney Island-Stillwell Avenue; F to Neptune Avenue; F, Q to West 8th Street-NY Aquarium.

Combining old-time fairground attractions, new amusement park rides and traditional seaside pleasures against a gritty urban backdrop, Coney Island is a strange hybrid undergoing a revitalisation plan that also includes improvements to the surrounding residential neighbourhood. In its heyday, from the turn of the century until World War II, Coney Island was New York City's playground, drawing millions each year to its seaside amusement parks Dreamland, Luna Park and Steeplechase Park. The first two were destroyed by fire (Dreamland in 1911 and Luna Park in 1944) and not rebuilt, while Steeplechase Park staggered on until 1964. Astroland was built in 1962 in the euphoria of the World's Fair, went up in flames in 1975 and was rebuilt, only to shutter in 2008.

A few years before, a developer had bought about half the area's entertainment district with a view to transforming it into a glitzy, Las Vegas-style resort, with hotels and condos, as well as restaurants, shops and rides. But a standoff with municipal planners halted progress. Then, in 2009, the city agreed to buy almost seven acres near the boardwalk that would form the core of a 27-acre amusement district. A new incarnation of **Luna Park** (1000 Surf Avenue, at W 10th Street, 1-718 373 5862, www.lunaparknyc.com, open Apr-Oct) opened in summer 2010. It now has more than 20 rides, including the new Thunderbolt – Coney Island's first custom-built rollercoaster since the **Cyclone** opened in 1927. That whiplash-inducing ride is still going strong, along with the 1918 **Deno's Wonder Wheel** – both are protected landmarks.

Nostalgic visitors will enjoy a stroll along the three-mile-long boardwalk, lined with corny carnival games and souvenir shops. The iconic 1939 **Parachute Jump** has been restored and is illuminated at night. Non-profit arts organisation Coney Island USA keeps the torch burning for 20th-century-style attractions at its **Coney Island Museum** with seasonal Circus Sideshows, as well as kitsch summer spectacle the **Mermaid Parade** (*see p34*). The local baseball team, **Brooklyn Cyclones**, play at the seaside **MCU Park**.

Walk left along the boardwalk from Coney Island and you'll reach **Brighton Beach**, New York's Little Odessa. Groups of Russian expats (the display of big hair and garish fashion can be jaw-dropping) crowd semi-outdoor eateries such as **Tatiana** (3152 Brighton 6th Street, at the Boardwalk, 1-718 891 5151) – on weekend nights, it morphs into a glitzy club.

Nathan's Famous.

Sights & Museums

Coney Island Museum

1208 Surf Avenue, at 12th Street, Coney Island (1-718 372 5159, www.coneyisland.com). Subway D, F, N, Q to Coney Island-Stillwell Avenue. **Open** *Museum* noon-6pm Sat, Sun. *Shows* vary. **Admission** *Museum* $5. *Shows* $12-$15.

Housed in a 1917 building, the Coney Island Museum acts as both a repository of the district's past and the focus of its current alternative culture. From Easter to the end of September, its venue, Sideshows by the Seashore, showcases the talents of such legendary freaks as human pincushion Scott Baker (aka the Twisted Shockmeister), and multi-talented sword swallower Betty Bloomerz, while Burlesque at the Beach slinks on to the stage on summer Thursday and Friday nights (see website for the schedule).

Restaurants & Cafés

Nathan's Famous

1310 Surf Avenue, at Stillwell Avenue, Coney Island (1-718 333 2202, www.nathansfamous.com). Subway D, F, N, Q to Coney Island-Stillwell Avenue. **Open** 9am-midnight Mon-Thur, Sun; 9am-1am Fri, Sat. **Hot dogs** $3.50. **American**

Opened in 1916, the famed frank joint has retained its subway tiles and iconic signage, as well as staples like crinkle-cut fries and thick-battered corn dogs. But there's one shiny 'new' addition: a curbside clam bar, a revival of the restaurant's 1950s raw bar. East Coast oysters and littlenecks are shucked over a mountain of ice, served with chowder crackers, lemon wedges, sinus-clearing horseradish and cocktail sauce.

Queens

While Queens is the point of arrival for visitors flying into JFK or La Guardia airports, the borough hasn't traditionally been on most tourists' must-see list. Now, however, cultural institutions, such as the Museum of Modern Art-affiliated MoMA PS1 and the revamped Museum of the Moving Image, are drawing both out-of-towners and Manhattanites across the Ed Koch Queensboro Bridge.

Queens is also an increasingly popular gastronomic destination. The city's largest borough is the country's most diverse urban area, with almost half its 2.3 million residents hailing from nearly 150 nations. Not for nothing is the elevated 7 subway line that serves these parts nicknamed the 'International Express'. **Astoria** is home to Greek tavernas and Brazilian *churrascarias*; **Jackson Heights** provides Indian, Thai and South American eateries; and **Flushing** boasts the city's second largest Chinatown.

M Wells Steakhouse

Don't Miss

1 **MoMA PS1** Adventurous shows and food, plus some of the best parties in the city (*p220*).

2 **M Wells Steakhouse** The full-scale follow-up to a much-missed cult spot (*p222*).

3 **Noguchi Museum** A serene sanctuary in industrial Queens (*p224*).

4 **Bohemian Hall & Beer Garden** Beer bars have returned to the borough, but this is the original (*p225*).

5 **Spicy & Tasty** If you like it hot, head to Flushing's Chinatown (*p227*).

Gantry Plaza State Park.

EXPLORE

LONG ISLAND CITY

Subway E, M to Court Square-23rd Street; G to Court Square or 21st Street; 7 to Vernon Boulevard-Jackson Avenue or Court Square.

Just across the East River from Manhattan, Long Island City has been touted as the 'next Williamsburg' (the hipster Brooklyn enclave; *see p209*) for so long that several other 'hoods have since claimed and passed on the mantle. In truth, LIC's proximity to midtown and the proliferation of modern apartment towers on the waterfront have proved more of a draw to upwardly mobile professionals and young families than cutting-edge cool hunters. Nevertheless, the neighbourhood has one of the city's most adventurous museums and several interesting galleries and performance spaces.

Fronting the main stretch of residential riverside development, **Gantry Plaza State Park** (48th Avenue, at Center Boulevard) commands an impressive panorama of midtown Manhattan. The 12-acre park takes its name from the hulking industrial gantries that still stand watch over the piers and were used to haul cargo from rail barges. Wavy deckchairs offer direct views of the United Nations across the East River. While Vernon Avenue is the neighbourhood's prime restaurant, retail and bar hub, the **Waterfront Crabhouse** (2-03 Borden Avenue, at 2nd Street, 1-718 729 4862), an old-time saloon and seafood restaurant in an 1880s brick building, evokes an earlier time with a jumble of bric-a-brac dangling from the dining room ceiling.

The neighbourhood's cultural jewel is the progressive art institution **MoMA PS1** (*see below*). In summer months, the courtyard of the museum becomes a dance-music hub with its Saturday-afternoon **Warm Up** parties (*see p267*). A well-preserved block of 19th-century houses constitutes the **Hunter's Point Historic District** (45th Avenue, between 21st & 23rd Streets).

With several artists' studio complexes lodged in Long Island City, a nascent art scene has taken hold. **SculptureCenter** (*see p222*), housed in a dramatic converted industrial space, is a great place to see new work, while the **Fisher Landau Center for Art** (38-27 30th Street, between 38th and 39th Avenues, 1-718 937 0727, www.flcart.org; closed Tue, Wed) showcases the 1,500-piece contemporary art collection of Emily Fisher Landau. For details of open-studio events in the neighbourhood, check out www.licartists.org.

IN THE KNOW
WHERE THE ACTION IS

Broadway Danny Rose (1984) and *Do the Right Thing* (1989) are among the movies shot at Long Island City's Silvercup Studios (42-22 22nd Street, between 43rd & 44th Avenues, www.silvercupstudios.com), a former bread factory in an industrial section by the Ed Koch Queensboro Bridge. The studios have also been home to some of the most iconic New York-set (and New Jersey-set) TV shows: *Sex and the City* (the series and both movies), *The Sopranos* and *Girls*. While you're in the neighbourhood, look out for its massive retro sign, which featured in the rooftop fight scene of 1986 flick *Highlander*.

Sights & Museums

For the Noguchi Museum, *see p224*.

★ MoMA PS1

22-25 Jackson Avenue, at 46th Avenue (1-718 784 2084, www.momaps1.org). Subway E, M to Court Square-23rd Street; G to 21st Street; 7 to Court Square. **Open** noon-6pm Mon, Thur-Sun. **Admission** $10; $5 reductions; under-17s free. **Map** p221 A5 ❶

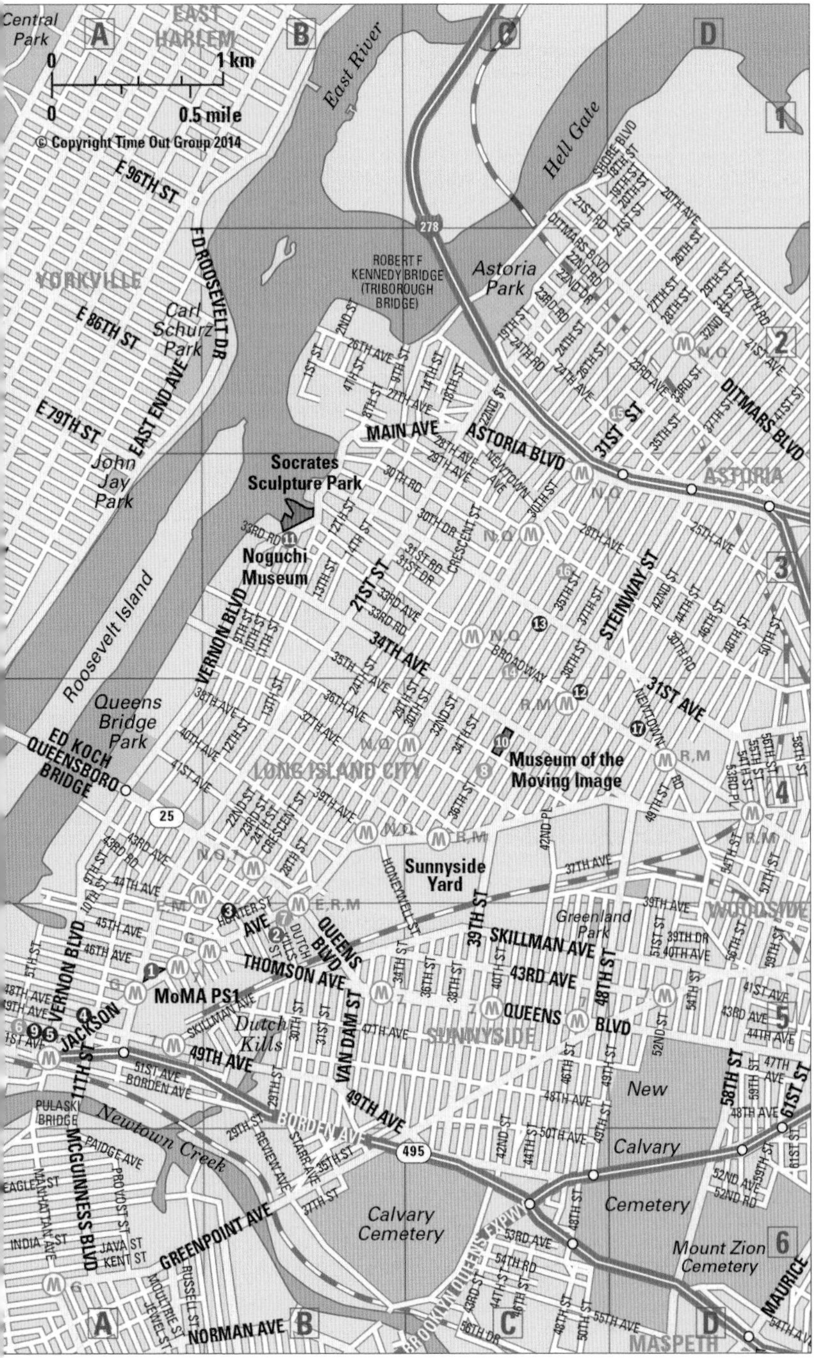
Central Park
East Harlem
0
1 km
0
0.5 mile
© Copyright Time Out Group 2014
E 96th St
FD Roosevelt Dr
Yorkville
E 86th St
Carl Schurz Park
East End Ave
E 79th St
John Jay Park
East River
Hell Gate
278
Robert F Kennedy Bridge (Triborough Bridge)
Astoria Park
Main Ave
Astoria Blvd
31st St
Ditmars Blvd
Astoria
Socrates Sculpture Park
Noguchi Museum
Vernon Blvd
21st St
34th Ave
Steinway St
31st Ave
Broadway
Roosevelt Island
Queens Bridge Park
Ed Koch Queensboro Bridge
Long Island City
Museum of the Moving Image
25
Sunnyside Yard
Greenland Park
Woodside
Skillman Ave
43rd Ave
Queens Blvd
Thomson Ave
Van Dam St
39th St
48th St
MoMA PS1
Dutch Kills
Jackson Ave
11th St
49th Ave
Sunnyside
Pulaski Bridge
Newtown Creek
Borden Ave
495
New Calvary Cemetery
Calvary Cemetery
Greenpoint Ave
McGuinness Blvd
Brooklyn Queens Expwy
Mount Zion Cemetery
Maurice
Norman Ave
Maspeth
58th St
61st St

EXPLORE

Housed in a distinctive Romanesque Revival building, MoMA PS1 mounts cutting-edge shows and hosts an acclaimed international studio programme. The contemporary art centre became an affiliate of MoMA in 1999, and the two institutions sometimes stage collaborative exhibitions. The DJed summer Warm Up parties are a fixture of the dance-music scene; eaterie M Wells Dinette is a foodie destination.

★ SculptureCenter

44-19 Purves Street, at Jackson Avenue (1-718 361 1750, www.sculpture-center.org). Subway E, M to Court Square-23rd Street; G, 7 to Court Square. **Open** 11am-6pm Mon, Thur-Sun. **Admission** *Suggested donation* $5; $3 reductions. **Map** p221 B5 ❷

One of the best places to see sculpture by blossoming and mid-career artists, this non-profit space – housed in an impressive former trolley-repair shop that was redesigned by acclaimed architect Maya Lin in 2002 – is known for its broad definition of the discipline.

Restaurants & Cafés

M Wells Steakhouse

43-15 Crescent Street, between 43rd Avenue & 44th Drive (1-718 786 9060, www.magasinwells.com). Subway N, Q, 7 to Queensboro Plaza. **Open** 5.30-11.30pm Mon, Wed-Sat; 5.30-10.30pm Sun. **Main courses** $17-$75. **Map** p221 B5 ❸ **Steakhouse/eclectic**

Just after we got hooked on the eccentric, carnivorous fare and penchant for excess at the original M Wells, the renegade LIC diner gave up its lease, and one of the most exciting restaurants New York had seen in years disappeared. Quirk power couple Hugue Dufour and Sarah Obraitis opened a more subdued venture – MoMA PS1's lunchtime cafeteria, M Wells Dinette – in 2012. But M Wells Steakhouse is their full-fledged return. Housed in a former autobody shop, the spot splices class with irreverence; black-tie waiters and a besuited sommelier dart around a room where trout swim in a concrete tank and Canadian-lumberjack movies project onto the wall. Charred iceberg salad, with creamy blue-cheese dressing and sweet dehydrated ketchup meringue chips, is a striking, whimsical wedge. The likes of dry-aged Nebraska côte de boeuf for two recall the gluttonous communal spirit of the first M Wells, while other dishes capture the madcap opulence that made it special.

Sweetleaf

10-93 Jackson Avenue, at 11th Street (1-917 832 6726, www.sweetleaflic.com). Subway 7 to Vernon Boulevard-Jackson Avenue. **Open** 7am-7pm Mon-Fri; 8am-7pm Sat; 9am-6pm Sun. **Coffee** $2-$4. **No credit cards. Map** p221 A5 ❹ **Café**

Long Island City's first speciality coffee shop serves direct-trade coffee, house-made pastries and artisan espresso in a cubbyhole-sized space.

Tournesol

50-12 Vernon Bouleveard, between 50th & 51st Avenues (1-718 472 4355, www.tournesolnyc.com). Subway 7 to Vernon Boulevard-Jackson Avenue. **Open** 5.30-11pm Mon; 11.30am-3pm, 5.30-11pm Tue-Thur; 11.30am-3pm, 5.30-11.30pm Fri; 11am-3.30pm, 5.30-11.30pm Sat; 11am-3.30pm, 5-10pm Sun. **Main courses** $16-$22. **No credit cards** (except AmEx). **Map** p221 A5 ❺ **French**

While Tournesol has fast become a local favourite for some steak frites and magret de canard, even Manhattanites are making the trip for beautifully executed south-western French cuisine at prices you'd be hard pressed to find across the East River. Squeeze into one of the red banquettes in the intimate one-room dining space outfitted with white tin ceilings and local artwork, and split an appetiser of the obscenely good house-made foie gras terrine.

Bars

Alewife

5-14 51st Avenue, between Vernon Boulevard & 5th Street (1-718 937 7494, www.alewifenyc.com). Subway 7 to Vernon Boulevard-Jackson Avenue. **Open** 4pm-1am Mon-Thur; 4pm-3am Fri; 11am-3am Sat; 11am-1am Sun. **Map** p221 A5 ❻

A serious craft-beer selection is the draw at this bi-level beer hall, which comes from a team of hops zealots with ties to Alewife Baltimore and the cultish Lord Hobo in Cambridge, MA. It's a generic-looking gastropub, and we could do without the poppy soundtrack and truffle oil on our fries. But the owners come through where it counts, curating a balanced and worldly beer list (28 taps and casks and 100-plus bottles) that can go toe-to-toe with the most pedigreed suds haunts. And while the pricey pub grub (a pulled pork sandwich with roasted corn and cabbage slaw) is hit-and-miss, late-night pizzas and weekend brunch service give Alewife anytime appeal.

Dutch Kills

27-24 Jackson Avenue, at Dutch Kills Street (1-718 383 2724, www.dutchkillsbar.com). Subway E, M, R to Queens Plaza. **Open** 5pm-2am Mon-Thur, Sun; 5pm-3am Fri, Sat. **Map** p221 B5 ❼

What separates Dutch Kills from other mixology temples modelled after vintage saloons is the abundance of elbow room. Settle into one of the deep, dark-wood booths in the front, or perch at the bar. Cocktails are mostly classic, with prices slightly lower than in similar establishments in Manhattan.

Garden at Studio Square

35-33 36th Street, between 35th & 36th Avenues (1-718 383 1001, www.studiosquarenyc.com). Subway M, R to 36th Street; N, Q to 36th Avenue. **Open** 1pm-3am Mon-Thur; 1pm-4am Fri-Sun. **Map** p221 D4 ❽

A contemporary interpretation of a classic beer garden, Studio Square's grand cobblestoned courtyard is lined with communal picnic tables. Three modern fire pits keep out evening chills, but there is also an indoor bar. The 20-strong list includes European classics and American microbrews. Basic pub grub is supplemented by sausages (kielbasas and brats), and the party-hearty ambience is fuelled by DJs and bands.

Shops & Services

LIC: living

5-35 51st Avenue, between Vernon Boulevard & 5th Street (1-718 361 5650, www.licliving.com). Subway 7 to Vernon Boulevard-Jackson Avenue. **Open** 11am-7pm Tue-Sat; 11am-5pm Sun. **Map** p221 A5 ❾ **Fashion/homewares**

Neighbours-turned-business-partners Rebekah Witzke and Jillian Tangen opened this lifestyle boutique, featuring women's clothing (including several hard-to-find Scandinavian brands) and accessories for both guys and gals, plus noteworthy household items; the latter, including Tocca candles and fun barware, are displayed inside a 1940s vintage cabinet.

ASTORIA

Subway R, M to Steinway Street; N, Q to Broadway, 30th Avenue, 36th Avenue or Astoria-Ditmars Boulevard.

A lively, traditionally Greek and Italian neighbourhood, Astoria has over the last few decades seen an influx of Brazilians, Bangladeshis, Eastern Europeans, Colombians and Egyptians; they've been joined by post-grads sharing row-house digs. A 15-minute downhill hike from Broadway subway station towards Manhattan brings you to the **Noguchi Museum** (*see p224*), which was created by the visionary sculptor. Nearby lies the **Socrates Sculpture Park** (Broadway, at Vernon Boulevard, www.socratessculpturepark.org), a riverfront art space in an industrial setting with great views of Manhattan.

In the early days of cinema, Astoria was a major celluloid star. Taking advantage of its proximity to talent-laden Broadway, Famous Players-Lasky (later Paramount Pictures) opened its first studios in the neighbourhood in 1920. Portions of Valentino's blockbuster *The Sheikh* (1921) were filmed there, and the studio produced the Marx Brothers' *The Cocoanuts* (1929) and *Animal Crackers* (1930) before Paramount moved its operations west. After years of neglect, the studios were declared a National Historic Landmark in 1976, and, in 1982, developer George S Kaufman bought the site and created **Kaufman Astoria Studios** (34-12 36th Street, between 34th & 35th Avenues, www.kaufmanastoria.com). Scenes for numerous films, including *The Taking of Pelham 1 2 3* (2009) and *Wall Street: Money Never Sleeps* (2010) were shot there, and the studios are also home to long-running kids' TV show *Sesame Street*. The recently expanded **Museum of the Moving Image** (*see p224*) is across the street.

Still New York's Greek-American stronghold, Astoria is well known for Hellenic eateries and cafés. One of the city's last central European beer gardens, **Bohemian Hall & Beer Garden** (*see p225*) offers Czech-style dining and drinking. Arrive early on warm weekends to nab a picnic table in the expansive, linden tree-shaded yard. You can puff on a shisha – a (legal) hookah pipe – with thick Turkish coffee in the cafés of 'Little Egypt' along Steinway Street, between 28th Avenue and Astoria Boulevard. At the end of the N and Q subway lines (Astoria-Ditmars Boulevard), walk west to **Astoria Park** (from Astoria Park South to Ditmars Boulevard, between Shore Boulevard & 19th Street) for its dramatic views of two bridges: the Robert F Kennedy Bridge (formerly the Triborough), Robert Moses's automotive labyrinth connecting Queens, the Bronx and Manhattan; and the 1916 Hell Gate Bridge, a steel single-arch tour de force and template for the Sydney Harbour Bridge. On the area's north-east fringes, you can take a tour (by appointment) of the still-thriving red-brick 1871 piano factory **Steinway & Sons** (1 Steinway Place, between 19th Avenue & 38th Street, 1-718 721 2600, www.steinway.com).

LIC: living.

EXPLORE

Sights & Museums

Museum of the Moving Image

36-01 35th Avenue, at 36th Street (1-718 777 6888, www.movingimage.us). Subway R, M to Steinway Street; N, Q to 36th Avenue. **Open** *Galleries* 10.30am-5pm Wed, Thur; 10.30am-8pm Fri; 11.30am-7pm Sat, Sun. **Admission** $12; $6-$9 reductions; under-3s free; free 4-8pm Fri. **Map** p221 C4 ⑩

The Museum of the Moving Image reopened in 2011 after a major renovation that doubled its size and made it one of the foremost museums in the world dedicated to TV, film and video. The museum, with its collection and state-of-the-art screening facilities and galleries, is housed on the campus of Kaufman Astoria Studios. The upgraded core exhibition, 'Behind the Screen', on the second and third floors, contains approximately 1,400 artefacts (including the super creepy stunt doll used in *The Exorcist*, with full head-rotating capabilities, and a miniature skyscraper from *Blade Runner*) and interactive displays. A new gallery devoted to Muppets creator Jim Henson is expected to open in early 2015.

★ Noguchi Museum

9-01 33rd Road, at Vernon Boulevard (1-718 204 7088, www.noguchi.org). Subway N, Q to Broadway, then 15min walk or Q104 bus to 11th Street; 7 to Vernon Boulevard-Jackson Avenue, then Q103 bus to 10th Street. **Open** 10am-5pm Wed-Fri; 11am-6pm Sat, Sun. **Admission** $10; $5 reductions; free under-12s; pay what you wish 1st Fri of the mth. No pushchairs/strollers. **Map** p221 B3 ⑪

When Japanese-American sculptor and designer Isamu Noguchi (1904-88) opened his Queens museum in 1985, he became the first living artist in the US to establish such an institution. The Noguchi Museum occupies a former photo-engraving plant across the street from the studio he had occupied since the 1960s; its location allowed him to be close to stone and metal suppliers along Vernon Boulevard. Noguchi designed the entire building to be a meditative oasis amid its gritty, industrial setting. Eleven galleries – spread over two floors – and an outdoor space are filled with his sculptures, as well as drawn, painted and collaged studies, architectural models, and stage and furniture designs.

ROCK ROCK ROCKAWAY

Summer hotspots are springing up around the urban surf hub.

Situated on a long peninsula, the 170-acre **Rockaway Beach**, popular with local surfers, has become a hip summer destination. Not only was the beach back in business the summer after the neighbourhood took a battering from Hurricane Sandy, but the 2013 season also saw the debut of new hotspots. Rockaway is an easy, if lengthy, subway ride from Manhattan: take the A train to Broad Channel, then transfer to the S.

Sayra's Wine Bar.

Get off at Beach 98 Street and swing by the superb seasonal **Rockaway Taco** (95-19 Rockaway Beach Boulevard, at Beach 96 Street, 1-347 213 7466, www.rockawaytaco.com) for fish, *carne*, chorizo or tofu tacos ($3 each) before hitting the sand.

Once you've had enough sun and surf, head to beloved dive **Connolly's** (155 Beach 95th Street, between Rockaway Beach Boulevard and Shore Front Parkway, 1-718 474 2374) for one of the bar's (in)famous frozen piña coladas. Or, for something a little more sophisticated, stop by **Sayra's Wine Bar** (91-11 Rockaway Beach Boulevard, between Beach 91st & 92nd Streets, 1-347 619 8009), the brainchild of local surfer Rashida Jackson and artist Patrick Flibotte. The 28-seat shoreside drinkery showcases seasonal vino from regions around the world, alongside tapas including smoked-paprika-rosemary chips, olives and barbecue pulled-pork sandwiches, piled on silver-dollar brioche from Brooklyn Bread. Out back is a 1,200-square-foot garden fitted with beach rocks and wooden picnic tables.

Those looking to make a night of it should try hipster haven **Playland Motel** (97-20 Rockaway Beach Boulevard, between Beach 97th & 98th Streets, 1-347 954 9063, www.playlandmotel.com). The restaurant, bar, late-night club, outdoor hangout, pizzeria and, yes, hotel (there are 12 creatively decorated rooms) is an arty-yet-casual oasis that attracts both fashion-conscious clubbers and weathered locals.

Restaurants & Cafés

$ The Queens Kickshaw

40-17 Broadway, between Steinway & 41st Streets (1-718 777 0913, www.thequeenskickshaw.com). Subway M, R to Steinway Street. **Open** 7.30am-1am Mon-Fri; 9am-1am Sat, Sun. **Sandwiches** $8-$11. **Map** p221 C4 ⑫ **Café**

Serious java draws caffeine fiends to this airy café, which also specialises in grilled cheese sandwiches. While the pedigreed beans – from Counter Culture Coffee – are brewed with Hario V60 drip cones and a La Marzocco Strada espresso machine, there's no coffee-snob attitude here. Fancy grilled cheese choices include a weekend-morning offering of soft egg folded with ricotta, a gruyère crisp and maple hot sauce between thick, buttery slices of brioche.

$ Zenon Taverna

34-10 31st Avenue, at 34th Street (1-718 956 0133, www.zenontaverna.com). Subway N, Q to Broadway. **Open** noon-11pm daily. **Main courses** $11-$18. **No credit cards**. **Map** p221 C3 ⑬ **Greek**

The faux-stone entryway and murals of ancient ruins don't detract from the Mediterranean charm of this humble place that's been serving Greek and Cypriot food for more than 25 years. Specials rotate daily, embracing all the classics – stuffed grape leaves, *keftedes* (Cypriot meatballs), *spanakopita* (spinach pie) – and less ubiquitous dishes such as rabbit stew and plump *loukaniko* (pork sausages). Filling sweets, such as *galaktopoureko* (syrupy layers of filo baked with custard cream), merit a taste.

Bars

Astoria Bier and Cheese

34-14 Broadway, between 34th & 35th Streets (1-718 545 5588, www.astoriabierandcheese.com). Subway M, R to Steinway Street; N, Q to Broadway. **Open** noon-11pm Mon-Thur; noon-midnight Fri, Sat; noon-10pm Sun. **Map** p221 C3 ⑭

Manhattan's hybrid bar-shop trend crosses the bridge to Queens with this funky curds-and-brew haven, which sports a bathroom mural of Kim Jong-il milking a cow. At the marble bar, grab one of the ten seasonal, mostly local drafts, like Greenport Harbor's Gobsmacked IPA, from Long Island. There are close to 300 bottles and cans – organised by style and offered in mix-and-match six packs – that can be purchased to go or opened on-site for a $2 corking fee. Fromage buff Mike Fisher (a Bedford Cheese Shop vet) culls close to 100 selections for the refrigerated case, some of which are worked into a sit-down menu that includes a selection of grilled cheese melts (like one stuffed with bleu, prosciutto and fig).

★ Bohemian Hall & Beer Garden

29-19 24th Avenue, between 29th & 31st Streets (1-718 274 4925, www.bohemianhall.com). Subway N, Q to Astoria Boulevard. **Open** 5pm-1am Mon-Thur; 5pm-3am Fri; noon-3am Sat; noon-1am Sun (hrs vary seasonally). **Map** p221 D2 ⑮

This authentic Czech beer garden features plenty of mingle-friendly picnic tables, where you can sample cheap, robust platters of sausage and 16 mainly European drafts. Though the huge, tree-canopied garden is open year-round (in winter, the area is tented and heated), summer is prime time to visit.

Sweet Afton

30-09 34th Street, between 30th & 31st Avenue (1-718 777 2570, www.sweetaftonbar.com). Subway N, Q to 30th Avenue. **Open** 4pm-4am Mon-Fri; 11am-4am Sat, Sun. **Map** p221 C3 ⑯

This Queens gastropub combines an industrial feel – lots of concrete and massive beams – with the dim, dark-wood cosiness of an Irish pub. The bar's smartly curated array of reasonably priced suds includes strong selections from craft breweries like Ommegang, Six Point and Captain Lawrence, but the bartender will just as happily mix a cocktail. The satisfying food menu is highlighted by the beer-battered McClure's pickles – an epic bar snack.

Shops & Services

Long Island City Kleaners

45-03 Broadway, between 45th & 46th Streets (1-718 606 0540, www.licknyc.com). Subway M, R to 46th Street. **Open** 11am-8pm Mon, Wed-Sat; noon-6pm Sun. **Map** p221 D4 ⑰ **Fashion**

Frustrated by the sparse streetwear options in his neighbourhood, Mark Garcia brought his favourite local brands together in this cosy lifestyle boutique. Inspired by gritty NYC storefronts from the 1980s and '90s that posed as dry cleaners but hosted illegal activities, Garcia decorated the space with vintage sewing machines and for-sale T-shirts displayed in plastic dry-cleaner bags. He sells clothing, skating goods and limited-edition collectibles.

JACKSON HEIGHTS

Subway E, F, M, R to Jackson Heights-Roosevelt Avenue; 7 to 74th Street-Broadway.

Dizzying even by Queens standards, Jackson Heights' multiculturalism gives it an energy all its own. Little India greets you with a cluster of small shops on 74th Street between 37th Road and 37th Avenue, selling Indian music, Bollywood DVDs, saris and glitzy jewellery. But the main appeal for visitors is culinary. The unofficial HQ of the Indian expat community, **Jackson Diner** (*see p226*) serves sumptuous curries. Along with neighbouring Elmhurst and Woodside, Jackson Heights has also welcomed waves of Latin American and South-east Asian immigrants. Fresh, meaty tacos – think broiled beef and steamed tongue – give **Taqueria Coatzingo** (76-05 Roosevelt Avenue, between 76th & 77th Streets, 1-718 424 1977) an edge over the other tempting holes-in-the-wall under the 7 train track.

Restaurants & Cafés

$ Jackson Diner

37-47 74th Street, between 37th Avenue & 37th Road (1-718 672 1232, www.jacksondiner.com). Subway E, F, M, R to Jackson Heights-Roosevelt Avenue; 7 to 74th Street-Broadway. **Open** 11.30am-10pm Mon-Thur, Sun; 11.30am-10.30pm Fri, Sat. **Main courses** $10-$22. **Map** p406 Y5 **Indian**

Harried waiters and Formica-topped tables evoke a diner experience at this weekend meet-and-eat headquarters for New York's Indian expat community. Watch Hindi soaps on Zee TV while enjoying *samosa chat* topped with chickpeas, yoghurt, onion, tomato, and a sweet-spicy mix of tamarind and mint chutneys. Specials such as *murgh tikka makhanwala*, tender pieces of marinated chicken simmered in curry and cream, are fiery and flavourful – ask for mild if you're susceptible to chilli.

★ $ Sripraphai

64-13 39th Avenue, between 64th & 65th Streets (1-718 899 9599, www.sripraphai restaurant.com). Subway 7 to 61st Street-Woodside. **Open** 11.30am-9.30pm Mon, Tue, Thur-Sun. **Main courses** $9-$17. **No credit cards. Map** p221 Y5 **Thai**

Woodside's destination eaterie offers distinctive, traditional dishes such as catfish salad or green curry with beef: a thick, piquant broth filled out with roasted Thai eggplant. The dining areas, which sprawl over two levels and a garden (open in summer), are packed with Manhattanites who can be seen eyeing the plates enjoyed by the Thai regulars, mentally filing away what to order the next time.

FLUSHING

Subway 7 to Flushing-Main Street, 103rd Street-Corona Plaza, 111th Street or Mets-Willets Point.

Egalitarian Dutchmen staked their claim to 'Vlissingen' in the 1600s and were shortly joined by pacifist Friends, or Quakers, seeking religious freedom in the New World. These religious settlers promulgated the Flushing Remonstrance, a groundbreaking 1657 edict extending 'the law of love, peace and liberty' to Jews and Muslims. It's now regarded as a forerunner of the United States Constitution's First Amendment. The plain wooden **Old Quaker Meeting House** (137-16 Northern Boulevard, between Main & Union Streets), built in 1694, creates a startling juxtaposition to the prosperous Chinatown that rings its weathered wooden walls. The neighbourhood has hundreds of temples and churches used by immigrants from Korea, China and south Asia. **St George's Church** (135-32 38th Avenue, between Main & Prince Streets, 1-718 359 1171, www.saintgeorgesflushing.org), an Episcopalian church with a striking steeple, chartered by King George III, was once a dominant site, but now competes for attention with restaurants and shops. The interior is worth a brief visit if only to see the two examples of Queens-made Tiffany stained glass and to hear church services in Caribbean-accented English, Chinese and Spanish.

Most visitors, however, come for the restaurants and dumpling stalls of Flushing's sprawling **Chinatown**, which has a more affluent demographic than its Manhattan counterpart – a case in point is the gleaming **New World Mall** (136-20 Roosevelt Avenue, at Main Street, 1-718 353 0551, www.newworld mallny.com) and its opulent third-floor dim sum palace, **Grand Restaurant** (1-718 321 8258). Downstairs, at the spacious **JMart** supermarket, peruse such exotic produce as the formidably prickled durian and the notoriously elusive mangosteen, or gawk at buckets full of live eels and frogs.

Flushing Town Hall (137-35 Northern Boulevard, at Linden Place, 1-718 463 7700, www.flushingtownhall.org), built during the Civil War in the highly fanciful Romanesque Revival style, showcases local arts groups, and hosts jazz and chamber music concerts. The most visited site in Queens is rambling **Flushing Meadows Corona Park** (from 111th Street to Van Wyck Expressway, between Flushing Bay & Grand Central Parkway, 1-718 760 6565, www.nycgovparks.org), where the 1939-40 and 1964-65 World's Fairs were held. Larger than Central Park, it's home to the **Queens Zoo** (1-718 271 1500, www.queenszoo.com); **Queens Theatre in the Park** (1-718 760 0064, www.queens theatre.org), an indoor amphitheatre designed by Philip Johnson; the **New York Hall of Science** (*see p244*), an acclaimed interactive museum; the **Queens Botanical Garden**, a 39-acre cavalcade of greenery; and the recently expanded **Queens Museum** (*see p226*). Also here are **Citi Field** (Roosevelt Avenue, near 126th Street, 1-718 507 8499, www.newyork.mets.mlb.com), the home of the Mets baseball team, and the **USTA (United States Tennis Association) National Tennis Center**. The US Open (*see p34*) raises an almighty racket at summer's end, but the general public can play here the other 11 months of the year.

Queens Museum.

Sights & Museums

Louis Armstrong House

34-56 107th Street, between 34th & 37th Avenues, Corona (1-718 478 8274, www.louisarmstronghouse.org). Subway 7 to 103rd Street-Corona Plaza. **Open** 10am-5pm Tue-Fri; noon-5pm Sat, Sun. *Tours* hourly (last tour 4pm). **Admission** $10; $6-$7 reductions; free under-4s.

Pilgrims to the two-storey house where the great 'Satchmo' lived from 1943 until his death in 1971 will find a shrine to the revolutionary trumpet player – as well as his wife's passion for wallpaper. Her decorative attentions extended to the interiors of cupboards, closets and even bathroom cabinets. The 40-minute tour is enhanced by audiotapes of Louis that give much insight into the tranquil domesticity he sought in the then suburban neighbourhood.

Queens Museum

New York City Building, park entrance on 49th Avenue, at 111th Street, Flushing Meadows-Corona Park (1-718 592 9700, www.queensmuseum.org). Subway 7 to 111th Street, then walk south on 111th Street, turning left on to 49th Avenue; continue into the park & over Grand Central Parkway Bridge. **Open** noon-6pm Wed-Sun. **Admission** *Suggested donation* $8; $4 reductions; under-12s free.

Facing the Unisphere, the 140ft stainless steel globe created for the 1964 World's Fair, in Flushing Meadows Corona Park, the Queens Museum occupies the former New York City Building, a Gotham-themed pavilion built for the earlier World's Fair in 1939. In the 1940s, the structure was the first home of the United Nations. During the 1964 World's Fair, the New York City Building showcased the Panorama of the City of New York, a 9,335sq ft scale model of the city dreamed up by powerful urban planner Robert Moses. Still on display in the museum, it includes every one of the 895,000 buildings constructed before 1992.

In autumn 2013, after more than two years, the Queens Museum wrapped up an expansion-cum-renovation project that doubled its size. The centrepiece of the 50,000sq ft addition, which used to house an ice-rink, is an airy atrium. The extra space accommodates studios for Queens-based artists, a café and a museum shop selling original World's Fair memorabilia. The Panorama has had a modest makeover of its own. Its day-to-night cycle, which allowed it to be viewed as a city at night, has been restored – wait for the room to darken to see the little Apple twinkle. The new World's Fair Visible Storage and Gallery displays more than 900 artefacts from the 1939 and 1964 fairs.

Restaurants & Cafés

Fu Run

40-09 Prince Street between Roosevelt Avenue and 40th Road (1-718 321 1363, www.furunflushing.com). Subway 7 to Flushing-Main Street. **Open** 11.30am-midnight daily. **Main courses** $10-$23. **Chinese**

Thanks to a change in immigration patterns, Flushing has seen an increase in Northern Chinese restaurants like Fu Run, whose owners are from Dongbei (what was once known as Manchuria). They call their justly celebrated dish the 'Muslim lamb chop', but it's more like a half rack of ribs: a platter of bone-in, fatty meat is braised, then battered and deep-fried, the whole juicy slab blanketed with cumin seeds, chilli powder and flakes, and black and white sesame seeds.

Spicy & Tasty

39-07 Prince Street, between Roosevelt & 39th Avenues (1-718 359 1601, www.spicyandtasty.com). Subway 7 to Flushing-Main Street. **Open** 11.30am-10.30pm Mon-Thur, Sun; 11.30am-11pm Fri, Sat. **Main courses** $9-$19. **No credit cards. Chinese**

Any serious trip to Flushing for spicy Szechuan food should begin here. Revered by in-the-know regulars, this brightly lit eaterie serves plates of peppercorn-laden pork and lamb swimming in a chilli sauce that's sure to set even the most seasoned palate aflame. Stock up on cold-bar options, like zesty sesame noodles, crunchy chopped cucumbers and smooth, delicate tofu – you'll need the relief. Service is speedy and mercifully attentive to water requests.

The Bronx

The only NYC borough that's physically attached to the mainland of America, the Bronx seems remote to most visitors – and, indeed, many New Yorkers. Part of this perceived distance is due to the lingering of the South Bronx's global reputation for urban strife in the 1970s, which means the borough's two best-known visitor attractions, Yankee Stadium and the Bronx Zoo, are generally covered in quick trips in and out. But there's more to the boogie-down borough than gritty cityscapes: the area offers art deco architecture on the Grand Concourse, an up-and-coming art scene, old-school Italian eateries on Arthur Avenue, and some of the most exquisite gardens in the city.

Visitors should note that although some parts of the Bronx are gentrifying, others, such as parts of the South Bronx and the northern swathe of the Grand Concourse, are still rough around the edges.

New York Botanical Garden.

Don't Miss

1 The Grand Concourse A fascinating parade of (somewhat faded) art deco architecture (*see p231*).

2 New York Botanical Garden The sprawling green space is an all-seasons oasis (*see p233*).

3 Mike's Deli Taste the 'real Little Italy' at this Arthur Avenue original (*see p234*).

4 Bronx Beer Hall For brewed-in-the-borough suds (*see p234*).

5 Wave Hill Lush gardens with stunning Hudson River views (*see p235*).

South Bronx.

THE SOUTH BRONX

Subway 4 to 161st Street-Yankee Stadium; 6 to Hunts Point Avenue or 138th Street-Third Avenue.

In the 1960s and '70s, the **South Bronx** was so ravaged by post-war 'white flight' and community displacement from the construction of the Cross Bronx Expressway that the neighbourhood became virtually synonymous with urban blight. Crime was rampant and arson became widespread, as landlords discovered that renovating decayed property was far less lucrative than simply burning it down to collect insurance. During a World Series game at Yankee Stadium in 1977, TV cameras caught a building on fire just blocks away. 'Ladies and gentlemen,' commentator Howard Cosell told the world, 'the Bronx is burning.'

These days, the South Bronx is rising from the ashes. In 2006, the South Bronx Initiative was formed to revitalise the area, while eco-sensitive outfits such as Sustainable South Bronx (www.ssbx.org) have helped to transform vacant lots into green spaces such as **Barretto Point Park** (between Tiffany & Barretto Streets) and **Hunts Point Riverside Park** (at the foot of Lafayette Avenue on the Bronx River). In 2005, Hunts Point became the new home to the city's **Fulton Fish Market** (1-718 378 2356, www.newfultonfishmarket.com), which moved from the site it had occupied for 180 years near South Street Seaport to a 400,000-square foot modern facility that is the largest consortium of seafood retailers in America.

Unsurprisingly, the rejuvenated area has also seen an influx of young professional refugees from overpriced Manhattan and Brooklyn: new condos are sprouting up, old warehouses are being redeveloped, once-crumbling tenements are being refurbished and, inevitably, chain stores are moving in. Young families have been snapping up the renovated townhouses on Alexander Avenue and furnishing them from the thoroughfare's antiques stores, while industrial lofts on Bruckner Boulevard have become homes to creatives. Yet despite developers' hopes for 'SoBro', the area has not quite turned into the Next Big Thing. Yet.

Hunts Point is also becoming a creative live-work hub. In 1994, a group of artists and community leaders converted an industrial building into the **Point** (940 Garrison Avenue, at Manida Street, 1-718 542 4139, www.thepoint.org, closed Sun), an arts-based community development centre with a much-used performance space and gallery, studios for dance, theatre and photography, an environmental advocacy group, and lively summer and after-school workshops for neighbourhood children. The Point also leads walking tours (call for reservations) that explore the history of locally born music, such as mambo and hip hop.

Another artistic South Bronx hotbed is simmering further south-west in **Mott Haven**. Here, **Longwood Art Gallery @ Hostos** (450 Grand Concourse, at 149th Street, 1-718 518 6728, www.bronxarts.org/lag.asp), the creation of the Bronx Council on the Arts, mounts top-notch exhibits in a variety of media.

IN THE KNOW
HIP HOP HISTORY

DJ **Kool Herc's old digs** at 1520 Sedgwick Avenue in the West Bronx is the acknowledged birthplace of hip hop, but the area in and around the **Bronx River Houses** (174th Street, between Bronx River & Harrod Avenue) is where Afrika Bambaataa and his Universal Zulu Nation developed it into a phenomenon.

Of course, the vast majority of visitors to the South Bronx are just stopping long enough to take in a baseball game at **Yankee Stadium**, where some of baseball's most famous legends, from Babe Ruth to Derek Jeter, have made history.

Sights & Museums

Yankee Stadium

River Avenue, at 161st Street (1-718 293 6000, www.yankees.com). Subway B, D, 4 to 161st Street-Yankee Stadium.

In 2009, the Yankees vacated the fabled 'House that Ruth Built' and moved into their new $1.3-billion stadium across the street. Monument Park, an open-air museum behind centre field that celebrates the exploits of past Yankee heroes, can be visited as part of a tour ($25, $23 reductions, $20 booked online; 1-646 977 8687), along with the New York Yankees Museum, the dugout, and – when the Yankees are on the road – the clubhouse.

Restaurants & Cafés

Mo Gridder's BBQ

565 Hunts Point Avenue, between Oak Point & Randall Avenues (1-718 991 3046, www.mogridder.com). Subway 6 to Hunts Point Avenue. **Open** 11am-5pm Mon-Fri; 11am-4pm Sat. **Main courses** $5-$18. **Barbecue**

On the lot of the Hunts Point Auto Sales & Service Station, surrounded by junked car yards and auto parts stores, Mo Gridder's BBQ operates out of a red Wells Cargo trailer that sports a serious-looking smoker on its open back half. If you're here for auto issues, get the oil change and ribs special for $35. Otherwise, park yourself at a picnic table for the sauce-shellacked ribs and barbecue chicken that's nicely charred on the outside and juicy on the inside. Sides like potato salad and collard greens are less stellar, but decent enough.

Bars

Bruckner Bar & Grill

1 Bruckner Boulevard, at Third Avenue (1-718 665 2001, www.thebrucknerbar.com). Subway 6 to Third Avenue-138th Street. **Open** 11am-1.30am daily.

This popular neighbourhood hangout has eight beers on tap, including Bronx Brewery Pale Ale, plus a wide range of bottled craft beers, and an eclectic menu of bar snacks, sandwiches and burgers. The local cultural hub also serves as a gallery spotlighting local talent.

THE GRAND CONCOURSE

Subway B, D to 167th Street; B, D, 4 to Kingsbridge Road; 4 to 161st Street-Yankee Stadium.

A few blocks east of Yankee Stadium runs the four-and-a-half-mile **Grand Concourse**, which begins at 138th Street in the South Bronx and ends at Mosholu Parkway just shy of **Van Cortlandt Park** (*see p234*). Once the most prestigious drag in the Bronx, the Grand Boulevard and Concourse (to give the artery's grandiose official title) is still a must for lovers of art deco. Engineer Louis Risse designed the boulevard in 1892, modelling it on Paris's Champs-Elysées, and it opened to traffic in 1909. Following the arrival of a new subway line nearly a decade later, rapid development along the Concourse began in the deco style so popular in the 1920s and '30s.

Starting at 161st Street and heading south, look for the permanent street plaques that make up the **Bronx Walk of Fame**, honouring famous Bronxites from Stanley Kubrick and Tony Orlando to Colin Powell and hip hop 'godfather' Afrika Bambaataa. Heading north, the buildings date mostly from the 1920s to the early '40s, and constitute the country's largest concentration of art deco housing outside Miami Beach. Erected in 1937 at the corner of 161st Street, **888 Grand Concourse** has a large concave entrance of gilded mosaic and is topped by a curvy metallic marquee. Inside, the mirrored lobby's central fountain and sunburst-patterned floor could rival those of any hotel on Miami's Ocean Drive. On the south side of **Joyce Kilmer Park**, at 161st Street, is the elegant white-marble fountain of Lorelei, built in 1893 in Germany in homage to Heinrich Heine, who wrote the poem of the same name. This was intended as the original entrance to the Concourse before it was extended south.

The grandest building on the Concourse is the landmark **Andrew Freedman Home**, a 1924 French-inspired limestone palazzo between

Bronx Museum of the Arts. *See p232.*

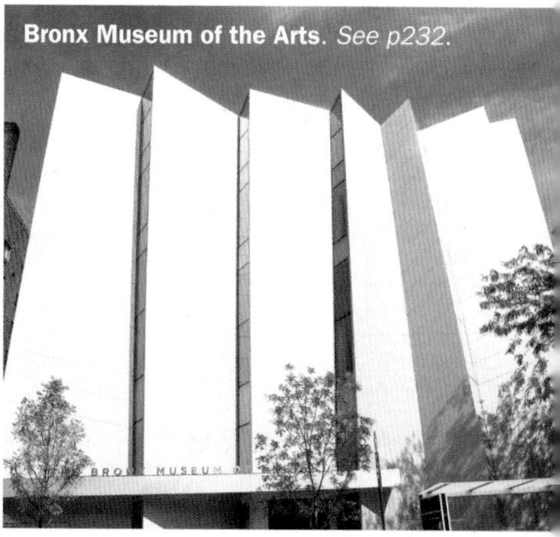

EXPLORE

McClennan and 166th Streets. Freedman, a millionaire subway contractor, left the bulk of his $7 million fortune with instructions to build a poorhouse for the rich – that is, those who had lost their fortunes and were suffering an impecunious old age. In 2012, it was reborn as a '20s-inspired B&B (1-718 588 8200, www.andrewfreedmancomplex.com), part of a local hospitality-training scheme, and a venue for arts events and exhibitions. The Family Preservation Center (FPC), a community-based social service agency, occupies the lower level. Across the street, the **Bronx Museum of the Arts** (*see below*), established in 1971 in a former synagogue, stages socially conscious, contemporary exhibitions.

A few blocks north, at **1150 Grand Concourse**, at McClellan Place, is a 1937 art deco apartment block commonly referred to as the 'fish building' because of the colourful marine-themed mosaic flanking its doors; pause inside the restored lobby for a glimpse of its two large murals depicting pastoral scenes. Near the intersection of Fordham Road, keep an eye out for the Italian rococo exterior of the **Paradise Theater** (2403 Grand Concourse, at 187th Street, www.paradisetheater.net), once the largest cinema in the city. To see the elaborate murals, fountains and grand staircase of the interior, which was restored in 2005, you'll need to buy a ticket for one of the concerts staged here. Just north is the ten-storey **Emigrant Savings Bank**, at 2526 Grand Concourse, worth ducking into for a glimpse of five striking murals by the artist Angelo Manganti, depicting scenes of the Bronx's past.

Further north to Kingsbridge Road lies the **Edgar Allan Poe Cottage** (*see below*), a small wooden farmhouse where the writer lived from 1846 to 1849. It was moved to the Grand Concourse from its original spot on Fordham Road in 1913.

EXPLORE

Sights & Museums

FREE ★ Bronx Museum of the Arts

1040 Grand Concourse, at 165th Street (1-718 681 6000, www.bronxmuseum.org). Subway B, D to 167th Street; 4 to 161st Street-Yankee Stadium. **Open** 11am-6pm Thur, Sat, Sun; 11am-8pm Fri. **Admission** free.

Featuring more than 1,000 works, this multicultural art museum shines a spotlight on 20th- and 21st-century artists who are either Bronx-based or of African, Asian or Latino ancestry. *Photo p231.*

Edgar Allan Poe Cottage

2640 Grand Concourse, at Kingsbridge Road (1-718 881 8900, www.bronxhistoricalsociety.org/poecottage). Subway B, D, 4 to Kingsbridge Road. **Open** 10am-4pm Sat; 1-5pm Sun. **Admission** $5; $3 reductions.

Pay homage to Poe in the house where he spent the last three years of his life and wrote such literary marvels as *Annabel Lee* and *The Bells*. After a major renovation, the cottage has been restored with period furnishings, including the author's rocking chair, and a new visitors' centre complete with a sloping shingle roof designed to resemble the wings of the bird from the poet's famous *The Raven*.

BELMONT & BRONX PARK

Subway B, D, 4 to Fordham Road, then Bx12 bus to Arthur Avenue.

Settled in the late 19th century by Italian immigrants hired to landscape nearby Bronx Zoo, close-knit **Belmont** is centred on Arthur Avenue, lined with delis, bakeries, restaurants and stores selling T-shirts proclaiming the locale to be New York's 'real Little Italy'. Still celebrating Mass in Italian, neoclassical **Our Lady of Mt Carmel Church** (627 E 187th Street, at Hughes Avenue, 1-718 295 3770) has been serving the community for more than a century. Aspects of Italian-American history and culture are highlighted in the modest, changing exhibits at the **Enrico Fermi Cultural Center** (in the Belmont Branch Library, 610 E 186th Street, between Arthur & Hughes Avenues, 1-718 933 6410, closed Sun).

Food, however, is the main reason to visit. **Arthur Avenue Retail Market** (2344 Arthur Avenue, between Crescent Avenue & E 186th Street) is a covered market built in the 1940s when Mayor Fiorello La Guardia campaigned to get the pushcarts off the street. Inside, you'll find **Mike's Deli** (*see p234*), where you can order enormous sandwiches bursting with Italian cold cuts. For a full meal, try old-school

Bronx Zoo.

Arthur Avenue Retail Market.

red-sauce joints such as **Mario's** (*see p234*), featured in several *Sopranos* episodes and Mario Puzo's novel *The Godfather*; or bare-bones canteen **Dominick's** (*see below*).

Belmont is within easy walking distance of **Bronx Park**, home to two of the borough's most celebrated attractions. Make your way east along 187th Street, then south along Southern Boulevard, and you'll come to the **Bronx Zoo** (*see below*). Opened in 1899 by Theodore Roosevelt, at 265 acres it's the largest urban zoo in the US. A 15-minute walk north of the zoo – and still in Bronx Park – brings you to the serene 250 acres of the **New York Botanical Garden** (*see right*), which offers respite from cars and concrete in the form of 50 different gardens.

Sights & Museums

Bronx Zoo/Wildlife Conservation Society

Bronx River Parkway, at Fordham Road (1-718 367 1010, www.bronxzoo.com). Subway 2, 5 to E Tremont/W Farms Square, then walk 2 blocks to the zoo's Asia entrance; or Metro-North (Harlem Line local) from Grand Central Terminal to Fordham, then take the Bx9 bus to 183rd Street and Southern Boulevard. **Open** *Apr-Oct* 10am-5pm Mon-Fri; 10am-5.30pm Sat, Sun. *Nov-Mar* 10am-4.30pm daily. **Admission** $17; $12-$15 reductions; pay what you wish Wed. Some rides & exhibitions cost extra.

The Bronx Zoo shuns cages in favour of indoor and outdoor environments that mimic natural habitats. There are more than 60,000 creatures and more than 600 species here. Monkeys, leopards and tapirs live inside the lush, steamy Jungle World, a recreation of an Asian rainforest inside a 37,000sq ft building, while lions, giraffes, zebras and other animals roam the African Plains. The popular Congo Gorilla Forest has turned 6.5 acres into a dramatic central African rainforest habitat. A glass-enclosed tunnel winds through the forest, allowing visitors to get close to the dozens of primate families in residence, including majestic western lowland gorillas. Tiger Mountain is populated by Siberian tigers, while the Himalayan Highlands features snow leopards and red pandas.

▶ *For other zoos, see p170, p206 and p226.*

★ New York Botanical Garden

Bronx River Parkway, at Fordham Road (1-718 817 8700, www.nybg.org). Subway B, D, 4 to Bedford Park Boulevard, then Bx26 bus to the garden's Mosholu Gate; or Metro-North (Harlem Line local) from Grand Central Terminal to Botanical Garden. **Open** *Jan, Feb* 10am-5pm Tue-Sun. *Mar-Dec* 10am-6pm Tue-Sun. **Admission** $20-$25; $8-$22 reductions. *Grounds only* $13; $3-$6 reductions; grounds free Wed, 9-10am Sat.

The serene 250 acres comprise 50 gardens and plant collections, including the Rockefeller Rose Garden, the Everett Children's Adventure Garden and the last 50 original acres of a forest that once covered the whole city area. In spring, clusters of lilac, cherry, magnolia and crab apple trees burst into bloom; in autumn you'll see vivid foliage in the oak and maple groves. The Azalea Garden features around 3,000 vivid azaleas and rhododendrons. The Enid A Haupt Conservatory – the nation's largest greenhouse, built in 1902 – contains the World of Plants, a series of environmental galleries that take you on an eco-tour through tropical rainforests, deserts and a palm tree oasis.

Restaurants & Cafés

Dominick's

2335 Arthur Avenue, between Crescent Avenue & E 186th Street, 1-718 733 2807). Subway B, D, 4 to Fordham Road, then Bx12 bus to Arthur Avenue. **Open** noon-10pm Mon, Wed, Thur, Sat; noon-11pm Fri; 1-9pm Sun. **Main courses** $15-$42. **No credit cards**. Italian

At Charlie DiPaolo's pinewood dining room – one of the most popular on Arthur Avenue – neighbourhood folks, out-of-towners and tracksuited wiseguys feast at long, crowded tables on massive platters of veal *parmigiana*, steaming bowls of mussels marinara and linguine with white clam sauce. There's no written menu, but you can trust your waiter's advice.

Mario's

2342 Arthur Avenue, between Crescent Avenue & E 186th Street (1-718 584 1188, www.mariosrestarthurave.com). Subway B, D, 4 to Fordham Road, then Bx12 bus to Arthur Avenue. **Open** noon-9pm Tue-Thur, Sun; noon-10pm Fri, Sat. **Main courses** $13.75-$35. **Italian**

The Migliucci family has stayed in business since 1919 by pleasing the customer; if you don't see what you want on the menu, feel free to ask for embellishments or modifications to the Neapolitan-inspired cuisine. Do as the regulars do and order the signature gnocchi, which arrive perfectly light and plump with a deliciously savoury and tangy sauce. For something more hearty, try the *saltimbocca alla romana* (veal braised in Marsala wine and served over spinach sautéed with prosciutto), or the generous lobster-tail *oreganata*, accompanied by a baked clam.

★ Mike's Deli

Arthur Avenue Retail Market, 2344 Arthur Avenue, between Crescent Avenue & E 186th Street (1-718 295 5033, www.arthuravenue.com). Subway B, D, 4 to Fordham Road, then Bx12 bus to Arthur Avenue. **Open** 7am-7pm Mon-Wed; 7am-9pm Thur-Sat; 10am-7pm Sun. **Sandwiches** $6.50-$13. **Café/deli**

This venerable delicatessen, overstocked butcher and café may leave you paralysed with indecision: the glossy menu lists more than 50 sandwiches, plus platters, pastas, soups, salads, stromboli (a kind of cheese turnover) and sides. Try the Yankee Stadium Big Boy hero sandwich, filled with prosciutto, soppressata, mozzarella, capicola, mortadella, peppers and lettuce.

Bars

★ Bronx Beer Hall

2344 Arthur Avenue, between Crescent Avenue & E 186th Street (1-347 396 0555, www.thebronxbeerhall.com). **Open** 11am-3am Mon-Sat; 11am-9pm Sun.

Surrounded by the cigar makers and meat and cheese counters of the septuagenarian Arthur Avenue Market, patrons can sit at BBH's standalone rustic wooden bar and imbibe one of five New York State choices on draft – there's a particular emphasis on the borough's own Jonas Bronck's Beer Co. Try the brewery's New York Chocolate Egg Cream Stout, a bi-borough creation made with Brooklyn's Fox's U-bet chocolate syrup, or another local favourite, City Island Beer Company's balanced pale ale. Mike's Deli supplies the grub, like cheese boards and sausages served with bread and sides such as hot peppers.

RIVERDALE & VAN CORTLANDT PARK

Subway D to Norwood-205th Street; 1 to 242nd Street-Van Cortlandt Park.

Riverdale, along the north-west coast of the Bronx, reflects the borough's suburban past; its huge homes perch on narrow, winding streets that meander towards the Hudson river. The only one you can actually visit is **Wave Hill** (*see p235*), an 1843 stone mansion set on a former private estate that has beautiful gardens and a gallery. The nearby 1,146-acre **Van Cortlandt Park** (entrance on Broadway, at 242nd Street) occasionally hosts cricket teams largely made up of West Indians and Indians. You can hike through a 100-year-old forest, play golf on the nation's first municipal course or ride horses hired from stables in the park.

The oldest building in the Bronx is **Van Cortlandt House Museum** (*see right*), a 1749 Georgian building that was commandeered by both sides during the Revolutionary War. Abutting the park is **Woodlawn Cemetery**, the resting place for such notable souls as Herman Melville, Duke Ellington, Miles Davis, FW Woolworth and Fiorello La Guardia. To help you to pay your respects, maps are available at the entrance at Webster Avenue and E 233rd Street. About five blocks south on Bainbridge Avenue, history buffs will also enjoy the **Museum of Bronx History**, set in a 1758 stone farmhouse.

Museum of Bronx History

Valentine-Varian House, 3266 Bainbridge Avenue, between Van Cortlandt Avenue East & 208th Street (1-718 881 8900, www.bronxhistoricalsociety.org/museumofbronxhistory.html). Subway D to Norwood-205th Street. **Open** 10am-4pm Sat; 1-5pm Sun. **Admission** $5; $3 reductions.

IN THE KNOW
THE BRONX CULTURE TROLLEY

To check out the South Bronx's burgeoning art scene, hop on the free **Bronx Culture Trolley** (www.bronxarts.org), which stops at about a half-dozen venues on the first Wednesday of each month, except September and January, and also selected Saturdays in spring and summer; see website for details.

Wave Hill.

Operated by the Bronx County Historical Society, the museum displays its collection of documents and photos in the Valentine-Varian House, a Federal-style fieldstone residence built in 1758.

► *The society also offers historical tours of the Bronx neighbourhoods.*

Van Cortlandt House Museum

Van Cortlandt Park, entrance on Broadway, at 246th Street (1-718 543 3344). Subway 1 to 242nd Street-Van Cortlandt Park. **Open** 10am-3pm Tue-Fri; 11am-4pm Sat, Sun. **Admission** $5; $3 reductions; free under-12s; free Wed.

A one-time wheat plantation that has since been turned into a colonial museum, Van Cortlandt House was alternately used as headquarters by George Washington and British General Sir William Howe during the Revolutionary War.

★ Wave Hill

W 249th Street, at Independence Avenue (1-718 549 3200, www.wavehill.org). Metro-North (Hudson Line local) from Grand Central Terminal to Riverdale. **Open** *Mid Mar-Oct* 9am-5.30pm Tue-Sun. *Nov-mid Mar* 9am-4.30pm Tue-Sun. **Admission** $8; $2-$4 reductions; free under-6s; free Tue, 9am-noon Sat.

Laze around in these 28 lush acres overlooking the Hudson River at Wave Hill, the setting of a Georgian Revival house that was home at various times to Mark Twain, Teddy Roosevelt and conductor Arturo Toscanini. Now open to the public, the grounds contain exquisite cultivated gardens and woodlands commanding excellent views of the river. The small on-site gallery hosts intriguing contemporary art shows inspired by nature, and the property is also a venue for concerts and other events.

PELHAM BAY PARK

Subway 6 to Pelham Bay Park.

Pelham Bay Park, in the borough's north-eastern corner, is NYC's largest park. Take a car or a bike if you want to explore the 2,765 acres; pick up a map at the Ranger Nature Center, near the entrance on Bruckner Boulevard at Wilkinson Avenue. The **Bartow-Pell Mansion Museum** (*see below*), in the park's south-eastern quarter, overlooks Long Island Sound. The park's 13 miles of coastline skirt the Hutchinson river to the west and the Long Island Sound and Eastchester Bay to the east. In summer, locals hit sandy **Orchard Beach**; set up in the 1930s, this 'Riviera of New York' is that rare beast – a Robert Moses creation not universally lamented.

Bartow-Pell Mansion Museum

895 Shore Road North, at Pelham Bay Park (1-718 885 1461, www.bartowpellmansion museum.org). Subway 6 to Pelham Bay Park, then Bee-Line bus 45 (ask driver to stop at Bartow-Pell Mansion). **Open** noon-4pm Wed, Sat, Sun. **Admission** $5; $3 reductions; free under-6s.

Operating as a museum since 1946, the origins of this impressive property date from 1654, when Thomas Pell bought the land from the Siwonay Indians. It was Robert Bartow, publisher and Pell descendant, who added the 1842 Greek Revival stone mansion, which faces a reflecting pool ringed by gardens.

► *Just east of Pelham Bay Park lies City Island (see p214), a rustic fishing village with a New England feel.*

Staten Island

With a largely suburban vibe, abundant parkland and beaches, New York's third largest – but least-populated – borough feels removed from the rest of the city. And physically it is. To visitors, Staten Island is best known for its ferry – the locals' sole public-transport link with Manhattan happens to pass by Lady Liberty. But the devastation wrought by Hurricane Sandy in autumn 2012 – the borough suffered more than half the city's total fatalities – trained the media spotlight on the island. Even more than a year later, South Shore communities were still struggling to get on their feet again. But the worldwide attention – combined with plans to build a $500 million retail and hotel complex near the ferry terminal, anchored by the world's tallest Ferris wheel – suggests a more prosperous future. After disembarking, stroll along the Esplanade or venture further to explore historic structures and sprawling green spaces.

Killmeyer's Old Bavaria Inn

Don't Miss

1 Alice Austen House Exquisite photographs and views (*p238*).

2 Fort Wadsworth An impressive panorama from one of the nation's oldest military sites (*p238*).

3 Greenbelt Go wild in suburban SI (*p238*).

4 Snug Harbor Quirky collections and gardens in a picturesque old sailors' home (*p239*).

5 Killmeyer's Old Bavaria Inn Raise a stein at this German hold-out (*p239*).

Ferry

Staten Island became one of the five boroughs in 1898, but remained a backwater until 1964, when the Verrazano-Narrows Bridge joined the island to Bay Ridge in Brooklyn. Many say that's when small-town Staten Island truly vanished.

Still, many quaint aspects remain – not least the free **Staten Island Ferry** (1-718 727 2508, www.nyc.gov/dot), which runs between the Financial District's Whitehall Terminal (4 South Street, at Whitehall Street) and the island's St George Terminal, where you can catch the buses noted in this chapter. The crossing takes 25 minutes. When you alight, head right along the new **Esplanade**, with its stirring views of lower Manhattan across the harbour, to pay your respects at *Postcards*, a memorial to the 274 Staten Islanders lost on 9/11. The fibreglass wings of the sculpture frame the spot where the Twin Towers used to stand.

Also near the terminal is the small **Staten Island Museum** (75 Stuyvesant Place, at Wall Street, 1-718 727 1135, www.statenisland museum.org). In late autumn 2014, it is moving some of its collections to Snug Harbor Cultural Center (*see p239*); check website for updates.

Sights & Museums

Alice Austen House

2 Hylan Boulevard, between Bay & Edgewater Streets (1-718 816 4506, www.aliceausten.org). S51 bus to Hylan Boulevard. **Open** *Mar-Dec* 11am-5pm Tue-Sun. **Admission** *Suggested donation* $3.

The beautiful photographs of Alice Austen (1866-1952) are the highlight at this 17th-century cottage – it contains 3,000 of her glass negative images. The restored house and grounds often host concerts and events, and offer breathtaking harbour views.

Conference House (Billopp House)

7455 Hylan Boulevard, at Satterlee Street (1-718 984 6046, www.conferencehouse.org). S78 bus to Craig Avenue & Hylan Boulevard. **Open** *Apr-mid Dec* 1-4pm Fri-Sun. **Admission** $4-$6; reductions free-$3.

In 1776, Britain's Lord Howe parlayed with John Adams and Benjamin Franklin in this 17th-century house, trying to forestall the American Revolution. Tours point out 18th-century furnishings, decor and daily objects. The lovely grounds command a terrific view over Raritan Bay, and provide a picturesque setting for free concerts and events.

FREE Fort Wadsworth

210 New York Avenue, on the east end of Bay Street (1-718 354 4500, www.nyharborparks.org). S51 bus to Fort Wadsworth. **Open** dawn-dusk daily. **Admission** free.

Explore the fortifications that guarded NYC for almost 200 years at Ford Wadsworth. The site was occupied by a blockhouse as far back as the 17th century.

FREE Greenbelt

Greenbelt Nature Center *700 Rockland Avenue, at Brielle Avenue (1-718 351 3450, www.sigreen belt.org). S61 bus to Forest Hill Road/Rockland*

WHEEL OF FORTUNE

The most-overlooked borough gets a destination attraction of its own.

New York City is building a brand-new landmark, but it's not a skyscraper or a monumental statue. In September 2014, construction starts on the New York Wheel on Staten Island's North Shore. This isn't your average carnival ferris wheel. Once complete in 2016, it will tower at an impressive 630 feet – almost 200 feet higher than the London Eye, which was the inspiration for the project. The wheel will be able to carry up to 1,440 passengers in its 36 pod-like capsules for each 38-minute rotation, offering unobstructed views of New York Harbor, lower Manhattan, the Statue of Liberty and the Verrazano-Narrows Bridge.

'We're expecting to target and achieve about four million visitors per year,' says Richard A Marin, New York Wheel CEO and president, citing the two million visitors who already ride the Staten Island Ferry annually

– the wheel will be in walking distance from the St George Ferry Terminal. Currently, many of those tourists don't explore the island, though they have to disembark before heading back to Manhattan. Further boosting the borough's attractions in 2016 is NYC's first outlet mall. Empire Outlets will feature 125 high-end retailers, plus restaurants and a 200-room hotel.

IN THE KNOW
THE STATEN ISLAND RAILWAY

Although it isn't connected to any of the city's other subway lines, the **Staten Island Railway** (SIR) does accept the MetroCard. The railway has one line, which runs from St George to Tottenville on the southern tip of the island.

Avenue. **Open** *Apr-Oct* 10am-5pm Tue-Sun. *Nov-Mar* 11am-5pm Wed-Sun. **Admission** free.
High Rock Park *200 Nevada Avenue, at Rockland Avenue. S62 bus to Manor Road, then S54 bus to Nevada Avenue.* **Open** dawn-dusk daily.
With 2,800 acres of open space, the Greenbelt offers 35 miles of trails through parks and woodland. Start your expedition at the Nature Center, where you can pick up a copy of the trail map (also on the website). A mile away, at the 90-acre High Rock Park, visitors can hike the mile-long Swamp Trail, climb Todt Hill or walk through forests, meadows and wetlands.

Jacques Marchais Museum of Tibetan Art

338 Lighthouse Avenue, off Richmond Road (1-718 987 3500, www.tibetanmuseum.org). S74 bus to Lighthouse Avenue. **Open** *Apr-Dec* 1-5pm Wed-Sun. *Feb-Mar* 1-5pm Fri-Sun. Closed Jan. **Admission** $6; $4 reductions; free under-6s.
This tiny museum contains a formidable Buddhist altar, tranquil meditation gardens and an extensive collection of Tibetan art and artefacts.

★ Snug Harbor Cultural Center & Botanical Garden

1000 Richmond Terrace, between Snug Harbor Road & Tysen Avenue (1-718 448 2500, www.snug-harbor.org). S40 bus to Richmond Terrace/Sailors SH Gate. **Open** *Grounds* dawn-dusk daily.
Stately Greek Revival structures form the nucleus of this former sailors' retirement home. Dating from 1833, the centre has been restored and converted into an arts complex that includes one of the city's oldest concert halls. In addition to the listings below, the **Staten Island Children's Museum** (1-718 273 2060, www.statenislandkids.org, closed Mon) and **Art Lab** (1-718 447 8667, www.artlab.info), a non-profit art school, are also based here.
Newhouse Center for Contemporary Art *1-718 425 3524, www.snug-harbor.org/newhouse.* **Open** noon-5pm Wed-Sun. **Admission** $3; $2 reductions; free under-13s. **No credit cards**.
Staten Island's premier venue for contemporary art holds several annual exhibitions from leading international sculptors, painters and mixed-media artists.
Noble Maritime Collection *1-718 447 6490, www.noblemaritime.org.* **Open** 1-5pm Thur-Sun. **Admission** Pay what you wish.
This museum is dedicated to the artist-seaman John A Noble, who had a 'floating studio' moored in the Kill van Kull, between Staten Island and New Jersey. As well as his maritime-themed paintings, Noble's houseboat is on display, restored to its appearance when the artist was featured in *National Geographic* magazine in 1954. Upstairs is a re-created dormitory room of the former Sailors' Snug Harbor, circa 1900.
Staten Island Botanical Garden *1-718 448 2500, www.snug-harbor.org.* **Open** 10am-5pm Tue-Sun. **Admission** *Chinese Scholar's Garden* $5; $4 reductions; free under-13s. *Grounds & other gardens* free.
Stroll through more than 13 themed gardens, including the traditional Chinese Scholar's Garden, with its pavilions, meandering paths and delicate footbridges, and the medieval-style children's Secret Garden, complete with a 38ft-high castle and a maze.

Restaurants & Cafés

Beso

11 Schuyler Street, between Richmond Terrace & Stuyvesant Place (1-718 816 8162, www.besonyc.com). **Open** 11.30am-11pm Mon-Thur; 11.30am-midnight Fri, Sat; noon-10pm Sun. **Main courses** $20-$30.
Although Beso is billed as a Spanish tapas bar, the menu at this little spot right by the ferry terminal goes far beyond Iberia (by way of Cuba, Mexico and Puerto Rico, for starters). Grab a fruity-sweet glass of tequila-spiked sangria and go straight for the sofrito-sprinkled Prince Edward Island mussels in a fish stock and white-wine broth; or the pork-loin-pickle-and-ham-stuffed Cuban sandwich with gooey, melted Mahon cheese.

Trattoria Romana

1476 Hylan Boulevard, at Benton Avenue (1-718 980 3113). Staten Island Railway to Old Town. **Open** noon-10pm Mon-Thur; noon-11pm Fri, Sat; 1-9.30pm Sun. **Main courses** $20-$25.
This casually elegant eaterie owes its popularity to the constant presence of chef-owner Vittorio Asoli as well as to the wood-burning brick oven that cooks everything from pizza to portobellos. The saltimbocca alla romana is a classic done right – tender veal scaloppine topped with salty prosciutto and accented with butter and sage.

Bars

Killmeyer's Old Bavaria Inn

4254 Arthur Kill Road, at Sharrotts Road (1-718 984 1202, www.killmeyers.com). S74 bus to Arthur Kill Road/Sharrotts Road. **Open** 11am-11.30pm Mon-Thur, Sun; 11am-1.30am Fri, Sat.
Semi-industrial Arthur Kill Road is home to this turn-of-the-century Bavarian beer garden. Sit outside and enjoy any of nearly 200 beers, plus sauerbraten, spicy goulash and potato pancakes.

Arts & Entertainment

Children

The crowded and fast-paced metropolis may not seem like the world's most child-friendly place at first glance, but its 21st-century baby boom has given rise to myriad cultural, culinary and just plain fun offerings for families. Such icons as the Ellis Island Immigration Museum and the American Museum of Natural History are not to be missed, but they are just the beginning. Among the most frequented corners of the city are its green spaces and playgrounds – seek one out when you're in need of a breather from the city's constant buzz. And for the latest child-centric events, visit www.timeout.com/newyorkkids.

SIGHTSEEING & ENTERTAINMENT

Animals & nature

See also pp246-247 **Central Park**.

★ Bronx Zoo

For listings, see p233.
Step aboard the Wild Asia Monorail (open May-Oct, admission $5), which tours 38 acres of exhibits housing elephants, Indo-Chinese tigers, antelope, Mongolian wild horses and more. Madagascar! is a permanent home to exotic animals from the lush island nation off the eastern coast of Africa. Among its residents are lemurs, giant crocodiles, lovebirds, radiated tortoises and, coolest (and grossest) of all, hissing cockroaches. Five lemurs were born in the exhibit in its first year.

► *There are also zoos in Central Park (see p170), Brooklyn (see p206) and Queens (see p226).*

New York Aquarium

610 Surf Avenue, at West 8th Street, Coney Island, Brooklyn (1-718 265 3474, www.nyaquarium.com). Subway D, N, Q to Coney Island-Stillwell Avenue; F, Q to W 8th Street-NY Aquarium. **Open** *Sept-May* 10am-4.30pm daily. *June-Aug* 10am-6pm daily. **Admission** $9.95; free under-3s. Pay what you wish after 3pm Fri.
Just weeks after announcing the construction of a 57,000sq ft building that will house a new 'Ocean Wonders: Sharks!' exhibition, slated to open in 2015, the seaside aquarium was hit hard by Hurricane Sandy, which unleashed its fury on New York in autumn 2012. It has since partially reopened with a new sea lion theatre and reduced pricing that reflects the institution's limited offerings during construction.

★ FREE Prospect Park Audubon Center

Prospect Park, enter from Ocean Avenue, at Lincoln Road, Brooklyn (1-718 287 3400, www.prospectpark.org/audubon). Subway B, Q to Prospect Park. **Open** *Feb, March, Nov, Dec* noon-4pm Sat, Sun. *Apr, June, Sept, Oct* noon-4pm Thur-Sun. *July, Aug* noon-5pm Thur-Sun. Closed Jan. **Admission** free. **Map** p404 U12.
Overlooking Prospect Lake, the child-oriented Audubon Center is dedicated to nature education and wildlife preservation. Start at the visitor centre, featuring a giant interactive microscope and live animal presentations, and stick around for woodland tours, storytelling and birdwatching walks.

Museums

Defying the stuffy cliché, many of Manhattan's most venerable institutions are extremely child-friendly. The **DiMenna Children's History Museum** inside the **New-York Historical Society** (*see p164*) engages kids with New York's past by looking at the childhoods of various residents, some famous (Alexander Hamilton), others anonymous (child newspaper sellers in the early 20th century). For years, workshops for kids of all ages have been offered at the **Museum of Modern Art** (*see p154*), the **Metropolitan Museum of Art** (*see p182*), the **Whitney Museum of American Art** (*see p176*), the **Rubin Museum** (*see p123*) and the **Museum of Arts and Design** (*see p164*); check their websites for schedules. The Met, with its mummies and Temple of Dendur, a real ancient Egyptian temple, is a particular hit with children, as long as you don't try to tackle too much of the massive collection.

Even very young kids love exploring the **American Museum of Natural History** (*see p164*). The Fossil Halls are home to the museum's huge, beloved dinosaurs – most reconstructed from actual fossils – and the myriad wildlife dioramas are a fascinating (and astonishingly lifelike) peek at the world's fauna. Firefighter wannabes will enjoy the **New York City Fire Museum**, housed in a historic fire station (*see p64*); kids can check out uniforms and equipment from the late 18th century to the present, including a hand-pumped fire engine. The highlight at the aircraft carrier-turned-attraction **Intrepid Sea, Air & Space Museum** (*see p147*) is the Space Shuttle Pavilion, housing the *Enterprise*, an original prototype. With 30-plus interactive exhibits, the new **Museum of Mathematics (MoMath)** (*see p135*) will probably win round those who claim to hate the subject.

In the boroughs, the excellent core exhibition 'Behind the Screen' at the **Museum of the Moving Image** (*see p224*), outfitted with state-of-the-art movie-making stations, makes it worth the trek to Astoria, Queens. Children and adults will be fascinated by the amazing scale-model Panorama of the City of New York at the recently renovated and expanded **Queens Museum** (*see p227*), while youngsters can pretend to drive a real bus and board vintage subway cars at Brooklyn's **New York Transit Museum** (*see p197*).

★ Brooklyn Children's Museum

145 Brooklyn Avenue, at St Marks Avenue, Crown Heights, Brooklyn (1-718 735 4400, www.brooklynkids.org). Subway A, C to Nostrand Avenue; C to Kingston-Throop Avenues; 3 to Kingston Avenue. **Open** 10am-5pm Tue-Sun; 10am-7pm 3rd Thur of each mth. **Admission** $9; free under-1s; free 3-5pm Thur (4-7pm 3rd Thur of each mth). **Map** p404 V11.

The city's oldest museum for kids is also one of its best after a major renovation that wrapped up in 2008. The star attraction, 'World Brooklyn', is an interactive maze of small mom-and-pop shops based on real-world Brooklyn businesses. 'Neighborhood Nature' puts the spotlight on the borough's diverse ecosystems with a collection of pond critters in terrariums and a tide-pool touch tank. Under-fives will delight in 'Totally Tots', a sun-drenched play space with a water station, a sand zone, and a special hub for babies aged 18 months and under.

Children's Museum of Manhattan

212 W 83rd Street, between Amsterdam Avenue & Broadway, Upper West Side (1-212 721 1234, www.cmom.org). Subway B, C to 81st Street-Museum of Natural History; 1 to 86th Street. **Open** 10am-5pm Tue-Fri, Sun; 10am-7pm Sat. **Admission** $11; $7 reductions; free under-1s. **Map** p399 C19.

An essential stop on every Upper West Side child's social agenda, this museum customises its themed exhibits by age group. 'PlayWorks', an imaginative play environment, is for babies and toddlers up to four; 'Adventures with Dora and Diego', a bilingual playspace that transports visitors to some of the Nickelodeon TV show's settings, is for ages two to six. 'EatSleepPlay: Building Health Every Day', for all ages, is an interactive exhibit that gives families strategies for taking up a more healthy lifestyle.

★ Children's Museum of the Arts

103 Charlton Street, between Greenwich & Hudson Streets, Soho (1-212 274 0986, www.cmany.org). Subway A, B, C, D, E, F, M to W 4th Street; C, E to Spring Street; 1 to Houston Street. **Open** noon-5pm Mon, Wed; noon-6pm Thur, Fri; 10am-5pm Sat, Sun. **Admission** $11; free under-1s; pay what you wish 4-6pm Thur. **Map** p397 E30.

The creativity-inspiring Soho mainstay, whose focus is on teaching, creating, collecting and exhibiting

Brooklyn Children's Museum.

kids' artwork, moved into a much larger (10,000sq ft) space in 2011. Engaging temporary exhibits are juxtaposed with works from the museum's collection of more than 2,000 pieces of children's art. For kids, the most exciting aspects of the museum are its hands-on art workshops, clay lab and interactive media lab, plus the ball pit for letting off steam.

★ New York Hall of Science

47-01 111th Street, at 47th Avenue, Flushing Meadows Corona Park, Queens (1-718 699 0005, www.nysci.org). Subway 7 to 111th Street. **Open** *Sept-Mar* 9.30am-5pm Tue-Fri; 10am-6pm Sat, Sun. *Apr-Aug* 9.30am-5pm Mon-Fri; 10am-6pm Sat, Sun. **Admission** $11; $8 reductions. *Sept-June* free 2-5pm Fri; 10-11am Sun. *Science playground* (open Mar-Dec) extra $4. *Rocket Park Mini Golf* extra $6; $5 reductions.

Known for the 1964 World's Fair pavilion in which it is housed and the rockets from the US space programme that flank it, this museum has always been worth a trek for its discovery-based interactive exhibits. A massive expansion in 2005 added a new building that houses such permanent exhibits as 'Hidden Kingdoms', where children can get their hands on microscopes, and 'Search for Life Beyond Earth', which investigates the solar system and the different planetary environments. From April through December, the 30,000sq ft outdoor Science Playground teaches children the principles of balance, gravity and energy, while a mini-golf course in Rocket Park lets families play outdoors surrounded by refurbished rockets from the 1960s space race.

Performing arts

Broadway is packed with excellent, if pricey, family fare, from long-runners like *The Lion King* and *Wicked* to London import *Matilda*, based on the book by Roald Dahl. *The Nutcracker* (*see p293* **David H Koch Theater**) is an annual Christmas family tradition. In summer, **Madison Square Park** (*see p130*) hosts regular children's concerts, and warm-weather events such as the **River to River Festival** (*see p34*) and **SummerStage** (*see p33*) always include music and theatre tailored to little ones.

> **IN THE KNOW IN-STORE FUN**
>
> If you're in the Theater District, don't miss the massive **Toys 'R' Us Times Square** (1514 Broadway at 44th Street, 1-646 366 8800, www.toysrus.com). With a 60-foot indoor Ferris wheel and a 20-foot-high animatronic T rex, it's more than a mere toy store.

Big Apple Circus

Damrosch Park, Lincoln Center, 62nd Street, between Columbus & Amsterdam Avenues, Upper West Side (1-212 268 2500, www.bigapplecircus.org). Subway 1 to 66th Street-Lincoln Center. **Shows** *Oct-Jan* times vary. **Tickets** $25-$175. **Map** p399 C21.

This travelling circus was founded in 1977 as an intimate answer to the scale of the Ringling Bros operation; it typically runs from October to mid January. The non-profit organisation's clowns are among the most creative in the country. If you've always wanted to run away to the circus, attend the special late show on New Year's Eve, at the end of which the entire audience joins the performers in the ring.

Carnegie Hall Family Concerts

For listings, see p285. **Tickets** $12-$18.

Even children who solemnly profess to hate classical music are usually impressed by a visit to Carnegie Hall. The Family Concert series builds on that, featuring first-rate classical, world music and jazz performers, plus a pre-concert workshop an hour before the show. It runs roughly monthly from November to May. Recommended for ages five to 12.

Galli Theater

347 W 36th Street, between Eighth & Ninth Avenues, Hell's Kitchen (1-212 731 0668, www.galliteaterny.com). Subway A, C, E to 34th Street-Penn Station. **Shows** 2pm Sat, Sun (see website for additional shows). **Tickets** $20; $15 under-18s. **Map** p398 C25.

Classic fairy tales such as *Rapunzel*, *Snow White* and *Hansel and Gretel* come to life through kid-oriented, often musical adaptations written by playwright and theatre founder Johannes Galli. A hallmark of each show is audience participation: children are frequently invited on stage during the performance.

★ Just Kidding at Symphony Space

For listings, see p290. **Shows** *Oct-early May* Sat (times vary). **Tickets** $20-$55; $15 reductions.

Tell your munchkins to forgo their weekly dose of cartoons. In Manhattan, children can spend their Saturday mornings grooving to live concerts or watching theatre, dance or a puppet show. Symphony Space's Just Kidding series features both local and nationally recognised talent, from kid rockers and bluegrass bands to hip hop storytellers and NYC star Gustaver Yellowgold.

★ New Victory Theater

For listings, see p305.

As New York's only full-scale young people's theatre, the New Victory presents international theatre and dance companies at junior prices. Recent shows have included Circus der Sinne, a Tanzanian troupe presenting a show of acrobatics, dance and live music with an African twist; Cre8ion, an Australia-based company, in a performance about a family

HORSING AROUND

Take your family for a spin on one of NYC's painted ponies.

Jane's Carousel.

New York City was an important carousel-building hub in the early 20th century, and merry-go-rounds seem to be having another moment with the 2011 opening of Jane's Carousel and Battery Park's sealife-inspired debut. Here's our pick of the best.

Central Park's classic **Friedsam Memorial Carousel** (mid-park at 64th Street, 1-212 439 6900, www.centralparknyc.org; open Apr-Oct; $3 per ride), built in 1908, is the fourth carousel on the site since 1871; the first was operated by a mule or horse hidden under the floorboards, and the next two were destroyed by fires in 1924 and 1950. Found in a Coney Island warehouse, the Friedsam belts out pop organ music for riders of its 57 steeds.

The winsome, pastel **Le Carrousel** in Bryant Park (W 40th Street, between Fifth & Sixth Avenues, www.bryantpark.org; $3) was built by the Brooklyn carousel company Fabricon. Installed in 2002, it pays homage to the Parisian design of the midtown park, with 14 animals that spin to the accompaniment of French cabaret music by the likes of Edith Piaf. Children will probably head for the prancing rabbit, leaping green frog, or orange cat. On weekend afternoons, Flaubert Frog and Friends, and the occasional magician, entertain youngsters with free stories, games and magic tricks.

Perched alongside the Brooklyn Bridge in the park of the same name, **Jane's Carousel** (Dock Street at the East River, Dumbo, Brooklyn, www.janescarousel.com; $2) takes its name from Jane Walentas, who spent nearly 25 years lovingly restoring its 48 hand-painted horses, scenery panels and crests. The 1922 spinner is surrounded by a simple Plexiglas box designed by French starchitect Jean Nouvel, so it can operate year-round. The structure was put to the test only a year after it was installed, by 2012's Hurricane Sandy.

The city's newest merry-go-round, the **SeaGlass**, opening in summer 2014 in the Financial District's Battery Park (www.batterypark.org), is also one of its most imaginative. The $12 million creation, spearheaded by the Battery Park Conservancy, features a glass-and-steel nautilus-shaped exterior filled with a panoply of Plexiglas sea life, including dolphins and angelfish, that children ride along four different tracks. An oceanic audio soundtrack completes the undersea illusion, and thanks to an LED lighting system, the interior glows with changing colours that also light up the park at night. The 30 creatures were ,made by George Tsypin, who knows a thing or two about sea life – the stage designer created the set for Broadway's *The Little Mermaid.*

Trump Rink.

that takes in all long-lost and misfit toys; and Hyperish, a presentation by the Netherlands-based ISH, a multidisciplinary troupe blending hip hop, acrobatics, martial arts and basketball to explore questions of identity. Shows often sell out well in advance, so reserve seats early.

Puppetworks

338 Sixth Avenue, at 4th Street, Park Slope, Brooklyn (1-718 965 3391, www.puppetworks.org). Subway F to Seventh Avenue. **Shows** 12.30pm, 2.30pm Sat, Sun. **Tickets** $9; $8 under-12s. **No credit cards. Map** p404 T11.

The Brooklyn company puts on musicals adapted from fairy tales and children's stories that feature a cast of marionettes operated by two puppeteers (the voice and music track is pre-recorded). The company also demonstrates how the puppets work at the beginning of each performance.

Vital Theatre Company

McGinn/Cazale Theatre, 4th floor, 2162 Broadway, at 76th Street, Upper West Side (1-212 579 0528, www.vitaltheatre.org). Subway 1 to 79th Street; 2, 3 to 72nd Street. **Shows** vary. **Tickets** $39.50-$89.50. **Map** p399 C19.

Founded in 1999, Vital has produced a series of original theatrical hits for kids, the biggest of which it reprises often – including *Angelina Ballerina* and *Fancy Nancy the Musical* – at its Upper West Side home. Its most popular creation, the ongoing *Pinkalicious*, about a girl who comes down with a case of 'pinkititis', tends to play at a location of its own, most recently midtown's Jacqueline Kennedy Onassis Theater, at 120 W 46th Street, between Sixth and Seventh Avenues.

PARKS & PLAY SPACES

Most New Yorkers don't have their own garden – instead, they run around and relax in parks. The most popular of all is **Central Park** (*see pp168-170*), which has places and programmes just for kids.

FREE Battery Park City Parks

Hudson River, between Chambers Street & Battery Place, Financial District (1-212 267 9700, www.bpcparks.org). Subway A, C, 1, 2, 3 to Chambers Street; 1 to Rector Street. **Open** 6am-1am daily. **Admission** free. **Map** p396 D32.

Besides watching the boats along the Hudson, kids can enjoy Teardrop Park, a hidden urban oasis with an enormous slide; Nelson A Rockefeller Park, with an open field for Frisbee and lazing, plus a playground with a unique pedal carousel and a charming duck pond. Don't miss Pier 25, just north of BPC: a top-to-bottom renovation added an excellent new playground, a mini-golf course and snack bar, an Astroturf area and a skate park.

Chelsea Piers

For listings, see p129.

This vast and hugely bustling complex on the Hudson River is ideal in the colder months, thanks to its bowling alley, roller rink, pool, toddler gym, ice-skating rink and climbing walls.

Central Park

For more information and a calendar of events, visit www.centralparknyc.org. Don't miss the antique **Friedsam Memorial Carousel** (*see p245* **Horsing Around**). There are 21 playgrounds in the park; the large **Heckscher Playground**, in the south-west corner (between Seventh Avenue & Central Park West, from 61st to 63rd Streets), sprawls over more than three acres and has an up-to-date adventure area and handy restrooms.

FREE Belvedere Castle

Midpark, off the 79th Street Transverse Road (1-212 772 0210, www.centralparknyc.org). Subway B, C to 81st Street-Museum of Natural History. **Open** 10am-5pm daily. **Admission** free. **Map** p399 D19.

Central Park designer Frederick Law Olmsted planned this fanciful structure to lend his masterful creation a pastoral, fairy tale-like quality. Three viewing platforms give little visitors a stunning view of Turtle Pond below and, in the distance, the expansive, tree-lined Great Lawn (the two higher terraces are accessed from within the castle's turret). During opening hours, budding naturalists can borrow nature kits equipped with binoculars and field guides with which to explore the castle's dominion.

Central Park Zoo

For listings, see p170.

The stars here are the penguins and the polar bear, which live in glass-enclosed habitats so you can watch their underwater antics. The creation of a snow leopard environment has added a breathtaking endangered animal to the zoo's menagerie and even changed the zoo's topography. Among the zoo's most engaging offerings for kids are the sea lion and penguin feedings, and the mist-filled Tropic Zone: the Rainforest, with free-flying birds, plus lots of tropical vegetation, monkeys and lemurs. The Tisch Children's Zoo, a stone's throw away, houses species that enjoy being petted – and fed – among them alpacas, sheep and goats.

Conservatory Water

Central Park, entrance on Fifth Avenue, at 72nd Street. Subway 6 to 68th Street-Hunter College. **Map** p399 E20.

Nicknamed Stuart Little Pond after EB White's storybook mouse, Conservatory Water is a mecca for model-yacht racers. When the boatmaster is around (daily from April through October, weather permitting), you can rent a remote-controlled vessel ($11/30mins; see www.centralparknyc.org for hours). Kids are drawn to two statues near the pond: the bronze rendering of Lewis Carroll's Alice, the Mad Hatter and the White Rabbit is an irresistible climbing spot, while the Hans Christian Andersen statue is a gathering point for free storytelling sessions (early June-late Sept 11am-noon Sat, www.hcastorycenter.org).

Swedish Cottage Marionette Theater

Central Park West, at 81st Street (1-212 988 9093). Subway B, C to 81st Street-Museum of Natural History. **Shows** *Oct-June* 10.30am, noon Tue, Thur, Fri; 10.30am, noon, 2.30pm Wed; 1pm Sat, Sun. *July, Aug* 10.30am, noon Mon-Fri. **Tickets** $10; $7 reductions. **Map** p399 D19.

Tucked just inside the western boundary of Central Park is a curiously incongruous old wooden structure. Designed as a schoolhouse, the building was Sweden's entry in the 1876 Centennial Exposition in Philadelphia (it was moved to NYC a year later). Inside is one of the best-kept secrets (and deals) in town: a tiny marionette theatre with regular shows. Reservations are recommended.

Trump Rink & Victorian Gardens

Trump Rink *Central Park, midpark at 62nd Street (1-212 439 6900, www.wollmanskatingrink.com). Subway N, Q, R to Fifth Avenue-59th Street.* **Open** *Late Oct-Apr* 10am-2.30pm Mon, Tue; 10am-10pm Wed, Thur; 10am-11pm Fri, Sat; 10am-9pm Sun. **Rates** $11.25-$18; $5-$9 reductions; $5 spectators. *Skate rental* $8. **No credit cards**.

Victorian Gardens *1-212 982 2229, www.victoriangardensnyc.com.* **Open** *Mid May-mid Sept* 11am-7pm Mon-Thur; 11am-8pm Fri; 10am-9pm Sat; 10am-8pm Sun. **Admission** $7 Mon-Fri; $8 Sat, Sun; free children under 36in tall. Games & rides cost extra. **Map** p399 D21.

Skating in Central Park amid snowy trees, with grand apartment buildings towering in the distance, is a New York tradition. This popular (read: crowded) skating rink offers lessons and skate rentals, plus a snack bar where you can warm up with hot chocolate. In summer, the site hosts Victorian Gardens, a quaint amusement park for younger children. It's hardly white-knuckle stuff, but the mini-teacup carousel and Rio Grande train will satisfy little thrill-seekers.

RESTAURANTS & CAFÉS

Alice's Teacup

102 W 73rd Street, at Columbus Avenue, Upper West Side (1-212 799 3006, www.alicesteacup.com). Subway B, C to 72nd Street. **Open** 8am-8pm daily. **Main courses** $10-$14. **Map** p399 C20.

IN THE KNOW SUMMER OUTING

Adults may dig the retro hipster tackiness of Coney Island's boardwalk and amusement parks (*see p217*), but kids unabashedly love the classic thrills: ogling sword swallowers, chowing down on hot dogs and screaming through adrenaline-pumping rides. If they're tall enough, take them on the teeth-rattling Cyclone rollercoaster; otherwise, try something a little tamer, like the Teacups or Balloon Expedition.

Beloved by Alice-loving and Disney-adoring children, this magical spot offers much more than tea (though the three-tiered version, comprising an assortment of sandwiches, scones and desserts, truly is a treat). The brunch menu is fit for royalty, with Alice's Curious French Toast (drenched in fruit coulis, crème anglaise and syrup) and scones in scrumptious flavours like blueberry and pumpkin. In the afternoons, the special after-school snack menu features house-made graham crackers and honey, and banana bread topped with jam. And at a little shop in the front of the eaterie, you can outfit your fairy princess in training with a pair of bright, glittery wings.
Other locations 156 E 64th Street, at Lexington Avenue, Upper East Side (1-212 486 9200); 220 E 81st Street, between Second & Third Avenues, Upper East Side (1-212 734 4832).

Cowgirl

519 Hudson Street, at 10th Street, West Village (1-212 633 1133, www.cowgirlnyc.com). Subway 1 to Christopher Street-Sheridan Square. **Open** 11am-11pm Mon-Thur; 11am-midnight Fri; 10am-midnight Sat; 10am-11pm Sun. **Main courses** $12-$21; $6 children's menu. **Map** p397 D28.

This neighbourhood favourite is one of those rare spots that appeals to both adults and children. Adults can unwind with a pitcher of potent margaritas amid the charming 1950s-era ranch decor. The whimsical setting, along with a small old-time candy shop and plenty of crayons, means the whole crowd will remain buoyant while waiting for rib-sticking fare such as quesadillas, pulled-pork sandwiches and gooey mac and cheese. Finish your meal with the unbelievable ice-cream sundae disguised as mashed potato.
Other locations Cowgirl Sea-Horse, 259 Front Street, at Dover Street, Financial District (1-212 608 7873, www.cowgirlseahorse.com).

Crema

111 W 17th Street, between Sixth & Seventh Avenues, Chelsea (1-212 691 4477, www.cremarestaurante.com). Subway F, M, 1, 2, 3 to 14th Street; L to Sixth Avenue. **Open** noon-10.30pm Mon-Wed; noon-11pm Thur; noon-midnight Fri; 11.30am-midnight Sat; 11.30am-10pm Sun. **Main courses** $11-$28. **Map** p397 D27.

Among the many child-friendly offerings to be found at Julieta Ballesteros's upscale Mexican restaurant are quesadillas. The versions here are grilled flour tortillas laced with chihuahua cheese and accented with black beans, shrimp, grilled chicken breast or steak. Other menu options include a *taco de carne asada* main and sides such as seasonal rice or *granielote* (corn kernels with cream). Tropical-flavoured lemonade, ice-cream and sorbet round out the à la carte offerings.

★ Ditch Plains

29 Bedford Street, at Downing Street, Greenwich Village (1-212 633 0202, www.ditch-plains.com). Subway A, B, C, D, E, F, M to W 4th Street; 1 to Houston Street. **Open** 11am-2am daily. **Main courses** $10-$29; $5-$12 children's menu. **Map** p397 D29.

This New England-style fish shack, named for chef-owner Marc Murphy's favourite surfing spot in Montauk, Long Island, is sophisticated and sleek: no seaside knick-knacks here. It's perfect for families at all times of day, as it excels at simple but upscale fare such as lobster roll (a mound of luscious chopped meat mixed with scallions, tarragon and aïoli, served on a soft roll with a side of sweet-potato chips), ceviche and soft tacos. The place offers kids a stellar menu of their own, packed with an array of hot dogs and health-conscious treats like whole-wheat quesadillas.
Other locations 100 W 82nd Street, at Columbus Avenue, Upper West Side (1-212 362 4815).

S'MAC

345 E 12th Street, between First & Second Avenues, East Village (1-212 358 7912, www.smacnyc.com). Subway L to First Avenue. **Open** 11am-11pm Mon-Thur, Sun; 11am-1am Fri, Sat. **Main courses** $8-$20. **Map** p397 F28.

A dozen varieties of mac and cheese range from simple all-American (mild enough for picky types) to a more complex dish with brie, roasted figs and shiitake mushrooms, or mac and manchego with fennel and shallots. There's a size for everyone: 'nosh' (great for kids), 'major munch' (a hearty adult serving), 'mongo' (if you want leftovers to take with you) and 'partay' (which serves eight to 12). Children are offered a regular bowl in lieu of the sizzling skillet in which meals are typically served.
Other locations 157 E 33rd Street, between Lexington & Third Avenues, Midtown East (1-212 383 3900).

BABYSITTING

Baby Sitters' Guild

1-212 682 0227, www.babysittersguild.com. **Bookings** 9am-9pm daily. **No credit cards** (except when paying through hotel).

Babysitters cost from $30 an hour and up (four-hour minimum), plus travel ($5, or $10 after midnight). Sitters are available around the clock, and between them speak 17 languages.

Pinch Sitters

1-212 260 6005, www.nypinchsitters.com. **Bookings** 8am-5pm Mon-Fri. **No credit cards**. Charges are $22/hr (four-hour minimum), plus a $15 travel charge after 9pm. A $45 fee is levied for cancellations given with less than 24 hours' notice.

Film & TV

Woody, Marty, Spike: by now the whole world is on first-name terms with New York's canonical legends. Even if this is your first visit to NYC, the cityscape will feel familiar; every corner has been immortalised on celluloid. It's easy to feel as if you've walked on to a massive movie set, especially when photogenic landmarks such as the Empire State Building pan into view. And you might even stumble upon an actual shoot – the thriving local film industry is based in Queens. Many high-profile TV shows are also produced here and, if you're organised (and lucky), you could snag tickets to a studio taping.

FILM

Few cities offer the film-lover as many options as New York. If you insist, you can check out the blockbusters at the multiplexes on 42nd Street. But Gotham's gems are its arthouses, museums and other film institutions. For current movie listings, see *Time Out New York* magazine or www.timeout.com/newyork.

Art & revival houses

Angelika Film Center
18 W Houston Street, at Mercer Street, Soho (1-212 995 2570, www.angelikafilmcenter.com). Subway B, D, F, M to Broadway-Lafayette Street; N, R to Prince Street; 6 to Bleecker Street. **Tickets** $14; $11 reductions. **Map** p397 E29.
When it opened in 1989, the Angelika immediately became a player in the then-booming Amerindie scene, and the six-screen cinema still puts the emphasis on edgier fare, both domestic and foreign. The complex is packed at weekends, so come extra early or visit the website to buy advance tickets.

Anthology Film Archives
32 Second Avenue, at 2nd Street, East Village (1-212 505 5181, www.anthologyfilmarchives.org). Subway F to Lower East Side-Second Avenue; 6 to Bleecker Street. **Tickets** $10; $8 reductions. **Map** p397 F29.
This red-brick building feels a bit like a fortress – and, in a sense, it is one, protecting the legacy of NYC's fiercest film experimenters. Dedicated to the preservation, study and exhibition of independent, avant-garde and artist-made work, Anthology houses two screens and a film museum.

★ BAM Rose Cinemas
Brooklyn Academy of Music, 30 Lafayette Avenue, between Ashland Place & St Felix Street, Fort Greene, Brooklyn (1-718 636 4100, www.bam.org). Subway B, D, N, Q, R, 2, 3, 4, 5 to Atlantic Avenue-Barclays Center; C to Lafayette Avenue; G to Fulton Street. **Tickets** $13; $9 reductions. **Map** p404 T10.
Brooklyn's premier art-film venue does double duty as a rep house for well-programmed classics on 35mm and as a first-run multiplex for indie films. June's annual BAMcinemaFest is an excellent showcase of new American work.

Cinema Village
22 E 12th Street, between Fifth Avenue & University Place, Greenwich Village (1-212 924 3363, www.cinemavillage.com). Subway L, N, Q, R, 4, 5, 6 to 14th Street-Union Square. **Tickets** $11; $6-$8 reductions. **Map** p397 E28.
A classic marquee that charmed Noah Baumbach long before he made *The Squid and the Whale*, this three-screener specialises in indie flicks, cutting-edge documentaries and foreign films.

★ Film Forum
209 W Houston Street, between Sixth Avenue & Varick Street, West Village (1-212 727 8110, www.filmforum.org). Subway 1 to Houston Street. **Tickets** $13; $7.50 reductions. **No credit cards** (except for online purchases). **Map** p397 D29.

The city's leading tastemaking venue for independent new releases and classic movies, Film Forum is programmed by festival-scouring staff who take their duties as seriously as a Kurosawa samurai. Born in 1970 as a makeshift screening space with folding chairs, Film Forum is still one of the few nonprofit cinemas in the United States – but thankfully its three screens are now furnished with comfortable seats.

★ IFC Center

323 Sixth Avenue, at W 3rd Street, Greenwich Village (1-212 924 7771, www.ifccenter.com). Subway A, B, C, D, E, F, M to W 4th Street. **Tickets** $13.50; $9.50 reductions. **Map** p397 D29.

The long-darkened 1930s Waverly was once again illuminated back in 2005 when it was reborn as a modern five-screen arthouse cinema, showing the latest indie hits, along with choice midnight cult items and occasional foreign classics. You may come face to face with the directors or the actors on the screen, as many introduce their work on opening night.

Landmark Sunshine Cinema

141-143 E Houston Street, between First & Second Avenues, East Village (1-212 260 7289, www.landmarktheatres.com). Subway F to Lower East Side-Second Avenue. **Tickets** $13.50; $10 reductions. **Map** p397 F29.

DINNER AT THE MOVIES

Gastro-cinemas are breaking free of the popcorn box.

After the Film Society of Lincoln Center (*see p251*) opened its stunning new **Elinor Bunin Munroe Film Center**, restaurateur Jason Denton premiered his smart and casual on-site street-level café attached to the cinema: Indie Food & Wine (144 W 65th Street, between Broadway & Amsterdam Avenue, 1-212 875 5456, www.indiefoodandwine.com). Movie-goers can stop in for Mediterranean-inflected fare such as salads and a milk-braised pork belly sandwich or pick up upgraded concession-stand snacks like organic hot dogs and parmesan-truffle popcorn – it's a far cry from the old spartan arthouse image.

The **Nitehawk Cinema** (136 Metropolitan Avenue, between Berry Street & Wythe Avenue, 1-718 384 3980, www.nitehawkcinema.com) in Williamsburg, Brooklyn, goes one better by serving food in the cinema itself. Seats are arranged in pairs with sturdy tables, and viewers order from a menu created by Michelin-starred chef Saul Bolton. Just write down your order at any point during the movie on a piece of paper for a server to pick up and ferry to the kitchen. The comfort-food grub includes meaty fish tacos and a tasty burger, but the real highlights are the chef's variations on concession-stand snacks, such as popcorn tossed with parmesan, black pepper and garlic butter. Two café-bars keep movie-goers loose.

Amid these shiny competitors, trailblazer **reRun Gastropub Theater** (147 Front Street, between Jay & Pearl Streets, Dumbo, Brooklyn, 1-718 766 9110, www.reruntheater.com) still feels original – both food and booze are served from a bar inside the theatre, and guests sit in repurposed minivan seats surrounded by a gritty mural of the city. The bar closes when the lights go down, but food orders placed beforehand – creative riffs on junk food such as mashed potato-stuffed pretzels and duck fat- and herb-tossed popcorn – will be delivered to your seat, and you can load up on discounted buckets of beer or carafes of wine and cocktails to tide you over through the show.

Nitehawk.

Once a renowned Yiddish theatre, this comfortable, date-friendly venue has snazz and chutzpah to spare. Intimate cinemas and excellent sound are a beautiful complement to the indie films; it also hosts New York's most consistently excellent midnight series on Fridays and Saturdays.

Leonard Nimoy Thalia

Symphony Space, 2537 Broadway, at 95th Street, Upper West Side (1-212 864 5400, www.symphonyspace.org). Subway 1, 2, 3 to 96th Street. **Tickets** $14; $12 reductions. **Map** p400 C17.

The famed Thalia arthouse, which featured in *Annie Hall* (when it was screening *The Sorrow and the Pity*), has since undergone an upgrade. The cinematic fare is an eclectic mix of international, arthouse and documentary films, plus HD screenings of plays and operas.

Maysles Documentary Center

343 Malcolm X Boulevard (Lenox Avenue), between 127th & 128th Streets, Harlem (1-212 582 6843, www.maysles.org/mdc). Subway A, B, C, D, 2, 3 to 125th Street. **Tickets** Suggested donation $10. **Map** p401 D13.

Harlem keeps it 'reel' with this intimate screening venue, run by veritable *cinema vérité* legend Albert Maysles and his extended family. Socially conscious documentaries, naturally, make up the bulk of the programming, but you're also likely to catch funky series of hip hop and jazz films, critics presenting personal esoteric favourites and plenty of uptown-centric flicks.

Paris Theatre

4 W 58th Street, between Fifth & Sixth Avenues, Midtown (1-212 688 3800, www.theparistheatre.com). Subway N, Q, R to Fifth Avenue-59th Street. **Tickets** $14; $11 reductions. **Map** p399 E22.

The elegant, single-screen Paris is one of the oldest continually operating movie houses in the country (it was founded in 1948). Its plush carpets and seats, tiny lobby and lack of any on-screen advertising set it apart even from the city's indie houses.

Quad Cinema

34 W 13th Street, between Fifth & Sixth Avenues, Greenwich Village (1-212 255 8800, www.quadcinema.com). Subway F, M to 14th Street; L to Sixth Avenue. **Tickets** $11; $8 reductions. **Map** p397 E28.

The Quad's four small screens show a wide range of foreign and American indie films. However, the real standout cinema at this Greenwich Village operation are the latest offerings related to gay sexuality and politics.

► *Another popular spot for gay-oriented cinema, the Bow Tie Chelsea Cinemas, offers drag queen-hosted classic films; see p255* **In the Know**.

Ziegfeld Theater

141 W 54th Street, between Sixth & Seventh Avenues, Midtown (1-212 307 1862, www.bowtiecinemas.com). Subway B, D, E to Seventh Avenue; F, N, Q, R to 57th Street; 1 to 50th Street. **Tickets** $14; $10.50 reductions. **Map** p399 D22.

Despite its Jazz Age moniker, this movie palace actually opened in 1969; since then, its red carpets and gilded staircases have served as a last stand against stadium-seated sameness. Temporarily endangered but saved by Bow Tie Cinemas, the largest single-screen theatre in the city seats 1,162 citizens under a vast ceiling of chandeliers, harking back to when going to motion pictures wasn't just idle entertainment but an aspirational experience.

Other institutions

★ Film Society of Lincoln Center

144 & 165 W 65th Street, between Broadway & Amsterdam Avenue, Upper West Side (1-212 875 5600, www.filmlinc.com). Subway 1 to 66th Street-Lincoln Center. **Tickets** $13; $9 reductions. **Map** p399 C21.

Founded in 1969, the FSLC hosts the prestigious New York Film Festival, among other annual fests, in addition to presenting diverse programming throughout the year. Series are usually thematic, with an international perspective or focused on a single auteur. The $40-million Elinor Bunin Munroe Film Center houses two plush cinemas that host frequent post-screening Q&As. Between these state-of-the-art screens and the operational Walter Reade Theater across the street, a small multiplex has been born. The Bunin also houses a café, Indie Food and Wine.

★ Museum of Modern Art

For listings, see p154. **Tickets** free with museum admission, or $12; $8-$10 reductions; free under-16s.

Renowned for its superb programming of art films and experimental work, MoMA draws from a vast vault. You have to buy tickets in person at the museum at the lobby desk or the film desk (see www.moma.org or call 1-212 708 9480 for more information). Note that while museum admission includes the day's film programme, a film ticket doesn't include admission to the museum galleries – although it can be applied towards the cost within 30 days.

Museum of the Moving Image

For listings, see p224. **Tickets** $12; $6-$9 reductions.

Like the rest of this Queens institution housed in the Astoria Studios complex, the museum's cinema has received a magnificent renovation, resulting in a state-of-the-art 267-seat cinema. Expect excellent prints and screenings of the classics.

Foreign-language specialists

You can catch the latest foreign-language flicks at art and revival houses, but there is a wealth of specialist venues as well, including the **French Institute Alliance Française** (22 E 60th Street, 1-212 355 6100, www.fiaf.org), the **Japan Society** (*see p158*) and **Scandinavia House** (*see p157*). The **Asia Society & Museum** (*see p174*) screens works from Asian countries plus Asian-American productions.

Film festivals

From late September to mid October, the Film Society of Lincoln Center hosts the **New York Film Festival** (1-212 875 5050, www.filmlinc.com), more than two weeks packed with premières, features and short flicks from around the globe. Together with Lincoln Center's *Film Comment* magazine, the FSLC also offers the popular **Film Comment Selects**, showcasing films that have yet to be distributed in the United States.

January brings the annual **New York Jewish Film Festival** (www.nyjff.org) to Lincoln Center's Walter Reade Theater. In early March, the **New York International Children's Film Festival** (1-212 349 0330, www.gkids.com) kicks off three to four weeks of anime, shorts and features made for kids and teens. Each spring, the Museum of Modern Art and the Film Society of Lincoln Center sponsor the highly regarded **New Directors/New Films** series, presenting works by on-the-cusp filmmakers. And in April, Robert De Niro's **Tribeca Film Festival** (1-212 941 2400, www.tribecafilmfestival.org) draws more than 400,000 fans to screenings of independent movies and other events. It's followed by the **New York Lesbian & Gay Film Festival** (1-646 290 8136, www.newfest.org) in summer. The season also brings several outdoor film festivals (*see below* **In the Know**).

IN THE KNOW OUTDOOR MOVIES

With summer arrives the wonderful New York tradition of free outdoor movie festivals. Look out for the **Bryant Park Summer Film Festival** in midtown (1-212 512 5700, www.bryantpark.org); **Central Park Conservancy Film Festival** (1-212 310 6600, www.centralparknyc.org); **Movies With a View** in Brooklyn Bridge Park (1-718 802 0603, www.brooklynbridgepark.org); the **River to River Festival** (*see p34*) across Lower Manhattan and Summer on the Hudson in Riverside Park South (1-212 870 3070).

TV STUDIO TAPINGS

Colbert Report

513 W 54th Street, between Tenth & Eleventh Avenues, Hell's Kitchen (www.colbertnation.com/tickets). Subway C, E to 50th Street. **Tapings** 7pm Mon-Thur. **Map** p399 C22.

In his cult parody of Bill O'Reilly's right-wing political talk-show, sarcastic correspondent Stephen Colbert tells viewers why everyone else's opinions are 'just plain wrong'. Reserve tickets online at least six months ahead, or try your luck for standby tickets on the day at 4pm. You must be 18 and have photo ID.

The Daily Show with Jon Stewart

733 Eleventh Avenue, between 51st & 52nd Streets, Hell's Kitchen (www.thedailyshow.com/tickets). Subway C, E to 50th Street. **Tapings** 6pm Mon-Thur. **Map** p399 C22.

Many viewers believe they get a fairer view of current affairs from Stewart's irreverent take than they do from the network news. Reserve tickets online at least three months ahead; as ticket distribution may be in excess of studio capacity, admission is not guaranteed. You must be over 18 and have photo ID.

Late Show with David Letterman

1697 Broadway, between 53rd & 54th Streets, Midtown (www.cbs.com/late_night/late_show/tickets). Subway B, D, E to Seventh Avenue. **Tapings** 4.30pm Mon-Wed; 3.30pm, 6pm Thur. **Map** p399 D22.

Despite periodic rumours of his impending retirement, Letterman is TV's longest-serving late-night talk-show host – his sardonic humour has been on the air for more than three decades. Seats are hard to get: fill out a request form online, or try to get a standby ticket by calling 1-212 247 6497 at 11am on the day. You must be 18 with photo ID.

Saturday Night Live

30 Rockefeller Plaza, Sixth Avenue, between 49th & 50th Streets, Midtown (1-212 664 3056, www.nbc.com/snl). Subway B, D, F, M to 47th-50th Streets-Rockefeller Center. **Tapings** *Dress rehearsal* 8pm. *Live show* 11.30pm. **Map** p399 D22.

Tickets to this long-running comedy sketch show are assigned by lottery every autumn. Check the website in August for ticket information, or try the standby lottery on the day. Line up by 7am (but get there much earlier) under the NBC Studio marquee (49th Street side of 30 Rockefeller Plaza). You must be over 16 with photo ID.

ESSENTIAL NEW YORK FILMS

Six celluloid visions of the great metropolis.

Manhattan.

DOG DAY AFTERNOON
SIDNEY LUMET (1975)
Al Pacino heads a stellar cast in this tense, moving tale of a first-time crook whose plan to rob a Brooklyn bank goes awry. The film brims with distinctly New York characters: John Cazale as a spaced-out partner in crime; Chris Sarandon as a fragile transsexual; and Charles Durning as a frazzled detective.

DO THE RIGHT THING
SPIKE LEE (1989)
Outraged by the 1986 Howard Beach incident, where a man died in a racially motivated incident, Lee responded with a 360-degree look at what can happen when New York's melting pot boils over. The film doubles as a vivid portrait of his native Brooklyn, where every stoop philosopher, nosy matriarch and beat-box-loving B-boy gets his or her moment in the spotlight.

MANHATTAN
WOODY ALLEN (1979)
Allen's love sonnet to his home city frames an edgy social comedy. The movie reminds you what a gorgeous sight the island really is from the moment the Gershwin-scored opening montage kicks in: the fish markets and basketball courts; the Fifth Avenue boutiques and Broadway theatres; the high-rise dwellers and lowlifes.

ROSEMARY'S BABY
ROMAN POLANSKI (1968)
This realistic supernatural drama was a transfusion of thick, urbane blood to the dated horror genre, and much of its revolutionary impact should be credited to the city of New York itself. A young couple, played by Mia Farrow and John Cassavetes, moves into the Dakota Building – as much of a Gothic pile as any Transylvanian mansion.

SWEET SMELL OF SUCCESS
ALEXANDER MACKENDRICK (1957)
This adaptation of a novella about a megalomaniacal gossip columnist (Burt Lancaster) – based on newspaperman Walter Winchell – and a parasitic press agent (Tony Curtis) encapsulates what once went down in the booths of the '21' Club.

TAXI DRIVER
MARTIN SCORSESE (1976)
'You talking to me?' Cracked hero Travis Bickle (Robert De Niro) cruises through Greenwich Village and Hell's Kitchen in his taxi. The story may be all in his head: a deranged man's dream of vanilla romance with Cybill Shepherd, unchecked fury at political impotence and the compulsive urge to right every wrong, no matter how slight.

Gay & Lesbian

In summer 2011, same-sex marriage became legal in New York State, marking a major civil rights victory in the birthplace of the modern gay rights movement. Two years later, New Yorker Edith Windsor was at the centre of the Supreme Court case that established same-sex marriage as a federal right. Even as gayness moves towards the mainstream, the city's queer scene is constantly finding ways to reinvent itself as an incubator of activism and innovative nightlife.

Offering much more than drag and piano bars (though, delightfully, these still thrive), today's LGBT New York has venues devoted to rock and country music and an abundance of arty, pan-queer events. Downtown cultural institutions such as Joe's Pub and Dixon Place stage performances by iconic artists like Sandra Bernhard and Justin Vivian Bond, as well as emerging stars.

THE QUEER CALENDAR

NYC Pride, New York's biggest queer event, takes place the last week of June, bringing with it a whirl of parties and performances. Capping the weekend, the **NYC LGBT Pride March**, which takes five hours to wind down Fifth Avenue from midtown to the West Village, draws millions of spectators and participants. The **Urban Bear Weekend** in May and **Black Party Weekend** in March also draw hordes to NYC, visibly upping the gay quotient around town. During the summer, the social scene extends to scenic **Fire Island**, home to the neighbouring beach resorts of Cherry Grove and the Pines (about a 90-minute train and ferry ride from Manhattan). In autumn, **Halloween** is a major to-do, with bars and clubs packed with costumed revellers. Culture buffs can check out summer's annual **Hot!** festival of lesbian and gay arts at Dixon Place, offering a wide variety of queer art, theatre, dance and comedy events. Film fans might like the offerings at the **NewFest** (www.newfest.org) in September.

INFORMATION, MEDIA & CULTURE

In what may be a sign of the times, there are no specifically gay bookstores left in New York. **Bluestockings** has a good selection of queer and feminist works, while most major bookstores have large LGBT sections.

To find out what's going on, refer to the Gay & Lesbian section of *Time Out New York* or www.timeout.com/newyork. Also popular is the gay entertainment magazine *Next* (www.nextmagazine.com), which offers extensive boy-centric information on bars, clubs, restaurants and events. The monthly *Go!* (www.gomag.com), 'a cultural road map for the city girl', gives the lowdown on the lesbian nightlife and travel scene. *Gay City News* (www.gaycitynews.com) provides feisty political coverage with an activist slant. All four are free and widely available in street boxes, gay and lesbian bars and stores. A number of popular gay blogs and websites are also based in the city, and feature attitude-filled thoughts on the queer scene. Among the best sites are sexy and occasionally gossipy Queerty (www.queerty.com), news-focused Joe. My. God (www.joemygod.com) and the wide-ranging Towleroad (www.towleroad.com).

Bluestockings

172 Allen Street, between Rivington & Stanton Streets, Lower East Side (1-212 777 6028, www.bluestockings.com). Subway F to Lower East Side-Second Avenue. **Open** 11am-11pm daily. **Map** p397 F29.

This radical bookstore, Fairtrade café and activist resource centre stocks LGBT literature and regularly hosts queer events (often with a feminist slant), including dyke knitting circles, trans-politics forums and women's open-mic nights.

★ Lesbian, Gay, Bisexual & Transgender Community Center

208 W 13th Street, between Seventh & Eighth Avenues, West Village (1-212 620 7310, www.gaycenter.org). Subway A, C, E, 1, 2, 3 to 14th Street; L to Eighth Avenue. **Open** 9am-10pm Mon-Sat; 9am-9pm Sun. **Map** p397 D27.

Founded in 1983, the Center provides information and a gay support network. As well as being a friendly resource that offers guidance to gay tourists, it is used as a venue for more than 300 groups. Public programming here includes everything from book signings to dance parties. The National Archive of Lesbian, Gay, Bisexual and Transgender History (open to the public 6-8pm Thur) and the Pat Parker/Vito Russo Library (6-9pm Mon-Fri; 1-4pm Sat) are housed here, as is an art gallery and a CyberCenter that offers internet access for $3 an hour (10am-9pm Mon-Fri; noon-9pm Sat, Sun).

IN THE KNOW MOVIE NIGHT

Once a week, the ever-bubbly green-topped drag queen Hedda Lettuce takes over the **Chelsea Bow Tie Cinema** (260 W 23rd Street, between Seventh & Eighth Avenues, 1-212 691 5519, www.bowtiecinemas.com) to provide a comedic fluffing before a (typically) campy flick. Past screenings have included Zsa Zsa Gabor vehicle *Queen of Outer Space*, horror classic *Carrie* and goofy '80s comedy *Elvira, Mistress of the Dark*.

Lesbian Herstory Archives

484 14th Street, between Eighth Avenue & Prospect Park West, Park Slope, Brooklyn (1-718 768 3953, www.lesbianherstoryarchives.org). Subway F to 15th Street-Prospect Park. **Open** varies; see website calendar. **Map** p404 T12.

The Herstory Archives contain more than 20,000 books (cultural theory, fiction, poetry, plays), 1,600 periodicals, 600 films and videos and assorted memorabilia. The cosy brownstone also hosts screenings, readings and social gatherings, plus an open house in June (during Brooklyn Pride) and December.

★ Leslie-Lohman Museum of Gay & Lesbian Art

26 Wooster Street, between Canal & Grand Streets, Soho (1-212 431 2609, www.leslielohman.org). Subway A, C, E to Canal Street. **Open** noon-6pm Tue-Sun. **Admission** free. **Map** p397 E30.

NYC Pride.

Formerly the Leslie-Lohman Gay Art Foundation, this institution was granted museum status by the state of New York in 2011. Founded in 1990 by Fritz Lohman and Charles Leslie, the museum seeks to preserve and highlight the contributions of LGBTQ artists throughout history up to the present. In addition to changing exhibitions, it has a large permanent collection and library, and hosts regular book signings, panel discussions and low-key parties.

WHERE TO STAY

While you'd be hard-pressed to find a gay-unfriendly hotel in New York, the following establishments are either exclusively gay or geared towards a queer clientele.

Chelsea Mews Guest House

344 W 15th Street, between Eighth & Ninth Avenues, Chelsea (1-212 255 9174, www.chelseamewsguesthouse.com). Subway A, C, E to 14th Street; L to Eighth Avenue. **Rooms** 8. **No credit cards. Map** p397 C27.

Built in 1840, this clothing-optional guesthouse caters to gay men. The rooms are comfortable and well furnished and, in most cases, share a bathroom. Bicycle tours and coffee are complimentary – as is access to a songbird aviary! An on-site massage therapist and soothing Tempur-Pedic beds in every room help to ensure a relaxing stay. New arrivals take note: the Chelsea Mews Guest House doesn't have a sign out front, so keep your eye on the building numbers.

★ Chelsea Pines Inn

317 W 14th Street, between Eighth & Ninth Avenues, Chelsea (1-212 929 1023, www.chelseapinesinn.com). Subway A, C, E to 14th Street; L to Eighth Avenue. **Rooms** 23. **Map** p397 C27.

On the border of Chelsea and the West Village, Chelsea Pines welcomes gay guests of all persuasions. The rooms are clean and comfortable, with classic-film themes; all have private bathrooms, and are equipped with a radio, a TV with satellite channels, a refrigerator and free Wi-Fi. Complimentary breakfast is offered daily.

Colonial House Inn

318 W 22nd Street, between Eighth & Ninth Avenues, Chelsea (1-212 243 9669, 1-800 689 3779, www.colonialhouseinn.com). Subway C, E to 23rd Street. **Rooms** 22 **Map** p398 C26.

This beautifully renovated 1850s townhouse sits on a quiet street in Chelsea. The hotel was founded by late dance-music legend Mel Cheren, and is still run by (and primarily for) gay men; it's a great place to stay, even if some of the cheaper rooms are a bit snug. Bonuses include fireplaces in three of the deluxe rooms and a rooftop deck (nude sunbathing is allowed).

Incentra Village House

32 Eighth Avenue, between Jane & W 12th Streets, West Village (1-212 206 0007, www.incentravillage.com). Subway A, C, E to 14th Street; L to Eighth Avenue. **Rooms** 11. **Map** p397 D28.

PARTY PEOPLE

Nightlife names you need to know.

To keep up with NYC's after-dark scene, just follow its top promoters. Upscale pretty boys tag along with **Josh Wood** (www.joshwoodproductions.com), the circuit crowd flocks to the legendary **Saint** soirées (www.saintatlarge.com) and the art-boy contingent is loyal to **Spank** dance parties (www.spankartmag.com). **Daniel Nardicio** (www.danielnardicio.com) can be counted on for sleazy, frisky bashes, and **Brandon Voss** (www.vossnyc.com) helps to run some of the most popular parties in town. Sarah Jenny and Avory Agony's monthly roving **Hey Queen!** fête (www.heyqueen.org) draws a mixed girl-boy-etc crowd, as do parties from the **Hot Rabbit** crew (facebook.com/thehotrabbit). Lesbians looking to dance and flirt should visit DJ **Whitney Day**'s website to check out her schedule (www.whitneyday.com).

Hey Queen!.

The Cock. *See p258.*

ARTS & ENTERTAINMENT

Two cute 1841 townhouses in the Village make up this nicely restored and gay-run guesthouse. The spacious rooms have private bathrooms and kitchenettes; some also have fireplaces. A 1939 Steinway baby grand graces the parlour and sets a tone of easy sophistication.

The Out NYC

510 W 42nd Street, between Tenth & Eleventh Avenues (1-212 947 2999, www.theoutnyc.com). Subway A, C, E to 42nd Street-Port Authority. **Rooms** 103. **Map** p398 C24.

This all-gay megacomplex is located just a few blocks from Times Square and the Theater District, and in convenient proximity to the Hell's Kitchen strip of gay bars. But there's actually no need to leave – the Out also houses BPM nightclub and the unremarkable but serviceable KTCHN restaurant, as well as a spa, gym and the Rosebud cocktail bar.

RESTAURANTS & CAFES

The sight of same-sex couples holding hands across a candlelit table is a pretty commonplace one in New York City. But if you want to increase the chances of being part of the majority when you dine, check out the following gay-friendly places.

Bamboo 52

344 W 52nd Street, between Eighth & Ninth Avenues, Hell's Kitchen (1-212 315 2777, www.bamboo52nyc.com). Subway C, E to 50th Street. **Open** 11am-2am daily. **Sushi rolls** $7-$14. **Map** p398 C23.

This sushi restaurant (with a bamboo garden to boot) feels more like a gay bar with an extended raw fish menu. There's loungey seating (patrons nestle on low banquettes and nibble off knee-high tables), a DJ and free-flowing drinks. The fun menu features such unorthodox combinations as buffalo chicken speciality rolls and a spicy sushi sandwich – a tasty triangle of seasoned rice layered with spicy tuna, avocado, eel and American cheese.

Elmo

156 Seventh Avenue, between 19th & 20th Streets, Chelsea (1-212 337 8000, www.elmorestaurant.com). Subway 1 to 18th Street. **Open** 11am-11pm Mon-Thur; 11am-midnight Fri; 10am-midnight Sat; 10am-11pm Sun. **Main courses** $17-$23. **Map** p397 D27.

The main attraction at this spacious, brightly decorated eaterie is the good, reasonably priced American comfort food which changes seasonally. Then there's the bar, which provides a view of the dining room jammed with guys in clingy tank tops. During warmer months, the sidewalk café is constantly bustling.

★ Empanada Mama

763 Ninth Avenue, between 51st & 52nd Streets, Hell's Kitchen (1-212 698 9008, www.empmamanyc.com). Subway C, E to 50th Street. **Open** 24hrs daily. **Empanadas** $3. **Map** p398 C23.

Massive flavours are crammed into tiny packages at this cute spot, right in the middle of Hell's Kitchen's boy-bar crawl. Savoury and sweet empanadas (both flour and corn varieties) make great on-the-go snacks, or combine several for a full meal. The joint tends to be packed from dinner time until the wee hours.

Manatus

340 Bleecker Street, between Christopher & 10th Streets, West Village (1-212 989 7042, www.manatusnyc.com). Subway 1 to Christopher Street-Sheridan Square. **Open** 7am-2am Sun-Thur; 24hrs Fri, Sat. **Main courses** $9-$25. **Map** p397 D28.

Manatus both is and isn't your typical greasy-spoon diner. There are the standard plastic-coated menus listing dozens of fried food items, but distinguishing the place is a full bar, flattering lighting and a very gay clientele, especially late at night when tipsy bar-goers pile in.

Rocking Horse Café

182 Eighth Avenue, between 19th & 20th Streets, Chelsea (1-212 463 9511, www.rockinghorse cafe.com). Subway C, E to 23rd Street. **Open** noon-11pm Mon-Thur; noon-midnight Fri; 11am-midnight Sat; 11am-11pm Sun. **Main courses** $17-$23. **Map** p397 D27.

Eclectic Mexican cuisine is what originally established the Rocking Horse Café as a unique place to eat in Chelsea, but the bar now holds a distinguished reputation for its tongue-numbingly stiff frozen margaritas (the Two Fruit version features prickly pear and mango).

Superfine

126 Front Street, between Jay & Pearl Streets, Dumbo, Brooklyn (1-718 243 9005). Subway A, C to High Street; F to York Street. **Open** 11.30am-3pm, 6-11pm Mon-Sat; 11.30am-3pm, 6-10pm Sun. **Main courses** $18-$30. **Map** p405 T9.

Owned by a couple of super-cool lesbians, this eaterie, bar and gallery serves Mediterranean cuisine in a massive, hip space. The mellow vibe and pool table draw a mixed local crowd. The Sunday brunch is justifiably popular.

> **IN THE KNOW**
> **NOT-SO-SQUARE DANCING**
>
> If throbbing house music isn't your style, one alternative to a club is the **Big Apple Ranch**, a lively gay and lesbian country and western bash held every Saturday night at a Flatiron District dance studio (5th Floor, 39 W 19th Street, between Fifth & Sixth Avenues, 1-212 358 5752, www.bigappleranch.com). Admission is $10 and an 8pm lesson is followed by the party at 9pm – offering a chance to don your chaps and do-si-do.

Vynl

754 Ninth Avenue, between 50th & 51st Streets, Hell's Kitchen (1-212 974 2003, www.vynl-nyc.com). Subway C, E to 50th Street. **Open** 11am-11pm Mon-Wed; 11am-midnight Thur, Fri; 9.30am-midnight Sat; 9.30am-11pm Sun. **Main courses** $14-$19. **Map** p398 C23.

The boys love this pop music-themed eaterie, where old albums adorn the walls above the cosy booths and mirrorballs are shoved into every available space. Menu items are an odd mishmash of comfort food (burgers, turkey meatloaf) and Asian cuisine (massaman curry, veggie-basil stir-fry). Cocktails are named after pop icons and the vibe is all-around fun.

BARS & CLUBS

'It ain't what it used to be,' grumble veterans of New York's gay nightlife. And they're right. The after-hours scene is continually morphing – sometimes for the better, sometimes not. Club nights such as **Viva Saturdays** at **Stage 48** (605 W 48th Street, between Eleventh & Twelfth Aves, www.vivasaturdays.com) and **Electro Pop Saturdays** at **BPM** (*see p257*) draw crowds of hot guys looking to dance to tunes from big-name DJs and even the occasional slumming pop star. But for serious dance music fans, the real action is at smaller venues. The basement disco at the **Monster** (*see p260*) features reliably sweaty (in a good way) parties most nights, and MEN's JD Samson hosts **Scissor Sundays** at the **Rusty Knot** (425 West Street, West Village, 1-212 645 5668), a top-notch tea dance that assembles an eclectic crowd.

East Village

The Cock

29 Second Avenue, between 2nd & 3rd Streets (no phone, www.thecockbar.com). Subway F to Lower East Side-Second Avenue. **Open** 11pm-4am daily. **Admission** free-$10. **No credit cards. Map** p397 F29.

This grungy hole-in-the-wall still holds the title of New York's sleaziest gay hangout, but nowadays it's hit-and-miss. At weekends, it's a packed grind-fest, but on other nights the place can often be depressingly under-populated. It's best to go very late when the cruising is at its peak. *Photo p257.*

Eastern Bloc

505 E 6th Street, between Avenues A & B (1-212 777 2555, www.easternblocnyc.com). Subway F to Lower East-Side-Second Avenue. **Open** 7pm-4am daily. **No credit cards. Map** p397 G28.

This cool little space has mostly shed its commie revolutionary decor for a funky living-room feel. The bartenders are cuties, and there are nightly themes, DJs and happy hours to get the ball rolling.

ARTS & ENTERTAINMENT

HOT AS HELL'S KITCHEN

Once again, NYC's gay scene has migrated north.

Out NYC

In the 1990s, New York's Chelsea neighbourhood was undisputedly the city's – perhaps the world's – queerest zone. The Village had the history (and still does), but Chelsea had cheaper rents and empty storefronts just begging to be filled with bars and shops that specialised in colourful underwear favoured by the waxed, buff 'Chelsea boys', whose aesthetic defined the era in gay New York.

But then history repeated itself. Like the Village, Chelsea became overpriced and clogged with wealthy straight people who lived in glass towers in the formerly industrial turf around the High Line. Soon, seemingly immortal queer businesses like the rough-and-tumble dive Rawhide and pioneering dance club Splash lost their leases. The area became a nightlife ghost town, and once again, things moved north.

Today, Hell's Kitchen reigns as the city's gayest gaybourhood, though it hasn't quite earned Chelsea's reputation outside of the five boroughs. Take a stroll through the area any night, and you'll see cute boys (and some girls) spilling out of bars, clubs and restaurants with rainbow flags proudly flapping outside. HK is even home to the city's first luxury gay hotel, the **Out NYC** (*see p257*), a sort of gay megaplex, which includes rooms arranged around a variety of themed courtyards, a 5,000-square-foot spa, the Rosebud NYC cocktail bar and BPM nightclub, which draws big-name DJs from around the world.

Unlike the intimidatingly fitness-focused '90s Chelsea scene, HK is relaxed and diverse. You'll find well-dressed businessmen drinking next to fanny-packed Midwestern tourists and bearded Brooklyn boys, and most venues welcome female patrons (gay and straight). Your hetero friends will feel right at home at bars like **Therapy** and **Industry** (for both, *see p262*) since HK bars rarely get overly cruisy or sexual – for that, you'll still have to head downtown.

★ Nowhere

322 E 14th Street, at First Avenue (1-212 477 4744, www.nowherebarnyc.com). Subway L to First Avenue. **Open** 3pm-4am daily. **No credit cards. Map** p397 F27.

Low ceilings and dim lighting help to create a speakeasy vibe at this subterranean bar. The place attracts everyone from young lesbians to bears, thanks to an entertaining line-up of theme nights. Tuesdays are especially fun, when DJ Damian's long-running Buddies party takes over. The pool table is another big draw.

West Village

★ Cubbyhole

281 W 12th Street, between 4th Street & Greenwich Avenue (1-212 243 9041, www.cubbyholebar.com). Subway A, C, E to 14th Street; L to Eighth Avenue. **Open** 4pm-4am Mon-Fri; 2pm-4am Sat, Sun. **No credit cards. Map** p397 E28.

This minuscule spot is filled with flirtatious girls (and their dyke-friendly boy pals), with the standard set of Melissa Etheridge or kd lang blaring. Chinese lanterns, tissue-paper fish and old holiday decorations emphasise the festive, homespun charm.

Henrietta Hudson

438 Hudson Street, at Morton Street (1-212 924 3347, www.henriettahudson.com). Subway 1 to Houston Street. **Open** 5pm-2am Mon, Tue; 4pm-4am Wed-Fri; 2pm-4am Sat; 2pm-2am Sun. **Admission** free-$10. **Map** p403 D29.

A much-loved lesbian hangout, this glam lounge attracts hottie girls from all over the New York area. Every night is different, with hip hop, pop, rock and live shows among the musical offerings.

The Monster

80 Grove Street, at Sheridan Square (1-212 924 3558, www.manhattan-monster.com). Subway 1 to Christopher Street-Sheridan Square. **Open** 4pm-4am Mon-Fri; 2pm-4am Sat, Sun. **No credit cards. Map** p397 D28.

Upstairs, locals gather to sing showtunes in the piano lounge, adorned with strings of lights and rainbow paraphernalia. The downstairs dancefloor has seen something of a renaissance lately, hosting top-notch house and disco events.

Rockbar

185 Christopher Street, at Weehawken Street (1-212 675 1864, www.rockbarnyc.com). Subway 1 to Christopher Street-Sheridan Square. **Open** 6pm-2am Mon-Wed; 4pm-2am Thur; 4pm-4am Fri, Sat; 1pm-2am Sun. **Map** p397 C29.

A burly, bearish crowd tends to congregate at this far-west dive with a rock 'n' roll theme. Various events include dance parties, game nights, comedy showcases and musical performances.

IN THE KNOW SEEKING SEX

While gay men in New York tend to organise encounters online or on mobile apps such as Grindr (www.grindr.com) and Scruff (www.scruffapp.com), those who favour an old-school approach can try the **West Side Club** (2nd floor, 27 W 20th Street, between Fifth & Sixth Avenues, 1-212 691 2700, www.westsideclubnyc.com) or the **East Side Club** (6th floor, 227 E 56th Street, between Second & Third Avenues, 1-212 753 2222, www.eastsideclubnyc.com). For between $18 and $22 (plus a $15 temporary membership, which entitles you to five visits within 30 days), each of these clubs gives you four hours of cruising dark hallways lined with nooks and private rooms.

Stonewall Inn

53 Christopher Street, at Waverly Place (1-212 488 2705, www.thestonewallinnnyc.com). Subway 1 to Christopher Street-Sheridan Square. **Open** 2pm-4am Mon-Sat; noon-4am Sun. **Map** p397 D28.

This gay landmark is the site of the 1969 gay rebellion against police harassment (though back then it also included the building next door). Special nights range from dance soirées and drag shows to burlesque performances and bingo gatherings.

► *While you're here, check out George Segal's sculptures in nearby Christopher Park; see p114.*

Chelsea & Flatiron District

Barracuda

275 W 22nd Street, between Seventh & Eighth Avenues (1-212 645 8613, www.facebook.com/barracudalounge). Subway C, E, 1 to 23rd Street. **Open** 4pm-4am daily. **No credit cards. Map** p398 D26.

This much beloved, slightly divey Chelsea institution is one of the most reliably bustling spots in the neighbourhood. Some of the city's most talented drag queens perform here nightly. Drinks are on the pricey side, but you'll often get a great show with no cover, so it balances out.

★ Eagle

554 W 28th Street, at Eleventh Avenue (1-646 473 1866, www.eaglenyc.com). Subway C, E to 23rd Street. **Open** 9pm-4am Mon-Sat; 5pm-4am Sun (extended hrs in summer). **No credit cards. Map** p398 C26.

You don't have to be a kinky leather daddy to enjoy this manly spot, but it definitely doesn't hurt. The fetish bar is home to an array of beer blasts, foot-worship fêtes and leather soirées, plus simple pool playing and cruising nights. Thursdays are gear night, so be sure to dress the part or you might not get past the doorman. In summer, the rooftop is a surprising oasis.

G Lounge

225 W 19th Street, at Seventh Avenue (1-212 929 1085, www.glounge.com). Subway 1 to 18th Street. **Open** 4pm-4am daily. **No credit cards.** **Map** p397 D27.

The neighbourhood's original slick boy lounge – a moodily lit cave with a cool brick-and-glass arched entrance – wouldn't look out of place in a boutique hotel. It's a favourite after-work cocktail spot, where a roster of DJs stays on top of the mood.

Gym Sports Bar

167 Eighth Avenue, between 18th & 19th Streets (1-212 337 2439, www.gymsportsbar.com). Subway A, C, E to 14th Street; L to Eighth Avenue. **Open** 4pm-2am Mon-Thur; 4pm-4am Fri; 1pm-4am Sat; 1pm-2am Sun. **Map** p397 D27.

This popular spot is all about games – of the actual sporting variety. Catch theme parties that revolve around gay sports leagues, play at the pool tables and video games, or watch the pro events from rodeo competitions to figure skating shown on big-screen TVs.

Hell's Kitchen & Theater District

Atlas Social Club

753 Ninth Avenue, between 50th & 51st Streets (1-212 762 8527, www.atlassocialclub.com). Subway C, E to 50th Street. **Open** 4pm-4am Mon-Sat; 3pm-4am Sun. **Map** p398 C23.

This drinkery, designed to look like a cross between an old-school athletic club and a speakeasy, is one of the more relaxed options on the HK strip – at least when it's not packed to the gills, which it can be on weekends. Be sure to check out the bathrooms, which are brightly papered with vintage beefcake and sports magazines.

★ FairyTail Lounge

500 W 48th Street, at Tenth Avenue (1-646 684 3897, www.fairytailnyc.com). Subway C, E to 50th Street. **Open** 5pm-2am Mon, Tue; 5pm-3am Thur-Sun. **Map** p398 B23.

An easy-to-miss entrance belies the psychedelic, pseudo-Victorian enchanted forest waiting inside this friendly watering hole. Whether you find a mellow happy-hour crowd or a hyper dance party, the vibe is more East Village arty than midtown pretty-boy scene.

Flaming Saddles

793 Ninth Avenue, at 53rd Street (1-212 713 0481, www.flamingsaddles.com). Subway C, E to 50th Street. **Open** 3pm-3am Mon-Thur,

FairyTail Lounge.

ARTS & ENTERTAINMENT

Sun; 3pm-4am Fri, Sat. **No credit cards**. **Map** p399 C23.
City boys can party honky-tonk-style at this country and western gay bar. It's outfitted to look like a Wild West bordello, with red velvet drapes, antler sconces and rococo wallpaper. Performances by bartenders dancing in cowboy boots add to the raucous vibe.

Industry

355 W 52nd Street, between Eighth & Ninth Avenues (1-646 476 2747, www.industrybar.com). Subway C, E to 50th Street. **Open** 4pm-4am daily. **No credit cards**. **Map** p399 C23.
Pretty boys flock to this appropriately named garage-like industrial-chic boite, which features a stage for regular drag shows and other performances, a pool table, and couches for lounging. DJs spin nightly to a sexy, fashionable crowd.

InFuse 51

331 W 51st Street, between Eighth & Ninth Avenues (1-212 974 8030, www.infuse51.com). Subway C, E to 50th Street. **Open** 4pm-4am daily. **Map** p398 C23.
Formerly Vlada, this vodka-focused drinkery has more than a dozen infused versions of the spirit, as well as food incorporating the concoctions. Drag shows take over the space Sunday to Wednesday, and skew more towards quirky and scary than campy.

Flaming Saddles. See p261.

Therapy

348 W 52nd Street, between Eighth & Ninth Avenues (1-212 397 1700, www.therapy-nyc.com). Subway C, E to 50th Street. **Open** 5pm-2am Mon-Wed, Sun; 5pm-4am Thur-Sat. **Map** p398 C23.
Therapy is just what your analyst ordered. The dramatic two-level space offers comedy and musical performances, some clever cocktails (including the Freudian Sip) and a crowd of well-scrubbed boys. You'll find good food and a cosy fireplace to boot.

Brooklyn

Excelsior

390 Fifth Avenue, between 6th & 7th Streets, Park Slope (1-718 832 1599, www.excelsiorbrooklyn.com). Subway F, R to Fourth Avenue-9th Street. **Open** 6pm-4am Mon-Fri; 2pm-4am Sat, Sun. **No credit cards**. **Map** p404 T11.
Homey Excelsior has a friendly neighbourhood crowd, an eclectic jukebox and plenty of beers on tap. This straight-friendly spot attracts gay men, lesbians and their hetero pals looking to catch up without the fuss found in trendy lounge bars.

Ginger's Bar

363 Fifth Avenue, between 5th & 6th Streets, Park Slope (1-718 788 0924, www.gingersbarbklyn.com). Subway F, R to Fourth Avenue-9th Street. **Open** 5pm-4am Mon-Fri; 2pm-4am Sat, Sun. **No credit cards**. **Map** p404 T11.
The front room of Ginger's, with its dark-wood bar, looks out on to a bustling street. The back, with an always-busy pool table, evokes a rec room, while the patio feels like a friend's yard. This local hangout is full of all sorts of dykes, many with their dogs – or favourite gay boys – in tow.

Metropolitan

559 Lorimer Street, at Metropolitan Avenue, Williamsburg (1-718 599 4444, www.metropolitanbarny.com). Subway G to Metropolitan Avenue; L to Lorimer Street. **Open** 3pm-4am daily. **Map** p405 V8.
Some Williamsburg spots are a little pretentious, but not this refreshingly unfancy bar, which resembles a 1960s ski lodge, complete with a brick fireplace. Guys dominate, but there's always a female contingent, and even some straight folks. There are weekend barbecues on the patio in summer.

★ This n' That (TNT)

108 North 6th Street, between Berry Street & Wythe Avenue, Williamsburg (1-718 599 5959, www.thisnthatbrooklyn.com). Subway L to Bedford Avenue. **Open** 4pm-4am daily. **Map** p405 U7.
This cavernous boite is parked in the middle of the most hipstery block of the city's most hipstery neighbourhood. Still, most nights you'll find a surprisingly unpretentious crowd here, enjoying various parties (trivia, movie nights, sweaty dance fests).

Nightlife

New York nightlife has an amazing history, and although the clubbing crown has passed to European cities, there's fun to be had here still. Roving parties are revitalising the after-dark landscape, and now that the Verboten gang is due to open an eponymous venue on North 11th Street, Williamsburg has officially become New York's clubland paradise.

The newest major music venue, the Barclays Center in Brooklyn, has attracted an unexpectedly cool list of acts. For smaller rock gigs, hit the Lower East Side or Williamsburg; the latter is the epicentre of the indie rock scene.

Classic cabaret took a hit in 2012 with the closure of the iconic Oak Room, but 54 Below stepped into the spotlight, and a boundary-pushing generation of performers is reinvigorating the genre. Comedy, meanwhile, is enjoying a moment, with thriving clubs and theatres across the city.

Clubs

Hallowed halls such as the Loft, Studio 54, the Paradise Garage and Area are imbedded in nightlife's collective consciousness as near-mythic ideals. But in this millennium? Well, the city can no longer claim to be the world's clubbing capital; the balance of power has shifted eastward to cities like London and Berlin. Still, with this much history (not to mention eight million people ready to party), New York nightlife can never be counted out – and the scene today is as strong as it's been in years. This is largely thanks to a burst of nomadic shindigs, often held in out-of-the-way warehouses and lofts; a visit to www.timeout.com/newyork should help to clue you in.

IN THE KNOW
WALLET ESSENTIALS

Most clubs operate an over-21 policy, and even if you're in the running for the World's Oldest Clubber award, you'll need a government-issued ID (such as a passport or driving licence) to gain admission. It's also worth carrying cash, as most clubs won't accept credit cards at the door.

DANCE CLUBS

Le Bain
The Standard, 444 W 13th Street, at Washington Street, Meatpacking District (1-212 645 4646, www.standardhotels.com). Subway A, C, E to 14th Street; L to Eighth Avenue. **Open** 11pm-4am Wed-Sun. **Admission** free. **Map** p397 C27.
Although an EDM-driven club scene is filling bigger and bigger venues, for a more intimate night out, head to this penthouse club and terrace atop the Standard hotel. In the swanky space, which offers spectacular Hudson River views from floor-to-ceiling windows, you can get within hugging distance of underground superstars that have included disco daddy Dimitri from Paris, deep-house kingpin Marques Wyatt and the aurally anarchic DJ Harvey.

Cielo.

★ Cielo

18 Little W 12th Street, at Ninth Avenue, Meatpacking District (1-212 645 5700, www.cieloclub.com). Subway A, C, E to 14th Street; L to Eighth Avenue. **Open** 10pm-4am Mon, Wed-Sat. **Admission** $12-$25. **Map** p397 C28.

You'd never guess from all the Kardashian wannabes hanging out in the neighbourhood that the attitude at this exclusive club is close to zero – at least once you get past the bouncers on the door. On the sunken dancefloor, hip-to-hip crowds gyrate to deep beats from top DJs, including NYC old-schoolers François K, Tedd Patterson and Louie Vega. Cielo, which features a crystal-clear sound system (by the legendary Funktion One), has won a bevy of 'best club' awards.

Marquee

289 Tenth Avenue, between 26th & 27th Streets, Chelsea (1-646 473 0202, www.marqueeny.com). Subway C, E to 23rd Street. **Open** 11pm-4am Wed-Sat. **Admission** varies **Map** p398 C26.

After shutting down for major renovations, the one-time models-and-bottles clubs Marquee has re-emerged…as a models-and-bottles club! In fairness, Marquee 2.0 is an entirely different – and in our opinion, far better – beast than it was in its original incarnation, with more open space, all manner of disco lights (including an impressive LCD screen behind the booth) and enough general razzle-dazzle to make your head spin. Most importantly, the Friday-night bookings have been taken over by NYC power couple Sleepy & Boo, who have been bringing in the world's house-and-techo elite – Slam, Marco Carola, Damian Lazarus, the Martinez Brothers and the like – to work their four-to-the-floor magic.

Output

74 Wythe Avenue, at North 12th Street, Williamsburg (no phone, www.outputclub.com). Subway L to Bedford Avenue. **Open** 10pm-4am Wed, Thur; 10pm-6am Fri, Sat. **Admission** varies. **Map** p405 U7.

With the opening of Output in early 2013, New York nightlife's centre of gravity continues its eastward push into Brooklyn. Akin in ethos to such underground-music headquarters as Berlin's Berghain/Panorama Bar complex or London's Fabric, the club boasts a warehouse-party vibe and a killer sound system. Top-shelf DJs (both international hotshots and local heroes) spin the kind of left-field house, techno and bass music you rarely hear in more commercially oriented spots. Head to the rooftop bar – the view of the Manhattan skyline is a stunner.

Pacha

618 W 46th Street, between Eleventh & Twelfth Avenues, Hell's Kitchen (1-212 209 7500, www.pachanyc.com). Subway C, E to 50th Street. **Open** 10pm-6am Fri; 10pm-8am Sat. **Admission** $10-$40. **No credit cards** (online purchases and bar only). **Map** p398 B23.

The worldwide glam-club chain Pacha, with outposts in nightlife capitals such as Ibiza, London and Buenos Aires, hit the US market back in 2005 with this swanky joint helmed by superstar spinner Erick Morillo. The spot attracts heavyweights ranging from local hero Danny Tenaglia to international crowd-pleasers such as Fedde Le Grande and Benny Benassi. Like most big clubs, it pays to check the line-up in advance if you're into underground (as opposed to lowest-common-denominator) beats.

★ Santos Party House

96 Lafayette Street, between Walker & White Streets, Tribeca (1-212 584 5492, www.santospartyhouse.com). Subway J, N, Q, R, Z, 6 to Canal Street. **Open** varies. **Admission** $10-$25. **No credit cards** (online purchases and bar only). **Map** p396 E31.

Launched by a team that includes rocker Andrew WK, Santos Party House – two black, square rooms done out in a bare-bones, generic club style – was initially hailed as a scene game-changer. While those too-high expectations didn't exactly pan out, it's still a rock-solid choice, particularly when Danny Krivit takes the spot over for the soulful house and classics-oriented 718 Sessions (www.dannykrivit.net).

Sapphire

249 Eldridge Street, between Houston & Stanton Streets, Lower East Side (1-212 777 5153, www.sapphirenyc.com). Subway F to Lower East Side-Second Avenue. **Open** 7pm-4am daily. **Admission** free-$10. **No credit cards** (bar only). **Map** p397 F29.

Sapphire's bare walls and minimal decor are as raw as it gets, yet the energetic, unpretentious clientele is oblivious to the (lack of) aesthetic. A dance crowd packs the place all week – various nights feature house, hip hop, reggae and disco. Admission is usually free, except for a small cover charge after 11pm on weekend nights.

Webster Hall

125 E 11th Street, at Third Avenue, East Village (1-212 353 1600, www.websterhall.com). Subway L to Third Avenue; L, N, Q, R, 4, 5, 6 to 14th Street-Union Square. **Open** 10pm-4am Thur-Sat. **Admission** free-$30. **Map** p397 F28.

The grand Webster Hall isn't exactly on clubland's A-list, due to a populist DJ policy and a crowd that favours muscle shirts and gelled hair. But hey, it's been open, on and off, since 1866, so it must be doing something right. Friday night's Girls & Boys bash attracts music makers of the stature of Grandmaster Flash and dubstep duo Nero.

BURLESQUE CLUBS

New York's burlesque scene is a winking throwback to the days when the tease was as important as the strip. Much of the scene tends to revolve around specific revues rather than dedicated venues; good bets include **Wasabassco Burlesque** (www.wasabassco.com) at the Bell House (*see p272*) and the Saturday-night **Floating Kabarette** at **Galapagos Art Space** (*see p273*) in Dumbo, Brooklyn. Some of the best producers and performers – they often cross over – are Shien

Santos Party House.

Lee (www.dancesofvice.com), Jen Gapay's Thirsty Girl Productions (www.thirstygirl productions.com), Angie Pontani of the World Famous Pontani Sisters (www.angiepontani.com) and Calamity Chang, 'the Asian Sexation' (www.calamitychang.com).

Duane Park

308 Bowery, between Bleecker & E Houston Streets (1-212 732 5555, www.duaneparknyc.com). Subway F to Lower East Side-Second Avenue; 6 to Astor Place. **Shows** 8pm Tue; 9pm Wed, Thur; 10pm Fri; 8pm, 10.30pm Sat. **Admission** varies. **Map** p397 F29.

Formerly the Bowery Poetry Club, the venue now operates as Southern-inflected supper club Duane Park from Tuesday to Saturday, but Bowery Poetry (www.bowerypoetry.com) still holds events on Sundays and Mondays. Get dinner and a show – burlesque, jazz, vaudeville or magic – in decadent surroundings featuring crystal chandeliers and Corinthian-topped columns.

Nurse Bettie

106 Norfolk Street, between Delancey & Rivington Streets, Lower East Side (1-212 477 7515, www.nursebettie.com). Subway F to Delancey Street; J, Z to Delancey-Essex Streets. **Open** 6pm-4am daily. **Admission** free. **Map** p397 G30.

The '50s-pinup-inspired venue – named after Bettie Page, one of the 20th century's premier hotsy-totsies – is a natural setting for burlesque. Weekly shows include Spanking of the Lower East Side, produced by Calamity Chang, which usually includes six or seven acts, as well as pre-show go-go dancers. Prepare to get up close and personal in the intimate space.

Slipper Room

167 Orchard Street, at Stanton Street, Lower East Side (1-212 253 7246, www.slipperroom.com). Subway F to Lower East Side-Second Avenue. **Open** varies Mon, Sun; 7pm-3am Tue-Thur; 8.30pm-4am Fri, Sat. **Admission** $10-$20. **No credit cards** (online purchases & bar only). **Map** p397 F29.

After being rebuilt from the ground up (which took a little more than two years), the Slipper Room reopened with a better sound system, new lighting and a mezzanine, among other swank touches, and reclaimed its place as the city's premier burlesque venue. Many of the shows that once called it home, including Mr. Choade's Upstairs Downstairs (which began in 1999), have returned, and the setting is as intimate and fun as ever – but with upgrades that make the experience better than before.

DANCE PARTIES

New York has a number of regular, peripatetic and season-specific bashes. Check the websites listed for dates and locations.

Blkmarket Membership

www.blkmarketmembership.com.

Competing with the Bunker for the unofficial title of NYC's best techno party, the Blkmarket crew hosts bashes in the city's established clubs as well as out-of-the-way warehouse spaces.

★ The Bunker

www.thebunkerny.com.

As befits the party that helped to kick off the current craze for all things techno in NYC, Bunker main man

Spanking of the Lower East Side at **Nurse Bettie**.

DJ Spinoza is still scoring at his Friday- or Saturday-night get-together once or twice a month. Big guns from such labels as Spectral Sound and Kompakt regularly pack spaces such as Output (*see p264*), and the bash is busier than ever despite running for more than a decade.

★ Body & Soul

www.bodyandsoul-nyc.com.

Some people call the long-running spiritual-house hoedown Body & Soul the best party ever to fill a dancefloor in NYC. The Sunday-night tea dance, helmed by the holy DJ trinity of Danny Krivit, Joe Claussell and François K, is certainly in the top ten. It's no longer a weekly affair – a few editions a year will have to do – but it's still a spectacle, with a few thousand sweaty revellers dancing their hearts out.

Mister Saturday Night/Mister Sunday

www.mistersaturdaynight.com.

Two of clubland's stalwart DJs, Justin Carter and Eamon Harkin, have pooled their years of experience to throw the friendliest of parties in venues ranging from intimate loft spaces and raw warehouses to tree-shaded meadows. The music runs the gamut too – deep disco, jacking house, and outer-fringes dubstep and techno – with some of the underground's top names stopping by for a date on the decks.

Turntables on the Hudson

www.turntablesonthehudson.com.

This ultra-funky affair lost its longtime home at the Lightship Frying Pan when the city put the kibosh on the vessel's parties, but resident Nickodemus and his crew still pop up at clubs and loft spaces all over the city (though rarely on the Hudson itself).

Verboten

www.verbotennewyork.com.

The house-music-loving Verboten crew have been tossing top-shelf, one-off affairs all over the city for more than ten years, but look out for a permanent 750-capacity club in Williamsburg, Brooklyn (no opening date had been confirmed at time of writing).

★ Warm Up

MoMA PS1 (for listings, *see p220*). **Open** July, Aug noon-9pm Sat. **Admission** call or see website. **Map** p406 V5.

Since 1997, PS1's courtyard has played host to one of the most anticipated, resolutely underground clubbing events in the city. Thousands of dance-music fanatics and alt-rock enthusiasts make the pilgrimage to Long Island City on summer Saturdays to drink and dance. The sounds range from spiritually inclined soul to full-bore techno.

Comedy

Beyond the dedicated venues, you'll find many worthwhile shows in the back rooms of pubs and other venues. Look out for **Big Terrific**, hosted by Max Silvestri, at Cameo (www.cameony.com) and **Comedy at the Knitting Factory** (*see p276*) with Hannibal Buress.

COMEDY VENUES

Broadway Comedy Club

318 W 53rd Street, between Eighth & Ninth Avenues, Theater District (1-212 757 2323, www.broadwaycomedyclub.com). Subway C, E to 50th Street. **Shows** 9pm, 11pm Mon-Thur, Sun; 9pm, 11pm, midnight, Sat, Sun. **Admission** $20 (2-drink min). **Map** p398 D23.

BCC features TV faces and club circuit regulars. On Friday and Saturday, it's home to Chicago City Limits (1-212 888 5233, www.chicagocitylimits.com); the group's format of topical sketches, songs and audience-inspired improv can seem a little dated.

★ Carolines on Broadway

1626 Broadway, between 49th & 50th Streets, Theater District (1-212 757 4100, www.carolines.com). Subway N, Q, R to 49th Street; 1 to 50th Street. **Shows** vary. **Admission** varies (2-drink min). **Map** p398 D23.

Carolines is a New York City institution. It's attained that status in part because of its long-term relationships with national headliners, sitcom stars and cable-special pros, which ensures that its stage always features marquee names. Although the majority of bookings skew towards mainstream, the club also makes time for undisputedly darker and edgier fare, such as Paul Mooney and Louis CK.

Comedy Cellar

117 MacDougal Street, between Bleecker & 3rd Streets, Greenwich Village (1-212 254 3480, www.comedycellar.com). Subway A, B, C, D, E, F, M to W 4th Street. **Shows** 8pm, 10pm Mon, Tue;

Greenwich Village Comedy Club.

8pm, 9.45pm, 11.30pm Wed; 8pm, 10pm, midnight Thur; 7pm, 8.45pm, 10.30pm, 12.15am Fri; 7.30pm, 9.15pm, 11pm, 12.45am Sat. **Admission** $12-$24 (2-item min). **Map** p397 E29.
Despite being dubbed one of the best stand-up clubs in the city year after year, the Comedy Cellar has maintained a hip, underground feel. It gets incredibly crowded, but the bookings, which typically include no-nonsense comics Dave Chapelle, Jim Norton and Marina Franklin, are enough to distract you from your bachelorette party neighbours.
Other locations Comedy Cellar at the Village Underground, 130 W 3rd Street, between Sixth Avenue & Macdougal Street, Greenwich Village (1-212 254 3480).

Comic Strip Live
1568 Second Avenue, between 81st & 82nd Streets, Upper East Side (1-212 861 9386, www.comicstriplive.com). Subway 4, 5, 6 to 86th Street. **Shows** 8.30pm Mon-Thur, Sun; 8pm, 10.30pm Fri, Sat. **Admission** $15-$20 (2-drink min). **Map** p399 F19.
The Upper East Side isn't a breeding ground for edgy entertainment, so cherish this fabled, long-running showcase. Established in 1975, CSL launched the careers of Eddie Murphy and Chris Rock. The fare is more standard these days, but the club does attract a lot of stand-ups from the late-night talk-show circuit.

The Creek & the Cave
10-93 Jackson Avenue, at 11th Street, Long Island City, Queens (1-718 706 8783, www.creeklic.com). Subway 7 to Vernon Boulevard-Jackson Avenue. **Shows** daily, times vary. **Admission** free-$5. **Map** p406 V5.
This hardworking Long Island City venue offers all the things comedians and their fans need to survive: multiple performance spaces, convivial environs, a fully stocked bar, cheap Mexican food and a patio on which to rant and laugh late into the night. As if this weren't enough, owner Rebecca Trent also shows her appreciation for all who make the trek to Queens by making nearly every show free.

Dangerfield's
1118 First Avenue, between 61st & 62nd Streets, Upper East Side (1-212 593 1650, www.dangerfields.com). Subway N, Q, R to Lexington Avenue-59th Street; 4, 5, 6 to 59th Street. **Shows** 8.30pm Mon-Thur, Sun; 8.30pm, 10.30pm, 12.30am Fri; 8pm, 10.30pm, 12.30am Sat. **Admission** $20 (2-item min). **Map** p399 F22.
The decor and gentility of the city's oldest comedy club are throwbacks to the era of its founder, the late great Rodney Dangerfield, who established it in 1969. Instead of putting eight to ten comics in a showcase, on weekends Dangerfield's gives three or four stand-ups the opportunity to settle into longer acts.

Gotham Comedy Club
208 W 23rd Street, between Seventh & Eighth Avenues, Chelsea (1-212 367 9000, www.gothamcomedyclub.com). Subway F, M, N, R to 23rd Street. **Shows** vary Mon-Thur, Sun; 8.30pm, 10.30pm Fri; 8pm, 10pm, 11.45pm Sat. **Admission** $10-$30 (2-drink min). **Map** p398 D26.
Chris Mazzilli's vision for his club involves elegant surroundings, professional behaviour and mutual respect. That's why the talents he fosters, such as Jim Gaffigan, Tom Papa and Ted Alexandro, keep coming back here after they've found national fame.

Greenwich Village Comedy Club
99 MacDougal Street, between Bleecker Street & Minetta Lane, Greenwich Village (1-212 777 5233, www.greenwichvillagecomedyclub.com). Subway A, B, C, D, E, F, M to W 4th Street. **Shows** 9.30pm Mon-Thur, Sun; 9pm, 11.30pm Fri; 8.30pm, 10.30pm, 12.30am Sat. **Admission** $20 (2-drink min). **Map** p397 E29.
Al Martin, the longtime owner of both the New York Comedy Club and Broadway Comedy Club, follows the same basic tenets in his latest venture, an intimate basement space below an Indian restaurant. Although a few pillars in the 60-seat room interfere with sight lines, the pub grub, extensive cocktail selection and long list of stars who just might do a spot while passing through town are drawing crowds every night.

Magnet Theater
254 W 29th Street, between Seventh & Eighth Avenues, Chelsea (1-212 244 8824, www.magnettheater.com). Subway A, C, E to 34th Street-Penn Station; 1 to 28th Street. **Shows** vary. **Admission** free-$10. **Map** p398 D25.

This comedy theatre exudes a distinctly Chicago vibe, from its DIY aesthetic to its performers, some of whom are from the Windy City. Even the local players here prefer theatrical to premise-based improvisation, and their shows give the impression they're not just seeking fame or commercial exposure, but pursue the craft simply for the joy of being on stage.

Peoples Improv Theater

123 E 24th Street, between Park & Lexington Avenues, Flatiron District (1-212 563 7488, www.thepit-nyc.com). Subway 6 to 23rd Street. **Shows** daily, times vary. **Admission** free-$20. **Map** p398 E26.

After inhabiting a black box in Chelsea for eight years, the PIT leapt across town into the former Algonquin Theatre space, where the improv and sketch venue has upgraded to a beautiful proscenium stage, an additional basement space for experimental shows or stand-up, and an elegant (if cluttered) full-service bar.

The Stand

239 Third Avenue, between 19th & 20th Streets, Gramercy Park (1-212 677 2600, www.thestandnyc.com). Subway L, N, Q, R, 4, 5, 6 to 14th Street-Union Square. **Open** 5.30pm-midnight Mon, Tue, Sun; 5.30pm-2am Wed-Sat. **Shows** 8.30pm

NYC COMEDY 101

A few tips from TONY's comedy editor, Matthew Love.

Whiplash.

FALL IN LINE

NYC's reputation as a stand-up hub is unquestioned, but it also boasts a strong long-form improv scene. Start with the best – the **Upright Citizens Brigade Theatre** (*see p270*). Its **ASSSSCAT 3000** on Sundays features a rotating cast making up scenes based on the stories of a celebrity monologuist. Tickets to the 7.30pm show are $10, and tend to sell out weeks in advance. The one at 9.30pm, however, is always free, and tickets are distributed at 8.15pm outside the theatre. (Psst, the line forms around 7pm.)

STAY UP LATE

Keep caffeinated – some of the top gigs go down way past bedtime. On Mondays at 11pm, the UCB throws **Whiplash**, a free show that speeds through up-and-coming and big-name comics. Reservations can be made online, but get there at least 15 minutes early. Stop by **Gotham Comedy Club** (*see p268*) on a Tuesday night at 9.30pm for **ComedyJuice**, in which national headliners practise new jokes. Tickets are $15 (plus a two-item minimum).

EXPLORE BROOKLYN

Head to Park Slope and Gowanus, where the **Bell House** (*see p272*), **Union Hall** (*see p279*) and art/performance space **Littlefield** (622 DeGraw Street, between Third & Fourth Avenues, Gowanus, Brooklyn, www.littlefieldnyc.com) are within a square mile of one another, and regularly host great events. Bonus: they all have cool bars and reasonable entry fees.

LOOK FOR SURPRISES

Watch for the phrase 'and special guests'. Famous comics often try out their material on unsuspecting crowds. It's not uncommon to see Jim Gaffigan or Mike Birbiglia drop in unannounced – or even Louis CK, Aziz Ansari, Chris Rock or a visiting Zach Galifianakis.

Mon-Thur; 8.30pm, 10.30pm, midnight Fri, Sat; 7pm, 9pm Sun. **Admission** $5-$40. **Map** p397 F27.
After producing popular stand-up shows for years, the four partners behind Cringe Humor (cringe humor.net) founded a venue in which to promote their favourite comics – think bawdy, raw and dark acts like Jim Norton and Dave Attell. The bi-level Gramercy spot offers cocktails and embellished comfort food upstairs, while shows take place seven nights a week in its long, narrow basement. The snug 80-seat room places the audience of frat guys and young professionals in close proximity to the performers, and they get pumped when one of their idols (Dane Cook, for instance) drops by.

Stand-up New York

236 W 78th Street, at Broadway, Upper West Side (1-212 595 0850, www.standupny.com). Subway 1 to 79th Street. **Shows** 8pm, 10pm Mon-Thur; 7pm, 9pm, 11pm Fri; 5pm, 7pm, 11pm Sat; 8pm, 10pm Sun. **Admission** $15-$20 (2-drink min). **Map** p399 C19.
After some managerial shifts, this musty uptown spot has begun to garner attention again. The line-ups (including stalwart club denizens such as Jay Oakerson and Godfrey) keep things pretty simple, but there's almost always one performer on the bill that makes it worth the trip.

Tribeca Comedy Lounge

22 Warren Street, between Broadway & Church Street, Tribeca (1-646 504 5653, www.tribeca comedylounge.com). Subway A, C, 1, 2, 3 to Chambers Street; N, R to City Hall. **Shows** 8pm Tue-Thur; 8pm, 10pm Fri, Sat. **Admission** $20 (2-drink min). **Map** p396 E32.
The atmosphere in this spot – not to be confused with the space's previous occupant, the Tribeca Comedy Club – is a congenial one. The brick walls and makeshift stage remind you that you're in a basement, but the doting waitstaff, haute Italian menu from Brick NYC upstairs and roomy layout will please fans of creature comforts. Adam Strauss, the owner-booker and a burgeoning comic himself, makes sure that his programming is packed with next-wave talent (young, funny stars such as Sara Schaefer, Dan St Germain and Kevin Barnett) while also saving stage time for himself.

★ Upright Citizens Brigade Theatre

307 W 26th Street, at Eighth Avenue, Chelsea (1-212 366 9176, www.ucbtheatre.com). Subway C, E to 23rd Street; 1 to 28th Street. **Shows** daily, times vary. **Admission** free-$10. **No credit cards**. **Map** p398 D26.
The most visible catalyst in New York's current alternative comedy boom. The improv troupes and sketch groups here are some of the best in the city. Stars of *Saturday Night Live* and writers for late-night talk-shows gather on Sunday nights to wow crowds in the long-running ASSSSCAT 3000. Other premier teams include the Stepfathers (Friday) and Death by Roo Roo (Saturday). Arrive early for a good seat – the venue has challenging sightlines.

UCBEast (153 E Third Street, East Village, 1-212 366 9231), which opened in 2011, gave the enormous community another space – and a bar. The warm lighting and low, rounded ceiling of the ex-arthouse cinema create immediate intimacy, whether the fare is improv or stand-up, and the venue snapped up some of the fledgling comedy variety shows that were scattered in East Side venues.

Tribeca Comedy Lounge.

Barclays Center.

Music

ROCK, POP & SOUL

Not only are venues offering increasingly eclectic fare, but gigs are also busting out of their usual club and concert hall confines: the **City Winery** (*see p273*) crushes and ferments grapes as well as staging shows, while bowling alley-music venue hybrid **Brooklyn Bowl** (61 Wythe Avenue, between North 11th & 12th Streets, Williamsburg, Brooklyn, 1-718 963 3369, www.brooklynbowl.com) has a 600-capacity space that features small acts for tiny cover charges, as well as a smattering of larger concerts (Art Brut, Sharon Jones & the Dap-Kings).

Information & tickets

Tickets are usually available from clubs in advance and at the door, though a few small and medium-size venues also sell tickets through local record stores. For larger events, buy online through the venue's website or through **Ticketmaster** or **TicketWeb** (for both, *see p296*). Phone ahead for information and show times, which often change without notice.

Major arenas & stadiums

★ Barclays Center

620 Atlantic Avenue, at Flatbush Avenue, Prospect Heights, Brooklyn (1-917 618 6700, www.barclays center.com) Subway B, D, N, Q, R, 2, 3, 4, 5 to Atlantic Avenue-Barclays Center. **Box office** noon-6pm Mon-Fri; noon-2pm Sat (varies on event days). **Tickets** vary. **Map** p404 T10.

The city's newest arena, home of the rechristened Brooklyn Nets basketball team, opened in autumn 2012 with a series of concerts by native son and Nets investor Jay-Z. Though its mere existence remains a point of contention for some Brooklynites, the arena has already been a success. The staff is efficient and amiable, the acoustics are excellent, and there's a top-notch view from nearly every one of the 19,000 seats. And since it opened, it has attracted an unexpectedly cool list of acts, with local luminaries like Vampire Weekend, Yeah Yeah Yeahs and MGMT gracing its stage.

★ Madison Square Garden

Seventh Avenue, between 31st & 33rd Streets, Garment District (1-212 465 6741, www.thegarden.com). Subway A, C, E, 1, 2, 3 to 34th Street-Penn Station. **Box office** 10am-6pm Mon-Sat; noon-6pm Sun (plus 1 hr after show starts). **Tickets** vary. **Map** p398 D25.

Some of music's biggest acts – Jay-Z, Lady Gaga, Rush – come out to play at the world's most famous basketball arena, home to the Knicks and also hockey's Rangers. Whether you'll actually be able to get a look at them depends on your seat number or the quality of your binoculars. While it is undoubtedly a part of the fabric of New York, the storied venue is too vast for a rich concert experience, but it has been improved by a major renovation. The three-year revamp brought new seating and food from top New York City chefs, among other improvements, while respecting the Garden's history. The striking circular ceiling has been restored, while the north and south corridors on the entry level have been returned to their original appearance, including advertisements and event posters from 1968. *Photo p272.*

Madison Square Garden. *See p271.*

Venues

★ Apollo Theater

253 W 125th Street, between Adam Clayton Powell Jr Boulevard (Seventh Avenue) & Frederick Douglass Boulevard (Eighth Avenue), Harlem (1-212 531 5300, www.apollotheater.org). Subway A, B, C, D, 1 to 125th Street. **Box office** 10am-6pm Mon-Fri; noon-5pm Sat. **Tickets** vary. **Map** p401 D13.

This 100-year-old former burlesque theatre has been a hub for African-American artists for decades, and launched the careers of Ella Fitzgerald and D'Angelo, among many others. The now-legendary Amateur Night showcase has been running since 1934. The venue, known for jazz, R&B and soul music, mixes veteran talents such as Dianne Reeves with younger artists such as John Legend.

Barbès

376 9th Street, between Sixth & Seventh Avenues, Park Slope, Brooklyn (1-347 422 0248, www.barbesbrooklyn.com). Subway F to Seventh Avenue. **Open** 5pm-2am Mon-Thur; 2pm-4am Fri, Sat; 2pm-2am Sun. **Tickets** free-$10. **Map** p404 T11.

IN THE KNOW
LOCAL (GUITAR) HEROES

Hometown band the **Strokes** began their fantastically quick rise with a residency at the modest Lower East Side rock club **Mercury Lounge** (*see p276*) in 2000 (the Moldy Peaches opened).

Show up early if you want to get into Park Slope's global-bohemian club – it's tiny. Run by musically inclined French expats, this boîte brings in traditional swing and jazz of more daring stripes – depending on the night, you could catch Colombian, Brazilian, African or French music or acts that often defy categorisation. Chicha Libre, a Brooklyn band reviving psychedelic Peruvian music, holds down Mondays.

Beacon Theatre

2124 Broadway, between 74th & 75th Streets, Upper West Side (1-212 465 6500, www.beacontheatrenyc.com). Subway 1, 2, 3 to 72nd Street. **Box office** 11am-7pm Mon-Sat (varies on event days). **Tickets** vary. **Map** p399 C20.

This spacious former vaudeville theatre hosts a variety of popular acts, from Aziz Ansari to ZZ Top; once a year, the Allman Brothers take over for a lengthy residency. While the vastness can be daunting to performers and audience alike, the baroque, gilded interior and uptown location make you feel as though you're having a real night out on the town.

The Bell House

149 7th Street, between Second & Third Avenues, Gowanus, Brooklyn (1-718 643 6510, www.thebellhouseny.com). Subway F, G, R to Fourth Avenue-9th Street. **Shows** vary. **Tickets** free-$27. **Map** p404 S11.

The pioneering venue offers a plethora of cool events each week, including concerts, nerdy lectures and dance parties. Regular fixtures on the schedule include Wasabassco Burlesque, off-the-cuff storytelling slam the Moth, trivia show Ask Me Another and the Rub, a funky long-running affair tossed by DJs Ayres and Eleven.

Best Buy Theater

1515 Broadway, at 44th Street, Theater District (1-212 930 1950, www.bestbuytheater.com). Subway N, Q, R, S, 1, 2, 3, 7 to 42nd Street-Times Square. **Box office** noon-6pm Mon-Sat. **Tickets** $20-$70. **Map** p398 D24.

This large, corporate club begs for character but finds redemption in its creature comforts. The sound and sightlines are both good, and there's even edible food. Those who wish to look into a musician's eyes can stand in the ample front section; foot-weary fans can sit in the cinema-like section at the back. It's a comfortable place to see a well-known band that hasn't (yet) reached stadium-filling fame.

★ Bowery Ballroom

6 Delancey Street, between Bowery & Chrystie Street, Lower East Side (1-212 533 2111, www.boweryballroom.com). Subway B, D to Grand Street; J, Z to Bowery; 6 to Spring Street. **Box office** at Mercury Lounge (*see p276*). **Tickets** $15-$35. **Map** p397 F30.

Bowery Ballroom is probably the best venue in the city for seeing indie bands, either on the way up or holding their own. But it also brings in a diverse range of artists from home and abroad, and you can expect a clear view and bright sound from any spot in the venue. The spacious downstairs lounge is a great place to hang out between sets.

★ Cake Shop

152 Ludlow Street, between Rivington & Stanton Streets, Lower East Side (1-212 253 0036, www.cake-shop.com). Subway F to Lower East Side-Second Avenue. **Open** 10am-4am daily. **Tickets** free-$12. **Map** p397 G29.

It can be difficult to see the stage in this narrow, stuffy basement space, but Cake Shop gets big points for its keen indie and underground-rock bookings, among the best and most adventurous in the city. The venue lives up to its name, selling vegan pastries and coffee upstairs, while the back room at street level sells record-store ephemera.

City Winery

155 Varick Street, at Vandam Street, Tribeca (1-212 608 0555, www.citywinery.com). Subway 1 to Houston Street. **Open** 11.30am-3pm, 5.30pm-midnight Mon-Fri; 5pm-midnight Sat; 10am-3pm, 5.30pm-midnight Sun. **Box office** 11am-6pm Mon-Fri. **Tickets** vary. **Map** p397 D30.

Unabashedly grown-up and yuppie-friendly, this slick, spacious club launched by oenophile Michael Dorf is New York's only fully functioning winery – as well as a 300-seat concert space. Acts tend to be on the quiet side – this is, after all, a wine bar – but that doesn't mean the shows lack bite. Younger singer-songwriters such as Laura Marling and Keren Ann have appeared, but the place is dominated by older artists (Steve Earle, Los Lobos).

▶ *Michael Dorf was also the founder of the Knitting Factory; see p276.*

Galapagos Art Space

16 Main Street, at Water Street, Dumbo, Brooklyn (1-718 222 8500, www.galapagosartspace.com). Subway A, C to High Street; F to York Street. **Shows** vary. **Tickets** free-$25. **Credit** AmEx, MC, V. **Map** p405 S9.

The Bell House.

Galapagos established itself in Williamsburg years before the neighbourhood's renaissance – and, like many colonisers, got squeezed out of the scene it had helped to create. The much larger space in Dumbo offers a grander mix of the cultural offerings for which Galapagos is known and loved: music, performance art, burlesque, drag queens and other weird stuff. Just be careful not to fall into the pools of water strategically placed throughout the club.

Glasslands Gallery

289 Kent Avenue, between South 1st & 2nd Streets, Williamsburg, Brooklyn (no phone, www.theglasslands.com). Subway L to Bedford Avenue. **Shows** vary (usually 8.30pm daily). **Tickets** free-$15. **No credit cards. Map** p405 U8.
If you're looking to catch a Brooklyn buzz band before it breaks, look here. Marvel at the cool DIY decor while nodding to sets from local indie faves such as Ducktails and Cults. The music/burlesque/party destination spotlights less-hyped acts; metal band Liturgy has rocked the house, and Canadian electro-rock crew Suuns have played here.

Goodbye Blue Monday

1087 Broadway, at Dodworth Street, Bushwick, Brooklyn (1-718 453 6343, www.goodbye-blue-monday.com). Subway J to Kosciuszko Street. **Open** 11am-2am Mon-Thur, Sun; 11am-3am Fri, Sat. **Admission** free. **Map** p405 W9.
Relax while taking in this cult Bushwick drinkery's distinct junkyard aesthetic (the walls are lined with old books, random lamps and retro radios). The acts that play here are pretty eclectic, ranging from anti-folk to experimental jazz, and, best of all, gigs are always free.

Highline Ballroom.

Gramercy Theatre

127 E 23rd Street, between Park & Lexington Avenues, Gramercy Park (1-212 614 6932, www.thegramercytheatre.com). Subway N, R, 6 to 23rd Street. **Box office** noon-6.30pm Mon-Fri (and 1 hr before weekend shows). **Tickets** $10-$100. **Map** p398 E26.
The Gramercy Theatre looks exactly like what it is, a run-down former movie theatre; yet it has a decent sound system and good sightlines. Concert-goers can lounge in raised seats on the top level or get closer to the stage. Bookings have included such Baby Boom underdogs as Loudon Wainwright III and Todd Rundgren, and the occasional hip hop show, but tilt towards niche metal and emo.

Hammerstein Ballroom

Manhattan Center, 311 W 34th Street, between Eighth & Ninth Avenues, Garment District (1-212 279 7740, Ticketmaster 1-800 745 3000, www.mcstudios.com). Subway A, C, E to 34th Street-Penn Station. **Tickets** vary. **Map** p398 C25.
Queues can wind across the block, drinks prices are high, and those seated in the balcony should bring binoculars if they want a clear view of the band. Still, this cavernous space regularly draws big performers in the limbo between club and arena shows, and it's ideal for theatrical blow-outs; Kylie, the Pet Shop Boys and Grace Jones have all wowed here.

Highline Ballroom

431 W 16th Street, between Ninth & Tenth Avenues, Chelsea (1-212 414 5994, www.highlineballroom.com). Subway A, C, E to 14th Street; L to Eighth Avenue. **Box office** 11am-end of show. **Tickets** free-$100 ($10 food/drink min at tables). **Map** p397 C27.
This West Side club is LA-slick and bland, in a corporate sense, but it has a lot to recommend it: the sound is top-of-the-heap and sightlines are pretty good. The bookings are also impressive, ranging from hip hop heatseekers such as Yelawolf and Wiz Khalifa, to singer-songwriter pop, world music and burlesque.

Irving Plaza

17 Irving Place, at 15th Street, Gramercy & Flatiron (1-212 777 6800, www.irvingplaza.com). Subway L, N, Q, R, 4, 5, 6 to 14th Street-Union Square. **Box office** noon-6.30pm Mon-Fri; 1-5pm Sat. **Tickets** $15-$75. **Map** p397 E27.
Lying just east of Union Square, this midsize rock venue has served as a Democratic Party lecture hall (in the 19th century), a Yiddish theatre and a burlesque house (Gypsy Rose Lee made an appearance). Most importantly, it's a great place to see big stars keeping a low profile (Jeff Beck, Jane's Addiction and Lenny Kravitz) and medium heavies on their way up.

Q&A: WALKER & ROYCE

TONY's Bruce Tantum talks to NYC's rising house-music stars.

Sam Walker and Gavin Royce have been producing their emotive, subdued and groove-heavy deep house for little more than two years – but almost from the start, they were touted as future stars. Now it's official, thanks to a certain UK tastemaker.

Time Out New York I've been hearing for a while that you guys are going to be the next big thing – and now it seems as though it's starting to happen.

Gavin Royce It's nice that you've been hearing that! *[Laughs]* When we started off a couple of years ago, we were kind of coming out of nowhere and it seemed we were getting noticed pretty quickly. But at the same time, we were just starting and had a long way to go, so we just kept at it. Things have started to fall in place nicely. [BBC Radio 1 DJ and longtime dance-music kingmaker] Pete Tong has taken notice of us, for instance.

TONY We'll get back to Mr Tong in a bit, but let's backtrack a little first. You guys were friends for quite a while before you teamed up as producers, right?

GR Yeah, we were friends for about ten years. We were both involved in this group of friends who were throwing parties in Williamsburg; we would help promote and occasionally DJ.

TONY How would you describe your current sound? Do you think you even have a specific sound?

GR We've been told we have a sound.

Sam Walker But we're not conscious of it.

GR We often try to do things that are a little different than what we've done before. For instance, last year we had a track called 'Connected' that did really well, and a lot of labels came to us and flat-out asked us for another 'Connected'. We pretty much refused; we're gonna write what we're gonna write, and if something like 'Connected' comes out of it, that's what will happen.

SW Our method of musical creation is happenstance; what comes out are happy accidents. It's like you might be feeling a vibe one day, and you won't be feeling it the next day. For us to try to recapture that vibe just doesn't work for us. But I would say that we're evolving with every track.

TONY Let's return to Pete Tong. He's named you as 'future stars', right?

GR Yeah! That's a segment he does on his show. A producer from his show hit us up and asked if we'd want to do it.

TONY And you said yes.

GR Of course! I've been listening to Pete Tong since I was raving.

Radio City Music Hall.

★ Joe's Pub

Public Theater, 425 Lafayette Street, between Astor Place & E 4th Street, East Village (1-212 967 7555, www.joespub.com). Subway N, R to 8th Street-NYU; 6 to Astor Place. **Box office** 1-6pm Mon, Sun; 1-7.30pm Tue-Sat. **Tickets** ($12 food or 2-drink minimum) $12-$30. **Map** p397 E28.

One of the city's premier small spots for sit-down audiences, the recently refurbished Joe's Pub brings in impeccable talent of all genres and origins. While some well-established names play here, Joe's also lends its stage to up-and-comers (this is where Amy Winehouse made her debut in the United States), drag acts and cabaret performers (Justin Vivian Bond is a mainstay). The food menu – a mix of snacks, shareable plates and main courses – has been revitalised by hot chef Andrew Carmellini.

Knitting Factory Brooklyn

361 Metropolitan Avenue, at Havemeyer Street, Williamsburg, Brooklyn (1-347 529 6696, www.knittingfactory.com). Subway L to Lorimer Street; G to Metropolitan Avenue. **Open** 5pm-3.30am Mon-Fri; 3pm-3.30am Sat, Sun. **Tickets** free-$25. **Map** p405 U8.

Once a downtown Manhattan incubator of experimental music – of both the jazz and the indie-rock variety – Knitting Factory now has outposts across the country. Its New York base, which relocated to Williamsburg, is a professional, well-managed club, with a happening front-room bar, and solid indie-rock and hip hop bills (Zola Jesus, Black Milk) designed to suit its hipster clientele.

► *For Knitting Factory founder Michael Dorf's latest venture, see p273 City Winery.*

Mercury Lounge

217 E Houston Street, between Essex & Ludlow Streets, Lower East Side (1-212 260 4700, www.mercuryloungenyc.com). Subway F to Lower East Side-Second Avenue. **Box office** noon-7pm Mon-Sat. **Tickets** $8-$20. **No credit cards** (online purchases & bar only). **Map** p397 G29.

The unassuming, boxy Mercury Lounge is an old standby, with solid sound and sightlines (and a cramped bar in the front room). There are four-band bills most nights, although they can seem stylistically haphazard and set times are often later than advertised. (It's a good rule of thumb to show up half an hour later than you think you should.) Some of the bigger shows sell out in advance, and the club thrives during autumn's CMJ Music Marathon; young hopefuls from years gone by include Mumford & Sons.

Music Hall of Williamsburg

66 North 6th Street, between Kent & Wythe Avenues, Williamsburg, Brooklyn (1-718 486 5400, www.musichallofwilliamsburg.com). Subway L to Bedford Avenue. **Box office** 11am-6pm Sat. **Tickets** $15-$35. **Map** p405 U7.

When, in 2007, the local promoter Bowery Presents found itself in need of a Williamsburg outpost, it gave the former Northsix a facelift and took over the bookings. It's basically a Bowery Ballroom in Brooklyn – and bands such as Sonic Youth, Hot Chip and Real Estate headline, often on the day after they've played Bowery Ballroom or Terminal 5.

★ Pete's Candy Store

709 Lorimer Street, between Frost & Richardson Streets, Williamsburg, Brooklyn (1-718 302 3770, www.petescandystore.com). Subway L to

Lorimer Street. **Open** 5pm-2am Mon-Wed; 5pm-4am Thur; 4pm-4am Fri, Sat; 4pm-2am Sun. **Admission** free. **Map** p405 V7.
An overlooked gem tucked away in an old candy shop, Pete's is beautifully ramshackle, tiny and almost always free. The performers are generally unknown and crowds can be thin, but it can be a charming place to catch a singer-songwriter. Worthy underdogs may stop by for casual sets.

Pianos

158 Ludlow Street, between Rivington & Stanton Streets, Lower East Side (1-212 505 3733, www.pianosnyc.com). Subway F to Delancey Street; J, M, Z to Delancey-Essex treets. **Open** 2pm-4am daily. **Admission** free-$12. **Map** p397 G29.
In recent years, a lot of the cooler bookings have moved down the block to venues such as Cake Shop or to Brooklyn. But while the sound is often lousy and the room can get uncomfortably mobbed, there are always good reasons to go back to Pianos – very often the under-the-radar, emerging rock bands that make local music scenes tick.

★ Le Poisson Rouge

158 Bleecker Street, at Thompson Street, Greenwich Village (1-212 505 3474, www.le poissonrouge.com). Subway A, B, C, D, E, F, M to W 4th Street. **Open** 5pm-2am Mon-Wed, Sun; 5pm-4am Thur-Sat. **Box office** 5pm-close daily. **Tickets** free-$30. **Map** p397 E29.
Tucked into the basement of the long-gone Village Gate – a legendary performance space that hosted everyone from Miles Davis to Jimi Hendrix – Le Poisson Rouge was opened in 2008 by a group of young music enthusiasts with ties to both the classical and the indie rock worlds. The cabaret space's booking policy reflects both camps, often on a single bill. No other joint in town books such a wide range of great music, whether from a feverish Malian band (Toumani Diabaté's Symmetric Orchestra), rising indie stars (Zola Jesus) or young classical stars (pianist Simone Dinnerstein).

★ Radio City Music Hall

1260 Sixth Avenue, at 50th Street, Midtown (1-212 247 4777, www.radiocity.com). Subway B, D, F, M to 47th-50th Streets-Rockefeller Center. **Box office** 10am-8pm Mon-Sat. **Tickets** vary. **Map** p398 D23.
Few rooms scream 'New York City!' more than this gilded hall, which in recent years has drawn Leonard Cohen, Drake and Bon Iver as headliners. The greatest challenge for any performer is to not be upstaged by the awe-inspiring art deco surroundings, although those same surroundings lend historic heft to even the flimsiest showing. Bookings are all over the map; expect everything from seasonal staples like the Rockettes to lectures with the Dalai Lama.

★ Rockwood Music Hall

196 Allen Street, between E Houston & Stanton Streets, Lower East Side (1-212 477 4155, www.rockwoodmusichall.com). Subway F to Lower East Side-Second Avenue. **Open** 5.30pm-3am Mon-Fri; 2.30pm-3am Sat, Sun. **Tickets** free-$20 (1-drink min per set). **No credit cards** (online purchases & bar only). **Map** p397 F29.
The cramped quarters are part of this club's appeal: there are no bad seats (or standing spots) in the house. You can catch multiple acts every night of the week on three separate stages, and it's likely that many of those performers will soon be appearing in much bigger halls. Multi-genre polymath Gabriel Kahane is a regular, as is bluegrass great Michael Daves.

Sidewalk Café

94 Avenue A, at 6th Street, East Village (1-212 473 7373, www.sidewalkny.com). Subway 6 to Astor Place. **Open** 5pm-3am Mon-Thur; 11am-4am Fri, Sat; 11am-2am Sun. **Shows** usually 7pm daily. **Admission** free (1-drink min). **Map** p397 G28.
Despite its cramped, awkward layout, the Sidewalk Café is the focal point of the city's anti-folk scene – although that category means just about anything from piano pop to wry folk. Nellie McKay, Regina Spektor and the Moldy Peaches all started here.

SOB's

204 Varick Street, at Houston Street, Tribeca (1-212 243 4940, www.sobs.com). Subway 1 to Houston Street. **Box office** 11am-6pm Mon-Fri. **Tickets** $5-$40. **No credit cards** (online purchases, food & bar only). **Map** p397 D29.
The titular Sounds of Brazil (SOB, geddit?) are just some of the many global genres that keep this venue hopping. Soul, hip hop, reggae and Latin beats figure in the mix, with Raphael Saadiq, Maceo Parker and Eddie Palmieri each appearing of late. The drinks are expensive, but the sharp-looking clientele doesn't seem to mind.

Terminal 5

610 W 56th Street, between 11th & 12th Avenues, Hell's Kitchen (1-212 582 6600, www.terminal5nyc.com). Subway A, B, C, D, 1 to 59th Street-Columbus Circle. **Box office** at Mercury Lounge (*see p276*). **Tickets** $15-$90. **Map** p399 C22.
Opened by Bowery Presents, this three-floor, 3,000-capacity place is the largest midtown venue to set up shop in more than a decade. Bookings include bands that only a short time ago were playing in the smaller Bowery confines (Odd Future), plus bigger stars (Florence and the Machine) and veterans with their loyal fan bases (Morrissey, Jane's Addiction). It's great for dancey acts (Chromeo, Matt & Kim), but be warned: sightlines from the T5 balconies are among the worst in the city.

ESSENTIAL NEW YORK ALBUMS

Want to feel the big city? Listen up.

THE COMPLETE SAVOY & DIAL MASTERS
Charlie Parker (1945-48)
No style of jazz more accurately captures New York City's edgy energy and take-no-prisoners attitude than bebop, the cerebral yet visceral style that saxophonist Parker, trumpeter Gillespie and their revolutionary comrades invented in Harlem joints and 52nd Street nightclubs.

BERNSTEIN CONDUCTS BERNSTEIN
New York Philharmonic (1961-65)
Leonard Bernstein made front-page news with his New York Philharmonic conducting debut in 1943. This sampling of his own buoyant and gritty New York-inspired music – *West Side Story*, *On the Town* and more – is the definitive example of the city firing a composer's imagination.

NEW YORK DOLLS
New York Dolls (1973)
Loud, snotty and outrageous in their quasi-drag regalia, David Johansen, Johnny Thunders and their raucous cohorts essentially invented shock rock (hello, Kiss!) and glam metal, while also giving punk rock a formative kick in the ass. Johansen is still making waves today, but this early album cemented his legend for all time.

SUICIDE
Suicide (1977)
Industrial music, techno and electroclash owe their existence to a confrontational slab of vinyl by caustic vocalist Alan Vega and stolid keyboardist Martin Rev. Misunderstood in its day, Suicide's debut was proclaimed the essential NYC platter by no less an expert than No Wave pioneer Lydia Lunch.

BOOGIE DOWN PRODUCTIONS
Criminal Minded (1987)
Rapper KRS-One and DJ Scott La Rock may not have invented hip hop, but on this still-exhilarating '87 LP the pair created the mould for underworld reportage, gangsta posturing, musical breadth and borough-proud brinksmanship that continues to define the best in NYC rap.

NEW YORK
Lou Reed (1989)
There's no Lou Reed album that couldn't be described as 'essential New York', so acute and unvarnished were his musical chronicles from the Velvet Underground days to the end of his life. But on the album he named for his long-time hometown, Reed leavens his caustic edge with wisdom, insight and grace.

★ Town Hall

123 W 43rd Street, between Sixth Avenue & Broadway, Theater District (1-212 840 2824, www.the-townhall-nyc.org). Subway B, D, F, M to 42nd Street-Bryant Park; N, Q, R, S, 1, 2, 3, 7 to 42nd Street-Times Square; 7 to Fifth Avenue. **Box office** noon-6pm Mon-Sat. **Tickets** vary. **Map** p398 D24.

Acoustics at the 1921 'people's auditorium' are superb, and there's no doubting the gravitas of the surroundings – the building was designed by illustrious architects McKim, Mead & White as a meeting house for a suffragist organisation. George Benson, Grizzly Bear and Lindsey Buckingham have performed here, and smart indie songwriters such as the Magnetic Fields have set up shop for a number of nights.

Union Hall

702 Union Street, between Fifth & Sixth Avenues, Park Slope, Brooklyn (1-718 638 4400, www.unionhallny.com). Subway R to Union Street. **Open** 4pm-4am Mon-Fri; 1pm-4am Sat, Sun. **Tickets** $5-$20. **Map** p404 T11.

The spacious main floor of this Brooklyn bar (*see p207*) has a garden, food service and a bocce ball court. Tucked in the basement is a comfortable space dominated by the more delicate side of indie rock, with infrequent sets by indie comics such as Mike Birbiglia and Eugene Mirman.

Union Pool

484 Union Avenue, at Meeker Avenue, Williamsburg, Brooklyn (1-718 609 0484, www.union-pool.com). Subway L to Lorimer Street; G to Metropolitan Avenue. **Open** 5pm-4am Mon-Fri; 1pm-4am Sat, Sun. **Tickets** free-$12. **No credit cards** (online purchases & bar only). **Map** p405 V8.

Wind through the kitschy backyard space of this modest but super-cool Williamsburg bar (which featured in the movie *Nick and Norah's Infinite Playlist*) and you'll find yourself back indoors, facing a small stage. Local stars check in from time to time (members of Yeah Yeah Yeahs have showed off their side projects here), but it's dominated by well-plucked smaller indie acts. For a rowdy, amusing Monday night, check out Reverend Vince Anderson and his Love Choir.

Webster Hall

125 E 11th Street, between Third & Fourth Avenues, East Village (1-212 353 1600, www.websterhall.com). Subway L to Third Avenue; L, N, Q, R, 4, 5, 6 to 14th Street-Union Square. **Box office** 10am-6pm Mon-Sat. **Tickets** $15-$50. **No credit cards** (online purchases & bar only). **Map** p397 F28.

A great-sounding alternative for bands (and fans) who've had their fill of the comparably sized Irving Plaza, Webster Hall is booked by Bowery Presents, the folks who run Bowery Ballroom and Mercury Lounge. Expect to find high-calibre indie acts (Animal Collective, Battles, Gossip), but be sure to arrive early if you want a decent view. A smaller space downstairs, the Studio at Webster Hall, hosts cheaper shows, mainly by local bands.

WORLD, COUNTRY & ROOTS

Among the cornucopia of live entertainment programmes at the **Brooklyn Academy of Music** (*p285*), the **BAMcafé** above the lobby comes to life on weekend nights with world music and other genres. *See also p277* **SOB's**, *p272* **Barbès** and *p280* **BB King Blues Club & Grill**.

Webster Hall.

ARTS & ENTERTAINMENT

BB King Blues Club & Grill.

Nublu

62 Avenue C, between 4th & 5th Streets, East Village (no phone, www.nublu.net). **Open** 9pm-4am daily. **Admission** $5-$10. **Map** p397 G28.

Nublu's prominence on the local globalist club scene has been inversely proportional to its size. A pressure-cooker of creativity, it gave rise to the Brazilian Girls, who started jamming at one late-night session and still occasionally bring their loungy electronic sounds back to the club. However, at time of writing, Nublu was looking for a new venue – call or see website for updates.

Rodeo Bar & Grill

375 Third Avenue, at 27th Street, Gramercy Park (1-212 683 6500, www.rodeobar.com). Subway 6 to 28th Street. **Shows** 9pm-midnight Mon-Wed, Sun; 9.30pm-12.30am Thur; 11pm-2am Fri, Sat. **Admission** free. **Map** p398 F26.

The unpretentious, if sometimes raucous crowd, roadhouse atmosphere and absence of a cover charge help to make the Rodeo the city's best roots club, with a steady stream of rockabilly, country and related sounds. Kick back with a beer from the bar – a funked-up trailer in the middle of the room.

JAZZ, BLUES & EXPERIMENTAL

Ever since Duke Ellington urged folks to take the A train up to Harlem, New York has been a hotbed of improvisational talent. While Harlem is no longer the centre of the jazz scene, in the Village, you can soak up the vibe at clubs that once provided a platform for the virtuoso experimentations of Miles Davis, John Coltrane and Thelonious Monk. Boundaries are still being pushed in eclectic avant-garde venues like **Roulette**, **Spectrum** (for both, *see p288*) and the **Stone**. For well-known jazz joints such as the **Village Vanguard** and **Birdland**, booking ahead is recommended.

55 Bar

55 Christopher Street, between Seventh Avenue South & Waverly Place, West Village (1-212 929 9883, www.55bar.com). Subway 1 to Christopher Street-Sheridan Square. **Open** 3pm-4am daily. **Tickets** free-$15. **No credit cards**. **Map** p397 D28.

This tiny Prohibition-era dive is one of New York's most artist-friendly rooms, thanks to its knowledgeable, appreciative audience. You can catch emerging talent almost every night at the free-of-charge early shows; late sets regularly feature established artists such as Mike Stern, Wayne Krantz and David Binney.

92nd Street Y

For listings, *see p287*.

Best known for the series Jazz in July and spring's Lyrics & Lyricists, this multidisciplinary cultural centre also offers cabaret, mainstream jazz and singer-songwriters. The small, handsome theatre provides a fine setting for the sophisticated fare.

BB King Blues Club & Grill

237 W 42nd Street, between Seventh & Eighth Avenues, Theater District (1-212 997 4144, www.bbkingblues.com). Subway A, C, E to 42nd Street-Port Authority; N, Q, R, S, 1, 2, 3, 7 to 42nd Street-Times Square. **Box office** 11am-midnight daily. **Tickets** $12-$150. **Map** p398 D24.

BB's Times Square joint hosts one of the most varied music schedules in town. Cover bands and tributes fill the gaps between big-name bookings such as George Clinton and Buddy Guy, but the venue also regularly hosts hip hop and the odd extreme-metal blowout. The best seats are often at the dinner tables in front, but the menu prices are steep (and watch out for drink minimums). The Harlem Gospel Choir's buffet brunch ($47, $44 booked in advance, 12.30pm Sun) raises the roof.

Birdland
315 W 44th Street, between Eighth & Ninth Avenues, Theater District (1-212 581 3080, www.birdlandjazz.com). Subway A, C, E to 42nd Street-Port Authority. **Open** 5pm-1am daily. **Tickets** $20-$50 ($10 food/drink min). **Map** p398 C24.
The flagship venue for midtown's jazz resurgence, Birdland takes its place among the neon lights of Times Square seriously. That means it's a haven for great jazz musicians (Joe Lovano, Kurt Elling) as well as performers like John Pizzarelli and Aaron Neville. The club is also notable for its roster of bands-in-residence. Sundays belong to the Arturo O'Farrill Afro Latin Jazz Orchestra.

Blue Note
131 W 3rd Street, between MacDougal Street & Sixth Avenue, Greenwich Village (1-212 475 8592, www.bluenote.net). Subway A, B, C, D, E, F, M to W 4th Street. **Shows** 8pm, 10.30pm Mon-Thur, Sun; 8pm, 10.30pm, 12.30am Fri, Sat. **Tickets** $10-$75 ($5 food/drink min). **Map** p397 E29.
The Blue Note prides itself on being 'the jazz capital of the world'. Bona fide musical titans (Jimmy Heath, Lee Konitz) rub against contemporary heavyweights (the Bad Plus), while the close-set tables in the club get patrons rubbing up against each other. The edgy Friday Late Night Groove series and the Sunday brunches (10.30am-3pm; $29.50 including show) are the best bargain bets.

Carnegie Hall
For listings, *see p285*.
Carnegie Hall means the big time. In recent years, though, the 599-seat, state-of-the-art Zankel Hall has greatly augmented the venue's pop, jazz and world music offerings. Between both halls, the complex has welcomed Keith Jarrett, Randy Newman and Bobby McFerrin, among other high-wattage names.

Cornelia Street Café
29 Cornelia Street, between Bleecker & 4th Streets, Greenwich Village (1-212 989 9319, www.corneliastreetcafe.com). Subway A, B, C, D, E, F, M to W 4th Street. **Open** 10am-midnight Mon-Thur, Sun; 10am-1am Fri, Sat. **Shows** 6pm, 8.30pm Mon-Thur, Sun; 6pm, 9pm, 10.30pm Fri, Sat. **Tickets** $10-$15 ($10 food/drink min). **No credit cards** (food & bar only). **Map** p397 D29.
Upstairs at the Cornelia Street Café is a cosy eaterie. Downstairs is an even cosier music space hosting adventurous jazz, poetry, world music and folk. Regular mini-festivals spotlight blues and songwriters. It's a good idea to arrive when the doors open for shows (5.45pm, 8.30pm or 10.15pm) because reservations are only held for 15 minutes after the set starts.

Iridium
1650 Broadway, at 51st Street, Theater District (1-212 582 2121, www.iridiumjazzclub.com). Subway 1 to 50th Street; N, R to 49th Street. **Shows** 8pm, 10pm daily. **Tickets** $25-$40 ($15 food/drink min). **Map** p398 D23.
Iridium lures upscale crowds with a line-up that's split between household names and those known only to the jazz-savvy. The sight lines and sound system are truly worthy of celebration. Long the site of a Monday-night residency by guitar icon Les Paul, the club now hosts a steady stream of veteran pickers who perform in his honour.

Jazz Gallery
5th floor, 1160 Broadway, between 27th and 28th Streets, Flatiron District (1-646 494 3625, www.jazzgallery.org). Subway N, R to 28th Street. **Shows** 9pm, 11pm Thur-Sat. **Tickets** $10-$35. **No credit cards** (online purchases only). **Map** p398 E26.
This beloved haunt, one of the city's premier incubators for progressive-jazz talent, relocated from its former Soho digs to a gallery-like space near the Flatiron Building. It's a place to witness true works of art from sometimes obscure but always interesting jazzers (Henry Threadgill and Vijay Iyer, to name a couple).

★ Jazz at Lincoln Center
Frederick P Rose Hall, Broadway, at 60th Street, Upper West Side (1-212 258 9800, www.jalc.org). Subway A, B, C, D, 1 to 59th Street-Columbus Circle.
Rose Theater & the Allen Room *CenterCharge 1-212 721 6500.* **Shows** vary. **Box office** 10am-6pm Mon-Sat; noon-6pm Sun. **Tickets** *Rose Theater* $30-$120. *The Allen Room* $55-$65.
Dizzy's Club Coca-Cola *1-212 258 9595.* **Shows** 7.30pm, 9.30pm Mon-Thur, Sun; 7.30pm, 9.30pm, 11.30pm Fri, Sat. **Tickets** $10-$35 ($5-$10 food/drink min). **Map** p399 D22.
The jazz arm of Lincoln Center is located several blocks away from the main campus, high atop the Time Warner Center. It includes three rooms: the Rose Theater is a traditional mid-size space, but the crown jewels are the Allen Room and the smaller Dizzy's Club Coca-Cola, with stages that are framed by enormous windows looking on to Columbus Circle and Central Park. The venues feel like a Hollywood cinematographer's vision of a Manhattan jazz club. Some of the best players in the business regularly grace the spot; among them is Wynton Marsalis, Jazz at Lincoln Center's famed artistic director.

Jazz Standard.

Jazz Standard
116 E 27th Street, between Park Avenue South & Lexington Avenue, Flatiron District (1-212 576 2232, www.jazzstandard.com). Subway 6 to 28th Street. **Shows** 7.30pm, 9.30pm Mon-Thur; 7.30pm, 9.30pm, 11.30pm Fri, Sat. **Tickets** $20-$35. **Map** p398 E26.
Renovation was just what the doctor ordered for the jazz den below restaurateur Danny Meyer's Blue Smoke barbecue joint. Now the room's marvellous sound matches its already splendid sight lines. The jazz is of the groovy, hard-swinging variety, featuring such musicians as organist Dr Lonnie Smith, Larry Goldings and Cedar Walton.

Merkin Concert Hall
For listings, *see p288*.
The Merkin provides a polished platform for classical and jazz composers, with chamber music, jazz, folk, cabaret and experimental music performers taking the stage at the intimate venue. Popular annual series include the New York Guitar Festival, WNYC's New Sounds Live (part of the Ecstatic Music Festival) and Broadway Close Up.

★ Smalls Jazz Club
183 W 10th Street, between Seventh Avenue South & W 4th Street, West Village (1-212 252 5091, www.smallsjazzclub.com). Subway 1 to Christopher Street-Sheridan Square. **Open** 6pm-3am Mon-Wed; 4pm-4am Thur-Sun. **Admission** $10-$20. **No credit cards. Map** p397 D28.
For those looking for an authentic jazz club experience – rather than the cheesy dinner-club vibe that prevails at too many other spots around town – Smalls is a must. The cosy basement space feels like a speakeasy, or more specifically, one of those hole-in-the-wall NYC jazz haunts of yore over which fans obsess. Best of all, the booking skews retro, yet not stubbornly so. You'll hear classic hardbop as well as more adventurous, contemporary approaches.

Smoke
2751 Broadway, between 105th & 106th Streets, Upper West Side (1-212 864 6662, www.smokejazz.com). Subway 1 to 103rd Street. **Shows** 7pm, 9pm, 10.30pm, midnight daily. **Admission** free ($10-$30 food/drink min). **Map** p400 C16.
Not unlike a swanky living room, Smoke is a classy little joint that acts as a haven for local jazz legends and touring artists looking to play an intimate space. Early in the week, evenings are themed: on Monday, it's big band; Tuesday, organ jazz; Wednesday, jazz-soul. On weekends, renowned jazzers hit the stage, relishing the chance to play informal gigs uptown.

★ The Stone
Avenue C, at 2nd Street, East Village (no phone, www.thestonenyc.com). Subway F to Lower East Side-Second Avenue. **Shows** 8pm, 10pm daily. **Admission** $15. **No credit cards. Map** p397 G29.
Don't call sax star John Zorn's not-for-profit venture a 'club'. You'll find no food or drinks here, and no nonsense, either: the Stone is an art space dedicated to 'the experimental and the avant-garde'. If you're down for some rigorously adventurous sounds (intense improvisers like Tim Berne and Okkyung Lee, or moonlighting rock mavericks such as Thurston Moore), Zorn has made it easy: no advance sales, and all ages admitted (under-19s get discounts, under-12s free). The bookings are left to a different artist-curator each month.

★ Village Vanguard
178 Seventh Avenue South, at Perry Street, West Village (1-212 255 4037, www.villagevanguard.com). Subway A, C, E, 1, 2, 3 to 14th Street; L to Eighth Avenue. **Shows** 9pm, 11pm daily. **Tickets** $25 (1-drink min). **Map** p397 D28.
Going strong for more than three-quarters of a century, the Village Vanguard is one of New York's legendary jazz centres. History surrounds you: the likes of John Coltrane, Miles Davis and Bill Evans have all grooved in this hallowed basement haunt. Big names – both old and new – continue to fill the schedule here, and the Grammy Award-winning Vanguard Jazz Orchestra has been the Monday-night regular here for almost 50 years. Reservations are recommended.

CABARET

In an age of globalism, cabaret is a fundamentally local art: a private party in a cosy club, where music gets stripped down to its bare essence. The intense intimacy of the experience can make it transformative if you're lucky, or mortifying if you're not. Expect consistently high-grade entertainment at Manhattan's fanciest venues, the **Café Carlyle** and the more theatre-oriented **54 Below**. Local clubs such as **Don't Tell Mama** and the **Duplex** are cheaper and more casual, but the talent is sometimes entry-level. The **Metropolitan Room** and the **Laurie Beechman Theatre** fall between these two poles.

★ 54 Below

254 W 54th Street, between Broadway & Eighth Avenue, Theater District (1-646 476 3551, www.54below.com). Subway B, D, E to Seventh Avenue; C, E, 1 to 50th Street; R to 57th Street. **Shows** vary. **Admission** $15-$95 ($25 food/drink min). **Map** p399 D22.

A team of Broadway producers is behind this swank supper club in the bowels of the legendary Studio 54 space. The schedule is dominated by big Broadway talent – such as Patti LuPone, Ben Vereen and Sherie Rene Scott – but there's also room for edgier talents like Justin Vivian Bond and Jackie Hoffman.

Café Carlyle

Carlyle, 35 E 76th Street, at Madison Avenue, Upper East Side (1-212 744 1600, www.thecarlyle.com). Subway 6 to 77th Street. **Shows** vary. **Admission** $65-$185 (dinner or $25 food/drink minimum required). **Map** p399 E20.

With its airy murals by Marcel Vertes, this elegant boîte in the Carlyle hotel remains the epitome of New York class, attracting such top-level singers as folk legend Judy Collins, Broadway star Sutton Foster and soul queen Bettye LaVette. Woody Allen often plays clarinet with Eddie Davis and his New Orleans Jazz Band on Monday nights.

► *Bemelmans Bar, across the hall, has an excellent pianist for those who want to drink in the atmosphere at a lower price; see p177.*

Don't Tell Mama

343 W 46th Street, between Eighth & Ninth Avenues, Theater District (1-212 757 0788, www.donttellmamanyc.com). Subway A, C, E to 42nd Street-Port Authority. **Open** *Piano bar* 9pm-2.30am Mon-Thur, Sun; 9pm-4am Fri, Sat. **Shows** vary; 2-4 shows per night. **Admission** $10-$25 (2-drink min). *Piano bar* free (2-drink min). **No credit cards**. **Map** p398 C23.

Showbiz pros and piano-bar buffs adore this dank but homey Theater District stalwart, where acts range from the strictly amateur to potential stars of tomorrow. The line-up may include pop, jazz and musical-theatre singers, as well as comedians and drag artists (including veteran Judy Garland impersonator Tommy Femia).

The Duplex

61 Christopher Street, at Seventh Avenue South, West Village (1-212 255 5438, www.theduplex.com). Subway 1 to Christopher Street-Sheridan Square. **Open** *Piano bar* 9pm-4am daily. **Shows** vary. **Admission** varies (2-drink min). **Map** p397 D28.

This cosy, brick-lined room, located in the heart of the West Village, is a good-natured testing ground for new talent. The eclectic offerings often come served with a generous dollop of good, old-fashioned camp. The no-cover downstairs piano bar provides an open mic until the wee hours of the morning.

Laurie Beechman Theatre

407 W 42nd Street, at Ninth Avenue, Theater District (1-212 695 6909, www.westbankcafe.com). Subway A, C, E to 42nd Street-Port Authority. **Shows** vary. **Admission** free-$45 ($15 food/drink min). **Map** p398 C24.

Tucked away beneath the West Bank Café on 42nd Street, the Beechman provides a stage for singers from the worlds of musical theatre and cabaret, including some of the city's most popular drag entertainers. It also hosts occasional comedy shows.

Metropolitan Room

34 W 22nd Street, between Fifth & Sixth Avenues, Flatiron District (1-212 206 0440, www.metropolitanroom.com). Subway F, M, N, R to 23rd Street. **Shows** vary. **Admission** $15-$35 (2-drink min). **Map** p398 E26.

The Metropolitan Room occupies a comfortable middle zone on the city's cabaret spectrum, being less expensive than the fancier supper clubs and more polished than the cheaper spots. Regular performers range from rising jazz artists to established cabaret acts such as Baby Jane Dexter and Annie Ross.

54 Below.

Performing Arts

An omnivorous approach to the arts is increasingly common on New York's cultural scene. The city is continuing to enjoy a classical music renaissance, with small genre-crossing venues such as Spectrum on the Lower East Side and Brooklyn's Roulette serving as laboratories for exciting new sounds.

Dance is also stepping beyond traditional boundaries, into venues such as the Museum of Modern Art while, in theatre, an Off-Broadway boom has resulted in several lower-priced offshoots of established theatres, including Lincoln Center's Claire Tow Theater and Brooklyn Academy of Music's Richard B Fisher Building. The latter, a seven-storey performing-arts centre, provides a space not only for theatre, but also dance, music and performance art. This corner of Brooklyn has evolved into a thriving arts district with the opening of several new venues.

Check out the weekly *Time Out New York* magazine or www.timeout.com/newyork for current cultural listings.

Classical Music & Opera

At the big institutions such as the New York Philharmonic, the Metropolitan Opera and Carnegie Hall, confident artistic leaders such as Alan Gilbert, Peter Gelb and Clive Gillinson are embracing new productions, living composers and innovative approaches to programming.

Meanwhile, some of the most exciting work is happening outside of Lincoln Center and Carnegie Hall. New-music groups like the International Contemporary Ensemble, Alarm Will Sound and So Percussion have grown from promising upstarts to become influential pillars of the artistic community. Genre-blind venues, including **Le Poisson Rouge** (*see p277*), the **Stone** (*see p282*) and **Spectrum** (*see p288*), are happy to give them space to do their thing. These days it's not rare for a Baroque opera to be followed by a DJ set or for an orchestra to interpret music by Mos Def or Sufjan Stevens. This is the postmodern aesthetic in full bloom and there's no better place to experience it right now than New York.

The standard New York concert season lasts from September to June, but there are plenty of summer events and performances (*see p289* **Everything Under the Sun**). Box office hours may change in summer, so phone ahead or check websites for times.

Information & tickets

You can buy tickets directly from most venues, whether by phone, online or at the box office. However, a surcharge is generally added to tickets not bought in person. For more on tickets, *see p296*.

MAJOR CONCERT HALLS

★ Brooklyn Academy of Music

Peter Jay Sharp Building *30 Lafayette Avenue, between Ashland Place & St Felix Street, Fort Greene, Brooklyn.*
BAM Harvey Theater *651 Fulton Street, at Rockwell Place, Fort Greene, Brooklyn.*
BAM Richard B Fisher Building *321 Ashland Place, between Ashland Place & Lafayette Avenue, Fort Greene, Brooklyn.*
All *1-718 636 4100, www.bam.org. Subway B, D, N, Q, R, 2, 3, 4, 5 to Atlantic Avenue-Barclays Center; C to Lafayette Avenue; G to Fulton Street.* **Box office** noon-6pm Mon-Sat. *Phone bookings* 10am-6pm Mon-Fri; noon-6pm Sat; noon-4pm Sun (show days). **Tickets** vary. **Map** p404 T10.

America's oldest performing-arts academy continues to present some of the freshest programming in the city. Every year from September through December, the Next Wave Festival brings avant-garde music, dance and theatre. The nearby BAM Harvey Theater offers a smaller and more atmospheric setting for multimedia creations by composers and performers such as Tan Dun, So Percussion and Meredith Monk. The newest facility, BAM Fisher, houses an intimate performance space and studios.

★ Carnegie Hall

154 W 57th Street, at Seventh Avenue, Midtown (1-212 247 7800, www.carnegiehall.org). Subway N, Q, R to 57th Street. **Box office** 11am-6pm Mon-Sat; noon-6pm Sun. *Phone bookings* 8am-8pm daily. **Tickets** vary. **Map** p399 D22.

Artistic director Clive Gillinson continues to put his stamp on Carnegie Hall. The stars – both soloists and orchestras – still shine brightly inside this renowned concert hall in the Isaac Stern Auditorium. But it's the spunky upstart Zankel Hall that has generated the most buzz, offering an eclectic mix of classical, contemporary, jazz, pop and world music. Next door, the Weill Recital Hall hosts intimate concerts and chamber music programmes. Keep an eye out for Ensemble ACJW, which is comprised of some of the city's most exciting young musicians and also performs at the Juilliard School of music, and the annual Spring for Music (a festival which features eclectic programmes from North America's most innovative regional orchestras, held at Carnegie Hall).

INSIDE TRACK
LUNCH WITH THE ORCHESTRA

A variety of free lunchtime concerts is held around New York by some of the city's brightest up-and-comers. The early music series **Midtown Concerts** presides over St Bartholomew's Church (*see p291*; www.midtownconcerts.org) every Thursday at 1.15pm. Downtown, stately sanctuary Trinity Wall Street (*see p291*) offers gratis Thursday afternoon recitals in its **Concerts at One** series (Mar-June, Sept-Dec). Also look out for **Bach at One** on Mondays and **Pipes at One** on Wednesdays.

Carnegie Hall.

ARTS & ENTERTAINMENT

Lincoln Center

Columbus Avenue, between 62nd & 65th Streets, Upper West Side (1-212 546 2656, www.lincolncenter.org). Subway 1 to 66th Street-Lincoln Center. **Map** p399 C21.

Built in the early 1960s, this massive complex is the nexus of Manhattan's – in fact, probably the whole country's – performing arts scene. The campus has undergone a major revamp, providing new performance facilities as well as more inviting public gathering spaces and restaurants. In addition to shows in its main concert halls, Lincoln Center stages lectures and symposia in the **Rose Building** and Sunday recitals at the **Walter Reade Theater** (*see p251*). Also here are the **Juilliard School** (*see p291*) and the **Fiorello H La Guardia High School of Music & Art and Performing Arts** (100 Amsterdam Avenue, between 64th & 65th Streets, www.laguardiahs.org), which frequently host performances by professional ensembles as well as students who may go on to be the stars of tomorrow.

Big stars such as Valery Gergiev and Emanuel Ax are Lincoln Center's meat and potatoes. Lately, though, the divide between the flagship Great Performers season and the more audacious, multidisciplinary **Lincoln Center Out of Doors festival** (*see p34*) continues to narrow. The **Mostly Mozart Festival** (late July-Aug), a formerly moribund four-week summer staple, has been thoroughly reinvented as a showcase of up-and-coming conductors and innovative performers. In autumn, the White Light Festival blends high-quality classical performers with world and popular musicians, all of whom angle to tap into the spiritually transcendent qualities of music.

The main entry point for Lincoln Center is from Columbus Avenue, at 65th Street, but the venues that follow are spread out across the square of blocks from 62nd to 66th Streets, between Amsterdam and Columbus Avenues. Tickets to most performances at Lincoln Center are sold through **Centercharge** (1-212 721 6500, 10am-9pm daily). There is now a central box office selling discounted tickets to same-day performances at the **David Rubenstein Atrium** (between W 62nd & W 63rd Streets, Broadway & Columbus Avenues).

IN THE KNOW
BACKSTAGE PASSES

It's possible to go behind the scenes at several of the city's major concert venues. **Metropolitan Opera Guild Backstage Tours** (1-212 769 7028, $22, $18 reductions) shows you around the famous opera house from October to mid May. A tour of **Carnegie Hall** (1-212 903 9765, $15, $5-$10 reductions, Oct-May) ushers you through what is perhaps the world's most famous concert hall. For $18, you may also watch an open rehearsal of the **New York Philharmonic** (1-212 875 5656, Sept-June).

Alice Tully Hall

1-212 875 5050. **Box office** 10am-6pm Mon-Sat; noon-6pm Sun. **Tickets** vary.
An 18-month renovation turned the cosy home of the Chamber Music Society of Lincoln Center (www.chambermusicsociety.org) into a world-class, 1,096-seat theatre. A new contemporary foyer with an elegant (if a bit pricey) café is immediately striking, but, more importantly, the revamp also brought dramatic acoustical improvements.

Avery Fisher Hall

1-212 875 5030. **Box office** 10am-6pm Mon-Sat; noon-6pm Sun; closes 30mins after performance time. **Tickets** vary.
This handsome, comfortable, 2,700-seat hall is the headquarters of the New York Philharmonic (1-212 875 5656, www.nyphil.org), the country's oldest symphony orchestra (founded in 1842) – and one of its finest. Depending on who you ask, the sound ranges from good to atrocious. A future renovation is planned, though the date hasn't been set. The ongoing Great Performers series – which also takes place at Alice Tully Hall and other Lincoln Center venues – features top international soloists and ensembles.

Metropolitan Opera House

1-212 362 6000, www.metoperafamily.org.
Box office 10am-8pm Mon-Sat; noon-6pm Sun. **Tickets** $25-$400.
The grandest of the Lincoln Center buildings, the Met is a spectacular place to see and hear opera. It hosts the Metropolitan Opera from September to May, with major visiting companies appearing in summer. Audiences are knowledgeable and fiercely devoted, with subscriptions remaining in families for generations. Opera's biggest stars appear here regularly, and music director James Levine has turned the orchestra into a true symphonic force.

The Met had already started becoming more inclusive before current impresario Peter Gelb took the reins in 2006. Now, the company is placing a priority on creating novel theatrical experiences with visionary directors (Robert Lepage, Bartlett Sher, Michael Grandage, David McVicar) and assembling a new company of physically graceful, telegenic stars (Anna Netrebko, Danielle de Niese, Jonas Kaufmann, Erwin Schrott). Its high-definition movie-theatre broadcasts continue to reign supreme outside the opera house. Although most tickets are expensive, 200 prime seats (50 of which are reserved for over-65s) for all are sold for a mere $20 apiece from Monday to Thursday, two hours before curtain up.

OTHER VENUES

92nd Street Y

1395 Lexington Avenue, at 92nd Street, Upper East Side (1-212 415 5500, www.92y.org). Subway 6 to 96th Street. **Box office** noon-8pm Mon-Thur, Sun; noon-5pm Fri. **Tickets** $25-$62. **Map** p400 F17.
The Y has always stood for solidly traditional orchestral, solo and chamber masterpieces. But the organisation also fosters the careers of young musicians and explores European and Jewish-American music traditions, with innovative results. In addition to showcasing several master classes (such as guitarist Eliot Fisk), the Y has recently lent its stage to the Takács Quartet and pianist Paul Lewis. And in an effort to make its concerts more affordable, $25 tickets to premium programmes are available to everyone age 35 and younger.

★ Bargemusic

Fulton Ferry Landing, between Old Fulton & Water Streets, Dumbo, Brooklyn (1-718 624 4924, www.bargemusic.org). Subway A, C to High Street; F to York Street; 2, 3 to Clark Street. **Tickets** $35; $15-$30 reductions. **No credit cards at venue. Map** p405 S9.
This former coffee bean barge usually presents four chamber concerts a week set against a panoramic view of lower Manhattan. It's a magical experience (and the programming has recently grown more ambitious), but be sure to dress warmly in the winter. In the less chilly months, admire the view from the upper deck during the interval. *Photo p288.*

Frick Collection

For listings, *see p174.* **Tickets** $35.
Concerts in the Frick Collection's elegantly appointed concert hall are a rare treat, generally featuring both promising debutants and lesser-known but world-class performers. Concerts are broadcast live in the Garden Court, where tickets aren't required.

ARTS & ENTERTAINMENT

Bargemusic. *See p287.*

Gilder Lehrman Hall

The Morgan Library & Museum, 225 Madison Avenue, at 36th Street, Murray Hill (1-212 685 0008, www.themorgan.org). Subway 6 to 33rd Street. **Tickets** vary. **Map** p398 E25.

This elegant, 264-seat gem of a concert hall is a perfect venue for song recitals and chamber groups. The St Luke's Chamber Ensemble was quick to establish a presence here.

Merkin Concert Hall

Kaufman Music Center, 129 W 67th Street, between Amsterdam Avenue & Broadway, Upper West Side (1-212 501 3330, www.kaufman-center.org). Subway 1 to 66th Street-Lincoln Center. **Box office** noon-7pm Mon-Thur, Sun; noon-4pm (until 3pm Nov-Jan) Fri. **Tickets** $15-$60. **Map** p399 C21.

On a side street in the shadow of Lincoln Center, this renovated 449-seat treasure offers a robust mix of early music and avant-garde programming, plus a healthy amount of jazz, folk and some more eclectic fare. The Ecstatic Music Festival, featuring the latest generation of composers and performers, heats up the space each January through March, and the New York Festival of Song regularly presents outstanding singers in appealingly quirky thematic programmes.

Metropolitan Museum of Art

For listings, *see p180.* **Tickets** $35-$60.

When it comes to established virtuosos and revered chamber ensembles, the Met's year-round programming is rich and full (and ticket prices can be correspondingly high). Under the leadership of Limor Tomer, the museum's programming has recently taken a sharp turn towards genre-flouting performers and intriguing artistic juxtapositions. Lately, performances by Alarm Will Sound and the Estonian Philharmonic Chamber Choir have transformed the museum's famous Temple of Dendur into an atmospheric spot to hear some mystical music.

▶ *At Christmas and Easter, early music concerts are held in the Fuentidueña Chapel at the Cloisters; see p193.*

★ Miller Theatre at Columbia University

2960 Broadway, at 116th Street, Morningside Heights (1-212 854 7799, www.millertheatre.com). Subway 1 to 116th Street-Columbia University. **Box office** noon-6pm Mon-Fri (also 2hrs before performance on show days). **Tickets** $25-$40. **Map** p401 C14.

Columbia University's Miller Theatre is at the forefront of making contemporary classical music sexy in New York City. The credit belongs to former executive director George Steel, who has proved that presenting challenging fare in a casual, unaffected setting could attract young audiences – and hang on to them. Director Melissa Smey seems to be continuing the tradition with programmes ranging from early music to contemporary, highlighted by musical upstarts such as Ensemble Signal and violinist Jennifer Koh. *Photo p290.*

Roulette

509 Atlantic Avenue, at Third Avenue, Boerum Hill, Brooklyn (1-917 267 0363, www.roulette.org). Subway B, D, N, Q, R, 2, 3, 4, 5 to Atlantic Avenue-Barclays Center. **Box office** 1-4pm Mon-Fri (also 1 hr before performances and during performances). **Tickets** vary. **Map** p404 T10.

This legendary experimental music institution recently moved from dingy Soho digs to a spectacularly redesigned art deco theatre in Brooklyn. The setting may have changed, but Roulette continues to offer a gold mine of far-out programming that could include anything from a John Cage Musicircus, where the audience is invited to wander through a forest of musical acts all playing at once, to a four-day festival of genre-defying fare from Anthony Braxton.

Spectrum

2nd Floor, 121 Ludlow Street, between Delancey & Rivington Streets, Lower East Side (no phone, www.spectrumnyc.com). Subway F to Lower East Side-Second Ave or Delancey Street; J, M, Z to Delancey-Essex Streets. **Tickets** $15; $10 reductions. **No credit cards**. **Map** p397 G30.

New York's newest contemporary-classical laboratory harks back to the days when the city's most

EVERYTHING UNDER THE SUN

When summer arrives, New York's music scene goes outside.

The main fixture on the summer calendar is **SummerStage** (*see p33*), a New York institution that has an ear for every sound under the sun, and also includes theatre, dance and spoken-word performances. Although the main stage is in Central Park, the series brings great world music to parks throughout the five boroughs. Most shows are free, with a handful of benefit concerts covering for them (recent headliners include Joan Baez and She & Him).

If your tastes veer more towards the classical, the **Metropolitan Opera** (www.metoperafamily.org) and the **New York Philharmonic** (www.nyphil.org) both stage free concerts in Central Park and other large greenspaces during the summer months.

Not far from Central Park is **Lincoln Center** (*see p286*), where the multi-tiered floorplan allows for several outdoor stages to be set up. The most popular venues are the North Plaza, which rolls out the red carpet for the likes of Sonny Rollins, and the Damrosch Park Bandshell, which houses the **Midsummer Night Swing** concerts (*see p34*).

There's also plenty of outdoors action downtown. During the **River to River Festival** (*see p34*), a variety of performers across all disciplines and styles take to waterside stages (Laurie Anderson, Leon Russell and Angélique Kidjo in 2013, for example).

River to River Festival.

innovative work was done in private lofts and similar spaces. Housed in a cosy Lower East Side walk-up, this busy venue largely relies on word of mouth and social media to publicise its ambitious chamber music, progressive jazz and avant-garde rock events.

Symphony Space

2537 Broadway, at 95th Streets, Upper West Side (1-212 864 5400, www.symphonyspace.org). Subway 1, 2, 3 to 96th Street. **Box office** Mon (times vary, show days only); 1-6pm Tue-Sun. **Tickets** vary. **Map** p400 C17.

Despite the name, programming at Symphony Space is anything but orchestra-centric: recent seasons have featured sax quartets, Indian classical music, a cappella ensembles and HD opera simulcasts from Europe. The annual Wall to Wall marathons (usually held in spring) provide a full day of music free of charge, all focused on a particular theme (for instance, a composer or period).

Churches

From sacred to secular, a thrilling variety of music is performed in New York's churches. Superb acoustics, out-of-this-world choirs and serene surroundings make these houses of worship particularly attractive venues. A bonus is that some concerts are free or very cheap.

Church of the Ascension

12 W 11th Street, between Fifth & Sixth Avenues, Greenwich Village (1-212 358 1469, tickets 1-212 358 7060, www.voicesofascension.org). Subway N, R to 8th Street-NYU. **Tickets** $10-$65. **Map** p397 E28.

There's a first-rate professional choir, the Voices of Ascension, at this little Village church. The choir has played at Lincoln Center, but home turf is the best place to hear it.

Church of St Ignatius Loyola

980 Park Avenue, between 83rd & 84th Streets, Upper East Side (1-212 288 2520, www.smssconcerts.org). Subway, 4, 5, 6 to 86th Street. **Tickets** voluntary donation-$75. **Map** p400 E18.

The 'Sacred Music in a Sacred Space' series is a high point of Upper East Side music culture. Lincoln Center and Carnegie Hall also hold concerts here, capitalising on the fine acoustics and prime location.

Corpus Christi Church

529 W 121st Street, between Amsterdam Avenue & Broadway, Morningside Heights (1-212 666 9266, www.mb1800.org). Subway 1 to 116th Street-Columbia Unversity. **Tickets** $10-$45. **Map** p401 C14.

Fans of early music can get their fix from 'Music Before 1800', a series that regularly imports the world's leading antiquarian artists and ensembles.

Holy Trinity Lutheran Church

65th Street & Central Park West, Upper West Side (1-212 877 6815, www.bachvespersnyc.org). Subway 1 to 66th Street-Lincoln Center. **Tickets** vary. **Map** p399 D21.

Miller Theater at Columbia University. *See p288.*

The choir, organist and period-instrument chamber orchestra of this church, located near Lincoln Center, perform free concerts of Baroque music every Sunday from October through April as part of the venerable Bach Vespers series.

St Bartholomew's Church

325 Park Avenue, at 51st Street, Midtown East (1-212 378 0248, www.stbarts.org). Subway E, M to Lexington Avenue-53rd Street; 6 to 51st Street. **Tickets** $15-$40. **Map** p398 E23.

This magnificent church hosts the Summer Festival of Sacred Music, one of the city's most ambitious choral music series. It fills the rest of the year with performances by resident ensembles and guests.

► *The church also hosts free lunchtime concerts; see p285* **In the know**.

St Thomas Church Fifth Avenue

1 W 53rd Street, at Fifth Avenue, Midtown East (1-212 757 7013, www.saintthomaschurch.org). Subway E, M to Fifth Avenue-53rd Street. **Tickets** free-$95. **Map** p399 E22.

The country's only residential boarding school for choir boys keeps the great Anglican choral tradition alive in Gotham. St Thomas's annual performance of Handel's *Messiah* is a must-hear that's worth the rather steep ticket price.

Trinity Wall Street

89 Broadway, at Wall Street, Financial District (1-212 602 0800, www.trinitywallstreet.org). Subway R, 1 to Rector Street; 4, 5 to Wall Street. **Tickets** vary. **Map** p399 E22.

This historic church has an ambitious music series and is home to one of the city's finest choirs, which regularly performs here and sometimes visits Carnegie Hall and Lincoln Center. Several times a week, Trinity hosts free lunchtime concerts in both the church and the nearby St Paul's Chapel (209 Broadway, between Fulton and Vesey Streets).

Schools

The **Juilliard School** and the **Manhattan School of Music** are renowned for their talented students, faculty and artists-in-residence, all of whom regularly perform for free or at low cost. Lately, **Mannes College of Music** has made great strides.

Juilliard School

60 Lincoln Center Plaza, W 65th Street, between Amsterdam Avenue & Broadway, Upper West Side (1-212 769 7406, www.juilliard.edu). Subway 1 to 66th Street-Lincoln Center. **Box office** 11am-6pm Mon-Fri. **Tickets** free-$30. **Map** p399 C21.

New York City's premier conservatory stages weekly concerts by student soloists, orchestras and chamber ensembles, as well as elaborate opera performances that can rival many professional productions. It's likely the singers you see here will be making their Met or other opera company debuts within the next few years.

Manhattan School of Music

120 Claremont Avenue, between Broadway and 122nd Street, Morningside Heights (1-917 493 4428, www.msmnyc.edu). Subway 1 to 125th Street. **Box office** 10am-5pm Mon-Fri. **Tickets** free-$20. **Map** p401 B14.

The School offers master classes, recitals and off-site concerts by its students and faculty as well as visiting professionals. The American String Quartet has been in residence here since 1984. Recently, MSM has also become known for performing opera rarities, such as John Corigliano's *The Ghosts of Versailles* and Virgil Thomson's *The Mother of Us All*.

Mannes College of Music

150 W 85th Street, between Columbus & Amsterdam Avenues, Upper West Side (1-212 580 0210 ext 4817, www.mannes.edu). Subway B, C, 1 to 86th Street. **Tickets** usually free. **Map** p400 C18.

In addition to student concerts and faculty recitals, Mannes also mounts its own ambitious, historically themed concert series; the summer is given over to festivals and workshops for instrumentalists. Productions by the Mannes Opera, whose fresh-faced members are drilled by seasoned opera professionals, are a perennial treat.

Opera companies

The **Metropolitan Opera** (*see p287*) may be the leader of the pack, but it's not the only game in town. Contact the organisations or check their websites for information and prices, schedules and venues.

American Opera Projects

South Oxford Space, 138 S Oxford Street, between Atlantic Avenue & Hanson Place, Fort Greene, Brooklyn (1-718 398 4024, www.operaprojects.org). Subway B, D, N, Q, R, 2, 3, 4, 5 to Atlantic Avenue-Barclays Center; C to Lafayette Avenue; G to Fulton Street. **Tickets** vary (average $20). **Map** p404 T10.

AOP is not so much an opera company as a living, breathing workshop that lets you follow a new work from gestation to completion. Shows, which can be anything from a table reading of a libretto to a complete orchestral production, are staged around the city and beyond.

Amore Opera Company

Connelly Theatre, 220 E 4th Street, between Avenues A & B, Lower East Side (OvationTix 1-866 811 4111, www.amoreopera.org). Subway F to Lower East Side-Second Avenue. **Tickets** $20-$40. **Map** p397 G29.

One of two successors to the late, great Amato Opera Company, the Amore has literally inherited the beloved former company's sets and costumes. Many of the cast members have migrated as well to keep the feisty Amato spirit alive. In previous seasons, they have presented US premières of lesser known or forgotten works – for example, Mercadante's 1835 opera *I due Figaro* in combination with two more famous Figaro incarnations, Mozart's *The Marriage of Figaro* and Rossini's *The Barber of Seville*.

Dicapo Opera Theatre
184 E 76th Street, between Lexington & Third Avenues, Upper East Side (1-212 759 7652, Smarttix 1-212 868 4444, www.dicapo.com). Subway 6 to 77th Street. **Box office** 11am-4pm Mon-Fri. **Tickets** $50. **Map** p399 F20.
This top-notch chamber opera troupe features high-quality singers performing in a delightfully intimate setting in the basement of St Jean Baptiste Church. Dicapo has recently augmented its diet of standard classics with a healthy dose of offbeat works and even premières.

★ Gotham Chamber Opera
1-212 868 4460, Ticket Central 1-212 279 4200, www.gothamchamberopera.org. **Tickets** $30-$175. **Map** p397 G30.
Although they perform in a variety of venues in the city – such as the Hayden Planetarium for a highly imaginative production of Haydn's *Il Mondo della Luna* – this fine young company often appears at John Jay College's Gerald W Lynch Theater on the Upper West Side. Expect a treasure trove of rarely staged shows (directed by the likes of Mark Morris and Tony-winner Diane Paulus) and new fare.

Dance

With its uptown and downtown divide, New York dance includes both luminous tradition and daring experimentation. While Lincoln Center remains the hub for traditional balletic offerings, with annual seasons by American Ballet Theatre and New York City Ballet, the deeper downtown you travel, the more you will encounter more subversive, modern voices – and it's not limited to Manhattan. In Brooklyn, Williamsburg, Bushwick and Bedford-Stuyvesant have sparked a new generation of dancers and choreographers, and Long Island City, Queens, is also pulsing with movement.

IN THE KNOW BANG ON A CAN

For nearly three decades, **Bang on a Can** (www.bangonacan.org) has kicked off its summer season with the Bang on a Can Marathon, 12 straight hours of non-stop free music in a convivial, kid-friendly atmosphere, often in the Winter Garden of Brookfield Place (*see p55*). Recent participants have included Pulitzer Prize winner (and BoaC co-founder) David Lang and Sonic Youth's Thurston Moore.

NOTABLE NAMES & EVENTS

The companies of modern dance icons such as Martha Graham, Alvin Ailey, Trisha Brown, Paul Taylor and Mark Morris are still based in the city, alongside a wealth of contemporary choreographers who create works outside the traditional company structure. The downtown performance world is full of singular voices, including Sarah Michelson, Trajal Harrell, Ralph Lemon, Maria Hassabi, Beth Gill and Ann Liv Young, as well as collectives such as AUNTS, a group of young artists who present performances in unlikely places.

Dance isn't relegated to devoted venues. Increasingly, the art form is making an appearance in museums, galleries and other venues. Multidisciplinary festivals such as **Crossing the Line** in autumn, presented by the **French Institute Alliance Française** (22 E 60th Street, between Madison & Park Avenues, 1-212 355 6100, www.fiaf.org), and **Performa** (1-212 366 5700, www.performa arts.org), a November biennial, showcase the latest developments in dance and performance. Autumn also brings **Fall for Dance** at City Center, which focuses on eclectic mixed bills.

MAJOR VENUES

Baryshnikov Arts Center
450 W 37th Street, between Ninth & Tenth Avenues, Hell's Kitchen (1-646 731 3200, www.bacnyc.org). Subway A, C, E to 34th Street-Penn Station. **Tickets** free-$35. **Map** p398 C25.
Mikhail Baryshnikov, former artistic director of American Ballet Theatre, is something of an impresario. His home base, on a stark overpass near the Lincoln Tunnel, includes several studios, the Howard Gilman Performance Space – a 136-seat theatre – and superb facilities for rehearsals and workshops. With 238 seats, the recently renovated Jerome Robbins Theatre is both intimate and refined.

Brooklyn Academy of Music
For listings, *see p285.*
With its Federal-style columns and carved marble, the 2,100-seat Howard Gilman Opera House is the Brooklyn Academy of Music's most regal dance venue, and has showcased the talents of Mark Morris and William Forsythe. The 1904 Harvey Theater hosts contemporary choreographers – past artists have included Wally Cardona, John Jasperse

David H Koch Theater.

and Sarah Michelson. Annual events include the DanceAfrica Festival, held each Memorial Day weekend (late May), and the Next Wave Festival, which features established groups from New York and abroad in autumn.

★ David H Koch Theater

Lincoln Center, 63rd Street and Columbus Avenue, Upper West Side (1-212 870 5570, www.davidkochtheater.com). Subway 1 to 66th Street-Lincoln Center. **Tickets** $10-$200. **Map** p399 C21.

The neoclassical New York City Ballet headlines at this opulent theatre, which Philip Johnson designed to resemble a jewellery box. During its spring, autumn and winter seasons, ballets by George Balanchine are performed by a wonderful crop of young dancers; there are also works by Jerome Robbins, Peter Martins (the company's ballet master in chief) and former resident choreographer Christopher Wheeldon. The company offers its popular *Nutcracker* from end of November, just into the new year. In the early spring, look for performances by the revered Paul Taylor Dance Company.

Joyce Theater

175 Eighth Avenue, at 19th Street, Chelsea (1-212 242 0800, www.joyce.org). Subway A, C, E to 14th Street; 1 to 18th Street; L to Eighth Avenue. **Tickets** $10-$59. **Map** p397 D27.

This intimate space houses one of the finest theatres – we're talking about sightlines – in town. Companies and choreographers that present work here, among them Ballet Hispanico, Pilobolus Dance Theater and Doug Varone, tend to be somewhat traditional. Regional ballet troupes, such as the Houston Ballet or Pacific Northwest Ballet, appear here too. The Joyce hosts dance throughout much of the year – Pilobolus is a summer staple.

Metropolitan Opera House

For listings, *see p287.*

A range of international companies, from the Paris Opera Ballet to the Kirov, performs here. In spring, the majestic space is home to American Ballet Theatre, which presents full-length traditional story ballets, contemporary classics by Frederick Ashton and Antony Tudor, and the occasional world première by the likes of Twyla Tharp. The acoustics are wonderful, but the theatre is immense: get as close to the stage as you can afford.

New York City Center

131 W 55th Street, between Sixth & Seventh Avenues, Midtown (1-212 581 1212, www.nycitycenter.org). Subway B, D, E to Seventh Avenue; F, N, Q, R to 57th Street. **Tickets** $10-$150. **Map** p399 D22.

Before Lincoln Center changed the city's cultural geography, this was the home of the American Ballet Theatre, the Joffrey Ballet and the New York City Ballet. City Center's lavish decor is golden – the theatre has recently been renovated – as are the companies that pass through here. Regular events include Alvin Ailey American Dance Theater in December and the popular Fall for Dance Festival, in autumn, which features mixed bills for just $15.

OTHER VENUES

★ Abrons Arts Center

466 Grand Street, at Pitt Street, Lower East Side (1-212 598 0400, www.henrystreet.org/arts). Subway B, D to Grand Street; F to Delancey Street; J, M, Z to Delancey-Essex Streets. **Tickets** $15-$25. **Map** p397 G30.

This venue, which features a beautiful proscenium theatre, focuses on a wealth of contemporary dance, courtesy of artistic director Jay Wegman; past artists have included Miguel Gutierrez, Jonah Bokaer, Ann Liv Young and Fitzgerald & Stapleton.

Ailey Citigroup Theater

Joan Weill Center for Dance, 405 W 55th Street, at Ninth Avenue, Hell's Kitchen (1-212 405 9000, www.alvinailey.org). Subway A, B, C, D, 1 to 59th Street-Columbus Circle; N, Q, R to 57th Street. **Tickets** vary. **Map** p399 C22.

The elegant home of Alvin Ailey American Theater contains this flexible downstairs venue; when not in use as rehearsal space by the company or for the home seasons of Ailey II, its junior ensemble, it is rented out to a range of groups of varying quality.

Brooklyn Arts Exchange

421 Fifth Avenue, between 7th & 8th Streets, Park Slope, Brooklyn (1-718 832 0018, www.bax.org). Subway F, G, R to Fourth Avenue-9th Street. **Tickets** $8-$15. **Map** p404 T11.

Brooklyn Arts Exchange holds classes and performances in its intimate theatre; the space hosts more than 50 performance evenings each season. Artists in residence have included choreographers Yasuko Yokoshi, Dean Moss and Jillian Peña; it's a great place to witness the creative process up close.

Center for Performance Research

Unit 1, 361 Manhattan Avenue, at Jackson Street, Williamsburg, Brooklyn (1-718 349 1210, www.cprnyc.org). Subway L to Graham Avenue. **Tickets** $10-$20. **Map** p405 V8.

CPR, founded by choreographers Jonah Bokaer and John Jasperse, represents a new trend of artists taking control of the means of production. It's based in an LEED-certified eco-conscious building with a performance space of approximately 40ft by 40ft. Presentations are sporadic.

★ Chocolate Factory Theater

5-49 49th Avenue, at Vernon Boulevard, Long Island City, Queens (1-718 482 7069, www.chocolatefactorytheater.org). Subway G to 21st Street; 7 to Vernon Boulevard-Jackson Avenue. **Tickets** $15. **Map** p406 V5.

Brian Rogers and Sheila Lewandowski founded this 5,000sq ft performance venue in Long Island City in 2005, converting a one-time hardware store into two spaces: a low-ceilinged downstairs room and a loftier, brighter upstairs white box that caters to the interdisciplinary and the avant-garde. Past choreographers include Beth Gill, Jillian Peña, Big Dance Theater and Tere O'Connor. Rogers, an artist in his own right, also presents work here.

Chocolate Factory Theater.

★ Danspace Project

St Mark's Church in-the-Bowery, 131 E 10th Street, at Second Avenue, East Village (1-212 674 8112 information, 1-866 811 4111 reservations, www.danspaceproject.org). Subway L to Third Avenue; 6 to Astor Place. **Tickets** free-$20. **Map** p397 F28.

A space is only as good as its executive director, and Judy Hussie-Taylor has injected new life into Danspace's programming by creating the Platform series, in which artists curate seasons based on a particular idea. Moreover, the space itself – a high-ceilinged sanctuary – is very handsome. Ticket prices are reasonable, making it easy to take a chance on unknown work.

Dixon Place

161 Chrystie Street, at Delancey Street, Lower East Side (1-212 219 0736, www.dixonplace.org). Subway F to Lower East Side-Second Avenue; J, Z to Bowery. **Tickets** free-$20. **Map** p397 F30.

Ellie Covan started hosting experimental performances in her living room in the mid 1980s; two decades later, this plucky organisation finally opened a state-of-the-art space on the Lower East Side. Along with a mainstage theatre, there is a cocktail lounge – perfect for post-show discussions. Dixon Place supports emerging artists and works in progress; summer events include the annual Hot! festival of queer arts.

Flea Theater

For listings, *see p303.*

Two stages here host a variety of offerings including the free June festival, Dance Conversations, with more than 30 performance pieces from both established and emerging choreographers.

Harlem Stage at the Gatehouse

150 Convent Avenue, at W 135th Street, Harlem (1-212 281 9240 ext.19, www.harlemstage.org). Subway 1 to 137th Street-City College. **Tickets** free-$45. **Map** p401 C12.

Performances at this theatre, formerly an operations centre for the Croton Aqueduct water system, celebrate African-American life and culture. Companies that have graced this flexible space, designed by Frederick S Cook and now designated a New York City landmark, include the Bill T Jones/Arnie Zane Dance Company and Kyle Abraham. Each spring, the space hosts the E-Moves Festival.

★ The Kitchen

512 W 19th Street, between Tenth & Eleventh Avenues, Chelsea (1-212 255 5793, www.thekitchen.org). Subway A, C, E to 14th Street; L to Eighth Avenue. **Tickets** free-$25. **Map** p397 C27.

The Kitchen, led by Tim Griffin, offers some of the best experimental dance around: inventive, provocative and rigorous. Some of the artists who have presented work here are the finest in New York, such as Sarah Michelson (who has served as a guest curator for specific programmes), Dean Moss, Ann Liv Young and Jodi Melnick.

La MaMa ETC

74A E 4th Street, between Bowery & Second Avenue, East Village (1-212 475 7710, www.lamama.org). Subway F to Lower East Side-Second Avenue; 6 to Astor Place. **Tickets** $10-$25. **Map** p397 F29.

This experimental theatre hosts the La MaMa Moves dance festival every spring, featuring a variety of up-and-coming artists, and presents international troupes throughout the year. While shows here can be worthwhile, some of the programming is marginal.

Movement Research at the Judson Church

55 Washington Square South, at Thompson Street, Greenwich Village (1-212 598 0551, www.movementresearch.org). Subway A, B, C, D, E, F, M to W 4th Street. **Tickets** free. **Map** p397 E28.

This free performance series is a great place to check out experimental works and up-and-coming artists. Performances are held roughly every Monday evening at 8pm, from September to June, but it's best to check the website. The group's autumn and spring festivals, which take place in December and May, feature a week-long series of performances held in venues across the city. Movement Research also offers a variety of classes and other events around town.

Movement Research at the Judson Church.

New York Live Arts

219 W 19th Street, between Seventh & Eighth Avenues, Chelsea (1-212 924 0077, www.newyorklivearts.org). Subway 1 to 18th Street. **Tickets** starts at $15. **Map** p397 D27.

In 2010, the Dance Theater Workshop and the Bill T Jones/Arnie Zane Dance Company merged to form New York Live Arts, which is dedicated to contemporary dance under Mr Jones and Carla Peterson. The company performs here regularly, along with local and international choreographers.

Performance Space 122

1-212 477 5829, www.ps122.org.

This venue – the public school where *Fame* was shot – is under renovation through 2015. In the meantime, Performance Space 122 is presenting work at other spaces (see website for info). Ronald K Brown and Doug Varone started out here; more recent artists include Maria Hassabi and Ishmael Houston-Jones.

Symphony Space

For listings, *see p290.*

The World Music Institute hosts traditional dancers from around the globe at this multidisciplinary performing arts centre, but Symphony Space also stages works by contemporary choreographers.

► *See p251 for details of the Thalia cinema.*

Theatre

Tom Hanks, Scarlett Johansson, Denzel Washington, Daniel Craig and Jessica Chastain are among the many boldface names that have shone on Broadway marquees lately. Major musicals tend not to have big stars above the title, but favour the familiar in a different way. In recent years, many of them have been adapted from pop-culture sources (such as *Once* and *The Lion King*) or have been built around existing catalogues of popular songs (such as *Jersey Boys* and *Motown – The Musical*).

Tickets and information

Nearly all Broadway and Off Broadway shows are served by one of the city's 24-hour ticketing agencies. For cheap seats, your best bet is one of the Theatre Development Fund's **TKTS** discount booths. If you're interested in seeing more than one Off-Off Broadway show or dance event, you might consider purchasing a set of four vouchers ($36) from the TDF, either online or at their offices. For more ticket tips, *see* **In the Know** *right* and *p305.*

TKTS

Father Duffy Square, Broadway & 47th Street, Theater District (www.tdf.org). Subway N, Q, R, S, 1, 2, 3, 7 to 42nd Street-Times Square. **Open** *For evening tickets* 3-8pm Mon, Wed-Sun; 2-8pm Tue. *For same-day matinée tickets* 10am-2pm Wed, Sat; 11am-3pm Sun. **Map** p398 D24.

At Times Square's architecturally striking TKTS base, you can get tickets on the day of the performance (or the evening before, in the case of matinées) for as much as 50% off face value. Although there is often a queue when it opens for business, this has usually dispersed one to two hours later, so it's worth trying your luck an hour or two before the show. The Downtown and Brooklyn branches, which are much less busy and open earlier (so you can secure your tickets on the morning of the show), also sell matinée tickets the day before a show (see website for hours). Never buy tickets from anyone who approaches you in the queue as they may have been obtained illegally.

TKTS.

IN THE KNOW CHEAP SEATS

Some of the cheapest tickets on Broadway are known as 'rush' tickets, purchased on the day of a show at a theatre's box office (not all theatres have them). On average, they cost $25. Some venues reserve them for students, while others use a lottery, which is held two hours before the performance.

Other locations: South Street Seaport, corner of Front and John Streets, Financial District; 1 Metrotech Center, corner of Jay Street & Myrtle Avenue Promenade, Downtown Brooklyn.

BROADWAY

Technically speaking, 'Broadway' is the theatre district that surrounds Times Square on either side of Broadway (the actual avenue), between 41st and 54th Streets (plus the Vivian Beaumont Theater, uptown at Lincoln Center). This is where you'll find the grandest theatres in town: wood-panelled, frescoed jewel boxes, mostly built between 1900 and 1930. Officially, 40 of them – those with more than 500 seats – are designated as being part of Broadway. Full-price tickets can easily set you back more than $100; the very best (so-called 'premium') seats can sell for almost $500 at the most popular shows.

The big musicals are still there, and hard to miss. At any given point, however, there are also a handful of new plays, as well as serious revivals of classic dramas ranging from William Shakespeare through Tennessee Williams and David Mamet. Each season also usually includes several small, artistically adventurous musicals to balance out the rafter-rattlers.

Long-running shows

Straight plays can provide some of Broadway's most stirring experiences, but they're less likely than musicals to enjoy long runs. Check *Time Out New York* magazine for current listings and reviews. (The shows listed below are subject to change.)

★ After Midnight

Brooks Atkinson Theatre, 256 W 47th Street, between Broadway & Eighth Avenues, Theater District (Telecharge 1-212 239 6200, aftermidnightbroadway.com). Subway C, E, 1 to 50th Street; N, R to 49th Street. **Box office** 10am-8pm Mon-Sat. **Tickets** $60-$142. **Map** p398 D24.

Evoking Harlem and the legendary Cotton Club, this raucous, joyous, white-hot revue features an array of fiercely talented dancers, singers and musicians (the latter handpicked by Wynton Marsalis). Warren Carlyle directs and choreographs this jazz phantasmagoria of tap, scatting and Duke Ellington classics.

★ The Book of Mormon

Eugene O'Neill Theatre, 230 W 49th Street, between Broadway & Eighth Avenue, Theater District (Telecharge 1-212 239 6200, www.bookofmormonbroadway.com). Subway C, E to 50th Street; N, Q, R, S, 1, 2, 3, 7 to 42nd Street-Times Square; N, R to 49th Street. **Box office** 10am-8pm Mon-Sat; noon-6pm Sun. **Tickets** $69-$477. **Map** p398 D23.

This gleefully obscene and subversive satire may be the funniest show to grace the Great White Way since *The Producers* and *Urinetown.* Writers Trey Parker and Matt Stone of *South Park*, along with composer Robert Lopez (*Avenue Q*), find the perfect blend of sweet and nasty for this tale of mismatched Mormon proselytisers in Uganda.

Chicago

Ambassador Theater, 219 W 49th Street, between Broadway and Eighth Avenue, Theater District, (Telecharge 1-212 239 6200, www.chicagothemusical.com). Subway C, E, 1 to 50th Street; N, R to 49th Street. **Box office** 10am-8pm Mon-Sat; noon-7pm Sun. **Tickets** $69-$200. **Map** p398 D23.

This John Kander-Fred Ebb-Bob Fosse favourite – revived by director Walter Bobbie and choreographer Ann Reinking – tells the saga of chorus girl Roxie Hart, who murders her lover and, with the help

After Midnight.

Kinky Boots.

of a huckster lawyer, becomes a vaudeville star. New headliners, sometimes including stunt-cast celebrities, rotate into the cast on a regular basis.

Jersey Boys

August Wilson Theatre, 245 W 52nd Street, between Broadway & Eighth Avenue, Theater District (Telecharge 1-212 239 6200, www.jerseyboysinfo.com/broadway). Subway C, E, 1 to 50th Street. **Box office** 10am-8pm Mon-Sat; noon-6pm Sun. **Tickets** $47-$297. **Map** p398 D23.

The Broadway musical finally does right by the jukebox with this nostalgic behind-the-music tale, presenting the Four Seasons' infectiously energetic 1960s tunes (including 'Walk Like a Man' and 'Big Girls Don't Cry') as they were intended to be performed. Sleek direction by Des McAnuff ensures that Marshall Brickman and Rick Elice's script feels canny instead of canned.

★ Kinky Boots

Al Hirschfeld Theatre, 302 W 45th Street, between Eighth & Ninth Avenues, Theater District (Telecharge 1-212 239 6200, kinkybootsthemusical.com). Subway A, C, E to 42nd Street-Port Authority; N, Q, R, S, 1, 2, 3, 7 to 42nd Street-Times Square. **Box office** 10am-8pm Mon-Sat; noon-6pm Sun. **Tickets** $87-$399. **Map** p398 D24.

Harvey Fierstein and Cyndi Lauper's fizzy crowd-pleaser, in which a sassy-dignified drag queen kicks an English shoe factory into gear, feels familiar at every step. But it has been manufactured with solid craftsmanship and care (Lauper is a musical-theatre natural), and is boosted by a heart-strong cast. The overall effect is nigh irresistible.

> **IN THE KNOW**
> **UNDERSTUDY REFUNDS**
>
> If you've come to see a particular performer on Broadway, you may be able to cash in your ticket if that star doesn't show up. As a general rule, you are entitled to a refund if the star's name appears above the title of the show. A card on the wall of the lobby will announce any absences that day – go to the box office if you want your money back.

The Lion King

Minskoff Theatre, 200 W 45th Street, between Broadway & Eighth Avenue, Theater District (Ticketmaster 1-866 870 2717, www.lionking.com). Subway A, C, E to 42nd Street-Port Authority; N, Q, R, S, 1, 2, 3, 7 to 42nd Street-Times Square. **Box office** 10am-8pm Mon-Sat; noon-6pm Sun. **Tickets** $89-$299. **Map** p398 D24.

Director-designer Julie Taymor surrounds the Disney movie's mythic plot and Elton John-Tim Rice score with African rhythm and music. Through elegant puppetry, Taymor populates the stage with a menagerie of African beasts; her staging has expanded a simple cub into the pride of Broadway.

★ Matilda

Shubert Theatre, 225 W 44th Street, between Broadway & Eighth Avenue, Theater District (Telecharge 1-212 239 6200, http://us.matildathemusical.com). Subway A, C, E to 42nd Street-Port Authority; N, Q, R, S, 1, 2, 3, 7 to 42nd Street-Times Square. **Box office** 10am-8pm Mon-Sat; noon-6pm Sun. **Tickets** $37-$167. **Map** p4398 D24.

Based on Roald Dahl's book about a child prodigy who must outwit horrid parents and a sadistic headmistress, this English musical delivers mischievous fun while hitting the requisite sentimental notes and smuggling in an anti-authoritarian message. Tim Minchin's cheeky Britpop score and Matthew Warchus's cartoonish staging offer sheer delight.

Newsies

Nederlander Theatre, 208 W 41st Street, between Broadway & Eighth Avenue (Ticketmaster 1-866 870 2717, www.newsiesthemusical.com). Subway A, C, E to 42nd Street-Port Authority; N, Q, R, S, 1, 2, 3, 7 to 42nd Street-Times Square. **Box office** 10am-8pm Mon-Sat. **Tickets** $67-$189. **Map** p398 D24.

Not since *Wicked* has there been a big-tent, family-friendly Broadway musical that gets so much so right. Disney's barnstorming, four-alarm delight focuses on the newsboy strike of 1899, in which spunky (and high-kicking) newspaper hawkers stand up to the media magnates of their day. The Alan Menken tunes are pleasing, the book is sharp, and the dances are simply spectacular.

★ Once

Bernard B Jacobs Theatre, 242 W 45th Street, between Broadway & Eighth Avenue (Telecharge 1-212 239 6200, www.oncemusical.com). Subway A, C, E to 42nd Street-Port Authority; N, Q, R, S, 1, 2, 3, 7 to 42nd Street-Times Square. **Box office** 10am-8pm Mon-Sat; noon-6pm Sun. **Tickets** $60-$252. **Map** p398 D24.

Known for big, splashy spectacles, Broadway also has room for more sincere and understated musicals. This touching hit, adapted from the 2006 indie flick about an Irish songwriter and the Czech immigrant who inspires and enchants him, has a brooding emo-folk score and a bittersweet sense of longing that make it an ideal choice for a romantic evening out.

The Lion King.

Matilda.

Wicked

Gershwin Theatre, 222 W 51st Street, between Broadway & Eighth Avenue, Theater District (Ticketmaster 1-800 982 2787, www.wickedthemusical.com). Subway C, E, 1 to 50th Street. **Box office** 10am-8pm Mon-Sat; noon-6pm Sun. **Tickets** $65-$301. **Map** p398 D23.

Based on novelist Gregory Maguire's 1995 riff on *The Wizard of Oz, Wicked* is a witty prequel to the classic children's book and movie. The show's combination of pop dynamism and sumptuous spectacle has made it the most popular show on Broadway. Teenage girls, especially, have responded to the story of how a green girl named Elphaba comes to be known as the Wicked Witch of the West.

OFF BROADWAY

As the cost of mounting shows on Broadway continues to soar, many serious playwrights (including major ones such as Edward Albee and Tony Kushner) are opening their shows in the less financially arduous world of Off Broadway, where many of the theatres are not-for-profit enterprises. The venues here have between 100 and 499 seats; tickets usually run from $30 to $80. Here, we've listed some reliable long-running shows, plus some of the best theatres and repertory companies.

ART OF BROOKLYN

A cultural district grows around BAM.

Theatre for a New Audience.

In the 1950s and '60s, city planner Robert Moses transformed a run-down portion of the Upper West Side into an artistic hub when he spearheaded the construction of Lincoln Center. Today, a portion of Brooklyn is undergoing a similar metamorphosis, as funds and support from the city are pouring in to build arts-centric spaces in a once-industrial patch at the nexus of Fort Greene, Boerum Hill and Downtown Brooklyn. Plans have been afoot since 2004, but it's only in the past few years that the so-called Downtown Brooklyn Cultural District, which will also include apartments, restaurants and retail, has truly come into its own, with performing arts spaces popping up like dandelions from the concrete.

The developments are centred on the **Brooklyn Academy of Music** (*see p301*), the oldest performing arts institution in America, which has been operating in one form or another since 1861. The BAM of today presents some of the most cutting-edge, progressive theatre, music, dance and film in the country. More than 150 years down the line, the venerable complex is now the nerve centre of an entire neighbourhood dedicated to performing arts of all stripes.

Longtime downtown Manhattan arts organisation Roulette moved further south to Kings County in 2011, setting up shop in a retooled art deco theatre (*see p288*). Here, you can see a variety of affordable performances in dance, music and more; in particular, it's become a haven for NYC's thriving new music scene.

A few blocks away is the most recent addition to the Cultural District, **Theatre for a New Audience** at the **Polonsky Shakespeare Center** (*see p308*). After 34 years of vagabonding, the powerhouse classical-theatre company finally opened this permanent home in 2013. Inside the striking modernist structure, audiences can see works by the Bard and other greats mounted by heavyweights such as *The Lion King* director Julie Taymor.

The other new kid on the block is **BRIC House** (647 Fulton Street, at Rockwell Place, Fort Greene, 1-718 683 5600, www.bricartsmedia.org), a multi-use arts centre housed in former vaudeville-circuit stop the Strand Theatre. Run by the cultural programmer behind much-loved outdoor festival Celebrate Brooklyn! (*see p33*), the space includes a theatre, a TV studio and a coffee shop overlooking an art gallery.

Long-running shows

Avenue Q

New World Stages, 340 W 50th Street, between Eighth & Ninth Avenues, Theater District (Telecharge 1-212 239 6200, www.avenueq.com). Subway C, E, 1 to 50th Street. **Box office** 1-8pm Mon, Thur, Fri; 1-7pm Tue; 10am-8pm Wed, Sat; 10am-7.30pm Sun. **Tickets** $72.50-$126.50. **Map** p398 D23.

After many years, which have included a Broadway run followed by a return to its Off Broadway roots, the sassy and clever puppet musical doesn't show its age. Robert Lopez and Jeff Marx's deft *Sesame Street*-esque novelty tunes about porn and racism still earn their laughs, and *Avenue Q* remains a sly and winning piece of metamusical tomfoolery.

Blue Man Group

Astor Place Theatre, 434 Lafayette Street, between Astor Place & 4th Street, East Village (1-800 258 3626, www.blueman.com). Subway N, R to 8th Street-NYU; 6 to Astor Place. **Box office** noon-7.45pm daily. **Tickets** $82-$106. **Map** p397 F28.

Three deadpan men with extraterrestrial imaginations (and head-to-toe blue body paint) carry this long-time favourite, which may be the world's most accessible piece of multimedia performance art. A weird, exuberant trip through the trappings of modern culture, the show is as smart as it is ridiculous.

★ Sleep No More

McKittrick Hotel, 530 W 27th Street, between Tenth & Eleventh Avenues, Chelsea (Ovationtix 1-866 811 4111, www.sleepnomorenyc.com). Subway 1 to 28th Street; C, E to 23rd Street. **Tickets** $75-$162.50. **Map** p398 C26.

A multitude of searing sights awaits at this bedazzling and uncanny installation by the English company Punchdrunk. Your sense of space is blurred as you wend through more than 90 discrete spaces, from a cloistral chapel to a ballroom floor. A Shakespearean can check off allusions to *Macbeth*; others can just revel in the haunted-house vibe.

Sleep No More.

Repertory companies & venues

59E59 Theaters

59 E 59th Street, between Madison & Park Avenues, Upper East Side (1-212 753 5959, Ticket Central 1-212 279 4200, www.59e59.org). Subway N, Q, R to Lexington Avenue-59th Street; 4, 5, 6 to 59th Street. **Box office** noon-6pm Mon; noon-7.30pm Tue-Thur; noon-8.30pm Fri, Sat; noon-3.30pm Sun. **Tickets** $18-$60. **Map** p399 E22.

This chic, state-of-the-art venue, which comprises an Off Broadway space and two smaller theatres, is home to the Primary Stages company. It's also where you'll find the annual Brits Off Broadway festival (www.britsoffbroadway.com), which imports some of the UK's best work for brief runs, and its newer offshoot, Americas Off Broadway.

Ars Nova

511 W 54th Street, between Tenth & Eleventh Avenues, Hell's Kitchen (1-212 489 9800, Ovationtix 1-866 811 4111, www.arsnovanyc.com). Subway C, E, 1 to 50th Street. **Box office** 30mins before show. **Tickets** $15-$35. **Map** p399 C22.

Committed to presenting innovative new theatre, music and comedy, this offbeat Hell's Kitchen space has been a boon to developing artists since it opened in 2002. Along with full productions, Ars Nova also presents an eclectic monthly special called Showgasm and the annual ANT Fest for emerging talents.

Atlantic Theater Company

336 W 20th Street, between Eighth & Ninth Avenues, Chelsea (1-212 691 5919, Ticket Central 1-212 279 4200, www.atlantictheater.org). Subway C, E to 23rd Street. **Box office** noon-6pm Mon-Fri. **Tickets** $35-$70. **Map** p397 D27.

Created in 1985 as an offshoot of acting workshops led by playwright David Mamet and actor William H Macy, the dynamic Atlantic Theater Company has presented dozens of new plays, including Steven Sater and Duncan Sheik's rock musical *Spring Awakening*, and Conor McPherson's *The Night Alive*. The Atlantic also has a smaller second stage deep underground at 330 W 16th Street.

★ Brooklyn Academy of Music

For listings, *see p285*.

BAM's beautifully distressed Harvey Theater – along with its grand old opera house in the Peter Jay Sharp Building – is the site of the Next Wave

Festival (*see p35*) and other international events. The spring season usually features high-profile productions of classics by the likes of Chekhov and Shakespeare, often shipped from England with major actors attached.

Classic Stage Company

136 E 13th Street, between Third & Fourth Avenues, East Village (1-212 677 4210, www.classicstage.org). Subway L, N, Q, R, 4, 5, 6 to 14th Street-Union Square. **Box office** noon-6pm Mon-Fri. **Tickets** $55-$125. **Map** p397 F27.

With a purview that runs from medieval mystery plays and Elizabethan standards to early modern drama and original period pieces, Classic Stage Company is committed to making the old new again. Under artistic director Brian Kulick, the company has a knack for attracting major stars, as recent productions of Chekhov plays with Maggie Gyllenhaal and Dianne Wiest attest.

Flea Theater

41 White Street, between Broadway & Church Street, Tribeca (1-212 226 2407, Ovationtix 1-866 811 4111, www.theflea.org). Subway A, C, E, J, M, N, Q, R, Z, 6 to Canal Street; 1 to Franklin Street. **Box office** noon-6pm Mon-Sat. **Tickets** $15-$60. **Map** p396 E31.

Founded in 1997, Jim Simpson's versatile and well-appointed venue has presented avant-garde experimentation and politically provocative satires. A second, basement theatre hosts the Flea's resident young acting company, the Bats. Construction recently started on a new theatre complex nearby, expected to open in 2015.

Irish Repertory Theatre

132 W 22nd Street, between Sixth & Seventh Avenues, Chelsea (1-212 727 2737, www.irishrep.org). Subway F, M, 1 to 23rd Street. **Box office** 10am-6pm Mon; 10am-8pm Tue-Fri; 11am-8pm Sat; 11am-6pm Sun. **Tickets** $55-$65. **Map** p398 D26.

Set in a cosily odd, L-shaped venue, the Irish Repertory Theatre puts on compelling shows by Irish and Irish-American playwrights. Fine revivals of classics by the likes of Oscar Wilde and George Bernard Shaw alternate with plays by lesser-known modern authors.

Lincoln Center Theater

Lincoln Center, 150 W 65th Street, at Broadway, Upper West Side (Telecharge 1-212 239 6200, www.lct.org). Subway 1 to 66th Street-Lincoln Center. **Box office** 10am-8pm Mon-Sat; noon-7pm Sun. **Tickets** $20-$200. **Map** p399 C21.

The majestic and prestigious Lincoln Center Theater complex has a pair of amphitheatre-style drama venues. The Broadway house, the 1,080-seat Vivian Beaumont Theater, is home to star-studded and elegant major productions. Downstairs is the 299-seat Mitzi E Newhouse Theater, an Off Broadway space devoted to new work by the upper layer of American playwrights. In 2008, in an effort to shake off its reputation for stodginess, Lincoln Center launched LCT3, which presents the work of emerging playwrights and directors at the new Claire Tow Theater, built on top of the Beaumont.

► *For music and festivals at Lincoln Center, see pp286-287 and p35, respectively.*

Claire Tow Theater, Lincoln Center.

ALWAYS
CHICAGO
THE MUSICAL
PHOTO BY JASON BELL
CHICAGOTHEMUSICAL.COM
TELECHARGE.COM/CHICAGO OR 212-239-6200
AMBASSADOR THEATRE • 49TH STREET AT BROADWAY

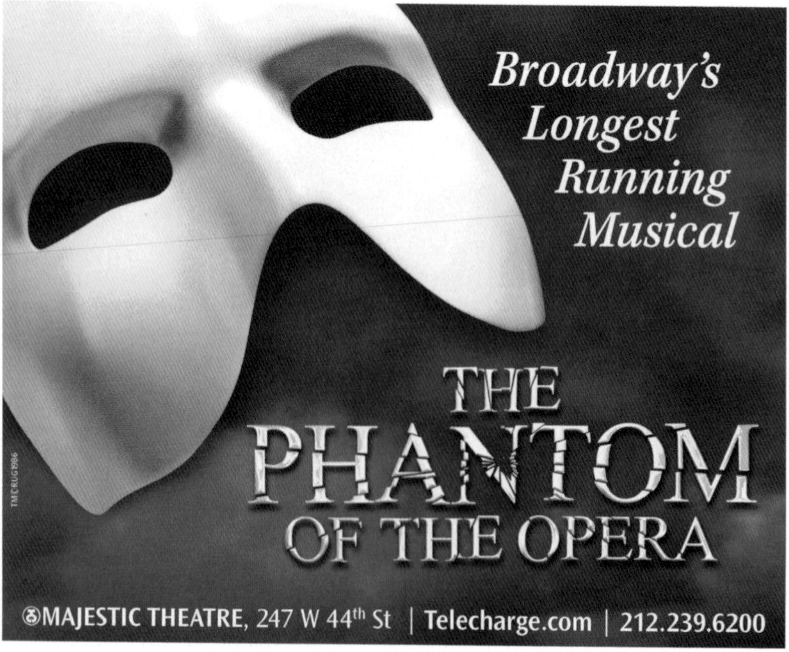
Broadway's Longest Running Musical
THE PHANTOM OF THE OPERA
MAJESTIC THEATRE, 247 W 44th St | Telecharge.com | 212.239.6200

Manhattan Theatre Club

Samuel J Friedman Theatre, 261 W 47th Street, between Broadway & Eighth Avenue, Theater District (Telecharge 1-212 239 6200, www.manhattantheatreclub.com). Subway N, Q, R, S, 1, 2, 3, 7 to 42nd Street-Times Square. **Box office** noon-6pm Tue-Sun. **Tickets** $30-$120. **Map** p398 D24.

One of the city's most important non-profit companies, Manhattan Theatre Club spent decades as an Off Broadway outfit before moving into the 622-seat Friedman Theatre in 2003. But it still maintains two smaller spaces at New York City Center (*see p293*), where it presents some of its best material – such as Lynn Nottage's 2009 Pulitzer Prize winner, *Ruined*. Twentysomethings and teens can sign up for the 30 Under 30 Club to get tickets at both theatres for $30.

New Victory Theater

209 W 42nd Street, between Seventh & Eighth Avenues, Theater District (1-646 223 3010, www.newvictory.org). Subway N, Q, R, S, 1, 2, 3, 7 to 42nd Street-Times Square. **Box office** 11am-5pm Mon, Sun; noon-7pm Tue-Sat. **Tickets** $14-$38. **Map** p398 D24.

The New Victory Theater is a perfect symbol of the transformation that has occurred in Times Square. Built in 1900, Manhattan's oldest surviving theatre became a strip club and adult cinema in the sleazy days of the 1970s and '80s. Renovated by the city in 1995, the building now functions as a kind of kiddie version of the Brooklyn Academy of Music, offering a full season of smart, adventurous, reasonably priced and family-friendly plays (including many international productions).

New World Stages

340 W 50th Street, between Eighth & Ninth Avenues, Theater District (1-646 871 1730, Telecharge 1-212 239 6200, www.newworldstages.com). Subway C, E, 1 to 50th Street. **Box office** 1-8pm Mon, Thur, Fri; 1-7pm Tue; 10am-8pm Wed, Sat; 10am-7.30pm Sun. **Tickets** $40-$150. **Map** p398 C23.

Formerly a movie multiplex, this centre – one of the last bastions of commercial Off Broadway in New York – boasts a shiny, space-age interior and five stages, presenting everything from family-friendly spectacles (like *Gazillion Bubble Show*) to downsized transfers of Broadway musicals (including the long-running *Avenue Q*).

★ New York Theatre Workshop

79 E 4th Street, between Bowery & Second Avenue, East Village (1-212 460 5475, www.nytw.org). Subway F to Lower East Side-Second Avenue; 6 to Astor Place. **Box office** 1-6pm Tue-Sun. **Tickets** $45-$85. **Map** p397 F29.

Founded in 1979, the New York Theatre Workshop works with emerging directors eager to take on challenging pieces. Besides presenting plays by world-class artists such as Caryl Churchill and Tony Kushner, this company also premièred *Rent*, Jonathan Larson's seminal 1990s musical. The iconoclastic Flemish director Ivo van Hove has made the NYTW his New York pied-à-terre.

IN THE KNOW HOT TICKETS

Buzzed-about shows, especially those with big stars on the bill, sell out fast. Keep on top of openings by checking sites such as www.playbill.com and www.theatermania.com, as well as the Theater section of www.timeout.com/newyork. All feature the latest news and interviews; Theatermania also has an online booking service and discounted tickets for some shows.

Pershing Square Signature Center

480 W 42nd Street, at Tenth Avenue, Hell's Kitchen (1-212 244 7529, www.signaturetheatre.org). Subway A, C, E to 42nd Street-Port Authority. **Box office** 11am-6pm Tue-Sun. **Tickets** $25-$65. **Map** p398 C24.

The award-winning Signature Theatre Company, founded by James Houghton in 1991, focuses on exploring and celebrating playwrights in depth, with whole seasons devoted to works by individual living writers. Over the years, the company has delved into the oeuvres of August Wilson, John Guare, Horton Foote and many more. Special programmes are designed to keep prices low. In 2012 the troupe expanded hugely into a new home – a theatre complex designed by Frank Gehry, with three major spaces and ambitious long-term commission programmes, cementing it as one of the city's key cultural institutions.

★ Playwrights Horizons

416 W 42nd Street, between Ninth & Tenth Avenues, Theater District (1-212 564 1235, Ticket Central 1-212 279 4200, www.playwrightshorizons.org). Subway A, C, E to 42nd Street-Port Authority. **Box office** noon-8pm daily. **Tickets** $50-$90. **Map** p398 C24.

More than 300 important contemporary plays have had their première here, including dramas (*Driving Miss Daisy, The Heidi Chronicles*) and musicals (Stephen Sondheim's *Assassins* and *Sunday in the Park with George*). More recent seasons have included new works by Edward Albee and Craig Lucas, as well as Bruce Norris's Pulitzer Prize-winning *Clybourne Park*.

★ Public Theater

425 Lafayette Street, between Astor Place & 4th Street, East Village (1-212 539 8500, tickets 1-212 967 7555, www.publictheater.org).

Subway N, R to 8th Street-NYU; 6 to Astor Place. **Box office** 1-6pm Mon, Sun; 1-7.30pm Tue-Sat. **Tickets** $15-$95. **Map** p397 F28.
Under the guidance of the civic-minded Oskar Eustis, this local institution – dedicated to producing the work of new American playwrights, but also known for its Shakespeare in the Park productions – has regained its place at the forefront of the Off Broadway world. The ambitious, multicultural programming ranges from new works by major playwrights to the annual Under the Radar festival for emerging artists. The company's home building, an Astor Place landmark, has five stages and has recently been extensively renovated.
► *The building is also home to Joe's Pub, see p276.*

Roundabout Theatre Company

American Airlines Theatre, 227 W 42rd Street, between Seventh & Eighth Avenues, Theater District (1-212 719 1300, www.roundabouttheatre.org). Subway N, Q, R, S, 1, 2, 3, 7 to 42nd Street-Times Square. **Box office** 10am-6pm Mon, Sun; 10am-8pm Tue-Sat. **Tickets** $20-$147. **Map** p398 D24.
Devoted mostly to revivals, the Roundabout often pairs beloved old chestnuts with celebrity casts. In addition to its Broadway flagship, the company also mounts shows at Studio 54 (254 W 54th Street, between Broadway & Eighth Avenue), the Stephen Sondheim Theatre (124 West 43rd Street, between Sixth & Seventh Avenues) and Off Broadway's Laura Pels Theatre (111 W 46th Street, between Sixth & Seventh Avenues).

St Ann's Warehouse

29 Jay Street, between John & Plymouth Streets, Dumbo, Brooklyn (1-718 254 8779, www.stannswarehouse.org). Subway A, C to High Street; F to York Street. **Box office** 1-7pm Tue-Sat. **Tickets** $25-$75. **Map** p405 T9.
The adventurous theatregoer's alternative to Brooklyn Academy of Music (*see p285*), St Ann's Warehouse offers an eclectic line-up of drama and music. The company recently left its longtime digs on Water Street for a nearby Dumbo location but is scheduled to move again in late 2015 to a converted space within Brooklyn Bridge Park's 1870s Tobacco Warehouse. Recent shows have included high-level work by the Wooster Group, Daniel Kitson and the National Theatre of Scotland.

Second Stage Theatre

307 W 43rd Street, at Eighth Avenue, Theater District (1-212 246 4422, www.2st.com). Subway A, C, E to 42nd Street-Port Authority. **Box office** 10am-6pm Mon-Sat; 10am-3pm Sun. **Tickets** $75-$125. **Map** p398 D24.

Public Theater. *See p305.*

Occupying a beautiful Rem Koolhaas-designed space near Times Square, Second Stage Theatre specialises in American playwrights, and hosted the New York première of Edward Albee's *Peter and Jerry*. It also provides a stage for serious new musicals, such as the Pulitzer Prize-winning *Next to Normal*.

Shakespeare in the Park at the Delacorte Theater

Park entrance on Central Park West, at 81st Street, then follow the signs (1-212 539 8750, www.shakespeareinthepark.org). Subway B, C to 81st Street-Museum of Natural History. **Tickets** free. **Map** p399 D19.

The Delacorte Theater in Central Park is the fair-weather sister of the Public Theater (*see p305*). When not producing Shakespeare in the East Village, the Public offers the best of the Bard outdoors during Shakespeare in the Park (June-Aug). Free tickets (two per person) are distributed at the Delacorte at noon on the day of the performance. Around 8am is usually a good time to begin waiting, although the queue can start forming as early as 6am when big-name stars are on the bill. There is also an online lottery for tickets.

★ Soho Rep

46 Walker Street, between Broadway & Church Street, Tribeca (TheaterMania 1-212 352 3101, www.sohorep.org). Subway A, C, E, N, R, 6 to Canal Street; 1 to Franklin Street. **Box office** 9am-9pm Mon-Fri; 10am-9pm Sat, Sun. **Tickets** 99¢-$35. **Map** p396 E31.

A few years ago, this Off-Off mainstay moved to an Off Broadway contract, but tickets for most shows have remained cheap. Artistic director Sarah Benson's programming is diverse and audacious: recent productions include works by Young Jean Lee, Sarah Kane and the Nature Theater of Oklahoma.

Theatre for a New Audience

Polonsky Shakespeare Center, 262 Ashland Place, between Fulton Street & Lafayette Avenue, Fort Greene, Brooklyn (Ovationtix 1-866 811 4111, www.tfana.org). Subway B, D, N, Q, R, 2, 3, 4, 5 to Atlantic Avenue-Barclays Center; C to Lafayette Avenue; G to Fulton Street. **Box office** 1-6pm Tue-Sat. **Tickets** $60-$85. **Map** p398 D24.

Founded in 1979, TFANA has grown steadily to become New York's most prominent classical-theatre company. Now, finally, it has a home of its own: the Polonsky Shakespeare Center (near BAM, in Brooklyn's cultural district). This flashy, glass-fronted 299-seat venue, designed by Hugh Hardy, opened its doors in 2013 with Julie Taymor's production of *A Midsummer Night's Dream*.

Theatre Row

410 W 42nd Street, between Ninth & Tenth Avenues, Theater District (1-212 714 2442, Telecharge 1-212 239 6200, www.theatrerow.org). Subway A, C, E to 42nd Street-Port Authority. **Box office** noon-6pm daily. **Tickets** $18-$95. **Map** p398 C24.

Soho Rep.

Comprising five main venues of various sizes, Theatre Row hosts new plays and revivals by the trendy and celebrity-friendly New Group (Ethan Hawke, Ed Harris, Bill Pullman and Matthew Broderick are among the recent stars), as well as scores of other productions by assorted theatre companies.

Vineyard Theatre

108 E 15th Street, at Union Square East, Union Square (1-212 353 0303, www.vineyardtheatre.org). Subway L, N, Q, R, 4, 5, 6 to 14th Street-Union Square. **Box office** 1-6pm Mon-Fri. **Tickets** $45-$100. **Map** p397 E27.

VT produces some excellent new plays and musicals, including *The Scottsboro Boys*, the wittily named *[title of show]* and the Tony Award-winning *Avenue Q*, all of which transferred to Broadway.

OFF-OFF BROADWAY

Technically, Off-Off Broadway denotes a show that is presented at a theatre with fewer than 100 seats, usually for less than $25. It's where some of the most daring writers and performers – who aren't necessarily card-carrying union professionals – create their edgiest work: **Radiohole** (www.radiohole.com), the **Debate Society** (www.thedebatesociety.org) and **Nature Theater of Oklahoma** (www.oktheater.org) are among many troupes that offer inspired theatre. The **New York International Fringe Festival** (1-212 279 4488, www.fringenyc.org), held every August, provides a wide opportunity to see the wacky side of the stage, and the **New York Musical**

Theatre Festival (www.nymf.org) in July has become an important testing ground for composers and lyricists.

Repertory companies & venues

For multidisciplinary **Dixon Place**, *see p294.*

The Brick

575 Metropolitan Avenue, between Lorimer Street & Union Avenue, Williamsburg, Brooklyn (1-718 907 6189, Ovationtix 1-866 811 4111, www.bricktheater.com). Subway G to Metropolitan Avenue; L to Lorimer Street. **Box office** opens 15mins before curtain. **Tickets** $15-$20. **No credit cards**. **Map** p405 V8.

This spunky, brick-lined venue presents a variety of boundary-pushing work. Its tongue-in-cheek themed summer series have included Moral Values, Hell, Pretentious and Antidepressant Festivals.

★ The Bushwick Starr

207 Starr Street, between Irving & Wyckoff Avenues, Bushwick, Brooklyn (Ovationtix 1-866 811 4111, www.thebushwickstarr.org). Subway L to Jefferson Street. **Box office** opens 30mins before curtain. **Tickets** $15-$25. **Map** p405 V8.

As small companies continue to be priced out of Manhattan, everyone's looking to Brooklyn to pick up the slack. This funky black box is one good option: some of the city's fiercest experimental troupes – Half Straddle, the TEAM and others – have made the Starr shine brightly.

HERE

145 Sixth Avenue, between Broome & Spring Streets, Soho (1-212 647 0202, TheaterMania 1-212 352 3101, www.here.org). Subway C, E to Spring Street. **Box office** 5-10pm daily. **Tickets** $20-$50. **Map** p397 E30.

Dedicated to not-for-profit arts enterprises, this thetre complex has been the launch pad for such well-known shows as Eve Ensler's *The Vagina Monologues*. More recently, HERE has showcased the talents of the brilliantly freaky playwright-performer Taylor Mac.

Incubator Arts Center

131 E 10th Street, at Second Avenue, East Village (TheaterMania 1-212 352 3101, www.incubatorarts.org). Subway L to First or Third Ave, 6 to Astor Place. **Box office** opens 45mins before curtain. **Tickets** $15-$25. **Map** p397 E30.

Located upstairs at the historic St Mark's Church-in-the-Bowery, this adventurous developmental venue has an eye for the best in local avant-garde theatre. Dave Malloy, Tina Satter and Julia Jarcho have done work there recently, negotiating the space's asymmetrical shape and weirdly placed columns to make exciting work; Incubator also produces the Other Forces festival each January.

La MaMa ETC

74A E Fourth Street, between Bowery & Second Avenue, East Village (1-212 475 7710, www.lamama.org). Subway 6 to Bleecker Street. **Box office** noon-6pm Mon-Sun. **Tickets** $10-$25. **Map** p397 F29.

Founded by the late Ellen Stewart, La MaMa has been a bastion of the Off-Off scene for more than half a century. The complex has helped to nurture such innovators as Sam Shepard, Charles Ludlam, Lanford Wilson and Ping Chong, and it continues to be an important rung in many rising artists' ladders.

Theatre for a New Audience.

Escapes & Excursions

Escapes & Excursions

Need a break from the city? New York is well situated for both coastal and countryside getaways, and there are plenty of worthwhile destinations within reach of the five boroughs. Bucolic areas such as New York State's Hudson Valley, north of Manhattan, are little more than an hour away; and although New Jersey is the butt of some unkind jokes, even hardened urbanites concede it has some lovely beaches that can be reached in little more time than it takes to get across town on a bus. What's more, many getaway spots are accessible by public transport, allowing you to avoid the often exorbitant car-rental rates and the heavy summer traffic in and out of town.

Hit the Trails

The city's parks are great for a little casual relaxation. But if you're hankering after a real fresh-air escape, set off on one of these day hikes, between one and three hours away. Bring water and snacks: refuelling options are scarce.

BREAKNECK RIDGE

The trek at Breakneck Ridge, in Hudson Highlands State Park, is a favourite of hikers for its accessibility, variety of trails and views of the Hudson Valley and the Catskill Mountains. The trail head is a half-mile walk along the highway from the Cold Spring stop on Metro-North's Hudson line (at weekends, the train stops closer to the trail, at the Breakneck Ridge stop).

You can spend anywhere from two hours to a full day hiking Breakneck, so plan your route in advance. The start of the trail is on the river's eastern bank, atop a tunnel that was drilled out for Route 9D: it's marked with small white paint splotches (called 'blazes' in hiking parlance) on nearby trees. Be warned, though, that Breakneck got its name for a reason. The initial trail ascends 500 feet in just a mile and a half, and gains another 500 feet via a series of dips and rises over the next few miles. If you're not in good shape, you might want to think about an alternative hike. But if you do choose this path, there are plenty of dramatic overlooks where you can stretch out on a rock and take in the majestic Hudson River below.

After the difficult initial climb, Breakneck Ridge offers options for all levels of hikers, and several crossings in the first few miles provide alternative routes back down the slope. Trail information and maps of all the paths, which

IN THE KNOW SLEEPY HOLLOW

South of Cold Spring is the small town of **Sleepy Hollow**. It's most famous as the putative location for Washington Irving's short story *The Legend of Sleepy Hollow*, later adapted into a movie by Tim Burton. Irving is buried in the village cemetery.

are clearly marked with different coloured blazes, are available from the New York-New Jersey Trail Conference; it's strongly recommended that you carry them with you.

Tourist information

Hudson Highlands State Park
1-845 225 7207, www.nysparks.state.ny.us.
New York-New Jersey Trail Conference
1-201 512 9348, www.nynjtc.org.

Getting there

By train Take the Metro-North Hudson train from Grand Central to the Cold Spring stop, or catch the early train to the Breakneck Ridge stop (Sat & Sun only). Journey time 1hr 15mins; round-trip ticket $26.50-$35.50 ($13.50-$17.50 reductions). Contact the MTA (www.mta.info/mnr) for schedules.

HARRIMAN STATE PARK

Across the Hudson River and south-west of the sprawling campus of West Point lies Harriman State Park (*photo p314*), containing more than 200 miles of trails and 31 lakes. It's accessible from stops on the Metro-North Port Jervis line. Of the various trails, our favourite is the **Triangle Trail**. Part of the White Bar Trail, this is an eight-mile jaunt that begins just past the parking lot at Tuxedo station (which is a little over an hour's journey from Penn Station). The route climbs steadily more than 1,000 feet towards the summit of Parker Cabin Mountain before turning south to offer lovely views of two lakes, Skenonto and Sebago. From there, it heads down steadily, although steeply at times, before ending after roughly five miles at a path marked with red dashes on white. It's a long distance to cover, but the terrain is varied and there are shortcuts. On a hot day, however, the best detour is to take a dip in one of the lakes followed by a nap in the sun.

Tourist information

Palisades Interstate Park Commission
1-201 768 1360, www.njpalisades.org.
New York-New Jersey Trail Conference
1-201 512 9348, www.nynjtc.org.

Getting there

By train Take the Metro-North/NJ Transit Port Jervis train from Penn Station to the Tuxedo stop (with a train switch in Secaucus, NJ). The journey takes 1hr 15mins, and a round-trip ticket costs $26. Contact the MTA (www.mta.info/mnr) for schedules.

OTIS PIKE WILDERNESS

If you're looking for ocean views and a less aggressive hike, consider Fire Island's Otis Pike Wilderness Area. The journey takes 90 minutes on the LIRR from Penn Station to Patchogue, on Long Island, followed by a 45-minute ferry ride south to the Watch Hill Visitor Center, but the pristine beaches and wildlife are worth the effort. The stretch of preserved wilderness from Watch Hill to Smith Point is home to deer, rabbits, foxes and numerous types of seabird, including the piping plover, which nests during

Breakneck Ridge.

the summer. Just be sure you stay out of the plovers' nesting grounds, which are marked with signs, and don't feed any wildlife you see along the way.

Apart from a few sand dunes, Fire Island is completely flat; even so, walking on the beaches and sandy paths can be slow going. After traversing the boardwalk leading from the Watch Hill Center, hike along Burma Road, a path that runs across the entire island, and in seven miles you'll arrive at the Wilderness Visitor Center (1-631 281 3010, hours vary by season, check www.nps.gov/fiis) at Smith Point.

Tourist information

Fire Island National Seashore
1-631 687 4750, www.nps.gov/fiis.

Getting there

By train/ferry Take the LIRR Montauk train from Penn Station to Patchogue; a round-trip ticket costs $25.50-$35 ($17.50 reductions). Contact the MTA (www.mta.info/lirr) for schedules. The cash-only Davis Park Ferry (1-631 475 1665, www.davisparkferry.com) from Patchogue to Watch Hill operates mid Mar-Nov, with reduced crossings in spring and autumn, and costs $16 round trip ($10.50-$15 reductions). Pets and freight cost extra. The journey should take about 2hrs 30mins in total.

Head for the Ocean

CITY ISLAND

It may look like a New England fishing village, but City Island, on the north-west edge of Long Island Sound, is part of the Bronx and accessible from anywhere in the city by public transport. With a population of fewer than 5,000, it formed the slightly gritty backdrop for films such as *Margot at the Wedding* and *A Bronx Tale*. Yet in its heyday, around World War II, it was home to no fewer than 17 shipyards. Seven America's Cup-winning yachts were built on the island – and, residents note, the Cup was lost in 1983, the very same year they stopped building the boats here. You'll find a room devoted to the island's nautical past at the free **City Island Historical Society & Nautical Museum** (190 Fordham Street, between Minnieford & King Avenues, 1-718 885 0008, www.cityisland museum.org, open 1-5pm Sat, Sun). Housed in a quaint former schoolhouse, it's stocked with model ships, Revolutionary War artefacts and tributes to such local heroes as Ruby Price Dill, the island's first kindergarten teacher.

With seafood spots on practically every corner and boats bobbing in the background, the small community exudes maritime charm. There are still a few sailmakers in the phone

Harriman State Park. *See p313.*

book, but City Islanders are far more likely to head into Manhattan for work nowadays.

If you're here at night, don't miss the eerie views of nearby Hart Island. The former site of an insane asylum, a missile base and a narcotics rehab centre, Hart is also home to NYC's public cemetery, where you can sometimes spot Rikers Island inmates burying the unnamed dead. How's that for a fishy tale?

Eating & drinking

Over on Belden Point are **Johnny's Reef** (2 City Island Avenue, 1-718 885 2086, www.johnnysreefrestaurant.com, open Mar-Nov) and **Tony's Pier Restaurant** (1 City Island Avenue, 1-718 885 1424, www.tonyspier.com); both have outdoor seating. Grab a couple of beers and a basket of fried clams, sit at one of the picnic tables and watch the boats sail by.

Getting there

By subway/bus Take the 6 line to Pelham Bay Park and transfer to the Bx29 bus to City Island.

LONG BRANCH

Although it's not the high-society retreat it was in 1869, when President Ulysses S Grant made it his summer base, this Jersey Shore enclave is in the midst of a revival that has nothing to do with girls with poufed hair or guys with overdeveloped abs. Years after a 1987 fire reduced its amusement pier to a charred skeleton, Jersey boys David and Michael Barry took over the decrepit boardwalk to create Pier Village, comprising apartments, restaurants, shops and a boutique hotel. Nearby, Asbury Park, with its rich rock 'n' roll legacy, is also poised for a comeback.

A day badge to access the pristine **Long Branch beach** costs just $5-$7 for adults (free-$3 reductions), available from the seasonal office at Ocean Boulevard and Melrose Terrace. But, for $25 per day, guests at the Bungalow hotel (*see p317*) can luxuriate at **Le Club** – an exclusive stretch open from Memorial Day through Labor Day. Lounge under imported palm trees and sip cocktails from the beach club's upscale eaterie Avenue (*see p317*). Atop the restaurant is a private pool deck and bar, which morphs into a slick nightclub.

For a grittier seaside vibe, catch the 837 bus from Long Branch Station to **Asbury Park**. Here, continuing redevelopment is bringing indie businesses to the boardwalk opposite the Boss's old stomping ground, **The Stone Pony** (913 Ocean Avenue, at Second Avenue, 1-732 502 0600, www.stoneponyonline.com). Across the street, you can join the pinheads at

City Island.

BOARDWALK EMPIRES

Atlantic City is regaining its glamour, thanks to glitzy new resorts.

Revel

Take a walk (or a ride in one of the iconic rolling chairs) along the famous four-mile-long seaside promenade in Atlantic City, New Jersey, and you'll be partaking in a tradition that goes back to 1870, when America's first boardwalk was a mere eight-foot-wide strip that was dismantled at the end of each season. Since then, the Boardwalk has been the subject of songs, starred in movies, lent a stage to showbiz legends, beauty queens, high-diving horses and boxing cats, and houses the most expensive property on the Monopoly board.

After the Camden and Atlantic Railroad was built in the mid-19th century and grand hotels sprang up along the seafront, hordes of visitors arrived in 'America's Playground' for its beach, sophisticated entertainment, quirky attractions and undercurrent of sin. Though AC has suffered a few turns of fortune over the past century and a half, some of the old excitement is back. A new generation of casino-hotels offer not just gambling, but also a dizzying range of diversions, from early-morning yoga to late-night burlesque.

It's all about the agua at AC's newest player. **Revel** (500 Boardwalk, between Metropolitan & New Jersey Avenues, 1-855 348 0500, www.revelcasino.com) offers 1,399 ocean-view rooms on 20 acres of prime beach frontage. If you actually want to get wet, take a dip in the year-round InOut Pool – perched more than 100 feet above sea level – which begins indoors and stretches into the open air. Revel's sprawling 32,000-square-foot health and relaxation complex is equipped with hydrotherapy pools and a healing salt room. The resort's theatrical casino, conceived by performing-arts design firm Scéno Plus, features more than 2,000 slot machines and 130 game tables. Among the $2.4 billion playground's many amenities are 13 eclectic eateries plus an entertainment line-up that includes Ivan Kane's Royal Jelly Burlesque Nightclub and the 5,000-seat Ovation Hall, which hosts the likes of Beyoncé.

Another luxury complex, **Borgata** (1 Borgata Way, at Huron Avenue, 1-609 317 1000, www.theborgata.com) offers a dozen dining options bearing the names of top chefs – including the closest Wolfgang Puck restaurant to NYC – plus two spas and six distinct drinkeries. But serious players come here with one thing on their minds: the 85-table poker room is the biggest in Atlantic City.

Away from the eclectic dining options in the big hotels, AC is traditionally known for Italian food. Try old-school spots such as the **White House Sub Shop** (2301 Arctic Avenue, at Mississippi Avenue, 1-609 345 1564, www.whitehousesubshop.net, no credit cards), which was opened in 1946 by returning World War II vet Anthony Basile (midday queues can stretch around the block). Ask your hotel concierge to secure you a table at **Chef Vola's** (111 S Albion Place, between Boardwalk & Pacific Avenues, 1-609 345 2022, no credit cards), a hidden dining room in a private home that requires a referral. You have to bring your own wine and be prepared for long waits and tight quarters, but the fish, pasta and luminous sauces render these inconveniences trivial.

GETTING THERE

Although the railway was key to the resort town's early development, there is no longer a direct train connecting NYC to Atlantic City. **Greyhound** (1-800 231 2222, www.luckystreakbus.com) runs bus services ($37-$44 round trip, 2½hrs each way).

Borgata

Silverball Museum Arcade (1000 Ocean Avenue, 1-732 774 4994, www.silverballmuseum.com), where collector Rob Ilvento lets the public play on 200 of his prize pinball machines, dating from 1932 to 2005 ($10/hour or $20/day). From the seafront, stroll along Cookman Avenue and browse the strip's vintage and interiors shops.

Eating & drinking

Order the spicy, orange-spiked lobster roll in a brioche bun ($18) at the David Collins-designed beachfront brasserie, **Avenue** (23 Ocean Avenue, at Pier Village, 1-732 759 2900, www.leclubavenue.com), which offers lovely ocean vistas and an outdoor deck. In Asbury Park, get a taste of exotic destinations at **Langosta Lounge** (1000 Ocean Avenue, at Second Avenue, 1-732 455 3275, www.langostalounge.com), where surfer-chef Marilyn Schlossbach's menu is inspired by 'vacation cuisine'.

Hotels

The design of **Bungalow** (50 Laird Street, at Landmark Place, Pier Village, 1-732 229 3700, www.bungalowhotel.net) may have been chronicled in a reality-TV show – *9 by Design*, about Robert and Cortney Novogratz, who juggle work and a large brood – but that doesn't dilute its cool factor. A hand-crafted wood bar by upstate New York artist John Houshmand, a vintage pool table, old board games and a 1960s foosball table encourage hanging out in the lobby. In the 24 guest rooms, whitewashed wood floors and mixed-media works by British artist Ann Carrington evoke the feel of a private beach house.

Getting there

By train Take the North Jersey Coast train from Penn Station to Long Branch. The journey takes 40mins and the fare is $15 one way ($6.75 reductions). Contact New Jersey Transit (1-973 275 5555, www.njtransit.com) for schedules. From the station, it's about a 10min walk to Pier Village and the boardwalk, or you can catch a cab.

SANDY HOOK

The first thing you should know about Sandy Hook, New Jersey, is that there's a nudist beach at its north end (Gunnison Beach, at parking lot G). The sights it affords compel boaters with binoculars to anchor close to shore, and there's also a cruisy gay scene – but there's much more to this 1,665-acre natural wonderland than sunbathers in the buff. With all that the expansive Hook has to offer, it's a little like an island getaway on the city's doorstep.

Along with seven miles of dune-backed ocean beach, the **Gateway National Recreation Area** is home to the nation's oldest lighthouse (which you can tour), as well as extensive fortifications from the days when Sandy Hook formed the outer line of defence for New York Harbor. You can explore the area's past at the **Fort Hancock Museum**, in the old post guardhouse, and at **History House**, located in one of the elegant century-old officer's houses that form an arc facing Sandy Hook Bay. The abandoned forts are worth a look as well.

Elsewhere, natural areas like the **Maritime Holly Forest** attract an astounding variety of birds. In fact, large stretches of beach are closed in summer to allow the endangered piping plover a quiet place to mate. In winter the Audubon Society offers bird walks in the forest.

There's even a cool way to get there: hop on the ferry from Manhattan and turn an excursion to the beach into a scenic mini-cruise. Once you dock at Fort Hancock, shuttle buses transport you to beaches along the peninsula.

Eating & drinking

Hot dogs and other typical waterside snacks are available from concession stands at the beach areas. Alternatively, picnics are permitted on the beach, so you can bring along goodies for dining alfresco. Guardian Park, at the south end of Fort Hancock, has tables and barbecue grills.

Tourist information

Sandy Hook Gateway National Recreation Area *1-732 872 5970, www.nps.gov/gate.*

Getting there

By boat The ferry operates from late May through September from E 35th Street at the East River or at Pier 11 in the Financial District (at the eastern end of Wall Street). Fares are $45 round trip (free-$30 reductions). Contact Sea Streak (1-800 262 8743, www.seastreak.com) for schedules. The ride takes 45 minutes.

Museum Escapes

DIA:BEACON

Take a model example of early 20th-century industrial architecture. Combine it with some of the most ambitious and uncompromising art of the past 50 years. What do you get? One of the finest aesthetic experiences on earth. Indeed, for the more than two dozen artists whose work is on view, and for the visiting public, Dia Art Foundation's outpost in the Hudson Valley is truly a blessing.

The foundation's founders, Heiner Friedrich and his wife Philippa de Menil (an heir to the Schlumberger oil fortune), acquired many of their holdings in the 1960s and '70s. The pair had a taste for the minimal, the conceptual and

Sandy Hook lighthouse.

Storm King Art Center.

the monumental, and supported artists with radical ideas about what art was, what it could do and where it should happen. Together with others of their generation, the Dia circle (Robert Smithson, Michael Heizer, Walter De Maria, Donald Judd and Dan Flavin) made it difficult to consider a work of art outside of its context – be it visual, philosophical or historical – ever again. Since 2003, that context has been the Riggio Galleries, a huge museum on a 31-acre tract of land overlooking the Hudson River, as Dia's hugely scaled collection had outgrown even its cavernous former galleries in Chelsea.

An 80-minute train ride from Grand Central Terminal, the 300,000-square foot complex of three brick buildings was erected in 1929 as a box-printing factory for Nabisco. No less than 34,000 square feet of north-facing skylights provide almost all the illumination within. The permanent collection also includes works by such 20th-century luminaries as Louise Bourgeois, Andy Warhol, Sol LeWitt and Joseph Beuys. But what really sets Dia:Beacon apart from other museums is its confounding intimacy. The design of the galleries and gardens by California light-and-space artist Robert Irwin, in collaboration with the Manhattan architectural collective OpenOffice, not only makes this enormous museum feel more like a private house, but it also allows the gallery's curators to draw correspondences between artworks into an elegant and intriguing narrative of connoisseurship.

If you're travelling by car, stop at **Storm King Art Center**, about 14 miles south-west of Beacon on the other side of the Hudson. The gorgeous sculpture park (open April-mid November), features works by Richard Serra, Alexander Calder and Maya Lin, among others.

IN THE KNOW CASTLE COUP

On the train to Beacon, which runs alongside the Hudson River, keep an eye out for the atmospheric ruins of **Bannerman Castle**, a recreation of a medieval Scottish pile built on tiny Pollepel Island in the early 1900s by an army-surplus heir. Tours are also available via kayak or passenger boat between April and October from Beacon and several other Hudson River locations (see www.bannermancastle.org for details).

Further information

Dia:Beacon Riggio Galleries *3 Beekman Street, Beacon, NY (1-845 440 0100, www.diaart.org).* **Open** *Jan-Mar* 11am-4pm Mon, Fri-Sun. *Apr-Oct* 11am-6pm Mon, Thur-Sun (until 8pm Sat June-Aug). *Nov, Dec* 11am-4pm Mon, Thur-Sun. **Admission** $12; $8-$10 reductions; free under-12s.

Storm King Art Center *1 Museum Road, New Windsor, NY (1-845 534 3115, www.stormking.org).* **Open** *Apr-Oct* 10am-5.30pm Wed-Sun. *Nov* 10am-4.30pm Wed-Sun. **Admission** $15; $8-$10 reductions; free under-6s.

Getting there

By train Take the Metro-North train from Grand Central Terminal to Beacon station. The journey takes 1hr 20mins, and the round-trip fare is $30.50-$40.50 (reductions $15.50-$20). Discount rail and admission packages are available; for details, see 'Deals & Getaways' at www.mta.info/mnr.

COOPERSTOWN

A mecca for baseball devotees, Cooperstown, north of NYC, isn't known for much besides its famous hall of rawhide ephemera, old pine

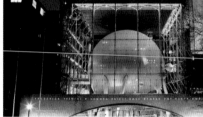

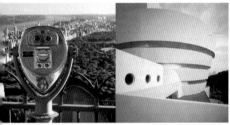

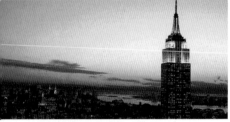

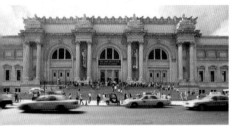

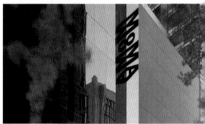

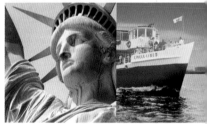

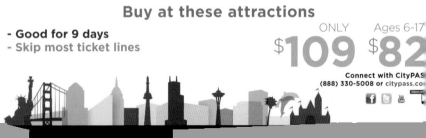

tar-stained lumber and October memories. Happily for those who don't care a lick about America's national pastime, there's more than Major League history to be found at this single-stoplight village (population 2,000) on the shores of Lake Otsego.

The **National Baseball Hall of Fame & Museum** draws around 300,000 visitors a year. The actual hall is exactly what it claims to be: a corridor full of plaques. And as such, it's the museum that's the real diamond here. You'll see everything from Babe Ruth's locker to racist hate mail sent to Jackie Robinson, and the glove worn by Willie Mays when he made his over-the-shoulder catch in the 1954 World Series.

Local shopping is devoted primarily to baseball, so if you're looking for memorabilia or limited-edition collectibles, the **Cooperstown Bat Company** (118 Main Street, at Chestnut Street, 1-607 547 2415, closed Sun Jan-Mar) is worth checking out. For a dose of non-sport history, take a walk through the **Christ Episcopal Churchyard Cemetery** (46 River Street, at Church Street, 1-607 547 9555, www.christchurchcooperstown.org), where the Cooper family is buried. A three-minute drive north along Route 80 brings you to the **Fenimore Art Museum**, which displays its fine collection of American art – including folk art and Native American works – in a 1930s mansion on Lake Otsego. Temporary shows have focused on such crowd-pleasing subjects as Modernism and Edward Hopper.

Heading south out of town, the **Brewery Ommegang** (656 County Highway 33, 1-800 544 1800, www.ommegang.com), set on a 136-acre farmstead, brews a half-dozen award-winning Belgian-style ales. You can see how the whole brewing process works on one of the hourly tours, which include a tasting.

Eating & drinking

On Cooperstown's Main Street, the **Doubleday Café** (no.93, at Pioneer Street, 1-607 547 5468) provides good American grub, while at **Alex & Ika** (no.149, at Chestnut Street, 1-607 547 4070, www.alexandika.com), hostess Ika Fognell and chef Alex Webster serve creative dishes such as sesame-crusted salmon with sesame noodle, arugula and cucumber salad. The local dive, **Cooley's Stone House Tavern** (49 Pioneer Street, at Main Street, 1-607 544 1311), is a beautifully restored tavern and a good spot for a nightcap.

Hotels

At the **Inn at Cooperstown** (16 Chestnut Street, at Main Street, 1-607 547 5756, www.innatcooperstown.com), many of the

National Baseball Hall of Fame & Museum.

18 uniquely decorated rooms feature four-poster beds, and you can play boardgames by the fire in the cosy parlour.

If you're looking for something a little more swanky, stay at the grand lakeside **Otesaga Resort Hotel** (60 Lake Street, at Pine Boulevard, 1-607 547 9931, www.otesaga.com) and play a round on the par-72 golf course.

Further information

Fenimore Art Museum *5798 Lake Road (State Highway 80) (1-607 547 1400, www.fenimore artmuseum.org).* **Open** *Apr-mid May, mid Oct-Dec* 10am-4pm Tue-Sun. *Mid May-mid Oct* 10am-5pm daily. Closed Jan-March. **Admission** $12; $10.50 reductions; free under-13s.

National Baseball Hall of Fame & Museum *25 Main Street, at Fair Street (1-888 425 5633, www.baseballhall.org).* **Open** *June-Aug* 9am-9pm daily. *Sept-May* 9am-5pm daily. **Admission** $19.50; $7-$12 reductions.

Tourist information

Cooperstown/Otsego County Tourism *1-607 643 0059, www.thisiscooperstown.com.*

Getting there

By car Take I-87N to I-90 to exit 25A. Take I-88W to exit 24. Follow Route 7 to Route 20W to Route 80S to Cooperstown. The journey takes about 4hrs.

A CENTENNIAL

In Context

History

Seeds of the Big Apple.

TEXT: KATHLEEN SQUIRES & RICHARD KOSS

More than 400 years ago, Henry Hudson, an English explorer in the service of the Dutch East India Company, sailed into New York Harbor, triggering events that would lead to the creation of the most dynamic and ethnically diverse city in the world. A steady flow of settlers, immigrants and fortune-seekers has seen New York evolve with the energy and aspirations of each successive wave of new arrivals. Intertwining cultural legacies have produced the densely layered character of the metropolis, from the wealthy and powerful Anglos who helped to build the city's riches to the fabled tired, poor huddled masses who arrived from far-off lands and faced a tougher struggle. From its beginnings, this forward-looking town has been shaped by a cast of hard-working, ambitious characters, and continues to be so today.

New York in 1874.

NATIVE NEW YORKERS

The area's first residents were the indigenous Lenape tribe. They lived among the forests, meadows and farms of the land they called Lenapehoking, pretty much undisturbed by outsiders – until the 16th century, when their idyll was interrupted by European visitors. The first to cast his eyes upon this land was Giovanni da Verrazano in 1524. An Italian explorer commissioned by the French to find a shortcut to the Orient, he found Staten Island instead. Recognising that he was on the wrong track, Verrazano hauled anchor nearly as quickly as he had dropped it, never setting foot on dry land.

Eighty-five years later, Henry Hudson, an Englishman in the service of the Dutch East India Company, found New York Harbor in the same way. After trading with the Lenape, he ventured up the river that now bears his name, thinking it offered a north-west passage to Asia, but halted just south of present-day Albany when its shallowness convinced him it didn't lead to the Pacific. Hudson turned back, and his tales of the lush, river-crossed countryside captured the Dutch imagination. In 1624, the Dutch West India Company sent 110 settlers to establish a trading post here, planting themselves at the southern tip of the island called Mannahata and caling the colony Nieuw Amsterdam (New Amsterdam). In many battles against the local Lenape, they did their best to drive the natives away from the little company town. But the tribe were immovable.

In 1626, Peter Minuit, New Amsterdam's first governor, thought he had solved the Lenape problem by pulling off the city's very first real-estate rip-off. He made them an offer they couldn't refuse: he 'bought' the island of Manhattan – all 14,000 acres of it – from the Lenape for 60 guilders' worth of goods. Legend famously values the purchase price at $24, but modern historians set the amount closer to $500. It was a slick trick, and one that set a precedent for countless future self-serving business transactions.

The Dutch quickly made the port of New Amsterdam a centre for fur trading. The population didn't grow as fast as the business, however, and the Dutch West India Company had a hard time finding recruits to move to this unknown island an ocean away. The company instead gathered servants, orphans and slaves, and other more unsavoury outcasts such as thieves, drunkards and prostitutes. The population grew to 400 within ten years, but drunkenness, crime and squalor prevailed. If the colony was to thrive, it needed a strong leader. Enter Dutch West India Company director Peter Stuyvesant.

PEG-LEG PETE

A one-legged, puritanical bully with a quick temper, Stuyvesant – or Peg-leg Pete, as he was known – may have been less than popular, but he was the colony's first effective governor. He made peace with the Lenape, formed the first policing force (consisting of nine men), cracked down on debauchery by shutting taverns and outlawing drinking on Sunday, and established the first school, post office, hospital, prison and poorhouse. Within a decade, the population had quadrupled, and the settlement had become an important trading port.

Lined with canals and windmills, and dotted with gabled farmhouses, New Amsterdam slowly began to resemble its namesake. Newcomers arrived to work in the fur and slave trades, or to farm. Soon, a dozen and a half languages could be heard in the streets – a fact that made Stuyvesant nervous. In 1654, he attempted to quash immigration by turning away Sephardic Jews who were fleeing the Spanish Inquisition. ut, surprisingly for the time, the corporate honchos at the Dutch West India Company reprimanded him for his intolerance and overturned his decision, leading to the establishment of the earliest Jewish community in the New World. It was the first time that the inflexible Stuyvesant was forced to mend his ways. The second time put an end to the 40-year Dutch rule for good.

BRITISH INVASION

In late August 1664, English warships sailed into the harbour, set on taking over the now prosperous colony. To avoid bloodshed and destruction, Stuyvesant surrendered quickly. Soon after, New Amsterdam was renamed New York (after the Duke of York, brother of King Charles II) and Stuyvesant quietly retired to his farm. Unlike Stuyvesant, the English battled with the Lenape; by 1695, those members of the tribe who hadn't been killed off were sent packing upstate, and New York's European population shot up to 3,000. Over the next 35 years, Dutch-style farmhouses and windmills gave way to stately townhouses and monuments to English royals. By 1740, the slave trade had made New York the third-busiest port in the British Empire. The city, now home to more than 11,000 residents, continued to prosper for a quarter-century. But resentment was beginning to build in the colony, fuelled by the ever-heavier burden of British taxation.

Fearing revolution, New York's citizenry fled the city in droves in 1775, causing the population to plummet from 25,000 to just 5,000. The following year, 100 British warships sailed into the harbour of this virtual ghost town, carrying with them an intimidating army of 32,000 men – nearly four times the size of Washington's militia. Despite the British presence, Washington organised a reading of the Declaration of Independence, and American patriots tore the statue of King George III from its pedestal. Revolution was inevitable.

The battle for New York officially began on 26 August 1776, and Washington's army sustained heavy losses; nearly a quarter of his men were slaughtered in a two-day period. As Washington retreated, a fire – thought to have been started by patriots – destroyed 493 buildings, including Trinity Church, the city's tallest structure. The British found a scorched city, and a populace living in tents.

The city continued to suffer for seven years. Eventually, of course, Washington's luck turned. As the British forces left, he and his troops marched triumphantly down Broadway to reclaim the city as a part of the newly established United States of America. A week and a half later, on 4 December 1783, the general bade farewell to his dispersing troops at Fraunces Tavern (*see p53*).

Meanwhile, Alexander Hamilton got busy in the rebuilding effort, laying the groundwork for New York City institutions that remain vital to this day. He started by establishing the Bank of New York, the city's first bank, in 1784. When Washington was inaugurated as the nation's first president in 1789, at Federal Hall on Wall Street, he brought Hamilton on board as the first secretary of the treasury. Thanks to Hamilton's business savvy, trade in stocks and bonds flourished, leading to the establishment in 1792 of what would eventually be known as the New York Stock Exchange.

THE CITY TAKES SHAPE...

New York continued to grow and prosper for the next three decades. Maritime commerce soared, and Robert Fulton's innovative steamboat made its maiden voyage on the Hudson River in 1807. Eleven years later, a group of merchants introduced regularly scheduled shipping (a novel concept at the time) between New York and Liverpool on the Black Ball Line. A boom in the maritime trades lured hundreds of European labourers, and the city, which was still entirely crammed in below Houston Street, grew more and more congested. Manhattan real estate became the most expensive in the world.

The first man to tackle the city's congestion problem was Mayor DeWitt Clinton, a protégé of Hamilton. Clinton's dream was to organise the entire island of Manhattan in such a way that it could cope with the eventual population creep northwards. In 1807, he created a commission to map out the foreseeable sprawl. It presented its work four years later, and the destiny of this new city was made manifest: it would be a regular grid of crossing thoroughfares, 12 avenues wide and 155 streets long. Then Clinton simply overstepped the city's boundaries. In 1811, he presented a plan to build a 363-mile canal linking the Hudson River with Lake Erie. Many of his contemporaries thought it was simply an impossible task: at the time, the longest canal in the world ran a mere 27 miles. But DeWitt pressed on and raised a staggering $6 million for the project.

Work on the Erie Canal began in 1817 and was completed in 1825 – three years ahead of schedule. It shortened the journey between New York City and Buffalo from three weeks to one, and cut the shipping cost per ton from about $100 to $4. Goods, people and money poured into New York, fostering a merchant elite that moved northwards in Manhattan to escape the urban crush. Estates multiplied above Houston Street – all grander and more imposing than their modest colonial forerunners. Once slavery was abolished n New York in 1827, free blacks became an essential part of the workforce. In 1831, the first public transport system began operating, with horse-drawn omnibuses.

...AND SO DO THE SLUMS

As the population multiplied (swelling to 240,000 by 1830 and 700,000 by 1850), so did the city's problems. Tensions bubbled between immigrant newcomers and those who could trace their American lineage back a generation or two. Crime rose and lurid tales filled the 'penny press', the city's proto-tabloids. While wealthy New Yorkers were moving as far 'uptown' as Greenwich Village, the infamous Five Points neighbourhood – the city's first slum – festered in the area now occupied by City Hall, the courthouses and Chinatown. Built on a fetid drained pond, Five Points became the ramshackle home of poor immigrants and blacks. Brutal gangs with colourful names such as the Forty Thieves, Plug Uglies and Dead Rabbits often met in bloody clashes in the streets, but what finally sent a mass of 100,000 people scurrying from lower Manhattan was an outbreak of cholera in 1832. In just six weeks, 3,513 New Yorkers died.

In 1837, a financial panic left hundreds of Wall Street businesses crumbling. Commerce stagnated at the docks, the real-estate market collapsed, and all but three city banks closed. Some 50,000 New Yorkers lost their jobs, while 200,000 teetered on the edge of poverty. The panic sparked civil unrest and violence. In 1849, a xenophobic mob of 8,000 protesting the performance of an English actor at the Astor Place Opera House was met by a militia that opened fire, killing 22. But the Draft Riots of 1863 were much worse. After a law was passed exempting men from the draft for a $300 fee, the (mostly Irish) poor rose up, forming a 15,000-strong force that rampaged through the city. Fuelled by anger about the Civil War (for which they blamed blacks), the rioters set fire to the Colored Orphan Asylum and vandalised black homes. Blacks were beaten in the streets, and some were lynched. A federal force of 6,000 men was sent to subdue the violence. After four days and at least 100 deaths, peace was finally restored.

ON THE MOVE

Amid the chaos of the mid 19th century, the pace of progress continued unabated. Compared to the major Southern cities, New York emerged nearly unscathed from the Civil War. The population ballooned to two million in the 1880s, and new technologies revolutionised daily life. The elevated railway helped New Yorkers to move into what are now the Upper East and Upper West Sides, while other trains connected the city with upstate New York, New England and the Midwest. By 1871, regional train traffic had grown so much that rail tycoon Cornelius Vanderbilt built the original Grand Central Depot (it was replaced in 1913 by the current Grand Central Terminal.)

One ambitious project was inspired by the harsh winter of 1867. The East River froze over, halting ferry traffic between Brooklyn and Manhattan. Brooklyn, by then, had become the nation's third most populous city, and its politicians and businessmen realised that the boroughs had to be linked. The New York Bridge Company's goal was to build the world's longest bridge, spanning the East River between downtown Manhattan and south-western Brooklyn. Over 16 years (four times longer than projected), 14,000 miles of steel cable were stretched across the 1,595-foot span, while the towers rose a staggering 276 feet above the river. The Brooklyn Bridge opened on 24 May 1883.

THE GREED OF TWEED

As New York recovered from the turmoil of the mid 1800s, William M 'Boss' Tweed began pulling the strings. Using his ample charm, the six-foot, 300-pound bookkeeper, chair-maker and volunteer firefighter became one of the city's most powerful politicians. He had been an alderman and district leader; he had served in the US House of Representatives and as a state senator; and he was a chairman of the Democratic General Committee and leader of Tammany Hall, a political organisation formed by local craftsmen ostensibly to keep the wealthy classes' political clout in check. But even though Tweed opened orphanages, poorhouses and hospitals, his good deeds were overshadowed by his and his cohort's gross embezzlement of city funds. By 1870, members of the 'Tweed Ring' had created a new city charter, granting themselves control of the City Treasury. Using fake leases and inflated bills for city supplies and services, Tweed and his cronies may ultimately have pocketed as much as $200 million.

Tweed was eventually sued by the city for $6 million, and charged with forgery and larceny. He escaped from debtors' prison in 1875, but was captured in Spain a year later and died in 1878. But his greed hurt many. As he was emptying the city's coffers, poverty spread. Then the stock market took a nosedive, factories closed and railroads went bankrupt. By 1874, New York estimated its homeless population at 90,000. That winter, *Harper's Weekly* reported, 900 New Yorkers starved to death.

IMMIGRANT DREAMS

In September 1882, a new era dawned brightly when Thomas Alva Edison lit up half a square mile of lower Manhattan with 3,000 electric lamps. One of the newly illuminated offices belonged to financier JP Morgan, who played an essential part in bringing New York's, and America's, economy back to life. By bailing out a number of failing railroads, then merging and restructuring them, Morgan jump-started commerce in New York once again. Goods, jobs and businesses returned to the city, and very soon such aggressive businessmen as John D Rockefeller, Andrew Carnegie and Henry Frick wanted a piece of the action. They made New York the HQ of Standard Oil and US Steel, corporations that went on to shape America's economic future.

'Many of these newcomers crowded into dark, squalid tenements on the Lower East Side.'

A shining symbol for less fortunate arrivals also made New York its home around that time. To commemorate the centennial of the Declaration of Independence, the French gave the United States the Statue of Liberty, which was dedicated in 1886. Between 1892 and 1954, the statue ushered more than 12 million immigrants into New York Harbor, and Ellis Island processed many of them. The island had opened as an immigration centre in 1892 with expectations of accommodating 500,000 people annually, but the number peaked at more than a million in 1907. In the 34-building complex, crowds of would-be Americans were herded through examinations, inspections and interrogations. About 98 per cent got through, turning New York into what British playwright Israel Zangwill optimistically called 'the great melting pot where all the races of Europe are melting and reforming'.

Many of these newcomers crowded into dark, squalid tenements on the Lower East Side, while millionaires such as Vanderbilt and Frick constructed huge French-style mansions along Fifth Avenue. Jacob A Riis, a Danish immigrant and police reporter for the *New York Tribune*, made it his business to expose this dichotomy, scouring filthy alleys and overcrowded tenements to research and photograph his 1890 book, *How the Other Half Lives*. Largely as a result of Riis's work, the state passed the Tenement House Act of 1901, calling for drastic housing reforms.

SOARING ASPIRATIONS

On 1 January 1898, the boroughs of Manhattan, Brooklyn, Queens, Staten Island and the Bronx consolidated to form New York City, the largest metropolis in America with over three million residents. More and more companies started to move their headquarters to this new city, increasing the demand for office space. With little land left to develop in lower Manhattan, New York embraced the steel revolution and grew steadily skywards. By 1920, New York boasted more than 60 skyscrapers (*see p341* **Race to the Top**).

If that weren't enough to demonstrate New Yorkers' unending ambition, the city burrowed below the streets at the same time, starting work on its underground transit system in 1900. The $35-million project took nearly four and a half years to complete. Less than a decade after opening, it was the most heavily travelled subway system in the world, carrying almost a billion passengers on its trains every year.

CHANGING TIMES

By 1909, 30,000 factories were operating in the city, churning out everything from heavy machinery to artificial flowers. Mistrusted, abused and underpaid, factory workers faced impossible quotas, had their pay docked for minor mistakes and were often locked in during working hours. In the end, it took the inevitable tragedy, in the form of the Triangle Shirtwaist Company fire (*see p331* **Sweatshop Inferno**), to bring about real changes in employment laws.

Another sort of rights movement was taking hold during this time. Between 1910 and 1913, New York City was the site of the largest women's suffrage rallies in the United States. Harriet Stanton Blatch (the daughter of famed suffragette Elizabeth Cady Stanton, and founder of the Equality League of Self-Supporting Women) and Carrie Chapman Catt (the organiser of the New York City Women's Suffrage Party) arranged attention-grabbing demonstrations intended to pressure the state into authorising a referendum on a woman's right to vote. The measure's defeat in 1915 only steeled the suffragettes' resolve. Finally, with the support of Tammany Hall, the law was passed in 1919, challenging the male stranglehold on voting throughout the country. With New York leading the nation, the 19th Amendment was ratified in 1920.

In 1919, as New York welcomed troops home from World War I with a parade, the city also celebrated its emergence on the global stage. It had supplanted London as the investment capital of the world, and had become the centre of publishing, thanks to two men: Joseph Pulitzer and William Randolph Hearst. *The New York Times* had become the country's most respected newspaper; Broadway was the focal point of American theatre; and Greenwich Village had become an international bohemian nexus, where flamboyant artists, writers and political revolutionaries gathered in galleries and coffeehouses.

The more personal side of the women's movement also found a home in New York City. A nurse and midwife who grew up in a family of 11 children, Margaret Sanger was a fierce advocate of birth control and family planning. She opened the first ever birth-control clinic in Brooklyn on 16 October 1916. Finding this unseemly, the police closed the clinic soon after and imprisoned Sanger for 30 days. She was not deterred, however, and, in 1921, formed the American Birth Control League – the forerunner of the organisation Planned Parenthood – which researched birth control methods and provided gynaecological services.

ALL THAT JAZZ

Forward-thinking women such as Sanger set the tone for an era when women, now a voting political force, were moving beyond the moral conventions of the 19th century. The country ushered in the Jazz Age in 1919 by ratifying the 18th Amendment, which outlawed the distribution and sale of alcoholic beverages. Prohibition turned

SWEATSHOP INFERNO

A reform movement rises from the ashes of tragedy.

As 25 March 1911 fell on a Saturday, the roughly 500 garment workers – many of them teenage girls – at the Triangle Shirtwaist Company were putting in only a seven-hour shift, as opposed to the nine demanded of them on weekdays. At 4.45pm, they were only 15 minutes from their brief weekend, when fire broke out on the eighth floor of the ten-storey building on the corner of Greene Street and Washington Place in Greenwich Village, where Triangle owned the top three floors. Fed by the fabrics, the flames spread rapidly up the building, engulfing the sewing room on the ninth floor. As the workers rushed to escape, they found many of the exits locked, and the single flimsy fire escape melted in the heat and fell uselessly away from the building. Roughly 350 made it out on to the adjoining rooftops before the inferno closed off all the exits. New Yorkers spending a leisurely Saturday in Washington Square Park a block away rushed to the scene, only to watch in horror as 54 workers jumped or fell to their deaths from the windows. A total of 146 perished.

The Triangle Shirtwaist Fire was one of the worst industrial disasters in New York City history. The two factory owners who were tried for manslaughter were acquitted, but the fire did at least spur labour and union organisations into seeking and winning major reforms. The Factory Commission of 1911 was established by the State Legislature, headed by Senator Robert F Wagner, Alfred E Smith and Samuel Gompers, president of the American Federation of Labour. It spawned the Fire Prevention division of the Fire Department, which enforced the creation and maintenance of fire escape routes in the workplace. The fire also garnered much-needed support for the Ladies Garment Workers Union – a major force in the 1920s and '30s.

the city into the epicentre of bootlegging, speakeasies and organised crime. By the early 1920s, New York boasted 32,000 illegal watering holes – twice the number of legal bars before Prohibition.

In 1925, New Yorkers elected the magnetic James J Walker as mayor. A charming ex-songwriter (as well as a speakeasy patron and skirt-chaser), Walker was the perfect match for his city's flashy style and hunger for publicity. Fame flowed in the city's veins: home-run hero Babe Ruth drew a million fans each season to baseball games at the newly built Yankee Stadium, and sharp-tongued Walter Winchell filled his newspaper columns with celebrity titbits and scandals. Alexander Woollcott, Dorothy Parker, Robert Benchley and other writers met up daily to trade witticisms around a table at the Algonquin Hotel; the result, in February 1925, was *The New Yorker*.

The Harlem Renaissance blossomed at the same time. Writers Langston Hughes, Zora Neale Hurston and James Weldon Johnson transformed the African-American experience into lyrical literary works, and white society flocked to the Cotton Club to see genre-defining musicians such as Bessie Smith, Cab Calloway, Louis Armstrong and Duke Ellington. (Blacks were only allowed into the club if they were performing on the stage, they could not be part of the audience.)

Downtown, Broadway houses were packed out with fans of George and Ira Gershwin, Irving Berlin, Cole Porter, Lorenz Hart, Richard Rodgers and Oscar Hammerstein II. Towards the end of the 1920s, New York-born Al Jolson wowed audiences in *The Jazz Singer*, the first talking picture.

AFTER THE CRASH

The dizzying excitement ended on 29 October 1929, when the stock market crashed. Corruption eroded Mayor Walker's hold on the city: despite a tenure that saw the opening of the Holland Tunnel, the completion of the George Washington Bridge and the construction of the Chrysler and Empire State Buildings, Walker's lustre faded in the growing shadow of graft accusations. He resigned in 1932, as New York, in the depths of the Great Depression, had one million unemployed inhabitants.

In 1934, an unstoppable force named Fiorello La Guardia took office as mayor, rolling up his sleeves to crack down on mobsters, gambling, smut and government corruption. La Guardia was a tough-talking politician known for nearly coming to blows with other city officials; he described himself as 'inconsiderate, arbitrary, authoritative, difficult, complicated, intolerant and somewhat theatrical'. His act played well: he ushered New York into an era of unparalleled prosperity over the course of his three terms. The 'Little Flower', as La Guardia was known, streamlined city government, paid down the debt and updated the transport, hospital,

Prohibition.

IN CONTEXT

reservoir and sewer systems. New highways made the city more accessible, and North Beach (now La Guardia) Airport became the city's first commercial landing field.

Helping La Guardia to modernise the city was Robert Moses, a hard-nosed visionary who would do much to shape – and in some cases, destroy – New York's landscape. Moses spent 44 years stepping on toes to build expressways, parks, beaches, public housing, bridges and tunnels, creating such landmarks as Lincoln Center, the United Nations complex and the Verrazano-Narrows Bridge, which connected Staten Island to Brooklyn in 1964.

PROTEST AND REFORM

Despite La Guardia's belt-tightening and Moses's renovations, New York began to fall apart financially. When World War II ended, 800,000 industrial jobs disappeared from the city. Factories in need of more space moved to the suburbs, along with nearly five million residents. But more crowding occurred as rural African-Americans and Latinos (primarily Puerto Ricans) flocked to the metropolis in the 1950s and '60s, to meet with ruthless discrimination and a dearth of jobs. Moses's Slum Clearance Committee reduced many neighbourhoods to rubble, forcing out residents in order to build huge, isolating housing projects that became magnets for crime. In 1963, the city also lost Pennsylvania Station, when the Pennsylvania Railroad Company demolished the site over the protests of picketers to make way for a modern station and new sports and entertainment venue Madison Square Garden. It was a wake-up call for New York: architectural changes were hurtling out of control.

But Moses and his wrecking ball couldn't knock over one steadfast West Village woman. Architectural writer and urban-planning critic Jane Jacobs organised local residents when the city unveiled its plan to clear a 14-block tract of her neighbourhood to make space for yet more public housing. Her obstinacy was applauded by many, including an influential councilman named Ed Koch (who would become mayor in 1978). The group fought the plan and won, causing Mayor Robert F Wagner to back down. As a result of Jacobs's efforts in the wake of Pennsylvania Station's demolition, the Landmarks Preservation Commission – the first such group in the US – was established in 1965.

At the dawning of the Age of Aquarius, the city harboured its share of innovative creators. Allen Ginsberg, Jack Kerouac and others gathered in Village coffeehouses to create a new voice for poetry. A folk music scene brewed in tiny clubs around Bleecker Street, showcasing musicians such as Bob Dylan. A former advertising illustrator named Andy Warhol turned images of mass consumerism into deadpan, ironic art statements. And in 1969, the city's long-closeted gay communities came out into the streets, as patrons at the Stonewall Inn on Christopher Street demonstrated against a police raid. The protests, known as the Stonewall riots, gave birth to the modern gay rights movement.

MEAN STREETS

By the early 1970s, deficits had forced heavy cutbacks in city services. The streets were dirty, and subway cars and buildings were scrawled with graffiti; crime skyrocketed as the city's debt deepened to $6 billion. Despite the huge downturn, construction commenced on the World Trade Center; when completed, in 1973, its twin 110-storey towers were the world's tallest buildings. Even as the WTC rose, the city became so desperately overdrawn that Mayor Abraham Beame appealed to the federal government for financial assistance in 1975. Yet President Gerald Ford refused to bail out the city.

Times Square had degenerated into a morass of sex shops and porn theatres, drug use rose and subway use hit an all-time low due to a fear of crime. In 1977, serial killer Son of Sam terrorised the city with six killings, and a blackout one hot August night that same year led to widespread looting and arson. The angst of the time fuelled the punk culture that rose in downtown clubs such as CBGB. At the same time, celebrities, designers and models converged on midtown to disco their nights away at Studio 54.

The Wall Street boom of the 1980s and fiscal petitioning by Mayor Ed Koch brought money flooding back into New York. Gentrification glamorised neighbourhoods such as Soho, Tribeca and the East Village, but deeper societal ills lurked. In 1988, a protest against the city's efforts to impose a strict curfew and displace the homeless from Tompkins Square Park erupted into a violent clash with the police. Crack use became endemic in the ghettos, homelessness rose and AIDS emerged as a new scourge.

By 1989, citizens were restless for change. They turned to David N Dinkins, electing him as the city's first African-American mayor. A distinguished, softly spoken man, Dinkins held office for only a single term, marked by a record murder rate, flaring racial tensions in Manhattan's Washington Heights and Brooklyn's Crown Heights and Flatbush neighbourhoods, and the explosion of a bomb in the basement parking garage of the World Trade Center in 1993 that killed six and injured 1,000.

Deeming the polite Dinkins ineffective, New Yorkers voted in former federal prosecutor Rudolph Giuliani. An abrasive leader, Giuliani used bullying tactics to get things done, as his 'quality of life' campaign cracked down on everything from drug dealing and pornography to unsolicited windshield washing. As cases of severe police brutality grabbed the headlines and racial polarisation was palpable, crime plummeted, tourism soared and New York became cleaner and safer than it had been in decades. Times Square was transformed into a family-friendly tourist destination, and the dot-com explosion brought young wannabes to the Flatiron District's Silicon Alley. Giuliani's second term as mayor would close, however, on a devastating tragedy.

9/11 AND BEYOND

On 11 September 2001, terrorists flew two hijacked passenger jets into the Twin Towers of the World Trade Center, collapsing the entire complex and killing nearly 3,000 people. Amid the trauma, the attack triggered a citywide sense of unity, as New Yorkers did what they could to help their fellow citizens – from feeding emergency crews to cheering on rescue workers en route to Ground Zero.

Two months later, billionaire Michael Bloomberg was elected mayor and took on the daunting task of repairing not only the city's skyline but also its battered economy. The stock market revived, downtown businesses re-emerged and plans for rebuilding the World Trade Center were drawn. True to form, however, New Yorkers debated the future of the site for more than a year until architect Daniel Libeskind was awarded the redevelopment job in 2003. The 9/11 Memorial opened on 11 September 2011 and, in autumn 2013, the WTC's centrepiece tower, 1 World Trade Center, was officially declared the tallest building in the Western Hemisphere (*see p58* **A Fitting Memorial**).

As Bloomberg's second term neared its end, he became increasingly frustrated that some of his pet proposals hadn't been realised. In the midst of 2008's deepening financial crisis, he proposed a controversial bill to extend the tenure of elected officials from two four-year terms to three. Although it was narrowly passed by the New York City Council in October 2008, many politicos (and citizens) opposed the law change. The encumbent poured a record sum of money into his campaign the following year, winning just 51 per cent of the vote to become the fourth mayor in New York's history to serve a third term. In October 2010, in a remarkable display of chutzpah, Bloomberg voted to restore the two-term limitation.

In June 2011, New York celebrated yet another civil rights milestone when it became the largest state in the US to legalise same-sex marriage. A few months later, a group of protesters set up camp in the Financial District's Zuccotti Park, demanding jobs and denouncing the financial industry. Occupy Wall Street demonstrators managed to hold their ground for almost two months until they were forced out by police in November. But the group had already inspired similar movements around the world, spreading the message of the '99 per cent'.

Just before Halloween 2012, the city was rocked by Hurricane Sandy, a disaster without modern precedent that flooded the subway system, plunged lower Manhattan and other parts of the metropolis into darkness and left thousands of New Yorkers homeless. The fallout was still being felt more than a year later; many businesses and landmarks – including the Statue of Liberty and Ellis Island – remained closed for months, others never recovered from the damage.

KEY EVENTS

New York in brief.

1524 Giovanni da Verrazano sails into New York Harbor.
1624 First Dutch settlers establish Nieuw Amsterdam.
1626 Peter Minuit purchases Manhattan for goods worth 60 guilders.
1639 The Broncks settle north of Manhattan.
1646 Village of Breuckelen founded.
1664 Dutch rule ends; Nieuw Amsterdam renamed New York.
1754 King's College (now Columbia University) founded.
1776 Battle for New York begins; fire ravages the city.
1783 George Washington's troops march triumphantly down Broadway.
1784 Alexander Hamilton founds the Bank of New York.
1785 City becomes nation's capital.
1789 President Washington inaugurated at Federal Hall.
1792 New York Stock Exchange opens.
1804 New York becomes country's most populous city, with 80,000 inhabitants.
1811 Mayor DeWitt Clinton's grid plan for Manhattan introduced.
1827 Slavery officially abolished in New York State.
1851 *The New-York Daily Times* (now *The New York Times*) launched.
1880 Metropolitan Museum of Art opens.
1883 Brooklyn Bridge opens.
1886 Statue of Liberty unveiled.
1891 Carnegie Hall opens.
1892 Ellis Island opens.
1898 The five boroughs are consolidated into the city of New York.
1900 Electric lights replace gas along lower Broadway.
1902 The Fuller (Flatiron) Building becomes the world's first skyscraper.
1904 New York's first subway line opens.
1908 First ball dropped in Times Square to celebrate the new year.
1911 Fire in the Triangle Shirtwaist Company kills 146.
1913 Woolworth Building completed; Grand Central Terminal opens.
1923 The first Yankee Stadium opens.
1929 Stock market crashes; Museum of Modern Art opens.
1931 George Washington Bridge completed; Empire State Building completed; Whitney Museum opens.
1934 Fiorello La Guardia elected mayor.
1939 New York hosts the World's Fair.
1950 United Nations complex finished.
1953 Robert Moses spearheads building of the Cross Bronx Expressway.
1957 Brooklyn Dodgers baseball team move to Los Angeles; New York Giants move to San Francisco.
1962 New York Mets debut at the Polo Grounds; Philharmonic Hall, first building in Lincoln Center, opens.
1964 Verrazano-Narrows Bridge completed; World's Fair held in Queens.
1970 First New York City Marathon.
1973 World Trade Center completed.
1975 On verge of bankruptcy, city is snubbed by federal government.
1977 Studio 54 opens; 4,000 arrested during citywide blackout.
1989 David N Dinkins elected city's first black mayor.
1993 Bomb explodes in World Trade Center, killing six and injuring 1,000.
2001 Hijackers fly two jets into World Trade Center, killing nearly 3,000.
2004 Statue of Liberty reopens for first time since 9/11.
2009 Yankees and Mets move into new state-of-the-art stadiums.
2010 Mayor Bloomberg is inaugurated as the fourth mayor in New York's history to serve a third term.
2011 Gay marriage is legalised in New York State; the 9/11 Memorial debuts.
2012 The Barclays Center, home to Brooklyn's first pro sports team since 1957, opens.
2012 Hurricane Sandy hits, paralysing the city and wreaking long-term damage.

Architecture

Tall stories.

TEXT: ERIC P NASH

Manhattan, of course, is synonymous with skyscrapers. Following advances in iron and steel technology in the middle of the 19th century, and the pressing need for space on an already overcrowded island, New York's architects realised that the only way was up. The race to reach the heavens in the early 20th century was supplanted by the minimalist post-war International Style, which saw a rash of towering glass boxes spread across midtown. Even now, despite less than favourable economic conditions, a surprising number of new high-rises are soaring skyward.

However, those with an architectural interest and an observant eye will be rewarded by the fascinating mix of styles and unexpected details closer to the ground in virtually every corner of the metropolis, from gargoyles crouching on the façade of an early 20th-century apartment building to extravagant cast-iron decoration adorning a humble warehouse. And it's worth remembering that under New York's gleaming exoskeleton of steel and glass lies the heart of a 17th-century Dutch city.

Federal Hall National Memorial.

LOWLAND LEGACY

The Dutch influence is still traceable in the downtown web of narrow, winding lanes. Because the Cartesian grid that rules the city was laid out by the Commissioners' Plan in 1811, only a few examples of Dutch architecture remain, mostly off the beaten path. One is the 1785 **Dyckman Farmhouse Museum** (4881 Broadway, at 204th Street, 1-212 304 9422, www.dyckmanfarmhouse.org; closed Mon-Thur) in Inwood, Manhattan's northernmost neighbourhood. Its decorative brickwork and gambrel roof reflect the fashion of the late 18th century. The oldest house still standing in the five boroughs, however, is the **Wyckoff House Museum** (5816 Clarendon Road, at Ralph Avenue, Flatbush, Brooklyn, 1-718 629 5400, www.wyckoffassociation.org; closed Mon Apr-Oct, Mon & Sun Nov-Mar). Erected around 1652, it's a typical Dutch farmhouse with deep eaves and roughly shingled walls.

In Manhattan, the only building left from pre-Revolutionary times is the stately columned and quoined **St Paul's Chapel** (*see p54*), completed in 1766 (a spire was added in 1796). George Washington, a parishioner here, was officially received in the chapel after his 1789 presidential inauguration. The Enlightenment ideals upon which the nation was founded influenced the church's non-hierarchical layout. **Trinity Church** (*see p54*) of 1846, one of the first and finest Gothic Revival churches in the country, was designed by Richard Upjohn. Its crocketed, finialed 281-foot spire held sway for decades as the tallest structure in Manhattan.

Holdouts remain from each epoch of the city's architectural history. An outstanding example of Greek Revival from the first half of the 19th century is the 1842 **Federal Hall National Memorial** (*see p50*), the mighty marble colonnaded structure on the site where George Washington took his oath of office. A larger-than-life statue of Washington by the sculptor John Quincy Adams Ward stands in front. The city's most celebrated blocks of Greek Revival townhouses, built in the 1830s, are known simply as the **Row** (1-13 Washington Square North, between Fifth Avenue & Washington Square West); they're exemplars of the more genteel metropolis of Henry James and Edith Wharton.

Greek Revival gave way to Renaissance-inspired Beaux Arts architecture, which itself reflected the imperial ambitions of a wealthy young nation during the Gilded Age of the late 19th century. Like Emperor Augustus, who boasted that he had found Rome a city of brick and left it a city of marble, the firm of McKim, Mead & White built noble civic monuments and palazzi for the rich. The best-known buildings of the classicist Charles Follen McKim include the main campus of **Columbia University** (*see p170*), begun in the 1890s, and the austere 1906 **Morgan Library** (*see p157*), which underwent an interior renovation completed in 2010. His partner, socialite and bon vivant Stanford White (scandalously murdered by his mistress's husband in 1906 on the roof of the original Madison Square Garden, which he himself designed), conceived more festive spaces, such as the **Metropolitan Club**

(1 E 60th Street, at Fifth Avenue) and the luxe Villard Houses of 1882, now part of the **New York Palace Hotel** (*see p365*).

Downtown, the old **Alexander Hamilton US Custom House**, which now houses the National Museum of the American Indian (*see p50*), was built by Cass Gilbert in 1907 and is a symbol of New York Harbor's significance in Manhattan's growth (before 1913, the city's chief source of revenue was customs duties). Gilbert's domed marble edifice is suitably monumental – its carved figures of the Four Continents are by Daniel Chester French, the sculptor of the Lincoln Memorial in Washington, DC. Another Beaux Arts treasure is Carrère & Hastings' sumptuous white marble **New York Public Library** of 1911 (*see p152*), built on the site of a former Revolutionary War battleground. The 1913 travertine-lined **Grand Central Terminal** (*see p155*) remains an elegant transportation hub, thanks to preservationists who saved it from the wrecking ball.

VERTICAL REALITY

Cast-iron architecture peaked in the latter half of the 19th century, coinciding with the Civil War. Iron and steel components freed architects from the bulk, weight and cost of stone, and allowed them to build taller structures. Cast-iron columns – cheap to mass-produce – could support enormous weight. The façades of many Soho buildings, with their intricate details of Italianate columns, were manufactured on assembly lines and could be ordered in pieces from catalogues. This led to an aesthetic of uniform building façades, which had a direct impact on later steel skyscrapers and continues to inform the skyline today. To enjoy one of the most telling vistas of skyscraper history, gaze north from the 1859 **Cooper Union** building (*see p94*) in the East Village, the oldest steel-beam-framed building in America.

The most visible effect of the move towards cast-iron construction was the way it opened up solid-stone façades to expanses of glass. In fact, window-shopping came into vogue in the 1860s. Mrs Lincoln bought the White House china at the **Haughwout Store** (488-492 Broadway, at Broome Street). The 1857 building's Palladian-style façade recalls Renaissance Venice, but its regular, open fenestration was also a portent of the future. (The cast-iron elevator sign is a relic of the world's first working safety passenger elevator, designed by Elisha Graves Otis in 1852.)

Once engineers perfected steel, which is stronger and lighter than iron, and created the interlocking steel-cage construction that distributed the weight of a building over its entire frame, the sky was the limit. New York has one structure by the great Chicago-based innovator Louis Sullivan: the 1898 **Bayard-Condict Building** (65-69 Bleecker Street, between Broadway & Lafayette Street). Though only 13 storeys tall, Sullivan's building, covered with richly decorative terracotta, was one of the earliest to have a purely vertical design rather than one that imitated the horizontal styles of the past. Sullivan wrote that a skyscraper 'must be tall, every inch of it tall... From bottom to top, it is a unit without a single dissenting line.'

The 21-storey **Flatiron Building** (*see p130*), designed by fellow Chicagoan Daniel H Burnham and completed in 1902, is another standout of the era. Its height and modern design combined with traditional masonry decoration was made possible only by its steel-cage construction.

The new century saw a frenzy of skyward construction, resulting in buildings of record-breaking height. When it was built in 1899, the 30-storey, 391-foot **Park Row Building** (15 Park Row, between Ann & Beekman Streets) was the tallest building in the world; by 1931, though, Shreve, Lamb & Harmon's 1,250-foot **Empire State Building** (*see p153*) had more than tripled its record. (For more on the battle for the city's tallest building, *see p341* **Race to the Top**.) Although they were retroactively labelled art deco (such buildings were then simply called 'modern'), the Empire State's setbacks were actually a response to the zoning code of 1916, which required a building's upper storeys to be tapered in order not to block out sunlight and air circulation to the streets. The code engendered some of the city's most fanciful architectural designs, such as the ziggurat-crowned 1926 **Paramount Building** (1501 Broadway, between 43rd & 44th Streets) and the romantically slender spire of the former **Cities Service Building** (70 Pine Street, at Pearl Street), illuminated from within like an enormous rare gem.

OUTSIDE THE BOX

The post-World War II period saw the rise of the International Style, pioneered by such giants as Le Corbusier and Ludwig Mies van der Rohe. The International Style relied on a new set of aesthetics: minimal decoration, clear expression of construction, an honest use of materials and a near-Platonic harmony of proportions. The style's most visible symbol was the all-glass façade, similar to that found on the sleek slab of the **United Nations Headquarters' Secretariat Building** (*see p158*).

Designed by Gordon Bunshaft of Skidmore, Owings & Merrill, **Lever House** (390 Park Avenue, between 53rd & 54th Streets) became the city's first all-steel-and-glass structure in 1952. It's almost impossible to imagine the radical vision this glass construction represented on the all-masonry corridor of Park Avenue, because nearly every building since has followed suit. Mies van der Rohe's celebrated bronze-skinned **Seagram Building** (375 Park Avenue, between 52nd & 53rd Streets), which reigns in isolation in its own plaza, is the epitome of the architect's cryptic dicta that 'Less is more' and 'God is in the details'. The detailing on the building is exquisite – the custom-made bolts securing the miniature bronze piers that run the length of the façade must be polished by hand every year to keep them from oxidising and turning green. With this heady combination of grandeur and attention to detail, it's the Rolls-Royce of skyscrapers.

High modernism began to show cracks in its façade during the mid 1960s. By then, New York had built too many such structures in midtown and below. The public had never fully warmed to the undecorated style, and the International Style's sheer arrogance in trying to supplant the traditional city structure didn't endear the movement to anyone. The **MetLife Building** (200 Park Avenue, at 45th Street), originally the Pan Am Building of 1963, was the prime culprit, not so much because of its design (by Walter Gropius of the Bauhaus) but because of its presumptuous location, straddling Park Avenue and looming over Grand Central. There was even a plan to raze Grand Central and construct a twin Pan Am in its place. The International Style had obviously reached its end when Philip Johnson, instrumental in defining the movement with his book *The International Style* (co-written with Henry-Russell Hitchcock), began disparaging the aesthetic as 'glass-boxitis'.

A different approach was provided by Boston architect Hugh Stubbins' triangle-topped **Citigroup Center** (Lexington Avenue, between 53rd & 54th Streets), which utilised contemporary engineering (the building cantilevers almost magically on high stilts above street level) while harking back to the decorative tops of yesteryear. Sly old Johnson turned the tables on everyone with the heretical Chippendale crown on his **Sony Building**, originally the AT&T Building (350 Madison Avenue, between 55th & 56th Streets), a bold throwback to decoration for its own sake.

Postmodernism provided a theoretical basis for a new wave of buildings that mixed past and present, often taking cues from the environs. Some notable examples include Helmut Jahn's **425 Lexington Avenue** (between 43rd & 44th Streets) of 1988; David Childs's retro diamond-tipped **Worldwide Plaza** (825 Eighth Avenue, between 49th & 50th Streets) of 1989; and the honky-tonk agglomeration of Skidmore, Owings & Merrill's **Bertelsmann Building** (1540 Broadway, between 45th & 46th Streets) of 1990. But even postmodernism became old hat after a while: too many architects relied on fussy fenestration and passive commentary on other styles, and too few were creating vital new building façades.

The electronic spectacle of **Times Square** (*see p146*) provided one possible direction for architects. Upon seeing the myriad electric lights of Times Square in 1922, British wit GK Chesterton remarked: 'What a glorious garden of wonder this would be, to anyone who was lucky enough to be unable to read.' The Crossroads of the World continues to be at the cybernetic cutting edge, with the 120-foot-tall, quarter-acre-in-area NASDAQ sign; the real-time stock tickers and jumbo TV screens; and the news ticker wrapping around the original 1904 New York Times HQ, **1 Times Square** (between Broadway & Seventh Avenue).

CONTEMPORARY VISION

Early 21st-century architecture is moving beyond applied symbolism to radical new forms, facilitated by computer-based design

RACE TO THE TOP

How NYC's architects egged each other onwards and upwards.

For nearly half a century after its 1846 completion, the 281-foot steeple of Richard Upjohn's Gothic Revival **Trinity Church** (*see p54*) reigned in lonely serenity at the foot of Wall Street as the tallest structure in Manhattan. The church was finally topped in 1890 by the since-demolished, 348-foot **New York World Building**. But it wasn't until the turn of the century that New York's architects started to reach for the skies. So began a mad rush to the top, with building after building capturing the title of the world's tallest.

When it was completed in 1899, the 30-storey, 391-foot **Park Row Building** (15 Park Row, between Ann & Beekman Streets) enjoyed that lofty distinction. However, its record was shattered by the 612-foot **Singer Building** in 1908 (which, in 1968, became the tallest building ever to be demolished); the 52-storey, 700-foot **Metropolitan Life Tower** (*see p130*) of 1909; and the 793-foot **Woolworth Building** (*see p60*), Cass Gilbert's Gothic 1913 masterpiece.

The Woolworth stood in solitary splendour until skyscraper construction reached a crescendo in the late 1920s, with a famed three-way race. The now largely forgotten **Bank of Manhattan Building** (now known as the Trump Building) at 40 Wall Street was briefly the record-holder, at 71 storeys and 927 feet in 1930. Soon after, William Van Alen, the architect of the **Chrysler Building** (*see p155*), unveiled his secret weapon: a 'vertex', a spire of chrome nickel steel put together inside the dome and raised from within, which brought the building's height to 1,046 feet. But then, 13 months later, Van Alen's homage to the Automobile Age was itself outstripped by Shreve, Lamb & Harmon's 1,250-foot **Empire State Building** (*see p153*). With its broad base, narrow shaft and needled crown, it remains the quintessential skyscraper, and one of the most famous buildings in the world.

Woolworth Building.

Incredibly, there were no challengers for the distinction of New York's – and the world's – tallest building for more than 40 years, until the 110-storey, 1,362- and 1,368-foot **Twin Towers** of Minoru Yamasaki's World Trade Center were completed in 1973. They were trumped by Chicago's Sears Tower a year later, but remained the city's tallest buildings until 11 September 2001, when the New York crown reverted to the Empire State Building. However, the World Trade Center has since regained the title. In spring 2012, **1 World Trade Center** (formerly known as the Freedom Tower), designed by David Childs of Skidmore, Owings & Merrill to replace the Twin Towers, overtook the ESB. It has since surpassed the original towers at a height of 1,776 feet, and NYC has beaten the Windy City as home to America's tallest skyscraper.

methods. A stellar example is Kohn Pedersen Fox's stainless steel and glass 'vertical campus', the **Baruch College Academic Complex** (55 Lexington Avenue, between 24th & 25th Streets). The phantasmagoric designs that curve and dart in sculptural space are so beyond the timid window-dressing of postmodernism that they deserve a new label.

Frank Gehry's ten-storey, white-glass mirage of a building in Chelsea, completed in 2007, is emblematic of the radical reworking of the New York cityscape. Gehry's first office building in New York, the headquarters for Barry Diller's Internet/media company **IAC** (555 W 18th Street, at West Side Highway) comprises tilting glass volumes that resemble a fully rigged tall ship. This area, once full of warehouses and industrial buildings, is being transformed by the **High Line**, a former elevated railroad viaduct that has been reconceived as a cutting-edge urban park. Striking residential structures are springing up, including Annabelle Selldorf's 19-storey apartment building at 200 Eleventh Avenue and 24th Street, which even has a car elevator. At the southern end, Renzo Piano's downtown satellite of the **Whitney Museum of American Art** (*see p113*) is expected to be finished in 2015. Down south, the **Urban Glass House** (330 Spring Street, at Washington Street), one of the late Philip Johnson's last designs, sprang up in 2006 amid Tribeca's hulking industrial edifices. The mini-skyscraper is a multiplication of his iconic Glass House in New Canaan, Connecticut.

In recent years, Midtown West has become a hotbed of construction. The area's architectural attractions were enhanced in 2006 by Norman Foster's elegant 46-storey, 597-foot crystalline addition to the art deco base of the **Hearst Magazine Building** (300 W 57th Street, at Eighth Avenue). The structure is a breathtaking combination of old and new, with the massive triangular struts of the tower penetrating the façade of the base and opening up great airy spaces within. Even as the age of superblock modernism seems to be coming to a close, a new era of green, eco-conscious architecture is emerging. Cook + Fox's **Bank of America Tower** at 1 Bryant Park (Sixth Avenue, between 42nd & 43rd Streets) bills itself as the greenest skyscraper in the city, with torqued, glass facets reaching 54 storeys. The structure has a thermal storage system, daylight dimmers, green roofs and double-wall construction to reduce heat build-up. Renzo Piano's 2007 tower for the *New York Times* at **620 Eighth Avenue** (between 40th & 41st Streets) also offers such green amenities as automatic shades that respond to the heat of the sun.

Further north, and among the more controversial facelifts of recent years, is Brad Cloepfil's renovation of Edward Durell Stone's 1964 modernism meets Venetian palazzo, **2 Columbus Circle**, originally the home of A&P heir Huntington Hartford's Gallery of Modern Art. In the same way that the gallery's collection of mostly figurative painting was seen as reactionary in the face of the abstract art movement, Stone's quotation of a historicist style was laughed into apostasy. However, Stone's work is being re-evaluated as a precursor to postmodernism, and many 20th-century architecture enthusiasts lamented the loss of the original façade after a lengthy, unsuccessful battle by the Landmarks Preservation Commission. The building is now the home of the Museum of Arts & Design (*see p164*).

BEST-LAID PLANS

Some of New York's more ambitious architectural projects have been scaled back in the face of new economic realities. The World Trade Center site, conceived by Daniel Libeskind, saw frustratingly little progress in the years after the tragedy of 9/11. The

Hearst Magazine Building.

IN CONTEXT

16-acre site's overseers, the Port Authority of New York and New Jersey, reported in 2008 that construction of the 26 interrelated projects was years behind schedule and billions of dollars over its $16 billion budget. However, it seems to be back on track: the **9/11 Memorial Plaza** opened in time for the tenth anniversary of the Twin Towers' fall and David Childs's 1,776-foot **1 World Trade Center** (formerly known as the Freedom Tower) is now the tallest building in the Western Hemisphere. Santiago Calatrava's spectacular plans for a shimmering, subterranean World Trade Center Transportation Hub, linking the suburban PATH trains to the subway, no longer feature retractable roof wings, but the ribbed ceiling will still let in the sun with a skylight. The station is expected to be completed in 2015.

Scaling back seems to be a key phrase in the second decade of the 21st century, and grandiose schemes have settled earthward. The transformation of Brooklyn's **Atlantic Yards** (*see p206*) into a mega-development started boldly as an architectural site for Frank Gehry and Enrique Norten, but Gehry's design for the Nets' arena was rejected as too expensive. Realised by SHoP Architects, the 19,000-seat **Barclays Center** (*see p207*), featuring a rust-coloured steel-panelled façade, was officially unveiled in autumn 2012, and work started on the first of 15 planned modular residential towers more than a year later. The proposed $1.5 billion renovation of **Lincoln Center** was also kept in check, leaving a team of top-notch architects to work with what was already there. Diller Scofidio + Renfro, one of the most creative teams on the scene, turned the travertine marble façade of Alice Tully Hall into a show window, integrating inside and out with glass walls; elsewhere, Billie Tsien and Tod Williams transformed a public atrium across from Lincoln Center, between Broadway and Columbus, and 62nd and 63rd Streets, into a sky-lit 'theatrical garden', lined with ferns, moss and flowering vines, for buying tickets and sipping refreshments.

Developers tend to overbuild commercial space until there's a bust – plans for the World Trade Center site alone call for new office space that equates to five times the amount in downtown Atlanta, but there have been difficulties attracting tenants. Setbacks have also met Pritzker Prize-winner Jean Nouvel's exciting plan for the sloped, crystalline **Tower Verre**, with an exoskeleton of irregularly crossing beams, that is planned to rise next door to the Museum of Modern Art. Initially proposed to reach 1,250 feet, the tower was opposed by activists who feared that its shadow would loom over Central Park and it was rejected by the city's Planning Commission. After 200 feet were snipped off the top, the plan received the green light and the tower should be a glamorous presence on the city skyline.

In a reversal of the city's historical pattern of development, much of the money is migrating downtown. The **Blue Building**, Bernard Tschumi's multifaceted, blue glass-walled condominium, is a startling breakaway from the low-rise brick buildings that make up the Lower East Side. Also noteworthy is the Japanese firm SANAA's **New Museum of Contemporary Art** (*see p84*); its asymmetrically staggered boxy volumes covered in aluminum mesh shake up the traditional streetfront of the Bowery. A block north, at **257 Bowery** (between Stanton & Houston Streets), Norman Foster's slender gallery building for Sperone Westwater art dealers – complete with a 12- by 20-foot lift that doubles as a moving exhibition space – has taken shape in a narrow gap. Meanwhile, Frank Gehry's boldly named 76-storey **New York by Gehry** (formerly known as the Beekman Tower), just south of City Hall, topped out at 870 feet in 2011. With a curled and warped stainless-steel façade, it has the unmistakable stamp of its creator and was briefly the city's tallest residential tower. However, it has since been surpassed by French architect Christian de Portzamparc's glassy midtown titan **One57** (157 W 57th Street, between Sixth & Seventh Avenues), which rises to more than 1,000 feet. Rafael Viñoly's **432 Park Avenue** will dwarf that at a lofty 1,398 feet when completed in 2015.

To keep up with what's going up, visit the **AIA Center for Architecture** (*see p109*), the **Skyscraper Museum** (*see p57*) and the **Storefront for Art and Architecture** (97 Kenmare Street, between Mulberry Street & Cleveland Place, 1-212 431 5795, www.storefrontnews.org, closed Mon & Sun), a non-profit organisation that hosts exhibitions, talks, screenings and more.

Essential Information

Hotels

Accommodation is more expensive in New York City than in the rest of the country and, while the average room rate dipped sharply in the wake of the financial crisis, it has been creeping up steadily since then, topping $300 in the autumn high season. The hotel business is booming and the citywide room count is nearly 100,000, an increase of nearly 25 per cent over the past five years. And most of them are full year-round.

There is now more boutique choice in popular areas like Chelsea and Greenwich Village with the arrival of the **High Line Hotel** (*see p355* **Divine Digs**) and the **Marlton** (*see p353*). But perhaps the strongest indication of the recovery is a cluster of new development on, or around, midtown's West 57th Street (*see p366* **The New 57**). It's also worth looking to the outer boroughs for competitive pricing – Brooklyn, especially, is an increasingly desirable place to stay. Even the Bronx now has a boutique hotel, a conversion of a former Beaux Arts opera house (*see p371*).

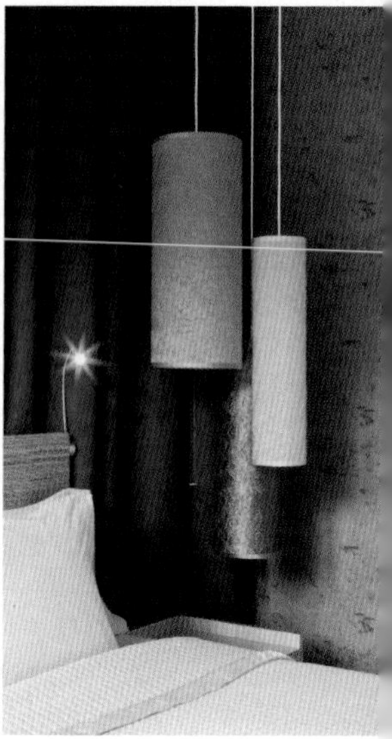

PRICES AND INFORMATION

Accommodation in this chapter has been organised by price level to give you an idea of what you can expect to pay at a given hotel, but note that rates can vary wildly according to season or room category within a single property. As a guide, you can expect to pay $500 or more per night in the deluxe category, $300-$500 for expensive hotels, $150-$300 for moderate accommodation and under $150 for properties listed as budget. Don't forget to factor in the hefty 14.75 per cent tax – which includes city, state and hotel-room occupancy tax – plus an extra $3.50 per night for most rooms.

Special deals are often available, especially in the low season between January and March, and you can frequently shave more off the price by booking on the hotel's website. Locally based discount agency **Quikbook** (www.quikbook.com) often has a good selection of the properties listed in this chapter on its website. For a budget option with a more personal touch, consider a B&B. Artist-run agency **City Sonnet** (1-212 614 3034, www.citysonnet.com) deals in downtown Manhattan locations. Expect to pay at least $135 for a double room in a private home. For gay-oriented hotels and B&Bs, *see pp256-257.*

FINANCIAL DISTRICT & BATTERY PARK

Expensive

★ Andaz Wall Street

75 Wall Street, between Water Street & Pearl Street, New York, NY 10005 (1-212 590 1234, www.wallstreetandaz.com). Subway 2, 3, 4, 5 to Wall Street. **Rooms** 253. **Map** p396 F33.

Although it's a subsidiary brand of global giant Hyatt, Andaz prides itself on giving each property a local flavour. Following launches in London and LA, the first New York outpost occupies the first 13 floors of a former Barclays bank building, outfitted by David Rockwell. The vibe inside is anything but corporate: upon entering the spacious, bamboo-panelled lobby-lounge, you're greeted by a free-range 'host', who acts as combination check-in clerk and concierge. The chic, loft-style rooms (starting at 350sq ft) are equally casual and user-friendly. A long, blond-wood unit doubles as desk, entertainment console and dressing table (the TV has a vanity mirror on the back); remote-controlled blackout blinds descend to cover the seven-foot windows; and Wi-Fi and non-alcoholic drinks and snacks are free. The local-centric restaurant (Wall & Water), bar and spa are welcome attributes in an area with little action at weekends.

Other location 485 Fifth Avenue, at 41st Street, Midtown (1-212 601 1234, www.5thavenue.andaz.com).

Conrad New York

102 North End Avenue, at Vesey Street, New York, NY 10282 (1-212 945 0100, www.conradnewyork.com). Subway A, C, 1, 2, 3 to Chambers Street; E to World Trade Center; R to Cortlandt Street; 2, 3 to Park Place. **Rooms** 88. **Map** p396 D31.

This sophisticated Hilton offshoot fronts Battery Park City's riverside Nelson A Rockefeller Park. West-facing guest quarters have views of the Hudson, but there's also plenty to see within the art-rich, all-suite property. Sol LeWitt's vivid 100ft by 80ft painting *Loopy Doopy (Blue and Purple)* graces the dramatic 15-storey, glass-ceilinged, marble-floored lobby, and coolly understated suites are adorned with pieces by the likes of Elizabeth Peyton and Mary Heilmann. Nespresso machines and marble bathrooms with Aromatherapy Associates products are indulgent touches. Above the rooftop bar (open May-Oct), with views of the Statue of Liberty, is a vegetable patch providing fresh produce for the North End Grill (*see p57*) next door.

TRIBECA & SOHO

Deluxe

★ Crosby Street Hotel

79 Crosby Street, between Prince & Spring Streets, New York, NY 10012 (1-212 226 6400, www.firmdalehotels.com). Subway N, R to Prince Street; 6 to Spring Street. **Rooms** 86. **Map** p397 E30.

In 2009, Britain's hospitality power couple, Tim and Kit Kemp, brought their super-successful Firmdale formula across the Atlantic with the 11-storey, warehouse-style Crosby Street Hotel – their first outside London. Design director Kit Kemp's signature style – a fresh, contemporary take on classic English decor characterised by an often audacious mix of patterns, bold colours and judiciously chosen antiques – is instantly recognisable. Other Firmdale imports include a carefully selected art collection, a guests-only drawing room as well as a public restaurant and bar, a slick, 99-seat screening room and a private garden.

★ Greenwich Hotel

377 Greenwich Street, between Franklin & North Moore Streets, New York, NY 10013 (1-212 941 8900, www.thegreenwichhotel.com). Subway 1 to Franklin Street. **Rooms** 88. **Map** p396 D31.

The design inspiration at this Tribeca retreat, co-owned by Robert De Niro, is as international as the jet-set clientele. Individually decorated rooms combine custom-made English leather seating, Tibetan rugs and gorgeous Moroccan or Carrara-marble-tiled bathrooms, most outfitted with capacious tubs that fill up in a minute flat (bath salts from Nolita spa Red Flower are provided). Breaststroke meditatively beneath the frame of a 250-year-old Kyoto farmhouse in the Shibui Spa's underground pool, then

ESSENTIAL INFORMATION

Conrad New York.

unwind with a bottle of wine by the water's edge. For dinner, there's no need to rub shoulders with the masses at the always-mobbed house restaurant, Locanda Verde. Have your meal delivered to the cloistered courtyard, where travertine floors and terracotta pots evoke a Florentine villa.

► *For more on Robert De Niro's Tribeca empire, see p69.*

The Mercer

147 Mercer Street, at Prince Street, New York, NY 10012 (1-212 966 6060, 1-888 918 6060, www.mercerhotel.com). Subway N, R to Prince Street. **Rooms** 75. **Map** p397 E29.

Opened in 2001 by trendsetting hotelier André Balazs, this pioneering boutique hotel still has ample attractions that appeal to a celeb-heavy clientele. The lobby, appointed with oversized couches and chairs, and shelves lined with colourful books, acts as a bar, library and lounge. The loft-like rooms are large by NYC standards and feature furniture by Christian Liaigre, enormous washrooms and Face Stockholm products. The restaurant, the Mercer Kitchen, serves Jean-Georges Vongerichten's stylish version of casual American cuisine.

Expensive

60 Thompson

60 Thompson Street, between Broome & Spring Streets, New York, NY 10012 (1-212 431 0400, 1-877 431 0400, www.thompsonhotels.com). Subway C, E to Spring Street. **Rooms** 100. **Map** p397 E30.

The first property of boutique chain Thompson has been luring film, fashion and media elites since it opened in 2001. British designer Tara Bernerd, who created the classy contemporary interiors for the group's London hotel, Belgraves, and the new Thompson Chicago, is behind a redesign planned for early 2014. Indulgent details in the guest rooms include Sferra linens and REN products. The hotel's acclaimed restaurant, Kittichai, serves creative Thai cuisine beside a pool filled with floating orchids, while A60, the exclusive guests-only rooftop bar, offers inspiring city views and a Moroccan-inspired decor. **Other locations** throughout the city.

► *For other Thompson hotels in New York City, visit www.thompsonhotels.com.*

The James New York

27 Grand Street, at Thompson Street, New York, NY 10013 (1-212 465 2000, 1-888 526 3778, www.jameshotels.com). Subway A, C, E to Canal Street. **Rooms** 114. **Map** p397 D30.

Hotel art displays are usually limited to some eye-catching lobby installations or forgettable in-room prints. Not so at the James, which maintains a substantial showcase of local talent. The corridor of each guest floor is dedicated to the work of an individual artist, selected by a house curator and complete with museum-style notes – which makes waiting for the lift a lot less tedious. The Chicago-based owners have given the property a distinctly Gotham vibe – even the doorstaff sport rakish uniforms (designed by Andrew Buckler) that look straight out of *Gangs of New York*. Although compact, bedrooms make the most of the available space with high ceilings, wall-spanning windows and glassed-off bathrooms (modesty is preserved by an artist-embellished, remote-controlled screen). Natural materials (wooden floors, linen duvet covers) warm up the clean contemporary lines, beds are piled with eco-friendly pillows, and bathroom products are courtesy of Intelligent Nutrients, the organic line created by Aveda founder Horst Rechelbacher. A two-level 'urban garden' (open May-Oct) houses an outdoor bar and eaterie. The rooftop bar, Jimmy, opens on to the (admittedly tiny) pool.

Mondrian Soho

9 Crosby Street, between Grand & Howard Streets, New York, NY 10013 (1-212 389 1000, www.mondriansoho.com). Subway J, N, Q, R, Z, 6 to Canal Street. **Rooms** 270. **Map** p396 E30.

Designed by Benjamin Noriega Ortiz, who created cool cribs for Lenny Kravitz and gave the Mondrian Los Angeles a glamorous makeover in 2008, Mondrian Soho has a distinctly un-Gotham vibe. An ivy-covered passageway leads to the 26-storey glass tower, set back from Crosby Street. Inspired by Jean Cocteau's *La Belle et la Bête*, Ortiz has created a fanciful interior in which lobby coffee tables have talons and floor lamps are shaded with petite parasols. Trippy, saturated-blue hallways lead to rooms that combine white minimalism with classic elements such as china blue arabesque-print upholstery and marble-topped vanity sinks that perch outside the bathroom. Floor-to-ceiling windows give rooms on higher floors spectacular vistas, especially in the suites, where double banks of glass provide a panoramic sweep. Going one better than Wi-Fi, every room is equipped with an in-room iPad that also connects to hotel services. The Italian restaurant, Isola Trattoria & Crudo Bar, offers seating in an adjacent greenhouse, fitted out with crystal chandeliers, ferns and ficus trees, while the dimly lit, cushion-strewn bar, Mister H, looks like a 1930s Shanghai opium den by way of *Casablanca*.

Soho Grand Hotel

310 West Broadway, between Canal & Grand Streets, New York, NY 10013 (1-212 965 3000,

IN THE KNOW LOFT LIVING

If you're in NYC for an extended period, accommodation agency **City Sonnet** (*see p346*) can set you up in your own private loft in arty Queens neighbourhood Long Island City. Rates start at $2,500 per month.

ESSENTIAL INFORMATION

Bowery House. *See p350.*

1-800 965 3000, www.sohogrand.com). Subway A, C, E, 1 to Canal Street. **Rooms** 363. **Map** p397 E30.
The Soho Grand, which pioneered the downtown hotel migration in 1996, is fresh from a revamp. The original designer, Bill Sofield, recently introduced new custom pieces to the elegant brown-and-beige guest rooms, including travel trunk-inspired minibars and natty houndstooth tuxedo chairs. Bathrooms feature charming wallpaper by the late illustrator Saul Steinberg (whose work was a long-time staple of the *New Yorker*) and CO Bigelow products. Endearingly, you can request a goldfish for the duration of your stay. Guests can also borrow old-fashioned bicycles in the warmer months to explore the city; after your exertions, claim a lounger in the hotel's seasonal outdoor bar-eaterie the Yard, or hole up with a cocktail by the fireplace in the Club Room, a glamorous year-round lounge.
Other locations Tribeca Grand Hotel, 2 Sixth Avenue, between Walker & White Streets, Tribeca (1-212 519 6600, www.tribecagrand.com).

Moderate

Cosmopolitan
95 West Broadway, at Chambers Street, New York, NY 10007 (1-212 566 1900, 1-888 895 9400, www.cosmohotel.com). Subway A, C, 1, 2, 3 to Chambers Street. **Rooms** 131. **Map** p396 E31.
Open continuously since the mid 19th century, the Cosmopolitan has long been a tourist favourite for its address, clean rooms and reasonable rates. In early 2014 the hotel embarks on a floor-by-floor revamp to upgrade its guest quarters and introduce a bar and restaurant. Other convenient facilities include a small gym and a business centre with two Macs that guests can use free of charge (if you don't have your own laptop to take advantage of the complimentary in-room Wi-Fi). A wide range of room configurations is available, including a suite with two queen beds and a sofa bed, ideal for families.

Duane Street Hotel
130 Duane Street, at Church Street, New York, NY 10013 (1-212 964 4600, www.duanestreethotel.com). Subway A, C, 1, 2, 3 to Chambers Street. **Rooms** 45. **Map** p396 E31.
In a city with a high tolerance for hype, the Duane Street Hotel stands out by its quiet dedication to doing the simple things well. Opened on a quiet Tribeca street in 2007, the boutique property takes its cues from its well-heeled residential neighbourhood, offering loft-inspired rooms with high ceilings, oversized triple-glazed windows and hardwood floors, and a chic, monochrome colour scheme. Free Wi-Fi, Ren products in the slate-tiled bathrooms, Nespresso machines in the deluxe-category accommodation and complimentary passes to the nearby swanky Equinox gym cement the value-for-money package – a rare commodity in this part of town. The chic Asian-inspired restaurant is helmed by *Iron Chef* regular Jehangir Mehta.

CHINATOWN, LITTLE ITALY & NOLITA

Expensive

Nolitan
30 Kenmare Street, at Elizabeth Street, New York, NY 10012 (1-212 925 2555, www.nolitanhotel.com). Subway J, Z to Bowery; 6 to Spring Street. **Rooms** 55. **Map** p397 F30.
To make like a Nolitan, check in to this boutique hotel. The rooms feature floor-to-ceiling windows, custom-made walnut beds, wooden floors and toiletries from Prince Street spa Red Flower. The emphasis on keeping it local is reflected in numerous guest perks: the luxuriously laid-back property lends out bikes and skateboards and lays on free local calls and discounts at neighbourhood boutiques. Complimentary wine and cheese is served Monday to Saturday in the lobby, which has a ceiling-height bookshelf stocked with tomes from nearby Phaidon Books. Admire views of

THE BEST CHEAP DIGS

For flophouse chic
Bowery House. *See p350.*

For an eye-popping art house
Carlton Arms Hotel. *See p359.*

For a deluxe sleeping compartment
The Jane. *See p354.*

For a designer dorm
New York Loft Hostel. *See p371.*

Nolita and beyond from the 2,400sq ft roof deck, complete with fire pit, or your private perch – more than half the guest quarters have balconies.

Budget

Bowery House

220 Bowery, between Prince & Spring Streets, New York, NY 10012 (1-212 837 2373, www.theboweryhouse.com). Subway J, Z to Bowery. **Rooms** 75. **Map** p397 F29.

Two young real-estate developers transformed a 1927 Bowery flophouse into a stylish take on a hostel. History buffs will get a kick out of the original wainscotted corridors leading to cubicles (singles are a cosy 35sq ft, and not all have windows) with latticework ceilings to allow air circulation. It might not be the best bet for light sleepers, but the place is hopping with pretty young things attracted to the hip aesthetic and the location (across the street from the New Museum and close to Soho and the Lower East Side). Quarters are decorated with vintage prints and historical photographs, and lit by lightbulbs encased in 1930s and '40s mason jars; towels and robes are courtesy of Ralph Lauren. The immaculate (gender-segregated) communal bathrooms have rain showerheads and products from local spa Red Flower, while the lounge is outfitted with chesterfield sofas, chandeliers and a huge LCD TV. There's also a 3,000sq ft roof terrace, and an eaterie serving eclectic small plates. To keep out the riff-raff and the rowdy, guests must be over 21 and reserve with a credit card. *Photo p349.*

Sohotel

341 Broome Street, between Elizabeth Street & Bowery, New York, NY 10013 (1-212 226 1482, www.thesohotel.com). Subway J, Z to Bowery; 6 to Spring Street. **Rooms** 98. **Map** p397 F30.

Established as an inn in 1805, but altered considerably since then, this is the oldest hotel in the city. By the time you read this, a renovation should be complete that will introduce a more industrial look while emphasising the building's period character with exposed-brick walls, ceiling beams and hardwood floors. While the rates put it at the upper end of the budget category, the hotel offers perks that place it a rung above similarly priced establishments, including bathroom products from CO Bigelow, complimentary morning tea and coffee served in the lobby and free in-room Wi-Fi. The Superior Family rooms, which can accommodate five, are the best bargain. Guests get a 10% discount at the on-site craft-brew emporium, Randolph Beer.

LOWER EAST SIDE

Expensive

Hotel on Rivington

107 Rivington Street, between Essex & Ludlow Streets, New York, NY 10002 (1-212 475 2600, www.hotelonrivington.com). Subway F to Delancey Street; J, Z to Delancey-Essex Streets. **Rooms** 108. **Map** p397 G29.

When the Hotel on Rivington opened in 2005, its ultra-modern glass-covered façade was a novelty on the largely low-rise Lower East Side. Now, with condos popping up everywhere, the building (designed by NYC firm Grzywinski & Pons) seems less out of place, but it remains one of the few luxury hotels in the neighbourhood. Rooms are super-sleek and minimalist, with black and white decorative touches, Frette bedlinen and robes, and floor-to-ceiling windows (even in the shower stalls) with views of Manhattan and beyond. A stylish crowd congregates in the hotel's two restaurants, Co-op Food & Drink, which serves sushi and modern American fare, and Viktor & Spoils, a contemporary taqueria and tequila bar.

Moderate

Off Soho Suites Hotel

11 Rivington Street, between Bowery & Chrystie Street, New York, NY 10002 (1-212 979 9808, 1-800 633 7646, www.offsoho.com). Subway B, D to Grand Street; F to Lower East Side-Second Avenue; J, Z to Bowery. **Rooms** 38. **Map** p397 F30.

These no-frills suites have become all the more popular in recent years due to the Lower East Side's burgeoning bar and restaurant scene. The rates are a decent value, especially as all have a sitting area and access to a kitchenette. Economy options have two twin beds and a shared kitchen or, if you're travelling in a group, book a deluxe suite – with a queen bed, plus a sleeper sofa in the living area, it can accommodate four. There's also free Wi-Fi, a gym and a handy coin-operated laundry.

EAST VILLAGE

Expensive

Bowery Hotel

335 Bowery, at 3rd Street, New York, NY 10003 (1-212 505 9100, www.theboweryhotel.com). Subway B, D, F, M to Broadway-Lafayette Street; 6 to Bleecker Street. **Rooms** 135. **Map** p397 F29.

This fanciful boutique hotel from prominent duo Eric Goode and Sean MacPherson is the capstone in the gentrification of the Bowery. Shunning minimalism, the pear have created plush rooms that pair old-world touches (oriental rugs, wood-beamed ceilings, marble washstands) with modern amenities (free Wi-Fi, flatscreen TVs, a DVD library). Tall windows offer views of historic tenements, and the property also includes an antique-looking trattoria, Gemma.

► *For the hoteliers' flamboyant take on a boarding house, the Jane, see p354.*

Budget

East Village Bed & Coffee

110 Avenue C, between 7th & 8th Streets, New York, NY 10009 (1-917 816 0071, www.bedandcoffee.com). Subway F to Lower East Side-Second Avenue; L to First Avenue.
Rooms 9. **Map** p397 G28.

Popular with European travellers, this East Village B&B (minus the breakfast) embodies quirky downtown culture. Each of the nine guest rooms has a unique theme: for example, the Black and White Room or the Treehouse (not as outlandish as it sounds: it has an ivory and olive colour scheme, animal-print linens and a whitewashed brick wall). Bathrooms are shared. Owner Anne Edris encourages guests to mingle in the communal areas, which include fully equipped kitchens and three loft-like living rooms with free Wi-Fi. When the weather's nice, sip your complimentary morning java in the private garden.

Hotel 17

225 E 17th Street, between Second & Third Avenues, New York, NY 10003 (1-212 475 2845, www.hotel17ny.com). Subway L to Third Avenue; L, N, Q, R, 4, 5, 6 to 14th Street-Union Square.
Rooms 125. **Map** p397 F27.

Shabby chic is the best way to describe this East Village hotel a few blocks from Union Square. Past the minuscule but well-appointed lobby, the rooms are a study in contrast, as antique dressers are paired with paisley bedspreads and mismatched patterned wallpaper. Bathrooms are generally shared between two to four rooms, but they're kept immaculately clean. Over the years, the building has been featured in numerous fashion mag layouts and films – including Woody Allen's *Manhattan Murder Mystery* – and has put up Madonna, and, more recently, transsexual downtown diva Amanda Lepore. Who knows who you might bump into on your way to the loo?

GREENWICH VILLAGE

Expensive

The Jade Hotel

52 W 13th Street, between Fifth & Sixth Avenues, New York, NY 10011 (1-212 375 1300, www.thejadenyc.com). Subway F, M, 1, 2, 3 to 14th Street; L to Sixth Avenue; L, N, Q, R, 4, 5, 6 to 14th Street-Union Square. **Rooms** 113. **Map** p397 E27.

With its Georgian-style portico and decorative brickwork, the Jade Hotel is indistinguishable from the

The Marlton. *See p353.*

ESSENTIAL INFORMATION

pre-war apartment buildings in its Greenwich Village locale. But the sensitively conceived 18-storey structure was built from scratch as a hotel a few years ago. The rooms, designed by Andres Escobar in an art deco style, feature marble-inlaid Macassar ebony desks, chrome period lamps and champagne satin poufs – to preserve the period illusion, the TV is hidden behind a decorative cabinet. The classic black-and-white tiled bathrooms are stocked with toiletries from venerable Village pharmacy CO Bigelow. Some rooms have private terraces, floor-to-ceiling windows or cosy window seats. The bar and restaurant, Grape & Vine, evokes snug glamour through distressed mirrors and plush red velvet banquettes.

► *A second Jade is tipped to open near midtown's Bryant Park in 2015.*

Moderate

The Marlton

5 W 8th Street, between Fifth and Sixth Avenues, New York, NY 10011 (1-212 321 0100, www.marltonhotel.com). Subway A, B, C, D, E, F, M to W 4th Street; N, R to 8th Street-NYU. **Rooms** 107. **Map** p397 E28.

Trendsetting hotelier Sean MacPherson, who co-owns the Bowery, the Maritime and the Jane, has sealed the transformation of this formerly run-down Village strip with this affordable boutique hotel. The 1900 building has plenty of local history – Beat icon Jack Kerouac wrote a couple of novellas while lodging there, and the place put up would-be Andy Warhol assassin Valerie Solanas – but the deceptively lived-in-looking interior, including the lobby's cunningly retro oak panelling, has largely been created from scratch. Here, you can lounge on a broken-in leather armchair while sipping a house-roasted Ferndell coffee, and flip through tomes on NYC history or local artists. Measuring a mere 150sq ft each, the bedrooms are miniaturised versions of a Paris grand hotel, with gilt-edged velvet headboards, crown mouldings and shaded sconces held by brass hands. The bathrooms feature petite marble sinks, antiquey brass rain showerheads and products by Provençal perfumer Côté Bastide. The classic decor is offset by midcentury touches: art by Berlin-based artist Stefano Castronovo, inspired by Abstract Expressionists like Franz Kline and Robert Motherwell, and Serge Mouille chandeliers that look like Anglepoise lamps on steroids. The sure-to-be-hot restaurant was opening as this guide went to press. *Photo p351.*

Washington Square Hotel

103 Waverly Place, between MacDougal Street & Sixth Avenue, New York, NY 10011 (1-212 777 9515, 1-800 222 0418, www.washingtonsquarehotel.com). Subway A, B, C, D, E, F, M to W 4th Street. **Rooms** 152. **Map** p397 E28.

Opened in 1902 as the Hotel Earle, this Village fixture has sheltered the likes of Ernest Hemingway, Dylan Thomas and Bob Dylan (who lodged in room 305 in 1964). Run by the same family since 1973, it has been restored in an art deco style but retains a personal air, reflected in artwork by one of the owners. The regularly updated rooms, currently sporting a cream-and-tan colour palette with black faux-leather headboards and plain, white-tiled bathrooms, may not be the height of fashion, but they offer comforts such as Keurig coffee makers, iPod docks and free Wi-Fi. Rates include continental breakfast. Many quarters have partial views of the park or picturesque Village streets from large windows. The North Square restaurant and lounge – an unsung secret with an eclectic menu – is popular with locals and NYU profs.

Budget

Larchmont Hotel

27 W 11th Street, between Fifth & Sixth Avenues, New York, NY 10011 (1-212 989 9333, www.larchmonthotel.com). Subway F, M to 14th Street; L to Sixth Avenue. **Rooms** 67. **Map** p397 E28.

Housed in a 1910 Beaux Arts building, the Larchmont is great value for this area. The basic decor has been spruced up with new IKEA furniture and flatscreen TVs, but with prices this reasonable, you can accept less than glossy-mag style. Except for the en-suite family room, with one double and one trundle bed, bathrooms are shared, but all guest quarters come with a washbasin, toiletries, bathrobe and slippers. Continental breakfast is included in the rate and Wi-Fi is thrown in free of charge.

WEST VILLAGE & MEATPACKING DISTRICT

Expensive

Gansevoort Meatpacking NYC

18 Ninth Avenue, at 13th Street, New York, NY 10014 (1-212 206 6700, www.hotelgansevoort.com). Subway A, C, E to 14th Street; L to Eighth Avenue. **Rooms** 186. **Map** p397 C28.

This Meatpacking District pioneer is known for its rooftop-pool-lounge playgrounds at two NYC locations (a Park Avenue property opened in 2010). By day, you can soak up the sun, and the Hudson River panorama, on a lounger by the 45ft heated open-air pool. After dark, the wraparound terrace bar becomes a DJed outdoor party with a glittering Manhattan backdrop. If you prefer a quieter night, admire the view through ample glass in your room – many feature contemporary bay windows or mini balconies. The guest quarters are outfitted with Studio 54-inspired photography that plays on the hotel's reputation as a party hub, plush feather-bed layers atop excellent mattresses and marble bathrooms. The Exhale spa is a dimly lit

Dream Downtown. *See p357.*

subterranean sanctuary, and the house restaurant, the Chester, serves American classics like Long Island oysters and steaks.
Other location 420 Park Avenue South, at 29th Street, enter on 29th Street, Flatiron District (1-212 317 2900, www.gansevoortpark.com).

Soho House

29-35 Ninth Avenue, at W 13th Street, New York, NY 10014 (1-212 627 9800, www.sohohouseny.com). Subway A, C, E to 14th Street; L to Eighth Avenue. **Rooms** 30. **Map** p397 C27.
Members of this British-born network of 11 clubs enjoy a slew of perks, and for the price of a room, so can you. Chief among them is the recently revamped roof deck, which feels more Montauk than Meatpacking District – in summer, you can hang out at the beach-shack-style bar or recline by the pool in the company of swimsuit-clad models, actors, and movers and shakers. (Don't be tempted to take any snaps, though: photography is strictly forbidden in the public spaces.) In the bedrooms, refined English furnishings – hand-carved beds, classic Colefax & Fowler wallpaper and vintage chandeliers – contrast with reclaimed barn-wood floors and exposed brick. You can get a bespoke pummelling in the Cowshed Spa, a diminutive version of the rural original at posh Babington House in Somerset, UK, and, if you time it right, catch a prerelease screening of a hotly anticipated flick in the 44-seat cinema.

The Standard

848 Washington Street, at 13th Street, New York, NY 10014 (1-212 645 4646, www.standardhotels.com). Subway A, C, E to 14th Street; L to Eighth Avenue. **Rooms** 337. **Map** p397 C27.
André Balazs's lauded West Coast mini-chain arrived in New York in early 2009. Straddling the High Line, the retro 18-storey structure has been configured to give each room an exhilarating view, of either the river or a midtown cityscape. Quarters are compact, but the combination of floor-to-ceiling windows, curving tambour wood panelling (think old-fashioned roll-top desks) and 'peekaboo' bathrooms (with Japanese-style tubs or huge showerheads and Kiss My Face products) give a sense of space. Eating and drinking options include a chop house, a beer garden and an exclusive top-floor bar with a massive jacuzzi and 180-degree views.
► *For more about the High Line, see p118.*
Other locations 25 Cooper Square, between 5th & 6th Streets (1-212 475 5700).

Moderate

★ The Jane

113 Jane Street, at West Street, New York, NY 10014 (1-212 924 6700, www.thejanenyc.com). Subway A, C, E to 14th Street; L to Eighth Avenue. **Rooms** 208. **Map** p397 D28.
Opened in 1907 as the American Seaman's Friend Society Sailors Home, the six-storey landmark was a residential hotel when hoteliers Eric Goode and Sean MacPherson of the Bowery and the Maritime took it over. The wood-panelled, 50sq ft rooms ($99-$115) were inspired by vintage train sleeper compartments: there's a single or bunk bed with built-in storage and brass hooks for hanging up your clothes – but also iPod docks, free Wi-Fi and wall-mounted flatscreen TVs. Alternatively, opt for a more spacious, wainscotted Captain's Cabin with private facilities – many have terraces or Hudson River views. If entering the hotel feels like stepping on to a film set, there's good reason. Inspiration came from various celluloid sources, including *Barton Fink*'s Hotel Earle for the lobby. The 'ballroom', decorated with mismatched chairs, oriental rugs and a fireplace topped with a stuffed ram, evokes an eccentric mansion, and there's an airy faux-vintage French-Moroccan café.

DIVINE DIGS

Stay in a serene sanctuary in the heart of the city.

In the early 19th century, Chelsea was a country estate owned by Clement Clarke Moore, author of the poem 'A Visit from St Nicholas' (''Twas the Night Before Christmas'). The man of letters gifted a chunk of land to the Episcopal Church to establish the General Theological Seminary, which remains a bastion of religious study. These days, however, it's across the street from one of the city's most popular attractions: the High Line. And the railway line-turned-park lends its name to a new boutique hotel on the seminary grounds.

The seminary's old guest wing and conference centre have been transformed into the **High Line Hotel** (*see p357*, with interiors by Roman and Williams, the firm behind the Ace Hotel New York's eclectic decor and the design of the sophisticated new Viceroy New York (*see p364*). In keeping with the seminary's intellectual purview, the lobby of the imposing 1895 neo-Gothic landmark is home to NYC's first outpost of Chicago's Intelligentsia Coffee. Exuding an old-fashioned residential vibe, the 60 rooms feature antique Persian rugs on hardwood floors, custom-designed wallpaper and a mix of vintage furnishings and reproductions of pieces sourced by the designers. Many

rooms retain original fireplaces – though these days the eco-friendly property is heated and cooled by a geothermal system. Rewired 1930s Western Electric rotary phones and desktop embossers for customising your snail mail may seem like an antidote to the digital age, but there's also free in-room Wi-Fi, and you can connect your iPod to the retro Tivoli radio by the bed.

CHELSEA

Expensive

Dream Downtown

355 W 16th Street, between Eighth & Ninth Avenues, New York, NY 10011 (1-212 229 2559, 1-877 753 7326, www.dreamdowntown.com). Subway A, C, E to 14th Street; L to Eighth Avenue. **Rooms** 316. **Map** p397 D27.

Be sure to pack your totem: staying at this surreal property from hotel wunderkind Vikram Chatwal may make you wonder if you're in a dream within a Dream. The expansive, tree-shaded lobby, furnished with curvy metallic-lizard banquettes, and presided over by a DJ nightly, provides an overhead view of swimmers doing laps in the glass-bottomed pool on the terrace above. Housed in the former annex of the New York Maritime Union (now the adjacent Maritime Hotel, *see p358*), the building is riddled with round windows. In the upper-floor rooms, these frame elements of the Manhattan skyline, such as the Empire State Building, in intriguing ways and are picked up by circular mirrors and wallpaper motifs. Rooms combine classic elements (white chesterfield chairs or sofas, Tivoli radios, Turkish rugs) with futuristic touches like shiny steel bathtubs in some rooms. The hotel recreates a 'beach club' experience on its pool deck with a sandy patch and suites that lead directly on to the pool area from ivy-concealed private spaces. To complete the indulgent vibe, guests can even book massages or other spa treatments in one of the outdoor cabanas. Also channelling the feel of a luxury resort, the rooftop PH-D (short for Penthouse Dream) bar-nightclub has a lushly planted terrace running the entire length of the building and overlooking the pool. *Photo p354.*

Eventi

851 Sixth Avenue, between 29th & 30th Streets, New York, NY 10001 (1-212 564 4567, 1-866 996 8396, www.eventihotel.com). Subway B, D, F, M, N, Q, R to 34th Street-Herald Square; N, R to 28th Street. **Rooms** 292. **Map** p398 D25.

This modern 23-floor hotel takes a light and playful approach to interior design, planting unexpected features in the lobby – a large-scale reproduction of 19th-century British artist Thomas Benjamin Kennington's *Autumn* peeks out tantalisingly from behind velvet drapes, for instance. Managed by Kimpton, a brand that's known for its informal, friendly ethos, flamboyant decor and nice perks like its free evening wine hour, the accommodation feels luxurious for the upper-mid-range rates. The spacious rooms (which feel even more open thanks to floor-to-ceiling outlooks) have either a king-size bed or two queens, outfitted with dapper grey fabric headboards and Frette linens. Cool marble bathrooms are stocked with CO Bigelow products. You can get an on-site bite at the sprawling, indoor-outdoor farm-to-table eaterie Humphrey and pampering in the spa.

High Line Hotel

180 Tenth Avenue, at 20th Street, New York,NY 10011 (1-212 929 3888, www.thehighlinehotel.com). Subway C, E to 23rd Street. **Rooms** 60. *See p355* **Divine Digs**.

Hôtel Americano

518 W 27th Street, between Tenth & Eleventh Avenues, New York, NY 10001 (1-212 216 0000, www.hotel-americano.com). Subway C, E to 23rd Street. **Rooms** 56. **Map** p398 C26.

You won't find any Talavera tiles in Grupo Habita's first property outside Mexico. Mexican architect Enrique Norten's sleek, mesh-encased structure stands alongside the High Line (*see p118*). The decor evokes classic midcentury American style, interpreted by a European (Colette designer Arnaud Montigny). The minimalist rooms have Japanese-style platform beds, iPads and, in one of several subtle nods to US culture, super-soft denim bathrobes. After a day of gallery-hopping, get an even more elevated view of the neighbourhood from the rooftop bar and grill, where a petite pool does double duty as a hot tub in winter. There's also an airy ground-floor eaterie and two subterranean bars.

► *For our picks of the many galleries in Chelsea, see p125.*

Hôtel Americano.

ESSENTIAL INFORMATION

Maritime Hotel
363 W 16th Street, between Eighth & Ninth Avenues, New York, NY 10011 (1-212 242 4300, www.themaritimehotel.com). Subway A, C, E to 14th Street; L to Eighth Avenue. **Rooms** 126. **Map** p397 C27.

Steve Zissou would feel at home at this nautically themed hotel (the former headquarters of the New York Maritime Union), which is outfitted with self-consciously hip details befitting a Wes Anderson film. Standard rooms are modelled on cruise cabins; lined with teak panelling and sporting a single porthole window, they're small but thoughtfully appointed (with CO Bigelow products in the bathroom, a Booty Parlor 'pleasure kit' in the minibar, and a well-curated list of DVDs that you can order from the front desk). The hotel's busy Italian restaurant, La Bottega, also supplies room service, and the adjoining bar hosts a crowd of models and mortals, who throng the umbrella-lined patio in warmer weather.

Moderate

The Inn on 23rd
131 W 23rd Street, between Sixth & Seventh Avenues, New York, NY 10011 (1-212 463 0330, www.innon23rd.com). Subway F, M, 1 to 23rd Street. **Rooms** 13. **Map** p398 D26.

This renovated 19th-century townhouse offers the charm of a traditional B&B with enhanced amenities (an elevator, pillow-top mattresses, private bathrooms, white-noise machines). Owners and innkeepers Annette and Barry Fisherman have styled the bedroom with a unique theme, such as the Asian-inspired Bamboo and the 1940s room, furnished with vintage Heywood-Wakefield pieces. One of its best attributes is the 'library', a cosy jumble of tables and chairs open 24/7 to guests for coffee and tea, which also hosts wine and cheese receptions on Friday and Saturday evenings. Another nice perk: guests receive 20% off the bill at the Guilty Goose, the owners' modern American brasserie on the ground floor.

Budget

Chelsea Lodge
318 W 20th Street, between Eighth & Ninth Avenues, New York, NY 10011 (1-212 243 4499, www.chelsealodge.com). Subway C, E to 23rd Street. **Rooms** 26. **Map** p397 D27.

Situated in a landmark brownstone blocks from the Chelsea gallery district, Chelsea Lodge is a long way from any arcadian idylls. Yet the rustic name is reflected in the mishmash of Americana that adorns the pine panelling of the inn's public spaces, such as rough-hewn duck decoys, cut-out roosters and early 20th-century photos. While all of the mostly tiny wood-floored rooms have TVs, sinks, showers and seasonal air-conditioning, most share toilets, so it's not for everyone. Still, the low prices and undeniable charm mean that it can fill up quickly. For more privacy and space, book one of the four suites down the block at 334 West 20th Street: all are former studio apartments with kitchenettes that sleep up to four people. The two at the back have direct access to the private garden.

The NoMad.

ESSENTIAL INFORMATION

FLATIRON DISTRICT & UNION SQUARE

Expensive

★ Ace Hotel New York
20 W 29th Street, at Broadway, New York, NY 10012 (1-212 679 2222, www.acehotel.com). Subway N, R to 28th Street. **Rooms** 265. **Map** p398 E26.

Founded in Seattle by a pair of DJs, this cool chainlet has expanded beyond the States to London and Panama. In its New York digs, the musical influence is clear: select rooms in the 1904 building have playful amenities such as functioning turntables, stacks of vinyl and gleaming Gibson guitars. And while you'll pay a hefty amount for the sprawling loft spaces, there are more reasonable options for those on a smaller budget. The respectable 'medium' rooms are fitted with vintage furniture and original art; even cheaper are the snug bunk-bed set-ups. Should you find the latter lodging stifling, repair to the buzzing lobby, where DJs or other music-makers are on duty nearly every night, and the bar is set within a panelled library salvaged from a Madison Avenue apartment. Guests can score a table at chef April Bloomfield's massively popular restaurants, the Breslin Bar & Dining Room (*see p132*) and the John Dory Oyster Bar (*see p133*). There's even an outpost of one of the city's hippest boutiques, Opening Ceremony, in case you find you haven't a thing to wear.

★ The NoMad
1170 Broadway, at 28th Street, New York, NY 10001 (1-212 796 1500, www.thenomadhotel.com). Subway N, R to 28th Street. **Rooms** 168. **Map** p398 E26.

Like nearby hipster hub the Ace Hotel, the NoMad is also a self-contained microcosm encompassing destination dining – courtesy of Daniel Humm and Will Guidara, of Michelin-three-starred Eleven Madison Park (*see p133*) – and the first stateside outpost of Parisian concept store Maison Kitsuné. Jacques Garcia, designer of Paris celeb hangout Hôtel Costes, transformed the interior of a 1903 New York office building into this convincing facsimile of a grand hotel. The chic rooms, furnished with vintage Heriz rugs and distressed- leather armchairs, are more personal – Garcia based the design on his old Paris apartment. Many feature old-fashioned claw-foot tubs for a scented soak in Côté Bastide bath salts.

GRAMERCY PARK

Deluxe

Gramercy Park Hotel
2 Lexington Avenue, at 21st Street, New York, NY 10010 (1-212 920 3300, 1-866 784 1300, www.gramercyparkhotel.com). Subway 6 to 23rd Street. **Rooms** 192. **Map** p398 F26.

Many NYC hotels have exclusive terraces or gardens, but only one boasts access to the city's most renowned private outdoor space: Gramercy Park. The hotel's interior resembles a baronial manor occupied by a rock star, with rustic wooden beams and a roaring fire in the lobby; a $65 million art collection, including works by Richard Prince, Damien Hirst and Andy Warhol; and studded velvet headboards and mahogany drink cabinets in the bedrooms. Get a taste of the Eternal City in the restaurant, Maialino, Danny Meyer's tribute to Roman trattorias.

> **IN THE KNOW CLOCK THIS**
>
> Fancy spending the night in one of the city's most iconic buildings, overlooking Madison Square Park? The Metropolitan Life tower (*see p130*), currently being converted to an all-suite property by Ian Schrager-Marriott brand Edition Hotels, is tipped to welcome guests in 2015.

Budget

★ Carlton Arms
160 E 25th Street, at Third Avenue, New York, NY 10010 (1-212 679 0680, www.carltonarms.com). Subway 6 to 23rd Street. **Rooms** 54. **Map** p398 F26.

The Carlton Arms Art Project started in the late 1970s, when a small group of creative types brought fresh paint and new ideas to a run-down shelter. Today, the site is a bohemian backpackers' paradise and a live-in gallery – every room, bathroom and hallway is festooned with outré artwork, including a couple of early stairwells by Banksy. Eye-popping themed quarters include the Money Room and a tribute to the traditional English cottage; new works are introduced regularly and artists return to restore their creations. Roughly half of the rooms have shared bathrooms. The place gets booked up early, so reserve well in advance.

HERALD SQUARE & GARMENT DISTRICT

Expensive

Refinery Hotel
63 W 38th Street, between Fifth & Sixth Avenues, New York, NY 10018 (1-646 664 0310, www.refineryhotelnewyork.com). Subway B, D, F, M, N, Q, R to 34th Street-Herald Square; B, D, F, M to Bryant Park; 7 to Fifth Avenue. **Rooms** 197. **Map** p398 E24.

The Garment District finally has a fittingly fashionable hotel. Stonehill & Taylor Architects, the firm behind this 1912 neo-Gothic building's conversion

Refinery Hotel. *See p359.*

and design, took inspiration from its former life as a hat-making hub. In the guest rooms, furnishings subtly reference the garment industry for a look that's more sophisticated than steampunk. Wall coverings riff on linen, super-soft bed throws mimic burlap, coffee tables are modelled on early-20th-century factory carts, and desks are reproductions of vintage Singer sewing-machine tables. Luxurious touches like Frette linens and walk-in showers with room for two offset the industrial elements. Eating and drinking options include Winnie's Lobby Bar, which takes its name from Winifred McDonald, who owned a ladies' tearoom in the building in the early 20th century, and a sprawling roof area, comprising three distinct spaces: an indoor bar with a fireplace, a semi-open atrium featuring a retractable skylight and a fountain, and an outdoor deck.

Moderate

Hotel Metro

45 W 35th Street, between Fifth & Sixth Avenues, New York, NY 10001 (1-212 947 2500, www.hotelmetronyc.com). Subway B, D, F, M, N, Q, R to 34th Street-Herald Square. **Rooms** 181. **Map** p398 E25.

It may not be trendy, but the Metro is a solid, good-value hotel that is extremely well maintained. Every two years, the owners start renovating the rooms, floor by floor, starting at the top; by the time they're finished it's almost time to start again. So even 'old' rooms are virtually new. The stylishly contemporary quarters feature marble-topped furniture and beige leather-effect headboards; premier rooms have luxurious rain showers. Unusually for New York, the hotel offers 18 family rooms, consisting of two adjoining bedrooms (one with two beds and a table) and a door that closes. Also rare: a generous continental breakfast buffet is offered in the guests' lounge (or take it to the homey adjoining library), outfitted with several large TVs. The rooftop bar (which is open from April to October) has views of the Empire State Building.

THEATER DISTRICT & HELL'S KITCHEN

Deluxe

The Chatwal New York

130 W 44th Street, between Sixth Avenue & Broadway, New York, NY 10036 (1-212 764 6200, www.thechatwalny.com). Subway N, Q, R, S, 1, 2, 3 to 42nd Street-Times Square. **Rooms** 76. **Map** p398 D24.

In a city awash with faux deco and incongruous nods to the style, the Chatwal New York occupies a Stanford White building that has been given a pitch-perfect art deco interior. Hotelier Sant Chatwal entrusted the design of this 1905 Beaux Arts building (formerly the clubhouse for the Lamb's Club, America's first professional theatre organisation) to Thierry Despont, who worked on the centennial restoration of the Statue of Liberty and the interiors of the J Paul Getty Museum in Los Angeles. The glamorous lobby is adorned with murals recalling the hotel's theatrical pedigree – past members of the Lamb's Club include Oscar Hammerstein, Charlie Chaplin, John Wayne and Fred Astaire. The theatrical past is further evoked by black and white photographs in the hotel's restaurant, helmed by Geoffrey Zakarian, which takes its name from the club. The elegant rooms feature vintage Broadway posters as well as hand-tufted Shifman mattresses,

400-thread count Frette linens and custom Asprey toiletries, and 15 rooms have spacious terraces. Unwind in the Elizabeth Arden Red Door Spa, which boasts a small saltwater lap pool.

Expensive

The London NYC

151 W 54th Street, between Sixth & Seventh Avenues, New York, NY 10019 (1-866 690 2029, www.thelondonnyc.com). Subway B, D, E to Seventh Avenue. **Rooms** 561. **Map** p399 D22.

This 54-storey high-rise was completely overhauled by David Collins (designer of some of London's most fashionable bars and restaurants) and reopened as the London NYC in 2007. The designer's sleek, contemporary-British style pervades the rooms, with attractive signature touches such as limed oak parquet flooring, embossed leather travel trunks at the foot of the beds, hand-woven throws and inventive coffee tables that adjust to dining-table height. But space is perhaps the biggest luxury: the London Suites (the starting-priced accommodation) are a minimum of 500sq ft and either open-plan or divided with mirrored French doors, and bathrooms feature double rain showerheads. Upper-floor Vista suites command impressive city views. The London is, appropriately, the site of two eateries from Britain's best-known celebrity chef, the eponymous Gordon Ramsay at the London and the less formal (and less expensive) Maze.

Moderate

★ 414 Hotel

414 W 46th Street, between Ninth & Tenth Avenues, New York, NY 10036 (1-212 399 0006, www.414hotel.com). Subway A, C, E to 42nd Street-Port Authority. **Rooms** 22. **Map** p398 C23.

Tucked into a residential yet central neighbourhood, this budget boutique hotel is a real find. The place is twice as big as it looks, as it consists of two walk-up buildings separated by a leafy courtyard, which in warmer months is a lovely place to eat your complimentary breakfast. Rooms are simple yet chic, with a modern colour scheme that pairs grey headboards with red accents, and equipped with fridges, flatscreen TVs and iPod docks.

Distrikt Hotel

342 W 40th Street, between Eighth & Ninth Avenues, New York, NY 10018 (1-212 706 6100, 1-888 444 5610, www.distrikthotel.com). Subway A, C, E to 42nd Street-Port Authority. **Rooms** 155. **Map** p398 C24.

Although it's on an unlovely street alongside Port Authority, this hotel has much to recommend it. Distrikt's subtle Manhattan theme is conceptual. Each of the 31 guest floors is named after one of the city's beloved 'hoods (Harlem, Soho, Chelsea and so on) and a backlit photo collage created by local artist Chris Rubino adorns the hallways; smaller framed versions liven up the rooms, which are otherwise coolly neutral, with luxury features such as Frette linens and marble in the bathrooms. Request a higher floor for Hudson River or Times Square views – the rates rise accordingly. A 14ft 'living wall' representing Central Park anchors the lobby, but what really impresses are the three big iMacs equipped with free Wi-Fi for guest use.

Hotel Edison

228 W 47th Street, at Broadway, New York, NY 10036 (1-212 840 5000, www.edisonhotelnyc.com). Subway N, Q, R to 49th Street; 1 to 50th Street. **Rooms** 800. **Map** p398 D23.

This 1931 art deco hotel retains enough original touches – such as gorgeous elevator doors and brass door handles – to evoke old New York. Its affordable rates and proximity to Broadway's theatres seal it as the ideal Gotham hotel for many guests. The no-frills rooms are standard in size, and clean, if also devoid of personality. For more upscale accommodation, the newly renovated Signature Collection quarters on the 19th through 22nd floors feature 32in flatscreen TVs, upgraded bedding, free Wi-Fi and Times Square or river views from some suites. Café Edison, a classic diner just off the lobby, is a long-time fave of Broadway actors – Neil Simon was so smitten that he put it in one of his plays.

Novotel New York Times Square

226 W 52nd Street at Broadway, New York, NY 10019 (1-212 315 0100, www.novotel.com). Subway B, D, E to Seventh Avenue; C, E to 50th Street; 1 to 50th Street; N, Q, R to 49th Street. **Rooms** 480. **Map** p398 D232.

If you want to immerse yourself in the pulsing heart of Times Square, check in to this redesigned hotel, part of the European Accor group (which also includes luxury brand Sofitel). Architecture and design firm Stonehill & Taylor brought elements of the dazzling, dynamic surroundings to the interiors of the 33-storey tower. Illuminated wall and ceiling

THE BEST HOTEL PERKS

For minibar freebies
Andaz Wall Street. *See p346.*

For a hot table
The NoMad. *See p359.*

For cult toiletries
The Quin. *See p363.*

For an in-room pet
Soho Grand Hotel. *See p348.*

panels in the check-in area riff on the hexagonal LEDs of the New Year's Eve ball. You can get a glimpse of the famed animated billboards from the glass-walled restaurant and bar, and its 5,700-square-foot wraparound terrace, which is warmed by two large fire pits. Wisely, the design team kept special effects out of the spare, contemporary guest rooms, which have a cool-beige colour scheme and sleek pear-wood-veneer furnishings. Room amenities include 46-inch flatscreen TVs, soundproof windows you can actually open and, instead of a costly minibar, a handy fridge to store your own drinks and snacks.

★ Yotel New York

570 Tenth Avenue, at 42nd Street, New York, NY 10036 (1-646 449 7700, www.yotel.com). Subway A, C, E to 42nd Street-Port Authority. **Rooms** 669. **Map** p398 C24.

The British team behind this futuristic hotel is known for airport-based capsule accommodation that gives long-haul travellers just enough space to get horizontal between flights. Yotel New York has ditched the 75sq ft cubbies in favour of 'premium cabins' more than twice the size. Adaptable furnishings (such as motorised beds that fold up futon-style) maximise space, and the bathrooms have streamlined luxuries such as heated towel rails and monsoon showers. Some first-class 'cabins' even have private terraces with hot tubs. If you want to unload excess baggage, the 20ft tall robot (or Yobot, in the hotel's playful lingo) will stash it away for you in a lobby locker. In contrast with the compact quarters, the sprawling public spaces include an eaterie serving Latin-Asian small plates and a wraparound terrace so large it's serviced by two bars.

IN THE KNOW
BEST FRIENDS WELCOME

New York hotels are increasingly pet-friendly. The **Benjamin** (*see p364*), **Eventi** (*see p357*), the **Surrey** (*see p369*) **Soho Grand Hotel** (*see p348*) and are among many that offer special beds, meals and treats – Soho Grand even debuted a dog park, compete with custom-made benches and 'fire hydrants'.

FIFTH AVENUE & AROUND

Deluxe

The Plaza

768 Fifth Avenue, at Central Park South, New York, NY 10019 (1-212 759 3000, 1-888 850 0909, www.theplazany.com). Subway N, Q, R to Fifth Avenue-59th Street. **Rooms** 282. **Map** p399 E22.

The closest thing to a palace in New York, this 1907 French Renaissance-style landmark reopened in spring 2008 after a two-year, $400-million renovation. Although 152 rooms were converted into private condo units, guests can still check into one of 282 elegantly appointed quarters with Louis XV-inspired furnishings and white-glove butler service. The opulent vibe extends to the bathrooms, which feature mosaic baths, 24-carat gold-plated sink fittings and even chandeliers – perhaps to make the foreign royals feel at home. Embracing the 21st century, the hotel has equipped every room with an iPad. The legendary Oak Room and Oak Bar, both

Novotel New York Times Square. *See p361.*

Yotel New York.

designated landmarks, are currently open only for private events, but you can still take afternoon tea in the restored Palm Court. There's also an upscale food hall conceived by celebrity chef Todd English, which includes both old and new cult NYC purveyors, such as William Greenberg Desserts and No. 7 Sub. The on-site Caudalie Vinothérapie Spa is the French grape-based skincare line's first US outpost.

The Quin
101 W 57th Street, at Sixth Avenue, New York, NY 10019 (1-212 245 7846, www.thequinhotel.com). Subway F, N, Q, R to 57th Street. **Rooms** 208. **Map** p399 D22.
See p366 **The New 57**.

Expensive

Algonquin Hotel
59 W 44th Street, between Fifth & Sixth Avenues, New York, NY 10036 (1-212 840 6800, www.algonquinhotel.com). Subway B, D, F, M to 42nd Street-Bryant Park; 7 to Fifth Avenue. **Rooms** 181. **Map** p398 E24.
Alexander Woollcott and Dorothy Parker swapped bon mots in the famous Round Table Room of this 1902 landmark – and you'll still find writer types holding court in the sprawling lobby. The Algonquin certainly trades on its literary past (quotes from Parker and other Round Table members adorn the door to each guest room and vintage *New Yorker* covers hang in the hallways), but a major 2012 renovation has spruced up the grande dame. Backlit vintage photographs of NYC in the rooms are nods to old New York but the sleek quarters could be in any corporate hotel, with faux-leather headboards, Frette linens, iHome clock radios and slate-floored bathrooms. Although it's now part of the Marriott-affiliated Autograph Collection, the hotel retains some of its quirky identity in the public spaces – in the lobby bar and restaurant, original panelling and some decorative fixtures remain and the hotel cat (always called Matilda or Hamlet depending on sex) still slumbers behind the check-in desk. Sadly, the iconic cabaret venue, the Oak Room, has closed, and the Blue Bar has been glitzed up with coloured lighting, but it retains the original Al Hirschfeld Broadway-themed drawings, donated by the late habitué's gallery.

Bryant Park Hotel
40 W 40th Street, between Fifth & Sixth Avenues, New York, NY 10018 (1-212 869 0100, 1-877 640 9300, www.bryantparkhotel.com). Subway B, D, F, M to 42nd Street-Bryant Park; 7 to Fifth Avenue. **Rooms** 128. **Map** p398 E24.
When the shows and the shoots are finished, the fashion and film folk flock to this luxe landing pad (it's particularly busy during Fashion Week). In its days as the American Radiator Building, the hotel was immortalised by Georgia O'Keeffe. Although the exterior (which you can appreciate up-close in one of several balconied rooms) is gothic art deco, the inside is all clean-lined and contemporary, with soft lighting, blanched hardwood floors, Tibetan rugs and soothing conveniences such as sleep-aiding sound machines and Bose Wave radios. A section of the room service menu is devoted to vibrators and other forms of adult recreation, but don't worry, you can also order in from the house restaurant, slick sushi destination Koi.

★ Chambers Hotel
15 W 56 Street, between Fifth & Sixth Avenues, New York, NY 10019 (1-212 974 5656, www.chambershotel.com). Subway E, M to Fifth Avenue-53rd Street. **Rooms** 77. **Map** p399 E22.
Although it opened in 2001, Chambers has a contemporary residential style that feels utterly current. The double-height lobby, with low seating and a gas fire, exudes Zen serenity. It also showcases some of the owners' 500-piece art collection, which is scattered around the public spaces and guest quarters

and includes works by John Waters, Eve Sussman and John Newsom. Room design takes its cue from upscale loft apartments, combining designer furniture with raw concrete ceilings, exposed pipes, floor-to-ceiling windows and either polished walnut floorboards or Tibetan wool carpeting. Everything is designed to make you feel at home, from the soft terrycloth slippers in bright colours to the architect's desks stocked with a roll of paper and coloured pencils should artistic inspiration hit. There's no need to leave the hotel for meals, since David Chang's Má Pêche and an outpost of his Milk Bar are on site.

★ Viceroy New York

120 W 57th Street, between Sixth and Seventh Avenues, New York, NY 10019 (1-212 830 8000, 1-855 647 1619, www.viceroyhotelsandresorts.com/newyork). Subway F, N, Q, R to 57th Street. **Rooms** 240. **Map** p399 D22.
See p366 **The New 57**.

WestHouse

201 W 55th Street, at Seventh Avenue, New York, NY 10019 (1-212 707 4888, www.westhousehotelnewyork.com). Subway F, N, Q, R to 57th Street. **Rooms** 172. **Map** p399 D22.
See p366 **The New 57**.

MIDTOWN EAST

Expensive

The Benjamin

125 E 50th Street, at Lexington Avenue, New York, NY 10022 (1-212 715 2500, www.thebenjamin.com). Subway E, M to Lexington Avenue-53rd Street; 6 to 51st Street. **Rooms** 209. **Map** p398 E23.

All rooms in this pet-friendly hotel have kitchenettes with microwaves and sinks (some suites have full-size fridges), so it's a hit with families as well as business travellers. The decor, in restful shades of beige and cream, is unfussy, with the emphasis on comfort: choose from a menu of ten pillows from Swedish memory foam and anti-snoring to a five-foot-long body cushion for side-slumberers. The list was devised in consultation with sleep expert Rebecca Robbins, who also advised on a selection of soothing before-bed snacks and treatments. Facilities include a hair salon and spa, a good-size gym and a chic, David Rockwell-designed bistro, the National Bar & Dining Rooms, from Iron Chef Geoffrey Zakarian.

IN THE KNOW
BUNKING WITH THE BAND

The **Wythe Hotel** (*see p370*) literally rocks. The hip Brooklyn hotel hosts Williamsburg's many touring bands in special quarters that sleep four to six – so keep your eyes open for familiar faces in the bar.

Chambers Hotel. *See p363.*

Hotel Elysée

60 E 54th Street, between Madison & Park Avenues, New York, NY 10022 (1-212 753 1066, www.elyseehotel.com). Subway E, M to Fifth Avenue-53rd Street; 6 to 51st Street. **Rooms** 100. **Map** p399 E22.

The former home of Tennessee Williams and Tallulah Bankhead, among other colourful figures, this small 1926 property is like a scaled-down grand hotel: rooms are furnished with antiques, gilt-framed paintings and old prints, and most of the marble-tiled bathrooms have tubs. Many suites are decked out with (non-functioning) fireplaces and crystal chandeliers. Stop by the sedate second-floor lounge for the complimentary wine and cheese served every evening on your way to dinner at the exclusive Monkey Bar (*see p156*), *Vanity Fair* editor Graydon Carter's restaurant that shares the building. Ask reception to reserve a table and your chances of eating among the power set rise from zilch to good – a few tables are set aside for guests every night.

Morgans

237 Madison Avenue, between 37th & 38th Streets, New York, NY 10016 (1-212 686 0300, www.morganshotel.com). Subway S, 4, 5, 6, 7 to 42nd Street-Grand Central. **Rooms** 113. **Map** p398 E24.

New York's original boutique hotel, Morgans opened in 1984. Some 25 years later, the hotel's designer,

octogenerian French tastemaker Andrée Putman, returned to officiate over a revamp that has softened its stark monochrome appearance. Unfussy bedrooms, cast in a calming palette of silver, grey, cream and white, are hung with original Robert Mapplethorpe prints; window seats piled with linen cushions encourage quiet reflection. The bathrooms, with classic black and white tiles, offer products from NYC's Malin + Goetz. The guests' living room, stocked with coffee and tea, is equally understated.

The New York Palace

455 Madison Avenue, between 50th & 51st Streets, New York, NY 10022 (1-212 888 7000, www.newyorkpalace.com). Subway E, M to Fifth Avenue-53rd Street. **Rooms** 893. **Map** p398 E23.

Modernity literally meets tradition here: a sleek 55-storey tower cantilevers over the landmark 1884 Villard Houses – the connected, courtyard-facing brownstones, commissioned by railroad tycoon and financier Henry Villard, were designed by McKim, Mead and White to look like a single Italian Renaissance mansion. In autumn 2013, the New York Palace officially unveiled the results of a $140 million rolling renovation that introduced six new bars and eateries – including a sleek cocktail lounge beneath the revamped gilt- and marble-bedecked lobby – and updated all the guest rooms. Rain showerheads, custom-made rosewood headboards and hand-picked art now enhance many quarters. Accommodation ranges from understated luxury in the original building, where many west-facing rooms overlook St Patrick's Cathedral, to a more contemporary, residential style in the Towers. Occupying the hotel's top 14 floors, these premium rooms and suites have a separate check-in and exclusive perks such as a private bar. The Palace is now home to James Beard Foundation Award-winning chef Michel Richard's first NYC restaurant, which stretches over several opulent rooms of Villard's old residence, including his dining room and parlour. The top toque also helms a casual café and patisserie, Pomme Palais.

Moderate

Library Hotel

299 Madison Avenue, at 41st Street, New York, NY 10017 (1-212 983 4500, www.libraryhotel.com). Subway S, 4, 5, 6, 7 to 42nd Street-Grand Central; 7 to Fifth Avenue. **Rooms** 60. **Map** p398 E24.

This bookish boutique hotel is organised on the principles of the Dewey decimal system – each of its ten floors is allocated a category, such as Literature, the Arts, and General Knowledge, and each elegantly understated guest room contains a collection of books and artwork pertaining to a subject within that category. The popular Love room (filed under Philosophy) has a king-size bed, an ivy-clad balcony overlooking the New York Public Library and reading matter ranging from Ovid's *The Art of Love* to Dr Ruth Westheimer's *The Art of Arousal* (the veteran sexpert is honorary curator of the room's book collection). Nightly receptions dish out wine and cheese, while upstairs in the rooftop bar, creative libations are inspired by Ernest Hemingway and Harper Lee. There's an extensive film library and in-room DVD players if you can't face reading another word.

Budget

Pod 39

145 E 39th Street, between Lexington & Third Avenues, New York, NY 10016 (1-212 865 5700, www.thepodhotel.com). Subway S, 4, 5, 6, 7 to 42nd Street-Grand Central. **Rooms** 366. **Map** p398 F24.

The city's second Pod occupies a 1918 residential hotel for single men – you can hang out by the fire or play ping-pong in the redesigned gents' sitting room. As the name suggests, rooms are snug, but not oppressively so; some have queen-size beds, others stainless-steel bunk beds with individual TVs and bedside shelves inspired by plane storage lockers. But you should probably know your roommate well since the utilitarian, subway-tiled bathrooms are partitioned off with sliding frosted-glass doors. Restaurant dream team April Bloomfield and Ken Friedman are behind on-site eaterie Salvation Taco (*see p159*), which also supplies the margaritas on the seasonal rooftop bar.

Other location Pod 51, 230 E 51st Street, at Third Avenue (212 355 0300, www,thepodhotel.com).

UPPER WEST SIDE

Moderate

Hotel Belleclaire
250 W 77th Street, at Broadway, New York, NY 10024 (1-212 362 7700, www.hotelbelleclaire.com). Subway 1 to 79th Street. **Rooms** 240. **Map** p399 C19.
This landmark Upper West Side hotel, a short walk from Lincoln Center, Central Park and the Museum of Natural History, debuted a complete renovation in early 2013, in time for its 100th birthday. The grand panelled lobby, which retains its original skylight and mosaic-tiled floor, now has a stylish coffee bar furnished with café tables and crushed-velvet chaise-style sofas. Guest quarters feature wooden floors and comfort-centric details such as padded headboards, Frette linens and iHome iPod docks. Snacks from gourmet grocer Dean & Deluca (complimentary in the premium rooms) and bath products courtesy of iconic East Village chemist CO Bigelow are further perks. Parents, in particular, will appreciate the refrigerators in every room and DVD players in the suites. Also family-friendly are the communal microwave and 'media lounge' housing two arcade stations loaded with thousands of games, in addition to three free-to-use iMacs.

NYLO New York City
2178 Broadway, at 77th Street, New York, NY 10024 (1-212 362 1100, 1-800 509 7598, www.nylohotels.com/nyc). Subway 1 to 79th Street. **Rooms** 285. **Map** p399 C20.

THE NEW 57

A midtown hotel boom is glamming up Carnegie Hall's staid strip.

When boutique hotels began springing up downtown in the 1990s and early noughties, cool-hunting visitors eschewed midtown for newly affluent neighbourhoods like Soho and Tribeca. But a cluster of sophisticated new properties on or around 57th Street signals a return to classic hotel luxury.

With its geometric structure, black-brick façade and muntined windows, **Viceroy New York** (*see p364*) would make a fitting HQ for a classic comic-book villain. Designed both inside and out by Roman and Williams, the hip local firm behind Ace Hotel New York's game-changing interiors, the NYC location of the luxury hotel group has a distinctly Gotham vibe. The double-height lobby suggests a midcentury aesthetic, with lavish use of contrasting Paonazzo marble, sleek leather seating in shades of putty and caramel, and brass-topped cocktail tables. In the snug standard quarters, custom-made iroko-wood cabinets flanking the bed evoke a first-class cabin back when ocean liners were glamorous. You'll find an Illy espresso maker tucked behind one of the tambour doors, while on the nightstand is a Beats by Dr Dre Beatbox Portable sound system that blows away standard iPhone docks. Visitors from abroad will appreciate the in-room tablet phone that you can tote around town during your stay. The capacious American eaterie Kingside, helmed by chef Marc Murphy (Landmarc, Ditch Plains), is bound to become a canteen for a media and performing-arts crowd – the Hearst Corporation HQ is just up 57th Street – and guests get preferential admittance to the sure-to-be-mobbed rooftop lounge, opening as this guide went to press.

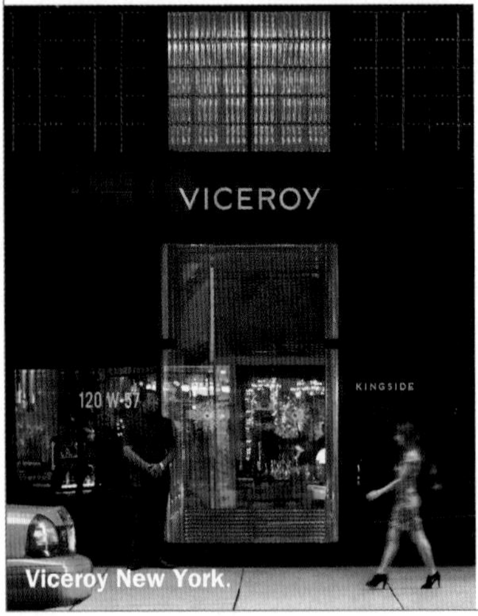

Viceroy New York.

Another key opening in the 57th Street luxury-hotel boom, the **Quin** (*see p363*) has an evocative past and some impressive perks. Less than a block from Carnegie Hall, the former Hotel Buckingham opened in 1929 and put up a colourful cast of divas, classical virtuosos and other artists. In the hotel's new incarnation, comforts and conveniences are to the fore. An automated system turns on the lights and raises the blinds as you open the door, and

The name is short for New York Loft, but the Texas-incubated hotel group launched by former W honcho Michael Mueller didn't have an NYC property until 2013, when it overhauled and rebranded the On the Ave Hotel. The airy guest quarters have stacked-plywood furnishings, original art – selected through a local competition – and 'brick' wallpaper that playfully references the loft-living archetype. The functional style doesn't skimp on comfort, though: beds have a cushy, custom-made pillow-top mattress and, in the bathroom, marble wall tiles contrast with capacious factory-style stainless-steel sink units. Deluxe rooms on the top three floors open on to terraces, some with views of the Hudson River or Central Park. Among the in-room amenities are free Wi-Fi and a Keurig coffeemaker to brew your free Wolfgang Puck joe, but you won't find a minibar – a selection of NYC-made snacks and drinks is available in the ground-level LOCL Bar. The bar is one element of a large, loosely divided space that also includes a low-lit, panelled piano lounge and a library furnished with an original 1910 fireplace and velvet sofas. In summer, garage doors open on to sidewalk seating, which will no doubt draw a local crowd; the uptown arm of acclaimed contemporary Chinese restaurant RedFarm is another strong pull. *Photo p368.*

Budget

Broadway Hotel & Hostel

230 W 101 Street, at Broadway, New York, NY 10024 (1-212 865 7710, www.broadwayhotelnyc.com). Subway 1, 2, 3 to 96th Street. **Rooms** 100. **Map** p400 C16.

The Quin.

the cushy Dux by Duxiana bed – topped with sumptuous Sferra linens – is an insomniac's dream. Further treats include a Nespresso machine, exclusive Fresh products in the roomy marble-tiled showers, and Bergdorf Goodman's personal-shopping department on speed dial. The house restaurant, the Wayfarer, puts a contemporary spin on high-class seafood and steak spots; or, if you've got your heart set on a hard-to-book table, one of the five specialised concierges can probably secure it for you.

WestHouse (*see p364*), meanwhile, aims to evoke the intimate atmosphere of a Manhattan townhouse. The 1920s-inspired decor, by Jeffrey Beers International, a firm known for lavish hospitality-industry interiors, feels like a hotel to us, but rooms do feature residential-style touches like marble-topped eucalyptus-wood desk-cum-vanity tables, alongside luxe details such as soft-grey leather tufted headboards, Sferra linens and Professional Hair Styling System products by GHD on top of the custom-made DayNa Decker toiletries. Perhaps the most impressive perk is the concept of a blanket 'residents' fee' ($30 per day) that entitles you to Wi-Fi, breakfast, snacks and hors d'oeuvres, barista-brewed coffee and, best of all, unlimited drinks in the 'den' off the lobby or the 23rd-floor guests-only terrace.

More openings are on the way: Beverly Hills-born brand **SLS** (www.slshotels.com) arrives at 444 Park Avenue, between 56th & 57th Streets, in late 2014, and Firmdale, the British company behind the Crosby Street Hotel (*see p347*), is opening a second NYC property on 56th Street, between Fifth & Sixth Avenues, in 2015.

Westhouse.

For those who have outgrown the no-frills backpacker experience but haven't quite graduated to a full-service hotel, the hybrid Broadway Hotel & Hostel, which has been given a 'boutique-style' makeover, fills the gap. On the ground floor, exposed brick, leather sofas and three large flatscreen TVs give the sprawling communal spaces a slick, urban veneer, but they still follow the traditional youth-hostel blueprint: TV room, shared kitchen, plus a computer area with eight credit card-operated terminals (if you have your own gadget, Wi-Fi is free). You won't find six-bed set-ups here, though: the cheapest option, the small, basic 'dormitory-style' rooms, jazzed up with striking colour schemes, mass-produced art and ceiling fans (there's AC in the summer too), accommodate a maximum of two in bunk beds. The good-value 'semi-private' rooms offer a queen bed or two doubles/twins, with luxuries like down comforters and flatscreen TVs, but you'll have to use the (well-scrubbed) shared bathrooms. There are also en suite quarters. The Broadway provides free linens and towels, daily housekeeping service and 24-hour reception.

Hostels

Hostelling International New York

891 Amsterdam Avenue, at 103rd Street, New York, NY 10025 (1-212 932 2300, www.hinewyork.org). Subway 1 to 103rd Street. **Rooms** 672 beds in dorms; 5 private rooms. **Map** p400 C16.

This budget lodging is actually the city's only 'real' hostel (a non-profit accommodation that belongs to the International Youth Hostel Federation). The handsome gabled, Gothic-inspired brick and stone building – the largest hostel in America – spans the length of an entire city block. Most of the accommodation is in four- to 12-bed dorms, which are spare but clean and air-conditioned with immaculate shared bathrooms. There is also a handful of private rooms that sleep up to four with en-suite facilities and standard hotel amenities including a 32-inch plasma TV, fridge and toiletries (but no in-room phone). You can get to know your fellow travellers in the on-site café, the large shared kitchen, and the backyard and patio. Linens and towels supplied free of charge as is the property-wide Wi-Fi.

UPPER EAST SIDE

Deluxe

The Pierre

2 E 61st Street, at Fifth Avenue, New York, NY 10065 (1-212 838 8000, www.tajhotels.com/thepierre). Subway N, Q, R to Fifth Avenue-59th Street. **Rooms** 189. **Map** p399 E22.

The 1930 landmark overlooking Central Park became part of the posh Indian Taj Hotels, Resorts and Palaces in 2005, setting in motion a $100-million overhaul – but it retains delightfully old-fashioned elements such as elevator operators and original fireplaces in some suites. In contrast to the glitzy public spaces, including the mural-clad Rotunda and the Grand Ballroom, the classic rooms are understated, dressed in a neutral colour palette and immaculate upholstery, with modern gadgets including Bose radio/iPod docks. The sumptuous Turkish marble bathrooms are generously stocked with Molton Brown bath products. The Asian influence is reflected in silk bedspreads from Bangalore and contemporary Indian art, but the hotel restaurant is a swanky Italian spot designed by Adam Tihany, Sirio Ristorante.

NYLO New York City. *See p366.*

★ The Surrey

20 E 76th Street, between Fifth & Madison Avenues, New York, NY 10021 (1-212 288 3700, 1-800 978 7739, www.thesurreyhotel.com). Subway 6 to 77th Street. **Rooms** 189. **Map** p399 E20.

Occupying an elegant 1920s building given a $60 million overhaul, the Surrey pitches at both traditionalists and the trend-driven. The coolly elegant limestone and marble lobby showcases museum-quality contemporary art – by the likes of Chuck Close, Jenny Holzer and William Kentridge – and rooms are dressed in a refined palette of cream, grey and beige, with luxurious white marble bathrooms. But the centrepiece is undoubtedly the incredibly comfortable DUX by Duxiana bed, swathed in sumptuous Sferra linens. The hotel is flanked by top chef Daniel Boulud's Café Boulud and his chic cocktail destination, Bar Pleiades; there's also a luxurious spa.

Moderate

Hotel Wales

1295 Madison Avenue, at 92nd Street, New York, NY 10128 (1-212 876 6000, www.hotelwalesnyc.com). Subway 4, 5, 6 to 86th Street; 6 to 96th Street. **Rooms** 89. **Map** p400 E18.

Purpose-built as a hotel in the early 1900s, the ten-storey Wales is a comfortable, convenient choice for a culture jaunt due to its proximity to Museum Mile. Tucked in the quietly affluent Carnegie Hill neighbourhood just above Madison Avenue's prime retail stretch, it's also well placed for a posh shopping spree. Standard double rooms are small, but high ceilings, large windows and an unfussy contemporary-classic style prevents them from seeming cramped; about half of the accommodation consists of suites. Guest quarters have been spruced up with designer wallpaper, sleek modern bathrooms and HD TVs. Higher-floor rooms on the east side have Central Park views, but all guests can enjoy them on the large roof terrace. Two on-site restaurants (Italian spot Paola's and mini-chain Sarabeth's) provide meals and snacks.

HARLEM

Moderate

Aloft Harlem

2296 Frederick Douglass Boulevard (Eighth Avenue), between 123rd & 124th Streets, New York, NY 10027 (1-212 749 4000, www.alofthotels.com). Subway A, B, C, D, 2, 3 to 125th Street. **Rooms** 124. **Map** p401 D13.

Starwood Hotels' fast-expanding Aloft brand pitches to a young, design-conscious traveller whose budget might not stretch to a room at one of the company's W properties. Launched in December 2010, Aloft Harlem was the first hotel to open in the area since the early 1960s. The public spaces combine high-tech amenities (a pair of iMacs, in addition to free hotel-wide Wi-Fi) with colourful, contemporary decor (a scrolling news ticker above the elevators, a pool table in the lobby-lounge). The industrial-edged w xyz bar hosts DJs, karaoke and jazz nights, while a slick, open-plan convenience store, re:fuel, dispenses coffee, sandwiches and snacks around the clock. A minimalist approach mitigates tight space in the bedrooms – despite 275sq ft dimensions, standard quarters are outfitted with king-size beds and 42in flatscreen TVs, while bathrooms feature oversize rainfall showerheads and products created by W collaborator Bliss Spa.

Other locations 216 Duffield Street, between Fulton Mall & Willoughby Street, Brooklyn (1-718 256 3833).

> **IN THE KNOW SECRET GARDEN**
>
> The **Gramercy Park Hotel**'s (*see p359*) greatest amenity is guest access to nearby Gramercy Park (*see p138*) – one of the most exclusive outdoor spaces in the city. A member of staff will escort you there and unlock the gate. If you want to linger, you'll have to call the hotel to be let out.

Budget

★ Harlem Flophouse

242 W 123rd Street, between Adam Clayton Powell Jr Boulevard (Seventh Avenue) & Frederick Douglass Boulevard (Eighth Avenue), New York, NY 10027 (1-917 720 3707, www.harlemflophouse.com). Subway A, B, C, D to 125th Street. **Rooms** 4. **Map** p401 D14.

The dark-wood interior, moody lighting and lilting jazz make musician Rene Calvo's Harlem inn feel more like a 1930s speakeasy than a 21st-century B&B. The airy suites, named for Harlem Renaissance figures such as Chester Himes and Cozy Cole, have restored tin ceilings, a quirky mix of junk-store furnishings and period knick-knacks, and working sinks in antique cabinets. There are just two suites per floor; each pair shares a bathroom.

Brooklyn

BOERUM HILL, CARROLL GARDENS & COBBLE HILL

Moderate

★ Nu Hotel

85 Smith Street, between Atlantic Avenue & State Street, Brooklyn, NY 11201 (1-718 852 8585, www.nuhotelbrooklyn.com). Subway A, C, F to Jay Street-Borough Hall; F, G to Bergen Street; R to Court Street; 2, 3, 4, 5 to Borough Hall. **Rooms** 93. **Map** p404 T10.

Conveniently placed for the shops and restaurants of BoCoCa, Nu Hotel has bundled quirky niceties into a classy, eco-friendly package. Rooms are decked out with wood flooring, organic linens and recycled teak furniture, 42in flatscreen TVs and Bluetooth-enabled iHome sound systems for wireless tunes. The standard accommodation is comfortably sized, but Friends Suites have bunk beds, and the lofty Urban Suites are outfitted with hammocks and a padded-leather sleeping alcove. Cyclists can borrow one of the hotel's loaner bikes to pedal around Brooklyn, and iPads are available for guest use. The lobby bar, which has outside tables in the warmer months, offers a tapas menu designed by *Iron Chef* regular Jehangir Mehta.

PARK SLOPE

Moderate

Hotel Le Bleu

370 Fourth Avenue, between 3rd & 5th Streets, Brooklyn, NY 11215 (1-718 625 1500, www.hotellebleu.com). Subway F, R to Fourth Avenue-9th Street; R to Union Street. **Rooms** 48. **Map** p404 T10.

The Manhattanisation of Park Slope hit new heights in late 2007, when Andres Escobar's steel and glass hotel popped up on industrial Fourth Avenue. Couples will find the open shower design a plus; more conventional draws include 42in plasma TVs with Bose system DVD/CD players, goose-down comforters, iPod docking stations and free Wi-Fi in every room.

WILLIAMSBURG & BUSHWICK

Expensive

King & Grove Williamsburg

160 North 12th Street, between Bedford Avenue & Berry Street, Williamsburg, Brooklyn, NY 11249 (1-718 218-7500, www.kingandgrove.com). Subway L to Bedford Avenue. **Rooms** 64. **Map** p405 U7.

Small boutique-hotel chain King & Grove, which operates an ironically retro retreat in Montauk, Long Island, brings resort style to Brooklyn. The place comes into its own in summer when the 40-foot saltwater pool opens to guests (and fee-paying locals) on the secluded back patio. The ninth-floor roof bar, furnished with cushion-strewn banquettes, comfy canvas sofas and rustic log stools, takes in an expansive panorama that includes McCarren Park across the street, the East River and Manhattan skyline. In winter, it's partially enclosed for year-round use. Guest rooms evoke midcentury minimalism with bamboo flooring, taupe leather platform beds, Frette linens and charcoal-grey accents. The Carrara-marble-tiled bathrooms are supplied with toiletries from NYC's Malin + Goetz. The hotel restaurant, the Elm, is helmed by Michelin-starred chef Paul Liebrandt, formerly of Corton in Tribeca.

Other locations 29 East 29th Street, between Madison & Park Avenues, Flatiron District (1-212 689 1900).

★ Wythe Hotel

80 Wythe Avenue, at North 11th Street, Williamsburg, Brooklyn, NY 11249 (1-718 460 8000, www.wythehotel.com). Subway L to Bedford Avenue. **Rooms** 72. **Map** p405 U7.

A 1901 cooperage near the waterfront topped with a three-storey glass-and-aluminium addition, the Wythe perfectly captures the neighbourhood's elusive hip factor. Since the launch team included Andrew Tarlow, the restaurateur behind popular local eateries Diner and Marlow & Sons, it's not surprising that the ground-floor restaurant, Reynard, was an instant hit. In many of the guest rooms, floor-to-ceiling windows offer a panorama of the Manhattan skyline. Heated concrete floors, exposed brick, reclaimed-timber beds and witty custom wallpaper create a rustic-industrial vibe, offset by fully plugged-in technology: a cable by the bed turns your iPhone into a surround-sound music system. For non-couple travelling companions, compact bunk rooms are equipped with individual TVs, and some even have cute terraces.

Z NYC Hotel.

Moderate

Hotel Le Jolie

235 Meeker Avenue, at Jackson Street, Williamsburg, Brooklyn, NY 11211 (1-718 625 2100, www.hotellejolie.com). Subway G to Metropolitan Avenue; L to Lorimer Street. **Rooms** 52. **Map** p405 V8.

This contemporary hotel is a reasonably priced option in Williamsburg – too bad it's right on top of the Brooklyn-Queens Expressway. Inside, though, the well-maintained rooms are enhanced with allergen-free goose-down comforters and Egyptian cotton sheets, 42in HD TVs and iPod docking stations. The property recently added a fitness centre.

Hostels

★ New York Loft Hostel

249 Varet Street, at Bogart Street, Bushwick, Brooklyn, New York, NY 11206 (1-718 366 1351, www.nylofthostel.com). Subway L to Morgan Avenue. **Rooms** 100 beds in dorms; 31 private rooms. **Map** p405 W9.

Set in an arty enclave, this budget lodging fuses the traditional youth hostel set-up (dorm-style rooms with single beds and lockers, communal lounging areas) with a fashionable loft aesthetic. In the former clothing warehouse, linen curtains billow in front of huge windows, and there's plenty of industrial-chic exposed brick and piping. Above the big shared kitchen is a mezzanine equipped with a large flatscreen TV. The spacious patio is the site of free summer barbecues and winter fondue parties. Unlike old-school hostels, there's no curfew; an electronic room-key card opens the front door after hours.

Queens

LONG ISLAND CITY

Moderate

Ravel

8-08 Queens Plaza South, at Vernon Boulevard, Queens, NY 11101 (1-718 289 6101, www.ravelhotel.com). Subway E, M, R to Queens Plaza; F to 21st Street-Queensbridge; N, Q, 7 to Queensboro Plaza. **Rooms** 63. **Map** p406 V4.

Perhaps in keeping with the Ravel's former incarnation as a motel, owner Ravi Patel gave Long Island City's first independent boutique hotel a vaguely 1960s feel; the lobby has cream leatherette seating, silver-bubble ceiling lights and paintings that recall those doe-eyed Spanish girl portraits. Ravel is also equipped with a 'virtual' wine bar: buy a card at the front desk and use it at a self-serve bank of more than 18 wines. An 8,000sq ft rooftop restaurant-bar has dazzling views of midtown and hosts film screenings, DJ nights and other events. Rooms are much larger than in similarly priced hotels in Manhattan, and most (many with private balconies) face the river – although a Con-Edison training facility directly below is less than picturesque. A new adjacent tower, scheduled for completion in autumn 2015, will add 54 more rooms and two one-bedroom suites, all with terraces.

Z NYC Hotel

11-01 43rd Avenue, at 11th Street, Queens, NY 11101 (1-212 319 7000, www.zhotelny.com). Subway E, M to Court Square-23rd Street; F to 21st Street-Queensbridge; N, Q, 7 to Queensboro Plaza. **Rooms** 100. **Map** p406 V5.

The Z shares a gritty industrial side street with tool suppliers and flooring wholesalers, but the Queensboro Bridge-side setting and largely low-rise neighbours facilitate its most stunning feature: knock-your-socks-off midtown views through floor-to-ceiling windows. Offbeat details, such as lightbulbs encased in mason jars dangling over the bed, wall stencils of iconic New York images and black flip-flops instead of the standard white slippers, enliven the stock boutique luxury of the accommodation. The public spaces are more dramatic: in the lobby, an old-school train-station-style 'departure board' spells out welcome in 18 languages, and the sprawling roof bar offers 360-degree panoramas.

The Bronx

Moderate

Opera House Hotel

436 E 149th Street, between Bergen & Brook Avenues, Bronx, New York NY 10455 (1-718 407 2800, www.operahousehotel.com). Subway 2, 5 to Third Avenue-149th Street. **Rooms** 60.

The Bronx Opera House showcased the big stars of the early 20th century, including the Marx Brothers and Harry Houdini. Now a hotel, the striking 1913 structure is still a draw for theatre lovers – steps from the subway, it's a mere 20-minute ride from the Great White Way, yet prices are a fraction of what you'd pay for similar digs in midtown. You get a lot more space too: ranging from about 275 to 450sq ft, rooms feature either one king-size or two queen beds. The decor isn't trendy, but comparable to an upscale chain hotel, with a warm, neutral colour scheme, beige leather padded headboards, and granite vanity tops and floors in the spacious bathrooms. All quarters are equipped with a refrigerator, microwave, flatscreen TV, iHome iPod dock and free Wi-Fi. Though little remains of the original building apart from the Beaux Arts facade, reproductions of playbills, architectural drawings, and photos of performers are reminders of its past. A complimentary continental-breakfast buffet spread is served on the mezzanine above the lobby, and a Crunch gym – free to guests – is due to open on the premises in autumn 2014.

Getting Around

ARRIVING & LEAVING

By air

John F Kennedy International Airport *1-718 244 4444, www.panynj.gov/airports/jfk.html.*
The subway (*see p373*) is the cheapest option. The **AirTrain** ($5, www.airtrainjfk.com) links to the A train at Howard Beach or the E, J and Z trains at Sutphin Boulevard-Archer Avenue ($2.50-$2.75).

NYC Airporter buses (1-718 777 5111, www.nycairporter.com; one way $16, round trip $29) connect JFK and Manhattan, with stops near Grand Central Terminal, Penn Station and Port Authority Bus Terminal. Buses run every 30mins from 5am to 11.30pm daily. **SuperShuttle** (1-800 258 3826, www.supershuttle.com) vans offer door-to-door service between NYC and the major airports.

A **yellow cab** to Manhattan will charge a flat $52.50 fare, plus toll (usually $5) and tip (15 per cent is the norm). The fare to JFK from Manhattan is not a set rate, but is usually roughly the same (*see p373*).

La Guardia Airport *1-718 533 3400, www.panynj.gov/airports/laguardia.html.*
Seasoned New Yorkers take the **M60 bus** ($2.50), to 106th Street at Broadway. The ride takes 40-60mins, depending on traffic, and buses run 24 hrs daily. The route crosses Manhattan at 125th Street in Harlem. Get off at Lexington Avenue for the 4, 5 and 6 trains; at Malcolm X Boulevard (Lenox Avenue) for the 2 and 3; or at St Nicholas Avenue for the A, B, C and D trains.

Less time-consuming options include **NYC Airporter buses** (one way $13, round trip $23). **Taxis** and **car services** charge about $30, plus toll and tip.

Newark Liberty International Airport *1-973 961 6000, www.panynj.gov/airports/newark-liberty.html.*
The best bet is the $12.50, half-hour trip via **New Jersey Transit** to or from Penn Station. The airport's monorail, AirTrain Newark (www.airtrainnewark.com), is linked to the NJ Transit and Amtrak train systems.

Bus services operated by **Coach USA** (1-877 894 9155, www.coachusa.com) run to Manhattan, stopping at Bryant Park in midtown, and inside the Port Authority Bus Terminal (one way $16, round trip $28); buses leave every 15-30mins. A **car** or **taxi** will run at $60-$75, plus toll and tip.

By bus

Most out-of-town buses come and go from the Port Authority Bus Terminal. **Greyhound** (1-800 231 2222, www.greyhound.com) runs long-distance travel to US destinations. The company's **BoltBus** (1-877 265 8287, www.boltbus.com), booked online, serves several East Coast cities. **New Jersey Transit** (1-973 275 5555, www.njtransit.com) runs services to most of New Jersey and parts of New York State. Finally, **Peter Pan** (1-800 343 9999, www.peterpanbus.com) runs extensive services to cities across the North-east; its tickets are also valid on Greyhound buses.

Port Authority Bus Terminal *625 Eighth Avenue, between 40th & 42nd Streets, Garment District (1-212 564 8484, www.panynj.gov/bus-terminals/port-authority-bus-terminal.html). Subway A, C, E to 42nd Street-Port Authority.* **Map** p398 S13.

By rail

America's national rail service is run by **Amtrak** (1-800 872 7245, www.amtrak.com). Nationwide routes are slow and infrequent (yet full of character), but there are some good fast services linking the eastern seaboard cities. (For commuter rail services, *see p373* **Public transport: Rail.**)

Grand Central Terminal *42nd to 44th Streets, between Vanderbilt & Lexington Avenues, Midtown East. Subway S, 4, 5, 6, 7 to 42nd Street-Grand Central.* **Map** p398 E24.
Grand Central is home to Metro-North, which runs trains to more than 100 stations in New York State and Connecticut.

Penn Station *31st to 33rd Streets, between Seventh & Eighth Avenues, Garment District. Subway A, C, E, 1, 2, 3 to 34th Street-Penn Station.* **Map** p398 D25.
Amtrak, Long Island Rail Road and New Jersey Transit trains depart from this terminal.

PUBLIC TRANSPORT

Changes to schedules can occur at short notice, especially at weekends – check the MTA's website before travelling and pay attention to the posters on subway station walls and announcements on trains and subway platforms.

Metropolitan Transportation Authority (MTA) *511 local, 1-877 690 5116 outside New York State, 1-212 878 7000 international, www.mta.info.*
The MTA runs the subway and bus lines, as well as services to points outside Manhattan. News of service interruptions and MTA maps are on its website. Be warned: backpacks, handbags and large containers may be subject to random searches.

Fares & tickets

Although you can pay with exact change (no dollar bills) on buses, to enter the subway system you'll need either a single-ride ticket ($2.75, available from station vending machines only) or a **MetroCard**. You can buy MetroCards from booths or vending machines in the stations, from the Official NYC Information Center (*see p382*), from the New York Transit Museum in Brooklyn (*see p197*) or Grand Central Terminal (*see left*), and from many hotels.

The standard base fare across the subway and bus network on a MetroCard is $2.50. Free transfers between the subway and buses are available only with a MetroCard (for bus-to-bus transfers on cash fares, *see p373*). Up to four people can use a pay-per-ride MetroCard, sold in denominations from $5 to $80. If you put $5 or more on the card, you'll receive a five per cent bonus – or 25 cents for every $5 – thus reducing the cost of each ride. However, if you're planning to use the subway or buses often, an

Unlimited Ride MetroCard is great value. These cards are offered in two denominations, available at station vending machines but not at booths: a seven-day pass ($30) and a 30-day pass ($112). Both are good for unlimited rides within those periods, but you can't share a card with your travelling companions.

Subway

Cleaner and safer than it has been for decades, the city's subway system is one of the world's largest and cheapest. For fares and MetroCards, *see p372*. Trains run around the clock. If you are travelling late at night, board the train from the designated off-peak waiting area, usually near the middle of the platform; this is more secure than the ends of the platform, which are often less populated in the wee hours.

Stations are most often named after the street on which they're located. Entrances are marked with a green and white globe (open 24 hours) or a red and white globe (limited hours). Many stations have separate entrances for the uptown and downtown platforms – look before you pay. Trains are identified by letters or numbers, colour-coded according to the line on which they run. Local trains stop at every station on the line; express trains stop at major stations only.

The most current Manhattan subway map is reprinted at the back of this guide; you can also ask MTA staff in service booths for a free copy, or refer to enlarged maps displayed in each subway station.

City buses

White and blue MTA buses are usually the best way to travel crosstown and a pleasant way to travel up- or downtown, as long as you're not in a hurry. They have a digital destination sign on the front, along with a route number preceded by a letter (M for Manhattan, B for Brooklyn, Bx for the Bronx, Q for Queens and S for Staten Island). Maps are posted on most buses and at all subway stops; they're also available from the Official NYC Information Center (*see p382*). The Manhattan bus map is printed in the back of this guide. All local buses are equipped with wheelchair lifts.

The fare is payable with a MetroCard (*see p372*) or exact change ($2.50 in coins only; no pennies or dollar bills). MetroCards allow for an automatic transfer from bus to bus, and between bus and subway. If you pay cash, and you're travelling uptown or downtown and want to go crosstown (or vice versa), ask the driver for a transfer when you get on – you'll be given a ticket for use on the second leg of your journey, valid for two hours. MTA's express buses usually head to the outer boroughs for a $6 fare.

Rail

The following commuter trains serve NY's hinterland.

Long Island Rail Road *511 local, 1-718 217 5477 outside New York State, www.mta.info/lirr.*
Provides rail services from Penn Station, Brooklyn and Queens to towns throughout Long Island.
Metro-North Railroad *511 local, 1-212 532 4900 outside New York State, www.mta.info/mnr.*
Commuter trains serve towns north of Manhattan and leave from Grand Central Terminal.
New Jersey Transit *1-973 275 5555, www.njtransit.com.*
Service from Penn Station reaches most of New Jersey, some points in New York State and Philadelphia.
PATH Trains *1-800 234 7284, www.panynj.gov/path.*
PATH (Port Authority Trans-Hudson) trains run from six stations in Manhattan to various New Jersey destinations, including Hoboken, Jersey City and Newark. The 24-hour service costs $2.50.

Boat

NY Waterway (1-800 533 3779, www.nywaterway.com) runs a water-transport service that connects Manhattan to Queens, Brooklyn and some New Jersey cities. The East River Ferry runs between Midtown East at 34th Street and downtown Manhattan at Pier 11, via Long Island City in Queens and Greenpoint, Williamsburg and Dumbo in Brooklyn (from $4 one way, $12 day pass). On the West Side of the island, NY Waterway's Hudson River ferries link Pier 79 on 39th Street and the World Financial Center in lower Manhattan to destinations in New Jersey, including Hoboken and Jersey City ($7-$21.50 one-way). Visit the website for ferry routes and schedules.

In addition to its hop-on hop-off service and tours, **New York Water Taxi** (*see p374*) offers a popular shuttle service connecting Pier 11 in Manhattan and IKEA in Red Hook, Brooklyn (2-8pm Mon-Fri; 11.20am-9.20pm Sat, Sun). The $5 fare is waived on weekends and for children under 12.

TAXIS

If the centre light atop the taxi is lit, the cab is available and should stop if you flag it down. Get in and then tell the driver where you're going. (New Yorkers generally give cross-streets rather than addresses.) By law, taxis cannot refuse to take you anywhere inside the five boroughs or to New York airports. Green Boro Taxis serving the outer boroughs can now be hailed on the street in the Bronx, Queens (excluding airports), Brooklyn, Staten Island and Manhattan north of West 110th and East 96th Streets. Use only yellow or green medallion (licensed) cabs.

Taxis will carry up to four passengers for the same price: $2.50 plus 50¢ per fifth of a mile or per minute idling, with an extra 50¢ charge (a new state tax), another 50¢ from 8pm to 6am and a $1 surcharge during rush hour (4-8pm Mon-Fri). The average fare for a three-mile ride is $14, but this will vary depending on the time and traffic.

If you have a problem, take down the medallion and driver's numbers, posted on the partition. Always ask for a receipt – there's a meter number on it. To complain or to trace lost property, call the Taxi & Limousine Commission (1-212 227 0700, 8.30am-5pm Mon-Fri) or visit www.nyc.gov/taxi. Tip 15-20 per cent, as in a restaurant. All taxis now accept major credit cards.

Car services

Car services are regulated by the Taxi & Limousine Commission. Unlike cabs, drivers can make only pre-arranged pickups. Don't try to hail one, and be wary of those that offer you a ride. These companies will pick you up anywhere in the city for a set fare.

Carmel *1-212 666 6666.*
Dial 7 *1-212 777 7777.*
GroundLink *1-877 227 7260.*

DRIVING

Car hire

You need a credit card to rent a car in the US, and usually must be at least 25 years old. Car hire is cheaper in the city's outskirts and further afield than in Manhattan. NYC companies add 19.875 per cent in taxes. If you just want a car for a few hours,

Zipcar (US: 1-866 494 7227, www.zipcar.com; UK: 0333 240 9000, www.zipcar.co.uk) is cost effective.
Alamo *US: 1-877 222 9075, www.alamo.com. UK: 0871 384 1086, www.alamo.co.uk.*
Avis *US: 1-800 230 4898, www.avis.com. UK: 0844 581 0147, www.avis.co.uk.*
Budget *US: 1-800 527 0700, www.budget.com. UK: 0844 581 2231, www.budget.co.uk.*
Enterprise *US: 1-800 261 7331, www.enterprise.com. UK: 0800 800 227, www.enterprise.co.uk.*
Hertz *US: 1-800 654 3131, www.hertz.com. UK: 0843 309 3099, www.hertz.co.uk.*

Parking

Make sure you read parking signs and never park within 15 feet of a fire hydrant (to avoid a $115 ticket and/or having your car towed). Parking is off-limits on most streets for at least a few hours daily. The Department of Transportation provides information on daily changes to regulations (dial 311). If precautions fail, call 1-212 971 0771 for Manhattan towing and impoundment information; go to www.nyc.gov for phone numbers in other boroughs.

CYCLING

While biking on NYC's streets is only recommended for experienced cyclists, the new **Citi Bike** system (www.citibikenyc.com, 1-855 245 3311) gives you temporary access to bikes at 600 stations in Manhattan and Brooklyn. Visitors can purchase a 24-hour ($9.95) or three-day ($25) Access Pass at a station kiosk with a credit or debit card. You'll then receive a 'ride code' that will allow you to undock and ride for 30 minutes at a stretch. A longer trip will incur an extra fee.

The Manhattan Waterfront Greenway, a 32-mile route that circumnavigates the island of Manhattan, is a fantastic asset: you can now ride, uninterrupted, along the Hudson River from Battery Park up to the George Washington Bridge, at 178th Street. The free NYC Cycling Map, covering cycle lanes in all five boroughs, is available from the **Department of City Planning Bookstore** (22 Reade Street, between Broadway & Elk Street, Civic Center, 1-212 720 3667, open noon-4pm Mon, 10am-1pm Tue-Fri), or you can download it from www.nyc.gov/planning.

Bike and Roll (1-212 260 0400, www.bikeandroll.com/newyork) is the city's biggest cycle-hire company, with 11 outposts. Rates (incl helmet) start at $10 per hour.

WALKING

One of the best ways to take in NYC is on foot. Most of the streets are laid out in a grid pattern and are relatively easy to navigate.

GUIDED TOURS

By bicycle

Bike the Big Apple *1-877 865 0078, www.bikethebigapple.com.* **Tickets** (incl bicycle & helmet rental) $80-$99.
Licensed guides lead cyclists through historic and newly hip hoods: tours include Harlem (the 'Sensational Park and Soul' tour), Chinatown ('From High Finance to Hidden Chinatown') and a twilight ride across the Brooklyn Bridge.

By boat

Circle Line Cruises *Pier 83, 42nd Street, at the Hudson River, Hell's Kitchen (1-212 563 3200, www.circleline42.com). Subway A, C, E to 42nd Street-Port Authority.* **Tickets** $27-$38; $21-$33 reductions. **Map** p398 B24.
The Circle Line's famed three-hour guided circumnavigation of Manhattan Island ($38; $25-$33 reductions) is a fantastic way to get your bearings and see many of the city's sights as you pass under its iconic bridges. The company also has a roster of themed tours. The separately run **Circle Line Downtown** (Pier 16, South Street Seaport, 1-212 742 1969, www.circlelinedowntown.com) has a more intimate vessel, the *Zephyr*, for tours of lower Manhattan (Apr-Dec, $30, $19 reductions). The two companies' rival speedboats – Circle Line's *Beast* (May-Sept, $27, $21 reductions) and Circle Line Downtown's *Shark* (May-Sept, $28, $19 reductions) – offer fun, adrenalin-inducing and splashy 30-minute rides.
New York Water Taxi *1-212 742 1969, www.nywatertaxi.com.* **Tickets** $28-$35; $16-$25 reductions.
Like their earthbound counterparts, New York water taxis are bright yellow. But unlike cabs, they run on a set schedule, and you can hop on and off with a day pass ($28, $16 reductions), enjoying neighbourhood attractions along the way.

By bus

Gray Line *777 Eighth Avenue, at 48th Street, Theater District (1-212 445 0848, www.newyorksightseeing.com). Subway A, C, E to 42nd Street-Port Authority; C, E to 50th Street; N, Q, R to 49th Street.* **Tickets** $39-$120. **Map** p398 D23.
Gray Line offers more than 20 bus tours, from a basic two-hour ride (with 40-plus hop-on, hop-off stops) to the guided 'Classic New York' tour, which includes lunch, admission to Top of the Rock or the Empire State Building, and a boat ride to Ellis Island and the Statue of Liberty.

On foot

Big Onion Walking Tours *1-888 606 9255, www.bigonion.com.* **Tickets** $18-$40; $15-$28 reductions.
New York was known as the Big Onion before it became the Big Apple. The tour guides will explain why, and they should know – all guides hold advanced degrees in history (or a related field). Among the offerings is the 'Official Gangs of New York' walk and a weekly 'Multi-Ethnic Eating Tour' that explores the history of the Lower East Side, Chinatown and Little Italy with a little cuisine sampling along the way.
Boroughs of the Dead *1-212 209 3370, www.boroughsofthedead.com.* **Tickets** $20-$25.
Horror writer Andrea Janes, author of *Boroughs of the Dead: New York City Ghost Stories*, explores the dark side of various neighbourhoods, and offers a spine-tingling tour of Brooklyn's Green-Wood Cemetery.
City Running Tours *1-877 415 0058, www.cityrunningtours.com.* **Tickets** from $35 group tour; $75 individual tour.
A guided four- to 26-mile jog around the city.
Municipal Art Society Tours *1-212 935 3960, www.mas.org/tours.* **Tickets** $20.
Walking tours led by architects, art historians and others reflect the society's focus on contemporary architecture, urban planning and historic preservation.
Urban Oyster *1-347 618-8687, www.urbanoyster.com.* **Tickets** $60-$85 (incl. food and drink).
Food-centric expeditions such as 'Brewed in Brooklyn' ($65), which illuminates the borough's suds-making legacy, and a 'Tenement, Tales and Taste' tour ($65) of the Lower East Side.

Resources A-Z

TRAVEL ADVICE

For up-to-date information on travel to a specific country – including the latest on safety and security, health issues, local laws and customs – contact your home country government's department of foreign affairs. Most have websites with useful advice for would-be travellers.

AUSTRALIA
www.smartraveller.gov.au

CANADA
www.voyage.gc.ca

NEW ZEALAND
www.safetravel.govt.nz

REPUBLIC OF IRELAND
www.foreignaffairs.gov.ie

UK
www.fco.gov.uk/travel

USA
www.state.gov/travel

ADDRESSES

Addresses follow the standard US format. The room, apartment or suite number usually appears after the street address, followed on the next line by the name of the city and the zip code.

AGE RESTRICTIONS

Buying/drinking alcohol 21
Driving 16
Sex 17
Smoking 18

ATTITUDE & ETIQUETTE

New Yorkers have a reputation for being rude, but 'outspoken' is more apt: they are unlikely to hold their tongues in the face of injustice or inconvenience, but they can also be very welcoming and will often go out of their way to offer advice or help.

Some old-fashioned restaurants and swanky clubs operate dress codes (jacket and tie for men, for example, or no baseball caps or ripped jeans – phone to check). However, on the whole, anything goes sartorially.

BUSINESS

Courier services

DHL *1-800 225 5345, www.dhl.com.*
FedEx *1-800 463 3339, www.fedex.com.*
UPS *1-800 742 5877, www.ups.com.*

Messenger services

A to Z Couriers *1-212 253 6500, www.atozcouriers.com.*
Breakaway *1-212 947 7777, www.breakawaycourier.com.*

Office services

All-Language Translation Services *77 W 55th Street, between Fifth & Sixth Avenues, Midtown (1-212 986 1688, www.all-language.com). Subway F to 57th Street.* **Open** 24hrs daily, by appt only. **Map** p399 E22.
Copy Specialist *44 E 21st Street, at Park Avenue South, Gramercy Park (1-212 533 7560, www.thecopyspecialist.com). Subway N, R, 6 to 23rd Street.* **Open** 8.30am-7pm Mon-Fri; Sat by appt. **Map** p398 E26.
FedEx Office *1-800 463 3339, www.fedex.com.*
There are outposts of this efficient computer and copy centre all over the city; many are open 24 hours.

CONSUMER

New York City Department of Consumer Affairs
Consumer Services Division, 9th Floor, 42 Broadway, New York, NY 10004 (311 local, 1-212 639 9675 outside New York State, www.nyc.gov/dca).
File complaints on consumer-related matters by email, mail or phone. The non-emergency, 24-hour three-digit number, 311, can also be used to get answers and register complaints about city issues, from parking regulations to real-estate auctions and consumer tips.

CUSTOMS

US Customs allows foreigners to bring in $100 worth of gifts (the limit is $800 for returning Americans) without paying duty. One carton of 200 cigarettes (or 100 cigars) and one litre of liquor (spirits) are allowed. Plants, meat and fresh produce of any kind cannot be brought into the country. You will have to fill out a form if you carry more than $10,000 in currency. You will be handed a white form on your inbound flight to fill in, confirming that you haven't exceeded any of these allowances.

If you need to bring prescription drugs into the US, make sure the container is clearly marked, and bring your doctor's statement or a prescription. Marijuana, cocaine and most opiate derivatives, along with a number of other drugs and chemicals, are not permitted: the possession is punishable by a stiff fine and/or imprisonment. Check in with the US Customs and Border Protection Service (www.cbp.gov) before you arrive if you're unsure.

HM Revenue & Customs allows returning visitors to the UK to bring £390 worth of 'gifts, souvenirs and other goods' into the country duty-free, along with the usual duty-free goods.

DISABLED

Under New York City law, facilities constructed after 1987 must provide complete access for the disabled – restrooms, entrances and exits included. In 1990, the Americans with Disabilities Act made the same requirement federal law. Many older buildings have added disabled-access features. There has been widespread compliance with the law, but call ahead to check facilities.

For information on accessible cultural institutions, contact the Mayor's Office for People with Disabilities (*see below*). All Broadway theatres are equipped with devices for the hearing-impaired; call Sound Associates (1-888 772 7686, www.soundassociates.com) for more information. For the visually impaired, HAI (1-212 284 4100, www.hainyc.org) offers live audio descriptions of selected theatre performances.

Lighthouse International
111 E 59th Street, between Park & Lexington Avenues, Upper East Side (1-212 821 9200, 1-212 821 9384 store, www.lighthouse.org). Subway N, R to Lexington Avenue-59th Street; 4, 5, 6 to 59th Street. **Open** 9am-5pm Mon-Fri. *Store* 10am-5.30pm Mon-Fri. **Map** p399 E29.
In addition to running a store that sells handy items for the vision-impaired, Lighthouse provides helpful information for blind people (residents and visitors).

Mayor's Office for People with Disabilities
2nd Floor, 100 Gold Street, between Frankfort & Spruce Streets, Financial District (1-212 788 2830). Subway J, Z to Chambers Street; 4, 5, 6 to Brooklyn Bridge-City Hall. **Open** 9am-5pm Mon-Fri. **Map** p396 F32.
This city office provides a broad range of services for the disabled.

New York Society for the Deaf
315 Hudson Street, between Vandam & Spring Streets, Soho (1-212 366 0066, www.fegs.org). Subway C, E to Spring Street; 1 to Houston Street. **Open** 8.30am-7pm Mon-Thur; 8.30am-5pm Fri. **Map** p397 D30.
Information and a range of services for the deaf and hearing-impaired.

Society for Accessible Travel & Hospitality
1-212 447 7284, www.sath.org.
This non-profit group educates the public about travel facilities for people with disabilities, and promotes travel for the disabled. Membership ($49/yr; $29 reductions) includes access to an information service and a quarterly newsletter.

DRUGS

Possession of marijuana can result in anything from a $100 fine and a warning (for a first offence, 25g or less) to felony charges and prison time (for greater amounts and/or repeat offenders). Penalties, ranging from class B misdemeanours to class C felonies, are greater for the sale and cultivation of marijuana.

Possession of 'controlled substances' (cocaine, ecstasy, heroin, etc) is not taken lightly, and charges come with stiff penalties – especially if you are convicted of possession with intent to sell. Convictions carry anything from a mandatory one- to three-year prison sentence to a maximum of 25 years.

ELECTRICITY

The US uses 110-120V, 60-cycle alternating current rather than the 220-240V, 50-cycle AC used in Europe. The transformers that power or recharge newer electronic devices such as laptops are designed to handle either current and may need nothing more than an adaptor for the wall outlet. Other appliances may also require a power converter. Adaptors and converters can be purchased at airport shops, pharmacies, department stores and at branches of electronics chain Radio Shack (www.radioshack.com).

EMBASSIES & CONSULATES

Check the phone book for a list of consulates and embassies. *See also p375* **Travel Advice.**

Australia *1-212 351 6500.*
Canada *1-212 596 1628.*
Great Britain *1-212 745 0200.*
Ireland *1-212 319 2555.*
New Zealand *1-212 832 4038.*

EMERGENCIES

In an emergency only, dial **911** for an ambulance, the police or the fire department, or call the operator (dial 0). For hospitals, *see right*; for helplines, *see p277*; for the police, *see p380.*

GAY & LESBIAN

For more gay and lesbian resources, including the Lesbian, Gay, Bisexual & Transgender Community Center, *see pp254-262.*

Gay, Lesbian, Bisexual & Transgender National Hotline
1-888 843 4564, www.glbtnationalhelpcenter.org. **Open** 4pm-midnight Mon-Fri; noon-5pm Sat.
This phone service offers excellent peer counselling, legal referrals, details of gay and lesbian organisations, and information on bars, restaurants and hotels. Younger callers can contact the toll-free GLBT National Youth Talk Line (1-800 246 7743, 4pm-midnight Mon-Fri; noon-5pm Sat).

HEALTH

Public health care is virtually nonexistent in the US, and private health care is very expensive. Make sure you have comprehensive medical insurance before you leave. For HIV testing and HIV/AIDS counselling, *see right* **Helplines**. For a list of hospitals, *see below*.

Accident & emergency

You will be billed for any emergency treatment. Call your travel insurance company before seeking treatment to find out which hospitals accept your insurance. The following hospitals have emergency rooms:

New York Presbyterian/Lower Manhattan Hospital
170 William Street, between Beeckman & Spruce Streets (1-212 312 5000). Subway 1 to Chambers Street; 2, 3 to Fulton Street; 4, 5, 6 to Brooklyn Bridge-City Hall. **Map** p396 F32.

Mount Sinai Hospital
Madison Avenue, at 100th Street, Upper East Side (1-212 241 6500). Subway 6 to 103rd Street. **Map** p400 E16.

New York-Presbyterian Hospital/Weill Cornell Medical Center
525 E 68th Street, at York Avenue, Upper East Side (1-212 746 5454). Subway 6 to 68th Street. **Map** p399 G21.

Roosevelt Hospital
1000 Tenth Avenue, at 59th Street, Upper West Side (1-212 523 4000). Subway A, B, C, D, 1 to 59th Street-Columbus Circle. **Map** p399 C22.

Clinics

Walk-in clinics offer treatment for minor ailments. Most clinics will require immediate payment for treatments and consultations, though some will send their bill directly to your insurance company if you're a US resident. You will have to file a claim to recover the cost of any prescription medication that is required.

Beth Israel Medical Group
55 E 34th Street, between Madison & Park Avenues, Murray Hill (1-212 252 6000, www.wehealny.org/services/bimg). Subway 6 to 33rd Street. **Open** walk-in 8am-5pm Mon-Fri; 9am-2pm Sat, Sun; also by appt. **Cost** from $125. **Map** p398 E25.
Primary-care facilities offering by-appointment and walk-in services.
Other locations 309 W 23rd Street, at Eighth Avenue (1-212 256 7000).

NY Hotel Urgent Medical Services
Suite 1D, 952 Fifth Avenue, between 76th & 77th Streets, Upper East Side (1-212 737 1212, www.travelmd.com). Subway 6 to 77th Street. **Open** 24hrs by appt only. **Cost** from $200. **Map** p399 E19.
Specialist medical attention, from a simple prescription to urgent medical care. House calls are available.

Dentists

New York County Dental Society
1-212 573 8500, www.nycdentalsociety.org. **Open** 9am-5pm Mon-Fri.
Can provide local referrals. An emergency line at the number above runs outside office hours; alternatively, use the search facility on the society's website.

Opticians

See also p104.

Morgenthal Frederics
399 W Broadway, at Spring Street, Soho (1-212 966 0099, www.morgenthalfrederics.com). Subway C, E to Spring Street. **Open** 11am-8pm Mon-Fri (10am-7pm in autumn & winter); 11am-7pm Sat; noon-6pm Sun. **Map** p397 E30.
The house-designed, handmade frames displayed in Morgenthal Frederics' David Rockwell-designed shops exude quality and subtly nostalgic style. Frames start from around $325 for plastic, but the buffalo horn and gold ranges are more expensive.
Other locations throughout the city.

Pharmacies

The fact that there's a **Duane Reade** pharmacy on almost every corner of Manhattan is lamented among chain-deriding locals; however, it is convenient if you need an aspirin pronto. Several branches, including the one at 250 W 57th Street, at Broadway (1-212 265 2101, www.duanereade.com), are open 24 hours. Competitor **Rite Aid** (with one of several 24-hour branches at 301 W 50th Street, at Eighth Avenue, 1-212 247 8384, www.riteaid.com) is also widespread. For New York's oldest apothecary, **CO Bigelow**, *see p112.*

STDs, HIV & AIDS

For the National STD & AIDS Hotline, *see right* **Helplines**.
NYC Department of Health Chelsea Health Center
303 Ninth Avenue, at 28th Street, Chelsea (no phone). Subway C, E to 23rd Street. **Open** walk-in 8.30am-3pm Tue-Sat. **Map** p398 B26.
Call 311 or visit www.nyc.gov for other free clinics.

Gay Men's Health Crisis
446 W 33rd Street, at Tenth Avenue, Hell's Kitchen (1-212 367 1000, 1-800 243 7692 HIV/AIDS helpline, www.gmhc.org). Subway A, C, E, 1, 2, 3 to 34th Street-Penn Station. **Open** *Centre* 10am-5pm Mon-Fri. *Hotline* 2-6pm Mon, Fri; 10am-2pm Wed; recorded information at other times. **Map** p398 C25.
GMHC was the world's first organisation dedicated to helping people with AIDS, and offers testing, counselling and other services on a walk-in and appointment basis, regardless of sexual orientation. The Testing Center is now located within the new Center for HIV Prevention (224 W 29th Street, between Seventh & Eighth Avenues, Chelsea, 1-212 367 1100). See website for separate walk-in and appointment-only hours.

Contraception & abortion

Parkmed Physicians Center
7th Floor, 800 Second Avenue, between 42nd & 43rd Streets, Midtown East (1-646 898 2135, www.parkmed.com). Subway S, 4, 5, 6, 7 to 42nd Street-Grand Central. **Open** by appt only 7am-8pm Mon-Fri; 7am-6pm Sat; 9am-5pm Sun. **Map** p398 F24.
Urine pregnancy tests are free. Counselling, contraception services and non-surgical abortions are also available at the centre.

Planned Parenthood of New York City *Margaret Sanger Center, 26 Bleecker Street, at Mott Street, Greenwich Village (1-212 965 7000, 1-800 230 7526, www.ppnyc.org). Subway B, D, F, M to Broadway-Lafayette Street; N, R to Prince Street; 6 to Bleecker Street.* **Open** 8am-4.30pm Mon, Tue; 8am-6.30pm Wed-Fri; 7.30am-4pm Sat. **Map** p397 F29.
The best-known network of family-planning clinics in the US. Counselling and treatment are available for a full range of needs, including abortion, contraception, HIV testing and treatment of STDs.
Other locations 44 Court Street, between Joralemon & Remsen Streets, Brooklyn Heights, Brooklyn (1-212 965 7000).

HELPLINES

All numbers are open 24 hours unless otherwise stated.

Addictions Hotline
1-800 522 5353.
Alcoholics Anonymous
1-212 647 1680.
Open 9am-2am daily.
Childhelp USA's National Child Abuse Hotline
1-800 422 4453.
Cocaine Anonymous
1-212 262 2463.
National STD & AIDS Hotline
1-800 232 4636.
Pills Anonymous
1-212 874 0700 recorded information.
Safe Horizon Crisis Hotline
1-800 621 4673, www.safehorizon.org.
Counselling for victims of domestic violence, rape or other crimes.
Samaritans
1-212 673 3000.
Counselling for suicide prevention.
Special Victims Liaison Unit of the NYPD Rape Hotline
1-212 267 7273.

ID

Always carry picture ID: even people well over 18 or 21 may be carded when buying tobacco or alcohol, ordering drinks in bars, or entering clubs.

INSURANCE

Non-nationals and US citizens should have travel and medical insurance before travelling. For a list of New York urgent-care facilities, *see p376.*

INTERNET

Cycle Café *250 W 49th Street, between Broadway & Eighth Avenue, Theater District (1-212 380 1204, www.cycle-cafe.com). Subway C, E, 1 to 50th Street; N, Q, R to 49th Street.* **Open** 8am-midnight daily. **Cost** from $3.15/15mins. **Map** p398 D23.
A bike-rental shop and internet café rolled into one.

FedEx Office *1-800 463 3339, www.fedex.com.*
Outposts of this ubiquitous and very efficient computer and copy centre are peppered throughout the city; many are open 24 hours a day.

New York Public Library
1-212 592 7000, www.nypl.org.
Branches of the NYPL are great places to get online for free, offering both Wi-Fi and computers for public use. (Ask for an out-of-state card, for which you need proof of residence, or a guest pass.) The Science, Industry & Business Library (188 Madison Avenue, at 34th Street, Midtown East), part of the Public Library system, has about 70 computers. All libraries have a computer limit of 45 minutes per day.

NYCWireless *www.nycwireless.net.*
This group has established dozens of hotspots in the city for free Wi-Fi access. (For example, most parks below 59th Street are covered.) Visit the website information and a map.
Starbucks *www.starbucks.com.*
Many branches offer free Wi-Fi; the website has a search facility.

LEFT LUGGAGE

There are luggage-storage facilities at arrivals halls in JFK Airport (Terminal 1: 7am-11pm, $4-$16 per bag per day; call 1-718 751 2947); (Terminal 4: 24hrs, $4-$16 per bag per day; call 1-718 751 4020). At Penn Station, Amtrak offers checked baggage services for a small fee for some of its ticketed passengers. Due to heightened security, luggage storage is not available at the Port Authority Bus Terminal, Grand Central, or LaGuardia or Newark airports.

One Midtown alternative is to leave bags with the private firm, located between Penn Station and Port Authority, listed below. Some hotels may allow you to leave suitcases with the front desk before check-in or after check-out; if so, be sure to tip the concierge.

Schwartz Travel Services
2nd Floor, 355 W 36th Street, between Eighth & Ninth Avenues (1-212 290 2626, www.schwartztravel.com). **Open** 8am-11pm daily. **Rates** $7-$10 per bag per day. **No credit cards.**
Other locations 4th Floor, 34 W 46th Street, between Fifth & Sixth Avenues (same phone).

LEGAL HELP

If you need a lawyer in NYC, contact the **New York City Bar Association** (1-212 382 6600; www.nycbar.org), which can provide referrals to attorneys practising in almost every area of the law, from personal injury to criminal defence. Outside the city, contact the **New York State Bar Association Lawyer Referral & Information Service** (1-800 342 3661, www.nysba.org). If you're arrested and held in custody, call your insurer's emergency number or contact your embassy or consulate (*see p376*).

Legal Aid Society *1-212 577 3300, www.legal-aid.org.* **Open** 9am-5pm Mon-Fri.
This non-profit organisation provides legal representation for low-income residents.

LIBRARIES

See left **New York Public Library**.

LOST PROPERTY

For lost credit cards or travellers' cheques, *see p380*.

Grand Central Terminal *Lower level, near Track 100. 1-212 532 4900.* **Open** 7am-6pm Mon-Fri.
You can call 24 hrs a day to file a claim if you've left something on a Metro-North train.
JFK Airport *1-718 244 4225,* or contact your airline.
La Guardia Airport *1-718 533 3988,* or contact your airline.
Newark Liberty International Airport *1-973 961 6243,* or contact your airline.
Penn Station: Amtrak *1-212 630 7389.* **Open** 6am-2.30pm daily.
Penn Station: Long Island Rail Road *1-718 217 5477.* **Open** 24hrs.
Penn Station: New Jersey Transit *1-973 275 5555.* **Open** 6am-10pm Mon-Fri; 8am-8pm Sat; 9am-8pm Sun.
Subway & Buses *New York City Metropolitan Transit Authority, 34th Street-Penn Station, near the A-train platform, Garment District (call 511).* **Open** 8am-3.30pm Mon, Tue, Fri; 11am-6.30pm Wed, Thur. **Map** p398 D25.
Call if you've left something on a subway train or a bus.
Taxis *311, www.nyc.gov/taxi.*
Call for items left in a cab.

MEDIA

Daily newspapers

Founded in 1801 by Alexander Hamilton, the **New York Post** is the nation's oldest continuously published daily newspaper. It has swerved sharply to the right under current owner Rupert Murdoch, includes more gossip than any other local paper, and its headlines are often sassy and sensational.

The **Daily News** has drifted politically from the Neanderthal right to a more moderate but always tough-minded stance under the ownership of noted real-estate mogul Mort Zuckerman.

Despite recent financial woes, **The New York Times** remains the city's, and the nation's, paper of record. Founded as the *New-York Daily Times* in 1851, it has the broadest and deepest coverage of world and national events and, as the masthead proclaims, it delivers 'All the News That's Fit to Print'. The hefty Sunday edition includes a very well-regarded magazine, as well as arts, book review, travel, real-estate and various other sections.

The **New York Amsterdam News**, one of the nation's longest-running black newspapers, offers a trenchant African-American viewpoint. New York also supports a Spanish-language daily: **El Diario La Prensa**. **Newsday** is a Long Island-based daily with a tabloid format but a sober tone. Free tabloids **AM New York** and **New York Metro** offer locally slanted news, arts and entertainment listings.

Weekly newspapers

Downtown journalism is a battlefield, with the **New York Press** pitted against the **Village Voice**. The *Press* is full of irreverence, as well as cynicism and self-absorption. The *Voice* is at turns passionate and ironic, but just as often strident and predictable. Both are free.

Many neighbourhoods have free publications featuring local news, reviews and gossip, such as **Our Town East Side** and **West Side Spirit**.

Magazines

New York magazine is part news weekly, part lifestyle reporting and part listings. Since the 1920s, the **New Yorker** has been known for its fine wit, elegant prose and sophisticated cartoons. It has also evolved into a respected forum for serious long-form journalism.

Based on the tried and trusted format of its London parent magazine, **Time Out New York** is an intelligent, irreverent, indispensable weekly guide to what's going on in the city: arts, restaurants, bars, shops and more.

Since its launch in 1996, the bimonthly **BlackBook Magazine** has covered New York's high fashion and culture with intelligent bravado. **Gotham**, a monthly from the publisher of glossy gab-rags *Hamptons* and *Aspen Peak*, unveiled its larger-than-life celeb-filled pages in 2001. And for more than two decades, **Paper** has offered buzz on bars, clubs, downtown boutiques and more.

Commercial radio

American commercial radio is rigidly formatted, which makes most pop stations extremely tedious and repetitive during the day. Tune in on evenings and weekends for more interesting programming. Always popular, **WQHT-FM 97.1**, 'Hot 97', is a commercial hip hop station with all-day rap and R&B. **WKTU-FM 103.5** is the premier dance music station. **WWPR-FM 105.1**, 'Power 105', plays top hip hop and a few old-school hits. **WBLS-FM 107.5** showcases classic and new funk, soul and R&B. **WBGO-FM 88.3** is strictly jazz, and **WAXQ-FM 104.3** offers classic rock.

WQEW-AM 1560, 'Radio Disney', has kids' programming. **WNYC-FM 93.9** (*see also below*) and **WQXR-FM 105.9** serve up a range of new and classical music. **WXNY-FM 96.3** and **WQBU-FM 92.7** spin Spanish and Latin sounds.

Public & college radio

The city's excellent NPR-affiliated public radio station, **WNYC-AM 820/FM 93.9**, provides news and current-affairs commentary and broadcasts the BBC World Service. **WBAI-FM 99.5** is a left-leaning community radio station.

College radio is innovative and commercial-free, but reception is often compromised by Manhattan's high-rise topography. **WNYU-FM 89.1** and **WKCR-FM 89.9** are, respectively, the stations of New York University and Columbia. **WFUV-FM 90.7**, Fordham University's station, airs a variety of shows, including Beale Street Caravan, the world's most widely distributed blues programme.

Talk radio & sports

WABC-AM 770, **WCBS-AM 880** and **WINS-AM 1010** offer news, plus traffic and weather reports. **WFAN-AM 660** airs Giants, Nets, Mets and Devils games, while **WCBS-AM 880** covers the Yankees. **WEPN-AM 1050** is devoted to news and sports talk and is the home of the Jets, Knicks and Rangers.

Television

Six major networks broadcast nationwide. All offer ratings-driven variations on a theme.

CBS (Channel 2 in NYC) has the top-rated investigative show, *60 Minutes*, on Sundays at 7pm; overall, programming is geared to a middle-aged demographic, but CBS also screens shows such as *CSI* and the reality series *Survivor*. **NBC** (4) is the home of *Law & Order*, the long-running sketch-comedy series *Saturday Night Live* (11.30pm Sat), and popular prime-time shows that include *The Office* and *30 Rock*. **Fox-WNYW** (5) is popular with younger audiences for shows such as *Glee*, *Family Guy*, *The Simpsons* and *The X Factor*. **ABC** (7) is the king of daytime soaps, family-friendly sitcoms and hits like *Modern Family*, *Grey's Anatomy* and *Dancing With the Stars*.

Public TV is on channels 13, 21 and 25. Documentaries, arts shows and science series alternate with *Masterpiece* (Anglo costume and contemporary dramas packaged for a US audience) and reruns of British sitcoms.

For channel numbers for cable TV providers, such as **Time Warner Cable**, **Cablevision** and **RCN**, check a local newspaper or the Web. **FSN (Fox Sports Network)**, **MSG (Madison Square Garden)**, **ESPN** and **ESPN2** are all-sports stations. **Comedy Central** is all comedy, airing *South Park*, *The Daily Show with Jon Stewart* and its hugely popular spin-off *The Colbert Report*. **Cinemax**, the **Disney Channel**,

SIZE CHARTS

WOMEN'S CLOTHES

British	French	US
4	32	2
6	34	4
8	36	6
10	38	8
12	40	10
14	42	12
16	44	14
18	46	16
20	48	18

WOMEN'S SHOES

British	French	US
3	36	5
4	37	6
5	38	7
6	39	8
7	40	9
8	41	10
9	42	11

MEN'S CLOTHES

British	French	US
34	44	34
36	46	36
38	48	38
40	50	40
42	52	42
44	54	44
46	56	46
48	58	48

MEN'S SHOES

British	French	US
6	39	7
7.5	40	7.5
8	41	8
8	42	8.5
9	43	9.5
10	44	10.5
11	45	11
12	46	11.5

the **Movie Channel**, **HBO** and **Showtime** are often available in hotels. They show uninterrupted feature films and exclusive specials; the latter two offer popular series such as *Boardwalk Empire, Girls, Homeland* and *Nurse Jackie*.

MONEY

Over the past few years, much of American currency has undergone a subtle facelift, partly to deter increasingly adept counterfeiters; all denominations except the $1 bill have recently been updated by the US Treasury. (However, 'old' money still remains in circulation.) Coins include copper pennies (1¢) and silver-coloured nickels (5¢), dimes (10¢) and quarters (25¢). Half-dollar coins (50¢) and the gold-coloured dollar coins are less common.

All paper money is the same size, so make sure you fork over the right bill. It comes in denominations of $1, $2, $5, $10, $20, $50 and $100 (and higher, but you'll never see those bills). The $2 bills are quite rare. Try to keep some low notes on you because getting change may be a problem with anything bigger than a $20 bill.

ATMs

The city is full of ATMs – in bank branches, delis and many small shops. Most accept Visa, MasterCard and major bank cards. Some UK banks charge up to £4 per transaction plus a variable payment to cover themselves against exchange rate fluctuations. Most ATM cards now double as debit cards, if they bear Maestro or Cirrus logos.

Banks & bureaux de change

Banks are generally open from 9am to 6pm Monday to Friday, though some stay open longer and/or on Saturdays. You need photo ID, such as a passport, to cash travellers' cheques. Many banks will not exchange foreign currency; many bureaux de change, limited to tourist-trap areas, close at around 6pm or 7pm. In emergencies, most large hotels offer 24-hour exchange facilities, but the rates won't be great.

Chase Bank
1-800 935 9935, www.chase.com.
Chase's website gives information on foreign currency exchange, branch locations and credit cards. For foreign currency delivered in a hurry, call the number listed above.

TD Bank
1-888 751 9000, www.tdbank.com.
All Manhattan branches (there are nearly 40) of the Canadian-owned bank are open seven days a week.

People's Foreign Exchange
60 E 42nd Street, between Madison & Park Avenues, Midtown East (1-212 883 0550, www.peoplesfx.com). Subway S, 4, 5, 6, 7 to 42nd Street-Grand Central. **Open** 9am-6pm Mon-Fri; 10.30am-4pm Sat, Sun.
Map p398 E23.
People's Foreign Exchange offers foreign currency exchange on travellers' cheques for one per cent commission or bank notes of any denomination for a flat fee of $5.
Other locations 3rd Floor, 575 Fifth Avenue, at 47th Street, Midtown East (same phone).

Travelex
1578 Broadway, at 47th Street, Theater District (1-212 265 6063, www.travelex.com). Subway N, Q, R to 49th Street. **Open** 9am-10pm daily. **Map** p398 D23.
Travelex offers a complete range of foreign-exchange services. The Times Square outpost stays open late; see website for other locations.
Other locations throughout the city.

Credit cards & travellers' cheques

Credit cards are essential for renting cars and booking hotels, and handy for buying tickets over the phone and the internet. The five major cards accepted in the US are **American Express** , **Diners Club**, **Discover**, **MasterCard** and **Visa**. MasterCard and Visa are the most popular; American Express is also widely accepted. Thanks to a 2004 deal between MasterCard and Diners Club, all businesses that accept the former can now in theory accept the latter, though in practice many business are unaware of this and may not comply.

If your cards or travellers' cheques are lost or stolen, call the following numbers:

American Express *1-800 528 2122, 1-800 221 7282 travellers' cheques.*
Diners Club *1-800 234 6377.*
Discover *1-800 347 2683.*
Mastercard/Maestro *1-800 826 2181, 1-800 223 9920 travellers' cheques.*
Visa/Cirrus *1-800 336 8472, 1-800 336 8472 travellers' cheques.*

Tax

Sales tax is 8.875 per cent in New York City, and is applicable to restaurant bills, services and the purchase of just about anything, except most store-bought foods, clothing and shoes under $110.

In the US, sales tax is almost never included in the price of the item, but added on to the final bill at the till. There is no tax refund option for foreign visitors.

Wire services

Funds can be wired from home through the following companies:

Moneygram *1-800 666 3947, www.moneygram.com.*
Western Union *1-800 325 6000, www.westernunion.com.*

OPENING HOURS

Banks and government offices, including post offices, close on federal holidays. Retail in the city shuts down on Christmas Day and New Year's Day, although movie theatres and some restaurants remain open. Most museums are closed on Mondays, but may open when a public holiday falls on a Monday. New York's subway runs 24 hours a day, 365 days a year, but always check station signs for track or schedule changes, especially during weekends and holidays.

Banks 9am-6pm Mon-Fri; generally also Sat mornings.
Businesses 9am or 10am to 5pm or 6pm Mon-Fri.
Post offices 9am-5pm Mon-Fri (a few open as early as 7.30am and close as late as 8.30pm); some are open Sat until 3pm or 4pm. The James A Farley Post Office (*see p381*) is open 24 hours daily for automated services.
Pubs & bars 4pm-2am Mon-Thur, Sun; noon-4am Fri, Sat (but hours vary widely).
Shops 9am, 10am or 11am to 7pm or 8pm Mon-Sat (some open at noon and/or close at 9pm). Many are also open on Sun, usually from 11am or noon to 6pm.

POLICE

In an emergency only, dial **911**. The NYPD stations below are in central, tourist-heavy areas of Manhattan. For the location of your nearest police precinct or information about police services, call 1-646 610 5000 or visit www.nyc.gov.

Sixth Precinct
233 West 10th Street, between Bleecker & Hudson Streets, West Village (1-212 741 4811).
Seventh Precinct
19½ Pitt Street, at Broome Street, Lower East Side (1-212 477 7311).
Midtown South Precinct
357 W 35th Street, between Eighth & Ninth Avenues, Garment District (1-212 239 9811).
Midtown North Precinct
306 W 54th Street, between Eighth & Ninth Avenues, Hell's Kitchen (1-212 767 8400).
17th Precinct
167 E 51st Street, between Third & Lexington Avenues, Midtown East (1-212 826 3211).
Central Park Precinct
86th Street & Transverse Road, Central Park (1-212 570 4820).

POSTAL SERVICES

Stamps are available at all US post offices, from drugstore vending machines and at most newsstands. It costs 49¢ to send a 1oz letter within the US. Each additional ounce costs 21¢. Postcards mailed within the US cost 34¢. Airmailed letters or postcards to Canada and Mexico cost 85¢ for the first ounce. The Global Forever Stamp ($1.15) can be used to send a postcard or 1oz letter anywhere in the world.

For faster **Express Mail**, you must fill out a form, either at a post office or by arranging a pick-up; 24-hour delivery to major US cities is guaranteed. International delivery takes two to three days, with no guarantee. Call 1-800 275 8777 for more information. For couriers and messengers, *see p375*.

James A Farley Post Office
421 Eighth Avenue, between 31st & 33rd Streets, Garment District (1-212 330 3296, 1-800 275 8777 24hr information, www.usps.com). Subway A, C, E to 34th Street-Penn Station. **Open** 24 hrs daily. *Counter service* 7am-10pm Mon-Fri; 9am-9pm Sat; 11am-7pm Sun. **Map** p398 D25.
In addition to operating a counter service, NYC's general post office has automated self-service machines for buying stamps and posting packages.

General Delivery
390 Ninth Avenue, between 31st & 33rd Streets, Garment District (1-212 330 3099). Subway A, C, E to 34th Street-Penn Station. **Open** 10am-1pm Mon-Fri; 10am-noon Sat. **Map** p398 C25.
US residents without local addresses and foreign visitors can receive their post here; it should be addressed to the recipient, General Delivery, 390 Ninth Avenue, New York, NY 10001. You will need to show a passport or ID card when picking up letters.

RELIGION

Here are just a few of New York's many places of worship. Check online or the telephone book for more listings.

Abyssinian Baptist Church
See p188.

Cathedral Church of St John the Divine *See p171.*

Church of St Paul & St Andrew, United Methodist
263 W 86th Street, between Broadway & West End Avenue, Upper West Side (1-212 362 3179, www.stpaulandstandrew.org). Subway 1 to 86th Street.
Map p400 C18.

Islamic Cultural Center of New York *1711 Third Avenue, between 96th & 97th Streets, Upper East Side (1-212 722 5234, www.icc-ny.org). Subway 6 to 96th Street.* **Map** p400 F17.

Madison Avenue Presbyterian Church *921 Madison Avenue, between 73rd & 74th Streets, Upper East Side (1-212 288 8920, www.mapc.com). Subway 6 to 72nd Street.* **Map** p399 E20.

New York Buddhist Church
331-332 Riverside Drive, between 105th & 106th Streets, Upper West Side (1-212 678 0305, www.newyorkbuddhistchurch.org). Subway 1 to 103rd Street.
Map p400 B16.

St Patrick's Cathedral
See p89.

UJA Federation of New York Information & Referral Center
1-877 852 6951, www.ujafedny.org.
Open 9am-5pm Mon-Fri.
This hotline provides referrals to temples, synagogues, other Jewish organisations and groups.

SAFETY & SECURITY

New York's crime rate, particularly for violent crime, has waned during the past two decades. Most crime occurs late at night and in low-income neighbourhoods. Don't arrive in NYC thinking your safety is at risk wherever you go; it is unlikely that you will ever be bothered.

Still, a bit of common sense won't hurt. Don't flaunt your money and valuables, keep phones and other electronic gadgets out of sight, and try not to look obviously lost. Avoid deserted and poorly lit streets; walk facing oncoming traffic so no one can drive up alongside you undetected, and close to or on the street; muggers prefer to hang back in doorways and shadows. If you are threatened, hand over your valuables at once, then dial 911.

Be extra alert to pickpockets and street hustlers – especially in crowded areas like Times Square.

SMOKING

The 1995 NYC Smoke-Free Air Act makes it illegal to smoke in virtually all indoor public places, including the subway and cinemas; for a few exceptions. As of May 2011, smoking is also prohibited in New York City parks, pedestrian plazas (such as the ones in Times Square and Herald Square) and on beaches. Violators could face a $50 fine.

STUDY

Those who study in NYC have access to an endless extracurricular education, as well as a non-stop playground. Foreign students should get hold of an International Student Identity Card (ISIC) in order to secure discounts. These cards can be purchased from your local student-travel agent (go to www.isic.org or ask at your student union or an STA Travel office).

Manhattan's main universities include: the **City University of New York**'s 24 colleges (1-212 794 5555, www.cuny.edu); **Columbia University** (2960 Broadway, at 116th Street, Morningside Heights, 1-212 854 1754, www.columbia.edu); the **Cooper Union** (30 Cooper Square, between 5th & 6th Streets, East Village, 1-212 353 4100, www.cooper.edu); **Fordham University**, which has campuses in the Bronx and on the Upper West Side (1-718 817 1000, 1-212 636 6000, www.fordham.edu);

the **New School** (55 W 13th Street, between Fifth & Sixth Avenues, Greenwich Village, 1-212 229 5600, www.newschool.edu); **New York University** (70 Washington Square South, Greenwich Village, 1-212 998 1212, www.nyu.edu); and performing arts school **Juilliard** (60 Lincoln Center Plaza, at Broadway, Upper West Side, 1-212 799 5000, www.juilliard.edu).

TELEPHONES

Dialling & codes

As a rule, you must dial 1 + the area code before a number, even if the place you are calling is in the same area code. The area codes for Manhattan are **212** and **646**; Brooklyn, Queens, Staten Island and the Bronx are **718** and **347**; **917** is now reserved mostly for mobile phones and pagers. Long Island area codes are 516 and 631; codes for New Jersey are 201, 551, 609, 732, 848, 856, 862, 908 and 973. Numbers preceded by **800, 877** and **888** are free of charge when dialled from within the US.

In an **emergency**, dial 911. All calls are free (including those from pay and mobile phones).

For the **operator**, dial 0. If you're not used to US phones, then note that the ringing tone is long; the engaged tone, or 'busy signal', consists of much shorter, higher pitched beeps.

Collect calls are also known as reverse-charge calls. To make one, dial 0 followed by the number, or dial AT&T's 1-800 225 5288, Sprint's 1-800 663 3463, or the aptly named 1-800-Collect's 1-800 265 5328.

For **directory assistance**, dial 411 or 1 + area code + 555 1212. Doing so may cost nothing, depending on the pay phone you are using; carrier fees may apply. Long-distance directory assistance may also incur long-distance charges. For a directory of toll-free numbers, dial 1-800 555 1212.

For **international calls**, dial 011 + country code (Australia 61; New Zealand 64; UK 44), then the number (omitting any initial zero).

Mobile phones

Most US mobile phones will work in NYC, but since the US doesn't have a standard national network, visitors should check with their provider that their phone will work here, and whether they need to unlock a roaming option. Visitors from other countries will need a tri-band handset and a roaming agreement, and may find charges so high that rental or purchase of a US phone (or SIM card) will make better economic sense. Phones can be hired from Jojo Talk (www.jojotalk.com).

If you carry a mobile phone, make sure you turn it off in museums and restaurants, and at plays, movies and concerts. New Yorkers are quick to show their annoyance at an ill-timed ring. Some establishments now even post signs designating a cellular-free zone.

Public phones

Functioning public pay phones are becoming increasingly hard to find. Phones take any combination of silver coins: local calls usually cost 50¢ for three minutes. To call long-distance or to make an international call from a pay phone, you need to go through a long-distance company. Most of the pay phones in New York automatically use AT&T, but phones in and around transportation hubs usually contract other long-distance carriers, and charges can be outrageous. MCI and Sprint are respected brand names.

Make the call by either dialling 0 for an operator or dialling direct, which is cheaper. To find out how much it will cost, dial the number, and a computerised voice will tell you how much money to deposit. You can pay for calls with your credit card. The best way to make long-distance calls is with a phone card, available from any post office branch, many newsagents and delis, or from chain stores such as Duane Reade and Rite Aid (*see p377* **Pharmacies**).

TIME & DATES

New York is on Eastern Standard Time, which extends from the Atlantic coast to the eastern shore of Lake Michigan and south to the Gulf of Mexico. This is five hours behind Greenwich Mean Time. Clocks are set forward one hour in early March for Daylight Saving Time (Eastern Daylight Time) and back one hour at the beginning of November. Going from east to west, Eastern Time is one hour ahead of Central Time, two hours ahead of Mountain Time and three hours ahead of Pacific Time.

In the United States, the date is written as month, day and year; so 6/9/14 is 9 June 2014. Forms that foreigners may need to fill in, however, are often the other way round.

TIPPING

In restaurants, it's customary to tip at least 15 per cent, and since NYC tax is 8.875 per cent, a quick way to calculate the tip is to double the tax. In many restaurants, when you are with a group of six or more, the tip will be included in the bill. For tipping on taxi fares, *see p373*.

TOILETS

The media had a field day when the first pay toilet to open in the city since 1975 received its 'first flush' by officials in a special ceremony in 2008. 'Public Toilet No.1', as the *New York Post* christened it, is in Madison Square Park (Madison Avenue, between 23rd & 24th Streets, Flatiron District) and was due to be followed by around 20 across the city within the following couple of years; progress, however, has been stalled. It costs 25¢ to enter the large stainless steel and tempered glass box (dawdlers and OCD sufferers, beware: the door opens after 15 minutes). Below is a list of other convenient rest stops.

Downtown

Battery Park Castle Clinton *Subway 1 to South Ferry; 4, 5 to Bowling Green.*
Tompkins Square Park *Avenue A, at 9th Street. Subway L to First Avenue; 6 to Astor Place.*
Washington Square Park *Thompson Street, at Washington Square South. Subway A, B, C, D, E, F, M to W 4th Street.*

Midtown

Bryant Park *42nd Street, between Fifth & Sixth Avenues. Subway B, D, F, M to 42nd Street-Bryant Park; 7 to Fifth Avenue.*
Grand Central Terminal *42nd Street, at Park Avenue, Lower Concourse. Subway S, 4, 5, 6, 7 to 42nd Street-Grand Central.*
Penn Station *Seventh Avenue, between 31st & 33rd Streets, Subway A, C, E, 1, 2, 3 to 34th Street-Penn Station.*

Uptown

Avery Fisher Hall *Broadway, at 65th Street. Subway 1 to 66th Street-Lincoln Center.*

Charles A Dana Discovery Center *Central Park, north side of Harlem Meer, 110th Street at Malcolm X Boulevard (Lenox Avenue). Subway 2, 3 to 110th Street-Central Park North.*
Delacorte Theater *Central Park, midpark, at 81st Street. Subway B, C to 81st Street-Museum of Natural History.*

TOURIST INFORMATION

Official NYC Information Center
810 Seventh Avenue, between 52nd & 53rd Streets, Theater District (1-212 484 1222, www.nycgo.com). Subway B, D, E to Seventh Avenue. **Open** 8.30am-6pm Mon-Fri; 9am-5pm Sat, Sun. **Map** p398 D23.
The city's official (private, non-profit) visitors' information centre recently got a high-tech renovation, complete with interactive map tables that allow visitors to navigate the city's attractions, hotels and restaurants, and send your itineraries to your email address or mobile device. The centre also doles out maps, leaflets, coupons and advice; and sells MetroCards and tickets to attractions such as Top of the Rock, the Statue of Liberty and the Empire State Building, potentially saving you time waiting in line. For other locations and information kiosks around the city, go to www.nycgo.com/articles/official-nyc-information-centers.
Other locations throughout the city.

Brooklyn Tourism & Visitors Center *Brooklyn Borough Hall, 209 Joralemon Street, between Court & Adams Streets (1-718 802 3846, www.visitbrooklyn.org). Subway A, C, F to Jay Street-Borough Hall; R to Court Street; 2, 3, 4, 5, to Borough Hall.*
Open 10am-6pm Mon-Fri.
A wealth of information on attractions, sites and events in the city's largest borough, plus local-interest books and gifts.

VISAS & IMMIGRATION

Visas

Currently, 37 countries participate in the Visa Waiver Program (VWP; www.cbp.gov/esta) including Australia, Ireland, New Zealand, and the UK. Citizens of these countries do not need a visa for stays in the US shorter than 90 days (business or pleasure) as long as they have a machine-readable passport (e-passport) valid for the full 90-day period, a return ticket, and authorisation to travel through he ESTA (Electronic System for Travel Authorization) scheme. Visitors must fill in the ESTA form at least 24 hours before travelling (72 hours is recommended) and pay a $14 fee; the form can be found at www.cbp.gov/xp/cgov/travel/id_visa/esta/).

If you do not qualify for entry under the VWP, you will need a visa; leave plenty of time to check before travelling.

Immigration

Your airline will give all visitors an immigration form to be presented to an official when you land. Fill it in clearly and be prepared to give an address at which you are staying (a hotel is fine).

Upon arrival in the US, you may have to wait an hour or, if you're unlucky, considerably longer, in Immigration, where, owing to tightened security, you can expect slow-moving queues. You may be expected to explain your visit; be polite and prepared. Note that all visitors to the US are now photographed and electronically fingerprinted on arrival on every trip.

WEIGHTS & MEASURES

Despite attempts to bring in metric measurements, you'll find imperial used in almost all contexts in New York and throughout the US. People think in ounces, inches, gallons and miles.

WHEN TO GO

There is no bad time to visit New York, and visitor numbers are fairly steady year-round. However, the weather can be unpleasantly hot and humid in summer (especially August) and, although winter snow (usually heaviest in January and February) is picturesque before it gets dirty and slushy, these months are often brutally cold. Late spring and early autumn bring pleasantly moderate temperatures that are perfect for walking and exploring.

Public holidays

New Year's Day 1 Jan
Martin Luther King, Jr Day 3rd Mon in Jan
Presidents Day 3rd Mon in Feb
Memorial Day last Mon in May
Independence Day 4 July
Labor Day 1st Mon in Sept
Columbus Day 2nd Mon in Oct
Veterans Day 11 Nov
Thanksgiving Day 4th Thur in Nov
Christmas Day 25 Dec

WORK

Non-nationals cannot work in the United States without the appropriate visa; these are hard to get and generally require you to prove that your job could not be done by a US citizen. Contact your local embassy for further details. Some student visas allow part-time work after the first academic year.

UK students who want to spend a summer vacation working in the US should contact the **British Universities North America Club** (BUNAC) for help in securing a temporary job and also the requisite visa (Priory House, 6 Wrights Lane, London W86TA, 020 7870 9570, www.bunac.org/uk).

THE LOCAL CLIMATE

Average temperatures and monthly rainfall in New York.

	High (°C/°F)	Low (°C/°F)	Rainfall (mm/in)
Jan	2 / 36	-5 / 23	94 / 3.7
Feb	4 / 40	-4 / 24	75 / 3.0
Mar	9 / 48	0 / 32	104 / 4.1
Apr	14 / 58	6 / 42	103 / 4.1
May	20 / 68	12 / 53	114 / 4.5
June	25 / 77	17 / 63	88 / 3.5
July	28 / 83	20 / 68	106 / 4.2
Aug	27 / 81	19 / 66	103 / 4.1
Sep	23 / 74	14 / 58	103 / 4.1
Oct	17 / 63	8 / 47	89 / 3.5
Nov	11 / 52	3 / 38	102 / 4.0
Dec	6 / 42	-2 / 28	98 / 3.9

Further Reference

BOOKS

Architecture

Richard Berenholtz
New York, New York
Miniature panoramic images of the city through the seasons.

Stanley Greenberg
Invisible New York
A photographic account of hidden architectural triumphs.

New York City Landmarks Preservation Commission
Guide to New York City Landmarks

Karl Sabbagh *Skyscraper*
How the tall ones are built.

Kevin Walsh *Forgotten New York*
Discover overlooked architectural gems and anachronistic remnants.

Norval White & Elliot Willensky *The AIA Guide to New York City*
A comprehensive directory of important buildings.

Culture & recollections

Irving Lewis Allen
The City in Slang
NYC-bred words and phrases.

Joseph Berger
The World in a City
The *New York Times* columnist explores the communities located within the five boroughs.

Andrew Blauner (ed)
Central Park: An Anthology
Writers reflect on the city's most celebrated green space.

Anatole Broyard
Kafka Was the Rage: A Greenwich Village Memoir
Vivid account of 1940s Village bohemia and its characters.

George Chauncey *Gay New York*
The evolution of gay culture from 1890 to 1940.

Martha Cooper & Henry Chalfant *Subway Art*
A definitive survey of city graffiti.

Naomi Fertitta & Paul Aresu
New York: The Big City and its Little Neighborhoods
This photojournalism/guidebook hybrid illuminates New York's immigrant populations.

Josh Alan Friedman
Tales of Times Square
Sleaze and decay in the old days.

Nelson George *Hip Hop America*
The real history of hip hop, from Grandmaster Flash to Puff Daddy.

Jane Jacobs *The Death and Life of Great American Cities*
A hugely influential critique of modern urban planning.

Chuck Katz
Manhattan on Film 1 & 2
On-location walking tours.

Gillian McCain & Legs McNeil
Please Kill Me
An oral history of the punk scene.

Joseph Mitchell
Up in the Old Hotel
Quirky recollections of New York from the 1930s to the 1960s.

Thurston Moore & Byron Coley *No Wave*
Musicians reminisce about the downtown post-punk underground scene in this nostalgia trip co-edited by the Sonic Youth frontman.

Adrienne Onofri
Walking Brooklyn
Thirty tours illuminate the culture and history of the borough.

Sam Stephenson *The Jazz Loft Project: Photographs and Tapes of W Eugene Smith from 821 Sixth Avenue, 1957-1965*
Images and transcripts of conversations from the jazz-obsessed photographer's loft, which became a rehearsal space for some of the era's greatest musicians.

Judith Stonehill *New York's Unique & Unexpected Places*
Fifty special yet less-visited spots.

Time Out
1000 Things To Do in New York
Original and inspirational ideas to appeal to jaded residents and newly arrived visitors.

EB White *Here is New York*
A clear-eyed love letter to Gotham.

History

Herbert Asbury *The Gangs of New York: An Informal History of the Underworld*
A racy journalistic portrait of the city at the turn of the 19th century.

Robert A Caro *The Power Broker*
A biography of Robert Moses, New York's mid 20th-century master builder, and his chequered legacy.

Federal Writers' Project
The WPA Guide to New York City
A wonderful evocation of the 1930s by writers who were employed under FDR's New Deal.

Sanna Feirstein
Naming New York
How Manhattan places got named.

Tom Folsom
The Mad Ones: Crazy Joe Gallo and the Revolution at the Edge of the Underworld
Engaging ride though the world of the Mafia during the 1960s.

Eric Homberger *The Historical Atlas of New York City*
Through maps, photographs, illustrations and essays, this hefty volume charts the metropolis's 400-year heritage.

Clifton Hood *722 Miles: The Building of the Subways and How They Transformed New York*
The birth of the world's longest rapid transit system.

Kenneth T Jackson (ed)
The Encyclopedia of New York City
An ambitious and useful reference guide.

David Levering Lewis
When Harlem Was in Vogue
A study of the Harlem Renaissance.

Jonathan Mahler *Ladies and Gentlemen, the Bronx is Burning*
A gritty snapshot of NYC in 1977.

Mitchell Pacelle *Empire*
The story of the fight to build the Empire State Building.

Clayton Patterson (ed)
Resistance
This collection of essays reflects on the Lower East Side's history as a radical hotbed.

Luc Sante *Low Life*
Opium dens and brothels in New York from the 1840s to the 1920s.

Russell Shorto *The Island at the Center of the World*
How the Dutch colony shaped Manhattan – and America.

Mike Wallace & Edwin G Burrows *Gotham: A History of New York City to 1898*
The first volume in a planned mammoth history of NYC.

Fiction & poetry

Kurt Andersen
Turn of the Century
Millennial Manhattan as seen through the eyes of media players.

Paul Auster
The New York Trilogy: City of Glass, Ghosts and *The Locked Room*
A search for the madness behind the method of Manhattan's grid.

Kevin Baker *Dreamland*
A poetic novel about Coney Island's glory days.

James A Baldwin
Another Country
Racism under the bohemian veneer of the 1960s.
Michael Chabon *The Amazing Adventures of Kavalier and Clay*
Jewish comic-book artists battling with crises of identity in the 1940s.
Ralph Ellison *Invisible Man*
Epic examination of race and racism in 1950s Harlem.
Jack Finney *Time and Again*
An illustrator travels back to 19th-century New York City.
Larry Kramer *Faggots*
A devastating satire of gay NYC.
Jonathan Lethem *Chronic City*
The author of *The Fortress of Solitude* packs his latest novel with pop-culture references.
Phillip Lopate (ed)
Writing New York
An excellent anthology of short stories, essays and poems.
Colum McCann
Let the Great World Spin
Interconnected stories set in 1970s New York.
Patrick McGrath *Trauma*
A first-person account of psychic decay that floats a critique of post-9/11 social and political amnesia.
Tim McLoughlin (ed)
Brooklyn Noir 1, 2 & 3
Second-borough crime tales.
Frank O'Hara *The Collected Poems of Frank O'Hara*
The great NYC poet found inspiration in his hometown.
Richard Price *Lush Life*
A contemporary murder story set on the Lower East Side.
David Schickler
Kissing in Manhattan
The lives of quirky tenants in a teeming Manhattan block.
Hubert Selby Jr
Last Exit to Brooklyn
Dockland degradation, circa 1950s.
Edith Wharton *Old New York*
Four novellas of 19th-century NYC.
Colson Whitehead *The Colossus of New York: A City in 13 Parts*
A lyrical tribute to city life.
Tom Wolfe
The Bonfire of the Vanities
Rich/poor, black/white – an unmatched slice of 1980s NYC.

FILM

Annie Hall (1977)
Woody Allen and Diane Keaton in this valentine to Manhattan.
Breakfast at Tiffany's (1961)
Audrey Hepburn as the cash-poor, time-rich socialite Holly Golightly.
Dog Day Afternoon (1975)
Al Pacino is a Brooklyn bank robber in Sidney Lumet's classic.
Do the Right Thing (1989)
Racial strife in Brooklyn's Bedford-Stuyvesant in Spike Lee's drama.
The French Connection (1971)
As detective Jimmy 'Popeye' Doyle, Gene Hackman chases down drug traffickers in William Friedkin's much-imitated thriller.
The Godfather (1972), **The Godfather: Part II** (1974)
Francis Ford Coppola's brilliant commentary on capitalism in America is told through the violent saga of Italian gangsters.
Mean Streets (1973)
Robert De Niro and Harvey Keitel shine as small-time Little Italy hoods in Martin Scorsese's breakthrough film.
Midnight Cowboy (1969)
Street creatures 'Ratso' Rizzo and Joe Buck face an unforgiving Times Square in John Schlesinger's darkly amusing classic.
Spider-Man (2002)
The comic book web-slinger from Forest Hills comes to life in Sam Raimi's pitch-perfect crowd-pleaser.
Superfly (1972)
Blaxploitation classic, propelled by legendary Curtis Mayfield soundtrack.
The Taking of Pelham 1 2 3 (2009)
The plot premise may be flawed – in this Denzel Washington/John Travolta remake, as well as in the 1974 original – but it stirs up strap-hangers' darkest fears.
Taxi Driver (1976)
Robert De Niro is a crazed cabbie who sees all of New York as a den of iniquity in Scorsese's drama.

MUSIC

Beastie Boys
'No Sleep Till Brooklyn'
The hip-hop troupe's on-the-road anthem exudes local pride
Leonard Cohen
'Chelsea Hotel #2'
Of all the songs inspired by the Chelsea, this bleak vision of doomed love is on a level of its own.
Jay-Z with Alicia Keys
"Empire State of Mind'
The Brooklyn rapper's ode to NYC is a 21st-century rival to Sinatra's classic anthem.
Billy Joel
'New York State of Mind'
This heartfelt ballad exemplifies the city's effect on the souls of its visitors and residents.
Charles Mingus *Mingus Ah Um*
Mingus brought the gospel to jazz and created an NYC masterpiece.
Public Enemy *It Takes a Nation of Millions to Hold Us Back*
A ferociously political tour de force from the Long Island hip hop group whose own Chuck D once called rap 'the CNN for black America'.
The Ramones *Ramones*
Four Queens roughnecks, a few buzzsaw chords, and musings on turning tricks and sniffing glue – it transformed rock 'n' roll.
Frank Sinatra 'Theme from *New York, New York*'
Ol' Blue Eyes' bombastic love letter melts those little-town blues.
Bruce Springsteen
'My City of Ruins'
The Boss praises the city's resilience post-September 11 with this track from *The Rising*.
The Strokes *Is This It*
The effortlessly hip debut of this hometown band garnered praise and worldwide attention.
The Velvet Underground
The Velvet Underground & Nico
Their first album is still the gold standard of downtown cool.
Wu Tang Clan
Few artists embodied '90s hip hop like the Wu, its members – RZA, GZA and the late ODB among them – coining a cinematic rap aesthetic that influences artists to this day.

WEBSITES

www.timeout.com/newyork
The recently relaunched *Time Out New York* website covers all the city has to offer, from upcoming museum exhibitions, shows and events to the latest shop openings, plus thousands of restaurant and bar reviews written by our critics.
www.clubplanet.com
Follow the city's nocturnal scene and buy tickets to big events.
www.forgotten-ny.com
Discover old New York here.
www.hopstop.com
Works out door-to-door directions on public transportation.
www.manhattanusersguide.com
An insiders' guide to what's going on around town.
www.mta.info
Subway and bus service news.
www.nyc.gov
City Hall's official New York City website has lots of useful links.
www.nycgo.com
The official New York City tourism organisation provides information on sights, attractions, hotels, restaurants, shops and more.
www.nytimes.com
'All the News That's Fit to Print' from *The New York Times* (limited access for non-subscribers).

Index

INDEX

INDEX

INDEX

INDEX

Advertisers' Index

Please refer to the relevant pages for contact details.

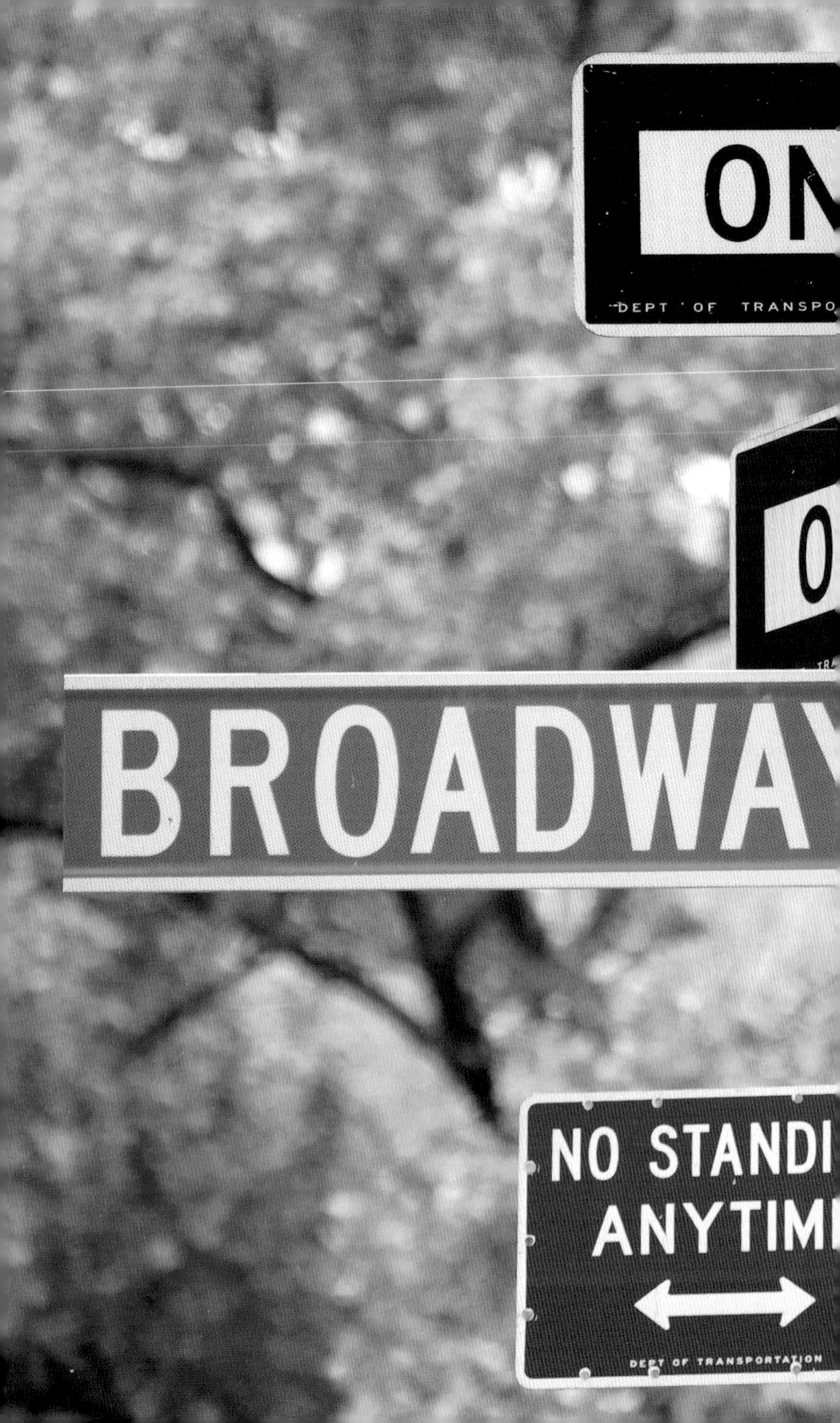
ON
DEPT OF TRANSPO
BROADWA
NO STANDI
ANYTIM
DEPT OF TRANSPORTATION

Maps

Hudson River
East River
TRIBECA
CHINATOWN
FINANCIAL DISTRICT
BATTERY PARK CITY
WEST SIDE HWY
HUDSON ST
WEST BROADWAY
CHURCH ST
BROADWAY
CENTRE ST
PARK ROW
VESEY ST
WALL ST
WHITEHALL ST
FRANKLIN D ROOSEVELT DR
BROOKLYN BRIDGE
MANHATTAN BRIDGE
BROOKLYN BATTERY TUNNEL
CHAMBERS ST
MURRAY ST
BARCLAY ST
PARK PL
READE ST
DUANE ST
THOMAS ST
WORTH ST
LEONARD ST
FRANKLIN ST
WHITE ST
WALKER ST
CORTLANDT AL
LAFAYETTE ST
NORTH MOORE ST
HARRISON ST
GREENWICH ST
STAPLE ST
JAY ST
BEACH ST
HUBERT ST
ERICSSON PL
WARREN ST
PARK PL W
RIVER TERR
VESEY PL
NORTH END AVE
VESEY ST
LIBERTY ST
CEDAR ST
ALBANY ST
CARLISLE ST
THAMES ST
RECTOR PL
RECTOR ST
S END AVE
W THAMES ST
WASHINGTON ST
GREENWICH ST
THIRD PL
SECOND PL
FIRST PL
MORRIS ST
WEST ST
BATTERY PL
CORTLANDT ST
DEY ST
FULTON ST
ANN ST
BEEKMAN ST
SPRUCE ST
FRANKFORT ST
GOLD ST
JOHN ST
PLATT ST
MAIDEN LN
NASSAU ST
PINE ST
WILLIAM ST
EXCHANGE PL
NEW ST
BROAD ST
BEAVER ST
MARKETFIELD ST
STONE ST
BRIDGE ST
MOORE ST
PEARL ST
WATER ST
HANOVER SQ
HANOVER ST
OLD SLIP
COENTIES SLIP
CUYLER'S SLIP
GOUVERNEUR LN
DEPEYSTER ST
FRONT ST
FLETCHER ST
PECK SLIP
DOVER ST
ST JAMES PL
OLIVER ST
CATHERINE ST
MONROE ST
MARKET ST
HENRY ST
CHATHAM SQ
DIVISION ST
FORSYTH ST
PIKE ST
MADISON ST
RUTGERS ST
JEFFERSON ST
CHERRY ST
CLINTON ST
MONTGOMERY ST
SOUTH ST
WAGNER PL
AVE OF THE FINEST
HAMILL PL
CARDINAL HAYES PL
MOSCO ST
PELL ST
BAYARD ST
ST ANDREWS PL
FOLEY SQ
Columbus Park
City Hall Park
City Hall
Rutgers Park
Battery Park
Bowling Green
Brookfield Place
1 World Trade Center
National September 11 Memorial & Museum
St Paul's Chapel
Federal Reserve Bank
Trinity Wall St
NY Stock Exchange
Museum of American Finance
Fraunces Tavern
National Museum of the American Indian
Skyscraper Museum
Museum of Jewish Heritage
Castle Clinton
Ferry to Statue of Liberty
Staten Island Ferry Terminal
South Street Seaport Museum
South Street Seaport
African Burial Ground
First Shearith Israel Graveyard
Confucius Plaza
Eldridge St Synagogue
34
33
32
31
C
D
E
F
G
H
0
300 m
300 yds
© Copyright Time Out Group 2014
See p406

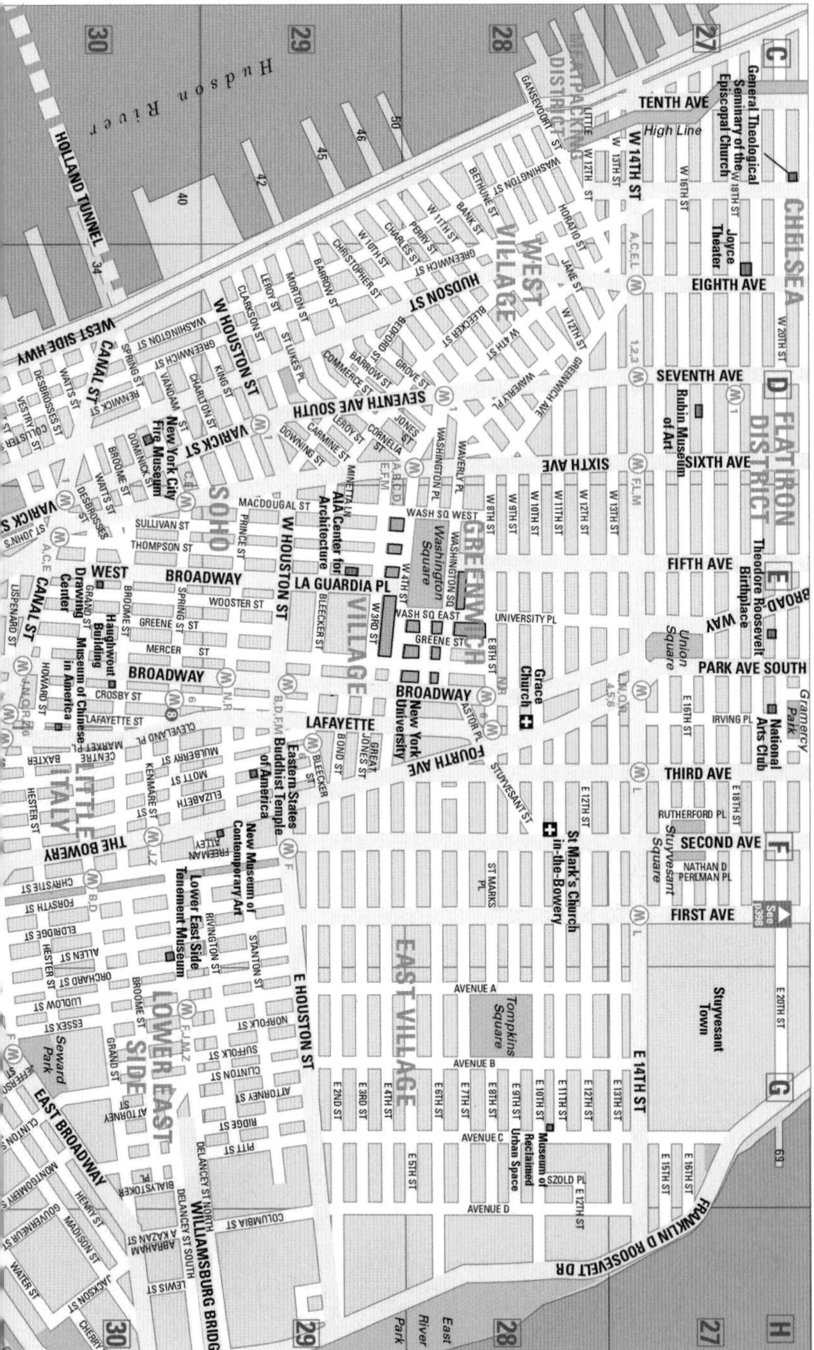
Hudson River
HOLLAND TUNNEL
WEST SIDE HWY
MEATPACKING DISTRICT
CHELSEA
FLATIRON DISTRICT
WEST VILLAGE
GREENWICH VILLAGE
SOHO
LITTLE ITALY
EAST VILLAGE
LOWER EAST SIDE
TENTH AVE
EIGHTH AVE
SEVENTH AVE
SIXTH AVE
FIFTH AVE
PARK AVE SOUTH
THIRD AVE
SECOND AVE
FIRST AVE
W 14TH ST
E 14TH ST
W HOUSTON ST
E HOUSTON ST
HUDSON ST
SEVENTH AVE SOUTH
VARICK ST
CANAL ST
BROADWAY
LA GUARDIA PL
LAFAYETTE
FOURTH AVE
THE BOWERY
EAST BROADWAY
WILLIAMSBURG BRIDGE
FRANKLIN D ROOSEVELT DR
High Line
General Theological Seminary of the Episcopal Church
Joyce Theater
Rubin Museum of Art
Theodore Roosevelt Birthplace
National Arts Club
Union Square
Gramercy Park
Washington Square
Tompkins Square
Stuyvesant Square
Stuyvesant Town
Seward Park
East River Park
New York City Fire Museum
AIA Center for Architecture
Drawing Center
Haughwout Building
Museum of Chinese in America
Grace Church
New York University
Eastern States Buddhist Temple of America
New Museum of Contemporary Art
Lower East Side Tenement Museum
St Mark's Church in-the-Bowery
Museum of Reclaimed Urban Space
See p398

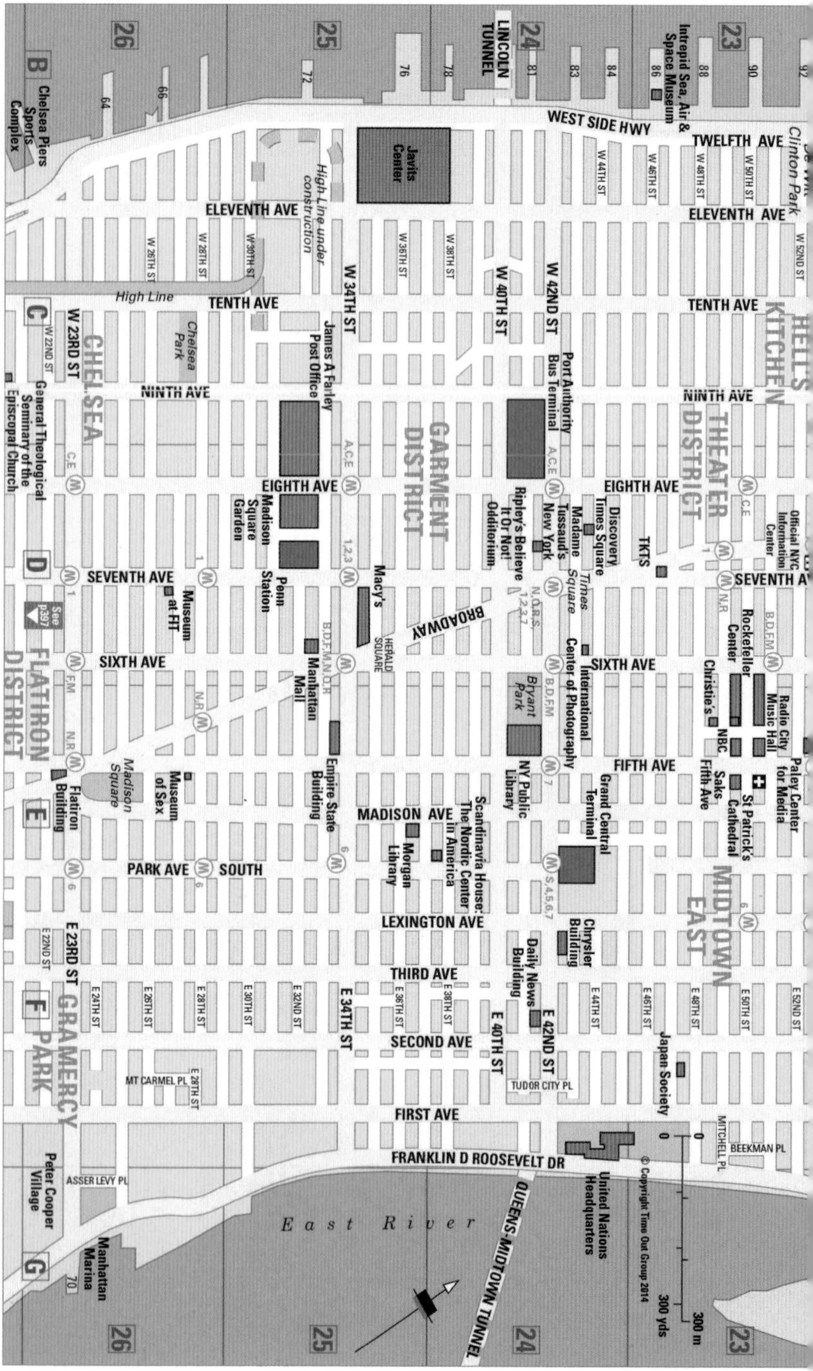

Clinton Park
Intrepid Sea, Air & Space Museum
LINCOLN TUNNEL
WEST SIDE HWY
TWELFTH AVE
Javits Center
High Line under construction
High Line
ELEVENTH AVE
TENTH AVE
NINTH AVE
EIGHTH AVE
SEVENTH AVE
SIXTH AVE
FIFTH AVE
MADISON AVE
PARK AVE SOUTH
LEXINGTON AVE
THIRD AVE
SECOND AVE
FIRST AVE
FRANKLIN D ROOSEVELT DR
BROADWAY
W 22ND ST
W 23RD ST
W 26TH ST
W 28TH ST
W 30TH ST
W 34TH ST
W 36TH ST
W 38TH ST
W 40TH ST
W 42ND ST
W 44TH ST
W 46TH ST
W 48TH ST
W 50TH ST
W 52ND ST
E 22ND ST
E 23RD ST
E 24TH ST
E 26TH ST
E 28TH ST
E 30TH ST
E 32ND ST
E 34TH ST
E 36TH ST
E 38TH ST
E 40TH ST
E 42ND ST
E 44TH ST
E 46TH ST
E 48TH ST
E 50TH ST
E 52ND ST
MT CARMEL PL
TUDOR CITY PL
MITCHELL PL
BEEKMAN PL
ASSER LEVY PL
HELL'S KITCHEN
THEATER DISTRICT
GARMENT DISTRICT
CHELSEA
FLATIRON DISTRICT
GRAMERCY PARK
MIDTOWN EAST
Chelsea Piers Sports Complex
Chelsea Park
General Theological Seminary of the Episcopal Church
James A Farley Post Office
Madison Square Garden
Penn Station
Museum at FIT
Macy's
HERALD SQUARE
Manhattan Mall
Empire State Building
Madison Square
Museum of Sex
Flatiron Building
Port Authority Bus Terminal
Ripley's Believe It Or Not! Odditorium
Madame Tussaud's New York
Discovery Times Square
Times Square
TKTS
International Center of Photography
Bryant Park
NY Public Library
Morgan Library
Scandinavia House: The Nordic Center in America
Grand Central Terminal
Chrysler Building
Daily News Building
Official NYC Information Center
Rockefeller Center
Radio City Music Hall
Christie's
NBC
Saks Fifth Ave
St Patrick's Cathedral
Paley Center for Media
Japan Society
United Nations Headquarters
QUEENS-MIDTOWN TUNNEL
East River
Peter Cooper Village
Manhattan Marina
See p397
© Copyright Time Out Group 2014
300 yds
300 m
B
C
D
E
F
G
23
24
25
26

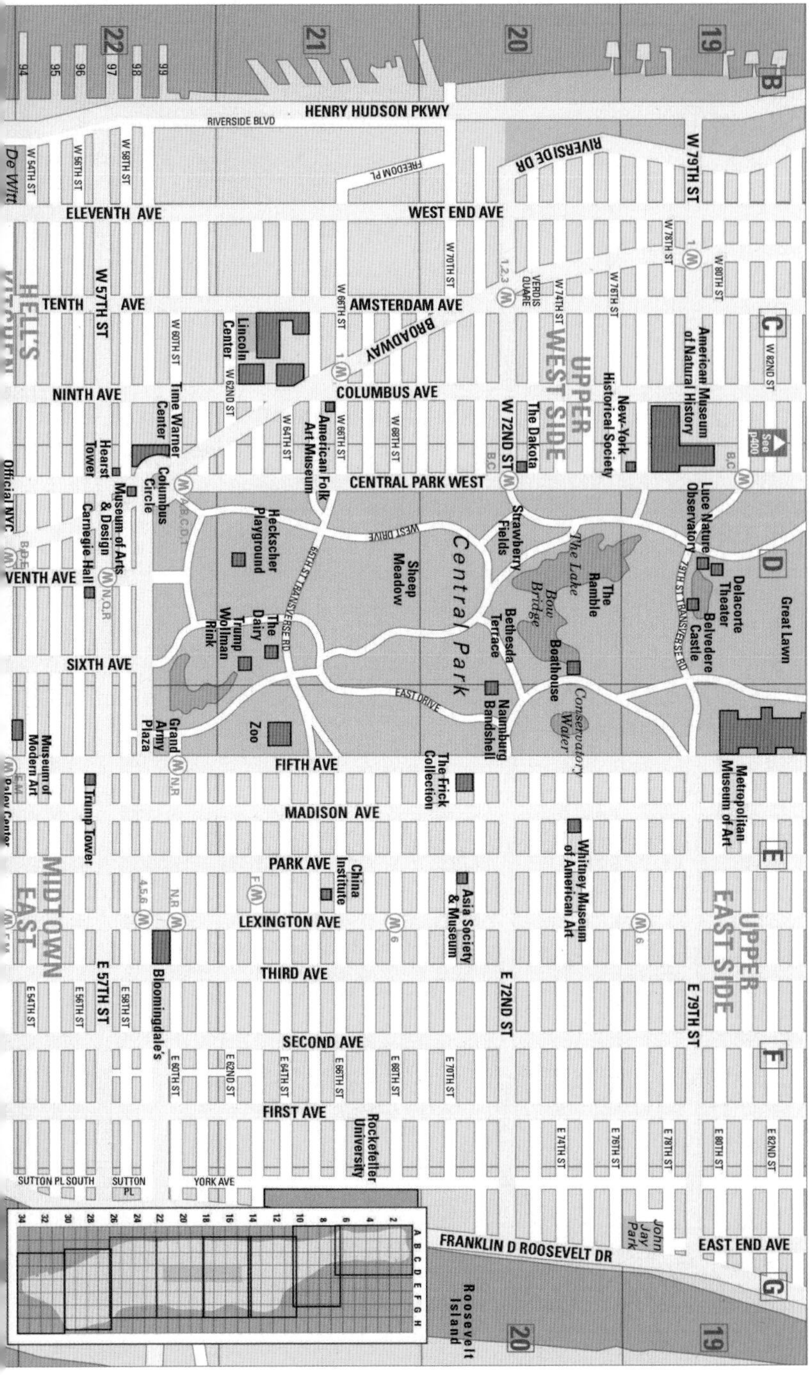
HENRY HUDSON PKWY
RIVERSIDE BLVD
RIVERSIDE DR
FREEDOM PL
W 79TH ST
W 54TH ST
W 56TH ST
W 58TH ST
De Witt
ELEVENTH AVE
WEST END AVE
W 70TH ST
W 78TH ST
W 80TH ST
VERDI SQUARE
W 74TH ST
W 76TH ST
W 66TH ST
W 57TH ST
HELL'S KITCHEN
TENTH AVE
AMSTERDAM AVE
BROADWAY
Lincoln Center
W 60TH ST
W 62ND ST
UPPER WEST SIDE
W 82ND ST
American Museum of Natural History
New-York Historical Society
NINTH AVE
COLUMBUS AVE
The Dakota
W 72ND ST
Time Warner Center
W 64TH ST
W 66TH ST
American Folk Art Museum
W 68TH ST
See p400
Hearst Tower
Columbus Circle
CENTRAL PARK WEST
Official NYC
Museum of Arts & Design
Carnegie Hall
Heckscher Playground
WEST DRIVE
Strawberry Fields
Luce Nature Observatory
Sheep Meadow
Central Park
The Lake
The Ramble
79TH ST TRANSVERSE RD
Delacorte Theater
Great Lawn
SEVENTH AVE
65TH ST TRANSVERSE RD
Bow Bridge
Belvedere Castle
The Dairy
Trump Wollman Rink
Bethesda Terrace
SIXTH AVE
Boathouse
EAST DRIVE
Conservatory Water
Naumburg Bandshell
Grand Army Plaza
Zoo
Museum of Modern Art
FIFTH AVE
The Frick Collection
Metropolitan Museum of Art
Trump Tower
MADISON AVE
Whitney Museum of American Art
MIDTOWN EAST
PARK AVE
China Institute
UPPER EAST SIDE
Asia Society & Museum
LEXINGTON AVE
Bloomingdale's
THIRD AVE
E 54TH ST
E 56TH ST
E 57TH ST
E 58TH ST
E 72ND ST
E 79TH ST
SECOND AVE
E 60TH ST
E 62ND ST
E 64TH ST
E 66TH ST
E 68TH ST
E 70TH ST
FIRST AVE
Rockefeller University
E 74TH ST
E 76TH ST
E 78TH ST
E 80TH ST
E 82ND ST
SUTTON PL SOUTH
SUTTON PL
YORK AVE
John Jay Park
FRANKLIN D ROOSEVELT DR
EAST END AVE
Roosevelt Island
B
C
D
E
F
G
19
20
21
22

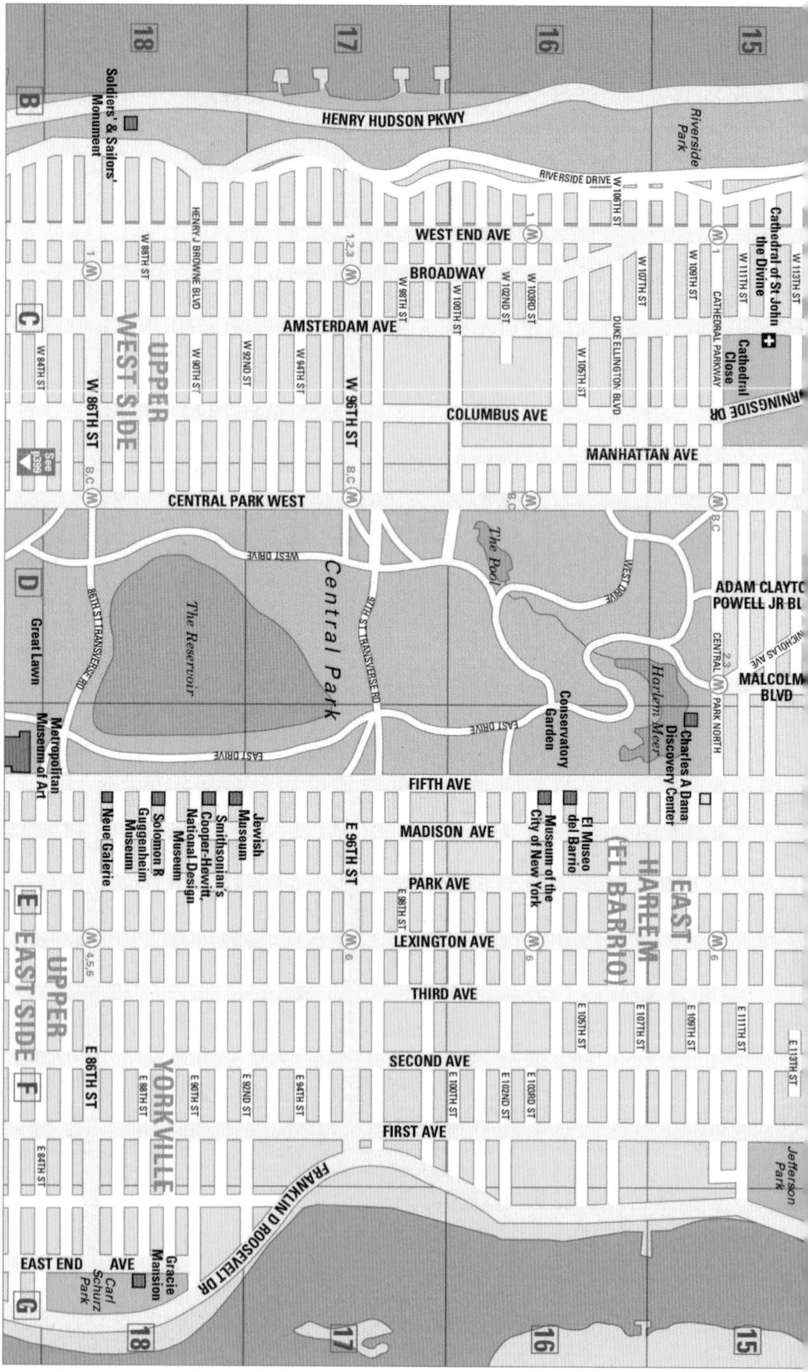
HENRY HUDSON PKWY
Riverside Park
Soldiers' & Sailors' Monument
RIVERSIDE DRIVE
Cathedral of St John the Divine
Cathedral Close
CATHEDRAL PARKWAY
WEST END AVE
BROADWAY
AMSTERDAM AVE
COLUMBUS AVE
MANHATTAN AVE
CENTRAL PARK WEST
UPPER WEST SIDE
W 84TH ST
W 86TH ST
W 88TH ST
HENRY J BROWNE BLVD
W 90TH ST
W 92ND ST
W 94TH ST
W 96TH ST
W 98TH ST
W 100TH ST
W 102ND ST
W 103RD ST
W 105TH ST
W 106TH ST
W 107TH ST
DUKE ELLINGTON BLVD
W 109TH ST
W 111TH ST
W 113TH ST
MORNINGSIDE DR
See p399
Central Park
The Reservoir
The Pool
WEST DRIVE
EAST DRIVE
86TH ST TRANSVERSE RD
97TH ST TRANSVERSE RD
Great Lawn
Conservatory Garden
Harlem Meer
Charles A Dana Discovery Center
ADAM CLAYTON POWELL JR BLVD
ST NICHOLAS AVE
CENTRAL PARK NORTH
MALCOLM X BLVD
Metropolitan Museum of Art
FIFTH AVE
MADISON AVE
PARK AVE
LEXINGTON AVE
THIRD AVE
SECOND AVE
FIRST AVE
EAST END AVE
Neue Galerie
Solomon R Guggenheim Museum
Smithsonian's Cooper-Hewitt, National Design Museum
Jewish Museum
Museum of the City of New York
El Museo del Barrio
EAST HARLEM (EL BARRIO)
UPPER EAST SIDE
YORKVILLE
E 84TH ST
E 86TH ST
E 88TH ST
E 90TH ST
E 92ND ST
E 94TH ST
E 96TH ST
E 98TH ST
E 100TH ST
E 102ND ST
E 103RD ST
E 105TH ST
E 107TH ST
E 109TH ST
E 111TH ST
E 113TH ST
Jefferson Park
FRANKLIN D ROOSEVELT DR
Gracie Mansion
Carl Schurz Park
B
C
D
E
F
G
15
16
17
18

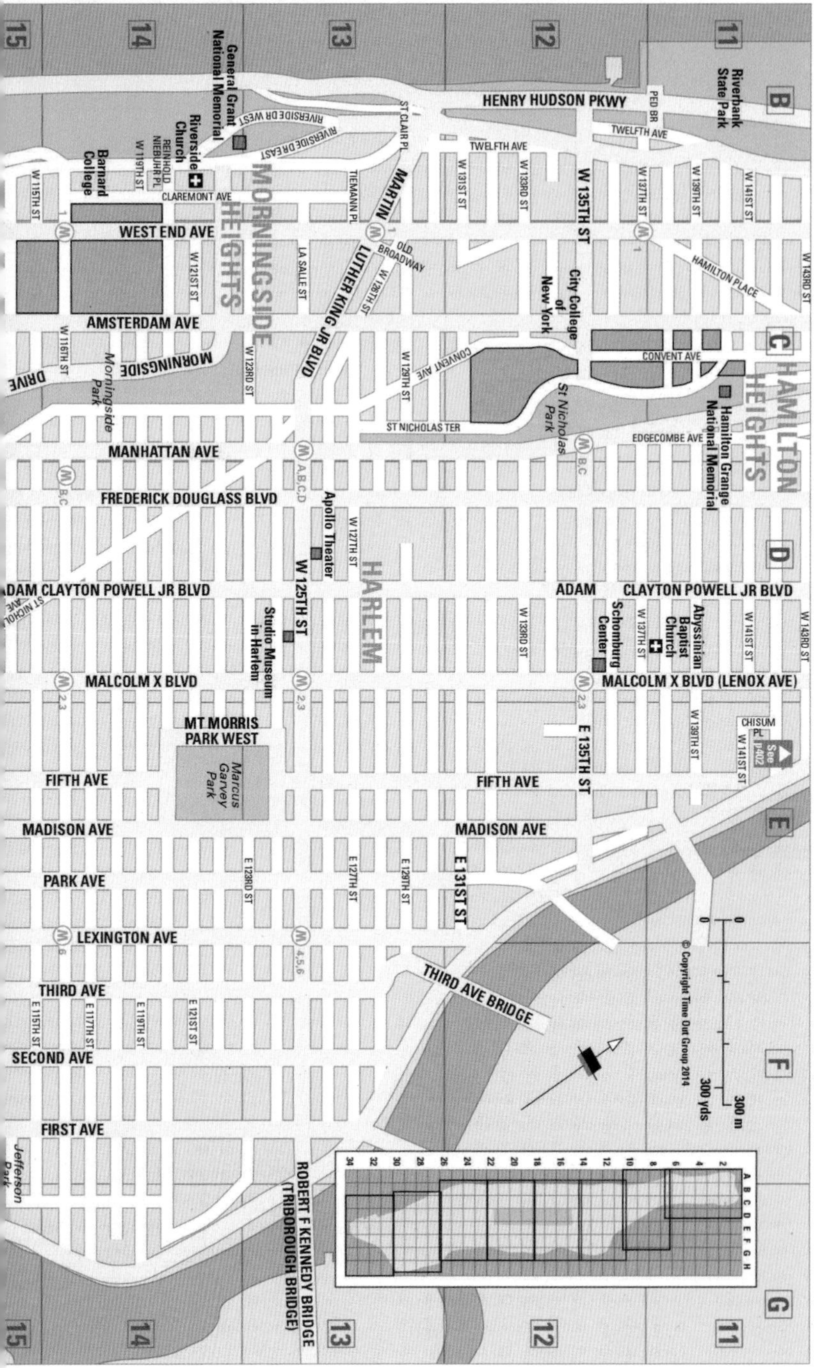
HENRY HUDSON PKWY
Riverbank State Park
PED BR
TWELFTH AVE
General Grant National Memorial
Riverside Church
RIVERSIDE DR WEST
RIVERSIDE DR EAST
ST CLAIR PL
REINHOLD NIEBUHR PL
W 119TH ST
Barnard College
CLAREMONT AVE
MORNINGSIDE HEIGHTS
TIEMANN PL
MARTIN LUTHER KING JR BLVD
W 131ST ST
W 133RD ST
W 135TH ST
W 137TH ST
W 139TH ST
W 141ST ST
W 143RD ST
W 115TH ST
WEST END AVE
OLD BROADWAY
HAMILTON PLACE
W 121ST ST
LA SALLE ST
W 128TH ST
City College of New York
AMSTERDAM AVE
W 116TH ST
MORNINGSIDE DRIVE
Morningside Park
W 123RD ST
W 129TH ST
CONVENT AVE
St Nicholas Park
HAMILTON HEIGHTS
Hamilton Grange National Memorial
ST NICHOLAS TER
EDGECOMBE AVE
MANHATTAN AVE
FREDERICK DOUGLASS BLVD
Apollo Theater
W 127TH ST
HARLEM
ADAM CLAYTON POWELL JR BLVD
ST NICHOLAS AVE
W 125TH ST
Studio Museum in Harlem
Schomburg Center
Abyssinian Baptist Church
MALCOLM X BLVD
MALCOLM X BLVD (LENOX AVE)
MT MORRIS PARK WEST
Marcus Garvey Park
CHISUM PL
See p402
E 135TH ST
FIFTH AVE
MADISON AVE
E 123RD ST
E 127TH ST
E 129TH ST
E 131ST ST
PARK AVE
LEXINGTON AVE
THIRD AVE BRIDGE
THIRD AVE
E 115TH ST
E 117TH ST
E 119TH ST
E 121ST ST
SECOND AVE
FIRST AVE
Jefferson Park
ROBERT F KENNEDY BRIDGE (TRIBOROUGH BRIDGE)
0 300 m
0 300 yds
© Copyright Time Out Group 2014

Hudson River
Riverbank State Park
HENRY HUDSON PKWY
RIVERSIDE DR WEST
RIVERSIDE DR EAST
RIVERSIDE DR
PED BR
Riverside Park
See p401
See p403
Hispanic Society of America
AUDUBON TERR
HAVEN AVE
FORT WASHINGTON AVE
ST NICHOLAS AVE
BROADWAY
W 143RD ST
W 145TH ST
W 147TH ST
W 149TH ST
W 151ST ST
W 153RD ST
W 155TH ST
W 157TH ST
W 159TH ST
W 161ST ST
W 163RD ST
W 165TH ST
W 167TH ST
W 169TH ST
W 171ST ST
AMSTERDAM AVE
CONVENT AVE
ST NICHOLAS AVE
ST NICHOLAS PL
MAHR CIRCLE
EDGECOMBE AVE
HARLEM RIVER DR
Morris-Jumel Mansion
Highbridge Park
HAMILTON HEIGHTS
Jackie Robinson Park
BROADHURST AVE
FREDERICK DOUGLASS BLVD
E 145TH ST
ADAM CLAYTON POWELL JR BLVD
145TH ST BRIDGE
© Copyright Time Out Group 2014
300 yds
300 m

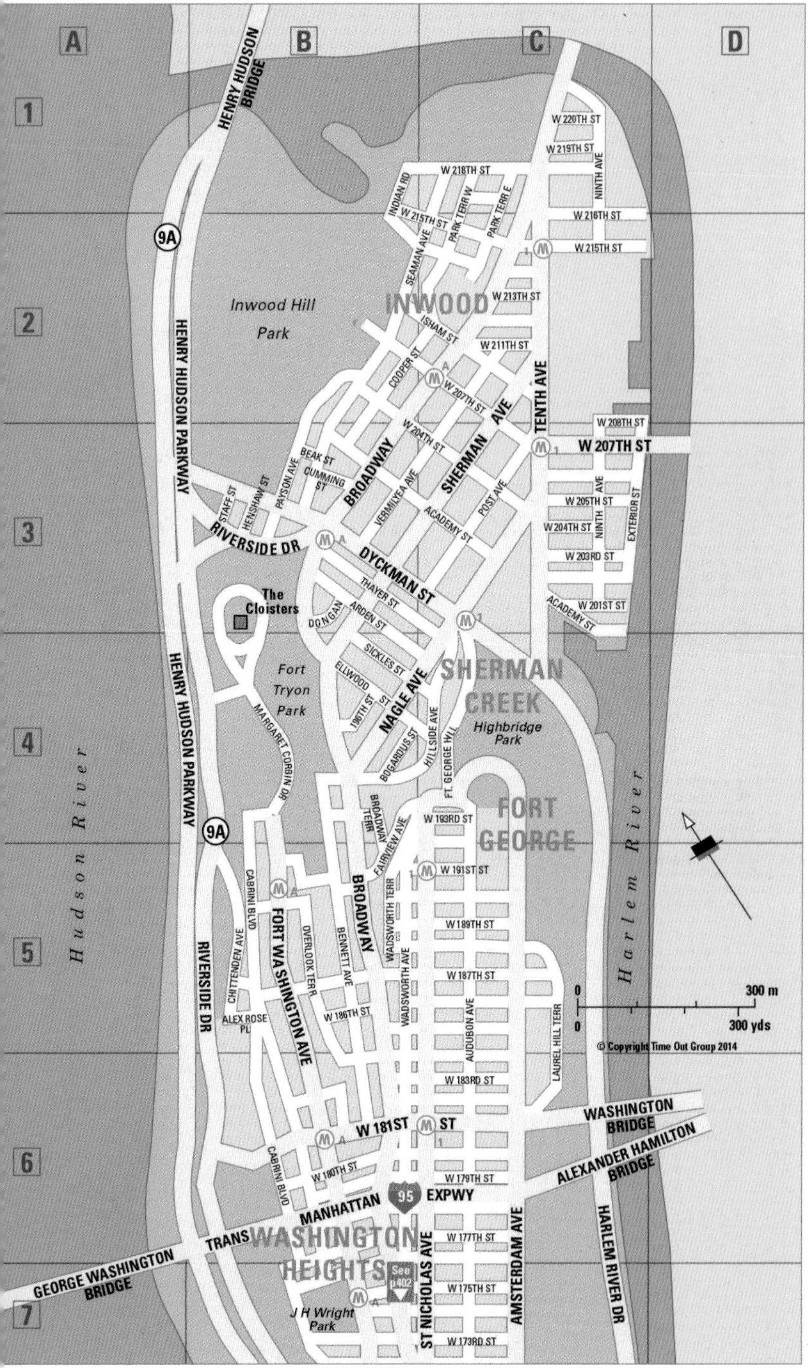
A
B
C
D
1
2
3
4
5
6
7
HENRY HUDSON BRIDGE
9A
Inwood Hill Park
INWOOD
W 220TH ST
W 219TH ST
W 218TH ST
NINTH AVE
INDIAN RD
W 215TH ST
PARK TERR W
PARK TERR E
W 216TH ST
W 215TH ST
SEAMAN AVE
W 213TH ST
ISHAM ST
W 211TH ST
COOPER ST
W 207TH ST
SHERMAN AVE
TENTH AVE
W 204TH ST
W 208TH ST
W 207TH ST
HENRY HUDSON PARKWAY
BEAK ST
CUMMING ST
BROADWAY
VERMILYEA AVE
PAYSON AVE
HENSHAW ST
STAFF ST
ACADEMY ST
POST AVE
W 205TH ST
W 204TH ST
NINTH AVE
EXTERIOR ST
RIVERSIDE DR
DYCKMAN ST
W 203RD ST
The Cloisters
THAYER ST
DONGAN
ARDEN ST
W 201ST ST
ACADEMY ST
Fort Tryon Park
SICKLES ST
ELLWOOD ST
196TH ST
NAGLE AVE
SHERMAN CREEK
HILLSIDE AVE
Highbridge Park
MARGARET CORBIN DR
BOGARDUS ST
FT. GEORGE HILL
Hudson River
Harlem River
BROADWAY TERR
FAIRVIEW AVE
W 193RD ST
FORT GEORGE
W 191ST ST
CABRINI BLVD
FORT WASHINGTON AVE
OVERLOOK TERR
BENNETT AVE
BROADWAY
WADSWORTH TERR
W 189TH ST
W 187TH ST
WADSWORTH AVE
AUDUBON AVE
CHITTENDEN AVE
W 186TH ST
ALEX ROSE PL
LAUREL HILL TERR
0
300 m
0
300 yds
© Copyright Time Out Group 2014
W 183RD ST
W 181ST ST
WASHINGTON BRIDGE
ALEXANDER HAMILTON BRIDGE
CABRINI BLVD
W 180TH ST
W 179TH ST
95
MANHATTAN EXPWY
TRANS
WASHINGTON HEIGHTS
W 177TH ST
AMSTERDAM AVE
HARLEM RIVER DR
GEORGE WASHINGTON BRIDGE
See p402
ST NICHOLAS AVE
W 175TH ST
J H Wright Park
W 173RD ST

MAPS

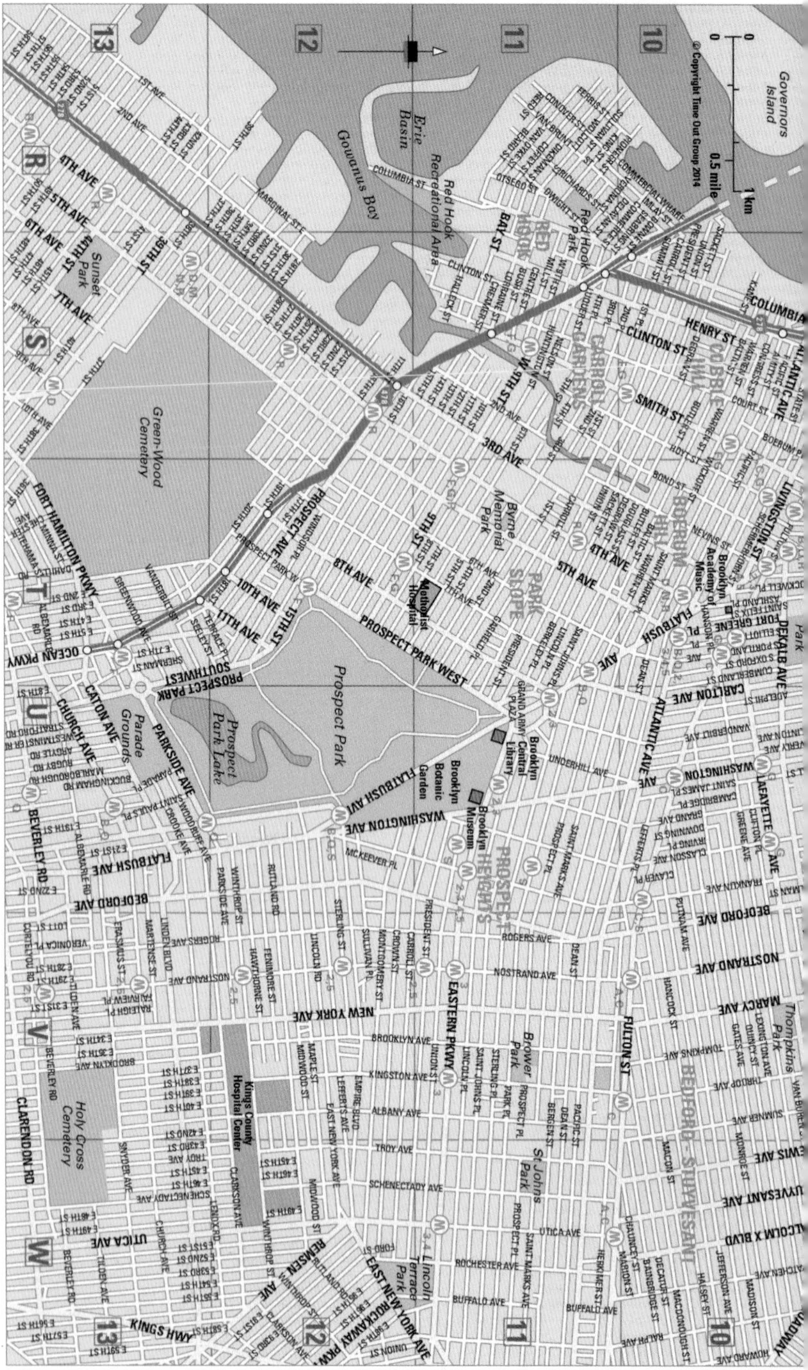
Governors Island
© Copyright Time Out Group 2014
0.5 mile
1 km
Erie Basin
Gowanus Bay
Red Hook Recreational Area
Red Hook Park
RED HOOK
CARROLL GARDENS
COBBLE HILL
BOERUM HILL
PARK SLOPE
PROSPECT HEIGHTS
FORT GREENE
BEDFORD - STUYVESANT
Green-Wood Cemetery
Sunset Park
Byrne Memorial Park
Methodist Hospital
Brooklyn Academy of Music
Prospect Park
Prospect Park Lake
Parade Grounds
Brooklyn Central Library
Brooklyn Botanic Garden
Brooklyn Museum
GRAND ARMY PLAZA
Brower Park
St Johns Park
Lincoln Terrace Park
Thompkins Park
Kings County Hospital Center
Holy Cross Cemetery
ATLANTIC AVE
FLATBUSH AVE
PROSPECT PARK WEST
PROSPECT PARK SOUTHWEST
OCEAN PKWY
FORT HAMILTON PKWY
EASTERN PKWY
FULTON ST
KINGS HWY
EAST NEW YORK AVE
NEW YORK AVE
WASHINGTON AVE
BEDFORD AVE
NOSTRAND AVE
UTICA AVE
CLARENDON RD
CHURCH AVE
CATON AVE
PARKSIDE AVE
BEVERLEY RD
4TH AVE
5TH AVE
6TH AVE
7TH AVE
8TH AVE
9TH ST
3RD AVE
SMITH ST
CLINTON ST
HENRY ST
COLUMBIA ST
LIVINGSTON ST
DEKALB AVE
LAFAYETTE AVE
MARCY AVE
MALCOLM X BLVD
REMSEN AVE
EAST NEW YORK AVE
10
11
12
13
R
S
T
U
V
W

Hudson River
East River
Upper Bay
Wallabout Bay
Newtown Creek
English Kills
Dutch Kills
BROOKLYN-BATTERY TUN
WHITEHALL
FINANCIAL DISTRICT
BATTERY PARK CITY
TRIBECA
WEST SIDE HWY
CHURCH ST
WEST BROADWAY
HUDSON ST
BROADWAY
CENTRE ST
PARK ROW
CHINATOWN
LITTLE ITALY
SOHO
GREENWICH VILLAGE
W HOUSTON ST
VARICK ST
AVENUE OF THE AMERICAS
FIFTH AVE
FLATIRON DISTRICT
LAFAYETTE
THE BOWERY
PARK AVE SOUTH
THIRD AVE
SECOND AVE
GRAMERCY PARK
E 23RD ST
W 14TH ST
E 14TH ST
E HOUSTON ST
EAST VILLAGE
LOWER EAST SIDE
EAST BROADWAY
WILLIAMSBURG BRIDGE
FRANKLIN D ROOSEVELT DR
FRANKLIN D ROOSEVELT DR
BROOKLYN BRIDGE
MANHATTAN BRIDGE
Brooklyn Bridge Park
DUMBO
Industrial Park
Brooklyn Navy Yard
NASSAU ST
FLUSHING AVE
LEE AVE
WILLIAMSBURG
BEDFORD AVE
BERRY ST
DRIGGS AVE
MARCY AVE
RODNEY ST
UNION AVE
GRAND STREET EXT
McCarren Park
NASSAU AVE
GREENPOINT
MCGUINNESS BLVD
PULASKI BRIDGE
HUMBOLDT ST
McGolrick Park
NORMAN AVE
KINGSLAND AVE
GREENPOINT AVE
BRIDGEWATER ST
VANDERVOORT AVE
Cooper Park
METROPOLITAN AVE
GRAND ST
BUSHWICK AVE
BROADWAY
BUSHWICK
MYRTLE AVE
FLUSHING AVE
NOSTRAND AVE
MARCY AVE
PARK AVE
KOSCIUSZKO BRIDGE
Calvary Cemetery
LAUREL HILL BLVD
See pp396-403
See p406

MAPS

U
V
W
X
Y
Z
1
2
3
4
5
6
7
8
9
0
1 km
0
0.5 mile
© Copyright Time Out Group 2014
Central Park
EAST HARLEM
Jefferson Park
East River
ROBERT F. KENNEDY BRIDGE (TRIBOROUGH BRIDGE)
Hell Gate
Astoria Park
YORKVILLE
UPPER EAST SIDE
Carl Schurz Park
John Jay Park
Roosevelt Island
Bowery Bay
LaGuardia Airport
Socrates Sculpture Park
Noguchi Museum
ASTORIA
St Michael's Cemetery
JACKSON HEIGHTS
ED KOCH QUEENSBORO BRIDGE
Queens Bridge Park
LONG ISLAND CITY
Museum of the Moving Image
Sunnyside Yard
Greenland Park
WOODSIDE
See pp396-403
MoMA PS1
SUNNYSIDE
See pp404-405
Dutch Kills
New Calvary Cemetery
Newtown Creek
Calvary Cemetery
Mount Zion Cemetery
MIDDLE VILLAGE
GREENPOINT
MASPETH
McCarren Park
English Kills
Mt Olivet Cemetery
Linden Hill Cemetery
Glen Ridge Park
Lutheran Cemetery
FIFTH AVE
PARK AVE
LEXINGTON AVE
THIRD AVE
SECOND AVE
FIRST AVE
E 96TH ST
E 86TH ST
E 79TH ST
E 72ND ST
EAST END AVE
FDR DRIVE
VERNON BLVD
21ST ST
34TH AVE
31ST AVE
STEINWAY ST
ASTORIA BLVD
DITMARS BLVD
31ST ST
MAIN AVE
NORTHERN BLVD
ROOSEVELT AVE
BROADWAY
QUEENS BLVD
SKILLMAN AVE
43RD AVE
48TH ST
39TH ST
VAN DAM ST
THOMSON AVE
JACKSON AVE
49TH AVE
WOODSIDE AVE
45TH AVE
GREENPOINT AVE
MCGUINNESS BLVD
NORMAN AVE
HUMBOLDT ST
LOMBARDY ST
KINGSLAND AVE
VANDERVOORT AVE
GRAND ST
MASPETH AVE
METROPOLITAN AVE
FLUSHING AVE
FRESH POND RD
MAURICE AVE
69TH ST
GRAND AVE
ELIOT AVE
CENTRAL AVE
BEDFORD AVE
DRIGGS AVE
BERRY ST
MARCY AVE
RODNEY ST
UNION AVE
MANHATTAN AVE
BUSHWICK AVE
LEE AVE
61ST ST
58TH ST
82ND ST
81ST ST

Street Index

MANHATTAN

map pp396-403

BROOKLYN

map pp404-405

STREET INDEX

QUEENS

map p406

STREET INDEX

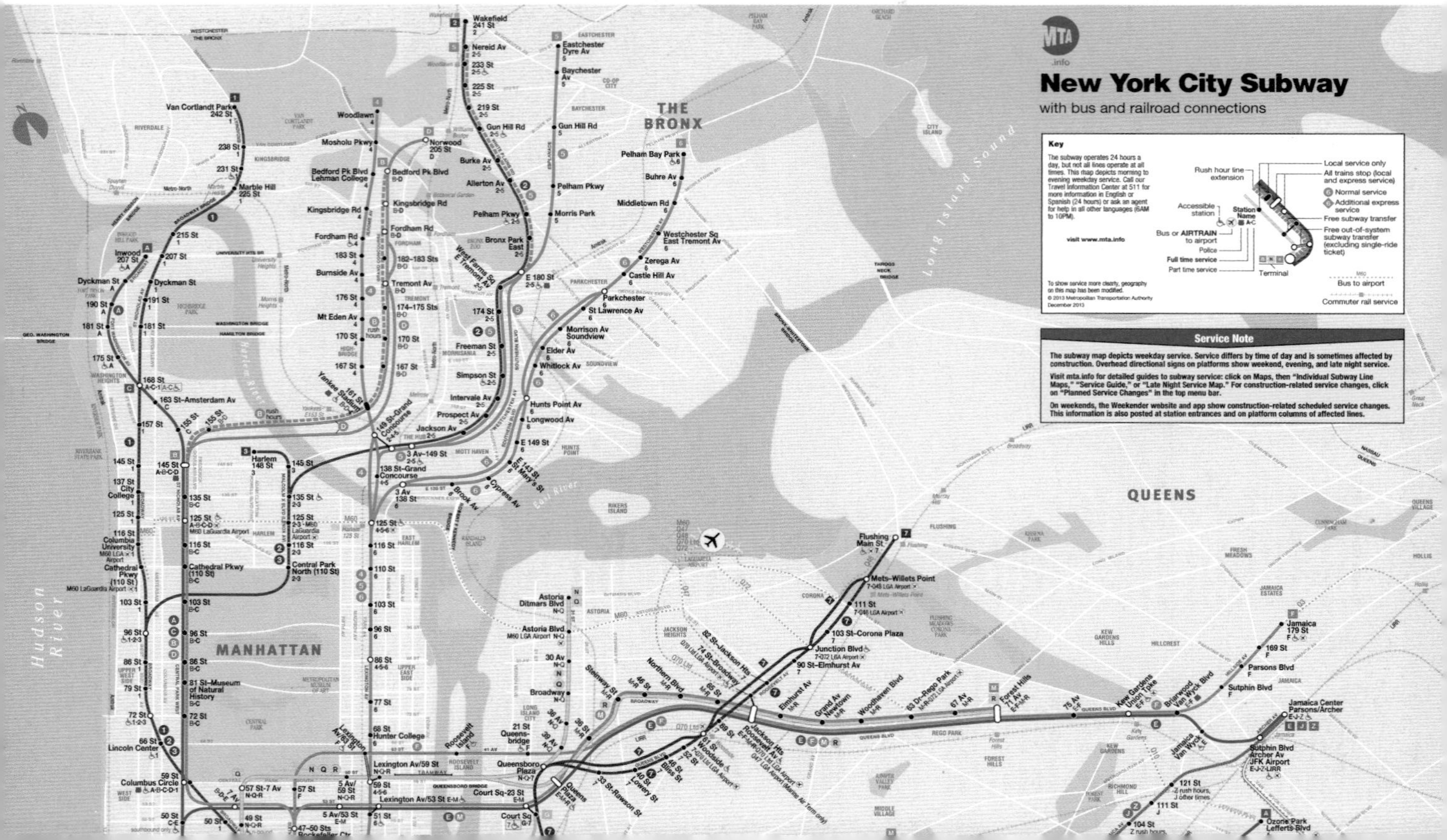
MTA .info
New York City Subway
with bus and railroad connections
Key
The subway operates 24 hours a day, but not all lines operate at all times. This map depicts morning to evening weekday service. Call our Travel Information Center at 511 for more information in English or Spanish (24 hours) or ask an agent for help in all other languages (6AM to 10PM).
visit www.mta.info
To show service more clearly, geography on this map has been modified.
© 2013 Metropolitan Transportation Authority
December 2013
Rush hour line extension
Accessible station
Station Name
Bus or AIRTRAIN to airport
Police
Full time service
Part time service
Terminal
Local service only
All trains stop (local and express service)
Normal service
Additional express service
Free subway transfer
Free out-of-system subway transfer (excluding single-ride ticket)
Bus to airport
Commuter rail service
Service Note
The subway map depicts weekday service. Service differs by time of day and is sometimes affected by construction. Overhead directional signs on platforms show weekend, evening, and late night service.
Visit mta.info for detailed guides to subway service: click on Maps, then "Individual Subway Line Maps," "Service Guide," or "Late Night Service Map." For construction-related service changes, click on "Planned Service Changes" in the top menu bar.
On weekends, the Weekender website and app show construction-related scheduled service changes. This information is also posted at station entrances and on platform columns of affected lines.
THE BRONX
QUEENS
MANHATTAN
Long Island Sound
Hudson River
Harlem River
East River

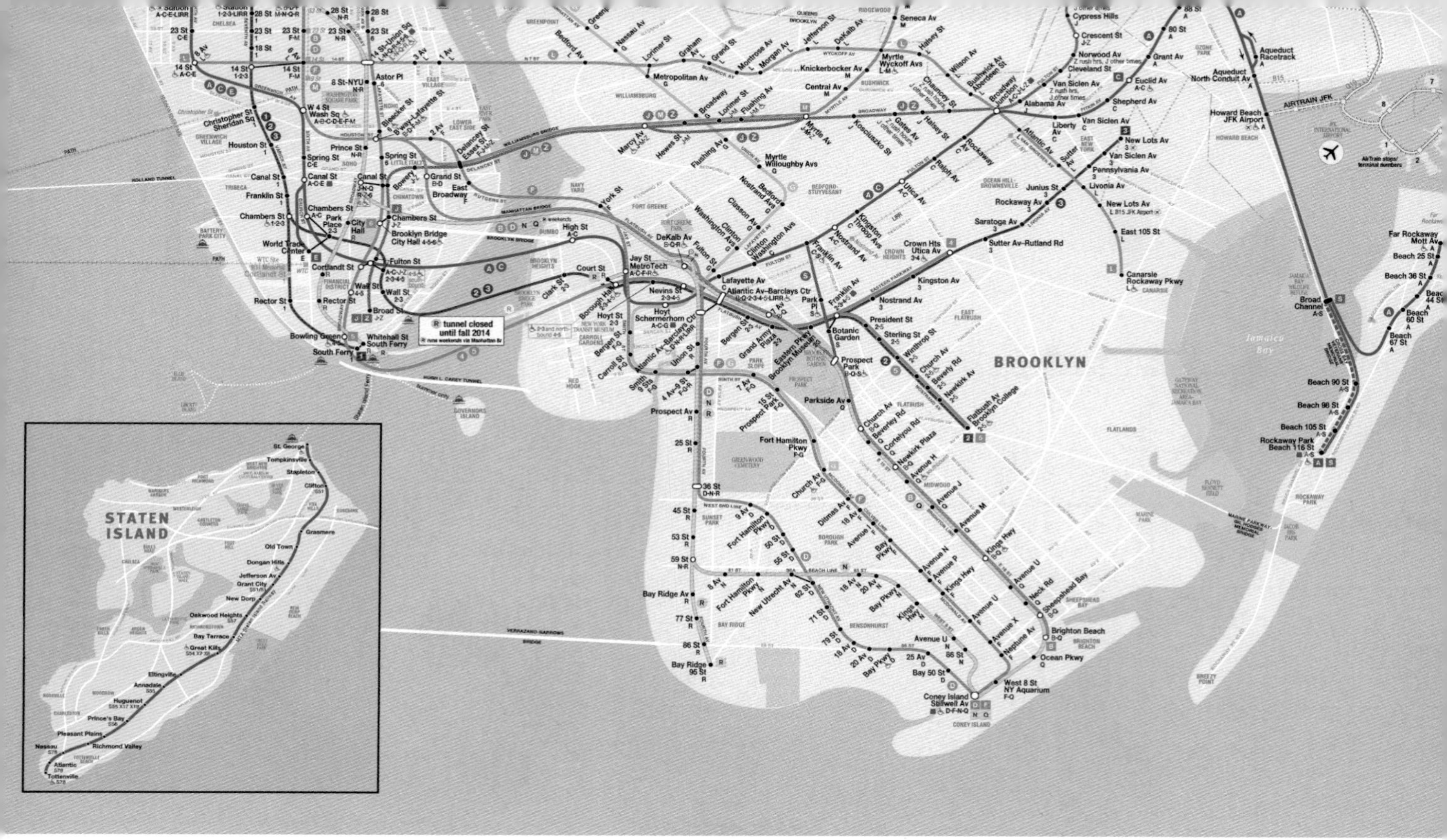
BROOKLYN
STATEN ISLAND
tunnel closed until fall 2014
AIRTRAIN JFK
Howard Beach JFK Airport
Jamaica Bay
Broad Channel
Far Rockaway Mott Av
Coney Island Stillwell Av
Brighton Beach
Bay Ridge 95 St
Atlantic Av–Barclays Ctr
Jay St MetroTech
Broadway Junction
Prospect Park
Botanic Garden
Flatbush Av Brooklyn College
Canarsie Rockaway Pkwy
Crown Hts Utica Av
Myrtle Wyckoff Avs
World Trade Center
South Ferry
Whitehall St South Ferry
Bowling Green
Fulton St
Chambers St
Canal St
14 St-Union Sq
St. George
Tottenville
VERRAZANO NARROWS BRIDGE
MANHATTAN BRIDGE
BROOKLYN BRIDGE
WILLIAMSBURG BRIDGE
HOLLAND TUNNEL
HUGH L. CAREY TUNNEL
MARINE PARKWAY GIL HODGES MEMORIAL BRIDGE

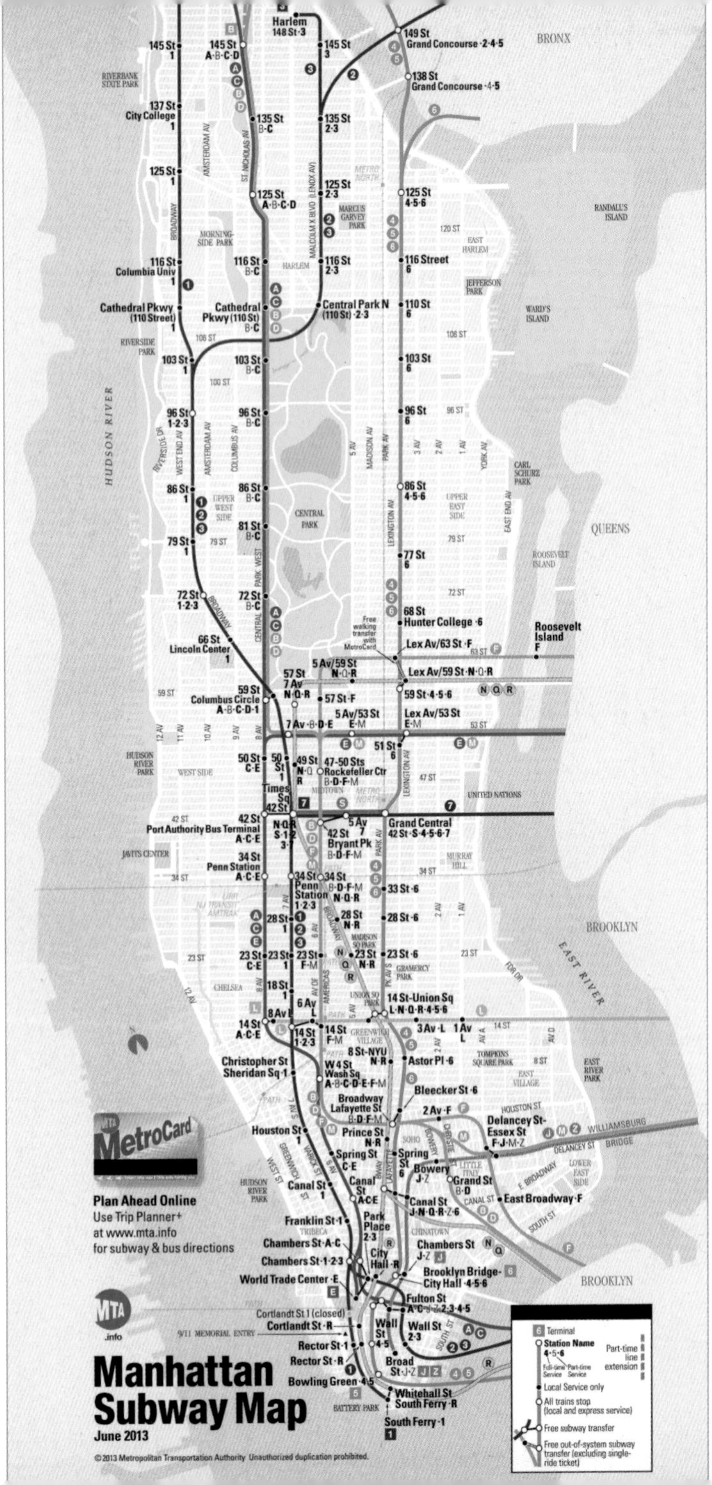
Manhattan Subway Map
June 2013
© 2013 Metropolitan Transportation Authority. Unauthorized duplication prohibited.
MetroCard
Plan Ahead Online
Use Trip Planner+
at www.mta.info
for subway & bus directions
MTA .info
Terminal
Station Name
4·5·6
Full-time Service
Part-time Service
Part-time line extension
Local Service only
All trains stop (local and express service)
Free subway transfer
Free out-of-system subway transfer (excluding single-ride ticket)
Harlem 148 St·3
145 St 1
145 St A·B·C·D
145 St 3
149 St Grand Concourse·2·4·5
138 St Grand Concourse·4·5
BRONX
137 St City College 1
135 St B·C
135 St 2·3
125 St 1
125 St A·B·C·D
125 St 2·3
125 St 4·5·6
116 St Columbia Univ 1
116 St B·C
116 St 2·3
116 Street 6
Cathedral Pkwy (110 Street) 1
Cathedral Pkwy (110 St) B·C
Central Park N (110 St)·2·3
110 St 6
103 St 1
103 St B·C
103 St 6
96 St 1·2·3
96 St B·C
96 St 6
86 St 1
86 St B·C
86 St 4·5·6
81 St B·C
79 St 1
77 St 6
72 St 1·2·3
72 St B·C
68 St Hunter College·6
66 St Lincoln Center 1
Lex Av/63 St·F
Roosevelt Island F
5 Av/59 St N·Q·R
Lex Av/59 St·N·Q·R
57 St 7 Av N·Q·R
57 St·F
59 St Columbus Circle A·B·C·D·1
59 St·4·5·6
5 Av/53 St E·M
Lex Av/53 St E·M
7 Av·B·D·E
51 St 6
50 St C·E
50 St 1
49 St N·Q·R
47-50 Sts Rockefeller Ctr B·D·F·M
Times Sq 42 St
42 St Port Authority Bus Terminal A·C·E
N·Q·R S·1·2 3·7
5 Av 7
42 St Bryant Pk B·D·F·M
Grand Central 42 St·S·4·5·6·7
34 St Penn Station A·C·E
34 St Penn Station 1·2·3
34 St B·D·F·M N·Q·R
33 St·6
28 St 1
28 St N·R
28 St·6
23 St C·E
23 St 1
23 St F·M
23 St N·R
23 St·6
18 St 1
14 St-Union Sq L·N·Q·R·4·5·6
6 Av L
8 Av L
14 St A·C·E
14 St 1·2·3
14 St F·M
3 Av·L
1 Av L
8 St-NYU N·R
Astor Pl·6
Christopher St Sheridan Sq·1
W 4 St Wash Sq A·B·C·D·E·F·M
Bleecker St·6
Broadway Lafayette St B·D·F·M
2 Av·F
Houston St 1
Prince St N·R
Delancey St-Essex St F·J·M·Z
Spring St C·E
Spring St 6
Bowery J·Z
Grand St B·D
Canal St 1
Canal St A·C·E
Canal St J·N·Q·R·Z·6
East Broadway·F
Franklin St·1
Park Place 2·3
Chambers St·A·C
Chambers St·1·2·3
City Hall·R
Chambers St J·Z
World Trade Center·E
Brooklyn Bridge-City Hall·4·5·6
Fulton St A·C·J·Z·2·3·4·5
Cortlandt St 1 (closed)
Cortlandt St·R
9/11 MEMORIAL ENTRY
Wall St 4·5
Wall St 2·3
Rector St·1
Rector St·R
Broad St·J·Z
Bowling Green·4·5
Whitehall St South Ferry·R
South Ferry·1
BATTERY PARK
HUDSON RIVER
EAST RIVER
QUEENS
BROOKLYN
RANDALL'S ISLAND
WARD'S ISLAND
ROOSEVELT ISLAND
CENTRAL PARK
HARLEM
EAST HARLEM
UPPER WEST SIDE
UPPER EAST SIDE
MIDTOWN
WEST SIDE
CHELSEA
GREENWICH VILLAGE
EAST VILLAGE
SOHO
LITTLE ITALY
CHINATOWN
TRIBECA
LOWER EAST SIDE
MURRAY HILL
GRAMERCY PARK
TOMPKINS SQUARE PARK
UNITED NATIONS
JAVITS CENTER
WILLIAMSBURG BRIDGE

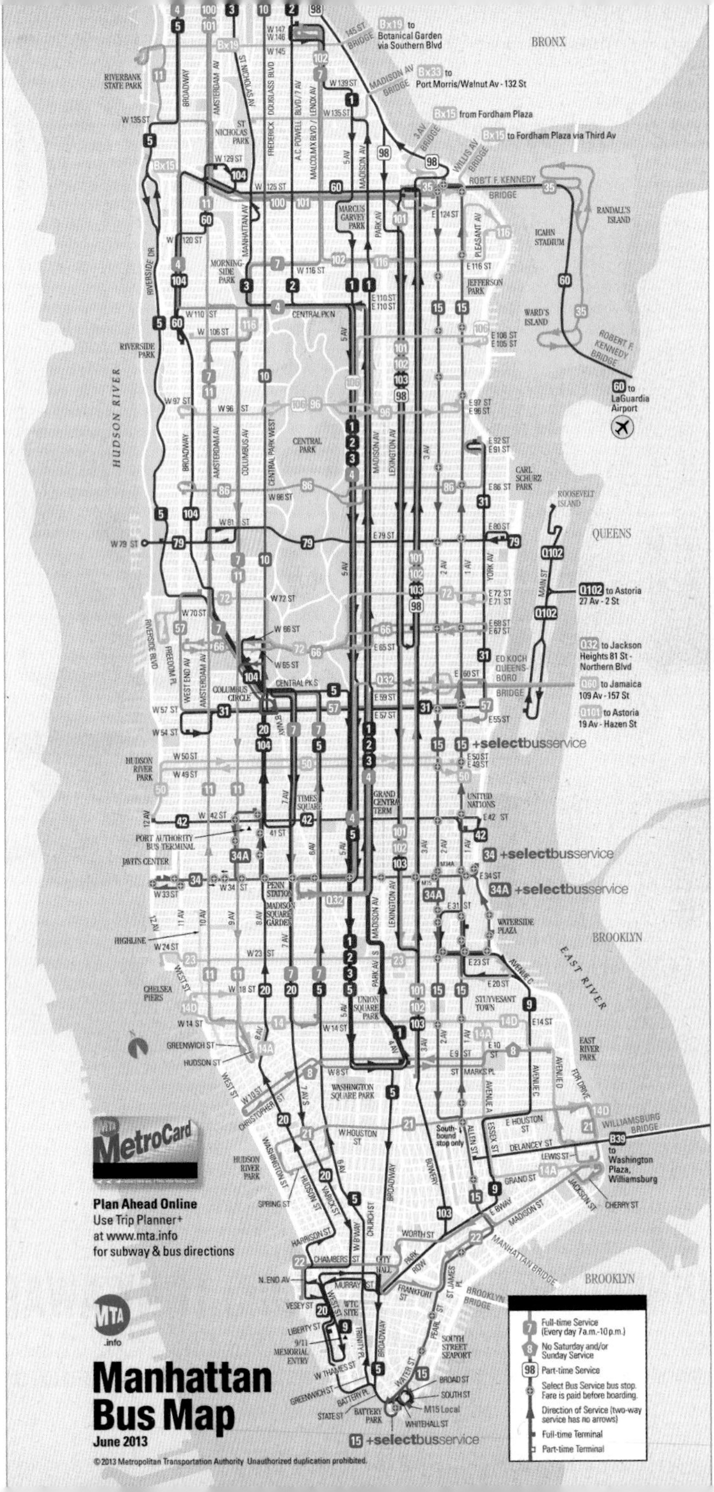
Manhattan Bus Map
June 2013
Plan Ahead Online
Use Trip Planner+
at www.mta.info
for subway & bus directions
MetroCard
MTA .info
Full-time Service (Every day 7 a.m.-10 p.m.)
No Saturday and/or Sunday Service
Part-time Service
Select Bus Service bus stop. Fare is paid before boarding.
Direction of Service (two-way service has no arrows)
Full-time Terminal
Part-time Terminal
Bx19 to Botanical Garden via Southern Blvd
Bx33 to Port Morris/Walnut Av - 132 St
Bx15 from Fordham Plaza
Bx15 to Fordham Plaza via Third Av
60 to LaGuardia Airport
Q102 to Astoria 27 Av - 2 St
Q32 to Jackson Heights 81 St - Northern Blvd
Q60 to Jamaica 109 Av - 157 St
Q101 to Astoria 19 Av - Hazen St
B39 to Washington Plaza, Williamsburg
15 +selectbusservice
34 +selectbusservice
34A +selectbusservice
HUDSON RIVER
EAST RIVER
BRONX
QUEENS
BROOKLYN
CENTRAL PARK
RANDALL'S ISLAND
WARD'S ISLAND
ROOSEVELT ISLAND
ROBERT F. KENNEDY BRIDGE
ED KOCH QUEENSBORO BRIDGE
WILLIAMSBURG BRIDGE
MANHATTAN BRIDGE
BROOKLYN BRIDGE
PORT AUTHORITY BUS TERMINAL
PENN STATION
GRAND CENTRAL TERM
TIMES SQUARE
COLUMBUS CIRCLE
UNITED NATIONS
WASHINGTON SQUARE PARK
UNION SQUARE PARK
SOUTH STREET SEAPORT
BATTERY PARK
CITY HALL
9/11 MEMORIAL ENTRY
© 2013 Metropolitan Transportation Authority Unauthorized duplication prohibited.